MyEconLab® Provides the Power of Practice

Optimize your study time with **MyEconLab**, the online assessment and tutorial system. When you take a sample test online, **MyEconLab** gives you targeted feedback and a personalized Study Plan to identify the topics you need to review.

Study Plan

The Study Plan shows you the sections you should study next, gives easy access to practice problems, and provides you with an automatically generated quiz to prove mastery of the course material.

Unlimited Practice

As you work each exercise, instant feedback helps you understand and apply the concepts. Many Study Plan exercises contain algorithmically generated values to ensure that you get as much practice as you need.

Learning Resources

Study Plan problems link to learning resources that further reinforce concepts you need to master.

- **Help Me Solve This** learning aids help you break down a problem much the same way as an instructor would do during office hours. Help Me Solve This is available for select problems.

- **eText links** are specific to the problem at hand so that related concepts are easy to review just when they are needed.

- A **graphing tool** enables you to build and manipulate graphs to better understand how concepts, numbers, and graphs connect.

Find out more at www.myeconlab.com

Real-Time Data Analysis Exercises

Up-to-date macro data is a great way to engage in and understand the usefulness of macro variables and their impact on the economy. Real-Time Data Analysis exercises communicate directly with the Federal Reserve Bank of St. Louis's FRED site, so every time FRED posts new data, students see new data.

End-of-chapter exercises accompanied by the Real-Time Data Analysis icon 🌐 include Real-Time Data versions in **MyEconLab**.

Select in-text figures labeled **MyEconLab** Real-Time Data update in the electronic version of the text using FRED data.

Current News Exercises

Posted weekly, we find the latest microeconomic and macroeconomic news stories, post them, and write auto-graded multi-part exercises that illustrate the economic way of thinking about the news.

Interactive Homework Exercises

Participate in a fun and engaging activity that helps promote active learning and mastery of important economic concepts.

Pearson's experiments program is flexible and easy for instructors and students to use. For a complete list of available experiments, visit *www.myeconlab.com*.

Microeconomics

PRINCIPLES, APPLICATIONS, AND TOOLS

EIGHTH EDITION

Arthur O'Sullivan
Lewis and Clark College

Steven M. Sheffrin
Tulane University

Stephen J. Perez
California State University, Sacramento

PEARSON

Boston   Columbus   Indianapolis   New York   San Francisco   Upper Saddle River
Amsterdam   Cape Town   Dubai   London   Madrid   Milan Munich   Paris   Montréal   Toronto
Delhi   Mexico City   São Paulo   Sydney   Hong Kong   Seoul   Singapore   Taipei   Tokyo

To Our Children
Conor, Maura, Meera, Kiran, Davis, and Tate

Editor in Chief: Donna Battista
Executive Editor: David Alexander
Senior Acquisitions Editor: Noel Seibert
Digital Publisher: Denise Clinton
Senior Editorial Project Manager: Carolyn Terbush
Managing Editor: Jeff Holcomb
Senior Production Project Manager: Meredith Gertz
Director of Marketing: Maggie Moylan
Executive Marketing Manager: Lori DeShazo
Marketing Assistant: Kim Lovato
Editorial Assistant: Emily Brodeur
Art Director/Cover Designer: Jonathan Boylan
Manager, Rights and Permissions, Text: Jill Dougan
Image Manager/Image Asset Services: Rachel Youdelman

Photo Researcher: Integra Software Services, Ltd.
Cover Illustration: Shutterstock/AlexRoz
Media Director: Susan Schoenberg
Senior Media Producer: Melissa Honig
Content Leads, MyEconLab: Noel Lotz, Courtney Kamauf
Senior Manufacturing Buyer: Carol Melville
Full-Service Project Management, Composition, Text Illustrations, and Text Design: GEX Publishing Services
Printer/Binder: Courier Kendallville
Cover Printer: Lehigh, Phoenix/Hagerstown
Text Font: 10/12 Janson Text

Credits and acknowledgments borrowed from other sources and reproduced, with permission, in this textbook appear on appropriate page within text (or on page 436).

Microsoft® and Windows® are registered trademarks of the Microsoft Corporation in the U.S.A. and other countries. Screen shots and icons reprinted with permission from the Microsoft Corporation. This book is not sponsored or endorsed by or affiliated with the Microsoft Corporation.

Many of the designations by manufacturers and seller to distinguish their products are claimed as trademarks. Where those designations appear in this book, and the publisher was aware of a trademark claim, the designations have been printed in initial caps or all caps.

FRED® is a registered trademark and the FRED Logo and ST. LOUIS FED are trademarks of the Federal Reserve Bank of St. Louis. http://research.stlouisfed.org/fred2. Licensee agrees not to and not to allow sublicensees to alter, modify, or create derivative works based upon the Licensed Material and agrees to display and require sublicensees to display all trademark notices present on the Licensed Material.

Library of Congress Cataloging-in-Publication Data
O'Sullivan, Arthur.
  Microeconomics: principles, applications, and tools / Arthur O'Sullivan, Steven M.Sheffrin, Stephen J.Perez. -- 8th ed.
    p. cm.
  Includes index.
  ISBN-13: 978-0-13-294886-9
  ISBN-10: 0-13-294886-9
1. Microeconomics. I. Sheffrin, Steven M. II. Perez, Stephen J. III. Title.

HB172.O85 2014
338.5--dc23

2012041604

10 9 8 7 6 5 4 3 2 1

www.pearsonhighered.com

ISBN 10: 0-13-294886-9
ISBN 13: 978-0-13-294886-9

About the Authors

ARTHUR O'SULLIVAN

is a professor of economics at Lewis and Clark College in Portland, Oregon. After receiving his B.S. in economics at the University of Oregon, he spent two years in the Peace Corps, working with city planners in the Philippines. He received his Ph.D. in economics from Princeton University in 1981 and has taught at the University of California, Davis, and Oregon State University, winning teaching awards at both schools. He is the author of the best-selling textbook *Urban Economics*, currently in its seventh edition.

Professor O'Sullivan's research explores economic issues concerning urban land use, environmental protection, and public policy. His articles have appeared in many economics journals, including the *Journal of Urban Economics*, *Journal of Environmental Economics and Management*, *National Tax Journal*, *Journal of Public Economics*, and *Journal of Law and Economics*.

Professor O'Sullivan lives with his family in Portland, Oregon. For recreation, he enjoys hiking, kiteboarding, and squash.

STEVEN M. SHEFFRIN

is professor of economics and executive director of the Murphy Institute at Tulane University. Prior to joining Tulane in 2010, he was a faculty member at the University of California, Davis, and served as department chairman of economics and dean of social sciences. He has been a visiting professor at Princeton University, Oxford University, London School of Economics, and Nanyang Technological University, and he has served as a financial economist with the Office of Tax Analysis of the United States Department of the Treasury. He received his B.A. from Wesleyan University and his Ph.D. in economics from the Massachusetts Institute of Technology.

Professor Sheffrin is the author of 10 other books and monographs and over 100 articles in the fields of macroeconomics, public finance, and international economics. His most recent books include *Rational Expectations* (second edition) and *Property Taxes and Tax Revolts: The Legacy of Proposition 13* (with Arthur O'Sullivan and Terri Sexton).

Professor Sheffrin has taught macroeconomics and public finance at all levels, from general introduction to principles classes (enrollments of 400) to graduate classes for doctoral students. He is the recipient of the Thomas Mayer Distinguished Teaching Award in economics.

He lives with his wife Anjali (also an economist) in New Orleans, Louisiana, and has two daughters who have studied economics. In addition to a passion for current affairs and travel, he plays a tough game of tennis.

STEPHEN J. PEREZ

is a professor of economics and NCAA faculty athletics representative at California State University, Sacramento. After receiving his B.A. in economics at the University of California, San Diego, he was awarded his Ph.D. in economics from the University of California, Davis, in 1994. He taught economics at Virginia Commonwealth University and Washington State University before coming to California State University, Sacramento, in 2001. He teaches macroeconomics at all levels as well as econometrics, sports economics, labor economics, and mathematics for economists.

Professor Perez's research explores most macroeconomic topics. In particular, he is interested in evaluating the ability of econometric techniques to discover the truth, issues of causality in macroeconomics, and sports economics. His articles have appeared in many economics journals, including the *Journal of Monetary Economics*; *Econometrics Journal*; *Economics Letters*; *Journal of Economic Methodology*; *Public Finance and Management*; *Journal of Economics and Business*; *Oxford Bulletin of Economics and Statistics*; *Journal of Money, Credit, and Banking*; *Applied Economics*; and *Journal of Macroeconomics*.

The Pearson Series in Economics

Abel/Bernanke/Croushore
*Macroeconomics**

Bade/Parkin
*Foundations of Economics**

Berck/Helfand
The Economics of the Environment

Bierman/Fernandez
Game Theory with Economic Applications

Blanchard
*Macroeconomics**

Blau/Ferber/Winkler
The Economics of Women, Men and Work

Boardman/Greenberg/Vining/ Weimer
Cost-Benefit Analysis

Boyer
Principles of Transportation Economics

Branson
Macroeconomic Theory and Policy

Brock/Adams
The Structure of American Industry

Bruce
Public Finance and the American Economy

Carlton/Perloff
Modern Industrial Organization

Case/Fair/Oster
*Principles of Economics**

Caves/Frankel/Jones
World Trade and Payments: An Introduction

Chapman
Environmental Economics: Theory, Application, and Policy

Cooter/Ulen
Law & Economics

Downs
An Economic Theory of Democracy

Ehrenberg/Smith
Modern Labor Economics

Farnham
Economics for Managers

Folland/Goodman/Stano
The Economics of Health and Health Care

Fort
Sports Economics

Froyen
Macroeconomics

Fusfeld
The Age of the Economist

Gerber
*International Economics**

González-Rivera
Forecasting for Economics and Business

Gordon
*Macroeconomics**

Greene
Econometric Analysis

Gregory
Essentials of Economics

Gregory/Stuart
Russian and Soviet Economic Performance and Structure

Hartwick/Olewiler
The Economics of Natural Resource Use

Heilbroner/Milberg
The Making of the Economic Society

Heyne/Boettke/Prychitko
The Economic Way of Thinking

Hoffman/Averett
Women and the Economy: Family, Work, and Pay

Holt
Markets, Games, and Strategic Behavior

Hubbard/O'Brien
*Economics**
*Money, Banking, and the Financial System**

Hughes/Cain
American Economic History

Husted/Melvin
International Economics

Jehle/Reny
Advanced Microeconomic Theory

Johnson-Lans
A Health Economics Primer

Keat/Young
Managerial Economics

Klein
Mathematical Methods for Economics

Krugman/Obstfeld/Melitz
*International Economics: Theory & Policy**

Laidler
The Demand for Money

Leeds/von Allmen
The Economics of Sports

Leeds/von Allmen/Schiming
*Economics**

Lipsey/Ragan/Storer
*Economics**

Lynn
Economic Development: Theory and Practice for a Divided World

Miller
*Economics Today**
Understanding Modern Economics

Miller/Benjamin
The Economics of Macro Issues

Miller/Benjamin/North
The Economics of Public Issues

Mills/Hamilton
Urban Economics

Mishkin
*The Economics of Money, Banking, and Financial Markets**
*The Economics of Money, Banking, and Financial Markets, Business School Edition**
*Macroeconomics: Policy and Practice**

Murray
Econometrics: A Modern Introduction

Nafziger
The Economics of Developing Countries

O'Sullivan/Sheffrin/Perez
*Economics: Principles, Applications, and Tools**

Parkin
*Economics**

Perloff
*Microeconomics**
*Microeconomics: Theory and Applications with Calculus**

Phelps
Health Economics

Pindyck/Rubinfeld
*Microeconomics**

Riddell/Shackelford/Stamos/ Schneider
Economics: A Tool for Critically Understanding Society

Ritter/Silber/Udell
*Principles of Money, Banking, & Financial Markets**

Roberts
The Choice: A Fable of Free Trade and Protection

Rohlf
Introduction to Economic Reasoning

Ruffin/Gregory
Principles of Economics

Sargent
Rational Expectations and Inflation

Sawyer/Sprinkle
International Economics

Scherer
Industry Structure, Strategy, and Public Policy

Schiller
The Economics of Poverty and Discrimination

Sherman
Market Regulation

Silberberg
Principles of Microeconomics

Stock/Watson
Introduction to Econometrics

Studenmund
Using Econometrics: A Practical Guide

Tietenberg/Lewis
Environmental and Natural Resource Economics
Environmental Economics and Policy

Todaro/Smith
Economic Development

Waldman
Microeconomics

Waldman/Jensen
Industrial Organization: Theory and Practice

Walters/Walters/Appel/ Callahan/Centanni/Maex/ O'Neill
Econversations: Today's Students Discuss Today's Issues

Weil
Economic Growth

Williamson
Macroeconomics

---

* denotes MyEconLab titles   Log onto www.myeconlab.com to learn more.

Brief Contents

PART 1   Introduction and Key Principles

1   Introduction: What Is Economics? 1

2   The Key Principles of Economics 28

3   Exchange and Markets 49

4   Demand, Supply, and Market Equilibrium 67

PART 2   A Closer Look at Demand and Supply

5   Elasticity: A Measure of Responsiveness 97

6   Market Efficiency and Government Intervention 127

7   Consumer Choice: Utility Theory and Insights from Neuroscience 152

PART 3   Market Structures and Pricing

8   Production Technology and Cost 185

9   Perfect Competition 207

10   Monopoly and Price Discrimination 233

11   Market Entry and Monopolistic Competition 254

12   Oligopoly and Strategic Behavior 270

13   Controlling Market Power: Antitrust and Regulation 297

PART 4   Externalities and Information

14   Imperfect Information: Adverse Selection and Moral Hazard 313

15   Public Goods and Public Choice 339

16   External Costs and Environmental Policy 356

PART 5   The Labor Market and Income Distribution

17   The Labor Market and the Distribution of Income 377

PART 6   The International Economy

18   International Trade and Public Policy 409

Contents

Preface xv

PART 1
Introduction and Key Principles

1 Introduction: What Is Economics? 1

What Is Economics 2
  Positive versus Normative Analysis 3
  The Three Key Economic Questions: What, How, and Who? 4
  Economic Models 4
Economic Analysis and Modern Problems 5
  Economic View of Traffic Congestion 5
  Economic View of Poverty in Africa 5
  Economic View of the Current World Recession 6
The Economic Way of Thinking 7
  Use Assumptions to Simplify 7
  Isolate Variables—*Ceteris Paribus* 7
  Think at the Margin 8
  Rational People Respond to Incentives 8
APPLICATION 1 Incentives to Buy Hybrid Vehicles 9
  Example: London Addresses Its Congestion Problem 9
APPLICATION 2 The Economic Solution to Spam 10
Preview of Coming Attractions: Macroeconomics 10
  Using Macroeconomics to Understand Why Economies Grow 11
  Using Macroeconomics to Understand Economic Fluctuations 11
  Using Macroeconomics to Make Informed Business Decisions 11
Preview of Coming Attractions: Microeconomics 12
  Using Microeconomics to Understand Markets and Predict Changes 12
  Using Microeconomics to Make Personal and Managerial Decisions 12
  Using Microeconomics to Evaluate Public Policies 12
* SUMMARY 13 * KEY TERMS 13
* EXERCISES 13

APPENDIX: Using Graphs and Percentages 15
USING GRAPHS 15
COMPUTING PERCENTAGE CHANGES AND USING EQUATIONS 23
APPLICATION 3 The Perils of Percentages 24

2 The Key Principles of Economics 28

The Principle of Opportunity Cost 29
  The Cost of College 29
  The Cost of Military Spending 30
  Opportunity Cost and the Production Possibilities Curve 31
APPLICATION 1 Don't Forget the Costs of Time and Invested Funds 32
The Marginal Principle 33
  How Many Movie Sequels? 34
  Renting College Facilities 35
  Automobile Emissions Standards 36
  Driving Speed and Safety 36
APPLICATION 2 How Fast to Sail? 36
The Principle of Voluntary Exchange 37
  Exchange and Markets 37
APPLICATION 3 Jasper Johns and Housepainting 38
  Online Games and Market Exchange 38
The Principle of Diminishing Returns 39
APPLICATION 4 Fertilizer and Crop Yields 39
The Real-Nominal Principle 40
  The Design of Public Programs 41
  The Value of the Minimum Wage 41
APPLICATION 5 Repaying Student Loans 42
* SUMMARY 43 * KEY TERMS 43
* EXERCISES 43
* ECONOMIC EXPERIMENT 47

3 Exchange and Markets 49

Comparative Advantage and Exchange 50
  Specialization and the Gains from Trade 50
  Comparative Advantage versus Absolute Advantage 52
  The Division of Labor and Exchange 53

Comparative Advantage and International Trade 53

APPLICATION 1 Absolute Disadvantage and Comparative Advantage in Latvia 54

Outsourcing 55

Markets 55

Virtues of Markets 56

APPLICATION 2 The Market for Meteorites 57

APPLICATION 3 Civil Liberties and Efficiency of Government 58

The Role of Entrepreneurs 59

Example of the Emergence of Markets: POW Camps 59

Market Failure and the Role of Government 60

Government Enforces the Rules of Exchange 61

Government Can Reduce Economic Uncertainty 62

* SUMMARY 62 * KEY TERMS 63
* EXERCISES 63

4 Demand, Supply, and Market Equilibrium 67

The Demand Curve 68

The Individual Demand Curve and the Law of Demand 68

From Individual Demand to Market Demand 70

APPLICATION 1 Law of Demand and Cigarettes 71

The Supply Curve 71

The Individual Supply Curve and the Law of Supply 72

Why Is the Individual Supply Curve Positively Sloped? 73

From Individual Supply to Market Supply 74

Why Is the Market Supply Curve Positively Sloped? 75

APPLICATION 2 Law of Supply and Woolympics 76

Market Equilibrium: Bringing Demand and Supply Together 76

Excess Demand Causes the Price to Rise 76

Excess Supply Causes the Price to Drop 77

APPLICATION 3 Shrinking Wine Lakes 78

Market Effects of Changes in Demand 78

Change in Quantity Demanded versus Change in Demand 78

Increases in Demand Shift the Demand Curve 79

Decreases in Demand Shift the Demand Curve 81

A Decrease in Demand Decreases the Equilibrium Price 82

APPLICATION 4 Chinese Demand and Pecan Prices 82

Market Effects of Changes in Supply 83

Change in Quantity Supplied versus Change in Supply 83

Increases in Supply Shift the Supply Curve 83

An Increase in Supply Decreases the Equilibrium Price 85

Decreases in Supply Shift the Supply Curve 86

A Decrease in Supply Increases the Equilibrium Price 87

Simultaneous Changes in Demand and Supply 87

APPLICATION 5 Honeybees and the Price of Ice Cream 89

Predicting and Explaining Market Changes 90

APPLICATION 6 Why Lower Drug Prices? 90

* SUMMARY 91 * KEY TERMS 91
* EXERCISES 91
* ECONOMIC EXPERIMENT 96

PART 2
A Closer Look at Demand and Supply

5 Elasticity: A Measure of Responsiveness 97

The Price Elasticity of Demand 98

Computing Percentage Changes and Elasticities 99

Price Elasticity and the Demand Curve 100

Elasticity and the Availability of Substitutes 101

Other Determinants of the Price Elasticity of Demand 102

APPLICATION 1 A Closer Look at the Elasticity of Demand for Gasoline 103

Using Price Elasticity 104

Predicting Changes in Quantity 104

Price Elasticity and Total Revenue 105

Using Elasticity to Predict the Revenue Effects of Price Changes 106

APPLICATION 2 Vanity Plates and the Elasticity of Demand 107

Elasticity and Total Revenue for a Linear
Demand Curve 108
Price Elasticity along a Linear Demand Curve 108
Elasticity and Total Revenue for a Linear
Demand Curve 109
APPLICATION 3 Trampolines and the Lower Half of a
Linear Demand Curve 110
Other Elasticities of Demand 110
Income Elasticity of Demand 110
Cross-Price Elasticity of Demand 111
APPLICATION 4 I Can Find that Elasticity in
Four Clicks! 112
The Price Elasticity of Supply 112
What Determines the Price Elasticity of
Supply? 113
The Role of Time: Short-Run versus Long-Run
Supply Elasticity 114
Extreme Cases: Perfectly Inelastic Supply and
Perfectly Elastic Supply 114
Predicting Changes in Quantity Supplied 115
APPLICATION 5 The Short-Run and Long-Run
Elasticity of Supply of Milk 116
Using Elasticities to Predict Changes
in Prices 116
The Price Effects of a Change in Demand 116
The Price Effects of a Change in Supply 118
APPLICATION 6 A Broken Pipeline and the Price of
Gasoline 120
* SUMMARY 120 * KEY TERMS 121
* EXERCISES 121

6   Market Efficiency and Government
Intervention 127

Consumer Surplus and Producer Surplus 128
The Demand Curve and Consumer Surplus 129
The Supply Curve and Producer Surplus 130
APPLICATION 1 Consumer Surplus of Internet
Service 131
Market Equilibrium and Efficiency 131
Total Surplus Is Lower with a Price below the
Equilibrium Price 132
Total Surplus Is Lower with a Price above the
Equilibrium Price 133
Efficiency and the Invisible Hand 133
Government Intervention in Efficient
Markets 133

APPLICATION 2 Rent Control and Mismatches 134
Controlling Prices—Maximum and Minimum
Prices 134
Setting Maximum Prices 134
Rent Control 135
Setting Minimum Prices 136
APPLICATION 3 Price Controls and the Shrinking
Candy Bar 137
Controlling Quantities—Licensing and Import
Restrictions 137
Taxi Medallions 137
Licensing and Market Efficiency 138
Winners and Losers from Licensing 139
Import Restrictions 139
APPLICATION 4 The Cost of Protecting a
Luggage Job 140
Who Really Pays Taxes? 141
Tax Shifting: Forward and Backward 141
Tax Shifting and the Price Elasticity of
Demand 142
Cigarette Taxes and Tobacco Land 143
The Luxury Boat Tax and Boat Workers 143
Tax Burden and Deadweight Loss 143
APPLICATION 5 Response to Lower Taxes in French
Restaurants 145
* SUMMARY 146 * KEY TERMS 146
* EXERCISES 146
* ECONOMIC EXPERIMENT 151

7   Consumer Choice: Utility Theory
and Insights from Neuroscience 152

Traditional Consumer Choice:
Utility Theory 153
Consumer Constraints: The Budget Line 153
Total and Marginal Utility 155
The Marginal Principle and the Equimarginal
Rule 156
Conditions for Utility Maximization 158
APPLICATION 1 Measuring Diminishing Marginal
Utility 160
The Law of Demand and the Individual
Demand Curve 160
Effect of a Decrease in Price 160
Income and Substitution Effects of a Decrease
in Price 162
The Individual Demand Curve 163

APPLICATION 2 A Revenue-Neutral Gasoline Tax 164

The Neuroscience of Consumer Choice 165

The Neuroscience of Benefit Valuation 165

The Neuroscience of Cost Valuation 166

The Wisdom of Gut Feelings 167

Cognition and Choice 167

Predicting Consumer Choice 168

Fuel for Cognition 168

APPLICATION 3 Stores vs. Online Retailers 169

Consumer Decisions: Insights from Neuroscience 170

Dietary Choice: Donut versus Apple 170
Present Bias: Spending versus Saving 171
Present Bias and Credit Cards 173
Present Bias and Smoking 174
Gambling as a Consumer Good 174

APPLICATION 4 Taxing Cigarettes to Offset Present Bias 176

* SUMMARY 176 * EXERCISES 177

APPENDIX to Chapter 7: Mental Shortcuts and Consumer Puzzles 181

PART 3
Market Structures and Pricing

8 Production Technology and Cost 185

Economic Cost and Economic Profit 186

APPLICATION 1 Opportunity Cost and Entrepreneurship 187

A Firm with a Fixed Production Facility: Short-Run Costs 187

Production and Marginal Product 187
Short-Run Total Cost 189
Short-Run Average Costs 190
Short-Run Marginal Cost 192
The Relationship between Marginal Cost and Average Cost 193

APPLICATION 2 Idle Capital and Short-Run Marginal Cost 194

Production and Cost in the Long Run 194

Expansion and Replication 195

Reducing Output with Indivisible Inputs 196
Scaling Down and Labor Specialization 197
Economies of Scale 197
Diseconomies of Scale 197
Actual Long-Run Average-Cost Curves 198
Short-Run versus Long-Run Average Cost 199

APPLICATION 3 Indivisible Inputs and the Cost of Fake Killer Whales 199

Examples of Production Cost 200

Scale Economies in Wind Power 200
The Average Cost of a Music Video 201
Solar versus Nuclear: The Crossover 201

* SUMMARY 202 * KEY TERMS 203
* EXERCISES 203

9 Perfect Competition 207

Preview of the Four Market Structures 208

APPLICATION 1 Wireless Women in Pakistan 210

The Firm's Short-Run Output Decision 210

The Total Approach: Computing Total Revenue and Total Cost 210
The Marginal Approach 212
Economic Profit and the Break-Even Price 213

APPLICATION 2 The Break-Even Price for Switchgrass, A Feedstock for Biofuel 214

The Firm's Shut-Down Decision 215

Total Revenue, Variable Cost, and the Shut-Down Decision 215
The Shut-Down Price 216
Fixed Costs and Sunk Costs 217

APPLICATION 3 Straddling the Zinc Cost Curve 217

Short-Run Supply Curves 218

The Firm's Short-Run Supply Curve 218
The Short-Run Market Supply Curve 218
Market Equilibrium 219

APPLICATION 4 Short-Run Supply Curve for Cargo 220

The Long-Run Supply Curve for an Increasing-Cost Industry 220

Production Cost and Industry Size 221
Drawing the Long-Run Market Supply Curve 221
Examples of Increasing-Cost Industries: Sugar and Apartments 222

APPLICATION 5 Chinese Coffee Growers Obey the Law of Supply 223

Short-Run and Long-Run Effects of Changes in Demand 223

The Short-Run Response to an Increase in Demand 223

The Long-Run Response to an Increase in Demand 224

APPLICATION 6 The Upward Jump and Downward Slide of Wine Prices 225

Long-Run Supply for a Constant-Cost Industry 225

Long-Run Supply Curve for a Constant-Cost Industry 225

Hurricane Andrew and the Price of Ice 226

APPLICATION 7 Economic Detective and the Case of Margarine Prices 227

* SUMMARY 227 * KEY TERMS 228
* EXERCISES 228

10 Monopoly and Price Discrimination 233

The Monopolist's Output Decision 234

Total Revenue and Marginal Revenue 235

A Formula for Marginal Revenue 236

Using the Marginal Principle 237

APPLICATION 1 Marginal Revenue from a Baseball Fan 239

The Social Cost of Monopoly 240

Deadweight Loss from Monopoly 240

Rent Seeking: Using Resources to Get Monopoly Power 242

APPLICATION 2 A Casino Monopoly in Creswell, Oregon? 242

Monopoly and Public Policy 243

Patents and Monopoly Power 243

Incentives for Innovation 243

Trade-Offs from Patents 243

APPLICATION 3 Bribing the Makers of Generic Drugs 244

Price Discrimination 245

Senior Discounts in Restaurants 246

Price Discrimination and the Elasticity of Demand 246

Examples: Movie Admission versus Popcorn, and Hardback versus Paperback Books 247

APPLICATION 4 Why Does Movie Popcorn Cost So Much? 248

* SUMMARY 248 * KEY TERMS 249
* EXERCISES 249

* ECONOMIC EXPERIMENT 252

11 Market Entry and Monopolistic Competition 254

The Effects of Market Entry 255

Entry Squeezes Profits from Three Sides 256

Examples of Entry: Car Stereos, Trucking, and Tires 257

APPLICATION 1 Satellite v Cable 258

Monopolistic Competition 258

When Entry Stops: Long-Run Equilibrium 259

Differentiation by Location 260

APPLICATION 2 Opening a Dunkin' Donuts Shop 261

Trade-Offs with Entry and Monopolistic Competition 261

Average Cost and Variety 262

Monopolistic Competition versus Perfect Competition 262

APPLICATION 3 Happy Hour Pricing 263

Advertising for Product Differentiation 264

APPLICATION 4 Picture of Man versus Picture of Woman 264

* SUMMARY 266 * KEY TERMS 266
* EXERCISES 266

* ECONOMIC EXPERIMENT 268

12 Oligopoly and Strategic Behavior 270

Cartel Pricing and the Duopolists' Dilemma 272

Price Fixing and the Game Tree 274

Equilibrium of the Price-Fixing Game 275

Nash Equilibrium 276

APPLICATION 1 Failure of the Salt Cartel 276

Overcoming the Duopolists' Dilemma 277

Low-Price Guarantees 277

Repeated Pricing Games with Retaliation for Underpricing 278

Price Fixing and the Law 279

Price Leadership 280

APPLICATION 2 Low-Price Guarantee Increases Tire Prices 280

Simultaneous Decision Making and the Payoff Matrix 281

Simultaneous Price-Fixing Game 281

The Prisoners' Dilemma 282

APPLICATION 3 Cheating On the Final Exam: The Cheaters' Dilemma 283

The Insecure Monopolist and Entry Deterrence 283

Entry Deterrence and Limit Pricing 284

Examples: Aluminum and Campus Bookstores 285

Entry Deterrence and Contestable Markets 286

When Is the Passive Approach Better? 286

APPLICATION 4 Microsoft as an Insecure Monopolist 287

The Advertisers' Dilemma 287

APPLICATION 5 Got Milk? 289

* SUMMARY 290 * KEY TERMS 290
* EXERCISES 290

* ECONOMIC EXPERIMENT 295

13 Controlling Market Power: Antitrust and Regulation 297

Natural Monopoly 298

Picking an Output Level 298

Will a Second Firm Enter? 300

Price Controls for a Natural Monopoly 301

APPLICATION 1 Public versus Private Waterworks 302

APPLICATION 2 Satellite Radio as a Natural Monopoly 303

Antitrust Policy 303

Breaking Up Monopolies 304

Blocking Mergers 304

Merger Remedy for Wonder Bread 306

Regulating Business Practices 307

A Brief History of U.S. Antitrust Policy 307

APPLICATION 3 Merger of Pennzoil and Quaker State 308

APPLICATION 4 FAQ about Predatory Pricing from the FTC 309

* SUMMARY 309 * KEY TERMS 310
* EXERCISES 310

PART 4
Externalities and Information

14 Imperfect Information: Adverse Selection and Moral Hazard 313

Adverse Selection for Buyers: The Lemons Problem 314

Uninformed Buyers and Knowledgeable Sellers 314

Equilibrium with All Low-Quality Goods 315

A Thin Market: Equilibrium with Some High-Quality Goods 316

APPLICATION 1 Are Baseball Pitchers Like Used Cars? 318

Evidence of the Lemons Problem 319

Responding to the Lemons Problem 319

Buyers Invest in Information 319

Consumer Satisfaction Scores from ValueStar and eBay 320

Guarantees and Lemons Laws 320

APPLICATION 2 Regulation of the California Kiwifruit Market 321

Adverse Selection for Sellers: Insurance 321

Health Insurance 321

Equilibrium with All High-Cost Consumers 323

Responding to Adverse Selection in Insurance: Group Insurance 324

The Uninsured 324

Other Types of Insurance 325

APPLICATION 3 Unisex Automobile Insurance in the European Union 325

Insurance and Moral Hazard 326

Insurance Companies and Moral Hazard 326

Deposit Insurance for Savings and Loans 327

APPLICATION 4 Car Insurance and Risky Driving 327

The Economics of Consumer Search 328

Search and the Marginal Principle 328

Reservation Prices and Searching Strategy 330

The Effects of Opportunity Cost and Product Prices on Search Effort 330

APPLICATION 5 Income and Consumer Search 332

* SUMMARY 332 * KEY TERMS 332
* EXERCISES 333

* ECONOMIC EXPERIMENT 337

15 Public Goods and Public Choice 339

External Benefits and Public Goods 342
Public Goods and the Free-Rider Problem 342
Overcoming the Free-Rider Problem 343
APPLICATION 1 Free Riders and the Three-Clock Tower 343
APPLICATION 2 Global Weather Observation 344
Private Goods with External Benefits 344
External Benefits from Education 344
External Benefits and the Marginal Principle 345
Other Private Goods That Generate External Benefits 346
APPLICATION 3 External Benefits from LoJack 346
APPLICATION 4 The Private and External Benefit of Trees 347
Public Choice and the Median Voter 347
Voting and the Median-Voter Rule 347
The Median Voter and the Median Location 349
Alternative Models of Government: Self-Interest and Special Interests 349
APPLICATION 5 The Median Voter in the NBA 351
Which Theory Is Correct? 351
* SUMMARY 351 * KEY TERMS 352
* EXERCISES 352
* ECONOMIC EXPERIMENT 355

16 External Costs and Environmental Policy 356

The Optimal Level of Pollution 357
Using the Marginal Principle 357
Example: The Optimal Level of Water Pollution 358
Coase Bargaining 359
APPLICATION 1 Reducing Methane Emissions 360
Taxing Pollution 360
A Firm's Response to a Pollution Tax 361
The Market Effects of a Pollution Tax 361
Example: A Carbon Tax 363
APPLICATION 2 Pollution Taxes in Rural and Urban Areas 364
Traditional Regulation 364
Uniform Abatement with Permits 364
Command and Control 365

Market Effects of Pollution Regulations 365
Lesson from Dear Abby: Options for Pollution Abatement 365
APPLICATION 3 Options for Reducing CO_2 Emissions from International Shipping 366
Marketable Pollution Permits 366
Voluntary Exchange and Marketable Permits 367
Supply, Demand, and the Price of Marketable Permits 368
APPLICATION 4 Weather and the Price of Pollution Permits 369
External Costs from Automobiles 369
External Costs from Pollution 369
External Costs from Congestion 371
External Costs from Collisions 371
APPLICATION 5 Young Drivers and Collisions 372
* SUMMARY 372 * KEY TERMS 373
* EXERCISES 373
* ECONOMIC EXPERIMENT 376

PART 5
The Labor Market and Income Distribution

17 The Labor Market and the Distribution of Income 377

The Demand for Labor 378
Labor Demand by an Individual Firm in the Short Run 378
Market Demand for Labor in the Short Run 381
Labor Demand in the Long Run 382
APPLICATION 1 Marginal Revenue Product in Major League Baseball 383
Short-Run versus Long-Run Demand 383
The Supply of Labor 384
The Individual Labor-Supply Decision: How Many Hours? 384
An Example of Income and Substitution Effects 385
The Market Supply Curve for Labor 385
APPLICATION 2 Cabbies Respond to an Increase in the Wage 386
Labor Market Equilibrium 387
Changes in Demand and Supply 387
The Market Effects of the Minimum Wage 388

Why Do Wages Differ across Occupations? 389

The Gender Pay Gap 390

Racial Discrimination 391

Why Do College Graduates Earn Higher Wages? 392

Labor Unions and Wages 393

APPLICATION 3 The Beauty Premium 393

The Distribution of Income 394

Income Distribution in 2007 394

Recent Changes in the Distribution of Income 396

APPLICATION 4 Trade-Offs from Immigration 397

Public Policy and the Distribution of Income 398

Effects of Tax and Transfer Policies on the Distribution of Income 398

Poverty and Public Policy 399

The Earned Income Tax Credit 401

APPLICATION 5 State Lotteries and the Distribution of Income 402

* SUMMARY 403 * KEY TERMS 403
* EXERCISES 404

PART 6
The International Economy

18 International Trade and Public Policy 409

Benefits from Specialization and Trade 410

Production Possibilities Curve 410

Comparative Advantage and the Terms of Trade 412

The Consumption Possibilities Curve 412

How Free Trade Affects Employment 413

Protectionist Policies 414

Import Bans 414

Quotas and Voluntary Export Restraints 415

Responses to Protectionist Policies 416

APPLICATION 1 The Impact of Tariffs on the Poor 417

What Are the Rationales for Protectionist Policies? 417

To Shield Workers from Foreign Competition 418

To Nurture Infant Industries until They Mature 418

To Help Domestic Firms Establish Monopolies in World Markets 418

APPLICATION 2 Chinese Imports and Local Economies 419

A Brief History of International Tariff and Trade Agreements 419

Recent Policy Debates and Trade Agreements 421

Are Foreign Producers Dumping Their Products? 421

APPLICATION 3 Are They Really Dumping? 421

Do Trade Laws Inhibit Environmental Protection? 422

APPLICATION 4 Trade, Consumption, and Inequality 424

Do Outsourcing and Trade Cause Income Inequality? 424

Why Do People Protest Free Trade? 425

* SUMMARY 426 * KEY TERMS 426
* EXERCISES 426

Glossary 430

Photo Credits 436

Index 437

ALTERNATIVE COURSE SEQUENCE

Alternative Microeconomics Sequence

		Mix of Theory and Policy	Supply, Demand, and Policy	Supply, Demand, and Market Structure	Challenging Theory	Short Policy Course
1	Introduction: What Is Economics?	X	X	X	X	X
2	The Key Principles of Economics	X	X	X	X	X
3	Exchange and Markets	X	X	X	X	
4	Demand, Supply, and Market Equilibrium	X	X	X	X	X
5	Elasticity: A Measure of Responsiveness	X	X	X	X	X
6	Market Efficiency and Government Intervention	X	X	X	X	X
7	Consumer Choice: Utility Theory and Insights from Neuroscience				X	
8	Production Technology and Cost	X	X	X	X	
9	Perfect Competition	X	X	X	X	
10	Monopoly and Price Discrimination	X		X	X	
11	Market Entry and Monopolistic Competition	X		X	X	
12	Oligopoly and Strategic Behavior	X		X	X	
13	Controlling Market Power: Antitrust and Regulation	X		X	X	
14	Imperfect Information: Adverse Selection and Moral Hazard	X	X		X	X
15	Public Goods and Public Choice		X			X
16	External Costs and Environmental Policy		X			X
17	The Labor Market and the Distribution of Income	X	X		X	X
18	International Trade and Public Policy	X	X		X	

Preface

In preparing this eighth edition, we had three primary goals. First, we wanted to incorporate the sweeping changes in the U.S. and world economies we have all witnessed in the last several years, and the difficulties that the world economics have experienced in recovering from the severe economic downturn. Second, we strived to update this edition to reflect the latest exciting developments in economic thinking and make these accessible to new students of economics. Finally, we wanted to stay true to the philosophy of the textbook—using basic concepts of economics to explain a wide variety of timely and interesting economic applications.

► WHAT'S NEW TO THIS EDITION

In addition to updating all the figures and data, we made a number of other key changes in this edition. They include the following:

- At the beginning of each chapter, we introduced a set of *Learning Objectives*. These give the students a preview of what they will learn in each section of the chapter, facilitating their learning.

- We revised our presentation of consumer theory in Chapter 7 to (a) use modern tools to present traditional utility theory and (b) incorporate recent insights from neuroscience. For instructors who choose not to cover the insights from neuroscience, that part of the chapter can be skipped without loss of continuity.

- We expanded and upgraded our discussion of poverty and the distribution of income in Chapter 17, including a discussion of reasons for recent changes in the distribution of income and the effects of government policy.

- We consolidated our presentation of labor economics into a single chapter (Chapter 17).

We also incorporated a total of 44 exciting new applications and 9 new chapter-opening stories,. These fresh applications and chapter openers show the widespread relevance of economic analysis. The new applications include incentives to purchase hybrid cars (Chapter 1), choosing how fast to sail a container ship (Chapter 2), the markets for meteorites (Chapter 3), the economic forces behind the proposal to include sheep shearing as an Olympic sport (Chapter 4), the effects of supply disruptions on the price of gasoline (Chapter 5), the use of a large cigarette tax to overcome consumers' present bias and make current low-income smokers better off (Chapter 7), the decision of some Chinese farmers to shift from growing tea to coffee (Chapter 9), the economic logic of low prices during "happy hour", a period of relatively high demand (Chapter 11), Microsoft as an insecure monopolist (Chapter 12), gender discrimination in insurance (Chapter 14), the economics of energy-efficient buildings (Chapter 16), and state lotteries as regressive taxes (Chapter 17).

▶ APPLYING THE CONCEPTS

This is an Applications-driven textbook. We carefully selected over 120 real-world Applications that help students develop and master essential economic concepts. Here is an example of our approach from Chapter 4, "Demand, Supply, and Market Equilibrium."

---

application 1

LAW OF DEMAND AND CIGARETTES

APPLYING THE CONCEPTS #1: What is the law of demand?

As price decreases and we move downward along the market demand for cigarettes, the quantity of cigarettes demanded increases for two reasons. First, people who smoked cigarettes at the original price respond to the lower price by smoking more. Second, some people start smoking.

A change in cigarette taxes in Canada illustrates the second effect, the new-smoker effect. In 1994, several provinces in eastern Canada cut their cigarette taxes in response to the smuggling of cigarettes from the U.S. (where taxes are lower), and the price of cigarettes in the provinces decreased by roughly 50 percent. Researchers tracked the choices of 591 youths from the Waterloo Smoking Prevention Program, and concluded that the lower price increased the smoking rate by roughly 17 percent. **Related to Exercises 1.6 and 1.8.**

SOURCE: Based on Anindya Sen and Tony Wirjanto, "Estimating the impacts of cigarette taxes on youth smoking partici-pation, initiation, and persistence: empirical evidence from Canada," *Health Economics* 19 (2010), pp. 1264–1280.

Each chapter includes three to five thought-provoking Applying the Concepts questions that convey important economic concepts, paired with and illustrated by an Application that discusses the concept and conveys its real-world use.

For each Application and Applying the Concepts question, we provide end-of-chapter exercises that test students' understanding of the concepts.

1.4 The market demand curve is the (horizontal/vertical) sum of the individual demand curves.

1.5 A change in price causes movement along a demand curve and a change in _____.

1.6 When several provinces in eastern Canada cut their cigarette taxes, the price of cigarettes decreased by roughly 50 percent, and the youth smoking rate increased by roughly _____ (1, 17, 50, 90) percent. (Related to Application 1 on page 71.)

1.7 **Draw a Demand Curve.** Your state has decided to offer its citizens vanity license plates for their cars and wants to predict how many vanity plates it will sell at different prices. The price of the state's regular license plates is $20 per year, and the state's per-capita income is $30,000. A recent survey of other states with approximately the same population (3 million people) generated the following data on incomes, prices, and vanity plates:

State	B	C	D	E
Price of vanity plate	$ 60	$ 55	$ 50	$ 40
Price of regular plates	20	20	35	20
Income	30,000	25,000	30,000	30,000
Quantity of vanity plates	6,000	6,000	16,000	16,000

a. Use the available data to identify some points on the demand curve for vanity plates and connect the points to draw a demand curve. Don't forget *ceteris paribus.*

b. Suppose the demand curve is linear. If your state sets a price of $50, how many vanity plates would be purchased?

1.8 **Youth Smoking.** Use a demand and supply graph of the youth smoking market to show the effects of the tax cut in eastern Canada. Assume that the initial price is $6.00, the initial quantity is 100 units, and each youth smoker smokes 5 cigarettes per day. (Related to Application 1 on page 71.)

4.2 The Supply Curve

2.1 Arrow up or down: According to the law of supply, an increase in price _____ the quantity supplied.

2.2 From the following list, choose the variables that are held fixed when drawing a market supply curve:
- The price of the product
- Wages paid to workers
- The price of materials used in production
- Taxes paid by producers
- The quantity of the product purchased

2.3 The minimum supply price is the _____ price at which a product is supplied.

2.4 The market supply curve is the (horizontal/vertical) sum of the individual supply curves.

2.5 A change in price causes movement along a supply curve and a change in _____.

2.6 Arrows up or down: In the 1990s, the world price of wool _____ and the quantity of wool supplied _____. (Related to Application 2 on page 76.)

2.7 **Marginal Cost of Housing.** When the price of a standard three-bedroom house increases from $150,000 to $160,000, a building company increases its output from 20 houses per year to 21 houses per year. What does the increase in the quantity of housing reveal about the cost of producing housing?

2.8 **Imports and Market Supply.** Two nations supply sugar to the world market. Lowland has a minimum supply price of 10 cents per pound, while Highland has a minimum supply price of 24 cents per pound. For each nation, the slope of the supply curve is 1 cent per million pounds.
a. Draw the individual supply curves and the market supply curve. At what price and quantity is the supply curve kinked?
b. The market quantity supplied at a price of 15 cents is _____ million pounds. The market quantity supplied at a price of 30 cents is _____ million pounds.

2.9 **Responses to Higher Soybean Prices.** Suppose that in initial equilibrium in the soybean market, each of the 1,000 farmers produces 50 units, for a total of 50,000 units of soybeans. Suppose the price of soybeans increases, and everyone expects the price to stay at the higher level for many years.
a. Arrows up or down: Over a period of several years, we expect the quantity of soybeans supplied to _____ as the number of soybean farmers _____ and the output per farmer _____.
b. A farmer who enters the market is likely to have a (higher/lower) marginal cost of production than an original firm.

2.10 **Response to Lower Wool Price.** Use a demand and supply graph of the wool market to show the effects of the decrease in the price of wool on the quantity supplied in New Zealand. Assume that the initial price is $20 per unit and the initial quantity is 100 units. Also assume that for each 1 percent decrease in price, the quantity supplied decreases by 1 percent. (Related to Application 2 on page 76.)

ECONOMIC EXPERIMENT

MARKET EQUILIBRIUM

This simple experiment takes about 20 minutes. We start by dividing the class into two equal groups: consumers and producers.

- The instructor provides each consumer with a number indicating the maximum amount he or she is willing to pay (WTP) for a bushel of apples: The WTP is a number between $1 and $100. Each consumer has the opportunity to buy one bushel of apples per trading period. The consumer's score for a single trading period equals the gap between the WTP and the price actually paid for apples. For example, if the consumer's WTP is $80 and he or she pays $30 for apples, the consumer's score is $50. Each consumer has the option of not buying apples. This will be sensible if the best price the consumer can get exceeds the WTP. If the consumer does not buy apples, his or her score will be zero.

- The instructor provides each producer with a number indicating the cost of producing a bushel of apples (a number between $1 and $100). Each producer has the opportunity to sell one bushel per trading period. The producer's score for a single trading period equals the gap between the selling prices and the cost of producing apples. So if a producer sells apples for $20, and the cost is

only $15, the producer's score is $5. Producers have the option of not selling apples, which is sensible if the best price the producer can get is less than the cost. If the producer does not sell apples, his or her score is zero.

Once everyone understands the rules, consumers and producers meet in a trading area to arrange transactions. A consumer may announce how much he or she is willing to pay for apples and wait for a producer to agree to sell apples at that price. Alternatively, a producer may announce how much he or she is willing accept for apples and wait for a consumer to agree to buy apples at that price. Once a transaction has been arranged, the consumer and producer inform the instructor of the trade, record the transaction, and leave the trading area.

Several trading periods are conducted, each of which lasts a few minutes. After the end of each trading period, the instructor lists the prices at which apples sold during the period. Then another trading period starts, providing consumers and producers another opportunity to buy or sell apples. After all the trading periods have been completed, each participant computes his or her score by adding the scores from the trading periods.

MyEconLab
For additional economic experiments, please visit www.myeconlab.com.

In addition, some chapters contain an Economic Experiment section that gives students the opportunity to do their own economic analysis.

▶ WHY FIVE KEY PRINCIPLES?

In Chapter 2, "The Key Principles of Economics," we introduce the following five key principles and then apply them throughout the book:

1. **The Principle of Opportunity Cost.** The opportunity cost of something is what you sacrifice to get it.

2. **The Marginal Principle.** Increase the level of an activity as long as its marginal benefit exceeds its marginal cost. Choose the level at which the marginal benefit equals the marginal cost.

3. **The Principle of Voluntary Exchange.** A voluntary exchange between two people makes both people better off.

4. **The Principle of Diminishing Returns.** If we increase one input while holding the other inputs fixed, output will increase, but at a decreasing rate.

5. **The Real-Nominal Principle.** What matters to people is the real value of money or income—its purchasing power—not the face value of money or income.

This approach of repeating five key principles gives students the big picture—the framework of economic reasoning. We make the key concepts unforgettable by using them repeatedly, illustrating them with intriguing examples, and giving students many opportunities to practice what they've learned. Throughout the text, economic concepts are connected to the five key principles when the following callout is provided for each principle:

PRINCIPLE OF OPPORTUNITY COST
The opportunity cost of something is what you sacrifice to get it.

▶ HOW IS THE BOOK ORGANIZED?

Chapter 1, "Introduction: What Is Economics?" uses three current policy issues—traffic congestion, poverty in Africa, and Japan's prolonged recession—to explain the economic way of thinking. Chapter 2, "The Key Principles of Economics," introduces the five principles we return to throughout the book. Chapter 3, "Exchange and Markets," is devoted entirely to exchange and trade. We discuss the fundamental rationale for exchange and introduce some of the institutions modern societies developed to facilitate trade.

Students need to have a solid understanding of demand and supply to be successful in the course. Many students have difficulty understanding movement along a curve versus shifts of a curve. To address this difficulty, we developed an innovative way to organize topics in Chapter 4, "Demand, Supply, and Market Equilibrium." We examine the law of demand and changes in quantity demanded, the law of supply and changes in quantity supplied, and then the notion of market equilibrium. After students have a firm grasp of equilibrium concepts, we explore the effects of changes in demand and supply on equilibrium prices and quantities.

Part 2, "A Closer Look at Demand and Supply," (Chapters 5 through 7), provides a closer look at demand and supply, including elasticity, market efficiency, and consumer choice. Part 3, "Market Structures and Pricing" (Chapters 8 through 13), starts with a discussion of production and costs, setting the stage for an examination of alternative market structures, including the extremes of perfect competition and monopoly, as well as the middle ground of monopolistic competition and oligopoly. The last chapter in Part 3 discusses antitrust policy and deregulation. Part 4, "Externalities and Information" (Chapters 14 through 16), discusses the circumstances under which markets break down, including imperfect information, public goods, and environmental degradation.

Part 5, "The Labor Market and Income Distribution" (Chapter 17), explores the labor market, unions, poverty, discrimination, and the distribution of income. Part 6, "The International Economy" (Chapter 18), covers trade and public policy.

▶ MyEconLab

Both the text and supplement package provide ways for instructors and students to assess their knowledge and progress through the course. MyEconLab, the new standard in personalized online learning, is a key part of O'Sullivan, Sheffrin, and Perez's integrated learning package for the eighth edition.

For the Instructor

MyEconLab is an online course management, testing, and tutorial resource. Instructors can choose how much or how little time to spend setting up and using MyEconLab. Each chapter contains two Sample Tests, Study Plan Exercises, and Tutorial Resources. The online Gradebook records each student's performance and time spent on the Tests and Study Plan and generates reports by student or by chapter. Instructors can assign tests, quizzes, and homework in MyEconLab using four resources:

- Preloaded Sample Test questions
- Problems similar to the end-of-chapter exercises
- Test Bank questions
- Self-authored questions using the Econ Exercise Builder

Exercises use multiple-choice, graph drawing, and free-response items, many of which are generated algorithmically so that each time a student works them, a different variation is presented. MyEconLab grades each of these problem types, even those with graphs. When working homework exercises, students receive immediate feedback with links to additional learning tools.

For the Student

MyEconLab puts students in control of their learning through a collection of tests, practice, and study tools tied to the online, interactive version of the textbook, and other media resources. Within MyEconLab's structured environment, students practice what they learn, test their understanding, and pursue a personalized Study Plan generated from their performance on Sample Tests and tests set by their instructors. At the core of MyEconLab are the following features:

- Sample Tests, two per chapter
- Personal Study Plan
- Tutorial Instruction
- Graphing Tool

Sample Tests Two Sample Tests for each chapter are preloaded in MyEconLab, enabling students to practice what they have learned, test their understanding, and identify areas in which they need further work. Students can study on their own, or they can complete assignments created by their instructor.

Personal Study Plan Based on a student's performance on tests, MyEconLab generates a personal Study Plan that shows where the student needs further study. The Study Plan consists of a series of additional practice exercises with detailed feedback and guided solutions that are keyed to other tutorial resources.

Tutorial Instruction Launched from many of the exercises in the Study Plan, MyEconLab provides tutorial instruction in the form of step-by-step solutions and other media-based explanations.

Graphing Tool A graphing tool is integrated into the Tests and Study Plan exercises to enable students to make and manipulate graphs. This feature helps students understand how concepts, numbers, and graphs connect.

Additional MyEconLab Tools MyEconLab includes the following additional features:

1. **Weekly News Update—** This feature provides weekly updates during the school year of news items with links to sources for further reading and discussion questions.

2. **eText—** While students are working in the Study Plan or completing homework assignments, part of the tutorial resources available is a direct link to the relevant page of the text so that students can review the appropriate material to help them complete the exercise.

3. **Glossary Flashcards—** Every key term is available as a flashcard, allowing students to quiz themselves on vocabulary from one or more chapters at a time.

Real-Time Data Analysis

New real-time data exercises that students can complete on MyEconLab.

 Real-Time Data Analysis Exercises allow instructors to assign problems which use up-to-the-minute data. Each RTDA exercise loads the appropriate and most currently available data from FRED®, a comprehensive and

up-to-date data set maintained by the Federal Reserve Bank of St. Louis. Exercises are graded based on that instance of data, and feedback is provided.

In the eText available in MyEconLab, select figures labeled MyEconLab Real-Time Data can upon student direction display a pop-up graph updated with real-time data from FRED.

MyEconLab content has been created over the years through the efforts of Charles Baum, Middle Tennessee State University; Peggy Dalton, Frostburg State University; Sarah Ghosh, University of Scranton; Russell Kellogg, University of Colorado, Denver; Bert G. Wheeler, Cedarville University; and Douglas A. Ruby, Noel Lotz, and Courtney Kamauf, Pearson Education.

▶ WHAT INSTRUCTOR'S SUPPLEMENTS DID WE DEVELOP?

A fully integrated teaching and learning package is necessary for today's classroom. Our supplement package helps you provide new and interesting real-world Applications and assess student understanding of economics. The supplements are coordinated with the main text through the numbering system of the headings in each section. The major sections of the chapters are numbered (1.1, 1.2, 1.3, and so on), and that numbering system is used consistently in the supplements to make it convenient and flexible for instructors to develop assignments.

Two Test Banks

There are two test banks for *Microeconomics*. Each test bank offers multiple-choice, true/false, and short-answer questions. The questions are referenced by topic and are presented in sequential order. Each question is keyed by degree of difficulty, with questions ranging on a scale of one to three. Easy questions involve straightforward recall of information in the text. Moderate questions require some analysis on the student's part. Difficult questions usually entail more complex analysis and may require the student to go one step further than the material presented in the text. Questions are also classified as *fact, definition, conceptual,* and *analytical*. Fact questions test the student's knowledge of factual information presented in the text. Definition questions ask the student to define an economic concept. Conceptual questions test the student's understanding of a concept. Analytical questions require the student to apply an analytical procedure to answer the question.

The test banks include tables and a series of questions asking students to solve for numeric values, such as profit or equilibrium output. There are also numerous questions based on graphs: Several questions ask students to interpret data presented in a graph, draw a graph on their own, and answer related questions.

In each chapter there are several questions that support the Applications in the main book. There are also new questions to support the updated and new content in the main book.

The Association to Advance Collegiate Schools of Business (AACSB) The authors of the test banks have connected questions to the general knowledge and skill guidelines found in the AACSB assurance of learning standards.

What Is the AACSB? AACSB is a not-for-profit corporation of educational institutions, corporations, and other organizations devoted to the promotion and improvement of higher education in business administration and accounting. A collegiate institution offering degrees in business administration or accounting may volunteer for AACSB accreditation review. The AACSB makes initial accreditation decisions and conducts periodic reviews to promote continuous quality improvement in management education. Pearson Education is a proud member of the AACSB and is pleased to provide advice to help you apply AACSB assurance of learning standards.

What Are AACSB Assurance of Learning Standards? One of the criteria for AACSB accreditation is quality of the curricula. Although no specific courses are required, the AACSB expects a curriculum to include learning experiences in the following areas:

- Communication
- Ethical Reasoning
- Analytic Skills
- Use of Information Technology
- Multiculturalism and Diversity
- Reflective Thinking

Questions that test skills relevant to these guidelines are appropriately tagged. For example, a question testing the moral questions associated with externalities would receive the Ethical Reasoning tag.

How Can Instructors Use the AACSB Tags? Tagged questions help you measure whether students are grasping the course content that aligns with the AACSB guidelines noted. In addition, the tagged questions may help instructors identify potential applications of these skills. This in turn may suggest enrichment activities or other educational experiences to help students achieve these skills.

For Microeconomics . . . Test Bank 1, prepared by Randy Methenitis of Richland College, includes approximately 3,000 multiple-choice, true/false, short-answer, and graphing questions. Test Bank 2, prepared by Robert Shoffner III of Central Piedmont Community College, contains over 2,000 multiple-choice, true/false, and short-answer questions. Both test banks are available in a computerized format using TestGen, test-generating software.

TestGen

Microeconomics test banks 1 and 2 appear in print and as computer files that may be used with TestGen test-generating software. This test-generating program permits instructors to edit, add, or delete questions from the test bank; analyze test results; and organize a database of tests and student results. This software allows for flexibility and ease of use.

It provides many options for organizing and displaying tests, along with a search and sort feature.

Instructor's Resource Manual

The instructor's resource manual, revised by Jeff Phillips of Colby-Sawyer College, follows the textbook's organization, incorporating extra Applications questions. The manual also provides detailed outlines (suitable for use as lecture notes) and solutions to all questions in the textbook. The instructor's resource manual is also designed to help the instructor incorporate applicable elements of the supplement package. The instructor's resource manual contains the following for each chapter:

- Summary: a bulleted list of key topics in the chapter
- Approaching the Material: student-friendly examples to introduce the chapter
- Chapter Outline: summary of definitions and concepts
- Teaching Tips on how to encourage class participation
- Summary and discussion points for the Applications in the main text
- New Applications and discussion questions
- Solutions to all end-of-chapter exercises

The instructor's resource manual is also available for download from the Instructor's Resource Center.

PowerPoint® Presentations

Three sets of PowerPoint slides are available for download from the Instructor's Resource Center at **www.pearsonhighered.com/irc**.

1. A comprehensive set of PowerPoint slides that can be used by instructors for class presentations. These PowerPoints, prepared by Brock Williams of Metropolitan Community College, include all the graphs, tables, and equations in the textbook, as well as lecture notes that outline the chapter.

2. A comprehensive set of PowerPoint slides with Classroom Response Systems (CRS) questions built in so that instructors can incorporate CRS "clickers" into their classroom lectures. This presentation is also prepared by Brock Williams of Metropolitan Community College. For more information on Pearson's partnership with CRS, see the following description. Instructors may download these PowerPoint presentations from the Instructor's Resource Center (www.pearsonhighered.com/irc).

3. A PDF version of the PowerPoint slides is also available as PDF files from the Instructor's Resource Center. This version of the PowerPoint slides can be printed and used in class.

Instructor's Resource Center on CD-ROM

The test banks, TestGen files, instructor's resource manuals, and PowerPoint slides are also available on this CD-ROM. Faculty can pick and choose from the various supplements and export them to their hard drive.

CourseSmart

The CourseSmart eTextbook for the text is available through **www.coursesmart.com**. CourseSmart goes beyond traditional expectations, providing instant, online access to the textbooks and course materials you need at a lower cost to students. And, even as students save money, you can save time and hassle with a digital textbook that allows you to search the most relevant content at the very moment you need it. Whether it's evaluating textbooks or creating lecture notes to help students with difficult concepts, CourseSmart can make life a little easier. See how when you visit www. coursesmart.com/instructors.

Instructor's Resource Center Online

This password-protected site is accessible from **www.pearsonshighered.com/irc** and hosts all of the resources previously listed: test banks, TestGen files, instructor's resource manuals, and PowerPoint slides. Instructors can click on the "Help downloading Instructor Resources" link for easy-to-follow instructions on getting access or contact their sales representative for further information.

Classroom Response Systems

Classroom Response Systems (CRS) is an exciting new wireless polling technology that makes large and small classrooms even more interactive because it enables instructors to pose questions to their students, record results, and display those results instantly. Students can answer questions easily using compact remote-control transmitters. Pearson has partnerships with leading CRS providers and can show you everything you need to know about setting up and using a CRS system. We'll provide the classroom hardware, text-specific PowerPoint slides, software, and support, and we'll also show you how your students can benefit! Learn more at **www.pearsonshighered.com/elearning**.

▶ WHAT STUDENT SUPPLEMENTS DID WE DEVELOP?

To accommodate different learning styles and busy student lifestyles, we provide a variety of print and online supplements.

Study Guide

The study guide, created by David Eaton of Murray State University, reinforces economic concepts and Applications from the main book and helps students assess their learning. Each chapter of the study guide includes the following features:

- Chapter Summary: Provides a summary of the chapter, key term definitions, and review of the Applications from the main book.
- Study Tip: Provides students with tips on understanding key concepts.

- Key Equations: Alerts students to equations they are likely to see throughout the class.
- Caution!: Alerts students to potential pitfalls and key figures or tables that deserve special attention.
- Activity: Encourages students to think creatively about an economic problem. An answer is provided so students can check their work.
- Practice Test: Includes approximately 25 multiple-choice and short-answer questions that help students test their knowledge. Select questions include a graph or table for students to analyze. Some of these questions support the Applications in the main book.
- Solutions to the practice test.

The student study guide is available as an additional resource in the MyEconLab course discussed earlier.

▶ REVIEWERS

A long road exists between the initial vision of an innovative principles text and the final product. Along our journey we participated in a structured process to reach our goal. We wish to acknowledge the assistance of the many people who participated in this process.

▶ REVIEWERS OF THE CURRENT EDITION

The guidance and recommendations from the following professors helped us develop the revision plans for this new edition:

Arizona

BASIL AL-HASHIMI, *Mesa Community College, Red Mountain*

Connecticut

STEPHEN RUBB, *Sacred Heart University*

Indiana

ROBERT B. HARRIS, *Indiana Univ. Purdue Univ. Indianapolis*

Minnesota

IHSUAN LI, *Minnesota State University, Mankato*

Mississippi

BILLY L. CARSON II, *Itawamba Community College*

Nebraska

DEBBIE GASPARD, *Southeast Community College*
BROCK WILLIAMS, *Metropolitan Community College*

North Carolina

JULIANNE TREME, *University of North Carolina, Wilmington*

Ohio

Kenneth C. Fah, *Ohio Dominican University*

Washington

Charles S. Wassell, Jr., *Central Washington University*

Colombia

Michael Jetter,

▶ REVIEWERS OF PREVIOUS EDITIONS

We benefited from the assistance of many dedicated professors who reviewed all or parts of previous editions in various stages of development:

Alabama

Jim Payne, *Calhoun Community College*
James Swofford, *University of South Alabama*

Alaska

Paul Johnson, *University of Alaska, Anchorage*

Arizona

Pete Mavrokordatos, *Tarrant County College/University of Phoenix*
Evan Tanner, *Thunderbird, The American Graduate School of International Management*
Donald Wells, *University of Arizona*

California

Antonio Avalos, *California State University, Fresno*
Collette Barr, *Santa Barbara Community College*
T. J. Bettner, *Orange Coast College*
Peter Boelman-Lopez, *Riverside Community College*
Matthew Brown, *Santa Clara University*
Jim Cobb, *Orange Coast College*
John Constantine, *Sacramento City College*
Peggy Crane, *San Diego State University*
Albert B. Culver, *California State University, Chico*
Jose L. Esteban, *Palomar College*
Gilbert Fernandez, *Santa Rosa Junior College*
E. B. Gendel, *Woodbury University*
Charles W. Haase, *San Francisco State University*
John Henry, *California State University, Sacramento*
George Jensen, *California State University, Los Angeles*
Janis Kea, *West Valley College*
Rose Kilburn, *Modesto Junior College*
Philip King, *San Francisco State University*
Anthony Lima, *California State University, Hayward*
Bret McMurran, *Chaffey College*
Jon J. Nadenichek, *California State University, Northridge*
Alex Obiya, *San Diego City College*
Jack W. Osman, *San Francisco State University*
Jay Patyk, *Foothill College*

Stephen Perez, *California State University, Sacramento*
Ratha Ramoo, *Diablo Valley College*
Greg Rose, *Sacramento City College*
Kurt Schwabe, *University of California, Riverside*
Terri Sexton, *California State University, Sacramento*
David Simon, *Santa Rosa Junior College*
Xiaochuan Song, *San Diego Mesa College*
Ed Sorensen, *San Francisco State University*
Susan Spencer, *Santa Rosa Junior College*
Linda Stoh, *Sacramento City College*
Rodney Swanson, *University of California, Los Angeles*
Daniel Villegas, *California Polytechnic State University*

Colorado

Steve Call, *Metropolitan State College of Denver*

Connecticut

John A. Jascot, *Capital Community Technical College*

Delaware

Lawrence Stelmach, *Delaware Valley College*

Florida

Irma de Alonso, *Florida International University*
Jay Bhattacharya, *Okaloosa-Walton Community College*
Edward Bierhanzl, *Florida A&M University*
Eric P. Chiang, *Florida Atlantic University*
Martine Duchatelet, *Barry University*
George Greenlee, *St. Petersburg College, Clearwater*
Martin Markovich, *Florida A&M University*
Thomas McCaleb, *Florida State University*
Barbara Moore, *University of Central Florida*
Stephen Morrell, *Barry University*
Carl Schmertmann, *Florida State University*
Garvin Smith, *Daytona Beach Community College*
Noel Smith, *Palm Beach Community College*
Michael Vierk, *Florida International University*
Joseph Ward, *Broward Community College, Central*
Virginia York, *Gulf Coast Community College*
Andrea Zanter, *Hillsborough Community College*

Georgia

Scott Beaulier, *Mercer College*
Ashley Harmon, *Southeastern Technical College*
Steven F. Koch, *Georgia Southern University*
L. Wayne Plumly, Jr., *Valdosta State University*
Greg Trandel, *University of Georgia*

Hawaii

Barbara Ross-Pfeiffer, *Kapiolani Community College*

Idaho

Charles Scott Benson, Jr., *Idaho State University*
Tesa Stegner, *Idaho State University*

Illinois

Diane Anstine, *North Central College*
Rosa Lea Danielson, *College of DuPage*

Sel Dibooglu, *Southern Illinois University*
Linda Ghent, *Eastern Illinois University*
Gary Langer, *Roosevelt University*
Nampeang Pingkarawat, *Chicago State University*
Dennis Shannon, *Belleville Area College*
Chuck Sicotte, *Rock Valley College*

Indiana

John L. Conant, *Indiana State University*
Mousumi Duttaray, *Indiana State University*
James T. Kyle, *Indiana State University*
Virginia Shingleton, *Valparaiso University*

Iowa

Dale Borman, *Kirkwood Community College*
Jonathan O. Ikoba, *Scott Community College*
Saul Mekies, *Kirkwood Community College, Iowa City*

Kansas

Carl Parker, *Fort Hays State University*
James Ragan, *Kansas State University*
Tracy M. Turner, *Kansas State University*

Kentucky

David Eaton, *Murray State University*
John Robertson, *University of Kentucky*

Louisiana

John Payne Bigelow, *Louisiana State University*
Sang Lee, *Southeastern Louisiana University*
Richard Stahl, *Louisiana State University*

Maine

George Schatz, *Maine Maritime Academy*

Maryland

Carey Borkoski, *Anne Arundel Community College*
Gretchen Mester, *Anne Arundel Community College*
Irvin Weintraub, *Towson State University*

Massachusetts

Hans Despain, *Nichols College*
Brian Deuriarte, *Middlesex Community College*
Dan Georgianna, *University of Massachusetts, Dartmouth*
James E. Hartley, *Mount Holyoke College*
Marlene Kim, *University of Massachusetts, Boston*
Mark Siegler, *Williams College*
Gilbert Wolfe, *Middlesex Community College*

Michigan

Christine Amsler, *Michigan State University*
Bharati Basu, *Central Michigan University*
Norman Cure, *Macomb Community College*
Susan Linz, *Michigan State University*
Scanlon Romer, *Delta College*
Robert Tansky, *St. Clair County Community College*
Wendy Wysocki, *Monroe Community College*

Minnesota

Mike Mcilhon, *Augsburg College*
Richard Milani, *Hibbing Community College*

Mississippi

Arlena Sullivan, *Jones County Junior College*

Missouri

Duane Eberhardt, *Missouri Southern State College*
David Gillette, *Truman State University*
Brad Hoppes, *Southwest Missouri State University*
Denise Kummer, *St. Louis Community College*
Steven M. Schamber, *St. Louis Community College, Meramec*
Elias Shukralla, *St. Louis Community College, Meramec*
Keith Ulrich, *Valencia Community College*
George Wasson, *St. Louis Community College, Meramec*

Nebraska

Theodore Larsen, *University of Nebraska, Kearney*
Timothy R. Mittan, *Southeast Community College*
Stanley J. Peters, *Southeast Community College*
Brock Williams, *Metropolitan Community College*

Nevada

Stephen Miller, *University of Nevada, Las Vegas*
Charles Okeke, *College of Southern Nevada*

New Jersey

Len Anyanwu, *Union County College*
Richard Comerford, *Bergen Community College*
John Graham, *Rutgers University*
Paul C. Harris, Jr., *Camden County College*
Calvin Hoy, *County College of Morris*
Taghi Ramin, *William Paterson University*
Brian de Uriarte, *Middlesex County College*

New Hampshire

Jeff Phillips, *Colby-Sawyer College*

New Mexico

Carl Enomoto, *New Mexico State University*

New York

Farhad Ameen, *State University of New York, Westchester County Community College*
Karijit K. Arora, *Le Moyne College*
Alex Azarchs, *Pace University*
Kathleen K. Bromley, *Monroe Community College*
Barbara Connelly, *Westchester Community College*
George Frost, *Suffolk County Community College*
Susan Glanz, *St. John's University*
Serge S. Grushchin, *ASA College of Advanced Technology*
Robert Herman, *Nassau Community College*
Christopher Inya, *Monroe Community College*
Marie Kratochvil, *Nassau Community College*
Marianne Lowery, *Erie Community College*

JEANNETTE MITCHELL, *Rochester Institute of Technology*
TED MUZIO, *St. John's University*
GRAY ORPHEE, *Rockland County Community College*
CRAIG ROGERS, *Canisius College*
FRED TYLER, *Fordham University*
EZGI UZEL, *SUNY-Maritime*
MICHAEL VARDANYAN, *Binghamton University*

North Carolina

KATIE CANTY, *Cape Fear Community College*
LEE CRAIG, *North Carolina State University*
HOSSEIN GHOLAMI, *Fayetteville Technical Community College*
MICHAEL G. GOODE, *Central Piedmont Community College*
CHARLES M. OLDHAM, JR., *Fayetteville Technical Community College*
RANDALL PARKER, *East Carolina University*
DIANE TYNDALL, *Craven Community College*
CHESTER WATERS, *Durham Technical Community College*
JAMES WHEELER, *North Carolina State University*

North Dakota

SCOTT BLOOM, *North Dakota State University*

Ohio

FATMA ABDEL-RAOUF, *Cleveland State University*
JEFF ANKROM, *Wittenberg University*
ERWIN EHRARDT, *University of Cincinnati*
KEN FAH, *Ohio Dominican University*
TAGHI T. KERMANI, *Youngstown State University*
DANDAN LIU, *Kent State University*

Oklahoma

JEFF HOLT, *Tulsa Community College*
MARTY LUDLUM, *Oklahoma City Community College*
DAN RICKMAN, *Oklahoma State University*

Oregon

TOM CARROLL, *Central Oregon Community College*
JIM EDEN, *Portland Community College*
JOHN FARRELL, *Oregon State University*
DAVID FIGLIO, *University of Oregon*
RANDY R. GRANT, *Linfield College*
LARRY SINGELL, *University of Oregon*

Pennsylvania

KEVIN A. BAIRD, *Montgomery County Community College*
CHARLES BEEM, *Bucks County Community College*
ED COULSON, *Pennsylvania State University*
TAHANY NAGGAR, *West Chester University*
ABDULWAHAB SRAIHEEN, *Kutztown University*

South Carolina

DONALD BALCH, *University of South Carolina*
CALVIN BLACKWELL, *College of Charleston*
JANICE BOUCHER BREUER, *University of South Carolina*
BILL CLIFFORD, *Trident Technical College*

FRANK GARLAND, *Tri-County Technical College*
CHARLOTTE DENISE HIXSON, *Midlands Technical College*
WOODROW W. HUGHES, JR., *Converse College*
MIREN IVANKOVIC, *Southern Wesleyan University*
CHIRINJEV PETERSON, *Greenville Technical College*
GARY STONE, *Winthrop University*
DENISE TURNAGE, *Midlands Technical College*
CHAD TURNER, *Clemson University*

South Dakota

JOSEPH SANTOS, *South Dakota State University*

Tennessee

CINDY ALEXANDER, *Pellissippi State University*
NIRMALENDU DEBNATH, *Lane College*
QUENTON PULLIAM, *Nashville State Technical College*
ROSE RUBIN, *University of Memphis*
THURSTON SCHRADER, *Southwest Tennessee Community College*

Texas

RASHID AL-HMOUD, *Texas Technical University*
MAHAMUDU BAWUMIA, *Baylor University*
STEVEN BECKHAM, *Amarillo College*
OMAR BELAZI, *Midland College*
JACK BUCCO, *Austin Community College*
CINDY CANNON, *North Harris College*
DAVID L. COBERLY, *Southwest Texas State University*
ED COHN, *Del Mar College*
DEAN DRAINEY, *St. Phillips College*
MICHAEL I. DUKE, *Blinn College*
GHAZI DUWAJI, *University of Texas, Arlington*
HARRY ELLIS, *University of North Texas*
S. AUN HASSAN, *Texas Tech University*
THOMAS JEITSCHKO, *Texas A&M University*
DELORES LINTON, *Tarrant County Community College, Northwest*
JESSICA MCCRAW, *University of Texas, Arlington*
RANDY METHENITIS, *Richland College*
WILLIAM NEILSON, *Texas A&M University*
MICHAEL NELSON, *Texas A&M University*
RHEY NOLAN, *Tyler Junior College*
PAUL OKELLO, *University of Texas, Arlington*
JOSHUA PICKRELL, *South Plains College*
JOHN PISCIOTTA, *Baylor University*
JOHN RYKOWSKI, *Kalamazoo Valley Community College*
DAVE SHORROW, *Richland College*
STEVE SCHWIFF, *Texas A&M University, Commerce*
JAMES R. VANBEEK, *Blinn College*
INSKE ZANDVLIET, *Brookhaven College*

Utah

REED GOOCH, *Utah Valley University*
ALI HEKMAT, *College of Eastern Utah*
GLENN LOWELL, *Utah Valley University*

Virginia

JAMES BRUMBAUGH, *Lord Fairfax Community College, Middleton Campus*
BRUCE BRUNTON, *James Madison University*
MICHAEL G. HESLOP, *North Virginia Community College*
GEORGE HOFFER, *Virginia Commonwealth University*
MELANIE MARKS, *Longwood College*
THOMAS J. MEEKS, *Virginia State University*
JOHN MIN, *Northern Virginia Community College, Alexandria*
SHANNON K. MITCHELL, *Virginia Commonwealth University*
BILL REESE, *Tidewater Community College, Virginia Beach*

Washington

WILLIAM HALLAGAN, *Washington State University*
MARK WYLIE, *Spokane Falls Community College*

Australia

HAK YOUN KIM, *Monash University*

► CLASS TESTERS

A special acknowledgment goes to the instructors who were willing to class-test drafts of early editions in different stages of development. They provided us with instant feedback on parts that worked and parts that needed changes:

SHERYL BALL, *Virginia Polytechnic Institute and State University*
JOHN CONSTANTINE, *University of California, Davis*
JOHN FARRELL, *Oregon State University*
JAMES HARTLEY, *Mt. Holyoke College*
KAILASH KHANDKE, *Furman College*
PETER LINDERT, *University of California, Davis*
LOUIS MAKOWSKI, *University of California, Davis*
BARBARA ROSS-PFEIFFER, *Kapiolani Community College*

► FOCUS GROUPS

We want to thank the participants who took part in the focus groups for the first and second editions; they helped us see the manuscript from a fresh perspective:

CARLOS AQUILAR, *El Paso Community College*
JIM BRADLEY, *University of South Carolina*
THOMAS COLLUM, *Northeastern Illinois University*
DAVID CRAIG, *Westark College*
JEFF HOLT, *Tulsa Junior College*
THOMAS JEITSCHKO, *Texas A&M University*
GARY LANGER, *Roosevelt University*
MARK McLEOD, *Virginia Polytechnic Institute and State University*
TOM McKINNON, *University of Arkansas*
AMY MEYERS, *Parkland Community College*
HASSAN MOHAMMADI, *Illinois State University*
JOHN MORGAN, *College of Charleston*

NORM PAUL, *San Jacinto Community College*
NAMPEANG PINGKARATWAT, *Chicago State University*
SCANLAN ROMER, *Delta Community College*
BARBARA ROSS-PFEIFFER, *Kapiolani Community College*
ZAHRA SADERION, *Houston Community College*
VIRGINIA SHINGLETON, *Valparaiso University*
JIM SWOFFORD, *University of South Alabama*
JANET WEST, *University of Nebraska, Omaha*
LINDA WILSON, *University of Texas, Arlington*
MICHAEL YOUNGBLOOD, *Rock Valley Community College*

► A WORLD OF THANKS . . .

We would also like to acknowledge the team of dedicated authors who contributed to the various ancillaries that accompany this book: Jeff Phillips of Colby-Sawyer College; David Eaton of Murray State University; Randy Methenitis of Richland College; Robert L. Shoffner III of Central Piedmont Community College; Brian Rosario of California State University, Sacramento; and Brock Williams of Metropolitan Community College.

For the eighth edition, Meredith Gertz was the senior production project manager who worked with Jacki Russell at GEX Publishing Services to turn our manuscript pages into a beautiful published book. Noel Seibert, senior acquisitions editor, and Carolyn Terbush, senior editorial project manager, guided the project and coordinated the schedules for the book and the extensive supplement package that accompanies the book. David Alexander, executive acquisitions editor, stepped in at the end to help wrap the project up and to support us and our users during the life of this edition.

From the start, Pearson provided us with first-class support and advice. Over the first seven editions, many people contributed to the project, including Leah Jewell, Rod Banister, P. J. Boardman, Marie McHale, Gladys Soto, Lisa Amato, Victoria Anderson, Cynthia Regan, Kathleen McLellan, Sharon Koch, David Theisen, Steve Deitmer, Christopher Bath, Ben Paris, Elisa Adams, Jodi Bolognese, David Alexander, Virginia Guariglia, and Lynne Breitfeller.

Last but not least, we must thank our families, who have seen us disappear, sometimes physically and other times mentally, to spend hours wrapped up in our own world of principles of economics. A project of this magnitude is very absorbing, and our families have been particularly supportive in this endeavor.

ARTHUR O'SULLIVAN

STEVEN SHEFFRIN

STEPHEN PEREZ

Introduction: What Is Economics?

Economics is the science of choice, exploring the choices made by individuals and organizations.

Over the last few centuries, these choices have led to substantial gains in the standard of living around the globe. In the United States, the typical person today has roughly seven times the income and purchasing power of a person 100 years ago. Our prosperity is the result of choices made by all sorts of people, including inventors, workers, entrepreneurs, and the people who saved money and loaned it to others to invest in machines and other tools of production. One reason we have prospered is greater efficiency: We have discovered better ways to use our resources—raw materials, time, and energy—to produce the goods and services we value.

As an illustration of changes in the standard of living and our growing prosperity, let's compare the way people listened to music in 1891 with how we listen today. You can buy an iPod shuffle® for $49 and fill it with 500 songs at $0.99 each. If you earn a wage of $15 per hour, it would take you about 36 hours of work to purchase and then fill an iPod. Back in 1891, the latest technological marvel was Thomas Edison's cylinder phonograph, which played music recorded on 4-inch cylinders. Imagine that you lived back then and wanted to get just as much music as you could fit on an iPod. Given the wages and prices in 1891, it would take you roughly 800 hours of work to earn enough money to buy the phonograph and all the cylinders. And if you wanted to keep your music with you, you would need 14 backpacks to carry the cylinders.

Although prosperity and efficiency are widespread, they are not universal. In some parts of the world, many people live in poverty. For example, in sub-Saharan Africa 388 million people—about half the population—live on less than $1.25 per day. And in all nations of the world, inefficiencies still exist, with valuable resources being wasted. For example, each year the typical urban commuter in the United States wastes more than 47 hours and $84 worth of gasoline trapped in rush hour traffic.

LEARNING OBJECTIVES

- List the three key economic questions.

- Discuss the insights from economics for a real-world problem such as congestion.

- List the four elements of the economic way of thinking.

- List three ways to use macroeconomics.

- List three ways to use microeconomics.

MyEconLab
MyEconLab helps you master each objective and study more efficiently.

*e*conomics provides a framework to diagnose all sorts of problems faced by society and then helps create and evaluate various proposals to solve them. Economics can help us develop strategies to replace poverty with prosperity, and to replace waste with efficiency. In this chapter, we explain what economics is and how we all can use economic analysis to think about practical problems and solutions.

1.1   What Is Economics?

Economists use the word **scarcity** to convey the idea that resources—the things we use to produce goods and services—are limited, while human wants are unlimited. Therefore, we cannot produce everything that everyone wants. As the old saying goes, you can't always get what you want. **Economics** studies the choices we make when there is scarcity; it is all about trade-offs. Here are some examples of scarcity and the trade-offs associated with making choices:

- You have a limited amount of time. If you take a part-time job, each hour on the job means one fewer hour for study or play.
- A city has a limited amount of land. If the city uses an acre of land for a park, it has one fewer acre for housing, retailers, or industry.
- You have limited income this year. If you spend $17 on a music CD, that's $17 fewer you have to spend on other products or to save.

People produce goods (music CDs, houses, and parks) and services (the advice of physicians and lawyers) by using one or more of the following five **factors of production**, also called *production inputs* or simply *resources*:

- **Natural resources** are provided by nature. Some examples are fertile land, mineral deposits, oil and gas deposits, and water. Some economists refer to all types of natural resources as *land*.
- **Labor** is the physical and mental effort people use to produce goods and services.
- **Physical capital** is the stock of equipment, machines, structures, and infrastructure that is used to produce goods and services. Some examples are forklifts, machine tools, computers, factories, airports, roads, and fiber-optic cables.
- **Human capital** is the knowledge and skills acquired by a worker through education and experience. Every job requires some human capital: To be a surgeon, you must learn anatomy and acquire surgical skills. To be an accountant, you must learn the rules of accounting and acquire computer skills. To be a musician, you must learn to play an instrument.
- **Entrepreneurship** is the effort used to coordinate the factors of production—natural resources, labor, physical capital, and human capital—to produce and sell products. An entrepreneur comes up with an idea for a product, decides how to produce it, and raises the funds to bring it to the market. Some examples of entrepreneurs are Bill Gates of Microsoft, Steve Jobs of Apple Computer, Howard Schultz of Starbucks, and Ray Kroc of McDonald's.

Given our limited resources, we make our choices in a variety of ways. Sometimes we make our decisions as individuals, and other times we participate in collective decision making, allowing the government and other organizations to choose for us. Many of our choices happen within *markets*, institutions or arrangements that enable us to buy and sell things. For example, most of us participate in the labor market, exchanging our time for money, and we all participate in consumer markets, exchanging money for food and clothing. But we make other choices outside

---

scarcity
The resources we use to produce goods and services are limited.

economics
The study of choices when there is scarcity.

factors of production
The resources used to produce goods and services; also known as *production inputs* or *resources*.

natural resources
Resources provided by nature and used to produce goods and services.

labor
Human effort, including both physical and mental effort, used to produce goods and services.

physical capital
The stock of equipment, machines, structures, and infrastructure that is used to produce goods and services.

human capital
The knowledge and skills acquired by a worker through education and experience and used to produce goods and services.

entrepreneurship
The effort used to coordinate the factors of production—natural resources, labor, physical capital, and human capital—to produce and sell products.

markets—from our personal decisions about everyday life to our political choices about matters that concern society as a whole. What unites all these decisions is the notion of scarcity: We can't have it all; there are trade-offs.

Economists are always reminding us that there is scarcity—there are trade-offs in everything we do. Suppose that in a conversation with your economics instructor you share your enthusiasm about an upcoming launch of the space shuttle. The economist may tell you that the resources used for the shuttle could have been used instead for an unmanned mission to Mars.

By introducing the notion of scarcity into your conversation, your instructor is simply reminding you that there are trade-offs, that one thing (a Mars mission) is sacrificed for another (a shuttle mission). Talking about alternatives is the first step in a process that can help us make better choices about how to use our resources. For example, we could compare the scientific benefits of a shuttle mission to the benefits of a Mars mission and choose the mission with the greater benefit.

Positive versus Normative Analysis

Economics doesn't tell us what to choose—shuttle mission or Mars mission—but simply helps us to understand the trade-offs. President Harry S. Truman once remarked,

> All my economists say, "On the one hand, . . . ; On the other hand, ..." Give me a one-handed economist!

An economist might say, "On the one hand, we could use a shuttle mission to do more experiments in the gravity-free environment of Earth's orbit; on the other hand, we could use a Mars mission to explore the possibility of life on other planets." In using both hands, the economist is not being evasive, but simply doing economics, discussing the alternative uses of our resources. The ultimate decision about how to use our resources—shuttle mission or Mars exploration—is the responsibility of citizens or their elected officials.

Most modern economics is based on **positive analysis**, which predicts the consequences of alternative actions by answering the question "What *is*?" or "What *will be*?" A second type of economic reasoning is normative in nature. **Normative analysis** answers the question "What *ought to be*?"

In Table 1.1, we compare positive questions to normative questions. Normative questions lie at the heart of policy debates. Economists contribute to policy debates by conducting positive analyses of the consequences of alternative actions. For example, an economist could predict the effects of an increase in the minimum wage on the number of people employed nationwide, the income of families with minimum-wage workers, and consumer prices. Armed with the conclusions of the economist's positive analysis, citizens and policymakers could then make a

positive analysis
Answers the question "What *is*?" or "What *will be*?"

normative analysis
Answers the question "What *ought to be*?"

TABLE 1.1 Comparing Positive and Normative Questions	
Positive Questions	**Normative Questions**
• If the government increases the minimum wage, how many workers will lose their jobs?	• Should the government increase the minimum wage?
• If two office-supply firms merge, will the price of office supplies increase?	• Should the government block the merger of two office-supply firms?
• How does a college education affect a person's productivity and earnings?	• Should the government subsidize a college education?
• How do consumers respond to a cut in income taxes?	• Should the government cut taxes to stimulate the economy?
• If a nation restricts shoe imports, who benefits and who bears the cost?	• Should the government restrict imports?

normative decision about whether to increase the minimum wage. Similarly, an economist could study the projects that could be funded with $1 billion in foreign aid, predicting the effects of each project on the income per person in an African country. Armed with this positive analysis, policymakers could then decide which projects to support.

Economists don't always reach the same conclusions in their positive analyses. The disagreements often concern the magnitude of a particular effect. For example, most economists agree that an increase in the minimum wage will cause unemployment, but disagree about how many people would lose their jobs. Similarly, economists agree that spending money to improve the education system in Africa will increase productivity and income, but disagree about the size of the increase in income.

The Three Key Economic Questions: What, How, and Who?

We make economic decisions at every level in society. Individuals decide what products to buy, what occupations to pursue, and how much money to save. Firms decide what goods and services to produce and how to produce them. Governments decide what projects and programs to complete and how to pay for them. The choices of individuals, firms, and governments answer three questions:

1 *What products do we produce?* Trade-offs exist: If a hospital uses its resources to perform more heart transplants, it has fewer resources to care for premature infants.

2 *How do we produce the products?* Alternative means of production are available: Power companies can produce electricity with coal, natural gas, or wind power. Professors can teach in large lecture halls or small classrooms.

3 *Who consumes the products?* We must decide how to distribute the products of society. If some people earn more money than others, should they consume more goods? How much money should the government take from the rich and give to the poor?

As we'll see later in the book, most of these decisions are made in markets, where prices play a key role in determining what products we produce, how we produce them, and who gets the products. In Chapter 3, we'll examine the role of markets in modern economies and the role of government in market-based economies.

Economic Models

economic model

A simplified representation of an economic environment, often employing a graph.

Economists use *economic models* to explore the choices people make and the consequences of those choices. An economic model is a simplified representation of an economic environment, with all but the essential features of the environment eliminated. An **economic model** is an abstraction from reality that enables us to focus our attention on what really matters. As we'll see throughout the book, most economic models use graphs to represent the economic environment.

To see the rationale for economic modeling, consider an architectural model. An architect builds a scale model of a new building and uses the model to show how the building will fit on a plot of land and blend with nearby buildings. The model shows the exterior features of the building, but not the interior features. We can ignore the interior features because they are unimportant for the task at hand—seeing how the building will fit into the local environment.

Economists build models to explore decision making by individuals, firms, and other organizations. For example, we can use a model of a profit-maximizing firm to predict how a firm will respond to increased competition. If a new car stereo store opens up in your town, will the old firms be passive and simply accept smaller market shares, or will they aggressively cut their prices to try to drive the new rival out of business? The model of the firm includes the monetary benefits and costs of doing business, and assumes that firms want to make as much money as possible. Although there may be other motives in the business world—to have fun or to help the world—the economic model ignores these other motives. The model focuses our attention on the profit motive and how it affects a firm's response to increased competition.

1.2 Economic Analysis and Modern Problems

Economic analysis provides important insights into real-world problems. To explain how we can use economic analysis in problem solving, we provide three examples. You'll see these examples again in more detail later in the book.

Economic View of Traffic Congestion

Consider first the problem of traffic congestion. According to the Texas Transportation Institute, the typical U.S. commuter wastes about 47 hours per year because of traffic congestion.[1] In some cities, the time wasted is much greater: 93 hours in Los Angeles, 72 hours in San Francisco, and 63 hours in Houston. In addition to time lost, we also waste 2.3 billion gallons of gasoline and diesel fuel each year.

To an economist, the diagnosis of the congestion problem is straightforward. When you drive onto a busy highway during rush hour, your car takes up space and decreases the distance between the vehicles on the highway. A driver's normal reaction to a shorter distance between moving cars is to slow down. So when you enter the highway, you force other commuters to slow down and thus spend more time on the highway. If each of your 900 fellow commuters spends just two extra seconds on the highway, you will increase the total travel time by 30 minutes. In deciding whether to use the highway, you will presumably ignore these costs you impose on others. Similarly, your fellow commuters ignore the cost they impose on you and others when they enter the highway. Because no single commuter pays the full cost (30 minutes), too many people use the highway, and everyone wastes time.

One possible solution to the congestion problem is to force people to pay for using the road, just as they pay for gasoline and tires. The government could impose a congestion tax of $8 per trip on rush-hour commuters and use a debit card system to collect the tax: Every time a car passes a checkpoint, a transponder would charge the commuter's card. Traffic volume during rush hours would then decrease as travelers (a) shift their travel to off-peak times, (b) switch to ride sharing and mass transit, and (c) shift their travel to less congested routes. The job for the economist is to compute the appropriate congestion tax and predict the consequences of imposing it.

Economic View of Poverty in Africa

Consider next the issue of poverty in Africa. In the final two decades of the twentieth century, the world economy grew rapidly, and the average per capita income (income per person) increased by about 35 percent. In contrast, the economies of poverty-stricken sub-Saharan Africa shrank, and per capita income *decreased* by about 6 percent. Africa is the world's second-largest continent in both area and population and accounts for more than 12 percent of the world's human population. Figure 1.1 shows a map of Africa. The countries of sub-Saharan Africa are highlighted in orange.

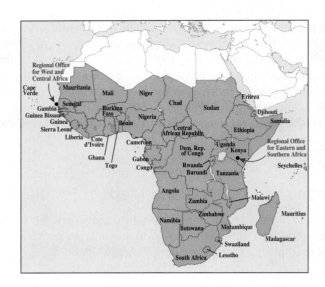

▲ **FIGURE 1.1**
Map of Africa
Africa is the world's second-largest continent in both area and population, and accounts for more than 12 percent of the world's human population. The countries of sub-Saharan Africa are highlighted in orange.
SOURCE: web.worldbank.org/WEBSITE/EXTERNAL/COUNTRIES/AFRICA

Economists have found that as a nation's economy grows, its poorest households share in the general prosperity.[2] Therefore, one way to reduce poverty in sub-Saharan Africa is to increase economic growth. Economic growth occurs when a country expands its production facilities (machinery and factories), improves its public infrastructure (highways and water systems), widens educational opportunities, and adopts new technology.

The recent experience of sub-Saharan Africa is somewhat puzzling because in the last few decades the region has expanded educational opportunities and received large amounts of foreign aid. Some recent work by economists on the sources of growth suggests that institutions such as the legal system and the regulatory environment also play key roles in economic growth.[3] In sub-Saharan Africa, a simple legal dispute about a small debt takes about 30 months to resolve, compared to 5 months in the United States. In Mozambique, it takes 174 days to complete the procedures required to set up a business, compared to just 2 days in Canada. In many cases, institutions impede rather than encourage the sort of investment and risk taking—called entrepreneurship—that causes economic growth and reduces poverty. As a consequence, economists and policymakers are exploring ways to reform the region's institutions. They are also challenged with choosing among development projects that will generate the biggest economic boost per dollar spent—the biggest bang per buck.

Economic View of the Current World Recession

Over the last several decades, the U.S. economy has performed well and has raised our standard of living. The general consensus was that our policymakers had learned to manage the economy effectively. Although the economy faltered at times, policymakers seemed to know how to restore growth and prosperity.

That is why the financial crisis and the recession that began in late 2007 has so shaken the confidence of people in the United States and around the world. The problems started innocently enough, with a booming market for homes that was fueled by easy credit from financial institutions. But we later discovered that many purchasers of homes and properties could not really afford them, and when many homeowners had trouble making their mortgage payments, the trouble spread to banks and other financial institutions. As a result, businesses found it increasingly difficult to borrow money for everyday use and investment, and economic activity around the world began to contract.

The major countries of the world have implemented aggressive policies to try to halt this downturn. Policymakers want to avoid the catastrophes that hit the global economy in the 1930s. Fortunately, they can draw on many years of experience in economic policy to guide the economy during this difficult time.

1.3   The Economic Way of Thinking

How do economists think about problems and decision making? The economic way of thinking is best summarized by British economist John Maynard Keynes (1883–1946):[4]

> The theory of economics does not furnish a body of settled conclusions immediately applicable to policy. It is a method rather than a doctrine, an apparatus of the mind, a technique of thinking which helps its possessor draw correct conclusions.

Let's look at the four elements of the economic way of thinking.

Use Assumptions to Simplify

Economists use assumptions to make things simpler and focus attention on what really matters. If you use a road map to plan a car trip from Seattle to San Francisco, you make two unrealistic assumptions to simplify your planning:

- The earth is flat: The flat road map doesn't show the curvature of the earth.
- The roads are flat: The standard road map doesn't show hills and valleys.

Instead of a map, you could use a globe that shows all the topographical features between Seattle and San Francisco, but you don't need those details to plan your trip. A map, with its unrealistic assumptions, will suffice because the curvature of the earth and the topography of the highways are irrelevant to your trip. Although your analysis is based on two unrealistic assumptions, that does not mean your analysis is invalid. Similarly, if economic analysis is based on unrealistic assumptions, that doesn't mean the analysis is faulty.

What if you decide to travel by bike instead of by automobile? Now the assumption of flat roads really matters, unless of course you are eager to pedal up and down mountains. If you use a standard map, and thus assume there are no mountains between the two cities, you may inadvertently pick a mountainous route instead of a flat one. In this case, the simplifying assumption makes a difference. The lesson is that we must think carefully about whether a simplifying assumption is truly harmless.

Isolate Variables—*Ceteris Paribus*

Economic analysis often involves *variables* and how they affect one another. A **variable** is a measure of something that can take on different values, for example, your grade point average. Economists are interested in exploring relationships between two variables—like the relationship between the price of apples and the quantity of apples consumers purchase. Of course, the quantity of apples purchased depends on many other variables, including the consumer's income. To explore the relationship between the quantity and price of apples, we must assume that the consumer's income—and anything else that influences apple purchases—doesn't change during the time period we're considering.

variable

A measure of something that can take on different values.

ceteris paribus
The Latin expression meaning that other variables are held fixed.

Alfred Marshall (1842–1924) was a British economist who refined the economic model of supply and demand and provided a label for this process.[5] He picked one variable that affected apple purchases (price) and threw the other variable (income) into what he called the "pound" (in Marshall's time, the "pound" was an enclosure for holding stray cattle; nowadays, a pound is for stray dogs). That variable waited in the pound while Marshall examined the influence of the first variable. Marshall labeled the pound *ceteris paribus*, the Latin expression meaning that other variables are held fixed:

> . . . the existence of other tendencies is not denied, but their disturbing effect is neglected for a time. The more the issue is narrowed, the more exactly can it be handled.

This book contains many statements about the relationship between two variables. For example, the quantity of computers produced by Dell depends on the price of computers, the wage of computer workers, and the cost of microchips. When we say, "An increase in the price of computers increases the quantity of computers produced," we are assuming that the other two variables—the wage and the cost of microchips—do not change. That is, we apply the *ceteris paribus* assumption.

Think at the Margin

marginal change
A small, one-unit change in value.

Economists often consider how a small change in one variable affects another variable and what impact that has on people's decision making. In other words, if circumstances change only slightly, how will people respond? A small, one-unit change in value is called a **marginal change**. The key feature of marginal change is that the first variable changes by only one unit. For example, you might ask, "If I study just one more hour, by how much will my exam score increase?" Economists call this process "thinking at the margin." Thinking at the margin is like thinking on the edge. You will encounter marginal thinking throughout this book. Here are some other marginal questions:

- If I keep my barber shop open one more hour, by how much will my revenue increase?
- If I stay in school and earn another degree, by how much will my lifetime earnings increase?
- If a car dealer hires one more sales associate, how many more cars will the dealer sell?

As we'll see in the next chapter, economists use the answer to a marginal question as a first step in deciding whether to do more or less of something, for example, whether to keep your barber shop open one more hour.

Rational People Respond to Incentives

A key assumption of most economic analysis is that people act rationally, meaning they act in their own self-interest. Scottish philosopher Adam Smith (1723–1790), who is also considered the founder of economics, wrote that he discovered within humankind[6]

> a desire of bettering our condition, a desire which, though generally calm and dispassionate, comes with us from the womb, and never leaves us until we go to the grave.

Smith didn't say people are motivated exclusively by self-interest, but rather that self-interest is more powerful than kindness or altruism. In this book, we will assume that people act in their own self-interest. Rational people respond to incentives. When the payoff, or benefit, from doing something changes, people change their behavior to get the benefit.

application 1

INCENTIVES TO BUY HYBRID VEHICLES

APPLYING THE CONCEPTS #1: How do people respond to incentives?

Consider the incentives to buy a hybrid vehicle, which is more fuel efficient but more expensive than a gas-powered vehicle. Between 2000 and 2007, the number of hybrid vehicles increased from fewer than 10,000 vehicles to more than 340,000 vehicles. Over this period, the price of gasoline increased significantly, and the higher price of gasoline was responsible for roughly one third of the hybrid vehicles purchased in 2007. An additional factor in hybrid purchases was a federal subsidy of up to $3,400 per hybrid vehicle. The subsidy was responsible for roughly one fifth of the hybrid vehicles purchased in 2007. The increase in the number of hybrid vehicles decreased the emission of the greenhouse gas carbon dioxide (CO_2).

How efficient is the hybrid subsidy in reducing CO_2? On average, the cost of abating one ton of CO_2 through the hybrid subsidy is $177. There are less costly ways to reduce CO_2 emissions, including building insulation, energy-efficient lighting, reforestation, and switching to electric power systems that use fuels that generate less CO_2. For example, a switch from coal to natural gas in power plants reduces CO_2 emissions at less than one third the cost associated with the hybrid subsidy. **Related to Exercise 3.4.**

SOURCE: Based on Arie Beresteanu and Shanjun Li, "Gasoline Prices, Government Support, and the Demand for Hybrid Vehicles in the United States," *International Economic Review* 52 (2011), pp. 161–182.

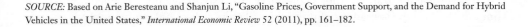

Example: London Addresses Its Congestion Problem

To illustrate the economic way of thinking, let's consider again how an economist would approach the problem of traffic congestion. Recall that each driver on the highway slows down other drivers but ignores these time costs when deciding whether to use the highway. If the government imposes a congestion tax to reduce traffic during rush hour, the economist is faced with a question: How high should the tax be?

To determine the appropriate congestion tax, an economist would assume that people respond to incentives and use the three other elements of the economic way of thinking:

- **Use assumptions to simplify.** To simplify the problem, we would assume that every car has the same effect on the travel time of other cars. Of course, this is unrealistic because people drive cars of different sizes in different ways. But the alternative—looking at the effects of each car on travel speeds—would needlessly complicate the analysis.

- **Isolate variables—use** *ceteris paribus***.** To focus attention on the effects of a congestion tax on the number of cars using the highway, we would make the *ceteris paribus* assumption that everything else that affects travel behavior—the price of gasoline, bus fares, and consumer income—remains fixed.

- **Think at the margin.** To think at the margin, we would estimate the effects of adding one more car to the highway. Now consider the marginal question: If we add one more car to the highway, by how much does the total travel time for commuters increase? Once we answer this question, we can determine the cost imposed by the marginal driver. If the marginal driver forces each of

THE ECONOMIC SOLUTION TO SPAM

APPLYING THE CONCEPTS #2: What is the role of prices in allocating resources?

Spam—unwanted commercial e-mail—torments people around the world, interrupting their work and congesting their computer networks. What's more, spam is spreading to cell phones, with annoying beeps to announce its arrival and sometimes a $0.20 charge to the recipient. A spammer pays nothing to send a million e-mail messages, but earns a profit if just a few people buy an advertised product. The first response to the spam problem was a system of e-mail filters to separate spam from legitimate e-mail. When that didn't work, many states passed laws that made spam illegal. Despite these efforts, the spam problem persists.

   The economic approach to spam is to establish a price for commercial e-mail. One idea is to follow the lead of snail mail and require a $0.01 electronic stamp for each commercial e-mail message. A bundle of one million e-mails would cost $10,000, so if a spammer expects just a few people to buy an advertised product, spamming won't be profitable. A second approach is to charge senders a penalty of $1 for each e-mail that is declared "unwanted" by a recipient. If each e-mail account has a credit limit of $200, the sender's internet service provider (ISP) would shut down an account once it receives 200 complaints. This actually solves the problem of viral spam because if a virus turns your grandmother's computer into a spam machine, her account will be shut down—and the spreading of the virus will stop—after 200 complaints. Of course, the ISP must be clever enough to quickly realize that grandma is not a spammer, and then reconnect her. **Related to Exercise 3.5.**

SOURCES: Based on "Make 'em Pay: The Fight against Spam," *Economist*, February 14, 2004, 58; Laura M. Holson, "Spam Moves to Cellphones and Gets More Invasive," *New York Times*, May 10, 2008.

the 900 commuters to spend two extra seconds on the highway, total travel time increases by 30 minutes. If the value of time is, say, $16 per hour, the appropriate congestion tax would be $8 (equal to $16 × 1/2 hour).

   If the idea of charging people for using roads seems odd, consider the city of London, which for decades had experienced the worst congestion in Europe. In February 2003, the city imposed an $8 tax per day to drive in the city between 7:00 A.M. and 6:30 P.M. The tax reduced traffic volume and cut travel times for cars and buses in half. Because the tax reduced the waste and inefficiency of congestion, the city's economy thrived. Given the success of London's ongoing congestion tax, other cities, including Toronto, Singapore, and San Diego, have implemented congestion pricing.

1.4   Preview of Coming Attractions: Macroeconomics

macroeconomics

The study of the nation's economy as a whole; focuses on the issues of inflation, unemployment, and economic growth.

The field of economics is divided into two categories: macroeconomics and microeconomics. **Macroeconomics** is the study of the nation's economy as a whole; it focuses on the issues of inflation (a general rise in prices), unemployment, and economic growth. These issues are regularly discussed on Web sites, in newspapers, and on television. Macroeconomics explains why economies grow and change and why economic growth is sometimes interrupted. Let's look at three ways we can use macroeconomics.

Using Macroeconomics to Understand Why Economies Grow

As we discussed earlier in the chapter, the world economy has been growing in recent decades, with per capita income increasing by about 1.5 percent per year. Increases in income translate into a higher standard of living for consumers—better cars, houses, and clothing and more options for food, entertainment, and travel. People in a growing economy can consume more of all goods and services because the economy has more of the resources needed to produce these products. Macroeconomics explains why resources increase over time and the consequences for our standard of living. Let's look at a practical question about economic growth.

Why do some countries grow much faster than others? Between 1960 and 2001, the economic growth rate was 2.2 percent per year in the United States, compared to 2.3 percent in Mexico and 2.7 percent in France. But in some countries, the economy actually shrunk, and per capita income dropped. Among the countries with declining income were Sierra Leone and Haiti. In the fastest-growing countries, citizens save a large fraction of the money they earn. Firms can then borrow the funds saved to purchase machinery and equipment that make their workers more productive. The fastest-growing countries also have well-educated workforces, allowing firms to quickly adopt new technologies that increase worker productivity.

Using Macroeconomics to Understand Economic Fluctuations

All economies, including those that experience a general trend of rising per capita income, are subject to economic fluctuations, including periods when the economy temporarily shrinks. During an economic downturn, some of the economy's resources—natural resources, labor, physical capital, human capital, and entrepreneurship—are idle. Some workers are unemployed, and some factories and stores are closed. By contrast, sometimes the economy grows too rapidly, causing prices to rise. Macroeconomics helps us understand why these fluctuations occur—why the economy sometimes cools and sometimes overheats—and what the government can do to moderate the fluctuations. Let's look at a practical question about economic fluctuations.

Should Congress and the president do something to reduce the unemployment rate? For example, should the government cut taxes to free up income to spend on consumer goods, thus encouraging firms to hire more workers to produce more output? If unemployment is very high, the government may want to reduce it. However, it is important not to reduce the unemployment rate too much, because, as we'll see later in the book, a low unemployment rate will cause inflation.

Using Macroeconomics to Make Informed Business Decisions

A third reason for studying macroeconomics is to make informed business decisions. As we'll see later in the book, the government uses various policies to influence interest rates (the price of borrowing money) and the inflation rate. A manager who intends to borrow money for a new factory or store could use knowledge of macroeconomics to predict the effects of current public policies on interest rates and then decide whether to borrow the money now or later. Similarly, a manager must keep an eye on the inflation rate to help decide how much to charge for the firm's products and how much to pay workers. A manager who studies macroeconomics will be better equipped to understand the complexities of interest rates and inflation and how they affect the firm.

1.5 Preview of Coming Attractions: Microeconomics

microeconomics

The study of the choices made by households, firms, and government and how these choices affect the markets for goods and services.

Microeconomics is the study of the choices made by households (an individual or a group of people living together), firms, and government and how these choices affect the markets for goods and services. Let's look at three ways we can use microeconomic analysis.

Using Microeconomics to Understand Markets and Predict Changes

One reason for studying microeconomics is to better understand how markets work and to predict how various events affect the prices and quantities of products in markets. In this book, we answer many practical questions about markets and how they operate. Let's look at a practical question that can be answered with some simple economic analysis.

How would a tax on beer affect the number of highway deaths among young adults? Research has shown that the number of highway fatalities among young adults is roughly proportional to the total amount of beer consumed by that group. A tax on beer would make the product more expensive, and young adults, like other beer drinkers, would therefore consume less of it. Consequently, a tax that decreases beer consumption by 10 percent will decrease highway deaths among young adults by about 10 percent, too.

Using Microeconomics to Make Personal and Managerial Decisions

On the personal level, we use economic analysis to decide how to spend our time, what career to pursue, and how to spend and save the money we earn. Managers use economic analysis to decide how to produce goods and services, how much to produce, and how much to charge for them. Let's use some economic analysis to look at a practical question confronting someone considering starting a business.

If the existing coffee shops in your city are profitable and you have enough money to start your own shop, should you do it? If you enter this market, the competition among the shops for consumers will heat up, causing some coffee shops to drop their prices. In addition, your costs may be higher than the costs of the stores that are already established. It would be sensible to enter the market only if you expect a small drop in price and a small difference in costs. Indeed, entering what appears to be a lucrative market may turn out to be a financial disaster.

Using Microeconomics to Evaluate Public Policies

Although modern societies use markets to make most of the decisions about production and consumption, the government does fulfill several important roles. We can use economic analysis to determine how well the government performs its roles in the market economy. We can also explore the trade-offs associated with various public policies. Let's look at a practical question about public policy.

Like other innovations, prescription drugs are protected by government patents, giving the developer the exclusive right to sell a new drug for a fixed period of time. Once the patent expires, other pharmaceutical companies can legally produce and sell generic versions of the drug, which causes its price to drop. Should drug patents be shorter? Shortening the patent has trade-offs. The good news is that generic versions of the drug will be available sooner, so prices will drop sooner and more people will use the drug to improve their health. The bad news is that the financial payoff from developing new drugs will be smaller, so pharmaceutical companies won't develop as many new drugs. The question is whether the benefit of shorter patents (lower prices) exceeds the cost (fewer drugs developed).

SUMMARY

Economics is about making choices when options are limited. Options in an economy are limited because the factors of production are limited. We can use economic analysis to understand the consequences of our choices as individuals, organizations, and society as a whole. Here are the main points of the chapter:

1 Most of modern economics is based on *positive analysis*, which answers the question "What *is*?" or "What *will be*?" Economists contribute to policy debates by conducting positive analyses about the consequences of alternative actions.

2 *Normative analysis* answers the question "What *ought to be*?"

3 The choices made by individuals, firms, and governments answer three questions: What products do we produce? How do we produce the products? Who consumes the products?

4 To think like an economist, we (a) use assumptions to simplify, (b) use the notion of *ceteris paribus* to focus on the relationship between two variables, (c) think in marginal terms, and (d) assume that rational people respond to incentives.

5 We use *macroeconomics* to understand why economies grow, to understand economic fluctuations, and to make informed business decisions.

6 We use *microeconomics* to understand how markets work, to make personal and managerial decisions, and to evaluate the merits of public policies.

KEY TERMS

ceteris paribus, p. 8

economic model, p. 4

economics, p. 2

entrepreneurship, p. 2

factors of production, p. 2

human capital, p. 2

labor, p. 2

macroeconomics, p. 10

marginal change, p. 8

microeconomics, p. 12

natural resources, p. 2

normative analysis, p. 3

physical capital, p. 2

positive analysis, p. 3

scarcity, p. 2

variable, p. 7

EXERCISES

All problems are assignable in MyEconLab.

1.1 What Is Economics?

1.1 The three basic economic questions a society must answer are _____ products do we produce? _____ do we produce the products? _____ consumes the products?

1.2 List the five factors of production.

1.3 Which of the following statements is true?

   a. Positive statements answer questions like "What will happen if . . .?" Normative economic statements answer questions like "What ought to happen to . . .?"

   b. Normative statements answer questions like "What will happen if . . .?" Positive economic statements answer questions like "What ought to happen to . . .?"

   c. Most modern economics is based on normative analysis.

1.4 Indicate whether each of the following questions is normative or positive.

   a. Should your city build levees strong enough to protect the city from Category Five hurricanes?

   b. How did Hurricane Katrina affect housing prices in New Orleans and Baton Rouge?

   c. Who should pay for a new skate park?

   d. Should a school district increase teachers' salaries by 20 percent?

   e. Would an increase in teachers' salaries improve the average quality of teachers?

Economic Analysis and Modern Problems

2.1 What is the economist's solution to the congestion problem?

    a. Require people to carpool.

    b. Charge a toll during rush hour.

    c. Require people to move closer to their jobs.

    d. No economist would suggest any of the above.

2.2 Some recent work by economists on the sources of growth suggests that institutions such as the _____ and the _____ play key roles in economic growth.

The Economic Way of Thinking

3.1 A road map incorporates two unrealistic assumptions: (1) _____ and (2) _____.

3.2 The four elements of the economic way of thinking are (1) use _____ to simplify the analysis, (2) explore the relationship between two variables by _____, (3) think at the _____, and (4) rational people respond to _____.

3.3 Which of the following is the Latin expression meaning *other things being held fixed*?

    a. *setiferous proboscis*

    b. *ceteris paribus*

    c. *e pluribus unum*

    d. *tres grand fromage*

3.4 The federal subsidy for hybrid cars was responsible for roughly _____ of the hybrid cars purchased in 2007. (Related to Application 1 on page 9.)

3.5 The economic approach to spam is to follow the lead of _____ and establish a _____ for e-mail. (Related to Application 2 on page 10.)

3.6 True or False: Adam Smith suggested that people are motivated solely by self-interest.

USING GRAPHS AND PERCENTAGES

Economists use several types of graphs to present data, represent relationships between variables, and explain concepts. In this appendix, we review the mechanics of graphing variables. We'll also review the basics of computing percentage changes and using percentages to compute changes in variables.

1A.1 Using Graphs

A quick flip through the book will reveal the importance of graphs in economics. Every chapter has at least several graphs, and many chapters have more. Although it is possible to do economics without graphs, it's a lot easier with them in your toolbox.

Graphing Single Variables

As we saw earlier in Chapter 1, a *variable* is a measure of something that can take on different values. Figure 1A.1 shows two types of graphs, each presenting data on a single variable. Panel A uses a pie graph to show the breakdown of U.S. music sales by type of music. The greater the sales of a type of music, the larger the pie slice. For example, the most popular type is rock music, comprising 24 percent of the market. The next largest type is country, followed by rap/hip-hop, R&B/urban, and so on. Panel B of Figure 1A.1 uses a bar graph to show the revenue from foreign sales (exports) of selected U.S. industries. The larger the revenue, the taller the bar. For example, the bar for computer software, with export sales of about $60 billion, is over three times taller than the bar for motion pictures, TV, and video, with export sales of $17 billion.

▼ **FIGURE 1A.1**
Graphs of Single Variables

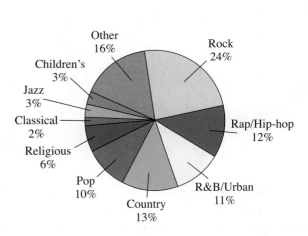

(A) Pie Graph for Types of Recorded Music Sold in the United States

SOURCE: Author's calculations based on Recording Industry Association of America, *"2004 Consumer Profile."*

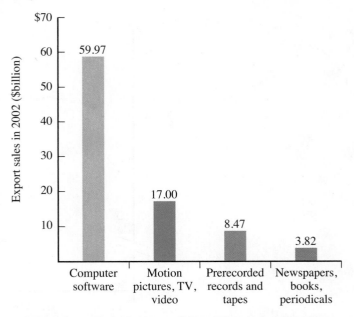

(B) Bar Graph for U.S. Export Sales of Copyrighted Products

SOURCE: Author's calculations based on International Intellectual Property Alliance, *"Copyright Industries in the U.S. Economy, 2004 Report."*

A third type of single-variable graph shows how the value of a variable changes over time. Panel A of Figure 1A.2 shows a time-series graph, with the total dollar value of a hypothetical industry for years 1 through 10. Time is measured on the horizontal axis, and sales are measured on the vertical axis. The height of the line in a particular year shows the value in that year. For example, in Year 1 the value was $12.32 billion. After reaching a peak of $14.59 billion in Year 5, the value dropped over the next several years.

(A) Total Sales of Industry

(B) Truncated Vertical Axis

▲ FIGURE 1A.2
Time-Series Graph

Panel B of Figure 1A.2 shows a truncated version of the graph in Panel A. The double hash marks in the lower part of the vertical axis indicate that the axis doesn't start from zero. This truncation of the vertical axis exaggerates the fluctuations in total sales.

Graphing Two Variables

We can also use a graph to show the relationship between two variables. Figure 1A.3 shows the basic elements of a two-variable graph. One variable is measured along the horizontal, or x, axis, while the other variable is measured along the vertical, or y, axis. The *origin* is the intersection of the two axes, where the values of both variables are zero. Dashed lines show the values of the two variables at a particular point. For example, for point a, the value of the horizontal, or x, variable is 10, and the value of the vertical, or y, variable is 13.

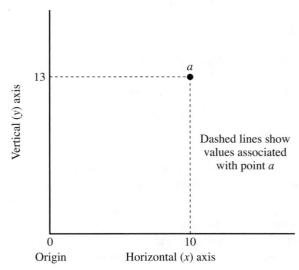

▲ FIGURE 1A.3
Basic Elements of a Two-Variable Graph
One variable is measured along the horizontal, or *x*, axis, while the other variable is measured along the vertical, or *y*, axis. The origin is defined as the intersection of the two axes, where the values of both variables are zero. The dashed lines show the values of the two variables at a particular point.

To see how to draw a two-variable graph, suppose that you have a part-time job and you are interested in the relationship between the number of hours you work and your weekly income. The relevant variables are the hours of work per week and your weekly income. In Figure 1A.4, the table shows the relationship between the hours worked and income. Let's assume that your weekly allowance from your parents is $40 and your part-time job pays $8 per hour. If you work 10 hours per week, for example, your weekly income is $120 ($40 from your parents and $80 from your job). The more you work, the higher your weekly income: If you work 20 hours, your weekly income is $200; if you work 30 hours, it is $280.

Hours Worked per Week	Income per Week	Point on the Graph
0	$ 40	a
10	120	b
20	200	c
30	280	d

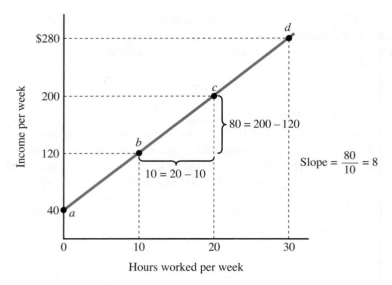

▲ FIGURE 1A.4

Relationship between Hours Worked and Income

There is a positive relationship between work hours and income, so the income curve is positively sloped. The slope of the curve is $8: Each additional hour of work increases income by $8.

Although a table with numbers is helpful in showing the relationship between work hours and income, a graph makes it easier to see the relationship. We can use data in a table to draw a graph. To do so, we perform five simple steps:

1 Draw a horizontal line to represent the first variable. In Figure 1A.4, we measure hours worked along the horizontal axis. As we move to the right along the horizontal axis, the number of hours worked increases, from 0 to 30 hours.

2 Draw a vertical line intersecting the first line to represent the second variable. In Figure 1A.4, we measure income along the vertical axis. As we move up along the vertical axis, income increases from $0 to $280.

3 Start with the first row of numbers in the table, which shows that with 0 hours worked, income is $40. The value of the variable on the horizontal axis is 0, and the value of the variable on the vertical axis is $40, so we plot point *a* on the graph. This is the *vertical intercept*—the point where the curve cuts or intersects the vertical axis.

4 Pick a combination with a positive number for hours worked. For example, in the second row of numbers, if you work 10 hours, your income is $120.

   4.1 Find the point on the horizontal axis with that number of hours worked— 10 hours—and draw a dashed line vertically straight up from that point.

   4.2 Find the point on the vertical axis with the income corresponding to those hours worked—$120—and draw a dashed line horizontally straight to the right from that point.

   4.3 The intersection of the dashed lines shows the combination of hours worked and income. Point *b* shows the combination of 10 hours worked and $120 in income.

5 Repeat step 4 for different combinations of work time and income shown in the table. Once we have a series of points on the graph (*a*, *b*, *c*, and *d*), we can connect them to draw a curve that shows the relationship between hours worked and income.

There is a **positive relationship** between two variables if they move in the same direction. As you increase your work time, your income increases, so there is a positive relationship between the two variables. In Figure 1A.4, as the number of hours worked increases, you move upward along the curve to higher income levels. Some people refer to a positive relationship as a *direct relationship*.

There is a **negative relationship** between two variables if they move in opposite directions. For example, there is a negative relationship between the amount of time you work and the time you have available for other activities such as recreation, study, and sleep. Some people refer to a negative relationship as an *inverse relationship*.

positive relationship

A relationship in which two variables move in the same direction.

negative relationship

A relationship in which two variables move in opposite directions.

Computing the Slope

How sensitive is one variable to changes in the other variable? We can use the slope of the curve to measure this sensitivity. To compute the **slope of a curve**, we pick two points and divide the vertical difference between the two points (the *rise*) by the horizontal difference (the *run*):

slope of a curve

The vertical difference between two points (the *rise*) divided by the horizontal difference (the *run*).

$$\text{Slope} = \frac{\text{Vertical difference between two points}}{\text{Horizontal difference between two points}} = \frac{\text{rise}}{\text{run}}$$

To compute the slope of a curve, we take four steps:

1 Pick two points on the curve, for example, points b and c in Figure 1A.4.

2 Compute the vertical difference between the two points (the rise). For points b and c, the vertical difference between the points is $80 ($200 – $120).

3 Compute the horizontal distance between the same two points (the run). For points b and c, the horizontal distance between the points is 10 hours (20 hours – 10 hours).

4 Divide the vertical distance by the horizontal distance to get the slope. The slope between points b and c is $8 per hour:

$$\text{Slope} = \frac{\text{Vertical difference}}{\text{Horizontal difference}} = \frac{\$200 - 120}{20 - 10} = \frac{\$80}{10} = \$8$$

In this case, a 10-hour increase in time worked increases income by $80, so the increase in income per hour of work is $8, which makes sense because this is the hourly wage. Because the curve is a straight line, the slope is the same at all points along the curve. You can check this yourself by computing the slope between points c and d.

We can use some shorthand to refer to the slope of a curve. The mathematical symbol Δ (delta) represents the change in a variable. So we can write the slope of the curve in Figure 1A.4 as

$$\text{Slope} = \frac{\Delta \text{ Income}}{\Delta \text{ Work hours}}$$

In general, if the variable on the vertical axis is y and the variable on the horizontal axis is x, we can express the slope as

$$\text{Slope} = \frac{\Delta y}{\Delta x}$$

Moving along the Curve versus Shifting the Curve

Up to this point, we've explored the effect of changes in variables that cause movement along a given curve. In Figure 1A.4, we see the relationship between hours of work (on the horizontal axis) and income (on the vertical axis). Because the total income also depends on the allowance and the wage, we can make two observations about the curve in Figure 1A.4:

1 To draw this curve, we must specify the weekly allowance ($40) and the hourly wage ($8).

2 The curve shows that an increase in time worked increases the student's income, *ceteris paribus*. In this case, we are assuming that the allowance and the wage are both fixed.

A change in the weekly allowance will shift the curve showing the relationship between work time and income. In Figure 1A.5, when the allowance increases from $40 to $90, the curve shifts upward by $50. For a given number of work hours, income increases by $50. For example, the income associated with 10 hours of work is $170 (point *f*), compared to $120 with the original allowance (point *b*). The upward shift also means that to reach a given amount of income, fewer work hours are required. In other words, the curve shifts upward and to the left.

▲ **FIGURE 1A.5**

Movement Along a Curve versus Shifting the Curve

To draw a curve showing the relationship between hours worked and income, we fix the weekly allowance ($40) and the wage ($8 per hour). A change in the hours worked causes movement along the curve, for example, from point *b* to point *c*. A change in any other variable shifts the entire curve. For example, a $50 increase in the allowance (to $90) shifts the entire curve upward by $50.

We can distinguish between movement along a curve and a shift of the entire curve. In Figure 1A.5, an increase in the hours worked causes movement along a single income curve. For example, if the allowance is $40, we are operating on the lower of the two curves, and if the hours worked increases from 10 to 20, we move from point *b* to point *c*. In contrast, if something other than the hours worked changes, we shift the entire curve, as we've seen with an increase in the allowance.

This book uses dozens of two-dimensional curves, each of which shows the relationship between *only two* variables. A common error is to forget that a single curve tells only part of the story. In Figure 1A.5, we needed two curves to explore the effects of changes in three variables. Here are some simple rules to keep in mind when you use two-dimensional graphs:

- A change in one of the variables shown on the graph causes movement along the curve. In Figure 1A.5, an increase in work time causes movement along the curve from point *a* to point *b*, to point *c*, and so on.
- A change in one of the variables that is not shown on the graph—one of the variables held fixed in drawing the curve—shifts the entire curve. In Figure 1A.5, an increase in the allowance shifts the entire curve upward.

Graphing Negative Relationships

We can use a graph to show a negative relationship between two variables. Consider a consumer who has an annual budget of $360 to spend on CDs at a price of $12 per CD and downloaded music at a price of $1 per song. The table in Figure 1A.6 shows the relationship between the number of CDs and downloaded songs. A consumer who doesn't buy any CDs has $360 to spend on downloaded songs and can get 360 of them at a price of $1 each. A consumer who buys 10 CDs at $12 each has $240 left to spend

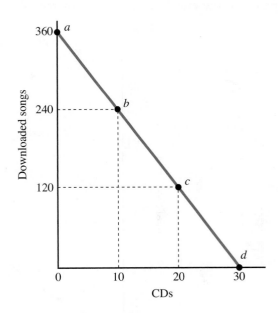

▲ FIGURE 1A.6

Negative Relationship between CD Purchases and Downloaded Songs

There is a negative relationship between the number of CDs and downloaded songs that a consumer can afford with a budget of $360. The slope of the curve is –$12: Each additional CD (at a price of $12 each) decreases the number of downloadable songs (at $1 each) by 12 songs.

Number of CDs Purchased	Number of Songs Downloaded	Point on the Graph
0	360	a
10	240	b
20	120	c
30	0	d

on downloaded songs (point *b*). Moving down through the table, as the number of CDs increases, the number of downloaded songs decreases.

The graph in Figure 1A.6 shows the negative relationship between the number of CDs and the number of downloaded songs. The vertical intercept (point *a*) shows that a consumer who doesn't buy any CDs can afford 360 downloaded songs. There is a negative relationship between the number of CDs and downloaded songs, so the curve is negatively sloped. We can use points *b* and *c* to compute the slope of the curve:

$$\text{Slope} = \frac{\text{Vertical difference}}{\text{Horizontal difference}} = \frac{120 - 240}{20 - 10} = \frac{-120}{10} = -12$$

The slope is 12 downloaded songs per CD: For each additional CD, the consumer sacrifices 12 downloaded songs.

Graphing Nonlinear Relationships

We can also use a graph to show a nonlinear relationship between two variables. Panel A of Figure 1A.7 shows the relationship between hours spent studying for an exam and the grade on the exam. As study time increases, the grade increases,

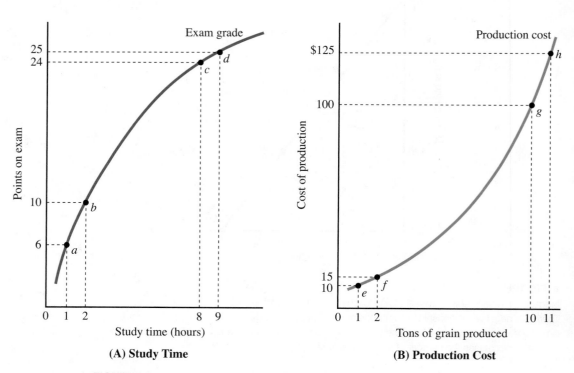

▲ FIGURE 1A.7

Nonlinear Relationships

(A) Study time There is a positive and nonlinear relationship between study time and the grade on an exam. As study time increases, the exam grade increases at a decreasing rate. For example, the second hour of study increased the grade by 4 points (from 6 points to 10 points), but the ninth hour of study increases the grade by only 1 point (from 24 points to 25 points).

(B) Production cost There is a positive and nonlinear relationship between the quantity of grain produced and total production cost. As the quantity increases, the total cost increases at an increasing rate. For example, to increase production from 1 ton to 2 tons, production cost increases by $5 (from $10 to $15) but to increase the production from 10 to 11 tons, total cost increases by $25 (from $100 to $125).

but at a decreasing rate. In other words, each additional hour increases the exam grade by a smaller and smaller amount. For example, the second hour of study increases the grade by 4 points—from 6 to 10 points—but the ninth hour of study increases the grade by only 1 point—from 24 points to 25 points. This is a nonlinear relationship: The slope of the curve changes as we move along the curve. In Figure 1A.7, the slope decreases as we move to the right along the curve: The slope is 4 points per hour between points *a* and *b* but only 1 point per hour between points *c* and *d*.

Another possibility for a nonlinear curve is that the slope increases as we move to the right along the curve. Panel B of Figure 1A.7 shows the relationship between the amount of grain produced on the horizontal axis and the total cost of production on the vertical axis. The slope of the curve increases as the amount of grain increases, meaning that production cost increases at an increasing rate. On the lower part of the curve, increasing output from 1 ton to 2 tons increases production cost by $5, from $10 to $15. On the upper part of the curve, increasing output from 10 to 11 tons increases production cost by $25, from $100 to $125.

1A.2 Computing Percentage Changes and Using Equations

Economists often express changes in variables in terms of percentage changes. This part of the appendix provides a brief review of the mechanics of computing percentage changes. It also reviews some simple rules for solving equations to find missing values.

Computing Percentage Changes

In many cases, the equations that economists use involve percentage changes. In this book, we use a simple approach to computing percentage changes: We divide the change in the variable by the initial value of the variable and then multiply by 100:

$$\text{Percentage change} = \frac{\text{New value} - \text{initial value}}{\text{Initial value}} \times 100$$

For example, if the price of a book increases from $20 to $22, the percentage change is 10 percent:

$$\text{Percentage change} = \frac{22 - 20}{20} \times 100 = \frac{2}{20} \times 100 = 10\%$$

Going in the other direction, suppose the price decreases from $20 to $19. In this case, the percentage change is −5 percent:

$$\text{Percentage change} = \frac{19 - 20}{20} \times 100 = -\frac{1}{20} \times 100 = -5\%$$

The alternative to this simple approach is to base the percentage change on the average value, or the midpoint, of the variable:

$$\text{Percentage change} = \frac{\text{New value} - \text{initial value}}{\text{Average value}} \times 100$$

For example, if the price of a book increases from \$20 to \$22, the computed percentage change under the midpoint approach is 9.52 percent:

$$\text{Percentage change} = \frac{22 - 20}{(20 + 22) \div 2} \times 100 = \frac{2}{42 \div 2} \times 100$$

$$= \frac{2}{21} \times 100 = 9.52\%,$$

If the change in the variable is relatively small, the extra precision associated with the midpoint approach is usually not worth the extra effort. The simple approach allows us to spend less time doing tedious arithmetic and more time doing economic analysis. In this book, we use the simple approach to compute percentage changes: If the price increases from \$20 to \$22, the price has increased by 10 percent.

If we know a percentage change, we can translate it into an absolute change. For example, if a price has increased by 10 percent and the initial price is \$20, then we add 10 percent of the initial price (\$2 is 10 percent of \$20) to the initial price (\$20), for a new price of \$22. If the price decreases by 5 percent, we subtract 5 percent

application 3

THE PERILS OF PERCENTAGES

APPLYING THE CONCEPTS #3: How do we compute percentage changes?

In the 1970s the government of Mexico City repainted the highway lane lines on the *Viaducto* to transform a four-lane highway into a six-lane highway. The government announced that the highway capacity had increased by 50 percent (equal to 2 divided by 4). Unfortunately, the number of collisions and traffic fatalities increased, and one year later, the government restored the four-lane highway and announced that the capacity had decreased by 33 percent (equal to 2 divided by 6). The government announced that the net effect of the two changes was an increase in the highway capacity by 17 percent (equal to 50 percent minus 33 percent).

This anecdote reveals a potential problem with using the simple approach to compute percentage changes. Because the initial value (the denominator) changes, the computation of percentage increases and decreases are not symmetric. In contrast, if the government had used the midpoint method, the percentage increase in capacity would be 40 percent (equal to 2 divided by 5), the same as the percentage decrease. In that case, we get the more sensible result that the net effect of the two changes is zero. **Related to Exercise A8.**

SOURCE: Based on "The Perils of Percentages," *Economist*, April 18, 1998, 70.

of the initial price ($1 is 5 percent of $20) from the initial price ($20), for a new price of $19.

Using Equations to Compute Missing Values

It will often be useful to compute the value of the numerator or the denominator of an equation. To do so, we use simple algebra to rearrange the equation to put the missing variable on the left side of the equation. For example, consider the relationship between time worked and income. The equation for the slope is

$$\text{Slope} = \frac{\Delta \text{ Income}}{\Delta \text{ Work hours}}$$

Suppose you want to compute how much income you'll earn by working more hours. We can rearrange the slope equation by multiplying both sides of the equation by the change in work hours:

$$\text{Work hours} \times \text{Slope} = \Delta \text{ Income}$$

By swapping sides of the equation, we get

$$\Delta \text{ Income} = \Delta \text{ Work hours} \times \text{Slope}$$

For example, if you work seven extra hours and the slope is $8, your income will increase by $56:

$$\Delta \text{ Income} = \Delta \text{ Work hours} \times \text{Slope} = \$7 \times \$8 = \$56$$

We can use the same process to compute the difference in work time required to achieve a target change in income. In this case, we multiply both sides of the slope equation by the change in work time and then divide both sides by the slope. The result is

$$\Delta \text{ Work hours} = \frac{\Delta \text{ Income}}{\text{Slope}}$$

For example, to increase your income by $56, you need to work seven hours:

$$\Delta \text{ Work hours} = \frac{\Delta \text{ Income}}{\text{Slope}} = \frac{\$56}{\$8} = 7$$

KEY TERMS

negative relationship, p. 19   positive relationship, p. 19   slope of a curve, p. 19

All problems are assignable in MyEconLab.

A.1 Suppose you belong to a tennis club that has a monthly fee of $100 and a charge of $5 per hour to play tennis.

   a. Using Figure 1A.4 on page 18 as a model, prepare a table and draw a curve to show the relationship between the hours of tennis (on the horizontal axis) and the monthly club bill (on the vertical axis). For the table and graph, use 5, 10, 15, and 20 hours of tennis.

   b. The slope of the curve is _____ per _____.

   c. Suppose you start with 10 hours of tennis and then decide to increase your tennis time by 3 hours. On your curve, show the initial point and the new point. By how much will your monthly bill increase?

   d. Suppose you start with 10 hours and then decide to spend an additional $30 on tennis. On your curve, show the initial point and the new point. How many additional hours can you get?

A.2 The following graph shows the relationship between the number of Frisbees produced and the cost of production. The vertical intercept is $_____, and the slope of the curve is $_____ per Frisbee. Point *b* shows that the cost of producing _____ Frisbees is $_____. The cost of producing 15 Frisbees is $_____.

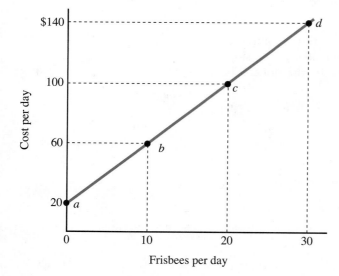

A.3 Suppose you have $120 to spend on CDs and movies. The price of a CD is $12, and the price of a movie is $6.

   a. Using Figure 1A.6 on page 21 as a model, prepare a table and draw a curve to show the relationship

between the number of CDs (on the horizontal axis) and movies (on the vertical axis) you can afford to buy.

   b. The slope of the curve is _____ per _____.

A.4 You manage Gofer Delivery Service. You rent a truck for $50 per day, and each delivery takes an hour of labor time. The hourly wage is $8.

   a. Draw a curve showing the relationship between the number of deliveries (on the horizontal axis) and your total cost (on the vertical axis). Draw the curve for between 0 and 20 deliveries.

   b. The slope of the cost curve is _____ per _____.

   c. To draw the curve, what variables are held fixed?

   d. A change in _____ would cause a movement upward along the curve.

   e. Changes in _____ would cause the entire curve to shift upward.

A.5 A change in a variable measured on an axis of a graph causes movement _____ a curve, while a change in a relevant variable that is not measured on an axis _____ the entire curve.

A.6 Compute the percentage changes for the following:

Initial Value	New Value	Percentage Change
10	11	
100	98	
50	53	

A.7 Compute the new values for the following changes:

Initial Value	Percentage Change	New Value
100	12%	
50	8	
20	15	

A.8 Suppose the price of an MP3 player decreases from $60 to $40. Using the midpoint approach, the percentage change in price is _____. Using the initial-value approach, the percentage change in price is _____. (Related to Application 3 on page 24.)

NOTES

1. Texas Transportation Institute, *2005 Urban Mobility Study*, http://mobility.tamu.edu/ums/

2. William Easterly, *The Elusive Quest for Growth* (Cambridge, MA: MIT Press, 2001), Chapter 1.

3. William Easterly, *The Elusive Quest for Growth* (Cambridge, MA: MIT Press, 2001); World Bank, *World Development Report 2000/2001: Attacking Poverty* (New York: Oxford University Press, 2000).

4. John Maynard Keynes, *The Collected Writings of John Maynard Keynes, Volume 7*, ed. Donald Moggridge (London: Macmillan, 1973), 856. Reproduced with permission of the publisher.

5. Alfred Marshall, *Principles of Economics*, 9th ed., ed. C.W. Guillebaud (1920; repr., London: Macmillan, 1961), 366. Reproduced with permission of the publisher.

6. Adam Smith, *An Inquiry into the Nature and Causes of the Wealth of Nations* (1776); Book 2, Chapter 3.

The Key Principles of Economics

What do we sacrifice by preserving tropical rainforests rather than mining or logging the land?

Recent experiences in Guyana and other tropical countries suggest that in some places, the answer is "not much"—only $1 per hectare per year ($0.40 per acre per year).[1] Conservation groups have a new strategy for conserving rainforests—bidding against loggers and miners for the use of the land. When the payoff from developing tropical forest land is relatively low, conservation groups can outbid developers at a price as low as $1 per hectare. When we add the cost of hiring locals to manage the ecosystems, the total cost of preservation is as low as $2 per hectare per year. A conservation group based in Amherst, New Hampshire, started by leasing 81,000 hectares of pristine forest in Guyana, and since then has leased land in Peru, Sierra Leone, Papua New Guinea, Fiji, and Mexico.

LEARNING OBJECTIVES

- Apply the principle of opportunity cost.
- Apply the marginal principle.
- Apply the principle of voluntary exchange.
- Apply the principle of diminishing returns.
- Apply the real-nominal principle.

MyEconLab
MyEconLab helps you master each objective and study more efficiently.

*i*n this chapter, we introduce five key principles that provide a foundation for economic analysis. A *principle* is a self-evident truth that most people readily understand and accept. For example, most people readily accept the principle of gravity. As you read through the book, you will see the five key principles of economics again and again as you do your own economic analysis.

2.1   The Principle of Opportunity Cost

Economics is all about making choices, and to make good choices we must compare the benefit of something to its cost. **Opportunity cost** incorporates the notion of scarcity: No matter what we do, there is always a trade-off. We must trade off one thing for another because resources are limited and can be used in different ways. By acquiring something, we use up resources that could have been used to acquire something else. The notion of opportunity cost allows us to measure this trade-off.

opportunity cost
What you sacrifice to get something.

> ## PRINCIPLE OF OPPORTUNITY COST
> The opportunity cost of something is what you sacrifice to get it.

In most decisions we choose from several alternatives. For example, if you spend an hour studying for an economics exam, you have one fewer hour to pursue other activities. To determine the opportunity cost of an activity, we look at what you consider the best of these "other" activities. For example, suppose the alternatives to studying economics are studying for a history exam or working in a job that pays $10 per hour. If you consider studying for history a better use of your time than working, then the opportunity cost of studying economics is the four extra points you could have received on a history exam if you studied history instead of economics. Alternatively, if working is the best alternative, the opportunity cost of studying economics is the $10 you could have earned instead.

We can also apply the principle of opportunity cost to decisions about how to spend money from a fixed budget. For example, suppose that you have a fixed budget to spend on music. You can buy your music either at a local music store for $15 per CD or online for $1 per song. The opportunity cost of 1 CD is 15 one-dollar online songs. A hospital with a fixed salary budget can increase the number of doctors only at the expense of nurses or physician's assistants. If a doctor costs five times as much as a nurse, the opportunity cost of a doctor is five nurses.

In some cases, a product that appears to be free actually has a cost. That's why economists are fond of saying, "There's no such thing as a free lunch." Suppose someone offers to buy you lunch if you agree to listen to a sales pitch for a timeshare condominium. Although you don't pay any money for the lunch, there is an opportunity cost because you could spend that time in another way—such as studying for your economics or history exam. The lunch isn't free because you sacrifice an hour of your time to get it.

The Cost of College

What is the opportunity cost of a college degree? Consider a student who spends a total of $40,000 for tuition and books. Instead of going to college, the student could have spent this money on a wide variety of goods, including housing, electronic devices, and world travel. Part of the opportunity cost of college is the $40,000 worth of other goods the student sacrifices to pay for tuition and books. Also, instead of going to college, the student could have worked as a bank clerk for $20,000 per year and earned $80,000 over four years. That makes the total opportunity cost of this student's college degree $120,000:

Opportunity cost of money spent on tuition and books	$ 40,000
Opportunity cost of college time (four years working for $20,000 per year)	80,000
Economic cost or total opportunity cost	$120,000

We haven't included the costs of food or housing in our computations of opportunity cost. That's because a student must eat and live somewhere even if he or she doesn't go to college. But if housing and food are more expensive in college, then we would include the extra costs of housing and food in our calculations.

There are other things to consider in a person's decision to attend college. As we'll see later, a college degree can increase a person's earning power, so there are benefits from a college degree. In addition, college offers the thrill of learning and the pleasure of meeting new people. To make an informed decision about whether to attend college, we must compare the benefits to the opportunity costs.

The Cost of Military Spending

We can use the principle of opportunity cost to explore the cost of military spending.[2] In 1992, Malaysia bought two warships. For the price of the warships, the country could have built a system to provide safe drinking water for 5 million citizens who lacked it. In other words, the opportunity cost of the warships was safe drinking water for 5 million people. The policy question is whether the benefits of the warships exceed their opportunity cost.

In the United States, economists have estimated that the cost of the war in Iraq will be at least $1 trillion. The economists' calculations go beyond the simple budgetary costs and quantify the opportunity cost of the war. For example, the resources used in the war could have been used in various government programs for children—to enroll more children in preschool programs, to hire more science and math teachers to reduce class sizes, or to immunize more children in poor countries. For example, each $100 billion spent on the war could instead support one of the following programs:

- Enroll 13 million preschool children in the Head Start program for one year.
- Hire 1.8 million additional teachers for one year.
- Immunize all the children in less-developed countries for the next 33 years.

The fact that the war has a large opportunity cost does not necessarily mean that it is unwise. The policy question is whether the benefits from the war exceed its opportunity cost. Taking another perspective, we can measure the opportunity cost of war in terms of its implications for domestic security. The resources used in the war in Iraq could have been used to improve domestic security by securing ports and cargo facilities, hiring more police officers, improving the screening of airline passengers and baggage, improving fire departments and other first responders, upgrading the Coast Guard fleet, and securing our railroad and highway systems. The cost of implementing the domestic-security recommendations of various government commissions would be about $31 billion, a small fraction of the cost of the war. The question for policymakers is whether money spent on domestic security would be more beneficial than money spent on the war.

Opportunity Cost and the Production Possibilities Curve

Just as individuals face limits, so do entire economies. As we saw in Chapter 1, the ability of an economy to produce goods and services is determined by its factors of production, including labor, natural resources, physical capital, human capital, and entrepreneurship.

Figure 2.1 shows a production possibilities graph for an economy that produces wheat and steel. The horizontal axis shows the quantity of wheat produced by the economy, and the vertical axis shows the quantity of steel produced. The shaded area shows all the possible combinations of the two goods the economy can produce. At point *a*, for example, the economy can produce 700 tons of steel and 10 tons of wheat. In contrast, at point *e*, the economy can produce 300 tons of steel and 20 tons of wheat. The set of points on the border between the shaded and unshaded area is called the **production possibilities curve** (or *production possibilities frontier*) because it separates the combinations that are attainable from those that are not. The attainable combinations are shown by the shaded area within the curve and the curve itself. The unattainable combinations are shown by the unshaded area outside the curve. The points on the curve show the combinations that are possible if the economy's resources are fully employed.

production possibilities curve
A curve that shows the possible combinations of products that an economy can produce, given that its productive resources are fully employed and efficiently used.

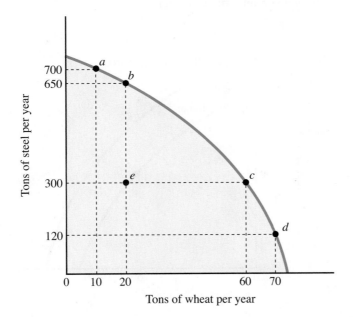

▲ **FIGURE 2.1**
Scarcity and the Production Possibilities Curve
The production possibilities curve illustrates the principle of opportunity cost for an entire economy.
An economy has a fixed amount of resources. If these resources are fully employed, an increase in the production of wheat comes at the expense of steel.

The production possibilities curve illustrates the notion of opportunity cost. If an economy is fully utilizing its resources, it can produce more of one product only if it produces less of another product. For example, to produce more wheat, we must take resources away from steel. As we move resources out of steel, the quantity of steel produced will decrease. For example, if we move from point *a* to point *b* along the production possibilities curve in Figure 2.1, we sacrifice 50 tons of steel (700 tons – 650 tons) to get 10 more tons of wheat (20 tons – 10 tons). Further down the curve, if we move from point *c* to point *d*, we sacrifice 180 tons of steel to get the same 10-ton increase in wheat.

Why is the production possibilities curve bowed outward, with the opportunity cost of wheat increasing as we move down the curve? The reason is that resources are not perfectly adaptable for the production of both goods. Some resources are more suitable for steel production, while others are more suitable for wheat production. Starting at point *a*, the economy uses its most fertile land to produce wheat. A 10-ton increase in wheat reduces the quantity of steel by only 50 tons, because plenty of fertile land is available for conversion to wheat farming. As the economy moves downward along the production possibilities curve, farmers will be forced to use land that is progressively less fertile, so to increase wheat output by 10 tons, more and more resources must be diverted from steel production. In the move from point *c* to point *d*, the land converted to farming is so poor that increasing wheat output by 10 tons decreases steel output by 180 tons.

The production possibilities curve shows the production options for a given set of resources. As shown in Figure 2.2, an increase in the amount of resources available to the economy shifts the production possibilities outward. For example, if we start at point *f*, and the economy's resources increase, we can produce more steel (point *g*), more wheat (point *h*), or more of both goods (points between *g* and *h*). The curve will also shift outward as a result of technological innovations that enable us to produce more output with a given quantity of resources.

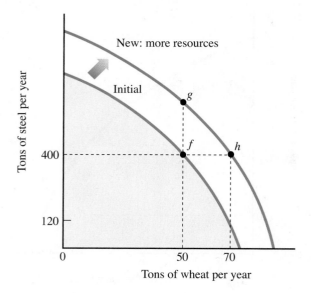

▲ FIGURE 2.2

Shifting the Production Possibilities Curve

An increase in the quantity of resources or technological innovation in an economy shifts the production possibilities curve outward. Starting from point *f*, a nation could produce more steel (point *g*), more wheat (point *h*), or more of both goods (points between *g* and *h*).

application 1

DON'T FORGET THE COSTS OF TIME AND INVESTED FUNDS

APPLYING THE CONCEPTS #1: What is the opportunity cost of running a business?

Suppose you run a lawn-cutting business and use solar-powered equipment (mower, edger, blower, truck) that you could sell tomorrow for $5,000. Instead of cutting lawns, you could work as a janitor for $300 per week. You have a savings account that pays a weekly interest rate of 0.20 percent (or $0.002 per dollar). What is your weekly cost of cutting lawns?

We can use the principle of opportunity cost to compute the cost of the lawn business. The opportunity cost of the $5,000 you have invested in the business is the $10 weekly interest you could have earned by selling the equipment and investing the $5,000 in your savings account. Adding in the opportunity cost of cutting lawns instead of earning $300 as a janitor, the weekly cost is $310. **Related to Exercise 1.7.**

2.2   The Marginal Principle

Economics is about making choices, and we rarely make all-or-nothing choices. For example, if you sit down to read a book, you don't read the entire book in a single sitting, but instead decide how many pages or chapters to read. Economists think in marginal terms, considering how a one-unit change in one variable affects the value of another variable and people's decisions. When we say *marginal*, we're looking at the effect of a small, or incremental, change.

The marginal principle is based on a comparison of the marginal benefits and marginal costs of a particular activity. The **marginal benefit** of an activity is the additional benefit resulting from a small increase in the activity. For example, the marginal benefit of keeping a bookstore open for one more hour equals the additional revenue from book sales. Similarly, the **marginal cost** is the additional cost resulting from a small increase in the activity. For example, the marginal cost of keeping a bookstore open for one more hour equals the additional expenses for workers and utilities for that hour. Applying the marginal principle, the bookstore should stay open for one more hour if the marginal benefit (the additional revenue) is at least as large as the marginal cost (the additional cost). For example, if the marginal benefit is $80 of additional revenue and the marginal cost is $30 of additional expense for workers and utilities, staying open for the additional hour increases the bookstore's profit by $50.

marginal benefit
The additional benefit resulting from a small increase in some activity.

marginal cost
The additional cost resulting from a small increase in some activity.

MARGINAL PRINCIPLE

Increase the level of an activity as long as its marginal benefit exceeds its marginal cost. Choose the level at which the marginal benefit equals the marginal cost.

Thinking at the margin enables us to fine-tune our decisions. We can use the marginal principle to determine whether a one-unit increase in a variable would make us better off. Just as a bookstore owner could decide whether to stay open for one more hour, you could decide whether to study one more hour for a psychology midterm. When we reach the level where the marginal benefit equals the marginal cost, we cannot do any better, and the fine-tuning is done.

How Many Movie Sequels?

To illustrate the marginal principle, let's consider movie sequels. When a movie is successful, its producer naturally thinks about doing another movie, continuing the story line with the same set of characters. If the first sequel is successful too, the producer thinks about producing a second sequel, then a third, and so on. We can use the marginal principle to explore the decision of how many movies to produce.

Figure 2.3 shows the marginal benefits and marginal costs for movies. On the benefit side, a movie sequel typically generates about 30 percent less revenue than the original movie, and revenue continues to drop for additional movies. In the second column of the table, the first movie generates $300 million in revenue, the second generates $210 million, and the third generates $135 million. This is shown in the graph as a negatively sloped marginal-benefit curve, with the marginal benefit decreasing from $300 for the first movie (point *a*), to $210 (point *b*), and then to $135 (point *c*). On the cost side, the typical movie in the United States costs about $50 million to produce and about $75 million to promote.[3] In the third column of the table, the cost of the first movie (the original) is $125 million. In the graph, this is shown as point *d* on the marginal-cost curve. The marginal cost increases with the number of movies because film stars typically demand

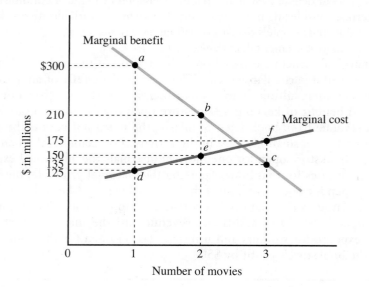

Number of Movies	Marginal Benefit ($ millions)	Marginal Cost ($ millions)
1	$300	$125
2	210	150
3	135	175

▲ **FIGURE 2.3**
The Marginal Principle and Movie Sequels
The marginal benefit of movies in a series decreases because revenue falls off with each additional movie, while the marginal cost increases because actors demand higher salaries. The marginal benefit exceeds the marginal cost for the first two movies, so it is sensible to produce two, but not three, movies.

higher salaries to appear in sequels. In the table and the graph, the marginal cost increases to $150 million for the second movie (point *e*) and to $175 million for the third (point *f*).

In this example, the first two movies are profitable, but the third is not. For the original movie, the marginal benefit ($300 million at point *a*) exceeds the marginal cost ($125 million at point *d*), generating a profit of $175 million. Although the second movie has a higher cost and a lower benefit, it is profitable because the marginal benefit still exceeds the marginal cost, so the profit on the second movie is $60 million ($210 million – $150 million). In contrast, the marginal cost of the third movie of $175 million exceeds its marginal benefit of only $135 million, so the third movie *loses* $40 million. In this example, the movie producer should stop after the second movie.

Although this example shows that only two movies are profitable, other outcomes are possible. If the revenue for the third movie were larger, making the marginal benefit greater than the marginal cost, it would be sensible to produce the third movie. Similarly, if the marginal cost of the third movie were lower—if the actors didn't demand such high salaries—the third movie could be profitable. Many movies have had multiple sequels, such as *Harry Potter and the Sorcerer's Stone* and *Star Wars*. Conversely, many profitable movies, such as *Wedding Crashers* and *Groundhog Day*, didn't result in any sequels. In these cases, the expected drop-off in revenues and run-up in costs for the second movie were large enough to make a sequel unprofitable.

Renting College Facilities

Suppose that your student film society is looking for an auditorium to use for an all-day Hitchcock film program and is willing to pay up to $200. Your college has a new auditorium that has a daily rent of $450, an amount that includes $300 to help pay for the cost of building the auditorium, $50 to help pay for insurance, and $100 to cover the extra costs of electricity and janitorial services for a one-day event. If your film society offers to pay $150 for using the auditorium, should the college accept the offer? The college could use the marginal principle to make the decision.

To decide whether to accept your group's offer, the college should determine the marginal cost of renting out the auditorium. The marginal cost equals the extra costs the college incurs by allowing the student group to use an otherwise vacant auditorium. In our example, the extra cost is $100 for additional electricity and janitorial services. It would be sensible for the college to rent the auditorium, because the marginal benefit ($150 offered by the student group) exceeds the marginal cost ($100). In fact, the college should be willing to rent the facility for any amount greater than $100. If the students and the college split the difference between the $200 the students are willing to pay and the $100 marginal cost, they would agree on a price of $150, leaving both parties better off by $50.

Most colleges do not use this sort of logic. Instead, they use complex formulas to compute the perceived cost of renting out a facility. In most cases, the perceived cost includes some costs that the university bears even if it doesn't rent out the facility for the day. In our example, the facility manager included $300 worth of construction costs and $50 worth of insurance, for a total cost of $450 instead of just $100. Because many colleges include costs that aren't affected by the use of a facility, they overestimate the actual cost of renting out their facilities, missing opportunities to serve student groups and make some money at the same time.

Automobile Emissions Standards

We can use the marginal principle to analyze emissions standards for automobiles. The U.S. government specifies how much carbon monoxide a new car is allowed to emit per mile. The marginal question is "Should the standard be stricter, with fewer units of carbon monoxide allowed?" On the benefit side, a stricter standard reduces health-care costs resulting from pollution: If the air is cleaner, people with respiratory ailments will make fewer visits to doctors and hospitals, have lower medication costs, and lose fewer work days. On the cost side, a stricter standard requires more expensive control equipment on cars and may also reduce fuel efficiency. Using the marginal principle, the government should make the emissions standard stricter as long as the marginal benefit (savings in health-care costs and work time lost) exceeds the marginal cost (the cost of additional equipment and extra fuel used).

Driving Speed and Safety

Consider the decision about how fast to drive on a highway. The marginal benefit of going one mile per hour faster is the travel time you'll save. On the cost side, an increase in speed increases your chances of colliding with another car, and also increases the severity of injuries suffered in a collision. A rational person will pick the speed at which the marginal benefit of speed equals the marginal cost.

In the 1960s and 1970s, the federal government required automakers to include a number of safety features, including seat belts and collapsible steering columns. These new regulations had two puzzling effects. Although deaths from automobile collisions decreased, the reduction was much lower than expected. In addition, more bicyclists were hit by cars and injured or killed.

We can use the marginal principle to explain why seat belts and other safety features made bicycling more hazardous. The mandated safety features decreased the marginal cost of speed: People who wear seat belts suffer less severe injuries in a collision, so every additional unit of speed is less costly. Drivers felt more secure because they were better insulated from harm in the event of a collision, and so they drove faster. As a result, the number of collisions between cars and bicycles increased, meaning that the safer environment for drivers led to a more hazardous environment for bicyclists.

application 2

HOW FAST TO SAIL?

APPLYING THE CONCEPTS #2: How do people think at the margin?

Consider the decision about how fast to sail an ocean cargo ship. As the ship's speed increases, fuel consumption increases. For example, a 70,000-ton cargo ship burns 16.5 tons of fuel per day at 11 knots, compared to 21.4 tons at 12 knots, 27.2 tons at 13 knots, and 33.9 tons at 14 knots. In other words, speed is costly. On the benefit side, an increase in speed means that the ship delivers more cargo per year. To decide the best speed, the ship operator must find the speed at which the marginal cost (the increase in fuel cost) equals the marginal benefit (the increase in revenue from delivered cargo). An increase in the price of fuel increases the marginal cost of speed, causing the shipper to slow the ship. **Related to Exercise 2.4.**

SOURCE: Based on Martin Stopard, *Maritime Economics*, 3rd edition (New York: Routledge, 2007).

2.3 The Principle of Voluntary Exchange

The principle of voluntary exchange is based on the notion that people act in their own self-interest. Self-interested people won't exchange one thing for another unless the trade makes them better off.

> ## PRINCIPLE OF VOLUNTARY EXCHANGE
> A voluntary exchange between two people makes both people better off.

Here are some examples.

- If you voluntarily exchange money for a college education, you must expect you'll be better off with a college education. The college voluntarily provides an education in exchange for your money, so the college must be better off, too.
- If you have a job, you voluntarily exchange your time for money, and your employer exchanges money for your labor services. Both you and your employer are better off as a result.

Exchange and Markets

Adam Smith stressed the importance of voluntary exchange as a distinctly human trait. He noticed[4]

> a propensity in human nature . . . to truck, barter, and exchange one thing for another . . . It is common to all men, and to be found in no other . . . animals . . . Nobody ever saw a dog make a fair and deliberate exchange of one bone for another with another dog.

As we saw in Chapter 1, a market is an institution or arrangement that enables people to exchange goods and services. If participation in a market is voluntary and people are well informed, both people in a transaction—buyer and seller—will be better off. The next time you see a market transaction, listen to what people say after money changes hands. If both people say "thank you," that's the principle of voluntary exchange in action: The double "thank you" reveals that both people are better off.

The alternative to exchange is *self-sufficiency*: Each of us could produce everything for him- or herself. As we'll see in the next chapter, it is more sensible to specialize, doing what we do best and then buying products from other people, who in turn are doing what they do best. For example, if you are good with numbers but an awful carpenter, you could specialize in accounting and buy furniture from Woody, who could specialize in making furniture and pay someone to do his bookkeeping. In general, exchange allows us to take advantage of differences in people's talents and skills.

Online Games and Market Exchange

As another illustration of the power of exchange, consider the virtual world of online games. Role-playing games such as *World of Warcraft* and *EverQuest* allow thousands of people to interact online, moving their characters through a landscape of survival challenges. Each player constructs a character—called an *avatar*—by choosing some initial traits for it. The player then navigates the avatar through the game's challenges, where it acquires skills and accumulates assets, including clothing, weapons, armor, and even magic spells.

The curious part about these role-playing games is that players use real-life auction sites, including eBay and Yahoo! Auctions, to buy products normally acquired in the game.[5] Byron, who wants a piece of armor for his avatar (say, a Rubicite girdle), can use eBay to buy one for $50 from Selma. The two players then enter the online game, and Selma's avatar transfers the armor to Byron's avatar. It is even possible to buy another player's avatar, with all its skills and assets. Given the time required to acquire various objects such as Rubicite girdles in the game and the prices paid for them on eBay, the implicit wage earned by the typical online player auctioning them off is $3.42 per hour: That's how much the player could earn by first taking the time to acquire the assets in the game and then selling them on eBay.

> ## application 3

JASPER JOHNS AND HOUSEPAINTING

APPLYING THE CONCEPTS #3: What is the rationale for specialization and exchange?

Jasper Johns is a contemporary American artist whose painting *False Start* sold for $80 million, the largest sum paid for a painting of a living artist. According to Skate's Art Market Research, Mr. Johns is among the top 30 artists in terms of the monetary value of art produced. Mr. Johns appears as a guest star in a 1999 episode of *The Simpsons* in which Homer uses a mangled barbeque to launch a career as a contemporary artist.

Mr. Johns is a very productive painter, and his painting skills presumably translate into house painting. If Mr. Johns is ten times more productive at house painting than a professional house painter, should he paint his own house? For example, suppose Mr. Johns can paint his house in one day, compared to 10 days for a professional. Should he take a day to paint his house, or hire someone who will take 10 days to complete the same task?

We can use the principle of voluntary exchange to explain why Mr. Johns should hire the less productive house painter to paint his house. If Mr. Johns can earn $5,000 per day painting works of art, the opportunity cost of house painting is $5,000—the income he sacrifices by spending a day painting the house rather than producing works of art. If the housepainter charges $150 per day, Mr. Johns could hire him to paint the house for only $1,500. By switching one day from house painting to art production, Mr. Johns earns $5,000 and incurs a cost of only $1,500, so he is better off by $3,500. Mr. Johns specializes in what he does best, and then buys goods and services from other people. **Related to Exercise 3.5.**

2.4   The Principle of Diminishing Returns

Xena has a small copy shop, with one copying machine and one worker. When the backlog of orders piled up, she decided to hire a second worker, expecting that doubling her workforce would double the output of her copy shop from 500 pages per hour to 1,000. Xena was surprised when output increased to only 800 pages per hour. If she had known about the principle of diminishing returns, she would not have been surprised.

> ## PRINCIPLE OF DIMINISHING RETURNS
> Suppose output is produced with two or more inputs, and we increase one input while holding the other input or inputs fixed. Beyond some point—called the *point of diminishing returns*—output will increase at a decreasing rate.

Xena added a worker (one input) while holding the number of copying machines (the other input) fixed. Because the two workers must share a single copying machine, each worker spent some time waiting for the machine to be available. As a result, adding the second worker increased the number of copies, but did not double the output. With a single worker and a single copy machine, Xena has already reached the point of diminishing returns: As she increases the number of workers, output increases, but at a decreasing rate. The first worker increases output by 500 pages (from 0 to 500), but the second worker increases output by only 300 pages (from 500 to 800).

This principle of diminishing returns is relevant when we try to produce more output in an existing production facility (a factory, a store, an office, or a farm) by increasing the number of workers sharing the facility. When we add a worker to the facility, each worker becomes less productive because he or she works with a smaller piece of the facility: More workers share the same machinery, equipment, and factory space. As we pack more and more workers into the factory, total output increases, but at a decreasing rate.

It's important to emphasize that diminishing returns occurs because one of the inputs to the production process is fixed. When a firm can vary all its inputs, including the size of the production facility, the principle of diminishing returns is not relevant. For example, if a firm doubled all its inputs, building a second factory and hiring a second workforce, we would expect the total output of the firm to at least double. The principle of diminishing returns does not apply when a firm is flexible in choosing all its inputs.

application 4

FERTILIZER AND CROP YIELDS

APPLYING THE CONCEPTS #4: Do farmers experience diminishing returns?

The notion of diminishing returns applies to all inputs to the production process. For example, one of the inputs in the production of corn is nitrogen fertilizer. Suppose a farmer has a fixed amount of land (an acre) and must decide how much fertilizer to apply. The first 50-pound bag of fertilizer will increase the crop yield by a relatively large amount, but the second bag is likely to increase the yield by a smaller amount, and the third bag is likely to have an even smaller effect. Because the farmer is changing just one of the inputs, the output will increase, but at a decreasing rate. Eventually, additional fertilizer will actually decrease output as the other nutrients in the soil are overwhelmed by the fertilizer.

Table 2.1 shows the relationship between the amount of fertilizer and the corn output. The first 50-pound bag of fertilizer increases the crop yield from 85 to 120 bushels per acre, a gain of 35 bushels. The next bag of fertilizer increases the yield by only 15 bushels (from 120 to 135), followed by a gain of 9 bushels (from 135 to 144) and then a gain of only 3 bushels (from 144 to 147). The farmer experienced diminishing returns because the other inputs to the production process are fixed. **Related to Exercises 4.5 and 4.6.**

TABLE 2.1 Fertilizer and Corn Yield	
Bags of Nitrogen Fertilizer	**Bushels of Corn per Acre**
0	85
1	120
2	135
3	144
4	147

2.5 The Real-Nominal Principle

One of the key ideas in economics is that people are interested not just in the amount of money they have but also in how much their money will buy.

> ### REAL-NOMINAL PRINCIPLE
> What matters to people is the real value of money or income—its purchasing power—not its "face" value.

To illustrate this principle, suppose you work in your college bookstore to earn extra money for movies and snacks. If your take-home pay is $10 per hour, is this a high wage or a low wage? The answer depends on the prices of the goods you buy. If a movie costs $4 and a snack costs $1, with one hour of work you could afford to see two movies and buy two snacks. The wage may seem high enough for you. But if a movie costs $8 and a snack costs $2, an hour of work would buy only one movie and one snack, and the same $10 wage doesn't seem so high. This is the real-nominal principle in action: What matters is not how many dollars you earn, but what those dollars will purchase.

Economists use special terms to express the ideas behind the real-nominal principle:

- The **nominal value** of an amount of money is simply its face value. For example, the nominal wage paid by the bookstore is $10 per hour.

- The **real value** of an amount of money is measured in terms of the quantity of goods the money can buy. For example, the real value of your bookstore wage would fall as the prices of movies and snacks increase, even though your nominal wage stayed the same.

nominal value
The face value of an amount of money.

real value
The value of an amount of money in terms of what it can buy.

The real-nominal principle can explain how people choose the amount of money to carry around with them. Suppose you typically withdraw $40 per week from an ATM to cover your normal expenses. If the prices of all the goods you purchase during the week double, you would have to withdraw $80 per week to make the same purchases. The amount of money people carry around depends on the prices of the goods and services they buy.

The Design of Public Programs

Government officials use the real-nominal principle when they design public programs. For example, Social Security payments are increased each year to ensure that the checks received by the elderly and other recipients will purchase the same amount of goods and services, even if prices have increased. The government also uses this principle when it publishes statistics about the economy. For example, its reports about changes in "real wages" in the economy over time take into account the prices of the goods workers purchase. Therefore, the real wage is stated in terms of its buying power, rather than its face value or nominal value.

The Value of the Minimum Wage

Between 1974 and 2011, the federal minimum wage increased from $2.00 to $7.25. Was the typical minimum-wage worker better or worse off in 2011? We can apply the real-nominal principle to see what's happened over time to the real value of the federal minimum wage.

As shown in the second row of Table 2.2, a full-time worker earning the minimum wage earned $80 in 1974 and $290 in 2011. The third row of Table 2.2 shows the cost of a standard basket of consumer goods, which includes a standard mix of housing, food, clothing, and transportation. In 1974, consumer prices were relatively low, and the cost of buying all the goods in the standard basket was only $47. Between 1974 and 2011, consumer prices increased, and the cost of this standard basket of goods increased to $225.

The last row in Table 2.2 shows the purchasing power of the minimum wage. In 1974, the $80 in weekly income could buy 1.70 standard baskets of goods. Between 1974 and 2011, the weekly income more than tripled, but the cost of the standard basket of goods more than quadrupled. As a result, the weekly income of $290 in 2011 could buy only 1.29 baskets of goods. Because prices increased faster than the nominal wage, the real value of the minimum wage actually decreased over this period.

TABLE 2.2 The Real Value of the Minimum Wage, 1974–2011		
	1974	**2011**
Minimum wage per hour	$ 2.00	$ 7.25
Weekly income from minimum wage	80	290
Cost of a standard basket of goods	47	225
Number of baskets per week	1.70	1.29

application 5

REPAYING STUDENT LOANS

APPLYING THE CONCEPTS #5: How does inflation affect lenders and borrowers?

Suppose you finish college with $20,000 in student loans and start a job that pays a salary of $40,000 in the first year. In 10 years, you must repay your college loans. Which would you prefer: stable prices, rising prices, or falling prices?

We can use the real-nominal principle to compute the real cost of repaying your loans. The first row of Table 2.3 shows the cost of the loan when all prices in the economy are stable—including the price of labor, your salary. In this case, your nominal salary in 10 years is $40,000, and the real cost of repaying your loan is the half year of work you must do to earn the $20,000 you owe. However, if all prices double over the 10-year period, your nominal salary will double to $80,000, and, as shown in the second row of Table 2.3, it will take you only a quarter of a year to earn $20,000 to repay the loan. In other words, a general increase in prices lowers the real cost of your loan. In contrast, if all prices decrease and your annual salary drops to $20,000, it will take you a full year to earn the money to repay the loan. In general, people who owe money prefer inflation (a general rise in prices) to deflation (a general drop in prices). **Related to Exercises 5.6 and 5.9.**

TABLE 2.3 Effect of Inflation and Deflation on Loan Repayment		
Change in Prices and Wages	**Annual Salary**	**Years of Work to Repay $20,000 Loan**
Stable	$40,000	1/2 year
Inflation: Salary doubles	80,000	1/4 year
Deflation: Salary cut in half	20,000	1 year

This chapter covers five key principles of economics, the simple, self-evident truths that most people readily accept. If you understand these principles, you are ready to read the rest of the book, which will show you how to do your own economic analysis.

1 Principle of opportunity cost. The opportunity cost of something is what you sacrifice to get it.

2 Marginal principle. Increase the level of an activity as long as its marginal benefit exceeds its marginal cost. Choose the level at which the marginal benefit equals the marginal cost.

3 Principle of voluntary exchange. A voluntary exchange between two people makes both people better off.

4 Principle of diminishing returns. Suppose that output is produced with two or more inputs, and we increase one input while holding the other inputs fixed. Beyond some point—called the *point of diminishing returns*—output will increase at a decreasing rate.

5 Real-nominal principle. What matters to people is the real value of money or income—its purchasing power—not the face value of money or income.

KEY TERMS

marginal benefit, p. 33
marginal cost, p. 33

nominal value, p. 41
opportunity cost, p. 29

production possibilities curve, p. 31
real value, p. 41

EXERCISES   All problems are assignable in MyEconLab; exercises that update with real-time data are marked with .

2.1   The Principle of Opportunity Cost

1.1 Consider Figure 2.1 on page 31. Between points *c* and *d*, the opportunity cost of _____ tons of wheat is _____ tons of steel.

1.2 Arrow up or down: An increase in the wage for high-school graduates _____ the opportunity cost of college.

1.3 Arrow up or down: An increase in the market interest rate _____ the economic cost of holding a $500 collectible for a year.

1.4 You just inherited a house with a market value of $300,000, and do not expect the market value to change. Each year, you will pay $1,000 for utilities and $3,000 in taxes. You can earn 6 percent interest on money in a bank account. Your cost of living in the house for a year is $ _____.

1.5 What is the cost of a pair of warships purchased by Malaysia?

1.6 Conservationists have a new strategy for preserving rainforests: _____ loggers and other developers for the land, paying as little as $ _____ per hectare per year.

1.7 **The Cost of a Flower Business.** Jen left a job paying $40,000 per year to start her own florist shop in a building she owns. The market value of the building is $200,000. She pays $30,000 per year for flowers and other supplies, and has a bank account that pays 8 percent interest. The annual economic cost of Jen's business is _____. (Related to Application 1 on page 33.)

1.8 **The Opportunity Cost of a Mission to Mars.** The United States has plans to spend billions of dollars on a mission to Mars. List some of the possible opportunity costs of the mission. What resources will be used to execute the mission, and what do we sacrifice by using these resources in a mission to Mars?

1.9 **Interest Rates and ATM Trips.** Carlos, who lives in a country where interest rates are very high, goes to an ATM every day to get $10 of spending money. Art, who lives in a country with relatively low interest rates, goes to the ATM once a month to get $300 of spending money. Why does Carlos use the ATM more frequently?

1.10 **Correct the Cost Statements.** Consider the following statements about cost. For each incorrect statement, provide a correct statement about the relevant cost.

    a. One year ago, I loaned a friend $100, and she just paid me back the whole $100. The loan didn't cost me anything.

    b. An oil refinery bought a million barrels of oil a month ago, when the price was only $75 per barrel, compared to $120 today. The cost of using a barrel of oil to produce gasoline is $75.

    c. Our new football stadium was built on land donated to the university by a wealthy alum. The cost of the stadium equals the $50 million construction cost.

    d. If a commuter rides a bus to work and the bus fare is $2, the cost of commuting by bus is $2.

1.11 **Production Possibilities Curve.** Consider a nation that produces baseball mitts and soccer balls. The following table shows the possible combinations of the two products.

Baseball mitts (millions)	0	2	4	6	8
Soccer balls (millions)	30	24	18	10	0

    a. Draw a production possibilities curve with mitts on the horizontal axis and balls on the vertical axis.

    b. Suppose the technology for producing mitts improves, meaning that fewer resources are needed for each mitt. In contrast, the technology for producing soccer balls does not change. Draw a new production possibilities curve.

    c. The opportunity cost of the first two million mitts is _____ million soccer balls and the opportunity cost of the last two million mitts is _____ million soccer balls.

1.12 **Cost of Antique Furniture.** Colleen owns antique furniture that she bought for $5,000 ten years ago.

Your job is to compute Colleen's cost of owning the furniture for the next year. To compute the cost, you need two bits of information: _____ and _____.

2.2 The Marginal Principle

2.1 A taxi company currently has nine cabs in its fleet, and its total daily cost is $4,000. If the company added a tenth cab, its daily total cost would be $4,200, or $420 per cab. Adding the tenth cab will increase the daily total revenue by $300. Should the company add the tenth cab? _____ (Yes/No)

2.2 In Figure 2.3 on page 34, suppose the marginal cost of movies is constant at $125 million. Is it sensible to produce the third movie? _____ (Yes/No)

2.3 Suppose that stricter emissions standards would reduce health-care costs by $50 million but increase the costs of fuel and emissions equipment by $30 million. Is it sensible to tighten the emissions standards? _____ (Yes/No)

2.4 Arrows up or down: The decision about how fast to sail a cargo ship is based on the _____ benefit and the _____ cost. (Related to Application 2 on page 36.)

2.5 **How Fast to Drive?** Suppose Duke is driving to a nearby town to attend a dance party, and must decide how fast to drive. The marginal benefit of speed is the extra dance time he will get by driving faster, and the marginal cost is the additional risk of a collision. The marginal-benefit curve is negatively sloped, and the marginal-cost curve is positively sloped.

    a. Draw a pair of curves that suggest Duke will drive 40 mph.

    b. Suppose the normal country band is replaced by Adam Smith and the Invisible Hands, Duke's favorite punk band. Duke's utility from slam dancing is twice his utility from the two-step. Use your curves to show how Duke's chosen speed will change.

    c. Suppose Duke's favorite dance partner, Daisy, is grounded for makeup violations. Use your curves to show how Duke's chosen speed will change.

    d. Suppose the legal speed limit is set at 35 mph, and there is a 50 percent chance that Duke will be caught if he speeds. Use your curves to show how Duke's chosen speed will change.

2.6 **Continental Airlines Goes Marginal.** In the 1960s, Continental Airlines puzzled observers of the airline industry and dismayed its stockholders by running flights with up to half the seats empty. The average cost of running a flight was $4,000, a figure that includes fixed costs such as airport fees and the cost of running the reservation system. A half-full aircraft generated only $3,100 of revenue.

    a. Use the marginal principle to explain why Continental ran half-empty flights.

    b. It will be sensible to run a half-empty flight if the marginal _____ of flight is _____ than $_____.

2.7 Marginal Airlines. Marginal Airlines runs 10 flights per day at a total cost of $50,000, including $30,000 in fixed costs for airport fees and the reservation system and $20,000 for flight crews and food service.

    a. If an 11th flight would have 25 passengers, each paying $100, would it be sensible to run the flight?

    b. If the 11th flight would have only 15 passengers, would it be sensible to run the flight?

2.8 How Many Police Officers? In your city, each police officer has a budgetary cost of $40,000 per year. The property loss from each burglary is $4,000. The first officer hired will reduce crime by 40 burglaries, and each additional officer will reduce crime by half as much as the previous one. How many officers should the city hire? Illustrate with a graph with a marginal-benefit curve and a marginal-cost curve.

2.9 How Many Hours at the Barber Shop? The opportunity cost of your time spent cutting hair at your barber shop is $20 per hour. Electricity costs $6 per hour, and your weekly rent is $250. You normally stay open nine hours per day.

    a. What is the marginal cost of staying open for one more hour?

    b. If you expect to give two haircuts in the 10th hour and you charge $15 per haircut, is it sensible to stay open for the extra hour?

2.10 How Many Pints of Blackberries? The pleasure you get from each pint of freshly picked blackberries is $2.00. It takes you 12 minutes to pick the first pint, and each additional pint takes an additional 2 minutes (14 minutes for the second pint, 16 minutes for the third pint, and so on). The opportunity cost of your time is $0.10 per minute.

    a. How many pints of blackberries should you pick? Illustrate with a complete graph.

    b. How would your answer to (a) change if your pleasure decreased by $0.20 for each additional pint ($1.80 for the second, $1.60 for the third, and so on)? Illustrate with a complete graph.

2.3 The Principle of Voluntary Exchange

3.1 When two people involved in an exchange say "thank you" afterwards, they are merely being polite. _____ (True/False)

3.2 Consider a transaction in which a consumer buys a book for $15. The value of the book to the buyer is at least $_____, and the cost of producing the book is no more than $_____.

3.3 Arrow up or down: Andy buys and eats one apple per day, and smacks his lips in appreciation as he eats it. The greater his satisfaction with the exchange of money for an apple, the larger the number of smacks. If the price of apples decreases, the number of smacks per apple will _____.

3.4 Sally sells one apple per day to Andy, and says "ca-ching" to show her satisfaction with the transaction. The greater her satisfaction with the exchange, the louder her "ca-ching." If the price of apples decreases, her "ca-ching" will become _____ (louder/softer).

3.5 Should a Heart Surgeon Do Her Own Plumbing? A heart surgeon is skillful at unplugging arteries and rerouting the flow of blood, and these skills also make her a very skillful plumber. She can clear a clogged drain in six minutes, about 10 times faster than the most skillful plumber in town. (Related to Application 3 on page 38.)

    a. Should the surgeon clear her own clogged drains? Explain.

    b. Suppose the surgeon earns $20 per minute in heart surgery, and the best plumber in town charges $50 per hour. How much does the surgeon gain by hiring the plumber to clear a clogged drain?

3.6 Fishing versus Boat Building. Half the members of a fishing tribe catch two fish per day and half catch eight fish per day. A group of 10 members could build a boat for another tribe in one day and receive a payment of 40 fish for the boat.

    a. Suppose the boat builders are drawn at random from the tribe. From the tribe's perspective, what is the expected cost of building the boat?

    b. How could the tribe decrease the cost of building the boat, thus making it worthwhile?

3.7 Solving a Tree Cutting Problem. Consider a hilly neighborhood where large trees provide shade but also block views. When a resident announces plans to cut down several trees to improve her view, her neighbors object and announce plans to block the tree cutting.

One week later, the trees are gone, but everyone is happy. Use the principle of voluntary exchange to explain what happened.

2.4 The Principle of Diminishing Returns

4.1 Consider the example of Xena's copy shop. Adding a second worker increased output by 300 pages. If she added a third worker, her output would increase by fewer than _____ pages.

4.2 If a firm is subject to diminishing marginal returns, an increase in the number of workers decreases the quantity produced. _____ (True/False)

4.3 Fill in the blanks with "at least" or "less than": If a firm doubles one input but holds the other inputs fixed, we normally expect output to _____ double; if a firm doubles all inputs, we expect output to _____ double.

4.4 Fill in the blanks with "flexible" or "inflexible": Diminishing returns is applicable when a firm is _____ in choosing inputs, but does not apply when a firm is _____ in choosing its inputs.

4.5 Arrows up or down: As a farmer adds more and more fertilizer to the soil, the crop yield _____, but at a _____ rate. (Related to Application 4 on page 40.)

4.6 **Feeding the World from a Flowerpot?** Comment on the following statement: "If agriculture did not experience diminishing returns, we could feed the world using the soil from a small flowerpot." (Related to Application 4 on page 40.)

4.7 **When to Use the Principle of Diminishing Returns?** You are the manager of a firm that produces memory chips for mobile phones.
  a. In your decision about how much output to produce this week, would you use the principle of diminishing returns? Explain.
  b. In your decision about how much output to produce two years from now, would you use the principle of diminishing returns? Explain.

4.8 **Diminishing Returns in Microbrewing?** Your microbrewery produces craft beer, using a single vat, various ingredients, and workers.
  a. If you double the number of workers and ingredients, but don't add a second vat, would you expect your output (gallons per hour) to double? Explain.
  b. If you double the number of workers and ingredients and add a second vat, would you expect your output (gallons per hour) to double? Explain.

4.9 **Diminishing Returns and the Marginal Principle.** Molly's Espresso Shop has become busy, and the more hours Ted works, the more espressos Molly can sell.

The price of espressos is $2 and Ted's hourly wage is $11. Complete the following table:

Hours for Ted	Espressos Sold	Marginal Benefit from Additional Hour	Marginal Cost from Additional Hour
0	100	—	—
1	130	$60 = $2 × 30 additional espressos	$11 = hourly wage
2	154		
3	172		
4	184		
5	190		
6	193		

If Molly applies the marginal principle, how many hours should Ted work?

2.5 The Real-Nominal Principle

5.1 Your savings account pays 4 percent per year: Each $100 in the bank grows to $104 over a one-year period. If prices increase by 3 percent per year, by keeping $100 in the bank for a year you actually gain $_____.

5.2 You earn 5 percent interest on funds in your money-market account. If consumer prices increase by 7 percent per year, your earnings on $1,000 in the money-market account is $_____ per year.

5.3 Suppose that over a one-year period, the nominal wage increases by 2 percent and consumer prices increase by 5 percent. Fill in the blanks: The real wage _____ by _____ percent.

5.4 Suppose you currently live and work in Cleveland, earning a salary of $60,000 per year and spending $10,000 for housing. You just heard that you will be transferred to a city in California where housing is 50 percent more expensive. In negotiating a new salary, your objective is to keep your real income constant. Your new target salary is $_____.

5.5 Between 1974 and 2011, the federal minimum wage increased from $2.00 to $7.25. Was the typical minimum-wage worker better off in 2011? _____ (Yes/No)

5.6 Suppose you graduate with $20,000 in student loans and repay the loans 10 years later. Which is better for you, inflation (rising prices) or deflation (falling prices)? _____ (Related to Application 5 on page 42.)

5.7 **Changes in Welfare Payments.** Between 1970 and 1988, the average monthly welfare payment to single mothers increased from $160 to $360. Over the same period, the cost of a standard basket of consumer goods (a standard bundle of food, housing, and other goods and services) increased from $39 to $118. Fill the blanks in the following table. Did the real value of welfare payments increase or decrease over this period?

	1970	1988
Monthly welfare payment	$160	$360
Cost of a standard basket of goods	39	118
Number of baskets per week		

5.8 **Changes in Wages and Consumer Prices.** The following table shows for 1980 and 2004 the cost of a standard basket of consumer goods (a standard bundle of food, housing, and other goods and services) and the nominal average wage (hourly earnings) for workers in several sectors of the economy.

Year	Cost of Consumer Basket	Nominal Wage: Manufacturing	Nominal Wage: Professional Services	Nominal Wage: Leisure and Hospitality	Nominal Wage: Information
1980	$ 82	$ 7.52	$ 7.48	$4.05	$ 9.83
2004	189	16.34	17.69	9.01	21.70
Percent change from 1980 to 2004					

a. Complete the table by computing the percentage changes of the cost of the basket of consumer goods and the nominal wages.

b. How do the percentage changes in nominal wages compare to the percentage change in the cost of consumer goods?

c. Which sectors experienced an increase in real wages, and which sectors experienced a decrease in real wages?

5.9 **Repaying a Car Loan.** Suppose you borrow money to buy a car and must repay $20,000 in interest and principal in five years. Your current monthly salary is $4,000. (Related to Application 5 on page 42.)

a. Complete the following table.

b. Which environment has the lowest real cost of repaying the loan?

Change in Prices and Wages	Monthly Salary	Months of Work to Repay $20,000 Loan
Stable	$4,000	
Inflation: Prices rise by 25%		
Deflation: Prices drop by 50%		

5.10 **Inflation and Interest Rates.** Len buys MP3 music at $1 per tune, and prefers music now to music later. He is willing to sacrifice 10 tunes today as long as he gets at least 11 tunes in a year. When Len loans $50 to Barb for a one-year period, he cuts back his music purchases by 50 tunes.

a. To make Len indifferent about making the loan, Barb must repay him _____ tunes or $_____. The implied interest rate is _____ percent.

b. Suppose that over the one-year period of the loan, all prices (including the price of MP3 tunes) increase by 20 percent, and Len and Barb anticipate the price changes. To make Len indifferent about making the loan, Barb must repay him _____ tunes or $_____. The implied interest rate is _____ percent.

ECONOMIC EXPERIMENT

PRODUCING FOLD-ITS

Here is a simple economic experiment that takes about 15 minutes to run. The instructor places a stapler and a stack of paper on a table. Students produce "fold-its" by folding a page of paper in thirds and stapling both ends of the folded page. One student is assigned to inspect each fold-it to be sure that it is produced correctly. The experiment starts with a single student, or worker, who has one minute to produce as many fold-its as possible. After the instructor records the number of fold-its produced, the process is repeated with two students, three students, four students, and so on. How does the number of fold-its change as the number of workers increases?

MyEconLab

For additional economic experiments, please visit
www.myeconlab.com.

1. "Rent a Tree," *The Economist*, March 3, 2008.

2. United Nations Development Program, *Human Development Report 1994* (New York: Oxford University Press, 1994); Linda Bilmes and Joseph Stiglitz, "The Economic Costs of the Iraq War: An Appraisal Three Years after the Beginning of the Conflict," *Faculty Research Working Papers*, Harvard University, January 2006; Center for American Progress, "The Opportunity Costs of the Iraq War," August 25, 2004; Scott Wallsten and Katrina Kosec, "The Economic Costs of the War in Iraq," AEI-Brookings Joint Center for Regulatory Studies, September 2005; Joseph Stiglitz and Linda Bilmes, *The Three Trillion Dollar War* (New York: WW Norton, 2008).

3. Colin Kennedy, "Lord of the Screens," in *Economist: The World in 2003* (London, 2003), 29.

4. Adam Smith, *An Inquiry into the Nature and Causes of the Wealth of Nations* (1776), Book 1, Chapter 2.

5. Edward Castronova, *Synthetic Worlds: The Business and Culture of Online Games* (Chicago: University of Chicago Press, 2005).

Exchange and Markets

The nation of Latvia is located on the shore of the Baltic Sea, and since the 14th century has been a major commercial hub between west and east.

Latvia was at the center of the Hanseatic League, the world's first Free Trade Area. But in the early 1990s, after several decades of being part of the Soviet Union, Latvia suffered from low labor productivity in the production of most goods. The following table shows output per worker for Latvia and the European Community (EC, a group of six nearby European countries).

	European Community	Latvia
Saw timber	1200	200
Milk	250	15
Livestock	100	4
Grain	200	10

Latvia's prospects for trade with the EC appear to be dim: Why would a member of the EC purchase goods produced by such low-productivity workers? Why not just use more productive EC workers to produce everything?

LEARNING OBJECTIVES

- Use opportunity cost to explain the rationale for specialization and trade.

- Explain how markets allow specialization and trade.

- List the roles of government in a market economy.

> MyEconLab
> MyEconLab helps you master each objective and study more efficiently.

*i*n Chapter 1, we saw that a society makes three types of economic decisions: what products to produce, how to produce them, and who gets them. In modern economies, most of these decisions are made in markets. Most of us participate in the labor market and are paid for jobs in which we produce goods and services for others. We participate in consumer markets, spending our incomes on food, clothing, housing, and other products. In this chapter, we explain why markets exist and then explore the virtues and the shortcomings of markets. We also examine the role of government in a market-based economy.

3.1 Comparative Advantage and Exchange

As we saw earlier in the book, a market is an institution or arrangement that enables people to buy and sell things. An alternative to buying and selling in markets is to be self-sufficient, with each of us producing everything we need for ourselves. Rather than going it alone, most of us specialize: We produce one or two products for others and then exchange the money we earn for the products we want to consume.

Specialization and the Gains from Trade

We can explain how people can benefit from specialization and trade with a simple example of two people and two products. Suppose that the crew of the television show *Survivor* finishes filming a season of episodes on a remote tropical island, and when the crew returns to the mainland two people miss the boat and are left behind. The two real survivors produce and consume two goods, coconuts and fish. The first row of Table 3.1 shows their production possibilities. Each day Fred can either gather 2 coconuts or catch 6 fish, while Kate can either gather 1 coconut or catch 1 fish.

TABLE 3.1 Productivity and Opportunity Costs				
	Fred		**Kate**	
	Coconuts	*Fish*	*Coconuts*	*Fish*
Output per day	2	6	1	1
Opportunity cost	3 fish	1/3 coconut	1 fish	1 coconut

We'll show that the two survivors will be better off if each person specializes in one product and then exchanges with the other person. We can use one of the key principles of economics to explore the rationale for specialization.

PRINCIPLE OF OPPORTUNITY COST
The opportunity cost of something is what you sacrifice to get it.

Fred's opportunity cost of 1 coconut is 3 fish—that's how many fish he could catch in the time required to gather 1 coconut. Similarly, his opportunity cost of a fish is 1/3 coconut, the number of coconuts he could gather in the time required to catch 1 fish. For Kate, the opportunity cost of 1 coconut is 1 fish, and the opportunity cost of 1 fish is 1 coconut.

To demonstrate the benefits of exchange, let's imagine that both people are initially self-sufficient, with each producing enough of both goods to satisfy their own desires. Suppose they devote six days per week to finding food. If Fred initially devotes two days per week to gathering coconuts and four days per week to catching fish, he will produce and consume 4 coconuts (2 per day times two days) and 24 fish (6 per day times four days) per week. This is shown in the first column of Figure 3.1. If Kate initially devotes one day per week to coconuts and five days per week to fish, she will produce and consume 1 coconut and 5 fish per week.

Self-Sufficient	Specialize: Fred in Fish, Kate in Coconuts	Exchange 10 Fish and 5 Coconuts
Fred produces and consumes 4 coconuts and 24 fish.	Fred specializes and produces 36 fish.	Fred gives Kate 10 fish for 5 coconuts. He gains 1 coconut and 2 fish.
(4)		(5)
(24)	(36)	(26)
Kate produces and consumes 1 coconut and 5 fish.	Kate specializes and produces 6 coconuts.	Kate gives Fred 5 coconuts for 10 fish. She gains 5 fish.
(1)	(6)	(1)
(5)		(10)

▲ FIGURE 3.1
Specialization and the Gains from Trade

comparative advantage
The ability of one person or nation to produce a good at a lower opportunity cost than another person or nation.

Specialization will increase the total output of our little survivor economy. It is sensible for each person to specialize in the good for which he or she has a lower opportunity cost. We say that a person has a **comparative advantage** in producing a particular product if he or she has a lower opportunity cost than another person:

- Fred has a comparative advantage in producing fish because his opportunity cost of fish is 1/3 coconut per fish, compared to 1 coconut per fish for Kate.

- Kate has a comparative advantage in harvesting coconuts because her opportunity cost of coconuts is 1 fish per coconut, compared to 3 fish per coconut for Fred.

The second column of Figure 3.1 shows what happens to production when the two people specialize: Fred produces 36 fish and Kate produces 6 coconuts. The total output of both goods increases: The number of coconuts increases from 5 to 6, and the number of fish increases from 29 to 36. Specialization increases the output of both goods because both people are focusing on what they do best.

If specialization is followed by exchange, both people will be better off. Suppose Fred and Kate agree to exchange 2 fish per coconut. Fred could give up 10 fish to get 5 coconuts. As shown in the third column of Figure 3.1, that leaves him with 5 coconuts and 26 fish. Compared to the self-sufficient outcome, he has more of both goods—1 more coconut and 2 more fish. If Kate gives up 5 coconuts to get 10 fish, that leaves her with 1 coconut and 10 fish, which is better than her self-sufficient outcome of 1 coconut and 5 fish. Specialization and exchange make both people better off, illustrating one of the key principles of economics:

PRINCIPLE OF VOLUNTARY EXCHANGE
A voluntary exchange between two people makes both people better off.

Comparative Advantage versus Absolute Advantage

We've seen that it is beneficial for each person to specialize in the product for which he or she has a comparative advantage—a lower opportunity cost. You may have noticed that Fred is more productive than Kate in producing both goods. Fred requires a smaller quantity of resources (in this case less labor time) to produce both goods, so he has an **absolute advantage** in producing both goods. Despite his absolute advantage, Fred gains from specialization and trade because he has a comparative advantage in fish. Fred is twice as productive as Kate in producing coconuts, but six times as productive in producing fish. By relying on Kate to produce coconuts, Fred frees up time to spend producing fish, the good for which he has the larger productivity advantage over Kate. The lesson is that specialization and exchange result from comparative advantage, not absolute advantage.

absolute advantage
The ability of one person or nation to produce a product at a lower resource cost than another person or nation.

The Division of Labor and Exchange

So far we've seen that specialization and trade exploit differences in productivity across workers and make everyone better off. We've assumed that the differences in productivity are innate, not acquired. In his 1776 book *An Inquiry into the Nature and Causes of the Wealth of Nations*, Adam Smith noted that specialization actually increased productivity through the division of labor. He used the example of the pin factory to illustrate how the division of labor increased output:[1]

> A workman . . . could scarce, perhaps with his utmost industry, make one pin a day, and certainly could not make twenty. But the way in which this business is now carried on . . . one man draws out the wire, another straightens it, a third cuts it, a fourth points it, a fifth grinds the top for receiving the head; to make the head requires two or three distinct operations. . . . The . . . making of a pin is, in this manner, divided into about eighteen distinct operations. . . . I have seen a small manufactory of this kind where ten men . . . make among them . . . upward of forty eight thousand pins in a day.

Smith listed three reasons for productivity to increase with specialization, with each worker performing a single production task:

1 *Repetition.* The more times a worker performs a particular task, the more proficient the worker becomes at that task.

2 *Continuity.* A specialized worker doesn't spend time switching from one task to another. This is especially important if switching tasks requires a change in tools or location.

3 *Innovation.* A specialized worker gains insights into a particular task that lead to better production methods. Smith believed that workers were innovators:[2]

> A great part of the machines made use of in those manufactures in which labour is most subdivided, were originally the inventions of common workmen, who, being each of them employed in some simple operation, naturally turned their thoughts toward finding out easier and readier methods of performing it.

To summarize, specialization and exchange result from differences in productivity that lead to comparative advantage. Differences in productivity result from differences in innate skills and the benefits associated with the division of labor. Adam Smith wrote that "every man thus lives by exchanging, or becomes in some measure a merchant, and the society itself grows to be what is properly a commercial society."[3]

Comparative Advantage and International Trade

The lessons of comparative advantage and specialization apply to trade between nations. Each nation could be self-sufficient, producing all the goods it consumes, or it could specialize in products for which it has a comparative advantage. Even if one nation is more productive than a second nation in producing all goods, trade will be beneficial if the first nation has a bigger productivity advantage in one

import

A good or service produced in a foreign country and purchased by residents of the home country (for example, the United States).

export

A good or service produced in the home country (for example, the United States) and sold in another country.

product—that is, if one nation has a comparative advantage in some product. An **import** is a product produced in a foreign country and purchased by residents of the home country. An **export** is a product produced in the home country and sold in another country.

Many people are skeptical about the idea that international trade can make everyone better off. President Abraham Lincoln expressed his discomfort with importing goods:[4]

> I know if I buy a coat in America, I have a coat and America has the money—If I buy a coat in England, I have the coat and England has the money.

What President Lincoln didn't understand is that when he buys a coat in England, he sends dollars to England, but the dollars don't just sit there. Eventually they are sent back to the United States to buy goods produced by U.S. workers. In the words of economist Todd Buchholz, the author of *New Ideas from Dead Economists*,[5]

> Money may not make the world go round, but money certainly goes around the world. To stop it prevents goods from traveling from where they are produced most inexpensively to where they are desired most deeply.

Outsourcing

When a domestic firm shifts part of its production to a different country, we say the firm is *outsourcing* or *offshoring*. In the modern global economy, transportation and communication costs are relatively low, so firms can spread production across many countries. By taking advantage of the comparative advantages of different countries, a firm can produce its product at a lower cost, charge a lower price, and sell more output.

Firms shift functions such as customer service, telemarketing, document management, and medical transcription overseas to reduce production costs, allowing them to sell their products at lower prices. Some recent studies of outsourcing have reached a number of conclusions:[6]

1 The loss of domestic jobs resulting from outsourcing is a normal part of a healthy economy because technology and consumer preferences change over time. The number of jobs lost to outsourcing is a small fraction of the normal job loss experienced by a healthy economy. For example, in the first three months of 2004, a total of 239,361 workers were laid off, with 9,985 jobs moving to another location within the United States, 4,633 outsourced to another country, and the rest simply lost to the economy. This means that roughly 2 percent of reported layoffs were caused by outsourcing.

2 The jobs lost to outsourcing are at least partly offset by jobs gained through *insourcing*, jobs that are shifted from overseas to the United States.

3 The cost savings from outsourcing are substantial, leading to lower prices for consumers and more output for firms. The jobs gained from increased output at least partly offset the jobs lost to outsourcing.

application 1

ABSOLUTE DISADVANTAGE AND COMPARATIVE ADVANTAGE IN LATVIA

APPLYING THE CONCEPTS #1: What is the rationale for specialization and trade?

Recall the chapter opener about the nation of Latvia, which in the 1990s was much less productive than nations in the European Community. The question is, Why would a member of the EC, whose workers are more productive than Latvian workers in the production of all goods, buy any products from Latvia? The following table shows worker productivity and the opportunity cost of production for two products, saw timber and grain.

	EC: Saw Timber	EC: Grain	Latvia: Saw Timber	Latvia: Grain
Output	1200	200	200	10
Opportunity Cost	1/6 Grain	6 Saw timber	1/20 Grain	20 Saw timber

Although the EC has an absolute advantage in both products, it has a comparative advantage (a lower opportunity cost) in grain: the opportunity cost of one unit of grain is 6 units of saw timber in the EC, compared to 20 units of saw timber in Latvia. Latvia has a comparative advantage in saw timber: the opportunity cost is 1/20 units of grain in Latvia, compared to 1/6 units of grain in the EC. Based on the notion of comparative advantage, we know that both the EC and Latvia can be made better off if the EC produces grain in exchange for saw timber produced by Latvia. The EC specializes in grain because that's the product for which it has the largest productivity advantage: the productivity ratio is 20:1 for grain, compared to only 6:1 for saw timber. **Related to Exercise 1.10.**

SOURCE: Based on Aleksandrs Fedotovs, "A small nation's comparative advantage: The case of Latvia," *Business and Economic Horizons* 1 (2010), pp. 51–57.

3.2   Markets

Earlier in the chapter, we used a simple example of direct exchange to show the benefits of specialization and exchange. In a modern economy, people don't directly exchange goods like fish and coconuts, but instead rely on all sorts of markets to exchange goods and services, trading what they have for what they want. In a **market economy**, most people specialize in one productive activity by picking

market economy

An economy in which people specialize and exchange goods and services in markets.

an occupation, and use their incomes to buy most of the goods they consume. In addition to the labor and consumer markets, many of us participate in the market for financial capital: We earn interest from savings accounts and money-market accounts and pay interest on mortgages, car loans, and student loans. Friedrich Hayek, a famous twentieth-century economist, suggested that if the market system hadn't arisen naturally, it would have been proclaimed the greatest invention in human history.[7]

Although it appears that markets arose naturally, a number of social and government inventions have made them work better:

- **Contracts specify the terms of exchange, facilitating exchange between strangers.** If you have a cell phone provider, you expect to have reliable phone service as long as you pay your bill. If you operate a bookstore, you expect book wholesalers to deliver the books you've purchased. In both cases, a contract specifies the terms of exchange.

- **Insurance reduces the risk entrepreneurs face.** If you operate a bagel shop, fire insurance reduces your losses in the event of a fire.

- **Patents increase the profitability of inventions, encouraging firms to develop new products and production processes.** Pharmaceutical companies such as Bayer Pharmaceutical and Merck spend billions of dollars to create, test, and bring new products to the market. A patent prevents other companies from copying a new product, making it more likely that the revenue from a new product will be large enough to cover research and development costs.

- **Accounting rules provide potential investors with reliable information about the financial performance of a firm.** If you are thinking about investing in Apple Inc., you can use publicly available information to examine the company's financial history.

Virtues of Markets

centrally planned economy
An economy in which a government bureaucracy decides how much of each good to produce, how to produce the good, and who gets the good.

To assess the virtues of the market system, imagine an alternative—a **centrally planned economy** in which a planning authority decides what products to produce, how to produce them, and who gets them. To make these decisions, a planner must first collect a huge amount of widely dispersed information about consumption desires (what products each individual wants), production techniques (what resources are required to produce each product), and the availability of factors of production (labor, human capital, physical capital, and natural resources). Then the planner must decide how to allocate the productive resources among the alternative products. Finally, the planner must divide the output among the economy's citizens. Clearly, a central planner has a formidable task.

Under a market system, decisions are made by the millions of people who already have information about consumers' desires, production technology, and resources. These decisions are guided by prices of inputs and outputs. To illustrate, suppose you buy a wool coat. The dozens of people who contributed to the production of the coat—including the farmers who manage the sheep, the workers who transform raw wool into cloth and the cloth into a coat, the truckers who transport the inputs and the actual coat, and the merchant who sold the coat—didn't know *you* wanted a coat:

- The farmer knew that the price of wool was high enough to justify raising and shearing sheep.
- The workers knew that wages were high enough to make their efforts worthwhile.
- The merchant knew that the retail price of the coat was high enough to make it worthwhile to acquire the coat in anticipation of selling it.

In a market system, prices provide individuals the information they need to make decisions.

Prices provide signals about the relative scarcity of a product and help an economy respond to scarcity. For example, suppose wool becomes scarcer, either because a new use for wool is discovered or an old source of wool disappears. The greater scarcity will increase the price of wool, and producers and consumers will respond in ways that diminish scarcity:

- The higher price encourages fabric producers to use the available wool more efficiently and encourages farmers to produce more of it.
- The higher price also encourages consumers to switch to coats made from alternative fabrics.

These two responses help the economy accommodate an increase in scarcity. Consumers and producers don't need to know why wool is scarcer for these mechanisms to kick in—they only need to know that the price is higher.

The decisions made in markets result from the interactions of millions of people, each motivated by his or her own interest. Adam Smith used the metaphor of the "invisible hand" to explain that people acting in self-interest may actually promote the interest of society as a whole:[8]

It is not from the benevolence of the butcher, the brewer, or the baker that we expect our dinner, but from their regard to their own interest. We address ourselves, not to their humanity but to their self-love, and never talk to them of our own necessities but of their advantages. . . [Man is] led by an invisible hand to promote an end which was no part of this intention. . . . By pursuing his own interest he frequently promotes that of the society more effectually than when he really intends to promote it. . . . Nobody but a beggar chooses to depend chiefly upon the benevolence of his fellow citizens.

The market system works by getting each person, motivated by self-interest, to produce products for other people.

The Role of Entrepreneurs

Entrepreneurs play a key role in a market economy. Prices and profits provide signals to entrepreneurs about what to produce. If a product suddenly becomes popular, competition among consumers to obtain it will increase its price and increase the profits earned by firms producing it. Entrepreneurs will enter the market and increase production to meet the higher demand, switching resources from the production of other products. As entrepreneurs enter the market, they compete for customers, driving the price back down to the level that generates just enough profit for them to remain in business. In contrast, if a product becomes less popular, the process is reversed. Producers will cut prices in order to be sure of selling the product to the smaller number of customers who want it. Entrepreneurs will leave the unprofitable market, finding other products to produce, and the price will eventually rise back to the level where profits are high enough for the remaining producers to justify staying in business.

Example of the Emergence of Markets: POW Camps

To illustrate the pervasiveness of exchange, consider the emergence of markets in prisoner of war (POW) camps during World War II.[9] During World War II, the International Red Cross gave each Allied prisoner a weekly parcel with the same mix of products—tinned milk, jam, butter, biscuits, corned beef, chocolate, sugar, and cigarettes. In addition, many prisoners received private parcels from family and friends. The prisoners used barter to exchange one good for another, and cigarettes emerged as the medium of exchange. Prisoners wandered through the camp calling out their offers of goods. For example, "cheese for seven" meant that the prisoner was willing to sell a cheese ration for 7 cigarettes. In addition to food, the prisoners bought and sold clothing (80 cigarettes per shirt), laundry services (2 cigarettes per garment), and hot cups of coffee (2 cigarettes per cup).

The prices of products reflected their scarcity. The tea-drinking British prisoners demanded little coffee. Because the British were confined to their compound, packets of coffee beans sold for just a few cigarettes. Enterprising British prisoners bribed prison guards to permit them to travel to the French compound, where they could sell coffee for dozens of cigarettes. Religious groups such as the Sikhs didn't eat beef, and the excess supply of beef in the Sikh compound led to low beef prices. One prisoner who knew the Sikh language bought beef at a low price in the Sikh compound and sold it at a higher price in other compounds. Eventually, other people entered the Sikh beef trade, and beef prices across compounds became roughly equal.

THE MARKET FOR METEORITES

APPLYING THE CONCEPTS #2: Why do markets develop?

When a meteoroid, a chunk of debris in the solar system, enters the earth's atmosphere it becomes a meteor, and if a meteor reaches the ground and survives impact, it becomes a meteorite. Meteorites are prized by private collectors and scientists, who study them for astronomical insights.

The market for meteorites is highly organized. Meteorites have been hitting the earth for millions of years, and they can still be found in many desert areas. In Morocco, people bring meteorites picked up in the desert to local dealers, who then sell them to the public through websites and eBay. And there are professional meteorite hunters, who listen for news of meteorite showers and then travel to the landfalls to gather fresh meteorites. Recently some scientists traveled to Morocco to purchase a meteorite from Mars for $17,400 ($300 per gram). The scientists will examine the meteorite to get insights into the geology of Mars. The market price of meteorites varies from a few dollars per gram for the most common types to hundreds of dollars per gram for the rarest, including objects that originated from Mars and the moon. **Related to Exercise 2.4.**

SOURCE: Based on Ira Flato, *Science Friday* January 20, 2012 (National Public Radio, 2012).

3.3   Market Failure and the Role of Government

Although markets often operate efficiently on their own, sometimes they do not. *Market failure* happens when a market doesn't generate the most efficient outcome. Later in the book, we'll explore several sources of market failure and discuss possible responses by government. Here is a preview of the topics:

- **Pollution.** For markets to work efficiently, the people making the decisions about production and consumption must bear the full costs of their decisions. In some cases, however, other people bear some of the costs. For example, people living downwind from a paper mill breathe dirty air. The people who decide how much paper to produce will ignore these other costs, so their decisions about how much paper to produce will be inefficient from the social perspective. Similarly, people with asthma suffer from the emissions of cars and

SUVs. Drivers ignore these other costs, so their decisions about how much to drive will be inefficient from the social perspective. The role of government is to ensure that polluters bear the full cost of their production and consumption decisions.

- **Public goods.** A public good is available for everyone to utilize, regardless of who pays and who doesn't. Another requirement for market efficiency is that decision makers must reap the full benefits from their decisions. In the case of a public good such as a levee, the benefits go to everyone in the area protected from flooding, not just the person who builds the levee. The role of government is to facilitate the collective decision making for public goods such as levees, national defense, parks, and space exploration.

- **Imperfect information.** For markets to operate efficiently, people must have enough information to make informed decisions about how much to produce or consume. When they don't, the role of government is to disseminate information and promote informed choices.

- **Imperfect competition.** Some markets are dominated by a few large firms, and the lack of competition leads to high prices and small quantities. For example, DeBeers dominates the diamond market. The role of government is to foster competition, which leads to lower prices and more choices.

What are the other roles of government in a market-based economy? The government enforces property rights by protecting the property and possessions of individuals and firms from theft. The government uses the legal system—police, courts, and prisons—to enforce those rights. The protection of private property guarantees that people will keep the fruits of their labor, encouraging production and exchange. The government has two additional roles to play in a market economy:

- Establishing rules for market exchange and using its police power to enforce the rules.
- Reducing economic uncertainty and providing for people who have lost a job, have poor health, or experience other unforeseen difficulties and accidents.

Government Enforces the Rules of Exchange

The market system is based on exchanges between strangers. These exchanges are covered by implicit and explicit contracts that establish the terms of trade. For example, real-estate transactions and other business dealings are sealed with explicit contracts that specify who pays what, and when. To facilitate exchange, the government helps to enforce contracts by maintaining a legal system that punishes people who violate them. This system allows people to trade with the confidence that the terms of the contracts they enter will be met.

In the case of consumer goods, the implicit contract is that the product is safe to use. The government enforces this implicit contract through product liability or tort law. If a consumer is harmed by using a particular product, the consumer can file a lawsuit against the manufacturer and seek compensation. For example, consumers who are injured in defective automobiles may be awarded settlements to cover the cost of medical care, lost work time, and pain and suffering.

The government also disseminates information about consumer products. The government requires firms to provide information about the features of their products, including warnings about potentially harmful uses of the product. For example, cigarettes have warning labels like "Quitting Smoking Now Greatly Reduces Serious Risks to Your Health." Some cold medications warn consumers to avoid driving while taking the medication.

We've already seen one of the virtues of a market system—competition among producers tends to keep prices low. As we'll see later, the government uses antitrust policy to foster competition by (a) breaking up monopolies (a single seller of a product), (b) preventing firms from colluding to fix prices, and (c) preventing firms that produce competing products from merging into a single firm. In some markets, the emergence of a single firm—a monopolist—is inevitable because the entry of a second firm would make both firms unprofitable. Some examples are cable television providers and electricity producers. Governments regulate these firms, controlling the price of the products they produce.

Government Can Reduce Economic Uncertainty

A market economy provides plenty of opportunities to people, but it has risks. Your level of success in a market economy—how much income you earn and how much wealth you accumulate—will depend on your innate intelligence as well as your efforts. But there is also an element of luck: Your fate is affected by where you were born, what occupation you choose, and your genetic makeup and health. Chance events, such as natural disasters and human accidents, also can affect your prosperity. Finally, some people lose their jobs when the national economy is in a slump and firms lay off workers. Given the uncertainty of market economies, most governments fund a "social safety net" that provides for citizens who fare poorly in markets. The safety net includes programs that redistribute income from rich to poor, from the employed to the unemployed. The idea behind having a social safety net is to guarantee a minimum income to people who suffer from job losses, poor health, or bad luck.

Of course, there are private responses to economic uncertainty. For example, we can buy our own insurance to cover losses from fire and theft, to cover our medical expenses, and to provide death benefits to our survivors in the event of an accident or disaster. Private insurance works because only a fraction of the people who buy insurance eventually file claims and receive reimbursements from insurance companies. In other words, the payments, or premiums, of many are used to pay the claims of a few. Private insurance works when enough low-risk people purchase insurance to cover the costs of reimbursing the high-risk people.

Some types of insurance are unavailable in the private insurance market. As a result, the government steps in to fill the void. For example, unemployment insurance (UI) is a government program that provides 26 weeks of compensation for people who lose their jobs. The insurance is financed by mandatory contributions from employers. Because all employers contribute to the system, the cost of the insurance stays low.

CIVIL LIBERTIES AND EFFICIENCY OF GOVERNMENT

APPLYING THE CONCEPTS #3: What is the role of government in a market economy?

One role of government is to promote civil liberties such as the freedom of expression, the freedom of religion, and the right to own personal property. Several organizations score different countries with respect to the strength of their civil liberties. For example, the Freedom House uses a checklist of 14 civil liberties to score countries on a scale of 1–7, and the Humana index scores countries on a scale of 0–100.

A recent study shows that countries with relatively strong civil liberties have relatively high rates of return on government investment projects. The World Bank funds all sorts of development projects, including roads, systems for electricity and water, and health services. If we move from a country with relatively weak civil liberties to a country with relatively strong civil liberties, the economic rate of return on World Bank projects increases by about 15 percentage points. For a less extreme comparison, if we move from a country with a Humana index of 32 to a country with a Humana index of 50, the average rate of return increases from 12 percent to 16 percent. The positive relationship between the strength of civil liberties and the economic rate of return suggests that civil liberties promote citizen participation and public accountability, increasing the efficiency of government projects. **Related to Exercise 3.5.**

SOURCE: Based on Jonathan Isham, Daniel Kaufmann, Lant Pritchett, "Civil Liberties, Democracy, and the Performance of Government Projects," *The World Bank Economic Review* 11 (1997), pp. 219–242.

SUMMARY

This chapter explored specialization and exchange and the virtues and shortcomings of markets. We also discussed the role of government in a market economy. Here are the main points of the chapter:

1 It is sensible for a person to produce the product for which he or she has a *comparative advantage*, that is, a lower opportunity cost than another person.

2 *Specialization* increases productivity through the division of labor, a result of the benefits of repetition, continuity, and innovation.

3 A system of international specialization and trade is sensible because nations have different opportunity costs of producing goods, giving rise to comparative advantages.

4 Under a *market system*, self-interested people, guided by prices, make the decisions about what products to produce, how to produce them, and who gets them.

5 Government roles in a market economy include establishing the rules for exchange, reducing economic uncertainty, and responding to market failures.

absolute advantage, p. 52

comparative advantage, p. 52

import, p. 54

centrally planned economy, p. 56

export, p. 54

market economy, p. 55

EXERCISES

All problems are assignable in MyEconLab; exercises that update with real-time data are marked with ⬤.

3.1 Comparative Advantage and Exchange

1.1 Consider an accounting firm with two accountants.

  a. Fill in the blanks in the following table.

	Quigley		Slokum	
	Financial Statements	*Tax Returns*	*Financial Statements*	*Tax Returns*
Output per hour	2	8	1	1
Opportunity cost				

  b. Quigley has a comparative advantage in _____, while Slokum has a comparative advantage in _____.

1.2 Mike, the manager of a car wash, is more productive at washing cars than any potential workers he could hire. Should he wash all the cars himself? _____ (Yes/No)

1.3 Pat and Terry run a landscaping firm that cuts lawns and prunes trees. Pat is more productive than Terry at both tasks. Pat should cut lawns and Terry should prune trees if Pat has a _____ in cutting lawns.

1.4 Adam Smith listed three reasons for specialization to increase productivity: (1)_____; (2) _____; and (3)_____.

1.5 President Lincoln's discomfort with imports resulted from his failure to recognize that money sent to England eventually_____.

1.6 Arrows up or down: Outsourcing _____ production costs and _____ consumer prices.

1.7 In the first three months of 2004, the number of jobs moving to another state was _____ (larger/smaller) than the number of jobs moving to another country.

1.8 Approximately what percentage of job losses in the first three months of 2004 were caused by outsourcing—2, 10, or 25 percent?

1.9 Consider a bicycle producer that initially employs 200 production workers and 10 customer-service workers. When the firm outsources its customer-service operation to India, the 10 customer-service workers lose their jobs.

  a. Explain why the net effect from outsourcing could be a loss of fewer than 10 jobs in the firm.

  b. Under what circumstances will there be a net gain in jobs in the firm?

1.10 Although Latvia had an absolute disadvantage in most products relative to EC countries, trade was mutually beneficial because Latvia had a _____ advantage in _____. (Related to Application 1 on page 55.)

1.11 **Exchange in an Island Economy.** Robin and Terry are stranded on a deserted island and consume two products, coconuts and fish. In a day, Robin can catch 2 fish or gather 8 coconuts, and Terry can catch 1 fish or gather 1 coconut.

  a. Use these numbers to prepare a table like Table 3.1 on page 50. Which person has a comparative advantage in fishing? Which person has a comparative advantage in gathering coconuts?

  b. Suppose that each person is initially self-sufficient. In a six-day week, Robin produces and consumes 32 coconuts and 4 fish, and Terry produces and consumes 3 coconuts and 3 fish. Show that specialization and exchange (at a rate of 3 coconuts per fish) allows Robin to consume more coconuts and the same number of fish and allows Terry to consume more coconuts and the same number of fish. Illustrate your answer with a graph like Figure 3.1 on page 51.

1.12 Technological Innovation and Exchange. Recall the example of Fred and Kate shown in Table 3.1 on page 50. Suppose a technological innovation, such as a rope ladder, increases the coconut productivity of both people: Fred can now produce three coconuts per day, while Kate can now produce two coconuts per day. Their productivity for fish has not changed. Suppose they agree to trade one coconut for each fish. Will both people gain from specialization and trade?

1.13 Comparative Advantage in Selling. Selma is a better salesperson than Mark in both city A and city B.

	Selma	Mark
Sales per day in city A	48	24
Sales per day in city B	40	10

a. If each person handles one city and the objective is to maximize total sales, which city should each person handle?

b. Is your answer to (a) consistent with the notion of exploiting comparative advantage?

1.14 Data on Exports and Imports. Access the *Statistical Abstract of the United States* on the Internet and download the tables in the section entitled "Foreign Commerce and Aid." One of the tables lists U.S. exports and imports by selected Standard Industrial Trade Classification (SITC) commodity. Fill in the blanks in the following table for the most recent year listed in the table.

Commodity	Export Value ($ millions)	Import Value ($ millions)	Net Exports = Exports – Imports ($ millions)
Coffee			
Corn			
Soybeans			
Airplanes			
Footwear			
Vehicles			
Crude oil			

1.15 Trade Balances by Country. Access the *Statistical Abstract of the United States* on the Internet and download the tables in the section entitled "Foreign Commerce and Aid." One of the tables lists U.S. exports and imports and merchandise trade balance by country. Fill in the blanks in the following table for the most recent year listed in the table.

Country	Exports ($ millions)	General Imports ($ millions)	Merchandise Trade Balance ($ millions)
Australia			
China			
Italy			
Japan			
Mexico			
Netherlands			
Saudi Arabia			
Singapore			

3.2 Markets

2.1 Four social inventions that support markets are (1) _____, which specify the terms of exchange; (2) _____, which reduce the risk of entrepreneurs; (3) _____ , which increases the profitability of inventions; and (4) _____ rules, which provide potential investors with reliable information about the financial performance of firms.

2.2 Arrow up or down: Trade between different POW compounds _____ the difference in the price of beef across the compounds.

2.3 To explain the virtues of markets, Adam Smith used the metaphor of the invisible pancreas. _____ (True/False)

2.4 Meteorites travel from Mars to science laboratories on Earth with the help of markets that involve _____. (Related to Application 2 on page 59.)

2.5 Coffee and Cheese Exchange in a POW Camp. Suppose that in the British compound of a POW camp, the price of cheese is 6 cigarettes per cheese ration and the price of coffee beans is 3 cigarettes per coffee ration. In the French compound, the price of coffee beans is 24 cigarettes per ration.

  a. Is there an opportunity for beneficial exchange?

  b. A British prisoner could exchange his cheese ration for _____ cigarettes, then exchange the extra cigarettes for _____ coffee rations in the British compound. If he travels to the French compound, he could exchange the extra coffee for _____ cigarettes. When he returns to the British compound, he can exchange the extra cigarettes for _____ cheese rations. In other words, his net gain from trade is _____ cheese rations.

2.6 Extending Trade outside the Camp. Late in World War II, a German guard exchanged bread and chocolate at the rate of one loaf for one chocolate bar. Inside the Allied POW camp, the price of chocolate was 15 cigarettes per bar, and the price of bread was 40 cigarettes per loaf.

  a. Is there an opportunity for beneficial exchange?

  b. With the guard, a POW could exchange three chocolate bars for _____ loaves of bread. In the camp, the POW could exchange the extra loaves for _____ cigarettes, and then exchange the extra cigarettes for chocolate bars. In other words, the POW's net gain from trade is _____ chocolate bars.

> **3.3** Market Failure and the Role of Government

3.1 For markets to operate efficiently, the people making consumption and production decisions must bear the full _____ and reap the full _____ from their decisions.

3.2 Pollution from a paper mill is an example of market failure because people living downwind of the mill bear part of _____ of production.

3.3 Some markets are dominated by a few large firms, leading to high _____ and small _____.

3.4 By promoting competition, the government generates _____ product prices.

3.5 There is a _____ (positive/negative) relationship between the strength of civil liberties and the economic rate of return on World Bank projects, suggesting that civil liberties lead to _____ (more/less) efficient government. (Related to Application 3 on page 62.)

3.6 Pirating Textbooks? The government protects intellectual property rights by enforcing copyright rules on textbooks. Suppose an organization scans the pages of this and other introductory economics textbooks and makes them available for downloading at no charge.

  a. As a current textbook consumer, would you be better off or worse off?

  b. What are the implications for the next generation of economics students?

3.7 Unemployment Insurance. Each worker employed by Risky Business has a 20 percent chance of losing his or her job in the next year. Each worker employed by Safe Business has a 2 percent chance of losing his or her job. You manage an insurance company that provides a lump sum of $10,000 to each unemployed worker.

  a. What is the minimum amount you would charge Risky Business for each employee covered by the unemployment policy?

  b. What is the minimum amount you would charge Safe Business for each employee covered by the unemployment policy?

  c. Suppose you charge the same premium to both businesses. The companies have the same number of workers and are required to purchase unemployment insurance. What is the minimum amount you would charge?

NOTES

1. Adam Smith, *An Inquiry into the Nature and Causes of the Wealth of Nations* (1776), Book 1, Chapter 1.

2. Ibid.

3. Adam Smith, *An Inquiry into the Nature and Causes of the Wealth of Nations* (1776), Book 4, Chapter 2.

4. Todd G. Buchholz, New Ideas from Dead Economists: *An Introduction to Modern Economic Thought* (New York: Penguin, 2007), 76.

5. Todd G. Buchholz, New Ideas from Dead Economists: *An Introduction to Modern Economic Thought* (New York: Penguin, 2007), 76–77.

6. U.S. Bureau of Labor Statistics, "Extended Mass Layoffs Associated with Domestic and Overseas Relocations, First Quarter 2004," June 2004.

7. Todd G. Buchholz, New Ideas from Dead Economists: *An Introduction to Modern Economic Thought* (New York: Penguin, 2007), 21.

8. Adam Smith, *An Inquiry into the Nature and Causes of the Wealth of Nations* (1776), Book 4, Chapter 2.

9. R. A. Radford, "The Economic Organization of a P.O.W. Camp," *Economica*, November 1945, 189–201.

Demand, Supply, and Market Equilibrium

In recent years, thousands of workers have moved to North Dakota to work in the oil industry, which uses hydraulic fracturing to extract oil from the Bakken formation, a 360-million-year-old shale bed.

Between 2009 and 2012, mining employment in the state increased by about 11,000 jobs and total employment increased by over 40,000 jobs. Given the limited options for increasing the housing stock in the short run, increased demand for housing caused housing prices to rise dramatically. In the town of Williston, the rent for a two-bedroom apartment increased from $350 per month to $2,000.

The housing industry is responding to higher housing prices in a number of ways. The number of building permits for homes and apartment complexes increased to record levels, and five new hotels are being built in Williston. One innovative response is the building of "man camps," dormitory-style housing complexes that accommodate up to 1,000 men. The daily rent of $100 includes three meals per day, and in many cases is paid by employers.

LEARNING OBJECTIVES

- Describe and explain the law of demand.

- Describe and explain the law of supply.

- Explain the role of price in reaching a market equilibrium.

- Describe the effect of a change in demand on the equilibrium price.

- Describe the effect of a change in supply on the equilibrium price.

- Use information on price and quantity to determine what caused a change in price.

MyEconLab
MyEconLab helps you master each objective and study more efficiently.

Our discussion of the virtues of exchange and markets in Chapter 3 has set the stage for this chapter, where we explore the mechanics of markets. We use the model of demand and supply—the most important tool of economic analysis—to see how markets work. We'll see how the prices of goods and services are affected by all sorts of changes in the economy, including bad weather, higher income, technological innovation, bad publicity, and changes in consumer preferences. This chapter will prepare you for the applications of demand and supply you'll see in the rest of the book.

perfectly competitive market

A market with many sellers and buyers of a homogeneous product and no barriers to entry.

The model of demand and supply explains how a perfectly competitive market operates. A **perfectly competitive market** has many buyers and sellers of a product, so no single buyer or seller can affect the market price. The classic example of a perfectly competitive firm is a wheat farmer who produces a tiny fraction of the total supply of wheat. No matter how much wheat an individual farmer produces, the farmer can't change the market price of wheat.

4.1   The Demand Curve

On the demand side of a market, consumers buy products from firms. We have one main question about this side of the market: How much of a particular product are consumers willing to buy during a particular period? Notice that we define *demand* for a particular period, for example, a day, a month, or a year.

We'll start our discussion of demand with the individual consumer. A consumer who is willing to buy a particular product is willing to sacrifice enough money to purchase it. The consumer doesn't merely have a desire to buy the good, but is also willing and able to sacrifice something to get it. How much of a product is an individual willing to buy? It depends on a number of variables. Here is a list of the variables that affect an individual consumer's decision, using the pizza market as an example:

- The price of the product (for example, the price of a pizza)
- The consumer's income
- The price of substitute goods (for example, the prices of tacos or sandwiches or other goods that can be consumed instead of pizza)
- The price of complementary goods (for example, the price of lemonade or other goods consumed with pizza)
- The consumer's preferences or tastes and advertising that may influence preferences
- The consumer's expectations about future prices

quantity demanded

The amount of a product that consumers are willing and able to buy.

Together, these variables determine how much of a particular product an individual consumer is willing and able to buy, the **quantity demanded**. We'll start our discussion of demand with the relationship between price and quantity demanded, a relationship we represented graphically by the demand curve. Later in the chapter, we will discuss the other variables that affect the individual consumer's decision about how much of a product to buy.

The Individual Demand Curve and the Law of Demand

demand schedule

A table that shows the relationship between the price of a product and the quantity demanded, *ceteris paribus*.

The starting point for a discussion of individual demand is a **demand schedule**, which is a table of numbers showing the relationship between the price of a particular product and the quantity that an individual consumer is willing to buy. The demand schedule shows how the quantity demanded by an individual changes with the price, *ceteris paribus* (everything else held fixed). The variables that are held fixed in the demand schedule are the consumer's income, the prices of substitutes and complements, the consumer's tastes, and the consumer's expectations about future prices.

The table in Figure 4.1 shows Al's demand schedule for pizza. At a price of $2, Al buys 13 pizzas per month. As the price rises, he buys fewer pizzas: 10 pizzas at a price of $4, 7 pizzas at a price of $6, and so on, down to only 1 pizza at a price of $10. Remember that in a demand schedule, any change in quantity results from a change in price alone.

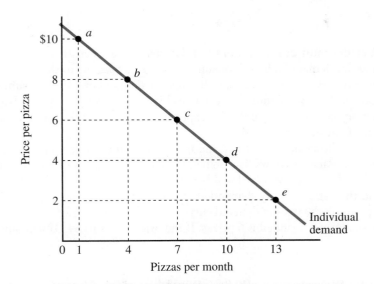

Point	Price	Quantity of Pizzas per Month
a	$10	1
b	8	4
c	6	7
d	4	10
e	2	13

▲ **FIGURE 4.1**

The Individual Demand Curve

According to the law of demand, the higher the price, the smaller the quantity demanded, everything else being equal. Therefore, the demand curve is negatively sloped: When the price increases from $6 to $8, the quantity demanded decreases from seven pizzas per month (point *c*) to four pizzas per month (point *b*).

The **individual demand curve** is a graphical representation of the demand schedule. By plotting the numbers in Al's demand schedule—various combinations of price and quantity—we can draw his demand curve for pizza. The demand curve shows the relationship between the price and the quantity demanded by an individual consumer, *ceteris paribus*. To get the data for a single demand curve, we change only the price of pizza and observe how a consumer responds to the price change. In Figure 4.1, Al's demand curve shows the quantity of pizzas he is willing to buy at each price.

Notice that Al's demand curve is negatively sloped, reflecting the **law of demand**. This law applies to all consumers:

There is a negative relationship between price and quantity demanded, *ceteris paribus*.

The words *ceteris paribus* remind us that in order to isolate the relationship between price and quantity demanded, we *must* assume that income, the prices of

individual demand curve

A curve that shows the relationship between the price of a good and quantity demanded by an individual consumer, *ceteris paribus*.

law of demand

There is a negative relationship between price and quantity demanded, *ceteris paribus*.

change in quantity demanded

A change in the quantity consumers are willing and able to buy when the price changes; represented graphically by movement along the demand curve.

market demand curve

A curve showing the relationship between price and quantity demanded by all consumers, *ceteris paribus*.

related goods such as substitutes and complements, and tastes are unchanged. As the price of pizza increases and nothing else changes, Al moves upward along his demand curve and buys a smaller quantity of pizza. For example, if the price increases from $8 to $10, Al moves upward along his demand curve from point *b* to point *a*, and buys only one pizza per month, down from four pizzas at the lower price. A movement along a single demand curve is called a **change in quantity demanded**, a change in the quantity a consumer is willing to buy when the price changes.

From Individual Demand to Market Demand

The **market demand curve** shows the relationship between the price of the good and the quantity demanded by *all* consumers, *ceteris paribus*. As in the case of the individual demand curve, when we draw the market demand curve we assume that the other variables that affect individual demand (income, the prices of substitute and complementary goods, tastes, and price expectations) are fixed. In addition, we assume the number of consumers is fixed.

Figure 4.2 shows how to derive the market demand curve when there are only two consumers. Panel A shows Al's demand curve for pizza, and Panel B shows Bea's demand curve. At a price of $8, Al will buy 4 pizzas (point *a*) and Bea will buy 2 pizzas (point *b*), so the total quantity demanded at this price is 6 pizzas. In Panel C, point *c* shows the point on the market demand curve associated with a price of $8. At this price, the market quantity demanded is 6 pizzas. If the price drops to $4, Al will buy 10 pizzas

QUANTITY OF PIZZA DEMANDED			
Price	Al +	Bea =	Market Demand
$8	4	2	6
6	7	4	11
4	10	6	16
2	13	8	21

▲ FIGURE 4.2

From Individual to Market Demand

The market demand equals the sum of the demands of all consumers. In this case, there are only two consumers, so at each price the market quantity demanded equals the quantity demanded by Al plus the quantity demanded by Bea. At a price of $8, Al's quantity is four pizzas (point *a*) and Bea's quantity is two pizzas (point *b*), so the market quantity demanded is six pizzas (point *c*). Each consumer obeys the law of demand, so the market demand curve is negatively sloped.

application 1

LAW OF DEMAND AND CIGARETTES

APPLYING THE CONCEPTS #1: What is the law of demand?

As price decreases and we move downward along the market demand for cigarettes, the quantity of cigarettes demanded increases for two reasons. First, people who smoked cigarettes at the original price respond to the lower price by smoking more. Second, some people start smoking.

A change in cigarette taxes in Canada illustrates the second effect, the new-smoker effect. In 1994, several provinces in eastern Canada cut their cigarette taxes in response to the smuggling of cigarettes from the U.S. (where taxes are lower), and the price of cigarettes in the provinces decreased by roughly 50 percent. Researchers tracked the choices of 591 youths from the Waterloo Smoking Prevention Program, and concluded that the lower price increased the smoking rate by roughly 17 percent. **Related to Exercises 1.6 and 1.8.**

SOURCE: Based on Anindya Sen and Tony Wirjanto, "Estimating the impacts of cigarette taxes on youth smoking participation, initiation, and persistence: empirical evidence from Canada," *Health Economics* 19 (2010), pp. 1264–1280.

(point *d*) and Bea will buy 6 pizzas (point *e*), for a total of 16 pizzas (shown by point *f* on the market demand curve). The market demand curve is the horizontal sum of the individual demand curves.

The market demand is negatively sloped, reflecting the law of demand. This is sensible, because if each consumer obeys the law of demand, consumers as a group will too. When the price increases from $4 to $8, there is a change in quantity demanded as we move along the demand curve from point *f* to point *c*. The movement along the demand curve occurs if the price of pizza is the only variable that has changed.

4.2   The Supply Curve

On the supply side of a market, firms sell their products to consumers. Suppose you ask the manager of a firm, "How much of your product are you willing to produce and sell?" The answer is likely to be "it depends." The manager's decision about how much to produce depends on many variables, including the following, using pizza as an example:

- The price of the product (for example, the price per pizza)
- The wage paid to workers
- The price of materials (for example, the price of dough and cheese)
- The cost of capital (for example, the cost of a pizza oven)
- The state of production technology (for example, the knowledge used in making pizza)
- Producers' expectations about future prices
- Taxes paid to the government or *subsidies* (payments from the government to firms to produce a product)

Together, these variables determine how much of a product firms are willing to produce and sell, the **quantity supplied**. We'll start our discussion of market supply

quantity supplied
The amount of a product that firms are willing and able to sell.

with the relationship between the price of a good and the quantity of that good supplied, a relationship we represent graphically by the supply curve. Later in the chapter we will discuss the other variables that affect the individual firm's decision about how much of a product to produce and sell.

The Individual Supply Curve and the Law of Supply

supply schedule

A table that shows the relationship between the price of a product and quantity supplied, *ceteris paribus*.

Consider the decision of an individual producer. The starting point for a discussion of individual supply is a **supply schedule**, a table that shows the relationship between the price of a particular product and the quantity that an individual producer is willing to sell. The supply schedule shows how the quantity supplied by an individual producer changes with the price, *ceteris paribus*. The variables we hold fixed in the supply schedule are input costs, technology, price expectations, and government taxes or subsidies.

The table in Figure 4.3 shows the supply schedule for pizza at Lola's Pizza Shop. At a price of $2, Lola doesn't produce any pizzas, indicating that a $2 price is not high enough to cover her cost of producing a pizza. In contrast, at a price of $4 she supplies 100 pizzas. In this example, each $2 increase in price increases the quantity supplied by 100 pizzas to 200 at a price of $6, 300 at a price of $8, and so on. Remember that in a supply schedule, a change in quantity results from a change in price alone.

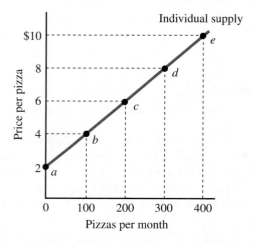

INDIVIDUAL SUPPLY SCHEDULE FOR PIZZA		
Point	Price	Quantity of Pizzas per Month
a	$2	0
b	4	100
c	6	200
d	8	300
e	10	400

▲ FIGURE 4.3

The Individual Supply Curve

The supply curve of an individual supplier is positively sloped, reflecting the law of supply. As shown by point *a*, the quantity supplied is zero at a price of $2, indicating that the minimum supply price is just above $2. An increase in price increases the quantity supplied to 100 pizzas at a price of $4, 200 pizzas at a price of $6, and so on.

individual supply curve

A curve showing the relationship between price and quantity supplied by a single firm, *ceteris paribus*.

The **individual supply curve** is a graphical representation of the supply schedule. By plotting the numbers in Lola's supply schedule—different combinations of price and quantity—we can draw her supply curve for pizza. The individual supply curve shows the relationship between the price of a product and the quantity supplied by a single firm, *ceteris paribus*. To get the data for a supply curve, we change only the price of pizza and observe how a producer responds to the price change.

Figure 4.3 shows Lola's supply curve for pizza, which shows the quantity of pizzas she is willing to sell at each price. The individual supply curve is positively sloped, reflecting the **law of supply**, a pattern of behavior that we observe in producers:

law of supply
There is a positive relationship between price and quantity supplied, *ceteris paribus*.

>   There is a positive relationship between price and quantity supplied, *ceteris paribus*.

The words *ceteris paribus* remind us that to isolate the relationship between price and quantity supplied we assume the other factors that influence producers are unchanged. As the price of pizza increases and nothing else changes, Lola moves upward along her individual supply curve and produces a larger quantity of pizza. For example, if the price increases from $6 to $8, Lola moves upward along her supply curve from point *c* to point *d*, and the quantity supplied increases from 200 to 300. A movement along a single supply curve is called a **change in quantity supplied**, a change in the quantity a producer is willing and able to sell when the price changes.

change in quantity supplied
A change in the quantity firms are willing and able to sell when the price changes; represented graphically by movement along the supply curve.

The **minimum supply price** is the lowest price at which a product is supplied. A firm won't produce a product unless the price is high enough to cover the marginal cost of producing it. As shown in Figure 4.3, a price of $2 is not high enough to cover the cost of producing the first pizza, so Lola's quantity supplied is zero (point *a*). But when the price rises above $2, she produces some pizzas, indicating that her minimum supply price is just above $2.

minimum supply price
The lowest price at which a product will be supplied.

Why Is the Individual Supply Curve Positively Sloped?

The individual supply curve is positively sloped, consistent with the law of supply. To explain the positive slope, consider how Lola responds to an increase in price. A higher price encourages a firm to increase its output by purchasing more materials and hiring more workers. To increase her workforce, Lola might be forced to pay overtime or hire workers who are more costly or less productive than the original workers. But the higher price of pizza makes it worthwhile to incur these higher costs.

The supply curve shows the marginal cost of production for different quantities produced. We can use the marginal principle to explain this.

> ## MARGINAL PRINCIPLE
> Increase the level of an activity as long as its marginal benefit exceeds its marginal cost. Choose the level at which the marginal benefit equals the marginal cost.

For Lola, the marginal benefit of producing a pizza is the price she gets for it. When the price is only $2.00, she doesn't produce any pizza, which tells us that the marginal cost of the first pizza must be greater than $2.00; otherwise, she would have produced it. But when the price rises to $2.01, she produces the first pizza because now the marginal benefit (the $2.01 price) exceeds the marginal cost. This tells us that the marginal cost of the first pizza is less than $2.01; otherwise, she wouldn't produce it at a price of $2.01. To summarize, the marginal cost of the first pizza is between $2.00 and $2.01, or just over $2.00. Similarly, point *b* on the supply curve in Figure 4.3 shows that Lola won't produce her 100th pizza at a price of $3.99, but will produce at a price of $4.00, indicating that her marginal cost of producing that pizza is between $3.99 and $4.00, or just under $4.00. In general, the supply curve shows the marginal cost of production.

From Individual Supply to Market Supply

market supply curve

A curve showing the relationship between the market price and quantity supplied by all firms, *ceteris paribus*.

The **market supply curve** for a particular good shows the relationship between the price of the good and the quantity that all producers together are willing to sell, *ceteris paribus*. To draw the market supply curve, we assume the other variables that affect individual supply are fixed. The market quantity supplied is simply the sum of the quantities supplied by all the firms in the market. To show how to draw the market supply curve, we'll assume there are only two firms in the market. Of course, a perfectly competitive market has a large number of firms, but the lessons from the two-firm case generalize to a case of many firms.

Figure 4.4 shows how to derive a market supply curve from individual supply curves. In Panel A, Lola has relatively low production costs, as reflected in her relatively low minimum supply price ($2 at point *a*). In Panel B, Hiram has higher production costs, so he has a higher minimum price ($6 at point *f*). As a result, his supply curve lies above Lola's. To draw the market supply curve, we add the individual supply curves horizontally. This gives us two segments for the market supply curve:

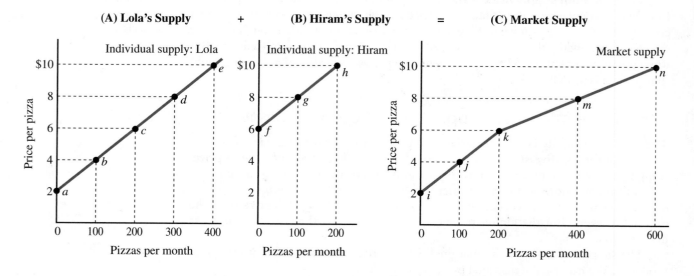

QUANTITY OF PIZZA SUPPLIED			
Price	Lola +	Hiram =	Market Supply
2	0	0	0
4	100	0	100
6	200	0	200
8	300	100	400
10	400	200	600

▲ **FIGURE 4.4**

From Individual to Market Supply

The market supply is the sum of the supplies of all firms. In Panel A, Lola is a low-cost producer who produces the first pizza once the price rises above $2 (shown by point *a*). In Panel B, Hiram is a high-cost producer who doesn't produce pizza until the price rises above $6 (shown by point *f*). To draw the market supply curve, we sum the individual supply curves horizontally. At a price of $8, market supply is 400 pizzas (point *m*), equal to 300 from Lola (point *d*) plus 100 from Hiram (point *g*).

• **Prices between $2 and $6:** Segment connecting points *i* and *k*. Hiram's high-cost firm doesn't supply any output, so the market supply is the same as the individual supply from Lola. For example, at a price of $4 Lola supplies 100 pizzas (point *b*) and Hiram does not produce any, so the market supply is 100 pizzas (point *j*).

- **Prices above $6:** Segment above point *k*. At higher prices, the high-cost firm produces some output, and the market supply is the sum of the quantities supplied by the two firms. For example, at a price of $8 Lola produces 300 pizzas (point *d*) and Hiram produces 100 pizzas (point *g*), so the market quantity supplied is 400 pizzas (point *m*).

A perfectly competitive market has hundreds of firms rather than just two, but the process of going from individual supply curves to the market supply curve is the same. We add the individual supply curves horizontally by picking a price and adding up the quantities supplied by all the firms in the market. In the more realistic case of many firms, the supply curve will be smooth rather than kinked. This smooth line is shown in Figure 4.5. In this case, we assume that there are 100 firms identical to Lola's firm. The minimum supply price is $2, and for each $2 increase in price, the quantity supplied increases by 10,000 pizzas.

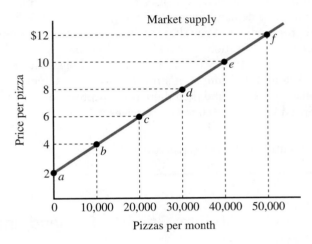

▲ **FIGURE 4.5**
The Market Supply Curve with Many Firms
The market supply is the sum of the supplies of all firms. The minimum supply price is $2 (point *a*), and the quantity supplied increases by 10,000 for each $2 increase in price to 10,000 at a price of $4 (point *b*), 20,000 at a price of $6 (point *c*), and so on.

Why Is the Market Supply Curve Positively Sloped?

The market supply curve is positively sloped, consistent with the law of supply. To explain the positive slope, consider the two responses by firms to an increase in price:

- **Individual firm.** As we saw earlier, a higher price encourages a firm to increase its output by purchasing more materials and hiring more workers.

- **New firms.** In the long run, new firms can enter the market and existing firms can expand their production facilities to produce more output. The new firms may have higher production costs than the original firms, but the higher output price makes it worthwhile to enter the market, even with higher costs.

Like the individual supply curve, the market supply curve shows the marginal cost of production for different quantities produced. In Figure 4.5, the marginal cost of the first pizza is the minimum supply price for the firm with the lowest cost (just over $2.00). Similarly, point *d* on the supply curve shows that the 30,000th pizza won't be produced at a price of $7.99, but will be produced at a price of $8.00. This indicates that the marginal cost of producing the 30,000th pizza is just under $8.00. Like the individual supply curve, the market supply curve shows the marginal cost of production.

application 2

LAW OF SUPPLY AND WOOLYMPICS

APPLYING THE CONCEPTS #2: What is the law of supply?

In the 1990s, the world price of wool decreased by about 30 percent, and prices have remained relatively low since then. Based on the law of supply, we would expect the quantity of wool supplied from New Zealand and other exporters to decrease, and that's what happened. Land formerly used to grow grass for wool-producing sheep has been converted into other uses, including dairy products, forestry, and the domestication of deer.

There have been several attempts to revive the wool industry by boosting the demand for wool and thus increasing its price. The United Nations General Assembly declared 2009 as the International Year of Natural Fibres, with the objective "to raise awareness and stimulate demand for natural fibres." In 2012, the Federated Farmers of New Zealand proposed that sheep shearing be added to the Commonwealth Games and Olympics as a demonstration sport. The favorites for Olympic titles are the current world record holders Ivan Scott (744 sheep in 24 hours) and Kerry-Jo Te Huia (507 sheep in 24 hours). Of course, it's not obvious that Olympic shearing would increase the demand for wool, and then there is the problem of what to do with all the sheared wool. Speed knitting? **Related to Exercises 2.6 and 2.10.**

SOURCE: Based on "Wait Wait Don't Tell Me." National Public Radio (January 21, 2012).

4.3 Market Equilibrium: Bringing Demand and Supply Together

In Chapter 3 we saw that a market is an arrangement that brings buyers and sellers together. So far in this chapter we've seen how the two sides of a market—demand and supply—work. Now we bring the two sides of the market together to show how prices and quantities are determined.

When the quantity of a product demanded equals the quantity supplied at the prevailing market price, we have reached a **market equilibrium**. When a market reaches an equilibrium, there is no pressure to change the price. If pizza firms produce exactly the quantity of pizza that consumers are willing to buy, each consumer will get a pizza at the prevailing price, and each producer will sell all its pizza. In Figure 4.6, the equilibrium price is shown by the intersection of the demand and supply curves. At a price of $8, the supply curve shows that firms will produce 30,000 pizzas, which is exactly the quantity that consumers are willing to buy at that price.

market equilibrium
A situation in which the quantity demanded equals the quantity supplied at the prevailing market price.

Excess Demand Causes the Price to Rise

If the price is below the equilibrium price, there will be excess demand for the product. **Excess demand** (sometimes called a *shortage*) occurs when, at the prevailing market price, the quantity demanded exceeds the quantity supplied, meaning that consumers are willing to buy more than producers are willing to sell. In Figure 4.6, at a price of $6, there is an excess demand equal to 16,000 pizzas: Consumers are willing to buy 36,000 pizzas (point *c*), but producers are willing to sell only 20,000 pizzas (point *b*) because the price is less than the marginal cost of producing pizza number 20,001 and beyond. This mismatch between demand and supply will cause the price of pizza to rise. Firms will increase the price they charge for their limited supply of pizza, and anxious consumers will pay the higher price to get one of the few pizzas available.

excess demand
A situation in which, at the prevailing price, the quantity demanded exceeds the quantity supplied.

An increase in price eliminates excess demand by changing both the quantity demanded and quantity supplied. As the price increases, the excess demand shrinks for two reasons:

- The market moves upward along the demand curve (from point *c* toward point *a*), decreasing the quantity demanded.
- The market moves upward along the supply curve (from point *b* toward point *a*), increasing the quantity supplied.

Because the quantity demanded decreases while the quantity supplied increases, the gap between the quantity demanded and the quantity supplied narrows. The price will continue to rise until excess demand is eliminated. In Figure 4.6, at a price of $8 the quantity supplied equals the quantity demanded, as shown by point *a*.

▲ **FIGURE 4.6**

Market Equilibrium

At the market equilibrium (point *a*, with price = $8 and quantity = 30,000), the quantity supplied equals the quantity demanded. At a price below the equilibrium price ($6), there is excess demand—the quantity demanded at point *c* exceeds the quantity supplied at point *b*. At a price above the equilibrium price ($12), there is excess supply—the quantity supplied at point *e* exceeds the quantity demanded at point *d*.

In some cases, government creates an excess demand for a good by setting a maximum price (sometimes called a *price ceiling*). If the government sets a maximum price that is less than the equilibrium price, the result is a permanent excess demand for the good. Later in the book we will explore the market effects of such policies.

Excess Supply Causes the Price to Drop

What happens if the price is *above* the equilibrium price? **Excess supply** (sometimes called a *surplus*) occurs when the quantity supplied exceeds the quantity demanded, meaning that producers are willing to sell more than consumers are willing to buy. This is shown by points *d* and *e* in Figure 4.6. At a price of $12, the excess supply is 32,000 pizzas: Producers are willing to sell 50,000 pizzas (point *e*), but consumers are willing to buy only 18,000 (point *d*). This mismatch will cause the price of pizzas to fall as firms cut the price to sell them. As the price drops, the excess supply will shrink for two reasons:

- The market moves downward along the demand curve from point *d* toward point *a*, increasing the quantity demanded.
- The market moves downward along the supply curve from point *e* toward point *a*, decreasing the quantity supplied.

excess supply

A situation in which the quantity supplied exceeds the quantity demanded at the prevailing price.

> **a p p l i c a t i o n   3**

SHRINKING WINE LAKES

APPLYING THE CONCEPTS #3: What are consequences of a price above the equilibrium price?

Under the Common Agricultural Policy (CAP) the European Union uses a number of policies to support the agricultural sectors of member countries. Under a minimum-price policy the government sets a price above the market-equilibrium price. The EU guarantees farmers minimum prices for products such as grain, dairy products, and wine. This policy causes artificial excess supply: if the minimum price exceeds the market-equilibrium price, the quantity supplied will exceed the quantity demanded. To support the minimum prices, the EU purchases any output that a farmer cannot sell at the guaranteed price and stores the excess supply in facilities labeled by the European press as "butter mountains" and "wine lakes." In recent years the EU has reformed its agriculture policy by reducing and in some cases eliminating minimum prices. As a result, the butter mountains and wine lakes are shrinking. **Related to Exercises 3.6 and 3.8.**

SOURCE: Europa, "Reform of the Common Agricultural Policy," *Summaries of EU Legislation* (europa.eu/legislation_summaries).

Because the quantity demanded increases while the quantity supplied decreases, the gap between the quantity supplied and the quantity demanded narrows. The price will continue to drop until excess supply is eliminated. In Figure 4.6, at a price of $8, the quantity supplied equals the quantity demanded, as shown by point *a*.

The government sometimes creates an excess supply of a good by setting a minimum price (sometimes called a *price floor*). If the government sets a minimum price that is greater than the equilibrium price, the result is a permanent excess supply. We'll discuss the market effects of minimum prices later in the book.

4.4 Market Effects of Changes in Demand

We've seen that market equilibrium occurs when the quantity supplied equals the quantity demanded, shown graphically by the intersection of the supply curve and the demand curve. In this part of the chapter, we'll see how changes on the demand side of the market affect the equilibrium price and equilibrium quantity.

Change in Quantity Demanded versus Change in Demand

Earlier in the chapter we listed the variables that determine how much of a particular product consumers are willing to buy. The first variable is the price of the product. The demand curve shows the negative relationship between price and quantity demanded, *ceteris paribus*. In Panel A of Figure 4.7, when the price decreases from $8 to $6, we move downward along the demand curve from point *a* to point *b*, and the quantity demanded increases. As noted earlier in the chapter, this is called a *change in quantity demanded*. Now we're ready to take a closer look at the other variables that affect demand besides price—income, the prices of related goods, tastes, advertising, and the number of consumers—and see how changes in these variables affect the demand for the product and the market equilibrium.

If any of these other variables change, the relationship between the product's price and quantity—shown numerically in the demand schedule and graphically in the demand curve—will change. That means we will have an entirely different demand schedule and an entirely different demand curve. In Panel B of Figure 4.7, we show this result as a *shift* of the entire demand curve from D_1 to D_2. This particular shift means that at any price consumers are willing to buy a larger quantity of the product. For example, at a price of $8 consumers are willing to buy 46,000 pizzas (point *c*), up from 30,000 with the initial demand curve. To convey the idea that changes in these other variables change the demand schedule and the demand curve, we say that a change in any of these variables causes a **change in demand**.

change in demand

A shift of the demand curve caused by a change in a variable other than the price of the product.

(A) A Change in Quantity Demanded   **(B) A Change in Demand**

▲ **FIGURE 4.7**

Change in Quantity Demanded versus Change in Demand

(A) A change in price causes a change in quantity demanded, a movement along a single demand curve. For example, a decrease in price causes a move from point *a* to point *b*, increasing the quantity demanded.
(B) A change in demand caused by changes in a variable other than the price of the good shifts the entire demand curve. For example, an increase in demand shifts the demand curve from D_1 to D_2.

Increases in Demand Shift the Demand Curve

What types of changes will increase the demand and shift the demand curve to the right, as shown in Figure 4.7? An increase in demand like the one represented in Figure 4.7 can occur for several reasons, listed in Table 4.1:

TABLE 4.1 Increases in Demand Shift the Demand Curve to the Right		
When this variable ...	increases or decreases ...	the demand curve shifts in this direction ...
Income, with normal good	↑	
Income, with inferior good	↓	
Price of a substitute good	↑	
Price of complementary good	↓	
Population	↑	
Consumer preferences for good	↑	
Expected future price	↑	

- **Increase in income.** Consumers use their income to buy products, and the more money they have, the more money they spend. For a **normal good**, there is a positive relationship between consumer income and the quantity consumed. When income increases, a consumer buys a larger quantity of a normal good. Most goods fall into this category—including new clothes, movies, and pizza.

normal good

A good for which an increase in income increases demand.

inferior good

A good for which an increase in income decreases demand.

substitutes

Two goods for which an increase in the price of one good increases the demand for the other good.

complements

Two goods for which a decrease in the price of one good increases the demand for the other good.

- **Decrease in income.** An **inferior good** is the opposite of a normal good. Consumers buy larger quantities of inferior goods when their income *decreases*. For example, if you lose your job you might make your own coffee instead of buying it in a coffee shop, rent DVDs instead of going to the theater, and eat more macaroni and cheese. In this case, homemade coffee, DVDs, and macaroni and cheese are examples of inferior goods.

- **Increase in price of a substitute good.** When two goods are **substitutes**, an increase in the price of the first good causes some consumers to switch to the second good. Tacos and pizzas are substitutes, so an increase in the price of tacos increases the demand for pizzas as some consumers substitute pizza for tacos, which are now more expensive relative to pizza.

- **Decrease in price of a complementary good.** When two goods are **complements**, they are consumed together as a package, and a decrease in the price of one good decreases the cost of the entire package. As a result, consumers buy more of both goods. Pizza and lemonade are complementary goods, so a decrease in the price of lemonade decreases the total cost of a lemonade-and-pizza meal, increasing the demand for pizza.

- **Increase in population.** An increase in the number of people means there are more potential pizza consumers—more individual demand curves to add up to get the market demand curve—so market demand increases.

- **Shift in consumer preferences.** Consumers' preferences or tastes can change over time. If consumers' preferences shift in favor of pizza, the demand for pizza increases. One purpose of advertising is to change consumers' preferences, and a successful pizza advertising campaign will increase demand.

- **Expectations of higher future prices.** If consumers think next month's pizza price will be higher than they had initially expected, they may buy a larger quantity today and a smaller quantity next month. That means the demand for pizza today will increase.

We can use Figure 4.8 to show how an increase in demand affects the equilibrium price and equilibrium quantity. An increase in the demand for pizza resulting from

▲ **FIGURE 4.8**

An Increase in Demand Increases the Equilibrium Price

An increase in demand shifts the demand curve to the right: At each price, the quantity demanded increases. At the initial price ($8), there is excess demand, with the quantity demanded (point *b*) exceeding the quantity supplied (point *a*). The excess demand causes the price to rise, and equilibrium is restored at point *c*. To summarize, the increase in demand increases the equilibrium price to $10 and increases the equilibrium quantity to 40,000 pizzas.

one or more of the factors listed in Table 4.1 shifts the demand curve to the right, from D_1 to D_2. At the initial price of $8, there will be excess demand, as indicated by points *a* and *b*: Consumers are willing to buy 46,000 pizzas (point *b*), but producers are willing to sell only 30,000 (point *a*). Consumers want to buy 16,000 more pizzas than producers are willing to supply, and the excess demand causes upward pressure on the price. As the price rises, the excess demand shrinks because the quantity demanded decreases while the quantity supplied increases. The supply curve intersects the new demand curve at point *c*, so the new equilibrium price is $10 (up from $8), and the new equilibrium quantity is 40,000 pizzas (up from 30,000).

Decreases in Demand Shift the Demand Curve

What types of changes in the pizza market will decrease the demand for pizza? A decrease in demand means that at each price consumers are willing to buy a smaller quantity. In Figure 4.9, a decrease in demand shifts the market demand curve from D_1 to D_0. At the initial price of $8, the quantity demanded decreases from 30,000 pizzas (point *a*) to 14,000 pizzas (point *b*). A decrease in demand like the one represented in Figure 4.9 can occur for several reasons, listed in Table 4.2:

▲ FIGURE 4.9

A Decrease in Demand Decreases the Equilibrium Price

A decrease in demand shifts the demand curve to the left: At each price, the quantity demanded decreases. At the initial price ($8), there is excess supply, with the quantity supplied (point *a*) exceeding the quantity demanded (point *b*). The excess supply causes the price to drop, and equilibrium is restored at point *c*. To summarize, the decrease in demand decreases the equilibrium price to $6 and decreases the equilibrium quantity to 20,000 pizzas.

- **Decrease in income.** A decrease in income means that consumers have less to spend, so they buy a smaller quantity of each normal good.
- **Increase in income.** Consumers buy smaller quantities of an inferior good when their income increases.
- **Decrease in the price of a substitute good.** A decrease in the price of a substitute good such as tacos makes pizza more expensive relative to tacos, causing consumers to demand less pizza.
- **Increase in the price of a complementary good.** An increase in the price of a complementary good such as lemonade increases the cost of a lemonade-and-pizza meal, decreasing the demand for pizza.

TABLE 4.2 Decreases in Demand Shift the Demand Curve to the Left		
When this variable ...	increases or decreases ...	the demand curve shifts in this direction ...
Income, with normal good	↓	
Income, with inferior good	↑	
Price of a substitute good	↓	
Price of complementary good	↑	
Population	↓	
Consumer preferences for good	↓	
Expected future price	↓	

D_1, Initial demand

D_0, New demand

Price

Quantity

- **Decrease in population.** A decrease in the number of people means that there are fewer pizza consumers, so the market demand for pizza decreases.
- **Shift in consumer tastes.** When consumers' preferences shift away from pizza in favor of other products, the demand for pizza decreases.
- **Expectations of lower future prices.** If consumers think next month's pizza price will be lower than they had initially expected, they may buy a smaller quantity today, meaning the demand for pizza today will decrease.

A Decrease in Demand Decreases the Equilibrium Price

We can use Figure 4.9 to show how a decrease in demand affects the equilibrium price and equilibrium quantity. The decrease in the demand for pizza shifts the demand curve to the left, from D_1 to D_0. At the initial price of $8, there will be an excess supply, as indicated by points *a* and *b*: Producers are willing to sell 30,000 pizzas (point *a*), but given the lower demand consumers are willing to buy only 14,000 pizzas (point *b*). Producers want to sell 16,000 more pizzas than consumers are willing to buy, and the excess supply causes downward pressure on the price. As the price falls, the excess supply shrinks because the quantity demanded increases while the quantity supplied decreases. The supply curve intersects the new demand curve at point *c*, so the new equilibrium price is $6 (down from $8), and the new equilibrium quantity is 20,000 pizzas (down from 30,000).

application 4

CHINESE DEMAND AND PECAN PRICES

APPLYING THE CONCEPTS #4: How does a change in demand affect the equilibrium price?

Between 2006 and 2009, Chinese imports of U.S. pecans increased from 9 million pounds per year to 88 million pounds. The increase in demand from China is roughly 30 percent of the total annual crop. The increase in demand was caused in part by widespread reports in the Chinese media that pecans promote brain and cardiovascular health. As a result of the increase in demand, the equilibrium price of pecans increased by about 50 percent, increasing the price of pecan pie, a holiday favorite. **Related to Exercises 4.6 and 4.10.**

4.5   Market Effects of Changes in Supply

We've seen that changes in demand shift the demand curve and change the equilibrium price and quantity. In this part of the chapter, we'll see how changes on the supply side of the market affect the equilibrium price and equilibrium quantity.

Change in Quantity Supplied versus Change in Supply

Earlier in the chapter we listed the variables that determine how much of a product firms are willing to sell. Of course, one of these variables is the price of the product. The supply curve shows the positive relationship between price and quantity, *ceteris paribus*. In Panel A of Figure 4.10, when the price increases from $6 to $8 we move along the supply curve from point *a* to point *b*, and the quantity of the product supplied increases. As noted earlier in the chapter, this is called a *change in quantity supplied*. Now we're ready to take a closer look at the other variables that affect supply—including wages, material prices, and technology—and see how changes in these variables affect the supply curve and the market equilibrium.

   If any of these other variables change, the relationship between price and quantity—shown numerically in the supply schedule and graphically in the supply curve—will change. That means that we will have an entirely different supply schedule and a different supply curve. In Panel B of Figure 4.10, this is shown as a shift of the entire supply curve from S_1 to S_2. In this case, the supply curve shifts downward and to the right:

- The shift to the right means that at any given price (for example, $6), a larger quantity is produced (25,000 pizzas at point *c*, up from 20,000 at point *a*).
- The shift downward means that the price required to generate a particular quantity of output is lower. For example, the new minimum supply price is just over $1 (point *f*), down from just over $2 (point *e*). Similarly, the price required to generate 20,000 pizzas is $5 (point *d*), down from $6 (point *a*).

To convey the idea that changes in these other variables change the supply curve, we say that a change in any of these variables causes a **change in supply**.

change in supply
A shift of the supply curve caused by a change in a variable other than the price of the product.

Increases in Supply Shift the Supply Curve

What types of changes increase the supply of a product, shifting the supply curve downward and to the right? Consider first the effect of a decrease in the wage paid to pizza workers. A decrease in the wage will decrease the cost of producing pizza and shift the supply curve:

- **Downward shift.** When the cost of production decreases, the price required to generate any given quantity of pizza will decrease. In general, a lower wage means a lower marginal cost of production, so each firm needs a lower price to cover its production cost. In other words, the supply curve shifts downward.
- **Rightward shift.** The decrease in production costs makes pizza production more profitable at a given price, so producers will supply more at each price. In other words, the supply curve shifts to the right.

A decrease in the wage is just one example of a decrease in production costs that shifts the supply curve downward and to the right. These supply shifters are listed in Table 4.3. A reduction in the costs of materials (dough, cheese) or capital (pizza oven) decreases production costs, decreasing the price required to generate any particular quantity (downward shift) and increasing the quantity supplied at any particular price (rightward shift). An improvement in technology that allows the firm to economize on labor or material inputs cuts production costs and shifts the supply curve in a similar fashion. The technological improvement could be a new machine or a new way of doing business—a new layout for a factory or store, or a more efficient system of ordering inputs and

(A) Change in Quantity Supplied

(B) Change in Supply

▲ FIGURE 4.10

Change in Quantity Supplied versus Change in Supply

(A) A change in price causes a change in quantity supplied, a movement along a single supply curve. For example, an increase in price causes a move from point *a* to point *b*. **(B)** A change in supply (caused by a change in something other than the price of the product) shifts the entire supply curve. For example, an increase in supply shifts the supply curve from S_1 to S_2. For any given price (for example, $6), a larger quantity is supplied (25,000 pizzas at point *c* instead of 20,000 at point *a*). The price required to generate any given quantity decreases. For example, the price required to generate 20,000 pizzas drops from $6 (point *a*) to $5 (point *d*).

distributing output. Finally, if a government subsidizes production by paying the firm some amount for each unit produced, the net cost to the firm is lowered by the amount of the subsidy, and the supply curve shifts downward and to the right.

Two other possible sources of increases in supply are listed in Table 4.3. First, if firms believe that next month's price will be lower than they had initially expected, they may try to sell more output now at this month's relatively high price, increasing supply this month. Second, because the market supply is the sum of the quantities supplied by all producers, an increase in the number of producers will increase market supply.

TABLE 4.3 Changes in Supply Shift the Supply Curve Downward and to the Right		
When this variable ...	increases or decreases ...	the supply curve shifts in this direction ...
Wage	↓	
Price of materials or capital	↓	
Technological advance	↑	
Government subsidy	↑	
Expected future price	↓	
Number of producers	↑	

As summarized in Table 4.3, the language of shifting supply is a bit tricky. An increase in supply is represented graphically by a shift to the right (a larger quantity supplied at each price) and down (a lower price required to generate a particular quantity). The best way to remember this is to recognize that the *increase* in "increase in supply" refers to the increase in quantity supplied at a particular price—the horizontal shift of the supply curve to the right.

An Increase in Supply Decreases the Equilibrium Price

We can use Figure 4.11 to show the effects of an increase in supply on the equilibrium price and equilibrium quantity. An increase in the supply of pizza shifts the supply curve to the right, from S_1 to S_2. At the initial price of $8, the quantity supplied increases from 30,000 pizzas (point *a*) to 46,000 (point *b*).

▲ FIGURE 4.11

An Increase in Supply Decreases the Equilibrium Price

An increase in supply shifts the supply curve to the right: At each price, the quantity supplied increases. At the initial price ($8), there is excess supply, with the quantity supplied (point *b*) exceeding the quantity demanded (point *a*). The excess supply causes the price to drop, and equilibrium is restored at point *c*. To summarize, the increase in supply decreases the equilibrium price to $6 and increases the equilibrium quantity to 36,000 pizzas.

The shift of the supply curve causes excess supply that eventually decreases the equilibrium price. At the initial price of $8 (the equilibrium price with the initial supply curve), there will be an excess supply, as indicated by points *a* and *b*: Producers are willing to sell 46,000 pizzas (point *b*), but consumers are willing to buy only 30,000 (point *a*). Producers want to sell 16,000 more pizzas than consumers are willing to buy, and the excess supply causes pressure to decrease the price. As the price decreases, the excess supply shrinks, because the quantity supplied decreases while the quantity demanded increases. The new supply curve intersects the demand curve at point *c*, so the new equilibrium price is $6 (down from $8) and the new equilibrium quantity is 36,000 pizzas (up from 30,000).

Decreases in Supply Shift the Supply Curve

Consider next the changes that cause a decrease in supply. As shown in Table 4.4, anything that increases a firm's production costs will decrease supply. An increase in production cost increases the price required to generate a particular quantity (an upward shift of the supply curve) and decreases the quantity supplied at each price (a leftward shift). Production costs will increase as a result of an increase in the wage, an increase in the price of materials or capital, or a tax on each unit produced. As we saw earlier, the language linking changes in supply and the shifts of the supply curve is tricky. In the case of a decrease in supply, the *decrease* refers to the change in quantity at a particular price—the horizontal shift of the supply curve to the left.

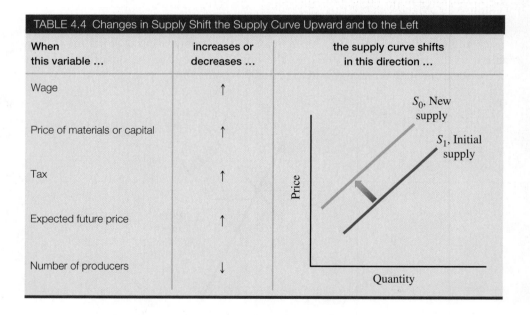

TABLE 4.4 Changes in Supply Shift the Supply Curve Upward and to the Left

When this variable ...	increases or decreases ...	the supply curve shifts in this direction ...
Wage	↑	
Price of materials or capital	↑	
Tax	↑	
Expected future price	↑	
Number of producers	↓	

A decrease in supply could occur for two other reasons. First, if firms believe next month's pizza price will be higher than they had initially expected, they may be willing to sell a smaller quantity today and a larger quantity next month. That means that the supply of pizza today will decrease. Second, because the market supply is the sum of the quantities supplied by all producers, a decrease in the number of producers will decrease market supply, shifting the supply curve to the left.

A Decrease in Supply Increases the Equilibrium Price

We can use Figure 4.12 to show the effects of a decrease in supply on the equilibrium price and equilibrium quantity. A decrease in the supply of pizza shifts the supply curve to the left, from S_1 to S_0. At the initial price of $8 (the equilibrium price with the initial supply curve), there will be an excess demand, as indicated by points a and b: Consumers are willing to buy 30,000 pizzas (point a), but producers are willing to sell only 14,000 pizzas (point b). Consumers want to buy 16,000 more pizzas than producers are willing to sell, and the excess demand causes upward pressure on the price. As the price increases, the excess demand shrinks because the quantity demanded decreases while the quantity supplied increases. The new supply curve intersects the demand curve at point c, so the new equilibrium price is $10 (up from $8), and the new equilibrium quantity is 24,000 pizzas (down from 30,000).

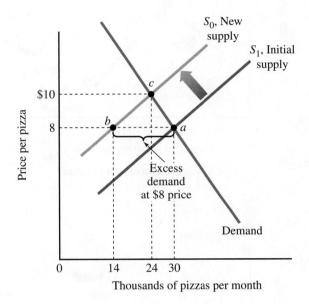

▲ **FIGURE 4.12**

A Decrease in Supply Increases the Equilibrium Price

A decrease in supply shifts the supply curve to the left. At each price, the quantity supplied decreases. At the initial price ($8), there is excess demand, with the quantity demanded (point a) exceeding the quantity supplied (point b). The excess demand causes the price to rise, and equilibrium is restored at point c. To summarize, the decrease in supply increases the equilibrium price to $10 and decreases the equilibrium quantity to 24,000 pizzas.

Simultaneous Changes in Demand and Supply

What happens to the equilibrium price and quantity when both demand and supply increase? It depends on which change is larger. In Panel A of Figure 4.13, the increase in demand is larger than the increase in supply, meaning the demand curve shifts by a larger amount than the supply curve. The market equilibrium moves from point a to point b, and the equilibrium price increases from $8 to $9. This is sensible because an increase in demand tends to pull the price up, while an increase in supply tends to push the price down. If demand increases by a larger amount, the upward pull will be stronger than the downward push, and the price will rise.

We can be certain that when demand and supply both increase, the equilibrium quantity will increase. That's because both changes tend to increase the equilibrium quantity. In Panel A of Figure 4.13, the equilibrium quantity increases from 30,000 to 44,000 pizzas.

Panel B of Figure 4.13 shows what happens when the increase in supply is larger than the increase in demand. The equilibrium moves from point *a* to point *c*, meaning that the price falls from $8 to $7. This is sensible because the downward pull on the price resulting from the increase in supply is stronger than the upward pull from the increase in demand. As expected, the equilibrium quantity rises from 30,000 to 45,000 pizzas.

(A) Larger Increase in Demand

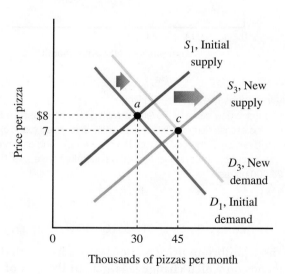

(B) Larger Increase in Supply

▲ **FIGURE 4.13**

Market Effects of Simultaneous Changes in Demand and Supply

(A) Larger increase in demand. If the increase in demand is larger than the increase in supply (if the shift of the demand curve is larger than the shift of the supply curve), both the equilibrium price and the equilibrium quantity will increase. **(B)** Larger increase in supply. If the increase in supply is larger than the increase in demand (if the shift of the supply curve is larger than the shift of the demand curve), the equilibrium price will decrease and the equilibrium quantity will increase.

What about simultaneous *decreases* in demand and supply? In this case, the equilibrium quantity will certainly fall because both changes tend to decrease the equilibrium quantity. The effect on the equilibrium price depends on which change is larger, the decrease in demand, which pushes the price downward, or the decrease in supply, which pulls the price upward. If the decrease in demand is larger, the price will fall because the force pushing the price down will be stronger than the force pulling it up. In contrast, if the decrease in supply is larger, the price will rise because the force pulling the price up will be stronger than the force pushing it down.

°application 5

HONEYBEES AND THE PRICE OF ICE CREAM

APPLYING THE CONCEPTS #5: How does a change in supply affect the equilibrium price?

In the last few years thousands of honeybee colonies have vanished, a result of bee colony collapse disorder (CCD). Roughly one-third of the U.S. food supply—including a wide variety of fruits, vegetables, and nuts—depends on pollination from bees. The decline of honeybees threatens $15 billion worth of crops in the United States. The decrease in pollination by bees has decreased the supply of strawberries, raspberries, and almonds, leading to higher prices. The higher prices for berries and nuts have increased the cost of producing food products such as ice cream, increasing their prices as well.

The collapsing of bee colonies is a mystery. The ice cream maker Haagen-Dazs donated money to Pennsylvania State University and the University of California, Davis to support research exploring the causes of CCD and possible solutions. To increase consumer awareness of the problem, Haagen-Dazs launched a new flavor, Vanilla Honey Bee. **Related to Exercises 5.8 and 5.15.**

SOURCE: Based on Parija Kavilanz, "Disappearing Bees Threaten Ice Cream Sellers," CNNMoney.com, February 20, 2008.

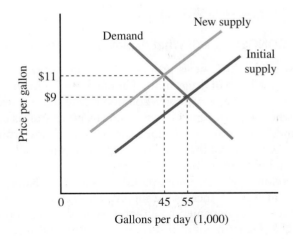

▲ FIGURE 4.14
Honeybees and the Price of Ice Cream
A decrease in pollination by bees decreases the output of fruit and nuts, increasing the prices of some ingredients for ice cream. The resulting increase in the cost of producing ice cream shifts the supply curve upward, increasing the equilibrium price and decreasing the equilibrium quantity.

4.6   Predicting and Explaining Market Changes

We've used the model of demand and supply to show how equilibrium prices are determined and how changes in demand and supply affect equilibrium prices and quantities. Table 4.5 summarizes what we've learned about how changes in demand and supply affect equilibrium prices and quantities:

- When demand changes and the demand curve shifts, price and quantity change in the *same* direction: When demand increases, both price and quantity increase; when demand decreases, both price and quantity decrease.
- When supply changes and the supply curve shifts, price and quantity change in *opposite* directions: When supply increases, the price decreases but the quantity increases; when supply decreases, the price increases but the quantity decreases.

TABLE 4.5 Market Effects of Changes in Demand or Supply

Change in Demand or Supply	How does the equilibrium price change?	How does the equilibrium quantity change?
Increase in demand	↑	↑
Decrease in demand	↓	↓
Increase in supply	↓	↑
Decrease in supply	↑	↓

We can use these lessons about demand and supply to predict the effects of various events on the equilibrium price and equilibrium quantity of a product.

We can also use the lessons listed in Table 4.5 to explain the reasons for changes in prices or quantities. Suppose we observe changes in the equilibrium price and quantity of a particular good, but we don't know what caused these changes. Perhaps it was a change

---

application 6

WHY LOWER DRUG PRICES?

APPLYING THE CONCEPTS # 6: What explains a decrease in price?

Ted Koppel, host of the ABC news program Nightline, once said, "Do you know what's happened to the price of drugs in the United States? The price of cocaine, way down, the price of marijuana, way down. You don't have to be an expert in economics to know that when the price goes down, it means more stuff is coming in. That's supply and demand." According to Koppel, the price of drugs dropped because the government's efforts to control the supply of illegal drugs had failed. In other words, the lower price resulted from an increase in supply.

Is Koppel's economic detective work sound? In Table 4.5, Koppel's explanation of lower prices is the third case—Increase in supply. This is the correct explanation only if a decrease in price is accompanied by an increase in the equilibrium quantity. But according to the U.S. Department of Justice, the quantity of drugs consumed actually decreased during the period of dropping prices. Therefore, the correct explanation of lower prices is the second case—Decrease in demand. In this case, lower demand—not a failure of the government's drug policy—was responsible for the decrease in drug prices. **Related to Exercises 6.5 and 6.13.**

SOURCES: Kenneth R. Clark, "Legalize Drugs. A Case for Koppel," *Chicago Tribune*, August 30, 1988, sec. 5, p. 8; U.S. Department of Justice, "Drugs, Crime, and the Justice System" (Washington, DC: U.S. Government Printing Office, 1992), p. 30.

in demand, or maybe it was a change in supply. We can use the information in Table 4.5 to work backward, using what we've observed about changes in prices and quantities to determine which side of the market—demand or supply—caused the changes:

- If the equilibrium price and quantity move in the same direction, the changes were caused by a change in demand.
- If the equilibrium price and quantity move in opposite directions, the changes were caused by a change in supply.

SUMMARY

In this chapter, we've seen how demand and supply determine prices. We also learned how to predict the effects of changes in demand or supply on prices and quantities. Here are the main points of the chapter:

1 A *market demand curve* shows the relationship between the quantity demanded and price, *ceteris paribus*.

2 A *market supply curve* shows the relationship between the quantity supplied and price, *ceteris paribus*.

3 *Equilibrium* in a market is shown by the intersection of the demand curve and the supply curve. When a market reaches equilibrium, there is no pressure to change the price.

4 A *change in demand* changes price and quantity in the same direction: An increase in demand increases the equilibrium price and quantity; a decrease in demand decreases the equilibrium price and quantity.

5 A *change in supply* changes price and quantity in opposite directions: An increase in supply decreases price and increases quantity; a decrease in supply increases price and decreases quantity.

KEY TERMS

change in demand, p. 79
change in quantity demanded, p. 70
change in quantity supplied, p. 73
change in supply, p. 83
complements, p. 80
demand schedule, p. 68
excess demand (shortage), p. 76
excess supply (surplus), p. 77

individual demand curve, p. 69
individual supply curve, p. 72
inferior good, p. 80
law of demand, p. 69
law of supply, p. 73
market demand curve, p. 70
market equilibrium, p. 76
market supply curve, p. 74

minimum supply price, p. 73
normal good, p. 79
perfectly competitive market, p. 68
quantity demanded, p. 68
quantity supplied, p. 71
substitutes, p. 80
supply schedule, p. 72

EXERCISES

All problems are assignable in MyEconLab.

 The Demand Curve

1.1 Arrow up or down: According to the law of demand, an increase in price _____ the quantity demanded.

1.2 From the following list, choose the variables that are held fixed in drawing a market demand curve:
- The price of the product
- Consumer income
- The price of other related goods

- Consumer expectations about future prices
- The quantity of the product purchased

1.3 From the following list, choose the variables that change as we draw a market demand curve:
- The price of the product
- Consumer income
- The price of other related goods
- Consumer expectations about future prices
- The quantity of the product purchased

1.4 The market demand curve is the (horizontal/vertical) sum of the individual demand curves.

1.5 A change in price causes movement along a demand curve and a change in _____ .

1.6 When several provinces in eastern Canada cut their cigarette taxes, the price of cigarettes decreased by roughly 50 percent, and the youth smoking rate increased by roughly_____ (1, 17, 50, 90) percent. (Related to Application 1 on page 71.)

1.7 **Draw a Demand Curve.** Your state has decided to offer its citizens vanity license plates for their cars and wants to predict how many vanity plates it will sell at different prices. The price of the state's regular license plates is $20 per year, and the state's per-capita income is $30,000. A recent survey of other states with approximately the same population (3 million people) generated the following data on incomes, prices, and vanity plates:

State	B	C	D	E
Price of vanity plate	$ 60	$ 55	$ 50	$ 40
Price of regular plates	20	20	35	20
Income	30,000	25,000	30,000	30,000
Quantity of vanity plates	6,000	6,000	16,000	16,000

    a. Use the available data to identify some points on the demand curve for vanity plates and connect the points to draw a demand curve. Don't forget *ceteris paribus*.

    b. Suppose the demand curve is linear. If your state sets a price of $50, how many vanity plates would be purchased?

1.8 **Youth Smoking.** Use a demand and supply graph of the youth smoking market to show the effects of the tax cut in eastern Canada. Assume that the initial price is $6.00, the initial quantity is 100 units, and each youth smoker smokes 5 cigarettes per day. (Related to Application 1 on page 71.)

4.2 The Supply Curve

2.1 Arrow up or down: According to the law of supply, an increase in price _____ the quantity supplied.

2.2 From the following list, choose the variables that are held fixed when drawing a market supply curve:
- The price of the product
- Wages paid to workers
- The price of materials used in production
- Taxes paid by producers
- The quantity of the product purchased

2.3 The minimum supply price is the _____ price at which a product is supplied.

2.4 The market supply curve is the (horizontal/vertical) sum of the individual supply curves.

2.5 A change in price causes movement along a supply curve and a change in _____ .

2.6 Arrows up or down: In the 1990s, the world price of wool _____ and the quantity of wool supplied _____ . (Related to Application 2 on page 76.)

2.7 **Marginal Cost of Housing.** When the price of a standard three-bedroom house increases from $150,000 to $160,000, a building company increases its output from 20 houses per year to 21 houses per year. What does the increase in the quantity of housing reveal about the cost of producing housing?

2.8 **Imports and Market Supply.** Two nations supply sugar to the world market. Lowland has a minimum supply price of 10 cents per pound, while Highland has a minimum supply price of 24 cents per pound. For each nation, the slope of the supply curve is 1 cent per million pounds.

    a. Draw the individual supply curves and the market supply curve. At what price and quantity is the supply curve kinked?

    b. The market quantity supplied at a price of 15 cents is _____ million pounds. The market quantity supplied at a price of 30 cents is _____ million pounds.

2.9 **Responses to Higher Soybean Prices.** Suppose that in initial equilibrium in the soybean market, each of the 1,000 farmers produces 50 units, for a total of 50,000 units of soybeans. Suppose the price of soybeans increases, and everyone expects the price to stay at the higher level for many years.

    a. Arrows up or down: Over a period of several years, we expect the quantity of soybeans supplied to _____ as the number of soybean farmers _____ and the output per farmer _____ .

    b. A farmer who enters the market is likely to have a (higher/lower) marginal cost of production than an original firm.

2.10 **Response to Lower Wool Price.** Use a demand and supply graph of the wool market to show the effects of the decrease in the price of wool on the quantity supplied in New Zealand. Assume that the initial price is $20 per unit and the initial quantity is 100 units. Also assume that for each 1 percent decrease in price, the quantity supplied decreases by 1 percent. (Related to Application 2 on page 76.)

3.1 The market equilibrium is shown by the intersection of the _____ curve and the _____ curve.

3.2 Excess demand occurs when the price is (less/greater) than the equilibrium price; excess supply occurs when the price is (less/greater) than the equilibrium price.

3.3 Arrow up or down: An excess demand for a product will cause the price to _____. As a consequence of the price change, the quantity demanded will _____ and the quantity supplied will _____.

3.4 Arrow up or down: An excess supply of a product will cause the price to _____. As a consequence of the price change, the quantity demanded will _____, and the quantity supplied will _____.

3.5 A minimum price above the equilibrium price generates excess _____ (supply/demand). (Related to Application 3 on page 78.)

3.6 **Interpreting the Graph.** The following graph shows the demand and supply curves for CD players. Complete the following statements.

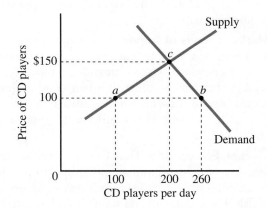

a. At the market equilibrium (shown by point _____), the price of CD players is _____ and the quantity of CD players is _____.

b. At a price of $100, there would be excess _____, so we would expect the price to _____.

c. At a price exceeding the equilibrium price, there would be excess _____, so we would expect the price to _____.

3.7 **Draw and Find the Equilibrium.** The following table shows the quantities of corn supplied and demanded at different prices.

Price per Ton	Quantity Supplied	Quantity Demanded
$ 80	600	1,200
90	800	1,100
100	1,000	1,000
110	1,200	900

a. Draw the demand curve and the supply curve.

b. The equilibrium price of corn is _____, and the equilibrium quantity is _____.

c. At a price of $110, there is excess (supply/demand) equal to _____.

3.8 **Relax Price Control.** Use a demand and supply graph to illustrate the effects of relaxing a minimum-price policy by allowing the price to decrease and narrow the gap between the controlled price and the equilibrium price. (Related to Application 3 on page 78.)

4.1 A change in demand causes a (movement along/shift of) the demand curve. A change in quantity demanded causes a (movement along/shift of) the demand curve.

4.2 Circle the variables that change as we move along the demand curve for pencils and cross out those that are assumed to be fixed.
- Quantity of pencils demanded
- Number of consumers
- Price of pencils
- Price of pens
- Consumer income

4.3 Consider the effects of online distribution of movies. A decrease in the price of online movies shifts the demand for DVD movies to the (left, right). A decrease in downloading time shifts the demand for DVD movies to the (left, right).

4.4 Arrow up or down: The market demand curve for a product will shift to the right when the price of a substitute good _____, the price of a complementary good _____, consumer income _____, and the population _____.

4.5 Arrow up or down: An increase in demand for a product _____ the equilibrium price and _____ the equilibrium quantity.

4.6 Between 2006 and 2009 the equilibrium price of pecans increased by roughly _____ (15, 50, 70) percent, a result of increased _____ (demand, supply) from China. (Related to Application 4 on page 82.)

4.7 **Market Effects of Increased Income.** Consider the market for restaurant meals. Use a demand and supply graph to predict the market effects of an increase in consumer income. Arrow up or down: The equilibrium price of restaurant meals will _____, and the equilibrium quantity of restaurant meals will _____.

4.8 **Public versus Private Colleges.** Consider the market for private college education. Use a demand and supply graph to predict the market effects of an increase in the tuition charged by public colleges. Arrow up or down: The equilibrium price of a private college education will _____, and the equilibrium quantity will _____.

4.9 **Gas Prices and New Gas Guzzlers.** Use a demand and supply graph to predict the implications for the market for new full-size SUVs. Arrow up or down: The equilibrium price of a full-size SUV will _____, and the equilibrium quantity will _____.

4.10 **Pecan Prices.** Use a demand and supply graph to illustrate the effects of the increase in the demand for pecans from Chinese consumers. Assume that the initial equilibrium price is $6 per unit. (Related to Application 4 on page 82.)

4.5	Market Effects of Changes in Supply

5.1 A change in supply causes a (movement along/shift of) the supply curve. A change in quantity supplied causes a (movement along/shift of) the supply curve.

5.2 Circle the variables that change as we move along the supply curve for pencils and cross out those that are assumed to be fixed:
  • Quantity of pencils supplied
  • Price of wood
  • Price of pencils
  • Production technology

5.3 Arrow up or down: An increase in the price of wood shifts the supply curve for pencils _____; an improvement in pencil-production technology shifts the supply curve for pencils _____; a tax on pencil production shifts the supply curve for pencils _____.

5.4 Arrow up or down: An increase in the supply of a product _____ the equilibrium price and _____ the equilibrium quantity.

5.5 If both demand and supply increase simultaneously, the equilibrium price will increase if the change in _____ is relatively large.

5.6 Arrow up or down: If supply increases while demand decreases, the equilibrium price will _____.

5.7 If supply increases while demand decreases, the equilibrium quantity will decrease if the change in (supply/demand) is relatively large.

5.8 Arrows up or down: The decrease in the number of bee colonies _____ the supply of fruits and berries, _____ the cost of producing ice cream, and _____ the equilibrium price of ice cream. (Related to Application 5 on page 89.)

5.9 **Effect of Weather on Prices.** Suppose a freeze in Florida wipes out 20 percent of the orange crop. How will this affect the equilibrium price and quantity of Florida oranges? Illustrate your answer with a graph.

5.10 **Immigration Control and Prices.** Consider the market for raspberries. Suppose a new law outlaws the use of foreign farm workers on raspberry farms, and the wages paid to farm workers increase as a result. Use a demand and supply graph to predict the effects of the higher wage on the equilibrium price and quantity of raspberries. Arrow up or down: The equilibrium price of raspberries will _____, and the equilibrium quantity of raspberries will _____.

5.11 **Market Effects of Import Ban.** Consider the market for shoes in a nation that initially imports half the shoes it consumes. Use a demand and supply graph to predict the market effect of a ban on shoe imports. Arrow up or down: The equilibrium price will _____, and the equilibrium quantity will _____.

5.12 **Market Effects of a Tax.** Consider the market for fish. Use a demand and supply graph to predict the effect of a tax paid by fish producers of $1 per pound of fish. Use a demand and supply graph to predict the market effect of the tax. Arrow up or down: The equilibrium price will _____, and the equilibrium quantity will _____.

5.13 **Innovation and the Price of Mobile Phones.** Suppose that the initial price of a mobile phone is $100 and that the initial quantity demanded is 500 phones per day. Use a graph to show the effects of a technological innovation that decreases the cost of producing mobile phones. Label the starting point with "*a*" and the new equilibrium with "*b*."

5.14 Used Cars: Gas Guzzlers versus Gas Sippers. Consider the market for used cars. In 2008, the price of gas rose while the price of used full-size SUVs dropped and the price of used compact cars increased.

a. Use a supply–demand graph to show the effects of a higher gasoline price on the market for used full-size SUVs.

b. Use a supply–demand graph to show the effects of a higher gasoline price on the market for used compact cars.

5.15 Honeybees and Ice Cream. Suppose the decline of bee colonies increases the prices of some ingredients used to produce ice cream. Consider two flavors of ice cream, strawberry and vanilla. The cost of producing strawberry ice cream increases by 20 percent, while the cost of producing vanilla ice cream increases by only 5 percent. Use a supply–demand graph to show the implications for the equilibrium prices and quantities of the two flavors of ice cream. (Related to Application 5 on page 89.)

4.6 Predicting and Explaining Market Changes

6.1 Fill in the blanks in the following table. Note that the ordering of the first column has been scrambled.

Change in Demand or Supply	How does the equilibrium price change?	How does the equilibrium quantity change?
Increase in supply		
Decrease in demand		
Decrease in supply		
Increase in demand		

6.2 When (supply/demand) changes, the equilibrium price and the equilibrium quantity change in the same direction. When (supply/demand) changes, the equilibrium price and the equilibrium quantity change in opposite directions.

6.3 Suppose the equilibrium price of accordions recently increased while the equilibrium quantity decreased. These changes were caused by a(n) (increase/decrease) in (supply/demand).

6.4 Suppose the equilibrium price of housing recently increased, and the equilibrium quantity increased as well. These changes were caused by a(n) (increase/decrease) in (supply/demand).

6.5 If a decrease in the price of drugs is accompanied by a decrease in quantity, the decrease in price was caused by a change in _____ (supply, demand). (Related to Application 6 on page 90.)

6.6 What Caused the Higher Gasoline Price? In the last month, the price of gasoline increased by 20 percent. Your job is to determine what caused the increase in price: a change in demand or a change in supply. Ms. Info has all the numbers associated with the gasoline market, and she can answer a single factual question. (She cannot answer the question "Was the higher price caused by a change in demand or a change in supply?")

a. What single question would you ask?

b. Provide an answer to your question that implies that the higher price was caused by a change in demand. Illustrate with a complete graph.

c. Provide an answer to your question that implies that the higher price was caused by a change in supply. Illustrate with a complete graph.

6.7 Rising Price of Milk. In 2007, the price of milk increased by roughly 10 percent while the quantity consumed decreased. Use a supply–demand graph to explain the changes in price and quantity.

6.8 Rising Price of Used Organs. Over the last few years, the price of transplantable human organs (livers, kidneys, hearts) has increased dramatically. Why? What additional information about the market for used organs would allow you to prove that your explanation is the correct one?

6.9 The Price of Summer Cabins. As summer approaches, the equilibrium price of rental cabins increases and the equilibrium quantity of cabins rented increases. Draw a demand and supply graph that explains these changes.

6.10 Simplest Possible Graph. Consider the market for juice oranges. Draw the simplest possible demand and supply graph consistent with the following observations. You should be able to draw a graph with no more than four curves. Label each of your curves as "supply" or "demand" and indicate the year (1, 2, or 3).

Year	1	2	3
Price	$5	$7	$4
Quantity	100	80	110

6.11 Zero Price for Used Newspapers. In 1987 you could sell a ton of used newspaper for $60. Five years later, you couldn't sell them at any price. In other words, the price of used newspapers dropped from $60 to zero in just five years. Over this period, the quantity of used newspapers bought and sold increased. What caused the drop in price? Illustrate your answer with a complete graph.

6.12 Koppel and Drug Prices. Use a demand and supply graph to show that Ted Koppel's proposed explanation of a decrease in drug prices is incorrect. (Related to Application 6 on page 90.)

MARKET EQUILIBRIUM

This simple experiment takes about 20 minutes. We start by dividing the class into two equal groups: consumers and producers.

- The instructor provides each consumer with a number indicating the maximum amount he or she is willing to pay (WTP) for a bushel of apples: The WTP is a number between $1 and $100. Each consumer has the opportunity to buy one bushel of apples per trading period. The consumer's score for a single trading period equals the gap between the WTP and the price actually paid for apples. For example, if the consumer's WTP is $80 and he or she pays only $30 for apples, the consumer's score is $50. Each consumer has the option of not buying apples. This will be sensible if the best price the consumer can get exceeds the WTP. If the consumer does not buy apples, his or her score will be zero.

- The instructor provides each producer with a number indicating the cost of producing a bushel of apples (a number between $1 and $100). Each producer has the opportunity to sell one bushel per trading period. The producer's score for a single trading period equals the gap between the selling prices and the cost of producing apples. So if a producer sells apples for $20, and the cost is only $15, the producer's score is $5. Producers have the option of not selling apples, which is sensible if the best price the producer can get is less than the cost. If the producer does not sell apples, his or her score is zero.

Once everyone understands the rules, consumers and producers meet in a trading area to arrange transactions. A consumer may announce how much he or she is willing to pay for apples and wait for a producer to agree to sell apples at that price. Alternatively, a producer may announce how much he or she is willing accept for apples and wait for a consumer to agree to buy apples at that price. Once a transaction has been arranged, the consumer and producer inform the instructor of the trade, record the transaction, and leave the trading area.

Several trading periods are conducted, each of which lasts a few minutes. After the end of each trading period, the instructor lists the prices at which apples sold during the period. Then another trading period starts, providing consumers and producers another opportunity to buy or sell apples. After all the trading periods have been completed, each participant computes his or her score by adding the scores from the trading periods.

MyEconLab

For additional economic experiments, please visit
www.myeconlab.com.

Elasticity: A Measure of Responsiveness

The city of Phoenix, Arizona gets its gasoline from two pipelines, one running from Texas and the other from the West Coast.

In summer of 2003, the Texas pipeline broke, cutting off 30 percent of the city's gasoline supply.

A reliable study of gasoline suggests that a 5 percent increase in price decreases the quantity demanded by 1 percent. Based on this study, it appears that to counteract the 30 percent decrease, the price would have to rise by 150 percent (5 times 30). But in fact the price increased by only 40 percent. What explains the relatively small increase in price?

LEARNING OBJECTIVES

- List the determinants of the price elasticity of demand.

- Use price elasticity of demand to predict changes in quantity and total revenue.

- Explain how the price elasticity of demand varies along a linear demand curve.

- Define the income elasticity and cross-price elasticity of demand.

- List the determinants of the price elasticity of supply.

- Use demand and supply elasticities to predict changes in equilibrium prices.

MyEconLab
MyEconLab helps you master each objective and study more efficiently.

*i*n Chapter 4 we discussed the law of demand, which states that an increase in price decreases the quantity demanded, *ceteris paribus*. The law of demand is useful, but sometimes we need to know the numbers behind the law of demand. That is, we need to know exactly how much less will be demanded at a higher price. In this chapter, we will quantify the law of demand, exploring the responsiveness of consumers to changes in price. Suppose your student film society has decided to increase the price for its tickets from $10 to $11. You know from the law of demand that you'll sell fewer tickets, but the question is "How many fewer tickets?" As we'll see, you can use the concept of elasticity to predict how many tickets you'll sell and how much money you'll collect in total.

Switching to the supply side of the market, the law of supply tells us that an increase in price increases the quantity supplied, *ceteris paribus*. Sometimes the question is "By how much?" We'll quantify the law of supply, showing how to predict just how much more of a product will be supplied at a higher price. For example, if the world price of oil increases from $70 to $80 per barrel, we know from the law of supply that domestic producers will supply more oil, but the question is "How much more?" We can use the concept of elasticity to predict how much more domestic oil will be supplied at the higher price.

5.1 The Price Elasticity of Demand

price elasticity of demand (E_d)
A measure of the responsiveness of the quantity demanded to changes in price; equal to the absolute value of the percentage change in quantity demanded divided by the percentage change in price.

The **price elasticity of demand (E_d)** measures the responsiveness of the quantity demanded to changes in price. To compute the price elasticity of demand, we divide the percentage change in the quantity demanded by the percentage change in price, and then take the absolute value of the ratio:

$$E_d = \left| \frac{\text{percentage change in quantity demanded}}{\text{percentage change in price}} \right|$$

The vertical bars indicate that we take the absolute value of the ratio, so the price elasticity is always a positive number. For example, suppose the price of milk *increases* by 10 percent and the quantity demanded *decreases* by 15 percent. The price elasticity of demand is 1.5:

$$E_d = \left| \frac{\text{percentage change in quantity demanded}}{\text{percentage change in price}} = \frac{-15\%}{10\%} = 1.50 \right|$$

The law of demand tells us that price and quantity demanded move in opposite directions. Therefore, the percentage change in quantity will always have the opposite sign of the percentage change in price. In our example, a positive 10 percent change in price results in a negative 15 percent change in quantity. The ratio of the percentage changes is –1.50, and taking the absolute value of this ratio, the elasticity is 1.50. Although it is conventional to use the absolute value to compute the price elasticity, the practice is not universal. So you may encounter a negative price elasticity, which means that the elasticity is reported as its numerical value rather than its absolute value.

When the price elasticity is listed as a positive number, the interpretation of the elasticity is straightforward. If the elasticity number is large, it means that the demand for the product is very elastic, or very responsive to changes in price. In contrast, a small number indicates that the demand for a product is very inelastic.

Computing Percentage Changes and Elasticities

As we saw in the appendix to Chapter 1, we can compute a percentage change in two ways. Using the initial-value method, we divide the change in the value of a variable by its initial value. For example, if a price increases from $20 to $22, the percentage change is $2 divided by $20, or 10 percent:

$$\text{percent change with initial value} = \frac{22 - 20}{20} \times 100 = \frac{2}{20} \times 100 = 10\%$$

Alternatively, we could use the midpoint method. We divide the change in the variable by its average value, that is, the midpoint of the two values. For example, if the price increases from $20 to $22, the average or midpoint value is $21 and the percentage change is $2 divided by $21, or 9.52 percent:

$$\text{percent change with midpoint value} = \frac{2}{\frac{20 + 22}{2}} \times 100 = \frac{2}{21} \times 100 = 9.52\%$$

The advantage of the midpoint approach is that it generates the same absolute percentage change whether the variable has increased or decreased. The reason is that the denominator is the same in both cases. In contrast, the initial-value computation is based on the initial value, so our answer there depends on the direction of the change—which of the two values is the initial value.

Table 5.1 shows the calculation of the price elasticity of demand with the two approaches. When the price increases from $20 to $22, the quantity demanded decreases from 100 to 80 units. Using the initial-value method, we get an elasticity of 2.0, equal to the 20 percent change in quantity divided by the 10 percent change in price. As shown in the lower part of the table, the midpoint method generates an elasticity of 2.33.

TABLE 5.1 Computing Price Elasticity with Initial Values and Midpoints

		Price	Quantity
Data	Initial	$20	100
	New	22	80
		Price	**Quantity**
Computation with initial-value method	Percentage change	$10\% = \frac{\$2}{\$20} \times 100$	$-20\% = -\frac{20}{100} \times 100$
	Price elasticity of demand	$2.0 = \left|\frac{-20\%}{10\%}\right|$	
		Price	**Quantity**
Computation with midpoint method	Percentage change	$9.52\% = \frac{\$2}{\$21} \times 100$	$-22.22\% = -\frac{20}{90} \times 100$
	Price elasticity of demand	$2.33 = \left|\frac{-22.22\%}{9.52\%}\right|$	

Why do the two approaches generate different elasticity numbers? The midpoint approach measures the percentage changes more precisely, so we get a more precise measure of price elasticity. In this case, the percentage changes are relatively small, so the two elasticity numbers are close to one another. If the percentage changes were larger, however, the elasticity numbers generated by the two approaches would be quite different, and it would be wise to use the midpoint approach. In this book, we use the initial-value approach because it generates nice round numbers and allows us to focus on economics rather than arithmetic. But any time you want to be more precise, you can use the midpoint formula.

Price Elasticity and the Demand Curve

Figure 5.1 shows five different demand curves, each with a different elasticity. We can divide products into five types, depending on their price elasticities of demand.

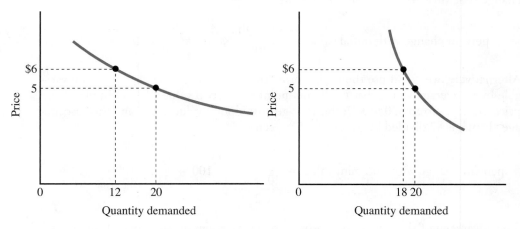

(A) Elastic Demand: $E_d = \left| \dfrac{-40\%}{20\%} \right| = 2.0 > 1$

(B) Inelastic Demand: $E_d = \left| \dfrac{-10\%}{20\%} \right| = 0.50 < 1$

(C) Unit Elastic Demand: $E_d = \left| \dfrac{-20\%}{20\%} \right| = 1$

(D) Perfectly Inelastic Demand: $E_d = \left| \dfrac{0\%}{20\%} \right| = 0$

(E) Perfectly Elastic Demand: $E_d = \infty$

▲ **FIGURE 5.1**
Elasticity and Demand Curves

- **Elastic demand** (Panel A). In this case, a 20 percent increase in price (from $5 to $6) decreases the quantity demanded by 40 percent (from 20 to 12), so the price elasticity of demand is 2.0. When the price elasticity is greater than 1.0, we say that demand is *elastic*, or highly responsive to changes in price. Some examples of goods with elastic demand are restaurant meals, air travel, and movies.

- **Inelastic demand** (Panel B). The same 20 percent increase in price decreases the quantity demanded by only 10 percent (from 20 to 18), so the price elasticity of demand is 0.50. When the elasticity is less than 1.0, we say that demand is *inelastic*, or not very responsive to changes in price. Some examples of goods with inelastic demand are salt, eggs, coffee, and cigarettes.

- **Unit elastic demand** (Panel C). A 20 percent increase in price decreases the quantity demanded by exactly 20 percent, so the price elasticity of demand is 1.0. Some examples of goods with *unit elasticity* are housing and fruit juice.

- **Perfectly inelastic demand** (Panel D). When demand is *perfectly inelastic*, the quantity doesn't change as the price changes, so the demand curve is vertical at the fixed quantity. The price elasticity of demand is zero. This extreme case is rare because for most products, consumers can either switch to a substitute good or do without. For example, although there are no direct substitutes for household water, as the price of water rises, people install low-flow showerheads and water their lawns and clean their cars less frequently. The rare cases of perfectly inelastic demand are medicines—such as insulin for diabetics—that have no substitutes.

- **Perfectly elastic demand** (Panel E). In the case of *perfect elasticity*, the price elasticity is infinite and the demand curve is horizontal, meaning that only one price is possible. At that price, the quantity demanded could be any quantity, from one unit to millions of units. If the price were to increase even a penny, the quantity demanded would drop to zero. As we'll see later in the book, firms in a perfectly competitive market face this sort of demand curve. For example, each wheat farmer can sell as much as he or she wants at the market price but would sell nothing at any price above the market price.

elastic demand
The price elasticity of demand is greater than one, so the percentage change in quantity exceeds the percentage change in price.

inelastic demand
The price elasticity of demand is less than one, so the percentage change in quantity is less than the percentage change in price.

unit elastic demand
The price elasticity of demand is one, so the percentage change in quantity equals the percentage change in price.

perfectly inelastic demand
The price elasticity of demand is zero.

perfectly elastic demand
The price elasticity of demand is infinite.

Elasticity and the Availability of Substitutes

The key factor in determining the price elasticity for a particular product is the availability of substitute products. Consider the substitution possibilities for insulin and cornflakes. There are no good substitutes for insulin, so diabetics are not very responsive to changes in price. When the price of insulin increases, they cannot switch to another medicine, so the demand for insulin is inelastic. In contrast, there are many substitutes for cornflakes, including different types of corn cereals, as well as cereals made from wheat, rice, and oats. Faced with an increase in the price of cornflakes, consumers can easily switch to substitute products, so the demand for cornflakes is relatively elastic.

Table 5.2 on page 102 shows the price elasticities of demand for various products. The different elasticities illustrate the importance of substitutes in determining the price elasticity of demand. Because there are no good substitutes for water and salt, it is not surprising that the elasticities are small. For example, the price elasticity of demand for water is 0.20, meaning that a 10 percent increase in price decreases the quantity demanded by 2 percent. The demand for coffee is inelastic (0.30), because although there are alternative beverages and caffeine-delivery systems (tea, infused soft drinks, sports drinks, and pills), coffee provides a unique combination of taste and caffeine. Although there is an artificial substitute for eggs (for people concerned about dietary cholesterol), there are no natural substitutes, so the demand for eggs is relatively inelastic (0.30).

TABLE 5.2 Price Elasticities of Demand for Selected Products[1]

	Product	Price Elasticity of Demand
Inelastic	Salt	0.1
	Food (wealthy countries)	0.15
	Weekend canoe trips	0.19
	Water	0.2
	Coffee	0.3
	Physician visits	0.25
	Sport fishing	0.28
	Gasoline (short run)	0.25
	Eggs	0.3
	Cigarettes	0.3
	Food (poor countries)	0.34
	Shoes and footwear	0.7
	Gasoline (long run)	0.6
Unit elastic	Housing	1.0
	Fruit juice	1.0
Elastic	Automobiles	1.2
	Foreign travel	1.8
	Motorboats	2.2
	Restaurant meals	2.3
	Air travel	2.4
	Movies	3.7
	Specific brands of coffee	5.6

Alternative brands of a product are good substitutes for one another, so the demand for a specific brand of a product is typically elastic. For example, the elasticity of demand for a specific brand of coffee is 5.6, compared to an overall elasticity for coffee of 0.30. This means that a 10 percent increase in the price of coffee in general (all brands) will decrease the quantity of coffee sold by 3 percent, but a 10 percent increase in the price of a specific brand will decrease the quantity of that brand sold by 56 percent. Each brand of coffee is a substitute for all the other brands, so consumers are very responsive to a change in the price of a specific brand. Similarly, the demand for specific brands of tires is more elastic than the demand for tires in general.

The availability of substitutes increases over time, so the longer the time consumers have to respond to a price change, the more elastic the demand. Because it often takes time for consumers to respond to price changes, the short-run price elasticity of demand is typically smaller than the long-run elasticity. For example, when the price of gasoline increases, consumers can immediately drive fewer miles in their existing cars or switch to public transportation. As shown in Table 5.2, the short-run price elasticity of demand for gasoline is 0.25. In the long run, consumers can buy more fuel-efficient cars and move closer to workplaces. As time passes, consumers have more options to cut gasoline consumption—more substitution possibilities—so demand becomes more elastic. In Table 5.2, the long-run price elasticity of demand for gasoline is 0.60, over twice as large as the short-run elasticity.

Other Determinants of the Price Elasticity of Demand

Two other factors help determine the price elasticity of demand for a product. First, the elasticity is generally larger for goods that take a relatively large part of a consumer's budget. If a good represents a small part of the budget of the typical consumer, demand is relatively inelastic. For example, suppose the price of pencils is 20 cents and then increases by 10 percent, or 2 cents. Because the price change is tiny compared to the income of the typical consumer, we would expect a relatively small decrease in the quantity of pencils demanded. In contrast, if the price of a car is $20,000 and then increases 10 percent ($2,000), we would expect a bigger response because the change in price is large relative to the income of the typical consumer.

International comparisons of the price elasticity of demand for food suggest that demand is more price elastic when the good represents a large part of the consumer's budget. As shown in Table 5.2, in wealthy countries the price elasticity of demand for food is around 0.15. In poor countries, people spend a larger fraction of their budget on food, so they are more responsive to changes in food prices. In these poor countries, the price elasticity of demand is around 0.34.

Another factor in determining the elasticity of demand is whether the product is a necessity or a luxury good. As shown in Table 5.2, the demand for food, a necessity, is relatively low in both wealthy and poor countries. Similarly, the demand for physician visits is inelastic (elasticity = 0.25). In contrast, the elasticity of demand for luxury goods such as restaurant meals, foreign travel, and motorboats is relatively elastic. Of course, not all goods that are considered luxuries have elastic demand. For example, the price elasticity of demand for weekend canoe trips is 0.19, and the demand elasticity for sport fishing is 0.28. These elasticities suggest that one person's luxury is another person's necessity.

Table 5.3 summarizes our discussion of the determinants of the price elasticity of demand. Demand is relatively elastic if there are many good substitutes, if we allow consumers a long time to respond, if spending on the product is a large part of the consumer's budget, and if the product is a luxury as opposed to a necessity.

TABLE 5.3 Determinants of Elasticity		
Factor	Demand is relatively elastic if ...	Demand is relatively inelastic if ...
Availability of substitutes	there are many substitutes.	there are few substitutes.
Passage of time	a long time passes.	a short time passes.
Fraction of consumer budget	is large.	is small.
Necessity	the product is a luxury.	the product is a necessity.

application 1

A CLOSER LOOK AT THE ELASTICITY OF DEMAND FOR GASOLINE

APPLYING THE CONCEPTS #1: How does the price elasticity of demand vary over time?

We've seen that the demand for gasoline is more elastic in the long run, when consumers have more opportunity to respond to changes in price. A recent study explores two sorts of responses to higher gasoline prices. First, when the price increases, people drive fewer miles, so there are fewer cars on the road. As shown in the following table, the elasticity of traffic volume is 0.10 in the short run (within one year) and 0.30 in the long run (after five years). In other words, a 10 percent increase in the price of gasoline decreases the number of cars on the road by 1 percent in the short run and 3 percent in the long run. A second response to higher prices is to switch to more fuel-efficient cars. As shown in the table, the elasticity of fuel efficiency is 0.15 in the short run and 0.40 in the long run. **Related to Exercises 1.6 and 1.7.**

TABLE 5.4 Gasoline Prices, Traffic Volume, and Fuel Efficiency		
Elasticity of	Short Run (1 year)	Long Run (5 years)
Traffic Volume	0.10	0.30
Fuel Efficiency	0.15	0.40

SOURCE: Based on Phil Goodwin, Joyce Dargay, and Mark Hanly, "Elasticities of Road Traffic and Fuel Consumption with Respect to Price and Income: A Review," *Transport Review* 24, no. 3 (2004): 275–292.

5.2 Using Price Elasticity

The price elasticity of demand is a very useful tool for economic analysis. If we know the price elasticity of demand for a particular good, we can quantify the law of demand, predicting the change in quantity resulting from a change in price. In addition, we can use an estimate of the price elasticity of demand to predict how a change in price affects a firm's total revenue.

Predicting Changes in Quantity

If we have values for two of the three variables in the elasticity formula, we can compute the value of the third. The three variables are (1) the price elasticity of demand itself, (2) the percentage change in quantity, and (3) the percentage change in price. So if we know the values for the price elasticity and the percentage change in price, we can compute the value for the percentage change in quantity. Specifically, we can rearrange the elasticity formula:

$$\text{percentage change in quantity demanded} = \text{percentage change in price} \times E_d$$

For example, suppose you run a campus film series and you've decided to increase your admission price by 15 percent. If you know the elasticity of demand for your movies, you could use it to predict how many fewer tickets you'll sell at the higher price. If the elasticity of demand is 2.0 and you increase the price by 15 percent, we would predict a 30 percent decrease in the quantity of tickets demanded:

$$\text{percentage change in quantity demanded} = \text{percentage change in price} \times E_d$$
$$= 15\% \times 2.0 = 30\%$$

We can use the concept of price elasticity to predict the effects of a change in the price of beer on drinking and highway deaths among young adults. The price elasticity of demand for beer among young adults is about 1.30.[2] If a state imposes a beer tax that increases the price of beer by 10 percent, we would predict that beer consumption will decrease by 13 percent:

$$\text{percentage change in quantity demanded} = \text{percentage change in price} \times E_d$$
$$= 10\% \times 1.30 = 13\%$$

The number of highway deaths among young adults is roughly proportional to their beer consumption, so the number of deaths will also decrease by 13 percent. According to a recent study, a doubling of the beer tax from $0.16 to $0.32 per six-pack would decrease highway deaths among 18- to 20-year-olds by about 12 percent. Raising the beer tax back to where it was in 1951 would cut highway deaths by 32 percent.

Another ongoing policy objective is to reduce smoking by teenagers. Under the 1997 federal tobacco settlement, cigarette prices increased by about 62 cents per pack, a percentage increase of about 25 percent. The demand for cigarettes by teenagers is elastic, with an elasticity of 1.3.[3] Therefore, a 25 percent price hike will reduce teen smoking by 32.5 percent:

$$\text{percentage change in quantity demanded} = 25\% \times 1.30 = 32.5\%$$

About half the decrease in consumption occurs because fewer teenagers will become smokers, and the other half occurs because each teenage smoker will smoke fewer cigarettes.

Price Elasticity and Total Revenue

Firms use the concept of price elasticity to predict the effects of changing their prices. A firm produces products to sell, and a firm's **total revenue** equals the money it generates from selling products. If a firm sells its product for the same price to every consumer, total revenue equals the price per unit times the quantity sold:

total revenue
The money a firm generates from selling its product.

$$\text{total revenue} = \text{price per unit} \times \text{quantity sold}$$

Suppose a firm increases the price of its product. Will its total sales revenue increase or decrease? The answer depends on the price elasticity of demand for the product. If you know the price elasticity, you can determine whether a price hike will increase or decrease the firm's total revenue.

Let's return to the example of the campus film series. Suppose you are thinking about increasing the price of tickets by 10 percent, from $10 to $11. An increase in the ticket price brings good news and bad news:

• Good news: You get more money for each ticket sold.

• Bad news: You sell fewer tickets.

Your total revenue will decrease if the bad news (fewer tickets sold) dominates the good news (more money per ticket). The elasticity of demand tells us how bad the bad news is. The more elastic the demand, the larger the reduction in the quantity sold—the worse the bad news.

The upper part of Table 5.5 shows an example of the effects of a price hike when the demand for a product is elastic. In this case, the price elasticity of demand is 2.0, so a 10 percent increase in price decreases the quantity demanded by 20 percent, from 100 to 80 tickets. Because the percentage decrease in quantity (the bad news) exceeds the percentage increase in price (the good news), total revenue decreases, from $1,000 to $880. In general, an elastic demand means that the percentage change in quantity (the bad news from a price hike) will exceed the percentage change in price (the good news), so an increase in price will decrease total revenue.

TABLE 5.5 Price and Total Revenue with Different Elasticities of Demand

	Elastic Demand: $E_d = 2.0$	
Price	Quantity Sold	Total Revenue
$10	100	$1,000
11	80	880

	Inelastic Demand: $E_d = 0.50$	
Price	Quantity Sold	Total Revenue
100	10	$1,000
120	9	1,080

We get the opposite result if the demand for the good is inelastic: An increase in price increases total revenue. The lower part of Table 5.5 shows an example of the effects of a price hike when demand is inelastic (equal to 0.50). Suppose that your campus bookstore starts with a textbook price of $100 and sells 10 books per minute. If the bookstore increases its price by 20 percent (from $100 to $120 per book), the quantity of textbooks sold will decrease by only 10 percent (from 10 to 9 per minute). Therefore, the store's total revenue will increase from $1,000 per minute ($100 × 10 books) to $1,080 per minute ($120 × 9 books). In general, an inelastic demand means that the percentage change in quantity will be smaller than the percentage change in price, so an increase in price will increase total revenue.

Table 5.6 shows, for different types of goods, the effects of changes in price on total revenue.

TABLE 5.6 Price Elasticity and Total Revenue		
Elastic Demand: $E_d > 1.0$		
If price …	Total revenue …	Because the percentage change in quantity is …
↑	↓	Larger than the percentage change in price.
↓	↑	Larger than the percentage change in price.
Inelastic Demand: $E_d < 1.0$		
If price …	Total revenue …	Because the percentage change in quantity is …
↑	↑	Smaller than the percentage change in price.
↓	↓	Smaller than the percentage change in price.

- *Elastic demand.* The relationship between price and total revenue is negative: An increase in price decreases total revenue; a decrease in price increases total revenue.
- *Inelastic demand.* The relationship between price and total revenue is positive: An increase in price increases total revenue; a decrease in price decreases total revenue.
- *Unit elastic demand.* Total revenue does not vary with price.

We can use the relationships summarized in Table 5.6 to work backward. If we observe the relationship between the price of a product and total sales revenue of the product, we can determine whether the demand for the product is elastic or inelastic. Suppose that when a music store increases the price of its CDs, its total revenue from CDs drops. The negative relationship between price and total revenue means that demand for the store's CDs is elastic: Total revenue decreases because consumers are very responsive to an increase in price, buying a much smaller quantity. In contrast, suppose that when a city increases the price it charges for water, the total revenue from water sales increases. The positive relationship between price and total revenue suggests that the demand for the city's water is inelastic: Total revenue increases because consumers are not very responsive to an increase in price.

Using Elasticity to Predict the Revenue Effects of Price Changes

If we know whether the demand for a product is elastic or inelastic, we can predict the effect of a change in price on total revenue. Here are four illustrations of the revenue consequences of changes in price.

1 **Market versus Brand Elasticity:** The demand for a specific brand of a product is more elastic than the demand for the product. Although the demand for coffee is inelastic (price elasticity of demand = 0.30), the demand for a specific brand of

coffee is elastic (price elasticity = 3.0). Therefore, a price cut on a specific brand of coffee will increase a firm's total revenue.

2 **Bus Fares and Deficits:** In every large city in the United States, the public bus system runs a deficit: Operating costs exceed revenues from passenger fares. The price elasticity of demand for bus ridership in the typical city is inelastic, about 0.33.[4] Therefore, the good news associated with a fare hike (more revenue per rider) will dominate the bad news (fewer riders), and total fare revenue will increase, reducing the bus deficit.

3 **A Bumper Crop Is Bad News for Farmers:** A bumper crop of soybeans (an unusually large harvest) brings good news and bad news for farmers. The good news is that they will sell more bushels of soybeans. The bad news is that the increase in supply will decrease the equilibrium price of soybeans, so farmers will get less money per bushel. Unfortunately for farmers, the demand for soybeans and many other agricultural products is inelastic, meaning that to sell the extra output, the price must fall by a relatively large amount. The bad news dominates the good news, so a bumper crop means less total revenue for farmers.

4 **Antidrug Policies and Property Crime:** What is the connection between antidrug policies and property crimes such as robbery, burglary, and auto theft? The government uses various policies to restrict the supply of illegal drugs, and the decrease in supply increases the equilibrium price. Because the demand for illegal drugs is inelastic, the increase in price will increase total spending on illegal drugs.[5] A drug addict who supports his or her habit by stealing personal property will commit more property crimes to pay for the pricier drugs. In other words, there is a trade-off: A policy that increases drug prices will reduce drug consumption, but will also increase the amount of property crime committed by addicts who continue to abuse drugs.

application 2

VANITY PLATES AND THE ELASTICITY OF DEMAND

APPLYING THE CONCEPTS #2: How does an increase in price affect total expenditures?

The radio quiz show *Wait Wait … Don't Tell Me!* recently asked the following question: Which state has the highest number of vanity license plates? The correct answer is Virginia, where over 10 percent of cars have vanity license plates such as 10SNE1 and GLBLWRMR. An economist might have extended the question to ask why there are so many vanity plates in Virginia. Although Virginians may be unusually vain, a more plausible explanation is that the price of vanity plates is only $10, or about one-third of the average price in the United States.

Is the low price in Virginia rational from the state's perspective? Suppose the state's objective is to maximize the revenue from vanity plates. According to a recent study, the demand for vanity plates in Virginia is inelastic, with a price elasticity of demand equal to 0.26. Therefore, if the state increased the price, the total revenue from vanity plates would increase. **Related to Exercises 2.4 and 2.14.**

SOURCE: Based on Erik Craft, "The Demand for Vanity (Plates): Elasticities, Net Revenue Maximization, and Deadweight Loss." *Contemporary Economic Policy* 20 (2002): 133–144.

5.3 Elasticity and Total Revenue for a Linear Demand Curve

It is often useful to represent the demand for a product with a linear demand curve. A linear demand curve—a straight line—has a constant slope, but that does not mean that it has a constant elasticity of demand. In fact, the price elasticity of demand decreases as we move downward along a linear demand curve. On the upper half of a linear demand curve, demand is elastic; on the lower half of the curve, demand is inelastic. At the midpoint of a linear demand curve, demand is unit elastic.

Price Elasticity along a Linear Demand Curve

We can use Panel A of Figure 5.2 to show how price elasticity varies along a linear demand curve. The slope of the demand curve is –$2 per unit quantity. We see this by picking any two points and computing the slope as the vertical difference between the two points (the "rise") divided by the horizontal difference between the two points (the "run"). For example, between points *e* and *u*, the vertical difference is –$30 and the horizontal difference is 15, so the slope is –$30/15 = –$2. That means a $2 decrease in price increases the quantity demanded by one unit.

► FIGURE 5.2
Elasticity and Total Revenue along a Linear Demand Curve
Demand is elastic along the upper half of a linear demand curve, so an increase in quantity from a decrease in price increases total revenue (between points *a* and *b* on the total-revenue curve). Demand is inelastic along the lower half of a linear demand curve, so an increase in quantity from a decrease in price decreases total revenue (between points *b* and *c*). Total revenue is maximized at the midpoint of a linear demand curve (point *u*), where demand is unit elastic.

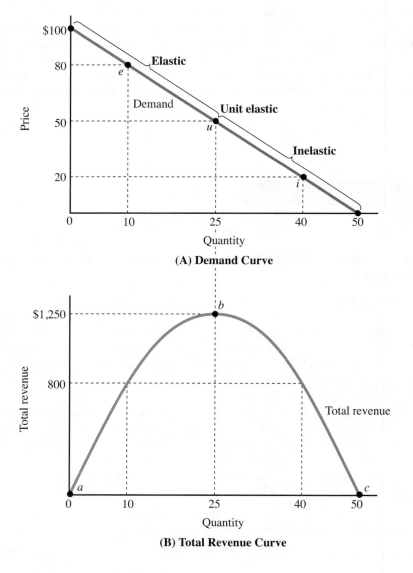
(A) Demand Curve

(B) Total Revenue Curve

Table 5.7 shows how to compute the price elasticity of demand with three starting points: e (for elastic demand), u (for unit elastic), and i (for inelastic). As shown in columns B and D, a $2 reduction in price increases the quantity demanded by one unit.

	A	B	C	D	E	F
	Starting Point	Change in Price	Percentage Change in Price	Change in Quantity	Percentage Change in Quantity	Elasticity of Demand
	e: Elastic	−$2	$\frac{-\$2}{\$80} = -2.5\%$	+1	$\frac{1}{10} = 10\%$	$\left\lvert\frac{10\%}{-2.5\%}\right\rvert = 4$
	u: Unit elastic	−$2	$\frac{-\$2}{\$50} = -4\%$	+1	$\frac{1}{25} = 4\%$	$\left\lvert\frac{4\%}{-4\%}\right\rvert = 1$
	i: Inelastic	−$2	$\frac{-\$2}{\$20} = -10\%$	+1	$\frac{1}{40} = 2.5\%$	$\left\lvert\frac{2.5\%}{-10\%}\right\rvert = 0.25$

TABLE 5.7 Elasticity of Demand along a Linear Demand Curve

- *Column C: Percentage change in price.* Starting from point e, we cut $2 off an $80 price, resulting in a 2.5 percent price cut. The same $2 price cut is larger in percentage terms farther down the demand curve, where the price is lower. For point u, the percentage change in price is −4 percent (equal to −$2/$50), and for point i the percentage change in price is −10 percent (equal to −$2/$20).

- *Column E: Percentage change in quantity.* At point e, we start with 10 units, so a one-unit increase in quantity is a 10 percent increase. Moving down the column, the same one-unit increase in quantity is smaller in percentage terms as we move down the demand curve, where the quantity is larger. For point u, the percentage change in price is 4 percent (equal to 1/25), and for point i the percentage change in quantity is 2.5 percent (equal to 1/40).

- *Column F: Price elasticity of demand.* Starting from point e, the price elasticity is large (4.0) because the percentage change in quantity (10 percent) is four times the percentage change in price (2.5 percent). Starting at point u, demand is unit elastic because the percentage change in quantity equals the percentage change in price. Starting from point i, demand is inelastic (0.25), because the percentage change in quantity is one-fourth the percentage change in price.

Why does the price elasticity vary along a linear demand curve? It's tempting to think the elasticity will be constant because a straight line has a constant slope. But that's incorrect, because we measure elasticity by percentage changes, not absolute changes. As we move downward along the demand curve, we're moving in the direction of larger quantities, so the same absolute change in quantity (one unit) becomes a smaller *percentage* change in quantity. At the same time, as we move downward along the curve, we are moving to lower prices, so a $2 price reduction leads to a larger *percentage* change in price. As a result, the elasticity (the ratio of the percentage changes) decreases as we move downward along the demand curve.

Elasticity and Total Revenue for a Linear Demand Curve

Panel B of Figure 5.2 shows the relationship between total revenue and the quantity sold for the linear demand curve. Demand is elastic along the upper half of a linear demand curve, which means that a decrease in price will increase the quantity sold by a larger percentage amount. As a result, total revenue will increase, as shown by the positively sloped total-revenue curve between points a and b. In contrast, demand is inelastic along the lower half of a linear demand curve, which means that a decrease in

TRAMPOLINES AND THE LOWER HALF OF A LINEAR DEMAND CURVE

APPLYING THE CONCEPTS #3: Will a firm choose a point on the lower half of a linear demand curve?

Suppose a firm that produces trampolines has a linear demand curve for its product, with a vertical intercept of $800. The firm currently charges a price of $300. Do you have any advice for the firm?

Your advice should be to increase the price. The price of $300 is certainly too low because it is less than the $400 price at the midpoint of the demand curve (half of $800). At a price of $300, the firm is below the midpoint of the demand curve, so the demand for its product is price-inelastic. If the firm increases its price from $300 to $400, its total revenue would increase because demand is inelastic (the percentage decrease in quantity is less than the percentage increase in price). At the same time, an increase in price would decrease the quantity of trampolines demanded (the law of demand), so the firm would produce fewer trampolines at a lower total cost. Because an increase in price increases total revenue and decreases total cost, the firm's profit would increase. The same logic applies to any price below the midpoint price of $400.

How much higher (how much above $400) should the price go? As we'll see later in the book, it depends on the cost of producing the product. Although we don't have the relevant cost information to pick the best price, we know for certain that it will be no less than $400 because a firm will never operate below the midpoint of a linear demand curve. **Related to Exercises 3.5 and 3.9.**

price will increase the quantity sold by a smaller percentage amount. As a result, total revenue will decrease, as shown by the negatively sloped total-revenue curve between points *b* and *c*. The total-revenue curve reaches its maximum at the midpoint of the linear demand curve, where demand is unit elastic. In Figure 5.2, demand is unit elastic at point *u* on the demand curve, so total revenue reaches its maximum at $1,250 at point *b* on the total-revenue curve.

5.4 Other Elasticities of Demand

We've seen that the price elasticity of demand measures the responsiveness of consumers to changes in the price of a particular good. Of course, the demand for a particular product also depends on other variables such as consumer income and the prices of related goods—substitutes and complements. We can use two other elasticities to measure the responsiveness of consumers to changes in these other variables that affect demand: income elasticity of demand and cross-price elasticity of demand.

Income Elasticity of Demand

We saw in Chapter 4 that the demand for a particular product depends in part on the consumer's income. The **income elasticity of demand** measures the responsiveness of demand to changes in income, indicating how much more or less of a particular product is purchased as income changes. The income elasticity of demand is defined as the percentage change in quantity demanded divided by the percentage change in income:

$$E_t = \frac{\text{percentage change in quantity demanded}}{\text{percentage change in income}}$$

income elasticity of demand
A measure of the responsiveness of demand to changes in consumer income; equal to the percentage change in the quantity demanded divided by the percentage change in income.

For example, if a 10 percent increase in income increases the quantity of books demanded by 15 percent, the income elasticity of demand for books is 1.50 (equal to 15% divided by 10%).

We can use the income elasticities of demand for various products to classify the products. Recall from Chapter 4 that when a consumer's income increases, he or she buys more of a "normal" good. If the income elasticity is positive—indicating a positive relationship between income and demand—we say that the good is normal. New cars and new clothes are products that have positive income elasticities and are thus considered normal goods. In contrast, if the income elasticity is negative—indicating a negative relationship between income and demand—we say the good is "inferior." Some examples of inferior goods are intercity bus travel, used clothing, and used cars.

Cross-Price Elasticity of Demand

We saw in Chapter 4 that the demand for a particular product also depends in part on the prices of related goods—substitutes and complements. The **cross-price elasticity of demand** measures the responsiveness of demand to changes in the prices of other goods, indicating how much more or less of a particular product is purchased as other prices change. The cross-price elasticity is defined as the percentage change in quantity demanded of one good (X) divided by the percentage change in the price of another good (Y):

cross-price elasticity of demand
A measure of the responsiveness of demand to changes in the price of another good; equal to the percentage change in the quantity demanded of one good (X) divided by the percentage change in the price of another good (Y).

$$E_{xy} = \frac{\text{percentage change in quantity of } X \text{ demanded}}{\text{percentage change in price of } Y}$$

As we saw in Chapter 4, two goods are considered substitutes if there is a positive relationship between the quantity demanded of one good and the price of the other good. For example, an increase in the price of bananas increases the demand for apples as consumers substitute apples for the now relatively expensive bananas. For substitute goods, the cross-price elasticity is positive. In contrast, two goods are considered complements if there is a negative relationship between the quantity demanded of one good and the price of the other. For example, an increase in the price of ice cream increases the cost of apple pie with ice cream, causing consumers to demand fewer apples. For complementary goods, the cross-price elasticity is negative. Table 5.8 summarizes the signs (positive or negative) for different types of goods.

TABLE 5.8 Income and Cross-Price Elasticities for Different Types of Goods		
This elasticity	**Is Positive for …**	**Is Negative for …**
Income elasticity	Normal goods	Inferior goods
Cross-price elasticity	Substitute goods	Complementary goods

Estimates of cross-price elasticity of demand are useful to retailers in their pricing decisions. For example, when a grocery store cuts the price of peanut butter by 10 percent, the store will sell more peanut butter but will also sell more complementary goods such as jelly and bread. If the cross-price elasticity of demand for jelly is 0.5, a 10 percent decrease in the price of peanut butter will increase the demand for jelly by 5 percent. Retailers use coupons for one product to promote sales of that good as well as sales of complementary goods. Armed with the relevant cross elasticities, retailers can predict just how much more of a complementary good consumers will buy.

application 4

I CAN FIND THAT ELASTICITY IN FOUR CLICKS!

APPLYING THE CONCEPTS #4: Where do I find estimates of elasticities of demand?

Suppose you want to find estimates of the elasticities of demand (own price, income, cross-price) for orange juice. The U.S. Department of Agriculture has a Web site that provides estimates of demand elasticities for hundreds of food products (from apples to yogurt) for dozens of countries (from Albania to Zimbabwe). Starting from (http:// www.ers.usda.gov/Data/Elasticities/), you are four clicks away from the following estimates of demand elasticities for orange juice in the United States: income elasticity = 2.212; own price elasticity = –1.391; cross-price elasticity for apple juice = 0.908. Here are the clicks: (1) Demand Elasticities from Literature; (2) Choose Country; Choose Commodity; (3) Cross Commodity; (4) Submit.

It's important to note two things about the reported elasticities. First, the regular price elasticity is reported as a negative number and labeled "own price elasticity" for "Marshallian Demand." Second, the reported "expenditure elasticity" is similar to the income elasticity, with the denominator of the elasticity equal to the percentage change in total consumer expenditure (versus percentage change in income). **Related to Exercise 4.9.**

5.5 The Price Elasticity of Supply

price elasticity of supply

A measure of the responsiveness of the quantity supplied to changes in price; equal to the percentage change in quantity supplied divided by the percentage change in price.

We've used the concept of elasticity to measure the responsiveness of consumers to changes in prices. We now look at elasticity on the supply side of the market. The **price elasticity of supply** measures the responsiveness of the quantity supplied to changes in price. We compute this elasticity by dividing the percentage change in quantity supplied by the percentage change in price:

$$E_s = \frac{\text{percentage change in quantity supplied}}{\text{percentage change in price}}$$

We can use some of the numbers in Figure 5.3 to compute the price elasticity of supply of milk. Consider Panel A, with a relatively steep supply curve. When the price of milk increases from $1.00 to $1.20, the quantity supplied increases from 100 million gallons (point *a*) to 102 million gallons (point *b*). The percentage change in quantity is the change (2) divided by the initial value (100), or 2 percent:

$$\text{percentage change in quantity supplied} = \frac{2}{100} = 2\%$$

The percentage change in price is the change ($0.20) divided by the initial value ($1.00), or 20 percent:

$$\text{percentage change in price} = \frac{\$0.20}{\$1.00} = 20\%$$

Dividing the percentage change in quantity supplied by the percentage change in price, the price elasticity of supply is 0.10:

$$E_s = \frac{\text{percentage change in quantity supplied}}{\text{percentage change in price}} = \frac{2\%}{20\%} = 0.10$$

▲ **FIGURE 5.3**
The Slope of the Supply Curve and Supply Elasticity
(*A*) The supply curve is relatively steep. A 20 percent increase in price increases the quantity supplied by 2 percent, implying a supply elasticity of 0.10. (*B*) The supply curve is relatively flat. A 20 percent increase in price increases the quantity supplied by 50 percent, implying a supply elasticity of 2.5.

What Determines the Price Elasticity of Supply?

What's the connection between the slope of the supply curve and the price elasticity of supply? With a steep curve, a given increase in price (in the denominator of the elasticity formula) generates a small increase in quantity supplied (in the numerator of the elasticity formula). In Panel A of Figure 5.3, an increase in price from $1.00 to $1.20 increases the quantity supplied from 100 to 102, so the price elasticity of supply is 0.10 (equal to 2% divided by 10%). In contrast, with a relatively flat supply curve the same increase in price generates a larger increase in quantity supplied, so the supply elasticity is relatively large. In Panel B of Figure 5.3, an increase in price from $1.00 to $1.20 increases the quantity supplied from 100 to 150, so the price elasticity of supply is 2.50 (equal to 50% divided by 20%).

Why is the market supply curve positively sloped? As we saw in Chapter 4, the market supply curve shows the marginal cost of production. A positively sloped supply curve tells us that the marginal cost of production increases as the total output of the industry increases. In other words, if we want to get more output out of an industry, the price must rise to cover the higher production costs associated with a larger industry. For example, as the total output of the gasoline industry increases, the worldwide demand for crude oil increases, pushing up its price. So to get more gasoline, the price of gasoline must increase to cover the higher cost of crude oil. The more rapidly crude-oil prices rise, the larger the increase in the gasoline price required to get more gasoline—and the steeper the gasoline supply curve.

The price elasticity of supply is determined by how rapidly production costs increase as the total output of the industry increases. If the marginal cost increases rapidly, the supply curve is relatively steep and the price elasticity is relatively low. For example, if crude-oil prices increase rapidly as the total amount of gasoline increases, the supply curve for gasoline will be relatively steep and the price elasticity of supply of gasoline will be relatively low. In contrast, the output of the pencil industry increases the prices of wood and other inputs used to produce pencils are unlikely to increase by much, so the supply curve will be relatively flat and the price elasticity of supply will be relatively large.

The Role of Time: Short-Run versus Long-Run Supply Elasticity

Time is an important factor in determining the price elasticity of supply for a product. As we saw in Chapter 4, the market supply curve is positively sloped because of two responses to an increase in price:

- *Short run.* A higher price encourages existing firms to increase their output by purchasing more materials and hiring more workers.
- *Long run.* New firms enter the market and existing firms expand their production facilities to produce more output.

The short-run response is limited because of the principle of diminishing returns.

PRINCIPLE OF DIMINISHING RETURNS

Suppose output is produced with two or more inputs, and

we increase one input while holding the other input or inputs fixed.

Beyond some point—called the *point of diminishing returns*—output

will increase at a decreasing rate.

In the short run, the fixed input is the firm's production facility. Although a higher price will induce firms to produce more, the response is limited by the fixed capacity of the firms' production facilities. As a result, the short-run supply curve is relatively steep and the short-run supply elasticity is relatively small. This case is illustrated by Panel A of Figure 5.4.

The long-run supply response to an increase in price is not limited by diminishing returns because production facilities are not fixed. Over time, new firms enter the market with new production facilities and old firms build new facilities. As a result, a given increase in price generates a larger increase in quantity supplied. The long-run supply curve will be relatively flat and the elasticity of supply will be relatively large. This case is illustrated by Panel B of Figure 5.4.

Extreme Cases: Perfectly Inelastic Supply and Perfectly Elastic Supply

Figure 5.4 shows the extreme cases of supply elasticity. The supply curve in Panel A is a vertical line, indicating that regardless of price, the quantity supplied is 50 units. This is the case of **perfectly inelastic supply**, with a price elasticity of supply equal to zero. The numerator in the elasticity expression (the percentage change in quantity supplied) is zero, regardless of the percentage change in the price of the good. Land is an example of a product that has a perfectly inelastic supply. In the words of American humorist and author Will Rogers, "The trouble with land is that they're not making it any more."

The supply curve in Panel B of Figure 5.4 is a horizontal line, indicating that the quantity supplied is infinitely responsive to any change in price. This is the case of **perfectly elastic supply**, with a price elasticity of supply equal to infinity. The numerator in the elasticity expression (the percentage change in quantity supplied)

perfectly inelastic supply
The price elasticity of supply equals zero.

perfectly elastic supply
The price elasticity of supply is equal to infinity.

▲ **FIGURE 5.4**
Perfectly Inelastic Supply and Perfectly Elastic Supply
In Panel A, the quantity supplied is the same at every price, so the price elasticity of supply is zero. In Panel B, the quantity supplied is infinitely responsive to changes in price, so the price elasticity of supply is infinite.

is infinite, regardless of the percentage change in the price. One implication of this supply curve is that if the price were to drop below $4, the quantity supplied would fall to zero.

What is the economic logic behind a horizontal supply curve? Recall that the supply curve shows the marginal cost of production. A horizontal supply curve indicates that the marginal cost of production doesn't change as the total output of the industry increases. For example, if the production cost per pencil is $0.20 no matter how many pencils the industry produces, the supply curve will be horizontal at $0.20.

Predicting Changes in Quantity Supplied

We can use the price elasticity of supply to predict the effect of price changes on the quantity supplied. For example, suppose that the elasticity of supply is 0.80 and the price increases by 5 percent. Rearranging the elasticity formula, we would predict a 4 percent increase in the quantity supplied:

$$\text{percentage change in quantity supplied} = E_s \times \text{percentage change in price}$$
$$= 0.80 \times 5\% = 4\%$$

As we saw in Chapter 4, many governments establish minimum prices for agricultural products. The higher the minimum price, the larger the quantity supplied, consistent with the law of supply. If we know the price elasticity of supply, we can predict just how much more will be supplied at a higher minimum price. For example, if the minimum price of cheese increases by 10 percent and the price elasticity is 0.60, the quantity of cheese supplied will rise by 6 percent:

$$\text{percentage change in quantity supplied} = E_s \times \text{percentage change in price}$$
$$= 0.60 \times 10\% = 6\%$$

application 5

THE SHORT-RUN AND LONG-RUN ELASTICITY OF SUPPLY OF MILK

APPLYING THE CONCEPTS #5: Why is supply more price-elastic in the long run?

The milk industry provides a good example of the difference between the short-run and long-run price elasticity of supply. The price elasticity of supply over a one-year period is about 0.10: If the price of milk increases by 20 percent and stays there for a year, the quantity of milk supplied will rise by only 2 percent. In the short run, dairy farmers can squeeze just a little more output from their existing production facilities. In the long run, dairy farmers can expand existing facilities and build new ones, so farmers are more responsive to a higher price—the supply curve is flatter and the supply elasticity is larger. The price elasticity of supply is 2.5, so the same 20 percent rise in price increases the quantity supplied by 50 percent. **Related to Exercises 5.5 and 5.6.**

SOURCE: Based on Richard Klemme and Jean-Paul Chavas, "The Effects of Changing Milk Price on Milk Supply and National Dairy Herd Size," *Economic Issues* 92 (June 1985).

5.6 Using Elasticities to Predict Changes in Prices

When demand or supply changes—that is, when the demand curve or the supply curve shifts—we can draw a demand and supply graph to predict whether the equilibrium price will increase or decrease. In many cases, the simple graph will show all we need to know about the effects of a change in supply or demand. But what if we want to predict *how much* a price will increase or decrease? We can use a simple formula to predict the change in the equilibrium price resulting from a change in demand or a change in supply.

The Price Effects of a Change in Demand

In Figure 5.5, an increase in demand shifts the demand curve to the right and increases the equilibrium price. We explained in Chapter 4 that a demand curve shifts as a result of a change in something other than the price of the product—for example, a change in income, tastes, or the price of a related good. When demand increases, the immediate effect is excess demand: At the original price ($1.00), the quantity demanded exceeds the quantity supplied by 35 million gallons (135 million – 100 million). As the price increases, both consumers and producers help to eliminate the excess demand: Consumers buy less (the law of demand), and firms produce more (the law of supply).

Under what conditions will an increase in demand cause a relatively small increase in price?

- *Small increase in demand.* If the shift of the demand curve is relatively small, the gap between the new demand and the old supply will be relatively small, and the small excess demand can be eliminated with a relatively small increase in price.

- *Highly elastic demand.* If consumers are very responsive to changes in price, the increase in price caused by excess demand will cause a large reduction in the quantity demanded. As a result, the excess demand will be eliminated with a relatively small increase in price.

▲ **FIGURE 5.5**
An Increase in Demand Increases the Equilibrium Price
An increase in demand shifts the demand curve to the right, increasing the equilibrium price. In this case, a 35 percent increase in demand increases the equilibrium price by 10 percent. Using the price-change formula, 10% = 35% / (2.5 + 1.0).

- *Highly elastic supply.* If producers are very responsive to changes in price, the increase in price caused by excess demand will cause a large increase in the quantity supplied. As a result, the excess demand will be eliminated with a relatively small increase in price.

We can use the following *price-change formula* to predict the change in the equilibrium price resulting from a change in demand. We divide the percentage change in demand by the sum of the price elasticities of supply and demand:

$$\text{percentage change in equilibrium price} = \frac{\text{percentage change in demand}}{E_s + E_d}$$

The numerator is the rightward shift of the demand curve in percentage terms. In Figure 5.5, the initial quantity demanded at a price of $1.00 is 100 million gallons (shown by the initial demand curve), and the new quantity demanded at the same price is 135 million gallons (shown by the new demand curve). The change in demand is 35 percent (35/100). The change in demand is in the numerator of the price-change formula, indicating that the larger the increase in demand (the larger the rightward shift of the demand curve), the larger the increase in the equilibrium price. The two price elasticities appear in the denominator. This is sensible because if consumers and producers are very responsive to changes in price (the elasticities are large numbers), excess demand will be eliminated with a relatively small increase in price.

We can illustrate the price-change formula with a simple example. Suppose that demand increases by 35 percent (the demand curve shifts to the right by 35 percent). If the supply elasticity is 2.5 and the demand elasticity is 1.0, the predicted change in the equilibrium price is 10 percent:

$$\text{percentage change in equilibrium price} = \frac{35\%}{2.5 + 1.0} = \frac{35\%}{3.5} = 10\%$$

In Figure 5.5, the equilibrium price increases by 10 percent, from $1.00 to $1.10. If either demand or supply were less elastic (if either of the elasticity numbers were smaller), the predicted change in price would be larger. For example, if the supply elasticity were 0.75 instead of 2.5, we would predict a 20 percent increase in price (35% divided by 1.75).

What about the direction of the price change? We know from Chapter 4 that an increase in demand increases the equilibrium price, and a decrease in demand decreases the equilibrium price. Therefore, the percentage change in price is positive when the change in demand is positive (when demand increases and the demand curve shifts to the right), and negative when the change in demand is negative (when demand decreases and the demand curve shifts to the left). For example, suppose the demand for a product decreases by 12 percent (the demand curve shifts to the left by 12 percent). If the supply elasticity is 1.6 and the demand elasticity is 0.40, the price-change formula shows that the equilibrium price will decrease by 6 percent:

$$\text{percentage change in equilibrium price} = \frac{-12\%}{1.6 + 0.4} = \frac{-12\%}{2.0} = -6\%$$

To illustrate the practical use of the price-change formula, consider the effect of population growth on housing prices. The Portland metropolitan area is expected to grow by 12 percent in the next decade. Suppose planners want to predict the effects of population growth on the equilibrium price of housing. At the metropolitan level, the price elasticity of supply is about 5.0 and the price elasticity of demand is 1.0. If the demand for housing is proportional to population, a 12 percent increase in population will increase the equilibrium price of housing by 2 percent:

$$\text{percentage change in equilibrium price} = \frac{12\%}{5.0 + 1.0} = \frac{12\%}{6.0} = 2\%$$

The Price Effects of a Change in Supply

Consider next the effects of a change in supply on the equilibrium price. In Figure 5.6, a decrease in supply shifts the supply curve to the left and increases the equilibrium price. We explained in Chapter 4 that a change in supply results from changes in something other than the price of the product—for example, a change in the cost of labor or raw materials, a change in production technology, or a change in the number of firms. The immediate effect of a decrease in supply is excess demand: At the original price, the quantity demanded exceeds the quantity supplied. In response to the excess demand, the price increases. Consumers respond to the higher price by purchasing less, and producers respond by producing more, so the gap between the quantity demanded and the quantity supplied narrows.

Under what conditions will a decrease in supply cause a relatively small increase in price?

- *Small decrease in supply.* If the shift of the supply curve is relatively small, the gap between the new supply and the old demand will be relatively small, and the small excess demand can be eliminated with a relatively small increase in price.

- *Highly elastic demand.* If consumers are very responsive to changes in price, the increase in price caused by excess demand will cause a large reduction in the quantity demanded. As a result, the excess demand will be eliminated with a relatively small increase in price.

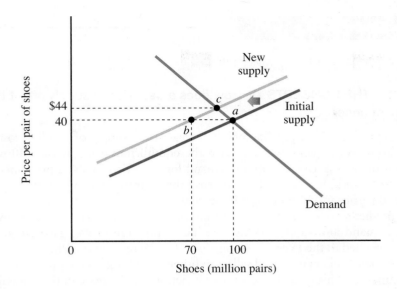

▲ **FIGURE 5.6**

A Decrease in Supply Increases the Equilibrium Price
An import restriction on shoes decreases the supply of shoes, shifting the market supply curve
to the left and increasing the equilibrium price from $40 to $44. In this case, a 30 percent
reduction in supply increases the equilibrium price by 10 percent. Using the price-change
formula, 10% = –(–30% / (2.3 + 0.70)).

- *Highly elastic supply.* If producers are very responsive to changes in price, the
  increase in price caused by excess demand will cause a large increase in the
  quantity supplied. As a result, the excess demand will be eliminated with a
  relatively small increase in price.

We can use a variation on the price-change formula to predict the price effects
of a change in supply. We modify the numerator of the formula by substituting the
percentage change in supply for the percentage change in demand and then add a
minus sign. The minus sign indicates a negative relationship between supply and the
equilibrium price: When supply decreases (when the supply curve shifts to the left),
the price increases; when supply increases, the price decreases:

$$\text{percentage change in equilibrium price} = -\frac{\text{percentage change in supply}}{E_s + E_d}$$

To illustrate the practical use of the price-change formula, consider the effects of
import restrictions on equilibrium prices. Suppose that import restrictions decrease
the supply of shoes by 30 percent. As shown in Figure 5.6, the policy shifts the supply
curve to the left by 30 percent: At the original price of $40, the quantity supplied
decreases from 100 million pairs (point *a*) to 70 million pairs (point *b*). The decrease in
supply increases the equilibrium price, and the price-change formula tells us just how
much the price will increase.

To use the price-change formula, we need the price elasticities of supply and
demand. Suppose the supply elasticity is 2.3 and, as shown in Table 5.2, the demand
elasticity is 0.70. Plugging these numbers into the price-change formula, we predict a
10 percent increase in price:

$$\text{percentage change in equilibrium price} = -\frac{-30\%}{2.3 + 0.70} = \frac{30\%}{3.0} = 10\%$$

In Figure 5.6, the price rises by 10 percent, from $40 to $44 per pair.

A BROKEN PIPELINE AND THE PRICE OF GASOLINE

APPLYING THE CONCEPTS #6: How does a decrease in supply affect the equilibrium price?

In the chapter opener, a pipeline break decreased the supply of gasoline to the city of Phoenix by 30 percent and increased the equilibrium price by only 40 percent. Given a short-run price elasticity of demand for gasoline of 0.20, a price increase of 150 percent would be required to decrease the quantity demanded by 30 percent. Why did the price increase by only 40 percent?

To predict a change in the equilibrium price, we must look at both sides of the market, demand and supply. When the Texas pipeline broke, gasoline sellers in Phoenix switched to the West Coast pipeline. The increase in the Phoenix retail price allowed Phoenix sellers to outbid sellers in other cities for gasoline produced by West Coast refineries. This is the law of supply in action: the increase in the Phoenix price diverted gasoline from other cities, reducing the impact of the pipeline break. As a result, the equilibrium price increased by only 40 percent, not the 150 percent that would have occurred in the absence of the supply boost from West Coast refineries.

We can use the price-change formula to illustrate this case. Suppose the price elasticity of supply is 0.55 and the price elasticity of demand is 0.20. In this case, a 30 percent decrease in supply generates a 40 percent increase in the equilibrium price:

$$\text{percentage change in equilibrium price} = -\frac{-30\%}{0.55 + 0.20} = \frac{30\%}{0.75} = 40\%$$

Related to Exercises 6.5 and 6.9.

SOURCE: Based on Federal Trade Commission, Gasoline Price Changes: The Dynamic of Supply, Demand, and Competition (Washington, DC: 2005).

SUMMARY

This chapter explored the numbers behind the laws of demand and supply. The law of demand tells us that an increase in price decreases the quantity demanded, *ceteris paribus*. If we know the price elasticity of demand for a particular product, we can determine just how much less of it will be purchased at the higher price. Similarly, if we know the price elasticity of supply for a product, we can determine just how much more of it will be supplied at a higher price. Here are the main points of the chapter:

1. The *price elasticity of demand*—defined as the percentage change in quantity demanded divided by the percentage change in price—measures the responsiveness of consumers to changes in price.

2. Demand is relatively elastic if there are good substitutes.

3. If demand is *elastic*, the relationship between price and total revenue is negative. If demand is *inelastic*, the relationship between price and total revenue is positive.

4. The *price elasticity of supply*—defined as the percentage change in quantity supplied divided by the percentage change in price—measures the responsiveness of producers to changes in price.

5. If we know the elasticities of demand and supply, we can predict the percentage change in price resulting from a change in demand or supply.

KEY TERMS

cross-price elasticity of demand, p. 111

elastic demand, p. 101

income elasticity of demand, p. 110

inelastic demand, p. 101

perfectly elastic demand, p. 101

perfectly elastic supply, p. 114

perfectly inelastic demand, p. 101

perfectly inelastic supply, p. 114

price elasticity of demand (E_d), p. 98

price elasticity of supply, p. 112

total revenue, p. 105

unit elastic demand, p. 101

EXERCISES

All problems are assignable in MyEconLab.

5.1 The Price Elasticity of Demand

1.1 To compute the price elasticity of demand, we divide the percentage change in _____ by the percentage change in _____ and then take the value of the ratio.

1.2 If a 10 percent increase in price decreases the quantity demanded by 12 percent, the price elasticity of demand is _____.

1.3 When the price of CDs increased from $10 to $11, the quantity of CDs demanded decreased from 100 to 80. The price elasticity of demand for CDs is _____, and demand is _____ (elastic/inelastic).

1.4 If demand is elastic, the percentage change in _____ exceeds the percentage change in _____.

1.5 As the number of substitutes for a particular product increases, the price elasticity of demand for the product _____ (increases/decreases).

1.6 Over time, the price elasticity of demand for gasoline _____ (increases/decreases). (Related to Application 1 on page 103.)

1.7 In the long run, a 20 percent increase in the price of gasoline will decrease traffic volume by _____ percent and increase fuel efficiency by _____ percent. (Related to Application 1 on page 103.)

1.8 Demand is relatively elastic if the product has _____ (many/few) substitutes, a _____ (long/short) time passes, and the consumer spends a _____ (large/small) fraction of his or her budget on the product.

5.2 Using Price Elasticity

2.1 Recall the example "Beer Prices and Highway Deaths" from the chapter. A doubling of the tax on beer will reduce the number of highway deaths among young adults by _____ percent.

2.2 Recall the example "Cigarette Prices and Teenagers" from the chapter. A 20 percent increase in the price of cigarettes will reduce the quantity of cigarettes demanded by teenagers by _____ percent.

2.3 If the price elasticity of demand is 0.60, a 10 percent increase in price will _____ the quantity demanded by _____ percent.

2.4 In the state of Virginia, the demand for vanity license plates is _____ (elastic/inelastic), so an increase in price would _____ (increase/decrease) total revenue from vanity plates. (Related to Application 2 on page 107.)

2.5 A policy that limits the supply of illegal drugs increases the number of burglaries and robberies because _____ is _____.

2.6 If demand is elastic, an increase in price (increases/decreases) total revenue; if demand is inelastic, an increase in price _____ (increases/decreases) total revenue.

2.7 Suppose that at the current price the price elasticity of demand for a campus film series is 2.0. If the price is cut, total revenue will _____ (increase/decrease).

2.8 **MADD Beer Tax.** Recall the example "Beer Prices and Highway Deaths" from the chapter. The organization Mothers Against Drunk Driving (MADD) has a goal of reducing the number of highway deaths among young adults by 39 percent. Assume that the number of highway deaths for young adults is proportional to their beer consumption. By what percentage must the price of beer increase to meet the MADD target?

2.9 **Meeting the Teenage Smoking Target.** Recall the example "Cigarette Prices and Teenagers" from the chapter. One of the stated objectives of the federal Tobacco Agreement of 1997 was to reduce teenage smoking by 60 percent. The price must increase by _____ percent to achieve this target.

2.10 **Use the Correct Elasticity.** Your company currently sells 50 units of salt per year and has decided to increase its price from $1.00 to $1.20. In a meeting, one person says, "As shown in Table 5.2 on page 102, the price elasticity of demand for salt is 0.10, so if we increase the price of salt by 20 percent, the quantity demanded will decrease by 2 percent." What's wrong with this statement?

2.11 Projecting Transit Ridership. As a transit planner, your job is to predict ridership and total fare revenue. Suppose the short-run elasticity of demand for commuter rail (over a one-month period) is 0.60, and the long-run elasticity (over a two-year period) is 1.60. The current ridership is 100,000 people per day. Suppose the transit authority decides to increase its fares from $2.00 to $2.20.

a. Predict the changes in train ridership over a one-month period (the short run) and a two-year period (the long run).

b. Over the one-month period, will total fare revenue increase or decrease? What about the two-year period?

2.12 Income and the Price Elasticity of Demand for Medical Care. Like many other developing nations, Peru subsidizes medical care, charging consumers a small fraction of the cost of providing services such as visits to medical clinics. The price elasticity of demand for medical care is 0.67 for poor households but only 0.03 for wealthy households. Suppose the government reduced its subsidies for medical care, and the price to consumers increased by 10 percent. Predict the changes in the quantity of medical care demanded (for example, the number of visits to clinics) for poor households and wealthy households.

2.13 Revenue Effects of a Bumper Crop. Your job is to predict the total revenue generated by the nation's corn crop. Last year's crop was 100 million bushels, and the price was $5 per bushel. This year's weather was favorable throughout the country, and this year's crop will be 110 million bushels, or 10 percent larger than last year's. The price elasticity of demand for corn is 0.50.

a. Predict the effect of the bumper crop on the price of corn. Assume that the entire crop is sold this year, meaning that the price elasticity of supply is zero. Illustrate with a complete graph.

b. Predict the total revenue from this year's corn crop.

c. Did the favorable weather increase or decrease the total revenue from corn? Why?

2.14 Elasticity and Vanity Plates. Suppose the price elasticity of demand for vanity plates in your state is 0.60. The initial price is $20 and the initial quantity is 1,000 plates per week. Suppose the state increases the price by 10 percent. (Related to Application 2 on page 107.)

a. Predict the new quantity per week and total revenue per week.

b. The increase in price _____ (increases, decreases) total revenue because _____ is _____.

2.15 The Price of Heroin and Property Crime. The price elasticity of demand for heroin is 0.27. Suppose that half of heroin users support their habits with property crime, so the loss from property crimes committed by heroin users equals half the total spending (total revenue) on the drug. Suppose the government reduces the supply of heroin, increasing the equilibrium price by 20 percent. Fill in the blanks in the following table.

Price	Quantity of Heroin	Total Spending (Total Revenue)	Property Crime
$10	1,000	$10,000	$5,000
12	-------------	-------------	-------------

2.16 Revenue from Mobile Phones. Consider the demand for mobile phones. Suppose the price elasticity of demand for the market as a whole is 0.80.

a. If all mobile-phone companies simultaneously increased their prices, will total revenue in the industry increase or decrease?

b. If a single mobile-phone company increased its price, would you expect the company's total revenue to increase or decrease? Explain.

2.17 Price Hikes and Cable TV Revenue. Four years ago the cable company in your city increased its price by 20 percent, and its total revenue increased. Last year, a new company started providing TV service with satellite dishes. This year, the cable company increased its price by 20 percent, but its total revenue decreased. Provide an explanation for the different revenue consequences of the cable company's price hikes.

3.1 Demand is _____ on the upper portion of a linear demand curve and _____ on the lower portion of a linear demand curve.

3.2 Suppose we are on the upper portion of a linear demand curve. If the price increases by 10 percent, the quantity demanded will decrease by _____ (more/less) than 10 percent and total revenue will _____ (increase/decrease).

3.3 At the midpoint of a linear demand curve, the price elasticity of demand is _____.

3.4 If we are on the lower part of a linear demand curve, a decrease in price _____ (increases/decreases) total revenue.

3.5 A firm will never operate _____ (above, below) the midpoint of a linear demand curve, where demand is _____ (elastic, inelastic). (Related to Application 3 on page 110.)

3.6 **Maximizing Revenue from Wilderness Passes.** Your state issues wilderness passes to people who hike, bike, and ski in wilderness areas. Its objective is to maximize the total revenue from the passes. The current price is $30. The demand for wilderness passes is linear, and a price of $90 would drive the quantity demanded to zero. What is the appropriate price? Illustrate with a complete graph.

3.7 **Where on the Demand Curve?** The demand curve for your firm's product is linear. Based on recent sales data, you have determined that at the current price, the price elasticity of demand is 0.80.
   a. Is the current price on the upper or lower portion of the demand curve?
   b. If you want to increase your total revenue, should you increase or decrease your price?
   c. Will you move upward or downward along the demand curve?

3.8 **Win-Win.** According to an economic consultant, "For your firm, an increase in price is a win-win situation. Your total revenue will increase and your total cost will decrease. Therefore, you'll earn more profit (equal to Total Revenue – Total Cost)."
   a. Concerning the revenue effect of a price hike, what is the consultant assuming about your firm and its customers?
   b. Concerning the cost effect of a price hike, what is the consultant assuming about your firm and its customers?

3.9 **Advice to Firm.** Suppose a firm that produces clown wigs has a linear demand for its product, with a vertical intercept of $6. If the firm currently charges a price of $1, what's your advice? (Related to Application 3 on page 110.)

4.1 The income elasticity of demand is _____ (positive/negative) for normal goods and _____ (positive/negative) for inferior goods.

4.2 If a 20 percent increase in income increases the quantity of iPods demanded by 30 percent, the income elasticity of demand is _____.

4.3 The cross-price elasticity of demand is _____ (positive/negative) for substitute goods and _____ (positive/negative) for complementary goods.

4.4 If a 10 percent increase in the price of natural gas increases the quantity of residential electricity demanded by 18 percent, the cross-price elasticity of demand is _____.

4.5 If a 10 percent increase in the price of tennis rackets decreases the quantity of tennis balls demanded by 15 percent, the cross-price elasticity of demand is _____.

4.6 **Income and Starbucks Coffee Shops.** Starbucks just hired you to determine whether your city could support a new Starbucks coffee shop. There are currently four Starbucks coffee shops in the city, and each has just enough customers to survive. The average household income in the city is expected to increase by 10 percent per year for the next few years. Suppose the income elasticity of demand for Starbucks' coffee products is 1.25. The population of the city is constant.
   a. By what percentage will the demand for coffee increase each year?
   b. How soon will the area have enough demand to support a fifth Starbucks?

4.7 **Gas Prices and Public Transit Ridership.** Consider the effect of higher gasoline prices on public transit ridership. The initial price of public transit is $2.00 per ride and the initial ridership is 100,000 people per day. Suppose the elasticity of transit ridership with respect to the price of gasoline is +0.667 (or 2/3) and the price of gasoline increases by 30 percent.
   a. Assume the price of public transit remains at $2. Use a graph to show the effect of the increase in the gas price on transit ridership.
   b. Suppose the transit authority matches the increase in the price of gasoline, increasing the transit fare by 30 percent. The price elasticity of demand for transit ridership is 0.333 (or 1/3). Use your graph to show the combined effect of the gas tax and higher transit fare.
   c. Explain why the net change in transit ridership is positive or negative.

4.8 iPods and iTunes. You have been hired to predict the effects of increasing the price of iTunes songs by 10 percent, from $0.99 to $1.09. You are interested in the effects of the price hike on the number of songs downloaded legally from iTunes, the number of songs downloaded legally from other online music stores, the number of iPod players sold, and the number of CDs sold in stores. Given the hypothetical elasticities in the following table, fill in the blanks. Recall that conventional practice for the price elasticity of demand of a product uses the absolute value of the elasticity.

Product	Price Elasticity or Cross-Price Elasticity	Predicted Percentage Change in Quantity Demanded
iTunes songs	1.50 (absolute value)	
Songs from other online stores	+2.00	
iPod players	−0.70	
CDs in stores	+1.80	

4.9 Find the following elasticities from the USDA Web site. (Related to Application 4 on page 112.)

a. Organic broccoli in the United States: own price elasticity = _____; expenditure (similar to income) = _____; cross-price of conventional broccoli = _____. If improved production techniques decreased the equilibrium price of organic broccoli by 10 percent, the quantity of organic broccoli would increase by _____ percent and the quantity of conventional broccoli would decrease by _____ percent.

b. Soft drinks in the United States: own price (Marshallian is regular demand) = _____. If a tax on soft drinks increased the equilibrium price by 10 percent, the quantity of soft drinks would decrease by _____ percent.

c. Fish in Tanzania. Own price = _____; income = _____. If the price of fish increases by 8.37 percent, the quantity demanded would decrease by _____ percent. If per-capita income increases by 20 percent, the quantity of fish demanded would increase by about _____ percent.

5.5 The Price Elasticity of Supply

5.1 When the price of paper increases from $100 to $104 per ton, the quantity supplied increases from 200 to 220 tons per day. The price elasticity of supply is _____.

5.2 Suppose the price elasticity of a supply of cheese is 0.80. If the price of cheese rises by 20 percent, the quantity of cheese supplied will increase by _____ percent.

5.3 Because the principle of diminishing returns is applicable only in the _____ (short/long) run, the _____ elasticity of supply is _____ (smaller/larger) than the _____ elasticity of supply.

5.4 As the supply curve becomes flatter, the price elasticity of supply _____ (increases/decreases).

5.5 The price elasticity of supply of milk is _____ (0.10, 0.70, 1.0, 2.5) over a one-year period, compared to _____ (0.10, 0.70, 1.0, 2.5) over a 10-year period. (Related to Application 5 on page 116.)

5.6 Short Run vs. Long Run in the Pear Market. Suppose in the production of pears, the short-run supply elasticity is 0.20, while the long-run supply elasticity is 3.5. Predict the effects of a 15% increase in price on the quantity of pears supplied in the short run and the long run. (Related to Application 5 on page 116.)

6.1 Assume that the elasticity of demand for chewing tobacco is 0.70 and the elasticity of supply is 2.30. Suppose an antichewing campaign decreases the demand for chewing tobacco by 18 percent. The equilibrium price of chewing tobacco will _____ (decrease/increase) by _____ percent.

6.2 Suppose the elasticity of demand for motel rooms is 1.0 and the elasticity of supply is 0.50. If the demand for motel rooms increases by 15 percent, the equilibrium price of motel rooms will _____ (decrease/increase) by _____ percent.

6.3 Suppose the price elasticity of demand for tomatoes is 0.70 and the supply elasticity is 3.30. If publicity about an outbreak of salmonella decreases demand by 12 percent, the equilibrium price will _____ (decrease/increase) by _____ percent.

6.4 Suppose the price elasticity of demand for accordions is 2.0 and the supply elasticity is 3.0. If a subsidy on accordions increases supply by 20 percent, the equilibrium price will _____ (decrease/increase) by _____ percent.

6.5 In the case of the broken gasoline pipeline, the decrease in supply and the resulting increase in price caused a decrease in _____ and an increase in _____. (Related to Application 6 on page 120.)

6.6 **College Enrollment and Apartment Prices.** Consider a college town where the initial price of rental apartments is $400 and the initial quantity is 1,000 apartments. The price elasticity of demand for apartments is 1.0, and the price elasticity of supply of apartments is 0.50. (Related to Application 4 on page 112.)

a. Use demand and supply curves to show the initial equilibrium, and label the equilibrium point *a*.

b. Suppose that an increase in college enrollment is expected to increase the demand for apartments in a college town by 15 percent. Use your graph to show the effects of the increase in demand on the apartment market. Label the new equilibrium point *b*.

c. Predict the effect of the increase in demand on the equilibrium price of apartments.

6.7 **Regulations and the Price of Housing.** Suppose local building regulations increase the cost of building new houses, decreasing supply by 12 percent. The initial price of new housing is $200,000, the price elasticity of demand is 1.0, and the price elasticity of supply is 3.0. Predict the effect of the regulations on the equilibrium price of new housing. Illustrate your answer with a graph that shows the initial point (*a*) and the new equilibrium (*b*). (Related to Application 4 on page 112.)

6.8 **Import Restrictions and the Price of Steel.** Suppose import restrictions on steel decrease the supply of steel by 24 percent. The initial price of steel is $100 per unit, the elasticity of demand is 0.70, and the elasticity of supply is 2.3. Predict the effect of the import restrictions on the equilibrium price of steel. Illustrate your answer with a graph that shows the initial point (*a*) and the new equilibrium (*b*).

6.9 **Price Effects of a Pipeline Break.** Consider a city that gets its natural gas from two pipelines, with each pipeline supplying half the city's natural gas. Suppose the price elasticity of supply is 0.70 and the price elasticity of demand is 0.55. If one pipeline breaks, by how much will the price of natural gas increase? (Related to Application 6 on page 120.)

1. Frank Chaloupka, "Rational Addictive Behavior and Cigarette Smoking," *Journal of Political Economy* (August 1991): 722–742; Gregory Chow, *Demand for Automobiles in the United States* (Amsterdam: North-Holland, 1957); David Ellwood and Mitchell Polinski, "An Empirical Reconciliation of Micro and Grouped Estimates of the Demand for Housing," *Review of Economics and Statistics* 61 (1979): 199–205; H. F. Houthakker and Lester B. Taylor, *Consumer Demand in the United States: Analysis and Projections*, 2nd ed. (Cambridge, MA: Harvard University Press, 1970); John R. Nevin, "Laboratory Experiments for Estimating Consumer Demand: A Validation Study," *Journal of Marketing Research* 11 (August 1974): 261–268; Herbert Scarf and John Shoven, *Applied General Equilibrium Analysis* (New York: Cambridge University Press, 1984); Phil Goodwin, "Review of New Demand Elasticities with Special Reference to Short and Long Run Effects of Price Changes," *Journal of Transport Economics* 26 (1992): 155–171; Chin-Fun Cling and James Peale, Jr., "Income and Price Elasticities," in *Advances in Econometrics Supplement*, ed. Henri Theil (Greenwich, CT: JAI Press, 1989); R. L. Adams, R. C. Lewis, and B. H. Drake, "Estimated Price Elasticity of Demand for Selected Outdoor Recreation Activities, United States," *Recreation Economic Decisions*, 2nd ed., ed. J. B. Loomis and R. G. Walsh (State College, PA: Venture Publishing, Inc., 1973), 20; U.S. Army Corps of Engineers, Walla Walla District, "Sport Fishery Use and Value on the Lower Snake River Reservoirs," May 1999; Rand Health, "The Elasticity of Demand for Health Care: A Review of the Literature and Its Application to the Military Health System" (Santa Monica, CA, 2001).

2. Henry Saffer and Michael Grossman, "Beer Taxes, the Legal Drinking Age, and Youth Motor Vehicle Fatalities," *Journal of Legal Studies* 16 (June 1987): 351–374; Frank Chaloupka, Henry Saffer, and Michael Grossman, "Alcohol Control Policies and Motor Vehicle Fatalities," *Journal of Legal Studies* 22 (January 1993): 161–183.

3. Michael M. Phillips and Suein L. Hwang, "Why Tobacco Pact Won't Hurt Industry," *Wall Street Journal*, September 12, 1997; Frank J. Chaloupka and Michael Grossman, "Price, Tobacco Control Policies, and Smoking Among Young Adults," *Journal of Health Economics* 16 (1997): 359–373.

4. Kenneth A. Small, *Urban Transportation Economics* (Philadelphia, PA: Harwood Academic Publishers, 1992).

5. L. P. Silverman and N. L. Sprull, "Urban Crime and the Price of Heroin," *Journal of Urban Economics* 4 (1977): 80–103.

Market Efficiency and Government Intervention

The housing market in New York City is highly regulated.

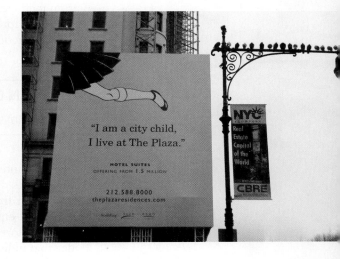

The city issues a relatively small number of permits for new condominium buildings, and rapid growth in the demand for condominiums has resulted in soaring condominium prices. To measure the effects of the city's supply restrictions on housing prices, we can compare the construction cost of a standard condominium to its market price. This is a sensible approach because in a competitive industry like housing, the equilibrium price in an unregulated market would equal the cost of construction. The construction cost for a Manhattan condominium is about $300 per square foot, while the market price is roughly $600 per square foot.[1] In other words, the city's supply restrictions double the price of the typical Manhattan condominium.

Other cities restrict the supply of housing and increase prices to varying degrees. The price effects are relatively large in highly restrictive cities such as San Francisco (53% gap between the market price and construction cost), Los Angeles (34%), Washington, DC (22%), and Boston (19%), and relatively small in less restrictive cities such as Chicago (6%) and Baltimore (2%). Many cities do not restrict the supply of housing, and housing prices in these cities (Houston, Minneapolis, Rochester, Tampa, Cincinnati, and Pittsburgh) match the construction cost of housing.

LEARNING OBJECTIVES

- Use demand and supply curves to compute the value of markets.

- Explain why the market equilibrium maximizes the value of a market.

- Describe the market effects of price controls.

- Describe the market effects of quantity controls.

- Explain how a tax is shifted to consumers and input suppliers.

MyEconLab

MyEconLab helps you master each objective and study more efficiently.

efficiency
A situation in which people do the best they can, given their limited resources.

*W*hen making choices, people strive for **efficiency**, trying to do the best they can, given their limited resources. The notion of efficiency applies to all sorts of decisions. A household decides how much to spend on consumer goods, how much to save, and how much to spend on a college education. The household tries to do the best it can, given its limited income. A Frisbee producer decides how many workers to hire and tries to make as much profit as possible, given the limitations of its factory. A government chooses between shuttle trips and Mars missions and tries to generate as much scientific information as possible, given its space exploration budget. As we'll see, economics provides a framework to guide us from inefficient choices to efficient ones.

In Chapter 3 we discussed the exchange principle, which conveys the simple idea that transactions make both the buyer and the seller better off.

PRINCIPLE OF VOLUNTARY EXCHANGE
A voluntary exchange between two people makes both people better off.

In this chapter, we will take a closer look at the benefits of exchange, examining the experiences of both buyers and sellers. We will see how to compute the surplus or net benefit from a market and see why the market equilibrium—where the quantity demanded equals the quantity supplied—*may* generate the largest possible surplus. We'll explore the logic behind Adam Smith's metaphor of the invisible hand—the idea that individual buyers and sellers, each acting in his or her own self-interest, *may* promote the social interest.

You'll notice that we use the word "may" in noting the virtues of markets and the invisible hand. A market equilibrium will generate the largest possible surplus when four conditions are met:

- *No external benefits:* The benefits of a product (a good or service) are confined to the person who pays for it.

- *No external costs:* The cost of producing a product is confined to the person who sells it.

- *Perfect information:* Buyers and sellers know enough about the product to make informed decisions about whether to buy or sell it.

- *Perfect competition:* Each firm produces such a small quantity that the firm cannot affect the price.

In this chapter, we discuss markets that meet these four conditions. As we'll see later in the book, when these conditions are not satisfied, free markets don't generate the largest possible surplus. A market that generates the largest possible surplus is efficient. A situation is *efficient* if we are doing the best we can, given our limited resources. In the case of a market, doing the best we can means getting the largest possible surplus. When that happens, we say that the market is efficient. Governments around the world intervene in markets, sometimes promoting efficiency, and other times preventing it. We'll see that when the four efficiency conditions are met, government intervention is inefficient in the sense that it decreases the total surplus of the market.

6.1 Consumer Surplus and Producer Surplus

We'll begin our discussion of market efficiency by showing how to measure the benefits experienced by consumers and producers. We'll start with consumers and then look at producers.

The Demand Curve and Consumer Surplus

If you said "thank you" the last time you purchased a book, did you mean it? If you were willing to pay more for the book than the price you actually paid, you probably really *did* mean it when you said "thank you," because you got what you considered to be a good deal. Your **willingness to pay** for a product (a good or a service) is the maximum amount you are willing to pay for the product. Your **consumer surplus** is equal to your willingness to pay minus the price you actually pay. For example, if you are willing to pay $21 for a book that you buy for $10, your consumer surplus is $11.

The market demand curve shows consumers' willingness to pay for a product. Consider the demand for lawn cutting in a small town; the market demand curve is shown in Figure 6.1. The demand curve shows that at a price of $25, no one will pay to have the lawn cut (point *t*), but if the price drops to $22, the first consumer (Juan) will pay for a lawn cut. This suggests that Juan is willing to pay up to $22 to have his lawn cut, but no more. Moving down the demand curve, the second consumer (Tupak) will pay for a lawn cutting when the price drops to $19, meaning that his willingness to pay is $19. As we continue to move downward along the demand curve, the price drops below the willingness to pay for more and more consumers, so more people have their lawns cut.

willingness to pay
The maximum amount a consumer is willing to pay for a product.

consumer surplus
The amount a consumer is willing to pay for a product minus the price the consumer actually pays.

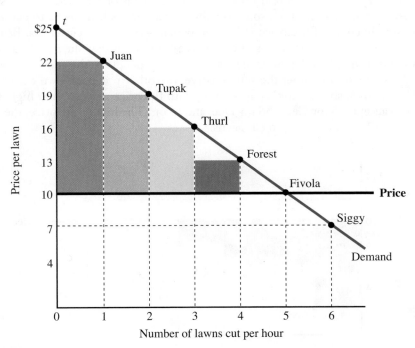

▲ **FIGURE 6.1**
The Demand Curve and Consumer Surplus
Consumer surplus equals the maximum amount a consumer is willing to pay (shown by the demand curve) minus the price paid. Juan is willing to pay $22, so if the price is $10, his consumer surplus is $12. The market consumer surplus equals the sum of the surpluses earned by all consumers in the market. In this case, the market consumer surplus is $30 = $12 + $9 + $6 + $3 + $0.

We can use the demand curve to measure just how much of a net benefit or surplus consumers get. Suppose that the price of a lawn cut is $10, and everyone in town pays this price. Juan's consumer surplus is $12, equal to his willingness to pay ($22) minus the price. Similarly, Tupak's consumer surplus is $9, equal to the difference between his willingness to pay ($19) and the market price. To compute the total consumer surplus in the lawn-cutting market, we simply add up the surpluses for each of the five consumers who buy lawn cutting at a price of $10. In this example, the market consumer surplus is $30, which is the sum of $12 (Juan) + $9 (Tupak) + $6 (Thurl) + $3 (Forest) + $0 (Fivola).

The fifth consumer (Fivola) gets no consumer surplus, because the price equals her willingness to pay. The sixth person (Siggy) doesn't have his lawn cut because the amount he is willing to pay is less than the price.

The Supply Curve and Producer Surplus

willingness to accept
The minimum amount a producer is willing to accept as payment for a product; equal to the marginal cost of production.

producer surplus
The price a producer receives for a product minus the marginal cost of production.

Like consumers, the people who produce goods and services say "thank you" when they sell their products. This suggests that they receive a net benefit or surplus from voluntary transactions. A seller's **willingness to accept** is the minimum amount he or she is willing to accept as payment for a product, and is equal to the marginal cost of production. For example, if your marginal cost of cutting a lawn is $4, you will be willing to accept any amount greater than or equal to $4. Of course, you'd prefer $10 to $4, but you'll accept as little as $4, because the lower amount covers all your costs, including the opportunity cost of your time. **Producer surplus** equals the price a producer receives for a product minus the marginal cost of production. For example, if your marginal cost for cutting a lawn is $4 and you do it for $10, your producer surplus is $6.

Figure 6.2 shows the market supply curve for lawn cutting in our small town. Let's imagine that up to six people are willing to cut lawns if the price is right, and each person can cut one lawn per hour. Each person incurs the same cost for renting a lawn mower but has a different opportunity cost for his or her time. The first producer (Abe) incurs a cost of $2, so he is willing to accept as little as $2 to cut a lawn. On the supply curve, if the price is $2, one person—Abe—will cut lawns. Bea has a higher opportunity cost of time, so her cost is $4, meaning that she won't cut a lawn unless she is paid at least $4. So if the price is $4, two people—Abe and Bea—will cut lawns. Moving upward along the supply curve, the other potential lawn cutters have even higher costs, so they don't start cutting until the price reaches their higher willingness to accept: $6 for Cecil, $8 for Dee, and so on. The higher the price, the larger the number of people willing to cut lawns.

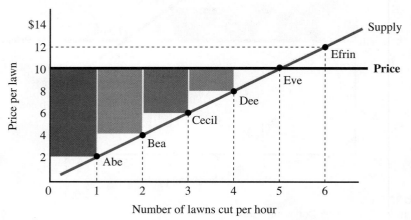

▲ **FIGURE 6.2**

The Supply Curve and Producer Surplus

Producer surplus equals the market price minus the producer's willingness to accept, or marginal cost (shown by the supply curve). Abe's marginal cost is $2, so if the price is $10, his producer surplus is $8. The market producer surplus equals the sum of the surpluses earned by all producers in the market. In this case, the market producer surplus is $20 = $8 + $6 + $4 + $2 + $0.

We can use the supply curve to measure just how much of a net benefit or surplus producers get. If the price of lawn cutting is $10, Abe's producer surplus for cutting the lawn is $8, the price he receives minus his cost ($2). Similarly, Bea's producer surplus is $6, equal to the difference between the price and her cost ($4). To compute the total producer surplus in the lawn-cutting market, we simply add up the surpluses for each of the five producers who cut lawns at a price of $10. In this example, the market

CONSUMER SURPLUS OF INTERNET SERVICE

APPLYING THE CONCEPTS #1: How do we compute consumer surplus?

What is the consumer surplus from Internet service? Two recent studies compute consumers' willingness to pay for Internet service. For Japanese consumers, the average willingness to pay for Internet service (email and web browsing delivered over personal computers) is ¥5,623 per month, compared to an average price of broadband Internet service of ¥4,000. In other words, the average consumer surplus is ¥1,623, or about 40 percent of the price. For US consumers, the average willingness to pay for Internet service is $85 per month, and with an average monthly price of $40, the consumer surplus is $45 per month. **Related to Exercises 1.8 and 1.9.**

SOURCE: Based on (1) Gregory Rosston, Scott Savage, Donal Waldman, "Household Demand for Broadband Internet Service," Final Report to the Broadband.gov Task Force of the Federal Communications Commission, February 2010; (2) Masanori Kondo, Akihiro Nakamura, Hitoshi Mitomo, "Quantifying the Benefits of the Internet and Its Applications," *Keio Communication Review* 31 (2009), pp. 37–50.

producer surplus is $20, which is the sum of $8 (Abe) + $6 (Bea) + $4 (Cecil) + $2 (Dee) + $0 (Eve). The fifth producer (Eve) gets no producer surplus because the price equals her cost, and the sixth potential producer (Efrin) doesn't cut any lawns because the price is less than his cost.

6.2   Market Equilibrium and Efficiency

Figure 6.3 puts the demand and supply curves together to show the equilibrium in the market for lawn cutting. The demand curve intersects the supply curve at a price of $10 per lawn. At this price, five lawns are cut, meaning that there are five buyers and five sellers. The **total surplus** of a market is the sum of consumer surplus and producer surplus. In Figure 6.3, the consumer surplus is $30 and the producer surplus is $20, so the total surplus of the market—shown by the shaded areas—is $50. As we'll see in this part of the chapter, the market equilibrium generates the highest possible total surplus. That's why we say that the market equilibrium is efficient: We can't do any better in terms of the total surplus.

total surplus
The sum of consumer surplus and producer surplus.

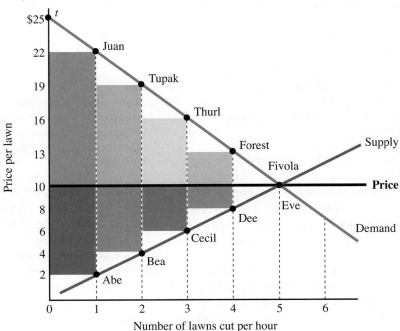

◀ **FIGURE 6.3**
Market Equilibrium and the Total Market Surplus
The total surplus of the market equals consumer surplus (the lightly shaded areas) plus producer surplus (the darkly shaded areas). The market equilibrium generates the highest possible total market value, equal to $50 = $30 (consumer surplus) + $20 (producer surplus).

Total Surplus Is Lower with a Price below the Equilibrium Price

price ceiling

A maximum price set by the government.

To see why the market equilibrium maximizes the total surplus of the market, let's look at the total surplus of the market when the price is less than the equilibrium price. The government could set a maximum price, also known as a **price ceiling**.

Suppose the government imposes a maximum price of $4 on lawn cutting. As shown in Panel A of Figure 6.4, at this price only two people cut lawns—Abe and Bea. Abe's producer surplus is shown by the darkly shaded area between the price line and the supply curve. For Bea, the price equals her willingness to accept, so she participates in the market but gets no producer surplus, receiving a price just high enough to keep her in the market. Consumers can buy only as much as producers are willing to sell, so the market consumer surplus equals the surpluses of just the first two consumers—Juan and Tupak. This is shown as the lightly shaded areas between the price line and the demand curve. By comparing Panel A in Figure 6.4 to Figure 6.3, we see that the maximum price reduces the total surplus of the market. For the first two lawns, consumers simply gain at the expense of producers. The maximum price also eliminates the surpluses from the third and fourth lawns because these transactions don't happen. Therefore, the total surplus decreases.

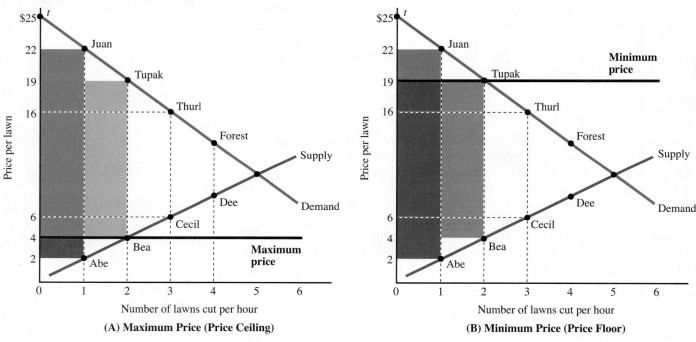

(A) Maximum Price (Price Ceiling) **(B) Minimum Price (Price Floor)**

▲ **FIGURE 6.4**

Price Controls Decrease the Total Surplus of the Market

(A) A maximum price of $4 reduces the total surplus of the market. The first two consumers gain at the expense of the first two producers. The consumer and producer surpluses for the third and fourth lawns are lost entirely, so the total value of the market decreases. (B) A minimum price of $19 reduces the total surplus of the market. The first two producers gain at the expense of the first two consumers. The consumer and producer surpluses for the third and fourth lawns are lost entirely, so the total value of the market decreases.

The maximum price reduces the total surplus of the market because it prevents some mutually beneficial transactions. For example, the third consumer, Thurl, is willing to pay $16 to have his lawn cut, and the third producer, Cecil, is willing to cut a lawn if he is paid at least $6. Thurl is willing to pay more than Cecil requires, so cutting Thurl's lawn would generate a net benefit of $10. If they split the difference, agreeing on a price of $11, each would get a surplus of $5. The maximum price prevents Thurl and Cecil from executing their transaction. The same logic applies to the fourth lawn: The maximum price prevents Forest and Dee from executing a transaction that would generate a net benefit of $5, equal to Forest's willingness to pay ($13) minus Dee's marginal cost ($8).

Total Surplus Is Lower with a Price above the Equilibrium Price

To reinforce the notion that the market equilibrium maximizes the total surplus of the market, let's look at the total surplus of the market when the price exceeds the equilibrium price. The government could set a minimum price, also known as a **price floor**. Suppose the government sets a minimum price for lawn cutting at $19. As shown in Panel B of Figure 6.4, the demand curve indicates that at a price of $19, only two consumers, Juan and Tupak, will have their lawns cut. The total surplus of the market is the sum of consumer and producer surplus for these first two lawns, the same as it was under the maximum price. Again, this is lower than the total surplus that the consumer and producer could have gained, as shown by Figure 6.3.

What's the difference between the two pricing policies? Under a maximum price, the first two consumers gain at the expense of the first two producers, whereas under the minimum price, the first two producers gain at the expense of the first two consumers. Like the maximum price, the minimum price prevents mutually beneficial transactions for the third, fourth, and fifth lawns.

price floor
A minimum price set by the government.

Efficiency and the Invisible Hand

The market equilibrium maximizes the total surplus of the market because it guarantees that all mutually beneficial transactions will happen. Once we reach the market equilibrium at the intersection of the supply curve and demand curve, there are no more transactions that would benefit a buyer and a seller. The market demand curve tells us that the potential buyer of the sixth lawn cut (Siggy) is willing to pay only $7 for a lawn cut, and the supply curve tells us that the potential seller of the sixth lawn cut (Efrin) has a marginal cost of $12. This transaction doesn't happen because the potential buyer is not willing to pay the cost of producing the good.

Our example of the market for lawn cutting illustrates a general lesson about markets. The typical market has thousands of buyers and thousands of sellers, each acting in his or her own self-interest. The market reaches the quantity that maximizes the total surplus of the market and is therefore efficient. Instead of using a bureaucrat to coordinate the actions of everyone in the market, we can rely on the actions of individual consumers and individual producers, each guided only by self-interest. This is Adam Smith's invisible hand in action.

Government Intervention in Efficient Markets

In most modern economies, governments take an active role. As we'll see later in the book, government action can be justified on efficiency grounds when one of the four efficiency conditions listed at the beginning of the chapter is not being met. But for a market that meets the four efficiency conditions, the market equilibrium generates the largest possible total surplus, so government intervention can only decrease the surplus and cause inefficiency. A government motivated exclusively by efficiency would not intervene in such a market, but instead would permit the invisible hand to guide consumers and producers to the market equilibrium.

So why would a government intervene in an efficient market? Sometimes the government's objective is not to promote efficiency—to maximize the size of the pie—but instead to slice the pie in favor of one group or another. For example, a government that restricts shoe imports prevents some domestic workers from losing their shoemaking jobs. Of course, limiting imports will decrease the supply of shoes, and consumers will pay higher prices. As we'll see, when the government intervenes in an efficient market to slice the pie in favor of one group, the pie shrinks, so there is a trade-off between efficiency (maximizing the size of the pie) and distributional concerns (slicing the pie).

What is the role of economic analysis in exploring government intervention in efficient markets? We will focus our attention on the inefficiencies of government intervention, looking at how much the pie shrinks. We will briefly discuss some of the distributional consequences of intervention—how the slices change. The decision about whether intervention in an efficient market is worthwhile—whether the changes in the slices are worth losing part of the pie—is made in the political sphere. Economic analysis shows the trade-offs associated with public policies.

Under some circumstances, groups of people who fare poorly in the market economy deserve special consideration. If a society decides that a particular group merits special treatment—for example, workers who lose their jobs because of imports—a more direct form of assistance is generally superior than intervention in efficient markets by the government. One alternative would be for the government to provide money for workers to get training for new jobs.

application 2

RENT CONTROL AND MISMATCHES

APPLYING THE CONCEPTS: Why does the market equilibrium maximize the value of a market?

Under rent control, the government sets a maximum price for housing, decreasing the quantity supplied and the total value of the market. Rent control and other maximum prices cause inefficiency of another sort. Consider a consumer living in a rent-controlled apartment who experiences a change in circumstances that would normally cause the consumer to a move to a different apartment. For example, when a single person renting a tiny apartment gets married, he or she is likely to move to a larger place. But a consumer in a rent-controlled apartment may stay in the tiny but inexpensive apartment, generating a housing mismatch. A recent study suggests that in New York City, about 20 percent of rent-controlled apartments are mismatched.

The most famous case of a mismatched tenant is former Mayor Koch of New York. When he was elected mayor and moved into the mayor's official residence, he held onto his rent-controlled apartment, presumably anticipating his post-mayor life in an apartment at a controlled rent that was roughly one-third the market rent. **Related to Exercise 2.7.**

SOURCE: Based on Edward Glaeser and Erzo Luttmer, "The Misallocation of Housing under Rent Control," *American Economic Review* 93 (2003), pp. 1027–1046.

6.3   Controlling Prices—Maximum and Minimum Prices

We'll start our discussion of government intervention with policies that control product prices. The government could set a maximum price or a minimum price. In both cases, if the market meets the four efficiency conditions listed at the beginning of the chapter, government intervention reduces the total surplus of the market and causes inefficiency.

Setting Maximum Prices

We've already seen two different effects of a maximum price or price ceiling. In Chapter 4 we saw that when the government sets a maximum price that is less than the equilibrium price, the result is permanent excess demand for the product. The maximum price encourages firms to supply *less* and encourages consumers to buy *more*. So at the maximum price there is excess demand because consumers want to buy more than producers want to sell. In this chapter, we saw from Panel A in Figure 6.4 that a maximum price decreases the total surplus of the market: Some consumers gain at the expense of producers, and the total surplus decreases. Here are some examples of goods that have been subject to maximum prices or may be subject to maximum prices in the near future:

- *Rental housing.* During World War II, the federal government instituted a national system of rent controls. Although only New York City continued rent control after the war, during the 1970s rent control spread to dozens of cities.

- *Gasoline.* In response to sharp increases in the price of gasoline in the 1970s, the national government set a maximum price on gasoline.

- *Medical goods and services.* Some proposals to control medical costs include price controls for prescription drugs.

In all three cases, a maximum price will cause excess demand and reduce the total surplus of the market.

Rent Control

Figure 6.5 shows the effects of rent control on consumer and producer surplus. Panel A shows the market equilibrium, with a price (monthly rent) of $400 per apartment and a quantity of 1,000 apartments. The total surplus is the sum of the consumer surplus and producer surplus, shown as the area between the demand curve and the supply curve. Panel B shows the effect of a maximum price of $300 per apartment. The decrease in price causes movement downward along the supply curve to point *b*, and the quantity of apartments supplied decreases to 700. Because the policy decreases the number of apartments from 1,000 to 700, the total surplus of the market decreases. For the first 700 apartments, consumers gain at the expense of producers, paying $300 per apartment rather than $400. Apartments 701 through 1,000 disappear from the market, so the surpluses associated with these apartments are lost entirely. The decrease in total surplus means that the market is inefficient.

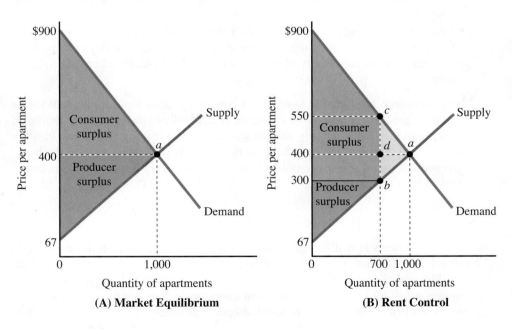

◀ **FIGURE 6.5**
Rent Control Decreases Total Surplus
(A) In the market equilibrium, with a price of $400 and 1,000 apartments, the total surplus is the area between the demand curve and the supply curve. (B) Rent control, with a maximum price of $300, reduces the quantity to 700 apartments and decreases the total surplus.

Because rent control decreases the total surplus of the market, the policy generates a **deadweight loss**. In Figure 6.5, the deadweight loss is shown by the yellow triangle *abc*, the decrease in the total surplus of the market. This is a deadweight loss in the sense that it is not offset by a gain to anyone else. The consumers and producers

deadweight loss
The decrease in the total surplus of the market that results from a policy such as rent control.

who are excluded from the market by rent control lose the surpluses they could have received in the market. The loss of consumer surplus is shown by triangle *cad*, and the loss of producer surplus is shown by triangle *dab*. Adding these together, we get the deadweight loss shown by triangle *abc*.

Another way to see the inefficiency of rent control is to apply the principle of voluntary exchange.

> ## PRINCIPLE OF VOLUNTARY EXCHANGE
> A voluntary exchange between two people makes both people better off.

As shown by the points between *c* and *a* on the demand curve, 300 consumers are willing to pay between $400 and $550 for an apartment. As shown by the points between points *b* and *a* on the supply curve, there are 300 producers who are willing to rent out an apartment for amounts between $300 and $400. Although the 300 excluded consumers are willing to pay more than these suppliers require to provide an apartment, the transactions are illegal under rent control. Because rent control outlaws transactions that would make both parties better off, it causes inefficiency.

Three more subtle effects associated with rent control add to its inefficiency:

- *Search costs.* At the artificially low maximum price, the number of people seeking apartments exceeds the number of apartments available. Consumers will spend more time searching for apartments, so an additional cost of rent control is the opportunity cost of the extra time spent searching for apartments.

- *Cheating.* Because rent control outlaws mutually beneficial transactions, many people violate the spirit and the letter of the law by cheating. In some rent-control cities, consumers pay extra money to property owners to outbid other consumers. These extra payments are often disguised as "nonrefundable security deposits" or as "key money"—thousands of dollars to get the keys to an apartment.

- *Decrease in quality of housing.* Given the lower payoff from providing apartments for rent, property owners will have less incentive to spend money on repair and maintenance, so the quality of apartments will decrease. In other words, lower rent is offset in part by lower housing quality.

Is rent control good for the poor? Rent control specifies a maximum rent for an apartment, regardless of who lives there. Rent-controlled apartments are occupied by the rich and the poor, so many wealthy people benefit from rent control. In other words, rent control is ineffective in helping the poor. As we explain later in the book, the government could use other policies to more effectively improve the economic circumstances of the poor.

Setting Minimum Prices

We've already seen two different effects of a minimum price, or price floor. In Chapter 4 we saw that when the government sets a minimum price that exceeds the equilibrium price, the result is permanent excess supply. The increase in price encourages producers to produce *more* and encourages consumers to buy *less*. So at the minimum price, there is excess supply because producers want to sell more than consumers want to buy. In this chapter, we saw from Panel A in Figure 6.4 that a minimum price decreases the total surplus of the market: Some producers gain at the expense of consumers, and the total surplus decreases.

Governments around the world establish minimum prices for agricultural goods. Under a price-support program, a government sets a minimum price for an agricultural product and then buys any resulting surpluses at that price.

application 3

PRICE CONTROLS AND THE SHRINKING CANDY BAR

APPLYING THE CONCEPTS #3: How do price controls affect the market?

During World War II, the U.S. government used a system of price controls to set maximum prices on all sorts of products, including candy bars. *Consumer Reports* compared the weights of candy bars in 1943 to their weights in 1939, before the maximum prices were imposed. In 19 of 20 cases, the candy bars had shrunk, causing the price per ounce to increase by an average of 23 percent. In other words, producers reacted to maximum prices by shrinking candy bars to match the relatively low maximum price. In the words of *Consumer Reports*, the shrinkage of candy bars is an example of "hidden price increases." **Related to Exercise 3.6.**

SOURCE: Based on foodtimeline.org, "Food Timeline FAQ: Historic Food Prices," (foodtimeline.org, accessed February 20, 2012).

6.4 Controlling Quantities—Licensing and Import Restrictions

What happens when the government controls the quantity of a particular product instead of its price? We'll consider two policies that control quantities. In the domestic economy, many state and local governments limit the number of firms in particular markets by limiting the number of business licenses to operate in those markets. Many national governments restrict imports, using import bans or quotas on the quantity of a product—for example, shoes or cheese—that can be imported.

The licensing of business by state and local government is extensive. For example, many cities and states limit the number of taxicabs, dry cleaners, tobacco farms, liquor stores, bars, and even dog groomers. Some people defend licensing programs on the grounds that they protect consumers from low-quality products and poor service. But studies have shown that most licensing programs increase prices without improving the quality of products and service.[2]

Another motive for cities to issue licenses is to limit the number of establishments that could be considered nuisances to some citizens, for example, bars, convenience stores, and gas stations.

Taxi Medallions

We can use the licensing of taxis to explain how the practice affects the market for taxi service and other markets in which licenses are common. Panel A of Figure 6.6 shows the market equilibrium in the taxi market. The demand curve intersects the supply curve at point *a*. The industry provides 10,000 miles of taxi service per day at a price of $3 per mile. Each taxi is capable of producing a maximum of 100 miles of service per day, and there are 100 taxicabs in the market. The total surplus of the market equals the sum of consumer surplus and producer surplus, shown by the area between the demand curve and the supply curve.

Now suppose that the city passes a law requiring each taxicab to have a license—also known as a taxi "medallion"—and limits the number of medallions to 80. The city then gives taxi medallions to the first 80 people who show up at city hall. In Panel B of Figure 6.6, the vertical line at 8,000 miles of service shows that this policy fixes the quantity of taxi service at 8,000 miles per day (80 taxis times 100 miles per taxi per

▶ **FIGURE 6.6**

The Market Effects of Taxi Medallions
(A) The market equilibrium is shown
by point *a*, with a price of $3.00 and a
quantity of 10,000 miles of service per
day (100 taxis and 100 miles per taxi).
The total surplus is the area between the
demand and supply curves. (B) A medallion policy reduces the quantity of taxi
service to 8,000 miles per day (80 taxis
and 100 miles per taxi) and increases the
price to $3.60 (point *c*). The producers of
the first 8,000 miles gain at the expense
of consumers, but the surpluses for
between 8,000 and 10,000 miles are
lost entirely. Therefore, the total surplus
decreases.

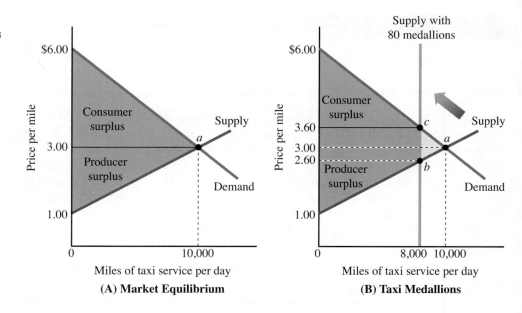

(A) Market Equilibrium   **(B) Taxi Medallions**

day). The medallion policy creates an excess demand for taxi service: At the original
price ($3.00), the quantity demanded is 10,000 miles, but the city's 80 taxicabs provide
only 8,000 miles of service. As a result, the market moves upward along the demand
curve to point *c*, where the price is $3.60 per mile of service. The medallion policy
increases the price and decreases the quantity of taxi services.

Licensing and Market Efficiency

The medallion policy decreases the total surplus of the taxi market. In Figure 6.6, we see
that the total surplus in Panel B is less than the total surplus in Panel A. The medallion
policy decreases consumer surplus, a result of the higher price and the smaller quantity
supplied. Producer surplus could increase or decrease, depending on the shapes of the
market supply and market demand curves. In this example, the producer surplus of
taxi drivers with medallions actually increases by a small amount. As in the cases of a
maximum price or a minimum price, the medallion policy decreases the quantity of goods
sold, decreasing the total surplus of the market. The producers of the first 8,000 miles of
service gain at the expense of consumers, but the surpluses that could have been gained
between 8,000 and 10,000 miles are lost entirely, so the total surplus of the market
decreases. The deadweight loss is shown by the area of yellow triangle *abc*.

   Another way to see the inefficiency of taxi medallions is to look at just the
consumers and producers who are excluded from the market and what they lose. Some
of the excluded consumers would gladly pay the cost of providing taxi service. As
shown by the points between points *c* and *a* on the demand curve, many consumers are
willing to pay between $3.00 and $3.60 per mile for taxi service. Although there are
plenty of drivers who would be willing to provide taxi service at these prices, they can't
do so without a medallion. Because the medallion policy prevents these riders and
drivers from executing mutually beneficial transactions, the policy causes inefficiency.

   Our analysis of taxi medallions applies to any market subject to quantity controls.
State and city governments use licensing to limit many types of small businesses. When
an establishment such as a convenience store or dry cleaner would cause a nuisance to
its neighbors, the inefficiency of the sort shown in Figure 6.6 may be offset at least
partly by the benefit of controlling nuisances. Of course, the alternative policy is to
control the nuisance directly by restricting the location of the establishment rather
than simply limiting the number of establishments. In general, a policy that limits
entry into a market increases price, decreases quantity, and causes inefficiency in
the market. In evaluating such a policy, we must compare the possible benefits from
controlling nuisances to the losses of consumer and producer surplus.

Winners and Losers from Licensing

Who benefits and who loses from licensing programs such as a taxi medallion policy? The losers are consumers, who pay more for taxi rides. The winners are the people who receive a free medallion and the right to charge an artificially high price for taxi service.

In some cities, people buy and sell taxi medallions. The market value of a medallion reflects the profits it can earn its owner. For example, the market price of a medallion is over $150,000 in New York City, $140,000 in Boston, and $100,000 in Toronto.[3] In cities such as Chicago, where medallions are more plentiful, the market price is much lower.

Why don't governments simply eliminate the taxi medallion system and allow free entry into the taxi market? Because doing so would decrease the price of taxi service and reduce the market value of medallions to zero. Some city governments are reluctant to eliminate medallions because owners use their political power to keep the system (and the value of their medallions) in place.

Import Restrictions

We've seen that the government can control the quantity of a good produced by issuing a limited number of business licenses to producers. Another way to control quantity is to limit the imports of a particular good. Like a licensing policy, an import restriction increases the market price and decreases the total surplus of the market.

To show the market effects of import restrictions, let's start with an unrestricted market. Panel A of Figure 6.7 shows the market equilibrium in the sugar market when there is free trade. The domestic supply curve shows the quantity supplied by domestic (U.S.) firms at different prices. Looking at point *m*, we see that U.S. firms

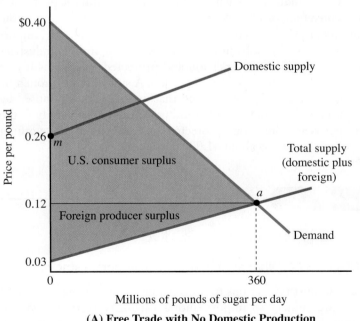

(A) **Free Trade with No Domestic Production**

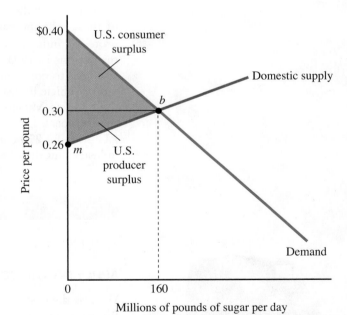

(B) **Import Ban and Domestic Production**

▲ **FIGURE 6.7**

The Effects of an Import Ban on U.S. Prices and Consumer and Producer Surplus

(A) With free trade, the demand intersects the total supply curve at point *a* with a price of $0.12 and a quantity of 360 million pounds. This price is below the minimum price of domestic suppliers ($0.26, as shown by point *m*), so domestic firms do not participate in the market. The total surplus is shown by the shaded areas (U.S. consumer surplus and foreign producer surplus). (B) If sugar imports are banned, the equilibrium is shown by the intersection of the demand curve and the domestic (U.S.) supply curve (point *b*). The price increases to $0.30. Although the ban generates a producer surplus for domestic producers, their gain is less than the loss of domestic consumers.

will not supply any sugar unless the price is at least $0.26 per pound. The total supply curve, which shows the quantity supplied by both domestic and foreign firms, lies to the right of the domestic curve. At each price, the total supply exceeds the domestic supply because foreign firms also supply sugar. Point *a* shows the free-trade equilibrium: The domestic demand curve (which shows the demand by U.S. consumers) intersects the total supply curve at a price of $0.12 per pound and a quantity of 360 million pounds per day. Because this price is below the minimum price for domestic firms, domestic firms do not supply any sugar to the U.S. market.

What would happen if the United States banned sugar imports? Foreign suppliers would disappear from the market, so the total supply of sugar would consist of only the domestic supply. In Panel B of Figure 6.7, the new equilibrium would be shown by point *b*: The demand curve would intersect the domestic supply curve at a price of $0.30 per pound and a quantity of 160 million pounds. The decrease in supply resulting from the import ban would increase the price and decrease the quantity. As a result, domestic firms would produce all the sugar for the domestic market.

The import ban would ultimately decrease the total surplus in the sugar market. The shaded areas in the two graphs show the consumer and producer surpluses that would result with and without free trade. The import ban decreases the U.S. consumer surplus, as shown by the two blue triangles in the two graphs. The ban would also eliminate the producer surplus of foreign suppliers (shown by the red triangle in Panel A of Figure 6.7) and generate a producer surplus for domestic suppliers (shown by the red triangle in Panel B of Figure 6.7). Therefore, the import ban would cause domestic producers to gain at the expense of domestic consumers. Because consumers would lose more than domestic producers would gain, the import ban would cause a net loss for people in the United States.

Import restrictions are often defended on the grounds that they increase employment in the "protected" industries, such as apparel and steel. But the protection of these jobs increases consumer prices, so there is a trade-off: more jobs in the protected industry, but higher prices for consumers.[4] According to one study, import restrictions in 1993 protected 56,464 jobs in the U.S. textile and apparel industries at a cost to consumers of about $178,000 per job and protected 3,419 jobs in the motor vehicle industry at a cost of about $271,000 per job. A study commissioned by the Swedish Ministry for Foreign Affairs concluded that import quotas imposed by the European Union (EU) increased the cost of clothing for the typical family in the EU by about 270 euros per year. The quotas protected jobs in the domestic clothing industry, but the cost per job saved was about 41,000 euros per year.

application 4

THE COST OF PROTECTING A LUGGAGE JOB

APPLYING THE CONCEPTS #4: What are the effects of import restrictions?

What is the cost of using import restrictions to protect jobs in the luggage industry? Luggage and handbags are subject to import quotas (quantity restrictions) and tariffs (import taxes) that decrease the supply of luggage and increase the price to consumers by 13 percent. These policies protect about 226 jobs in the industry and reduce consumer surplus by $290 million, so the cost per job protected is roughly $1.29 million per year. Similar calculations show that the cost per job protected is $826,000 for the sugar industry, $685,000 for the dairy industry, and $199,000 for the apparel industry. **Related to Exercise 4.5.**

SOURCE: Based on (1) Federal Reserve Bank of Dallas, The Fruits of Free Trade (2002); (2) United States International Trade Commission, The Economic Effects of Significant U.S. Import Restraints (2002).

6.5   Who Really Pays Taxes?

In this part of the chapter, we'll look at the market effects of taxes and answer two important questions. First, who really bears the burden of a tax? As we'll see, it is not necessarily the person who actually pays the tax to the government. Second, is the total burden of a tax equal to the revenue collected by the government? As we'll see, a tax changes people's behavior, so the total burden actually exceeds the revenue collected.

Tax Shifting: Forward and Backward

We can use supply and demand curves to look at the market effects of taxes. Suppose that your city imposes a tax of $100 per apartment and collects the tax from housing firms—the firms that own apartment buildings and rent out the apartments. You may think the burden of the tax falls exclusively on the housing firm, because that's who mails the check to the government. But some simple supply and demand analysis will show why this is incorrect. The housing firm will charge more for apartments and pay less for its inputs, such as labor and land, so the tax will actually be paid by consumers and input suppliers.

Figure 6.8 shows the market effects of a $100 tax on apartments. As we saw earlier in the chapter, the market supply curve tells us how high the price must be to get producers to supply a particular quantity of output. The price must be high enough to cover all the costs of production. A unit tax increases the cost of production, so we need a higher price to get firms to produce any given quantity. In other words, the supply curve shifts upward by the amount of the tax. A unit tax of $100 per apartment increases a property owner's cost per apartment by $100, so the supply curve shifts upward by $100.

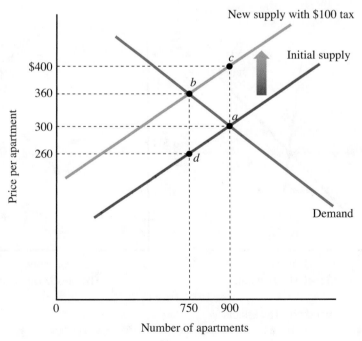

▲ FIGURE 6.8
The Market Effects of an Apartment Tax
A tax of $100 per apartment shifts the supply curve upward by the $100 tax, moving the market equilibrium from point a to point b. The equilibrium price increases from $300 to $360, and the equilibrium quantity decreases from 900 to 750 apartments.

The shift of the supply curve increases the equilibrium price of apartments. At the $300 price, there will be an excess demand for apartments, and the price will increase to eliminate the excess demand. In Figure 6.8, the market moves from point *a* to point *b*: The demand curve intersects the new supply curve at a price of $360, compared to $300 before the tax. In other words, housing firms shift part of the tax forward onto consumers, who pay $60 of the $100 tax. Although housing firms pay the entire $100 tax in a legal sense, they get some of the money to pay the tax by charging consumers $60 more for apartments.

The apartment tax also affects the people who supply inputs such as land and labor to the housing industry. The tax decreases the output of the industry, so the industry needs smaller quantities of the inputs used to produce apartments. The resulting excess supply of inputs like labor and land will decrease land and labor prices, decreasing the cost of producing apartments. As a result, part of the $100 tax gets shifted backward onto input suppliers. Although housing firms pay the apartment tax in a legal sense, they get some of the money to pay the tax by paying less to workers and landowners.

Tax Shifting and the Price Elasticity of Demand

The amount of the tax shifted forward to consumers depends on the price elasticity of demand for the taxed good. If the demand for a taxed good is inelastic—meaning that consumers are not very responsive to price changes—we need a large price hike to eliminate the excess demand caused by the tax. Therefore, consumers will be hit by a large increase in price, and so they will pay the bulk of the tax. This is shown in Panel A of Figure 6.9. Demand is inelastic—that is, the demand curve is steep—so a $5 tax increases the equilibrium price by $4 (from $10 to $14). In other words, consumers pay four-fifths of the tax. In Panel B of Figure 6.9, demand is elastic—that is, the demand curve is relatively flat—so consumers pay just a small part of the tax. A $5 tax increases the equilibrium price by only $1 (from $10 to $11). In this case, consumers pay only one-fifth of the tax.

▲ FIGURE 6.9

Elasticities of Demand and Tax Effects

If demand is inelastic (Panel A), a tax will increase the market price by a large amount, so consumers will bear a large share of the tax. If demand is elastic (Panel B), the price will increase by a small amount and consumers will bear a small share of the tax.

Why should we care about tax shifting? We've seen that a tax increases consumer prices and decreases input prices, so to determine who actually pays a tax, we must look beyond the actual taxpayer. As shown in the following application, the subtleties of tax shifting are often revealed by the objections of people who don't actually pay a tax in a legal sense.

Cigarette Taxes and Tobacco Land

In 1994, President Clinton proposed an immediate $0.75 per pack increase in the cigarette tax. The tax had two purposes: to generate revenue for Clinton's health-care reform plan and to decrease medical costs by discouraging smoking. Based on our discussion of the market effects of a tax, we would predict that the tax would be shared by consumers, who would pay higher prices, and the owners of land where tobacco is grown. It appears tobacco farmers and landowners understand the economics of cigarette taxes. Led by a group of representatives and senators from tobacco-growing areas in North Carolina, Kentucky, and Virginia, Congress scaled back Clinton's proposed tax hike from $0.75 to $0.05. Although the government would have collected the tax from cigarette manufacturers, savvy tobacco farmers realized the tax would decrease the price of their tobacco-growing land.

The Luxury Boat Tax and Boat Workers

A lesson on backward shifting occurred when Congress passed a steep luxury tax on boats and other luxury goods in 1990. Under the new tax, a person buying a $300,000 boat paid an additional $20,000 in taxes. The burden of the tax was actually shared by consumers and input suppliers, including people who worked in boat factories and boatyards. The tax increased the price of boats, and consumers bought fewer boats. The boat industry produced fewer boats, and the resulting decrease in the demand for boat workers led to layoffs and lower wages for those who managed to keep their jobs. Although the idea behind the luxury tax was to "soak the rich," the tax actually harmed low-income workers in the boat industry. The tax was repealed a few years later.

Tax Burden and Deadweight Loss

We've seen that people respond to a tax by changing their behavior. As a result, the total burden of a tax will exceed the total amount of money the government actually collects from the tax. To see why, suppose the government imposes a tax on no. 3 pencils, and the tax is large enough that everyone who initially used no. 3 pencils switches to other types of pencils or other writing implements. If no one purchases no. 3 pencils, the tax won't raise any revenue for the government, but the tax still generates a burden because some people who would prefer to use no. 3 pencils have switched to other writing implements.

We'll use the fish market to explore the total burden of a tax. To simplify matters, let's assume that the supply curve for fish is horizontal, as shown in Figure 6.10. As we'll see later in the book, a supply curve will be horizontal if the prices of the inputs used in the industry don't change as the total output of the industry changes. For the fish market, this means that wages and the prices of bait and fuel don't change as the total fish harvest changes. The demand curve intersects the initial supply curve at point *a*, so the price is $2 per pound and the quantity is 60,000 pounds of fish per day.

▲ **FIGURE 6.10**

The Deadweight Loss or Excess Burden of a Tax

When the supply curve is horizontal, a tax increases the equilibrium price by the tax ($1 per pound in this example). Consumer surplus decreases by the areas *B* and *C*. Total tax revenue collected is shown by rectangle *B*, so the total burden exceeds tax revenue by triangle *C*. Triangle *C* is sometimes known as the deadweight loss or excess burden of the tax.

Suppose the government imposes a tax of $1 per pound of fish, and the tax is paid in legal terms by producers. As we saw earlier, a unit tax shifts the market supply upward by the amount of the tax. As shown in Figure 6.10, a $1 tax on fish producers shifts the supply curve up by $1: Each firm now needs $3, not $2, to cover all of its costs, including the tax.

In Figure 6.10 the fish tax increases the equilibrium price of fish from $2 to $3. Why does the price increase by an amount equal to the tax? The supply curve is horizontal because input prices are fixed, regardless of how much output is produced. There is no opportunity to shift the tax backward onto input suppliers, so consumers bear the full cost of the tax.

We can use the concept of consumer surplus to determine just how much consumers lose as a result of the tax. Before the fish tax, the consumer surplus is shown by the area between the initial price line (and horizontal supply curve) and the demand curve, or areas *A*, *B*, and *C*. When the price increases to $3, the consumer surplus shrinks to the area of triangle *A*, so the loss of consumer surplus (the total burden of the tax) is shown by rectangle *B* and yellow triangle *C*. Let's take a closer look at these two areas.

- Rectangle *B* shows the extra money consumers must pay for the 40,000 pounds of fish they purchase. The tax increases the price by $1 per pound, so consumers pay an extra $40,000.

• Triangle *C* shows the loss of consumer surplus on the fish that are not consumed because of the tax. Consumers obey the law of demand, so when the price rises, they cut their purchases, buying 20,000 fewer pounds of fish. As a result, they give up the consumer surplus they would have received on these 20,000 pounds of fish.

How does the total burden of the tax compare to the tax revenue raised by the government? The total tax revenue is the tax per pound ($1) times the quantity consumed (40,000 pounds), or $40,000. This is shown by rectangle *B*: Part of the loss experienced by consumers is the revenue gain for government. But in addition to losing rectangle *B*, consumers also lose triangle *C*, so the consumer's total burden of the tax exceeds the tax revenue. Triangle *C* is sometimes known as the **deadweight loss from taxation** or the **excess burden of a tax**.

In the example shown in Figure 6.10, we used a horizontal supply curve to simplify matters and make the analysis of deadweight loss transparent. In a market with a positively sloped supply curve, a tax generates a deadweight loss, but the analysis is a bit more complex. For students interested in a challenge, one of the problems at the end of the chapter deals with deadweight loss for the apartment market, a market with a positively sloped supply curve.

deadweight loss from taxation
The difference between the total burden of a tax and the amount of revenue collected by the government.

excess burden of a tax
Another name for deadweight loss.

application 5

RESPONSE TO LOWER TAXES IN FRENCH RESTAURANTS

APPLYING THE CONCEPTS #5: How does a tax cut affect prices?

In France, regular restaurants pay a 20 percent value-added tax (VAT) on sit-down meals, while fast-food restaurants pay just a 5 percent tax on take-away meals. A group of large restaurant owners made the following pledge. If the nation were to cut its VAT rate on restaurant meals to 5 percent, the owners would

• cut the prices of restaurant meals by 5 percent, and
• increase the wages paid to waiters and dishwashers by 10 percent.

The owners predicted that these changes would increase the quantity of restaurant meals sold by 14 percent and increase restaurant employment by 40,000 workers.

Does the pledge of the restaurant owners make economic sense? We know that firms shift taxes forward to consumers in higher prices and backward to workers in lower wages. A tax cut will of course have the opposite effects. The restaurant market is highly competitive, so any decrease in cost will lead to lower prices as restaurants compete for customers. And lower prices will increase the quantity of meals served, increasing the demand for restaurant workers and their wages. So although the actual numbers in the owners' pledge for lower prices and higher wages may not be correct, the pledge is consistent with the economics of tax shifting. **Related to Exercises 5.1, 5.2, and 5.7.**

SOURCE: Based on "Better Value, Lower Tax: French Restaurants," *Economist*, January 25, 2003.

SUMMARY

In this chapter, we discussed the efficiency of markets and the consequences of government intervention in perfectly competitive markets. In a market without external benefits or costs, government intervention prevents consumers and producers from executing beneficial transactions and thus decreases the total surplus of the market. We also saw that taxes affect the prices of consumer goods and inputs. To determine who actually bears the cost of a tax, we must look beyond the taxpayer. Here are the main points of the chapter:

1 The *total surplus* of a market equals the sum of consumer surplus and producer surplus.

2 In a market that meets the four efficiency conditions (no external cost, no external benefit, perfect information, perfect competition), the market equilibrium maximizes the total surplus and is therefore efficient.

3 Price controls reduce the total surplus of a market because they prevent mutually beneficial transactions.

4 Quantity controls (such as licensing and import restrictions) decrease consumer surplus and the total surplus of the market.

5 A tax on a good may be shifted forward onto consumers and backward onto input suppliers.

6 Because a tax causes people to change their behavior, the total burden of the tax exceeds the revenue generated by the tax.

KEY TERMS

consumer surplus, p. 129

deadweight loss, p. 135

deadweight loss from taxation, p. 145

efficiency, p. 128

excess burden of a tax, p. 145

price ceiling, p. 132

price floor, p. 133

producer surplus, p. 130

total surplus, p. 131

willingness to accept, p. 130

willingness to pay, p. 129

EXERCISES

All problems are assignable in MyEconLab.

6.1 Consumer Surplus and Producer Surplus

1.1 Consumer surplus equals _____ minus _____.

1.2 Producer surplus equals _____ minus _____.

1.3 In Figure 6.1 on page 129, Tupak's consumer surplus is _____, compared to _____ for Thurl.

1.4 In Figure 6.1 on page 129, Tupak's consumer surplus is _____ (greater/less) than Thurl's because Tupak has a _____ (lower, higher) willingness to pay.

1.5 In Figure 6.2 on page 130, Bea's producer surplus is _____ (greater/less) than Dee's because Dee has a _____ (lower, higher) marginal cost of production.

1.6 As the market price increases, consumer surplus _____ (increases/decreases) and producer surplus _____ (increases/decreases).

1.7 For a given market price, a consumer who is on the high end of the demand curve has a _____ consumer surplus than a consumer on the low end of the demand curve.

1.8 For U.S. consumers, the average consumer surplus for Internet service is $_____ (10, 45, 80, 100) per month. (Related to Application 1 on page 131.)

1.9 Consider the demand for Internet service in the U.S. Assume that the demand curve is linear, the monthly price is $40, and the equilibrium number of consumers is 50 million. For the average consumer, show willingness to pay and the consumer surplus. (Related to Application 1 on page 131.)

6.2 Market Equilibrium and Efficiency

2.1 You are willing to pay $2,000 to have your house painted, and Pablo's marginal cost of painting a house is $1,400. If you agree to split the difference, the price is _____, your consumer surplus is _____, and Pablo's producer surplus is _____.

2.2 In Figure 6.3 on page 131, Forest is willing to pay _____ for the fourth cut lawn, and Dee's marginal cost is _____. If they split the difference, the price would be _____ and each would get a surplus of _____.

2.3 In Figure 6.4 on page 132, a maximum price of $4 prevents mutually beneficial transactions between Thurl and _____ and between Forest and _____.

2.4 Fill in the blanks with "consumers" or "producers": A maximum price below the equilibrium price generates benefits for some _____ and imposes costs on some _____ and some _____.

2.5 Fill in the blanks with "consumers" or "producers": A minimum price above the equilibrium price generates benefits for some _____ and imposes costs on some _____ and some _____.

2.6 In Figure 6.3 on page 131, the sixth lawn is not cut because the _____ of the sixth consumer (Siggy, in Figure 6.1) is _____ the _____ of the sixth producer (Efrin, in Figure 6.2).

2.7 A recent study suggests that in New York City, rent control causes roughly _____ percent of rent-controlled apartments are mismatched. (Related to Application 2 on page 134.)

2.8 **Identify the Surpluses.** The following graph shows a supply curve and a demand curve and several areas between the curves. Identify the areas on the figure that represent the following:
   a. Consumer surplus in the market equilibrium
   b. Producer surplus in the market equilibrium
   c. Total surplus in the market equilibrium
   d. Consumer surplus under a maximum price of $10
   e. Producer surplus under a maximum price of $10
   f. Total surplus under a maximum price of $10
   g. Consumer surplus under a maximum quantity of 70
   h. Producer surplus under a maximum quantity of 70
   i. Total surplus under a maximum quantity of 70

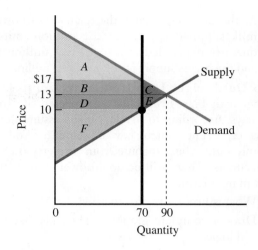

6.3 Controlling Prices—Maximum and Minimum Prices

3.1 Arrow up or down: In Figure 6.5 on page 135, rent control _____ the quantity of apartments, _____ producer surplus, _____ consumer surplus, and _____ the total market surplus.

3.2 In Figure 6.5 on page 135, rent control prevents a total of _____ mutually beneficial transactions for consumers on the demand curve between points and producers on the supply curve between points _____ and _____.

3.3 In Figure 6.5 on page 135, suppose rent control is partly relaxed, with the maximum price rising from $300 to $350. The quantity of apartments on the market will increase from _____ to _____.

3.4 In Figure 6.5 on page 135, a consumer who is on the demand curve halfway between points *c* and *a* would be willing to pay $_____ above the controlled price to get an apartment. A producer who is on the supply curve halfway between points *b* and *a* would be willing to supply an apartment at a price of $_____, or _____ above the maximum price.

3.5 The deadweight loss from rent control is shown by the area between the _____ curve and the _____ curve from the quantity _____ to the quantity _____.

3.6 During World War II, candy producers responded to maximum prices by _____, leading to _____ prices per ounce. (Related to Application 3 on page 137.)

3.7 **Excess Supply from a Minimum Milk Price.** In the equilibrium in the powdered milk market, the quantity is 100 million units and the price is $9.00 per unit. The price elasticity of demand is 0.80 and the price elasticity of supply is 2.50. Suppose the government imposes a minimum price of $9.90.
   a. Draw a graph to show the market effects of the minimum price.

b. At the minimum price, the quantity of powdered milk supplied is —————— million units, the quantity demanded is —————— million units, and the excess supply is —————— million units.

3.8 No Deadweight Loss from Rent Control? Like other fruit flies, Frudo has an expected life span of 37 days. According to Frudo, "If my assumptions are correct, a rent-control law implemented today will simply redistribute income from property owners to consumers. There will be no deadweight loss, at least not in my lifetime."

    a. What is Frudo's key assumption?

    b. Draw a complete graph to show his assumption and logic.

    c. The typical elephant has an expected life span of 60 years. How would its analysis of rent control differ from Frudo's? Illustrate with a complete graph.

3.9 Price Controls for Medical Care. Consider a town where the equilibrium price of a doctor's visit is $60 and the equilibrium quantity supplied is 90 patient visits per hour. For suppliers (doctors), each $1 increase in price increases the quantity supplied by two visits. For consumers, each $1 increase in price decreases the quantity demanded by one visit. Suppose that in an attempt to control the rising costs of medical care the government imposes price controls, setting a maximum price of $50 per visit.

    a. Use a completely labeled graph to show the effects of the maximum price on (a) the quantity of visits to doctors and (b) the total surplus of the market.

    b. What sort of inefficiencies does the price control cause?

    c. Would you expect patients and doctors to find ways around the maximum price?

3.10 Gasoline Price Controls. The equilibrium price of gasoline is $3, and the equilibrium quantity is 100 million gallons per day. Suppose the government sets a maximum price of $2.90. For producers, each $0.01 increase in price increases the quantity supplied by 3 million gallons.

    a. Draw a graph to show the effects of the maximum price on the gasoline market. Label the initial equilibrium point as *a* and the point that shows the quantity supplied under the maximum price as *b*.

    b. How does the maximum price affect the quantity of gasoline sold?

3.11 Maximum Rent on Land. Consider a state where all land is occupied by mobile-home parks, and each household rents one padacre (a standard pad for a mobile home). In the market equilibrium, the rent is $200 per padacre. Suppose the government sets a maximum rent of $150 per padacre, regardless of how the land is used. Recall the old saying "The trouble with land is that they're not making it anymore."

    a. Use a supply-demand graph to depict the market with the maximum rent.

    b. Does the rent maximum affect the equilibrium quantity of land?

    c. Does the rent maximum generate a deadweight loss? If not, why not?

3.12 Supply Elasticity and Deadweight Loss. Consider the following statement: As the price elasticity of supply increases, the deadweight loss from a maximum price changes.

    a. Draw two sets of supply-demand curves, one with a more elastic supply curve.

    b. In the case of more elastic supply, is the deadweight loss larger or smaller?

6.4   Controlling Quantities—Licensing and Import Restrictions

4.1 In Figure 6.6 on page 138, the taxi medallion policy prevents mutually beneficial transactions for consumers on the demand curve between points —————— and —————— and producers on the supply curve between points —————— and ——————.

4.2 In Figure 6.6 on page 138, a consumer who is on the demand curve halfway between points *c* and *a* would be willing to pay $—————— for a mile of taxi service, while a supplier who is halfway between points *b* and *a* on the supply curve would be willing to supply a mile of taxi service at a price of $——————.

4.3 In Figure 6.7 on page 139, domestic firms will produce —————— tons of sugar at a price of $0.15, —————— tons at a price of $0.30, and —————— tons at a price of $0.28.

4.4 Arrow up or down: An import ban —————— the price of sugar, —————— the total (market) quantity of sugar, and —————— the quantity of sugar produced by domestic firms.

4.5 Import restrictions for luggage increase —————— and decrease ——————, and the cost per protected job is roughly $—————— (10,000, 50,000, 1,290,000). (Related to Application 4 on page 140.)

4.6 Compute the Changes. Consider the example of taxi medallions shown in Figure 6.6 on page 138.

    a. The policy changes consumer surplus from $—————— to $——————.

    b. The policy changes producer surplus from $—————— to $——————.

    c. The policy changes the total surplus of the market from $—————— to $——————.

    d. The deadweight loss is shown by the area of triangle ——————, which equals $——————.

4.7 Effects of Relaxing the Medallion Policy. Consider the example of taxi medallions shown in Figure 6.6 on page 138. Suppose the government relaxes the policy, increasing the number of medallions from 80 to 90.

  a. The price of taxi service will change from $_____ to $_____.

  b. The miles of taxi service will change from _____ miles to _____ miles.

  c. At the margin an excluded consumer would be willing to pay up to $_____ for a mile of taxi service, while an excluded supplier would be willing to supply a mile of taxi service at a price as low as $_____.

4.8 Equilibrium and Surplus in a Liver Market. The following table shows different points on the linear supply curve and linear demand curve for livers for transplant.

Price	Quantity Supplied	Quantity Demanded
$ 0	50	200
2,000	70	160
5,000	100	100
7,000	120	60
10,000	150	0

  a. Draw the two curves and show the market equilibrium. The equilibrium price is $_____, and the equilibrium quantity is _____ livers.

  b. On your graph, show the total surplus of the liver market—the sum of consumer and producer surplus.

  c. Suppose the government bans the buying and selling of livers. On your graph, show the new equilibrium quantity of livers and the resulting loss in the total value of the market.

4.9 Barber Licensing. Consider the market for haircuts in a city. In the market equilibrium, the price per haircut is $6 and the quantity is 240 haircuts per day. For consumers, each $1 increase in price decreases the quantity demanded by 20 haircuts. For producers, each $1 increase in price increases the quantity supplied by 60 haircuts. In the market equilibrium, there are 24 barbers, each of whom produces 10 haircuts per day. Suppose the city passes a law requiring all barbers to have a license and then issues only 18 barber licenses. Each licensed barber continues to provide 10 haircuts per day. Use a completely labeled graph to show the effects of licensing on (a) the price of haircuts and (b) the total surplus in the haircut market.

4.10 Bidding for a Boston Taxi Medallion. In 1997, there were 1,500 taxi medallions in the city of Boston, and each medallion generated a profit of about $14,000 per year. In 1998, the city announced that it would issue 300 new taxi medallions, auctioning the new medallions to the highest bidders.[5] Even with the new medallions, the number of taxis in the city would still be less than the number that would occur in an unregulated market. Your job is to predict the annual profit from a medallion after the new medallions were issued. To predict the new annual profit, assume the following:

  • The cost of providing taxi service is constant at $2.00 per mile of service.

  • The initial price of taxi service (with 1,500 medallions issued) is $2.14 per mile.

  • Each taxi (or medallion) provides 100,000 miles of service per year, so issuing the 300 new medallions increases the total quantity of taxi service from 150 million miles to 180 million miles.

  • The slope of the demand curve is –$0.001 per million miles: For each $0.001 decrease in the price of taxi service, the quantity demanded increases by one million miles.

  a. Compute the new price of taxi service.

  b. Compute the new profit per medallion.

4.11 Eliminate the Mango Market? Draw a supply-demand graph depicting a situation in which banning mango imports drives the quantity of mangos sold to zero.

4.12 Import Ban for Kiwi Fruit. Initially, there are no restrictions on importing kiwi fruit. The minimum supply price of domestic producers is $0.26, while the minimum supply price of foreign suppliers is $0.08. Each supply curve is linear, with a slope of $0.01 per million pounds. In the initial equilibrium, the price is $0.18 and the quantity is 10 million pounds. The demand curve has a vertical intercept of $0.38 and a slope of –$0.02 per million pounds.

  a. Draw a graph showing the initial equilibrium.

  b. Suppose imports are banned, raising the price to $0.30. Draw a graph to show the new equilibrium and identify the new equilibrium quantity.

  c. Compute the consumer surplus before the import ban and after the ban.

  d. Suppose the import ban protects 10 jobs in the kiwi fruit industry. What is the cost to consumers for each job protected?

5.1 The lobby group of French restaurant owners pledged that if the VAT tax on restaurant meals was cut, they would increase _____ and decrease _____. (Related to Application 5 on page 145.)

5.2 According to the numbers provided by the lobby group of French restaurant owners, the price elasticity of demand for restaurant meals is _____. (Related to Application 5 on page 145.)

5.3 A tax paid in legal terms by producers will be partly shifted forward onto _____ and partly shifted backward onto _____.

5.4 Arrow up or down: As the price elasticity of demand increases, the size of the price increase resulting from a tax _____ and the share of the tax borne by consumers _____.

5.5 The demand for coffee is relatively inelastic. Therefore, we would expect _____ to pay a relatively large share of a tax on coffee.

5.6 **The Employment and Wage Effects of a Luxury Boat Tax.** Suppose the luxury boat industry initially employs 1,000 workers and produces 100 boats per month. Suppose a tax on luxury boats increases the equilibrium price from $300,000 to $345,000. The price elasticity of demand for luxury boats is 2.0.

a. The luxury tax increases the equilibrium price of boats by _____ percent, so it decreases the quantity of boats demanded from 100 to _____. If builders continue to employ 10 workers for each boat, the number of boat workers decreases from 1,000 to _____.

b. Suppose the workers in the industry respond to the luxury boat tax by agreeing to take a wage cut that decreases the cost of producing boats by 5 percent. In addition, suppose firms pass on the savings in labor costs to boat consumers. The wage reduction decreases the price of boats by _____ percent and increases the quantity of boats demanded from _____ to _____. If builders continue to employ 10 workers for each boat, the number of boat workers is _____.

5.7 **Cutting the Hotel Tax.** Suppose your city initially has a $20-per-night tax on hotel rooms, paid in a legal sense by the hotel. Under the tax, the equilibrium price of hotel rooms is $80 per night. (Related to Application 5 on page 145.)

a. Draw a supply-demand graph to show the effects of eliminating the tax.

b. How does the elimination of the tax affect the equilibrium price of hotel rooms?

c. How does the elimination of the tax affect the wages of hotel workers?

d. Is the change in the price greater than, less than, or equal to $20? Why?

5.8 **Shifting a Housecleaning Tax.** Consider a city where poor people clean the houses of rich people. Initially, housecleaning firms charge their customers $10 per hour, keep $1 per hour for administrative costs, and pay their workers $9 per hour. Like many luxury goods, the demand for housecleaning service is very elastic. Housecleaning workers are not very responsive to changes in the wage.

a. Use supply and demand curves to show the initial equilibrium in the market for cleaning services (price = $10 per hour; quantity = 1,000 hours of cleaning per week), and label the equilibrium as point *a*.

b. Suppose the city imposes a tax of $3 per hour on cleaning services, and one-third of the tax is shifted forward to consumers. Use your graph to show the effects of the tax on the housecleaning market. Label the new equilibrium as point *b*. What is the new price?

c. Is it reasonable that only one-third of the tax is shifted forward? Explain.

d. Suppose that firms continue to keep $1 per hour for administrative costs. Predict the new wage.

e. Who bears the bulk of the housecleaning tax, wealthy households or poor ones?

5.9 **Effects of a Higher Fish Tax.** In Figure 6.10 on page 144, suppose the fish tax is $2 per pound of fish instead of $1. Draw a graph to show the effect of the $2 tax. In the new equilibrium, the price is $_____, the quantity is _____, and the deadweight loss from the tax is $_____.

5.10 **Tax Eliminates a Market?** Use a supply and demand graph to show a situation in which a tax on no. 3 pencils reduces the equilibrium quantity of no. 3 pencils to zero.

ECONOMIC EXPERIMENT

GOVERNMENT INTERVENTION

Recall the market equilibrium experiment from Chapter 4. We can modify that experiment to show the various forms of government intervention in the market. After several trading periods without any government intervention, you can change the rules as follows:

- The instructor sets a maximum price for apples.
- The instructor sets a minimum price for apples.
- The instructor issues licenses to a few lucky producers.
- The instructor divides producers into domestic producers and foreign producers, and some of the foreign producers are excluded from the market.

NOTES

1. Edward L. Glaeser, Joseph Gyourko, Raven Saks, "Why is Manhattan So Expensive? Regulations and the Rise in Housing Prices," *Journal of Law and Economics* 48 (2005), pp. 331–369.

2. J. K. Smith, "An Analysis of State Regulations Governing Liquor Store Licensees," *Journal of Law and Economics* (October 1982): 301–319; David Kirp and Eileen Soffer, "Taking Californians to the Cleaners," *Regulation* (September–October 1985): 24–26.

3. D. W. Taylor, "The Economic Effects of Direct Regulation of Taxicabs in Metropolitan Toronto," *Logistics and Transportation Review* (June 1989): 169–182; Laura Brown, "Hub Cabbie Hopefuls Cry: The Russians Are Coming!" *Boston Herald*, December 16, 1998.

4. *The Economic Effects of Significant U.S. Import Restraints* (Washington, D.C.: U.S. International Trade Commission), initial report in 1993, update in 1996; Joseph F. François, Hans-Hinrich Glismann, Dean Spinanger, "The Cost of EU Trade Protection in Textiles and Clothing," Kiel Institute for the World Economy, March 2000, 49.

5. Laura Brown, "Hub Cabbie Hopefuls Cry: The Russians Are Coming!" *Boston Herald*, December 16, 1998.

Consumer Choice: Utility Theory and Insights from Neuroscience

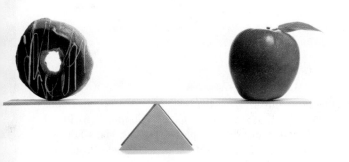

Consumer choice often involves a battle between instant and delayed gratification. For example, a consumer might choose between a donut, with its immediate taste and sugar sensations, and an apple, with its contribution to future health.

In fact, the very act of consumption involves a choice of spending money now rather than saving for the future. The outcome of the battle between instant and delayed gratification is determined by a person's self-control.

Scientists have been exploring the mental processes involved in self-control. One line of inquiry led to the following question: *Why do societies have curse words that everyone knows but no one is supposed to use?* One possibility is that suppressing the urge to use a curse word strengthens our self-control systems in the same way that calisthenics like jumping jacks strengthen our muscles. Calisthenics are not useful by themselves, but they build up our muscles for tasks that really matter. Perhaps resisting the urge to curse builds up our willpower to help resist the urge to eat unhealthy food, smoke tobacco, and go into debt.

A number of experiments have shown that seemingly trivial exercises improve self-control. In one experiment, subjects were told to improve their posture, sitting up straight rather than slouching. After two weeks of resisting the urge to slouch, the subjects performed much better on tasks that required self-control. By overriding their habit of slouching, the subjects boosted their willpower and stamina in tasks that had nothing to do with posture. Similar improvements in self-control occurred for right-handed subjects who switched to the left hand to perform everyday tasks.[1]

LEARNING OBJECTIVES

- Explain the equimarginal principle and apply it to consumer choice.

- Describe the income and substitution effects of a price change.

- Describe the general process involved in the valuation of the benefits and costs of a consumer good.

- Apply the insights from neuroscience to consumer decisions about nutrition and saving.

MyEconLab
MyEconLab helps you master each objective and study more efficiently.

*i*n Chapter 4, we introduced the law of demand, which is shown graphically by a negatively sloped demand curve. In this chapter, we'll use the theory of consumer choice to provide the economic logic behind the law of demand. The theory is based on the notion that consumers maximize their level of satisfaction, or utility, given the constraints dictated by their income and the prices of consumer goods. As we'll see, every point on a demand curve represents the best affordable choice for a consumer at a particular price.

The first two parts of this chapter use traditional utility theory to explore consumer decision-making. Under the utilitarian framework developed by Jeremy Bentham and John Stuart Mill in the eighteenth century, every action generates a benefit ("pleasure" to the utilitarians) and a cost ("pain" to the utilitarians), and taking an action is sensible if the benefit exceeds the cost. Applying the marginal principle to the consumer choice problem, a consumer will buy a product if the marginal benefit exceeds the marginal cost. We will use this utilitarian logic to explain the law of demand and the negatively sloped demand curve.

The first two parts of the chapter provide a self-contained treatment of traditional consumer choice and demand theory. So it is possible to stop at the end of Part 2 and still get a thorough understanding of consumer decision making and the law of demand. In other words, the third and fourth parts of the chapter can be skipped without loss of continuity.

The third part of the chapter introduces recent advances in neuroscience that are relevant to consumer decision-making. In the last few decades, neuroscientists have explored the brain activity associated with making decisions, and can now map and measure the neural activity involved in consumer choice. Specifically, neuroscientists observe neural activity representing both the benefit and the cost of consuming a product. Based on the observed neural activity, neuroscientists can predict consumer choice: if the benefit activity is stronger than the cost activity, a consumer is likely to buy the product. In other words, the utilitarians got it right: consumers base their decisions on the benefits and costs of a particular product. And the utilitarians were correct in imagining that some day it would be possible to actually measure the utility associated with consuming a product.

The fourth part of the chapter integrates some insights from neuroscience into our model of consumer choice. We can use the integrated model to address the following questions.

- Why do consumers eat unhealthy food? Why so many donuts and so few apples?
- Why do people save so little money for the future?
- Why do most people who want to quit smoking fail in their efforts to quit?
- Why do people play lotteries when the typical player pays $10 to get an average payoff of about $5?

The lessons from neuroscience help explain puzzling consumer behavior. In addition, we can use the insights from neuroscience to identify strategies to change consumer behavior—to eat fewer donuts, to save more money, and to quit smoking.

7.1   Traditional Consumer Choice: Utility Theory

Consider a consumer who has a fixed budget to spend on movies (m) and books (b). The consumer's objective is to maximize its level of utility (satisfaction), subject to its budget constraint. In other words, the consumer wants to find the best affordable bundle of movies and books.

Consumer Constraints: The Budget Line

A consumer's ability to purchase movies and other goods is limited by her income and the prices of movies and other products. Suppose the consumer has a fixed income of $27 per month, which she spends entirely on movies and books. The price of movies is $3 and the price of books is $1.

A consumer's budget line shows all the combinations of two goods that exhaust the budget. In Figure 7.1, if the consumer spends her entire $27 budget on books, she gets 27 books and no movies (point *r*). At the other extreme, she can spend her entire budget on movies, getting 9 movies at a price of $3 per movie (point *v*). The points between these two extremes are possible too. For example, she could reach point *s* (1 movie and 24 books) by spending $3 on movies and $24 on books, or point *u* (6 movies and 9 books) by spending $18 on movies and $9 on books.

The slope of the budget line is the opportunity cost of a movie in terms of books. Mathematically, the slope is the ratio of the price of the good shown on the horizontal axis (movies, with a price of $3), to the price of the good shown on the vertical axis (books, with a price of $1). In this example, the slope is 3 books per movie: a movie is three times as expensive as a book, so the opportunity cost of a movie is the three books that could be purchased instead.

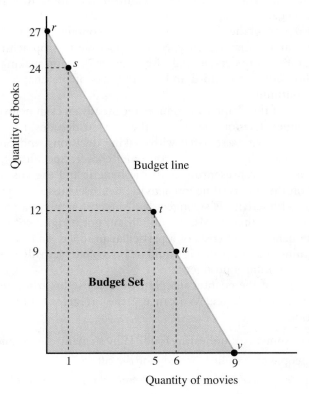

▲ **FIGURE 7.1**
Budget Set and Budget Line
The budget set (the shaded triangle) shows all the affordable combinations of books and movies, and the budget line (with endpoints *r* and *v*) shows the combinations that exhaust the budget.

A consumer's budget set is the set of affordable combinations of two goods. The budget set includes the budget line—combinations that exhaust the budget—as well as combinations that cost less than the consumer has to spend, leaving the consumer with leftover money. In Figure 7.1, the consumer's budget set is shown as a shaded triangle. She can afford any combination on or below the budget line, but cannot afford combinations above it.

It's important to distinguish the budget line from a demand curve. Although the budget line may look similar to a consumer's demand curve, they are very different graphical tools. The budget line shows the different combinations of two goods that a consumer can buy. In contrast, the demand curve shows the quantity of a single good that a consumer is willing to buy at different prices.

Total and Marginal Utility

The consumer's objective is to maximize its utility. The upper panel of Figure 7.2 shows the relationship between the number of movies watched and the total utility from movies. As the number of movies increases, total utility increases. The utility from 5 movies (point *a*) is 225 utils and the utility from 6 movies (point *b*) is 261 utils, so the marginal utility of the sixth movie is 36 utils (261 – 225). This is shown in the lower panel of Figure 7.1 by point *e*, where the marginal utility of the sixth movie is 36 utils. As the number of movies increases, utility increases, but at a decreasing rate. The utility from 9 movies (point *d*, 351 utils) is 27 utils greater than the utility from 8 movies (point *c*, 324 utils). This is shown in the lower panel by point *f*, where the marginal utility of the ninth movie is 27 utils. As the number of movies increases, utility will continue to increase, but at a decreasing rate.

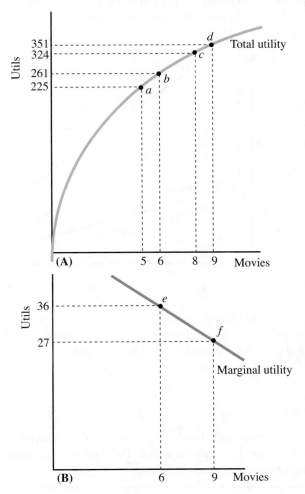

▲ **FIGURE 7.2**
Total Utility and Marginal Utility
A: The total utility or satisfaction from movies increases with the number of movies, but at a decreasing rate. B: The marginal utility from movies decreases as the number of movies increases.

The shapes of the utility curves reflect the law of diminishing marginal utility. The basic idea is that the first unit of a product generates more additional satisfaction or utility than the second unit, which generates more additional utility than the third, and so on. In graphical terms, this means that as the number of movies increases, the total utility curve becomes progressively flatter: the slope of the total utility curve decreases. The marginal utility curve shows the slope of the total utility curve, so by the law of diminishing marginal utility, it is negatively sloped.

It will be useful to derive one more utility curve. In Figure 7.3, the upper curve is the familiar marginal-utility curve, with a marginal utility of 36 utils for the 6th movie, compared to 27 utils for the 9th movie. The lower curve shows the marginal utility per dollar on movies, assuming that the price of movies is $3. For the 6th movie, the marginal utility per dollar spent on movies is 12 utils (36 utils/$3). At the margin, each dollar spent on movies (each dollar spent on the 6th movie) increases the consumer's utility by 12 utils. In popular language, this is the marginal bang per buck spent on movies: the increase in consumer utility (bang) per dollar (buck). As shown by point d, the marginal utility per dollar spent on the 9th movie is 9 utils (27 utils/$3). The marginal bang per buck decreases from 12 utils for the 6th movie to 9 utils for the 9th movie, reflecting the law of diminishing marginal utility.

▲ **FIGURE 7.3**

Marginal Utility and Marginal Utility per Dollar

The marginal utility of movies decreases as the number of movies increases, reflecting the assumption of diminishing marginal utility. The marginal utility per dollar equals the marginal utility divided by the price of movies.

The Marginal Principle and the Equimarginal Rule

Consider a consumer who has a fixed budget to spend on movies (m) and books (b). We can use the marginal principle to model the consumer's decision about how to allocate the budget between the two products.

MARGINAL PRINCIPLE

Increase the level of an activity as long as its marginal benefit exceeds its marginal cost. Choose the level at which the marginal benefit equals the marginal cost.

To maximize utility, a consumer picks the quantity of a product at which the marginal benefit of the product equals its marginal cost. For a movie, the benefit is the utility generated by the movie, so the marginal benefit is simply the marginal utility of a movie.

$$MB(movie) - MU_m$$

The law of diminishing returns tells us that the marginal benefit decreases as the number of movies increases.

Consider next the cost associated with consuming a product. To compute the marginal cost of a movie, we use the principle of opportunity cost.

THE PRINCIPLE OF OPPORTUNITY COST
The opportunity cost of something is what you sacrifice to get it.

For a consumer who buys movies and books, the opportunity cost of a movie is the utility sacrificed by getting one movie rather than some number of books. The number of books sacrificed per movie is determined by the prices of the two goods. The number of books sacrificed per movie equals the price of movies divided by the price of books:

$$Books\ per\ Movie - \frac{p_m}{p_b}$$

For example, if $p_m = 3$ and $p_b = 1$, movies are three times as expensive as books, so the consumer sacrifices three books per movie. In utility terms, the marginal cost of a movie (the utility lost from getting one movie rather than some number of books) equals the number of books sacrificed times the marginal utility of books (the utility lost per book):

$$MC(movie) - \frac{p_m}{p_b}MU_b$$

For example, if the price ratio is 3 and the marginal utility of a book is 12 utils, the marginal cost of a movie is 3 books sacrificed per movie times the 12 utils lost per book not purchased, or 36 utils.

To satisfy the marginal principle, the marginal benefit of movies equals the marginal cost. Using the expressions for the marginal benefit and the marginal cost of movies, the marginal benefit equals the marginal cost if

$$MU_m - \frac{p_m}{p_b}MU_b$$

We can rewrite this in a more convenient way. If we divide both sides of the equation by p_m we get

$$\frac{MU_m}{p_m} - \frac{MU_b}{p_b}$$

To satisfy the marginal principle, a consumer chooses the quantities of movies and books such that the marginal utility per dollar spent on movies equals the marginal utility per dollar spent on books. This is the equimarginal rule:

EQUIMARGINAL RULE
Pick the combination of two activities where the marginal benefit per dollar for the first activity equals the marginal benefit per dollar for the second activity.

In other words, the consumer chooses the quantities of movies and books such that the two products have the marginal bang per buck (the same marginal utility per dollar).

Conditions for Utility Maximization

The consumer's objective is to maximize the utility generated by a fixed budget. Utility is maximized when the chosen bundle of goods satisfies two conditions.

1 *Equimarginal rule.* The equimarginal rule is satisfied: the marginal utility per dollar on movies equals the marginal utility per dollar on books.

2 *Affordability.* The money spent on the two goods adds up to the fixed budget for the two goods: the chosen bundle is just affordable, meaning that it is on the budget line.

To summarize, the consumer chooses the affordable bundle that satisfies the equimarginal rule.

Figure 7.4 illustrates utility maximization for a consumer with a budget of $27 for movies and books. The left panel shows the marginal utility per dollar on movies, assuming a movie price of $3. The right panel shows the marginal utility per dollar on books, assuming a book price of $1. Points *a* and *b* show the utility-maximizing bundle of 6 movies and 9 books.

▲ FIGURE 7.4

The Equimarginal Rule: Equalize the Marginal Benefit per Dollar

The consumer picks the affordable bundle at which the marginal utility per dollar on movies equals the marginal utility per dollar on books. This is shown by point *a* (6 movies) and point *b* (9 books). Starting from any other affordable combination, the consumer can do better by reallocating the budget in favor of the good with the larger marginal utility per dollar. For example, starting from points *c* and *d*, movies have a larger marginal utility per dollar, so the consumer can increase utility by choosing more movies and fewer books.

1 *Equimarginal rule.* For each good, the marginal utility per dollar is 12 utils.

2 *Affordability.* The consumer spends $18 on movies ($3 × 6 movies) and $9 on books ($1 × 9 books), for a total of $27. This corresponds to point *u* in Figure 7.1.

The bundle is affordable and satisfies the equimarginal rule, so it generates the highest affordable utility level.

We can illustrate the logic of the equimarginal rule by showing what happens when it is violated. Consider another bundle, the one shown by points *c* (fewer than 6 movies), and *d* (more than 9 books). This bundle does not satisfy the equimarginal rule: the marginal utility per dollar for movies (greater than 12 utils per dollar) exceeds the marginal utility per dollar for books (less than 12 utils per dollar). For one dollar switched from books to movies, the gain in movie utility (the marginal utility per dollar of movies) exceeds the loss in book utility (the marginal utility per dollar of books), so the consumer's utility increases. Starting from points *c* and *d*, a consumer can do better by spending more on movies, the product with the larger marginal bang per buck. In general, whenever the equimarginal rule is violated—whenever the marginal utility per dollar of one good exceeds the marginal utility per dollar on a second good—the consumer can increase utility by shifting the budget in favor of the good with the larger marginal bang per buck.

Table 7.1 provides a detailed view of the utility-maximization process. The first two columns show the affordable bundles of movies and books, that is, the bundles on the consumer's budget line shown in Figure 7.1. Columns 3 and 4 show the marginal utility numbers for movies and books. Moving down through the table, the number of movies increases, and, consistent with the law of diminishing marginal utility, the marginal utility of movies decreases, from 51 utils for the first movie to 48 utils for the second movie, and so on. As we move down through the table, the number of affordable books decreases, so the marginal utility of books increases, from 2 utils for the 24th book, to 4 utils for the 21st book, and so on. Columns 5 and 6 show the numbers for the marginal utility per dollar for movies and books, assuming a movie price of $3 and a book price of $1. As we move down through the table, the marginal bang per buck of movies decreases, from 17 utils to 16 utils, and so on, while the marginal bang per buck of books increases, from 2 utils to 4 utils, and so on.

TABLE 7.1 Utility Maximization

Movies	Books	Marginal Utility: Movies	Marginal Utility: Books	Marginal Utility per $: Movies	Marginal Utility per $: Books	Utility from Movies	Utility from Books	Total Utility
1	24	51	2	17	2	51	216	267
2	21	48	4	16	4	99	210	309
3	18	45	6	15	6	144	198	342
4	15	42	8	14	8	186	180	366
5	12	39	10	13	10	225	156	381
6	**9**	**36**	**12**	**12**	**12**	**261**	**126**	**387**
7	6	33	14	11	14	294	90	384
8	3	30	16	10	16	324	48	372

The last three columns of Table 7.1 show that utility is maximized when the equimarginal rule is satisfied. In column 7, the utility from movies increases from 51 utils for one movie to 99 utils for two movies (51 from the first movie + 48 from the second movies), to 144 for three movies (51 + 48 + 45), and so on. To compute the

application 1

MEASURING DIMINISHING MARGINAL UTILITY

APPLYING THE CONCEPTS #1: How does marginal utility change with the quantity consumed?

Neuroscientists have used brain imaging techniques to provide some insights into the law of diminishing marginal utility. The scientists offered subjects in an experiment varying monetary rewards, and observed the neural activity in a subject's striatum, the region of the brain responsible for the valuation of rewards. As the monetary reward increased, the subjective benefit (the utility value, as measured in neuron activity) increased, but at a decreasing rate. In other words, the larger the reward, the lower the marginal utility of the reward money. For example, starting with a $15 reward, the marginal utility was 1 util per dollar, but starting with a $150 reward, the marginal utility was only 0.25 utils per dollar. Although this experiment does not provide a direct demonstration of the law of diminishing marginal utility for a particular product, it does show that general rewards are subject to diminishing marginal utility. **Related to Exercise 1.10.**

numbers in Column 8, we work from the bottom up. From the bottom of Column 2, for the first three books, the marginal utility per book is 16 utils, so the utility from the first 3 books is 48 utils. Working upward, the additional utility from the next trio of books is 42 (equal to 14 utils per book times 3 books), so the utility from 6 books is 90 utils (48 + 42). Continuing to move upward in Column 8, the utility from books increases to 126 utils for 9 books, 156 for 12 books, and so on. Column 9 shows total utility, the sum of utility from movies and books. Moving down through the column, total utility increases from 267 (equal to 51 + 216), to 309, and so on until we reach a total of 387 utils with the bundle of 6 movies and 9 books. Beyond that point, total utility decreases. As shown by the bold numbers in the row associated with 6 movies and 9 books, utility is maximized when the equimarginal rule is satisfied: the marginal utility per dollar of movies (12 utils = 36 utils/$3) equals the marginal utility per dollar of books (12 utils = 12 utils/$1).

7.2 The Law of Demand and the Individual Demand Curve

We can use our model of consumer choice to demonstrate the law of demand and derive an individual demand curve. In addition, we can decompose the effect of a change in price into two effects: the substitution effect and the income effect.

Effect of a Decrease in Price

Suppose the price of movies decreases from $3 to $2. In the left panel of Figure 7.5, the curve shifts upward: a decrease in price increases the marginal utility per dollar of movies. In other words, the lower the price of movies, the larger the marginal bang per buck for movies. For the original choice of 6 movies, the marginal bang per buck increases from 12 utils (36 utils/$3, shown by point *a*) to 18 utils (36 utils/$2, shown by point *c*).

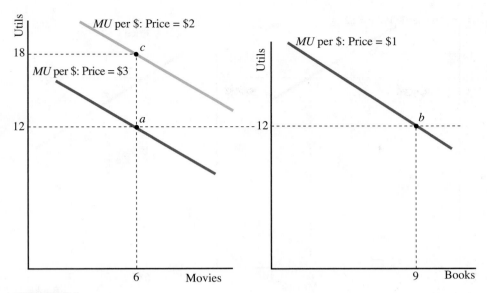

▲ **FIGURE 7.5**

A Decrease in the Price of Movies Increases the Utility-Maximizing Number of Movies

A decrease in the price of movies shifts the movie benefit curve (MU per $ of movies) upward.
At the original bundle (6 movies and 9 books), the MU per $ of movies (18 utils at point *c*) exceeds
the MU per $ of books (12 utils at point *b*), so the consumer increases the number of movies.

The decrease in the price of movies means that the original bundle violates the equimarginal rule. As shown by points *c* and *b*, the marginal utility per dollar on movies (18 utils) now exceeds the marginal utility per dollar on books (12 utils). Given the larger marginal bang per buck for movies, the rational consumer will reallocate the budget in favor of movies. In other words, a decrease in the price of movies increases the quantity of movies demanded: the consumer obeys the law of demand.

How far will the consumer go in response to a decrease in the price of movies? In Figure 7.6, the consumer chooses points *d* and *e*, with 10 movies and 7 books. This bundle satisfies the two conditions for utility maximization.

1 *Equimarginal rule.* For each good, the marginal utility per dollar is 14 utils.

2 *Affordability.* The consumer spends $20 on movies ($2 × 10 movies) and $7 on books, for a total of $27.

In this case, a decrease in the movie price from $3 to $2 increases the quantity of movies demanded from 6 to 10, consistent with the law of demand.

The same logic applies, in reverse, to an increase in the price of movies. An increase in price decreases the marginal utility per dollar on movies, shifting the marginal-bang-per-buck curve downward. At the original bundle of 6 movies and 9 books, the marginal bang per buck of movies will be less than the marginal bang per buck of books (12 utils). The consumer will respond by reallocating the budget away from movies, consistent with the law of demand: An increase in price decreases the quantity of movies demanded.

▲ **FIGURE 7.6**

Income and Substitution Effects of a Decrease in Price

For a price of movies of $2, utility is maximized at points *d* and *e*, with 10 movies and 7 books. The move from point *c* to point *s* is the substitution effect of the decrease in price, and the move from point *s* to point *d* is the income effect of the decrease in price.

Income and Substitution Effects of a Decrease in Price

We've seen that a decrease in price increases the quantity of movies demanded. We can break down the increase in the quantity demanded into two separate effects. The first is the substitution effect.

- **Substitution effect.** A decrease in the price of movies decreases the price of movies relative to the price of books, causing the consumer to substitute movies for books.

We can show the substitution effect with a simple thought experiment. Suppose that when price of movies decreases from $3 to $2, we decrease the consumer's nominal income from $27 to $21. In other words, the consumer's nominal income drops by $6, leaving just enough money to afford the original bundle of 6 movies (a cost of $12) and 9 books (a cost of $9). The price reduction is exactly offset by the $6 decrease in nominal income, meaning that the consumer's real income hasn't changed.

If the original bundle of movies and books is just affordable at the lower price, will the consumer choose it? As shown by points *c* and *b* in Figure 7.6, the still-affordable original bundle of 6 movies and 9 books violates the equimarginal rule: the marginal bang per buck of movies is 18 utils, compared to 12 utils for books. The consumer will reallocate the $21 budget in favor of movies. The new movie price is twice the book price, so for each additional movie, the consumer sacrifices 2 books. In Figure 7.6, the consumer moves downward along the movie curve, starting from point *c*, and moves upward along the book curve, starting from point *b*.

The consumer will continue to shift money toward movies at a 2:1 rate until the equimarginal rule is satisfied. In Figure 7.6, this happens at point *s* for movies and point *t* for books, with a marginal utility per dollar of 16 utils for both movies and books. In the movie panel, the move from point *c* to point *s* is the substitution effect of the decrease in price. Holding the consumer's real income constant (by cutting the nominal income to make the original bundle just affordable), movie consumption increases from 6 to 8 movies.

The substitution effect is not the end of the consumer response to a decrease in price. The second response is the income effect.

- **Income effect.** A decrease in the price of movies increases the consumer's real income (purchasing power), and the consumer will buy more of all "normal" goods, including movies.

Recall that our thought experiment for the substitution effect cut nominal income by $6 to keep real income constant. To show the income effect of a decrease in price, we simply undo the $6 cut in nominal income. In other words, we give back the $6 and see how the consumer responds to the additional income.

The consumer will use the equimarginal rule to allocate the additional income. For each additional dollar, the consumer will spend the dollar on the good with the larger marginal utility per dollar. When the additional income is all spent, the marginal utility per dollar on movies will equal the marginal utility per dollar on books. In Figure 7.6, the consumer moves downward along the movie curve starting from point *s*, and moves downward along the book curve starting from point *t*. The movement downward along the curves continues until all the additional $6 is spent. In Figure 7.6, this happens at points *d* for movies and e for books.

- **Movies:** The quantity increases from 8 to 10, meaning that the consumer spends $4 of the additional $6 on movies. The income effect is the increase in movies from 8 to 10.
- **Books.** The quantity increases from 7 to 9, meaning that the consumer spends $2 of the additional $6 on books.

At points *d* and *e*, the equimarginal rule is satisfied: for both goods, the marginal utility per dollar is 14 utils.

We can summarize the two effects of a decrease in the price of movies. The substitution effect causes the move from point *c* to point *s*, an increase in movie consumption from 6 to 8 movies. The income effect causes the move from point *s* to point *d*, an increase in movie consumption from 8 to 10 movies. In this simple example, the substitution effect is equal to the income effect. In general, the substitution effect will not be the same as the income effect. But for normal goods, the two effects operate in the same direction. A decrease in price increases the relative attractiveness of the good, causing substitution in favor of the good (the substitution effect). In addition, a decrease in price increases the consumer's purchasing power (real income), increasing the quantity demanded of all normal goods (the income effect).

The Individual Demand Curve

Figure 7.7 shows the individual demand curve for our hypothetical consumer. At the initial price of $3, the consumer maximizes utility with 6 movies (point *i*). A decrease in price to $2 increases the quantity demanded to 10 movies (point *j*). The move from point *i* to point *j* reflects both the substitution effect and the income effect of a decrease in price. The consumer observes the law of demand, consuming a larger quantity of movies because (a) movies are less costly relative to books and other goods (the substitution

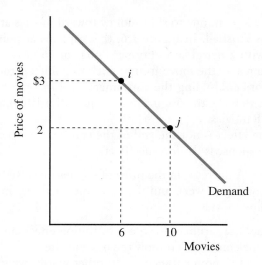

▲ **FIGURE 7.7**

The Individual Demand Curve

When the price of a movie is $3, the consumer maximizes utility at point *i*, with 6 movies. At a price of $2, utility is maximized at point *j*, with 10 movies.

application 2

A REVENUE-NEUTRAL GASOLINE TAX

APPLYING THE CONCEPTS #2: How would a simultaneous increase in the gasoline tax and a decrease in the income tax affect gasoline consumption?

Suppose the national government imposes a new tax of $3 per gallon gasoline, which will bring gasoline taxation in the U.S. closer to the levels experienced in European countries. And suppose the gasoline tax is combined with a cut in income taxes to ensure that total tax revenue doesn't change. In other words, the gasoline tax is revenue neutral. How will such a tax policy affect total gasoline consumption?

It may be tempting to conclude that the change in tax policy will not change gasoline consumption. After all, the policy doesn't change the tax liability of the typical taxpayer: the increase in gasoline taxes is offset by a decrease in income taxes. This was the logic of Ronald Reagan in his campaign for president against John Anderson, who proposed a revenue-neutral increase in the gasoline tax. Reagan said that the idea was silly because it simply took money from one of the taxpayer's pockets and put it back into the other pocket.

This logic is faulty because it ignores the substitution effect of a price change. For example, consider the typical taxpayer Mr. Evgeny Slutsky, who buys 300 gallons of gasoline per year. He will pay $900 in gasoline taxes per year, while his income taxes will be cut by $900 per year. So Evgeny can still afford to do what he did before the change in taxes: his original bundle of gasoline and other goods is still affordable. Although Evgeny can still afford his original choice, that's not the best choice. As we've seen in our discussion of the substitution effect, the gas tax decreases the marginal utility per dollar spent on gasoline, which is now less than the marginal utility per dollar spent on other goods. Gasoline now generates a lower marginal bang per buck, and the rational response for Evgeny is to buy less gasoline and more of the other goods, which now have a larger marginal bang per buck. This is the substitution effect in action, and we know for sure that a revenue-neutral increase in the gasoline tax will decrease gasoline consumption. **(Related to Exercise 2.8.)**

effect) and (b) the decrease in price increases the consumer's real income, increasing the quantity of all "normal" goods, including movies (the income effect).

We could use the same process to derive other points on the individual demand curve. For example, an increase in price would generate substitution and income effects that decrease the quantity of movies demanded.

- **Substitution effect.** An increase in the price of movies increases the price of movies relative to the price of books, causing the consumer to substitute books for movies.
- **Income effect.** An increase in the price of movies decreases the consumer's real income (purchasing power), and the consumer will buy less of all "normal" goods, including movies.

The key lesson is that each point on a demand curve shows the utility-maximizing choice for a particular price.

7.3   The Neuroscience of Consumer Choice

In this part of the chapter we explore the mental processes involved in consumer decision-making. Neuroscientists have developed techniques to map and measure the brain activity involved in the valuation of the benefits and costs of various actions, including a consumer's product choice. By integrating the insights from neuroscience into our economic model of consumer choice, we can gain a deeper understanding of how consumers make decisions and why consumers sometimes make choices that appear to be irrational.

The Neuroscience of Benefit Valuation

Recent work in neuroscience shows that different regions of the brain are involved in the valuation of the benefits and costs of possible actions. Starting on the benefit side, the key region for the valuation of benefits is the Nucleus Accumbens (NAcc), the main part of the ventral striatum. When a person considers taking an action, the NAcc is activated, and the greater the anticipated benefit from the action, the stronger the NAcc activity. For example, if you think about buying an apple, your NAcc will be activated, and the more you expect to enjoy an apple, the stronger the brain activity. The strength of the NAcc activity associated with a particular product is determined by past experience. If you've had good apple experiences in the past, the NAcc activity generated by thinking about eating an apple will be relatively strong.

The calibration of the regions of the brain involved in benefit valuation comes from the brain's dopamine system. Dopamine is the reward chemical of the brain—when it flows over receptors in your brain, you feel good. When you consider buying a product such as an apple, your brain uses its past experience to form a conjecture about the likely pleasure and satisfaction from eating the apple. The greater the conjectured satisfaction, the greater the flow of dopamine to the receptors in your brain. It's important to note that the dopamine flow starts before you eat the apple. When you actually eat the apple, your brain will check its reward systems to see if its conjecture about the pleasure from the apple is realized. If the conjectures are realized—if the brain correctly predicted the pleasure—the (correct) dopamine flow continues.

Learning happens when a consumer's conjectures about the pleasure of consuming a product are wrong. For example, suppose you anticipate a sweet apple and thus have a large dopamine flow, but the first bite generates a sour taste. The invalidation of the brain's conjecture causes an abrupt decrease in the dopamine flow, causing an abrupt reduction of the good feelings produced by dopamine. The brain is especially sensitive to a decrease in the flow of dopamine, so the sour apple provides a memorable lesson: Some apples are sour. The next time you consider eating an apple, your conjectured pleasure—and dopamine flow—will be lower. In the other direction, if you are pleasantly surprised by the wonderful taste of an apple, you will update and upgrade your conjectures for the next time you consider eating an apple. Over years or decades of consumption, errors in benefit conjectures allow the brain to fine-tune its valuation of the benefits of different products. In effect, the dopamine system allows us to learn from our mistakes, honing our valuation of the benefit of all sorts of products.

How does your brain assess the benefit of a product you've never consumed? For a new product, the brain uses the notion of association, basing its benefit valuation on past experiences with similar products. For example, the first time you consider eating a pear, your brain may associate the pear with a look-alike fruit such as an apple, triggering NAcc activity of a similar strength. Over decades of choices, the NAcc uses the dopamine system to learn the benefits of a wide variety of products, providing an inventory of benefit valuations that can be used directly for repeat purchases and used indirectly for new products.

It's important to note that these benefit valuations are gut feelings that occur without any thinking or reflection. When you see an apple, the NAcc benefit valuation is instantaneous, without any conscious thought of the taste and the rewards from reducing your hunger. These gut feelings are calibrated by the dopamine trial and error system. Given the discomfort of the penalty for an error (the interruption of the dopamine flow), the brain quickly hones its benefit conjectures to more closely match the actual benefits from consuming the product.

The Neuroscience of Cost Valuation

On the cost side, the key regions for cost valuation are the insular cortex (insula for short) and the amygdala. These interconnected regions express aversion to various actions. For example, activity in the insula increases when you see someone in pain or imagine a foul odor. Insula activity also increases when you consider losing something of value such as money. The aversion to spending money is consistent with the principle of opportunity cost.

PRINCIPLE OF OPPORTUNITY COST
The opportunity cost of something is what you sacrifice to get it.

The money spent on one product cannot be used on another product, so it is natural that the brain reacts in a negative way (in the region that expresses aversion) to the thought of spending money. The higher the price of a product, the greater the opportunity cost of the product, and thus the stronger the activity of the insula.

It is not yet clear to neuroscientists how the insula is calibrated to represent, in neuron activity, the cost of buying a product. The leading theory is that the value of money is learned from conditioned association. For example, suppose you lose $10 (by misplacing it, giving it away, or spending it on a product), and that means you can't buy a $10 book you really want. You will experience a gut-feeling sense of loss from not getting the book. This gut feeling comes from a certain level of neuron activity, which you then associate with the $10 loss. If you lose $20 and then cannot go to a $20 concert, the loss of the concert opportunity will generate neuron activity that you will associate with the $20 loss. Over time, you will learn from experience what it means, in terms of neuron activity, to lose different amounts of money. This learning process incorporates the cost of spending money into your gut feelings. When you imagine spending a particular dollar amount, you will have an instantaneous gut-feeling reaction, a result of neuron activity that is based on learning from past experience. This learning process essentially builds opportunity cost into your gut feelings and neuron activity.

To summarize, neuron activity in the insula represents the dollar cost of buying a product. Although the mechanism that calibrates the insula has so far been elusive, we do know that the higher the price of a product, the stronger the insula activity. It's important to note that these cost valuations are gut feelings that occur without any thinking or reflection. When you look at the price tag on apple, the cost valuation in your insula is instantaneous.

The Wisdom of Gut Feelings

Scientists use a classic experiment, the Iowa Gambling Task, to demonstrate the power and wisdom of gut feelings. The subjects in the experiment draw cards from four different decks, and each card triggers either a monetary reward or a penalty. Two of the decks have favorable cards (on average, a positive payoff), and two have unfavorable cards (on average, a negative payoff and relatively large penalties). The subjects don't have any prior knowledge of the features of the decks, but they learn as they draw cards. The key question is, How long will it take for the subjects to start drawing exclusively from the favorable decks?

Scientists use skin-conductivity sensors attached to the subjects' hands to track their gut feelings. When the brain senses that a person is about to take a harmful action, it sends an alarm in the form of increased sweat production that increases the electrical conductivity of a subject's skin. In this case, the harmful action is reaching for an unfavorable deck and the possibility of a relatively large penalty. By observing the conductivity of the subjects' hands, scientists observe the timing of the gut-feeling alarm. On average, the alarm for the unfavorable decks starts after a subject has drawn only 10 cards. Based on only 10 trials, the dopamine learning system has seen enough: when the subject reaches for an unfavorable deck, the brain activates the sweat glands as a warning of an imminent harmful action.

Most subjects don't immediately heed the gut-feeling warning. On average, it takes a subject about 50 cards to respond to the warning and stop drawing from the unfavorable decks. At this point, the typical subject cannot explain why he or she started avoiding the unfavorable decks. Although the subjects' choices are affected by their gut feelings, they cannot articulate the reasons. After about 60 cards, the typical subject can finally explain their avoidance of the unfavorable decks.

The Iowa Gambling Task reminds us that the brain quickly processes lots of information without our knowledge. The dopamine learning system is unconscious, and generates gut feelings that are useful in assessing the benefits and costs of actions. Although the expression of the gut feelings is instantaneous, the feelings are based on experiences that go back hours or years. The brain is continuously monitoring our actions, using its dopamine learning system to hone its valuation of benefits and costs. Although we may not be able to articulate our gut feelings, these feelings reflect the wisdom of experience.

Scientists have used the Iowa Gambling Task to study the brain's learning system. They observed the choices of subjects whose amygdala (part of the cost-valuation system) was disabled. These subjects never learned to draw exclusively from the favorable deck. The data from skin conductivity tests explained their choices: the alarm system that warned normal subjects to avoid the unfavorable decks did not work in the disabled subjects. The disabling of the amygdala prevented the brain from learning which decks were unfavorable, so there were no gut-feeling alarms.

Cognition and Choice

To decide whether to take an action, a person compares the anticipated benefit of the action to its anticipated cost. The principal decision-making region of the brain is the prefrontal cortex (PFC). The PFC observes the benefit-valuation activity in various regions of the brain, and uses these activity levels as inputs into the decision-making process. In other words, the PFC uses gut feelings as inputs into the decision-making process.

Scientists have used variations on the Iowa Gambling Task to demonstrate the role of the PFC in decision-making. Scientists gave the task to people whose PFCs were disabled in the regions responsible for comparing gut-feeling benefits to gut-feeling costs. The subjects with disabled PFCs never learned to avoid the unfavorable decks, despite the fact that the regions of their brains responsible for valuing gut-feeling benefits and costs (NAcc and insula) functioned normally. This experiment shows the role of the PFC in processing benefit and cost information that originates in other regions of the brain.

The PFC is not a simple calculator of gut-feeling benefits and costs, but incorporates other factors into the decision-making process. The PFC uses cognition (conscious thought) to consider a broad set of possible consequences of an action. For example, suppose you have decided to buy either a donut or an apple, each of which costs $1. At the gut-feeling level, the consideration of each product will trigger activity in your NAcc in anticipation of the benefit of consumption, and this gut-feeling benefit will be transmitted to the PFC. Suppose the donut generates a stronger gut-feeling benefit, reflecting its delightful sugar and fat content. If you rely exclusively on your gut feeling, you will choose the donut. But you could use your PFC to incorporate other considerations into the decision. For example, you could stop to think about the health consequences of the high-fat donut. If the unfavorable health consequences of the donut seem large enough, you will ignore your gut feelings and choose the apple instead.

The dorsal-lateral portion of the PFC (DLPFC) is responsible for introducing other factors into the decision-making process. In particular, the DLPFC incorporates the possible future consequence of an action. Neuroscientists use transcranial magnetic stimulation (TMS) to down-regulate (partially disable) the DLPFC of subjects, and then observe their choices. The subjects with disabled DLPFCs make impulsive choices based on gut feelings rather than thoughtful choices based on cognition. For example, the subjects grab a small immediate reward rather than waiting a relatively short time for a larger reward. The general effect of disabling the DLPFC is to make the subjects more selfish and impulsive. In our example of the apple versus the donut, a person with a disabled DLPFC is more likely to choose the donut because he or she will ignore the long-term health consequences.

Why do people make different choices? People differ in two ways that are relevant to consumer decisions.

- **Strength of their gut feelings.** On the benefit side, consumers differ in the gut-feeling benefit of consuming a product, as represented by the strength of activity in the NAcc. On the cost side, consumers differ in the gut-feeling cost of spending money, as represented by the strength of activity in the insula. Consumers with relatively active insulas are tightwads (reluctant to spend money), while consumers with relatively quiet insulas are looser with their money.
- **Cognitive weighting.** Consumers who are relatively inactive in a cognitive sense tend to make impulsive purchases (the donut). In contrast, cognitively active consumers tend to exercise more self-control and make more thoughtful purchases (the apple). In one experiment, scientists were able to divide subjects into two groups: the self-controllers had relatively active DLPFCs, indicating lively cognition that generated non-impulsive behavior; the non-self-controllers had less active DLPFCs, indicating cognitive passivity that generated impulsive behavior.

Predicting Consumer Choice

We've seen that neuroscientists map and measure the brain activity associated with consumer decisions. After observing a consumer's brain activity while he or she considers different options, scientists can actually predict the consumer's choice. In the SHOP experiment (save holdings or purchase), scientists showed a consumer different products and prices, and observed the levels of activity in the NAcc (for benefit valuation), insula (for cost valuation), and PFC (benefit-cost analysis). The scientists used the observed activity levels to predict which product the consumer actually purchased. Although the scientists' predictions were not perfect, they were much better than would occur by chance.

Fuel for Cognition

As we've seen, the decision-making process that occurs in the PFC is complex. As a result, the cognitive process consumes a large amount of energy in supporting neurons as they perform their various tasks. The brain gets most of its energy from glucose (aka blood sugar), and operates effectively only when it has a plentiful supply of glucose.

To demonstrate the importance of glucose as brain fuel, scientists perform the following experiment. A subject is forced to make a series of decisions, each of which engages the cognitive process (considering benefits and costs and then making a choice). This engagement of the cognitive process burns glucose. After a long series of challenging decisions, the subject is asked to perform a task that requires cognition, for example solving a difficult puzzle. Compared to a control group (people who had not depleted their glucose by making decisions), the subjects were less persistent in trying to solve the puzzle. The simple lesson is that the depletion of cognitive fuel makes people less inclined to engage their cognitive systems.

The fuel requirements of cognition have important implications for consumer decision making. As we've seen, cognition can replace impulsive decisions (simply go with your gut) with thoughtful decisions that consider both gut feelings and other factors. A person with a low level of glucose is more likely to skip the energy-consuming cognitive process and make an impulsive decision. It doesn't take much energy to go with your gut feelings, and if you're low on fuel, that is the natural response.

Cognitive processing is particularly important in making consumer decisions that involve many options. To illustrate, consider the process of buying a new car, which typically involves a series of choices about style (color), performance (acceleration, fuel economy), and features (seats, sound systems). As a customer goes through a long series of decisions about style, performance, and features, each decision engages the cognitive process and consumes brain fuel. Eventually, the depletion of cognitive fuel causes decision fatigue, and the consumer is more likely to rely exclusively on gut feelings, making impulsive rather than thoughtful decisions.

The same logic applies when a consumer faces a large number of options for a single product. For example, consider a consumer who faces a display with 50 different types of toothbrushes. The consumer will naturally engage the cognitive process, assessing the benefits and costs of each toothbrush and weighing the trade-offs. Given the large number of options, the deliberative process will burn a lot of brain fuel and reduce the consumer's ability to effectively engage the cognitive process. A consumer may respond to the depletion of brain fuel in one of three ways: (a) simplify matters by focusing on a single dimension of the product (price, color, shine), (b) abandon cognition and make an impulse buy, or (c) abandon the decision-making process altogether and refrain from buying a toothbrush.

application 3

STORES VS. ONLINE RETAILERS

APPLYING THE CONCEPTS #3: How do the sales strategies of conventional stores and online retailers differ?

Conventional stores encourage shoppers to buy products by boosting the neural activity in the NAcc, the region of the brain responsible for the valuation of the benefit of a product. Some of the benefit boosting comes from tactile stimulation—feeling the softness of a cashmere sweater or the bounce of an athletic shoe. Conventional stores also down-regulate the insula, the region of the brain responsible for the valuation of the cost of a product. The suppression of insula activity comes from price reductions and low-price guarantees. On-line retailers can work with the insula by offering discounted prices and low-price guarantees, but they are at a disadvantage in boosting the neural activity in the NAcc. There is currently no substitute for the tactile sensations available in physical stores, so online retailers have an incentive to focus on products for which the stimulation of the NAcc is less critical to making a sale. **Related to Application 3.7.**

SOURCE: Based on Jonah Lehrer, "The Neuroscience of Groupon," *Wired*, September 8, 2011.

The problems caused by having too many options are illustrated by the famous jam experiment. Researchers ran the experiment in a fancy food store in Menlo Park, California. They set up a table with samples of jam, sometimes offering 6 different flavors, and other times offering 24 flavors. Although shoppers were more likely to stop by the table with more flavors, they were less likely to actually buy jam. After the taste test, only 3 percent of the shoppers at the 24-flavor table bought jam, compared to 30 percent at the 6-flavor table. The simple lesson is that sometimes having too many options makes it difficult to choose.

7.4 Consumer Decisions: Insights from Neuroscience

In this part of the chapter, we incorporate the key insights from neuroscience into our model of consumer choice. Specifically, we apply the equimarginal rule to several consumer decisions in which the engagement of the cognitive process—the forward-looking DLPFC—may change behavior as consumers switch from impulsive choices to more thoughtful choices. Some scientists speculate that the evolutionary development of the DLPFC in humans increased our fitness (likelihood of survival) because it gave us the ability to incorporate long-term considerations into the decision-making process.

Dietary Choice: Donut versus Apple

Consider the decision between healthy and unhealthy food. Suppose a consumer has a fixed budget of $10 to spend on apples and donuts, each of which has a price of $1. The gut-feeling benefit of the high-fat donut is relatively high: neuroscientists have shown that the subjective pleasantness of the oral texture of fat generates a high level of neural activity in the NAcc. In the left panel of Figure 7.8, the upper curve shows the gut-feeling marginal utility per dollar of donuts.

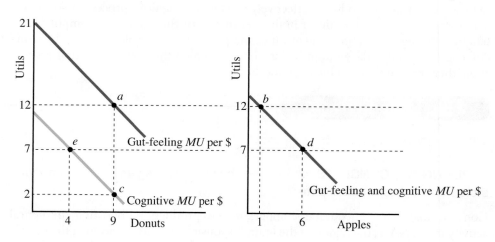

▲ FIGURE 7.8

Gut Feelings versus Cognition: Donuts versus Apples

For a decision based exclusively on gut feelings, a consumer using the equimarginal rule chooses points a and b (9 donuts and 1 apple). The engagement of the cognitive process decreases the perceived MU per $ of donuts, so at the original bundle (9 donuts, 1 apple), the MU per $ is 2 utils for donuts (point c), compared to 12 utils for apples (point b). The new utility-maximizing choice is shown by points e and d: cognitive engagement decreases donut consumption from 9 to 4 and increases apple consumption from 1 to 6.

Consider first the outcome for a consumer who relies exclusively on gut feelings. In this case, utility is maximized with point *a* (9 donuts) and point *b* (1 apple). This bundle satisfies the two conditions for utility maximization.

1   *Equimarginal rule.* For each good, the marginal utility per dollar is 12 utils.

2   *Affordability.* The consumer spends $9 on donuts and $1 on apples, for a total of $10.

In this case, a consumer who simply goes with his or her gut feelings eats a lot of donuts.

How does cognition affect the consumer's choice? Recent experiments by neuroscientists have shown that the more a person thinks about the health consequences of an unhealthy food like a donut, the lower the perceived benefit of the unhealthy food. In terms of neural activity, the DLPFC modulates (in this case reduces) the neural activity that signals the benefit of the donut. In the left panel of Figure 7.8, the lower curve shows the cognitive marginal utility per dollar: the incorporation of health concerns shifts the benefit curve downward. For the 9th donut, the marginal utility per dollar decreases from 12 utils (point *a*) to 2 utils (point *c*). The marginal utility per dollar of donuts (2 utils) is now less than the marginal utility per dollar of apples (12 utils, as shown by point *b*). The consumer's rational response is to buy more apples and fewer donuts. In other words, cognition that incorporates long-term health concerns decreases donut consumption and increases apple consumption.

How far will the consumer go in substituting apples for donuts? Since the price of each good is $1, the consumer trades off one donut for each additional apple, moving upward along the donut benefit curve (starting at point *c*) and downward along the apple curve (starting from point *b*). The consumer will continue substituting apples for donuts until the two products generate the same marginal utility per dollar (the same marginal bang per buck). This occurs at point *e* (4 donuts) and point *d* (6 apples), with a common marginal utility per dollar of 7 utils. The switch from impulsive choice (based on gut feelings) to thoughtful choice (based on cognition that incorporates health consequences) increases apple consumption at the expense of donuts.

What are the implications of brain fueling for dietary choices? Our gut feelings for food and nutrition are biased toward high-fat and high-calorie foods, meaning that impulsive choices generally lead to unhealthy choices. Although the cognitive process can counteract this bias by introducing health concerns, this requires cognitive fuel. So the best way to make healthy food choices is to shop when your brain is fully fueled and ready for impulse control, not when you are hungry and thus susceptible to impulsive decisions. An added problem with shopping while hungry is that a glucose-depleted brain seeks immediate refueling, and the quickest refueling comes from sugary food.

Present Bias: Spending versus Saving

Consider the broad consumer decision about how much income to spend now, and how much to save for the future. Since any money saved will eventually be spent, this is essentially a decision about the timing of consumption, now versus later. We can use the utilitarian framework to explore decisions about spending and saving.

Gut feelings are visceral, in-the-moment sensations, and humans are myopic with respect to gut feelings. In other words, humans do a poor job imagining the strength of future gut feelings, including the gut-feeling benefits of future consumption. Experiments by psychologists and neuroscientists have consistently shown that people systematically underestimate the strength of future gut feelings, both positive (benefits of consumption) and negative (monetary cost). Our underestimation of future consequences means that humans are subject to present bias: we accurately incorporate the present consequences of an action, but either ignore or underestimate the future consequences. This present bias can lead to misguided decisions, but the bias can be counteracted by cognitive processing.

Figure 7.9 illustrates utility maximization with respect to spending versus saving. In the left panel, the benefit curve shows the marginal utility per dollar spent in the present. For current consumption, gut feelings accurately represent the benefit of consumption. In the right panel, the lower curve shows the benefit of saving (the benefit of future consumption) for a consumer subject to present bias: the consumer systematically underestimates the future benefit of consumption. In the case of a consumer subject to present bias, utility is maximized with point *a* (spend $19 now) and point *b* (save $1 for the future). This bundle satisfies the two conditions for utility maximization.

1 *Equimarginal rule.* For both spending and saving, the marginal utility per dollar is 14 utils.

2 *Affordability.* The consumer spends $19 now and saves $1, for a total of $20.

In this case, a consumer who goes with his or her gut feelings doesn't save much.

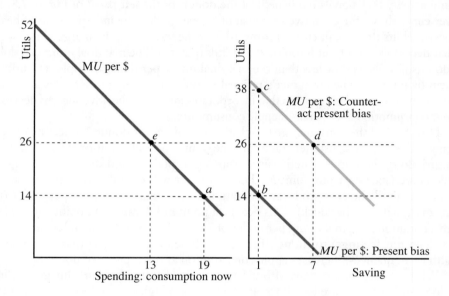

▲ **FIGURE 7.9**
Present Bias and Spending versus Saving
A consumer subject to present bias chooses points *a* and *b* (spend $19 and save $1). Cognition that reduces present bias increases the perceived MU per $ of saving, so at the original bundle (spend $19, save $1), the MU per dollar is higher for saving (point *c* versus point *a*). The new utility-maximizing choice shown by points *e* and *d*: cognitive engagement increases saving from $1 to $7 and decreases spending (consumption now) from $19 to $13.

Consider next a consumer who uses cognition to offset present bias. In the right panel of Figure 7.9, the upper curve shows the benefit curve for a consumer who engages the DLPFC and thus increases the perceived benefit of future consumption: cognition offsets present bias and shifts the benefit curve upward. For example, for the first dollar saved, the marginal utility per dollar increases from 14 utils (point *b*) to 38 utils (point *c*). The marginal utility per dollar of saving (38 utils) now exceeds the marginal utility per dollar of spending (14 utils). The consumer's rational response is to save more and thus have more to spend on future consumption. As in the case of the apple versus the donut, the engagement of the DLPFC incorporates the future consequences of a present action, and thus reduces impulsive behavior (spend most of the money now).

How much more will the consumer save? As current spending decreases and saving increases, the consumer moves upward along the spending benefit curve (starting at point *a*) and downward along the saving curve (starting from point *c*). The consumer will continue to increase saving until the marginal utility per dollar of saving equals the marginal utility per dollar of spending. This occurs at point *e* ($13 spent now) and point *d* ($7 saved), with a common marginal utility per dollar of 26 utils. The switch from impulsive choice (based on gut feelings) to thoughtful choice (based on cognition) increases saving and future consumption at the expense of current consumption.

Consumers use a number of strategies to counteract present bias and increase saving. Some workers pre-commit to regular saving programs, directing their employers to take out a fixed amount of money from each paycheck. This approach eliminates the monthly decision of how much to save, reducing the cognitive effort required to overcome present bias. Another commitment strategy is to join savings clubs such as a Christmas saving club that saves a fixed amount each month leading up to Christmas. In micro-finance programs in the less developed world, participants band together in small groups to monitor each others' savings programs and enforce commitments to save. The basic strategy behind these programs is for the consumer/saver to pre-commit to a saving program, and then get someone else to enforce the rules. This approach economizes on cognitive effort and reduces impulsive spending.

Present bias occurs because there is a mismatch in the timing of benefits and costs. In the case of saving for retirement, the cost occurs in the present (lower current consumption), while the benefit occurs in the future. One approach to counteracting present bias is to shift the cost of contributing to retirement accounts from the present to the future. For example, some employers allow new employees to delay their investment in a retirement account for a year or two. This approach avoids the powerful gut-feeling cost of contributing now, and puts the costs and the benefits of saving for retirement on an equal temporal footing: they are both in the future. By simply shifting the cost into the near future (even if the cost occurs sooner than the benefit), the employer counteracts present bias, increasing investment in retirement accounts.

Present Bias and Credit Cards

Consider next the implications of present bias for a consumer who purchases a product with a credit card. Credit cards cause a different sort of temporal mismatch between benefits and costs. In this case, the benefit of a product will be experienced now, but the cost will be delayed until some future date. Neuroscientists have measured the brain activity associated with cash purchases (pay now) and credit-card purchases (pay later). Consistent with the notion of present bias, credit-card purchases generate much weaker activity than cash purchases: the insula, which indicates cost (the degree of aversion or disgust), is relatively quiet for credit-card purchases. In other words, using a credit card weakens our gut-feeling aversion to spending money.

We can use cognition to counteract the failure of our gut feelings to represent future costs. Once the PFC recognizes the under-representation of the future cost, we can upgrade the perceived cost of a credit-card purchase, perhaps by imagining how it would feel to pay with cash. Alternatively, we can remind ourselves that a credit-card charge will eventually require a cash payment. In one experiment, people making credit-card purchases were simply shown their credit-card statements. A quick look at the credit-card balance triggered activity in the insula that was similar to the activity associated with cash purchases, thus eliminating present bias. Some organizations have developed mobile apps that send reminders to consumers about their credit-card balances, thereby activating the insula and mitigating present bias.

Present Bias and Smoking

The decision to smoke cigarettes is subject to present bias because there is a temporal mismatch between the present benefit (the good feeling from nicotine) and a future cost (health problems). Some people continue to smoke even when smoking is not in their long-term interest. One response to this case of present bias is to use self-imposed penalties to move the cost of smoking to the present. This allows a direct comparison of present benefit and present cost. For example, a smoker could commit to contribute $50 to a charitable organization for each cigarette smoked, and get someone else to enforce the commitment. Under this approach, when someone considers lighting up a cigarette, he or she instantaneously experiences both a gut-feelings benefit and a gut-feeling cost of losing $50. The increase in the present cost of smoking increases the likelihood that a smoker will quit.

Experiments with self-imposed penalties demonstrate their effectiveness. In one experiment, each subject voluntarily deposited the money that he or she would normally spend on cigarettes into a bank account that paid no interest. After six months, any subject who tested positive for nicotine forfeited the money in the account. Compared to a control group that was offered an alternative stop-smoking program, the smokers in the bank-account program were about 40 percent more likely to be nonsmokers after a year (six months after the program ended).

Another approach to pre-commitment comes from stickK.com. You start by picking your goal (stop smoking, lose weight, exercise regularly), and then pick your penalty and choose a referee to monitor your progress and impose any penalties. The penalty could be as light as emails from stickK.com to your friends informing them you are falling short of your goal, or it could be a financial penalty such as $50 deducted from your bank account and paid to your favorite charity. For extra incentive, you can send your penalty money to an anti-charity, an organization whose goals you vehemently oppose. In late 2011, nearly $9 million in potential penalties was in play, with over 120,000 commitments and over 2 million cigarettes not smoked. For people who pre-commit to a monetary penalty, the reported success rate is 80%, compared to only 35% for people without a monetary penalty.

Gambling as a Consumer Good

Why do people gamble when the expected reward is negative? For example, the typical state-run lottery pays out roughly half of what it takes in, so on average a person who plays the lottery for $10 can expect a payoff of roughly $5. Neuroscientists have discovered a possible reason for this seemingly irrational behavior.

Consider a simple gambling game. You put on a blindfold and draw a single ball from an urn that has three balls, marked #1, #2, and #3. As shown in the first row of the table in Figure 7.10, you win $12 if you draw #3, but get nothing if you draw #1 or #2. In this case, the expected monetary payoff equals the probability of winning (1/3) times the $12 prize, or $4. Suppose the cost of the gamble is $6: Each time you draw a ball from the urn you pay $6. If you draw a ball repeatedly, on average the payoff will be $4 per draw, or two-thirds the $6 cost per draw. This doesn't sound like a very attractive gamble: why pay $6 for an average payoff of $4?

A near miss is defined as an outcome that seems to be close to a winning outcome (a better label might be "near win"). In the case of drawing a ball from the urn, a person might consider drawing ball #2 a near miss in the sense 2 is close to 3, the winning number. Neuroscientists have discovered that the brain's dopamine reward system treats a near miss almost the same as a real win: the flow of dopamine generated by a near miss is almost the same as the flow generated by an actual win. In the second row of numbers in Figure 7.10, the dopamine benefit for a near miss (drawing #2) is 9 utils, which is almost as large as the 12-util reward for an actual win.

	Draw			Expected benefit
	#1	#2	#3	
Monetary benefit ($)	0	0	12	$4 = 1/3 × $12
Dopamine benefit (utils)	0	9	12	7 utils = 1/3 × 9 + 1/3 × 12

▲ **FIGURE 7.10**

Near-Miss Benefits and Gambling as a Consumer Good

If you draw ball #3, you win $12. The expected monetary value of drawing a ball from the urn is $4 = 1/3 × $12. Suppose the dopamine benefit of winning is 12 utils, while the dopamine benefit for a near win (drawing ball #2) is 9 utils. The expected dopamine value of drawing a ball is 7 utils = 1/3 × 9 + 1/3 × 12.

The consideration of the dopamine benefits of near misses makes the gamble more attractive. There is a two-thirds chance of drawing #2 or #3, meaning that there is a two-thirds chance of getting a dopamine reward of at least 9 utils. More precisely, the expected dopamine reward is 7 utils, computed as the sum of two components:

- 4 utils = 1/3 × 12: a one-in-three chance of getting 12 utils by drawing #3
- 3 utils = 1/3 × 9: a one-in-three chance of getting 9 utils by drawing #2

On average, the dopamine reward is 7 utils, compared to a cost of $6 per draw from the urn. The consumer will take the gamble if the average reward of 7 utils exceeds the cost—the utility loss associated with paying $6 to draw a ball.

Because the brain rewards near misses with pleasure-generating dopamine, gambling can be considered a consumer good. The expected monetary payoff of the gamble is negative: the consumer pays $6 for an average payoff of $4, so the "price" of the gamble is the $2 lost, on average, on each ball draw. The consumer can buy dopamine brain rewards, exchanging a monetary loss of $2 per ball draw for a dopamine reward that averages 7 utils per draw.

Although the dopamine reward for near misses seems puzzling, scientists suggest that there is evolutionary rationale for this feature of the learning system. The reward for a near miss encourages skill acquisition. Suppose you are a basketball novice, and you want to learn how to shoot the basketball successfully. As a beginner, you are unlikely to make many shots, but you might occasionally hit the rim. If there are rewards only for successful shots, you may get discouraged and give up after a few dozen shots. As a result, you may never acquire the skill. In contrast, if you are rewarded for your occasional near miss (a rim shot) the rewards will encourage you to keep trying. In addition, the reward for a near basket will provide important feedback on what it takes to get close, and you can use this feedback to adjust your actions and get even closer. The reward for near baskets encourages you to keep trying, making it more likely that you will develop your shooting skills. In other words, rewards for near misses promote the acquisition of skills.

The dopamine rewards for near misses are problematic in truly random environments like gambling. In the case of drawing balls from an urn, rolling dice, or playing a slot machine, there are no skills to master: no matter how much you practice, you cannot increase your probability of drawing ball #3, rolling snake eyes, or getting a triple on the slot machine. But if the brain reward for a near miss is almost the same as a reward for an actual win, you have an incentive to keep playing (and losing money) despite the lack of skill acquisition. In a sense, you are buying the brain reward (pleasurable dopamine flow) with the money you leave behind.

application 4

TAXING CIGARETTES TO OFFSET PRESENT BIAS

APPLYING THE CONCEPTS #4: What is the appropriate cigarette tax?

The present bias that leads some people to smoke cigarettes raises an important policy question: Can we use taxes on cigarettes to offset present bias and actually make people better off in the process? A recent study concludes that to fully offset the present bias that underlies the decision to smoke, the appropriate tax is roughly $11 per pack of cigarettes.

The authors of the study focused on the effects of smoking on premature death. Smoking cuts the lifespan of the typical smoker by roughly 6 years, and given the economic value of one year of life, we can translate the cost associated with premature death into a cost of roughly $36 per pack of cigarettes. If smokers did not suffer from present bias, their present choices would fully reflect this future cost, meaning that they would compare the benefit of smoking (the nicotine experience) to the full cost of a pack of cigarettes (the purchase price plus the $36 cost associated with premature death). But present bias is sufficiently strong that a tax of roughly $11 per pack is required to ensure that the typical smoker considers the full cost associated with premature death. This tax put the benefits and costs of smoking on an equal temporal footing: a tax of $11 moves the neglected future cost to the present, allowing a person to make choices that consider the full benefits and costs of smoking.

How would the cigarette tax affect low-income households? Because smoking is more prevalent among the poor, a cigarette tax imposes a relatively large tax burden on low-income households: lower-income households spend a much larger fraction of their income on cigarettes and cigarette taxes. The authors of the study suggest that the cigarette tax would actually be beneficial for low-income households. The reason is that low-income households are relatively responsive to changes in the price of cigarettes, so they would experience a relatively large reduction in smoking, and a relatively large increase in lifespan. Of course, the whole idea of the tax is to reduce smoking, and anyone who quits gets the benefit of a longer lifespan and avoids paying the $11 tax too. **Related to Exercise 4.7.**

SOURCE: Based on Jonathan Gruber, Botond Koszegi, "A Modern Economic View of Tobacco Taxation," (Paris: International Union against Tuberculosis and Lung Disease, 2008).

SUMMARY

This chapter uses traditional utility theory, which originated with the utilitarians of the eighteenth century, to explain the economic logic behind the law of demand. We also use the insights of modern neuroscience to explore the distinction between impulsive and thoughtful consumer decisions. Here are the main points of the chapter.

1 The law of diminishing marginal utility: As the consumption of a product increases, utility increases at a decreasing rate.

2 The equimarginal rule: To maximize utility, choose the affordable bundle of goods such that the marginal utility per dollar spent on one good equals the marginal utility per dollar spent on a second good.

3 The individual demand curve is negatively sloped because a decrease in price (a) decreases the relative price of the good, causing consumers to substitute the good for other goods (the substitution effect) and (b) increases the consumer's real income, increasing the consumption of all normal goods (the income effect).

4 For some goods, thoughtful decisions (based on cognition) differ from impulsive decisions (based on gut feelings). Some examples are food choices (donut vs. apple) and saving decisions (consume now vs. later).

5 One explanation for consumers taking gambles that have a negative expected monetary payoff is that there are brain rewards (dopamine) for near misses as well as actual wins.

7.1 Traditional Consumer Choice: Utility Theory

1.1 Based on Figure 7.1, fill the blanks in the following table to identify different points on the consumer's budget line.

Quantity of movies	2	4	6	8
Quantity of books	__	__	__	__

1.2 In Figure 7.1, suppose the price of movies increases to $9. Draw a new budget line. The horizontal intercept of the budget line is _____ and the slope of the budget line is _____ .

1.3 In Figure 7.2, if the total utility from seven movies is 294 utils, the marginal utility of the seventh movie is _____ utils, which is _____ than the marginal utility of the sixth movie.

1.4 As the consumption of a product increases, utility _____ (increases/decreases) at a _____ (increasing/decreasing/constant) rate, so the marginal utility curve is _____ sloped. This illustrates the law of _____ .

1.5 In Figure 7.3, suppose the price of movies decreases to $2. The marginal utility per dollar of the sixth movie is _____ utils.

1.6 Suppose the marginal utility of a video game is 48 utils and the marginal utility of an iTunes song is 2 utils. The price of a video game is $12 and the price of a song is $1. The opportunity cost of a video game is _____ songs and the marginal cost of a video game is _____ utils. The marginal benefit of a video game is _____ utils.

1.7 According to the equimarginal rule, a consumer chooses the combination of two goods that equalizes the _____ per _____ on each product consumed.

1.8 The conditions for utility maximization are
   a. _____
   b. _____

1.9 Suppose a consumer has a fixed amount to spend each week on iTunes songs ($1 each) and movies ($6 each). For the combination she chose this week, the marginal utility of movies is 30 and the marginal utility of songs is 3. For next week she should _____ (increase/decrease) the number of songs and _____ (increase/decrease) the number of movies.

1.10 Brain imaging provides evidence for the law of _____ utility. (Based on Application 1 on page 160.)

1.11 *Change in Marginal Utility.* In Table 7.1, suppose the marginal utility numbers for books change: for each quantity of books, the marginal utility is 6 utils higher. For example, for 24 books, the marginal utility is 8 utils instead of 2 utils, and for 21 books, the marginal utility is 10 utils instead of 4 utils. Determine the new utility-maximizing bundle.

1.12 *Utility-Maximizing Rides and Games.* Suppose the price of amusement rides is $2 and the price of a video arcade game is $1. The following table shows points on the budget line (given an income of $30) and the associated marginal utilities. Fill in the blanks in the table and find the utility-maximizing combination of rides and games. Illustrate with a figure like Figure 7.3.

Quantity		Marginal Utility		Marginal Utility per Dollar	
Rides	Games	Rides	Games	Rides: Price = $2	Games: Price = $1
1	28	50	10		
2	26	42	14		
3	24	36	18		
4	22	26	26		

1.13 *Consumer Consultant.* You have been hired to determine whether a consumer is maximizing his utility. He has a fixed budget of $2,500 per month to spend on food and housing. The price of food is $1 per pound, and the price of housing is $3 per square foot of living space. He currently lives in a 600-square foot apartment and spends $700 on food.
   a. You can ask your client two questions—only two. What are your questions?
   b. Your client's answers indicate that he is indeed maximizing utility. What are his answers?

7.2 The Law of Demand and the Individual Demand Curve

2.1 In Figure 7.5, suppose the price of movies increases from $3 to $6. The increase in price shifts the benefit curve (marginal utility per dollar) for movies _____ (upward/downward). For the initial quantity of 6 movies, the marginal utility per dollar becomes _____ utils, which is _____ (greater/less) than the marginal utility per dollar of books.

2.2 Suppose a consumer has a budget of $100 to spend on concerts (price = $6) and carnival rides (price = $2). For each of the following pairs of points in the figure below, indicate whether the pair (i) satisfies the budget constraint, (ii) satisfies the equimarginal rule, (iii) is the best affordable bundle.
   a. Points *a* and *e*.

b. Points *b* and *h*.

c. Points *c* and *f*.

d. Points *d* and *g*.

e. Points *d* and *e*.

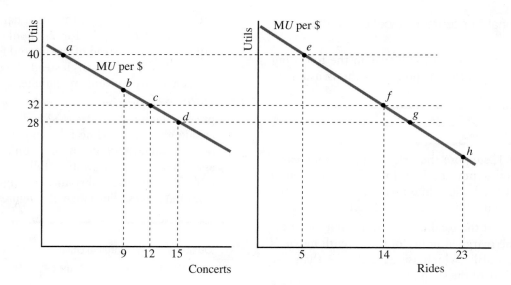

2.3 Arrow up or down: The income effect of a price change is that a decrease in price _____ a consumer's real income and _____ the consumption of a normal good.

2.4 Arrow up or down: The substitution effect is that a decrease in the price of movies _____ the relative price of movies and _____ the consumption of movies.

2.5 To show the substitution effect of a decrease in price, we _____ (increase/decrease) a consumer's nominal income so the consumer can just afford _____.

2.6 Suppose Maxine initially watches six movies at a price of $3 each and buys 9 books at a price of $1 each, and then the price of movies increases to $5. To make Maxine's original bundle just affordable, her income must _____ (increase/decrease) by _____. Her utility-maximizing consumption of movies will _____ (increase/decrease) because at the original bundle, _____ is now less than _____.

2.7 If the typical consumer buys 200 gallons of gasoline and the gasoline tax increases by $3, revenue neutrality requires that the consumer's income tax must _____ (increase/decrease) by _____. (Related to Application 1 on page 160.)

2.8 **Response to the Gas Tax.** Petrov initially pays $2,200 in income taxes and consumes 600 gallons of gasoline per year at a price of $3 per gallon. The price of the other good is $1. For Petrov's initial product bundle, the marginal utility of gas is 30 utils and the marginal utility of the other good is 10 utils. (Related to Application 2 on page 164.)

a. For his initial bundle, the marginal utility per dollar on gasoline is _____ utils.

b. Suppose the government imposes a new gasoline tax that increases the price of gas to $5. To make his initial consumer bundle just affordable, Petrov's income must _____ (increase/decrease) by _____.

c. Suppose the government cuts Petrov's income tax by the amount computed in (b). Given the new gas tax and the income tax cut, at his initial bundle, the marginal utility per dollar of gasoline is _____ utils, compared to _____ for the other good. To satisfy the marginal principle, Petrov will _____ (increase/decrease) his gasoline consumption.

2.9 *Shipping the Good Apples Out?* Suppose apples come in two quality levels, low and high. At a store in the apple-growing region, the price of low-quality apples is $1 per pound, and the price of high-quality apples is $4 per pound. Johnny lives in the apple-growing region and buys eight pounds of each type. His marginal utility of apples is 3 utils for low-quality apples and 12 utils for high-quality apples.

a. Is Johnny maximizing his utility?

b. Suppose Johnny moves to an area outside the apple-growing region. Shipping the apples to his new area adds $2 to the price of a pound of apples, for both low-quality and high-quality apples. To simplify matters, assume Johnny's income increases by an amount large enough to fully offset the higher prices of apples. In other words, he can still afford the original bundle of eight pounds of each type of apples. If he continues to buy eight pounds of apples of each type, is he maximizing his utility? If not, how should he change his mix of high- and low-quality apples?

c. What are the implications for the mix of high-quality and low-quality apples in apple-growing areas and other regions?

7.3 Neuroscience of Consumer Choice

3.1 The key region of the brain for the valuation of benefits is the _____.

3.2 In the dopamine learning system, learning happens when the _____ about the pleasure from a product are _____ (correct/wrong).

3.3 The key region of the brain for the valuation of costs is the _____.

3.4 In the Iowa Gambling Task, the brain sends an alarm to avoid drawing from the unfavorable decks after about _____ (3, 10, 25, 50, 75) cards, but the typical subject doesn't switch to the favorable decks until about _____ (3, 10, 25, 50, 75) cards.

3.5 The key region of the brain responsible for comparing benefits and costs is the _____.

3.6 The fuel for cognition is _____, and the depletion of this fuel increases the likelihood that a person will base a decision on _____.

3.7 Conventional stores encourage shoppers to buy products by boosting neural activity in _____ and reducing neural activity in the _____. (Related to Application 3 on page 169.)

7.4 Consumer Decisions

4.1 The introduction of cognition into a consumer's choice between healthy and unhealthy food shifts the _____ curve downward, causing the marginal utility per dollar of _____ to be less than the marginal utility per dollar of _____.

4.2 Consumers are subject to present bias in the sense that they systematically underestimate the strength of _____.

4.3 The introduction of cognition into a consumer's choice between consumption now and saving shifts the _____ curve upward, causing the marginal utility per dollar of _____ to exceed the the marginal utility per dollar of _____.

4.4 Compared to a cash purchase, a credit-card purchase generates _____ activity in the _____, which is responsible for valuation of the _____ (benefits/costs) of a product.

4.5 The organization stickK.com gives people the opportunity to exercise self-control by _____.

4.6 Neuroscientists have discovered that the brain's dopamine reward system of a gambler treats a _____ almost the same as a real _____. The evolutionary purpose is that the reward encourages _____.

4.7 To counteract the effects of present bias in smoking behavior, the tax per pack of cigarettes is roughly _____ ($1, $3, $11, $35) per pack. (Related to Application 4 on page 176.)

4.8 One possible reason for curse words is that they give us opportunities to exercise our _____.

4.9 *How Many Donuts?* Using Figure 7.8 as a starting point, suppose cognition shifts the MU per $ curve downward by a larger amount, as shown in the figure below. How many donuts and how many apples will the consumer choose?

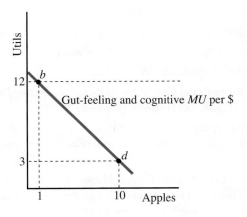

4.10 *Effects of a Donut Tax.* Using Figure 7.8 as a starting point, consider the effect of a donut tax equal to $2 per donut, which increases the price of a donut from $1 to $3. In the figure below, assume that the new (post-tax) equilibrium is shown by points *e* and *d*. Fill the blanks (shown by horizontal lines) with numbers. The marginal utility per dollar associated with point *c* is _____ utils. The number of apples associated with point *d* is _____.

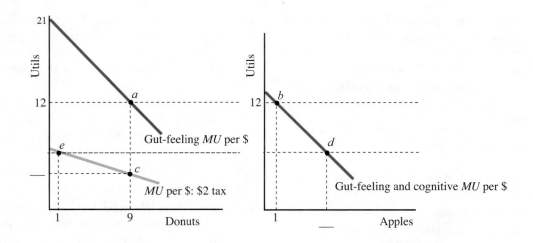

4.11 ***Effect of Consumption Tax.*** Using Figure 7.9 as a starting point, suppose the consumer chooses point *e* (spend $13 now) and point *d* (save $7). Suppose the government imposes a 20% tax on spending (consumption now), meaning that for every dollar spent now, $0.20 goes to the government, leaving only $0.80 to purchase products.

a. Use a graph to show the effect of the consumption tax on the relevant curves.

b. On your graph, show, for the initial bundle ($13, $7), the tax-induced gap between the marginal utility per dollar on spending and the marginal utility per dollar of saving.

c. Which direction will the consumer go—more spending or more saving?

NOTES

1. Baumeister, Ray, and John Tierney. Willpower (Penguin, 2011).

Our discussion of the neuroscience of consumer choice is based on a wide variety of material in books and scientific journals. In the following books, the authors explain many of the key insights from neuroscience in a non-technical fashion.

i. Lehrer, Jonas. *How We Decide* (Houghton Mifflin, 2009).

ii. Baumeister, Ray, and John Tierney. *Willpower* (Penguin, 2011).

iii. Ariely, Daniel. *Predictable Irrational* (Harper, 2008).

iv. Thaler, Richard, and Cass Sunstein. *Nudge: Improving Decisions about Health, Wealth, and Happiness* (Penguin, 2008).

The following articles from scientific journals present some key neuroscience research results that are relevant for consumer decision making.

i. Bastena, Ulrike, Guido Bieleb, Hauke R. Heekerenb, and Christian J. Fiebach. "How the brain integrates costs and benefits during decision making." *Proceedings of the National Academy of Science* 107 (50), pp. 21767–21772 (2010).

ii. Baumgartner, Thomas, Daria Knoch, Philine Hotz, Christoph Eisenegger & Ernst Fehr. "Dorsolateral and ventromedial prefrontal cortex orchestrate normative choice." *Nature Neuroscience* 14, pp. 1468–1474 (2011).

iii. Chasel, Henry and Luke Clark, Gambling Severity Predicts Midbrain Response to Near-Miss Outcomes, *Journal of Neuroscience* 30 (2010), pp. 6180–6187.

iv. Grabenhorst, Fabian, and Edmund T. Rolls. "Value, pleasure and choice in the ventral prefrontal cortex." *Trends in Cognitive Sciences* 15 (2011).

v. Hare, Todd, Colin Camerer, Antonio Rangel. "Self Control in Decision-Making Involves Modulation of the vmPFC Valuation System." *Science* 324, pp. 646–648 (2009).

vi. Hare, Todd, Jonathan Malmaud, Antonio Rangel, "Focusing attention on the health aspects of foods changes value signals in vmPFC and improves dietary choice." *Journal of Neuroscience* 31 (2011), pp. 11077–11087.

vii. Kable, Joseph and Paul W. Glimcher. "The Neurobiology of Decisions: Consensus and Controversy." *Neuron* 63 (2), pp. 733–745 (2009).

viii. Knoch, Daria and Ernst Fehr. "Resisting the Power of Temptations." *Annals of the New York Academy of Science* 1104, pp. 123–134 (2007).

ix. Knutson, Brian, Scott Rick, G. Elliott Wimmer, Drazen Prelec, and George Loewenstein. "Neural Predictors of Purchases." *Neuron* 53, pp. 147–156 (2007).

x. Pine, Alex, Ben Seymour, Jonathan P. Roiser, Peter Bossaerts, Karl J. Friston, H. Valerie Curran, and Raymond J. Dolan, "Encoding of Marginal Utility across Time in the Human Brain." *Journal of Neuroscience* 29 (2009), pp. 9575–9581.

xi. Winstanley, C., Dopamine modulates reward expectancy during performance of a slot machine task in rats: Evidence for a near-miss effect. *Neuropsychopharmacology* 36 (2011) pp. 913–925.

The following books contain collections of articles that relate recent advances in neuroscience to consumer choice

i. Dolan, Raymond, and Tali Sharot (editors). *Neuroscience of Preference and Choice* (Academic Press, 2012).

ii. Glimcher, Paul, Colin Camerer, Ernst Fehr, Russell Poldrack (editors). *Neuroeconomics: Decision Making and the Brain* (Academic Press and Elsevier, 2009).

APPENDIX TO CHAPTER 7

MENTAL SHORTCUTS AND CONSUMER PUZZLES

Although the brain has billions of cells and trillions of synapses to process information and make decisions, the decision-making process is far from perfect. Mental processing takes time and energy, and the brain uses a number of time-saving shortcuts that sometimes lead to puzzling and misguided decisions. Economists and psychologists have identified several types of puzzling consumer behavior.

- Spending choices sometimes depends on the source of income.
- The willingness to pay for a product sometimes is affected by irrelevant information.
- Product choices are sometimes influenced by irrelevant alternatives.
- Decisions are sometimes based on percentage differences rather than absolute differences.

These are ongoing puzzles in the sense that we do not fully understand the mental processes behind what appears to be misguided consumer behavior.

One possible explanation for a consumer puzzle is that people sometimes base their decisions on heuristics. A heuristic is a simple rule for dealing with a complex situation, and provides a "fast and frugal" decision. A simple rule may work well in most circumstances, but in some cases may generate misguided choices. In the case of misguided choices generated by heuristics, a key question concerns the motivation for the heuristic: What are the advantages of using a heuristic rather than a more thoughtful and deliberative decision-making process?

7A.1 Mental Accounting and Bundling

One way to economize on decision making is to separate decisions into different type or accounts. For example, a consumer could establish separate accounts for food ($300 per month) and entertainment ($100 per month). If the price of a particular food increases, the consumer would reallocate its fixed food budget, but would not consider changing its entertainment budget. This shortcut—known as mental accounting—simplifies the decision-making process because it limits the calculation of tradeoffs.

An important application of mental accounting concerns the classification of money from different sources. Consider the treatment of income that comes unexpectedly, for example, a $50 birthday gift or $50 found on the street. For many people, unexpected income is "play money" that is frequently spent on fun or frivolous purchases. In contrast, people are more careful with regular income, allocating it to buying regular goods, paying bills, and saving. Who would blame you for spending birthday cash on a restaurant meal rather than paying down your credit card or putting the money into your savings account? Similarly, money picked up off the street is considered "fun money" and not spent in the same way as regular income.

Another mental shortcut is to monitor consumption by bundles rather than individual units. People tend to track consumption by the bundles in which a product is delivered rather than the actual consumption of the product. In a famous experiment, people had the opportunity to use a scoop to get free M&Ms from a bowl. When the experimenters switched to a larger scoop, people continued to get roughly the same number of scoops, but of course a lot more M&Ms. In other words, people monitor their consumption by scoops (bundles) of the product, not the actual quantity of the product. In another experiment, diners were provided a bottomless bowl of soup: using a secret tube, the experimenters refilled the bowl every time the diner consumed some soup. The result was consistent with the notion of consumer bundling: the subjects drank much more soup than people drawing from a normal bowl of soup.

7A.2 Anchoring

Another mental shortcut is called anchoring. Suppose the brain is asked to compute the numerical value of something, for example, the amount you are willing to pay for a car or a house. In computing a numerical value, the brain tends to latch onto numbers in a seemingly random way. In the classic experiment, each participant writes down the last two digits of his or her social security number, and then bids (expresses a willingness to pay) for a t-shirt. The bizarre result is the larger the participant's social-security number, the higher the bid on the t-shirt. In other words, the social-security number provides an anchor for an unrelated mental task.

There are some important implications of the anchoring effect. A person's expressed valuation of a product is affected by the numbers in his or her head. In a negotiation over the price of a product, the seller has an incentive to plant a relatively large number in the buyer's head, while the buyer has incentive to plant a low number in the seller's head. One way to plant an anchoring number is to be the first to state a price. In other words, there is a first-mover advantage in negotiations over price. This provides one reason for relatively high (and negotiable) sticker prices on new and used cars. Using a high price as an anchor, a buyer can negotiate a lower price and feel good about getting a bargain, while the seller can get less than the anchor price but more than his or her true willingness to accept.

The notion of anchoring helps explain the large effects of "sales" for retail goods. The regular price of a product provides an anchor for your underlying value of the product. When a product goes on sale at a 20% discount, it looks like a great deal, given your anchor, the regular price. So a store that has a 20% off sale is likely to experience a relatively large increase in the quantity sold.

7A.3 The Decoy Effect

One of the most puzzling quirks of consumer decision making is the decoy effect. Consider the options for an mp3 player represented in Figure 7A.1. In the left panel, there are two options: a low-price player with a capacity of 8 GB (option A), and a high-price player with a capacity of 16 GB (option B). Suppose that in a direct comparison of A versus B, a consumer chooses A: when the consumer considers the trade-offs between price and capacity, the extra 8GB of capacity is not worth the additional $100. In a direct comparison, A is superior to B.

▶ FIGURE 7A.1

The right panel introduces a third option, a decoy. Option C has the same capacity as option B, but its price is $20 higher. The comparison of B versus C is quick and easy: the consumer doesn't have to think about any trade-offs, but simply recognizes that the extra $20 spent on C doesn't buy anything. The typical consumer will then choose option B over options A and C. The consumer focuses on the easy comparison of B versus C, and neglects the more difficult task of comparing B to A. The introduction of a clearly inferior option (the decoy C) changes the consumer's choice from A to B.

The decoy effect occurs for all sorts of preferences and decisions. In a standard decoy-effect experiment, each person in a control group is shown three faces (A, B, C) and asked to choose the most attractive face. Suppose the control group chooses A as the most attractive and C as the least attractive. For the treatment group, a fourth face (C–) is introduced, one that is similar to face C (the least attractive face) but just a bit less attractive. When the treatment group looks at four faces (A, B, C, C–) the participants tend to focus on the comparable faces C and C–, and ignore faces A and B. As a result, the treatment group picks C, not A, as the most attractive face. The decoy focuses attention on comparable faces and diverts attention from the most attractive face and thus changes the outcome.

The decoy effect has important implications for consumer decision-making. Marketers have an incentive to introduce products that are not designed to sell, but are designed to manipulate consumers into choosing a similar but superior product. A savvy consumer can use cognition to avoid being affected by the decoy effect. If you can identify a decoy and recognize the slightly better product, you could then continue evaluating the other options, rather than stopping your valuation prematurely. Assessing tradeoffs is cognitively challenging, but may be worthwhile.

7A.4 The Appeal of Percentage Changes

People use another mental shortcut to assess numerical changes, for example an increase in price. The natural inclination is to translate a numerical change into a percentage change. For example, a change in price from $1.00 to $0.90 is a 10 percent change, and so is a change from $200 to $180. The translation into percentages means that all 10% changes appear to be alike, despite the fact that 10% of $200 is much larger than 10% of $1.00.

The percentage shortcut can lead to misguided decisions. In the classic demonstration of percentage bias, we ask a consumer two questions.

1 Would you drive a dozen miles to save 10% on a quart of milk?

2 Would you drive a dozen miles to save 3% on a new chair?

The typical consumer responds "yes" to the first question, and "no" to the second question. In other words, the 10% saving on milk is worthwhile, but the 3% saving on a new chair is not. This is puzzling and illogical because a chair is much more expensive than milk. The numerical saving associated with 10% off a $1.00 quart of milk is only $0.10, but the numerical savings associated with 3% off a $200 chair is $6.00. If it is sensible to drive a dozen miles to save $0.10, why isn't it sensible to drive the same distance to save $6.00? In assessing numerical changes, the brain appears to be naturally inclined to work in percentage or relative terms rather than absolute terms, leading to misguided decisions.

As an application of the percentage shortcut, consider the provision of Internet service in hotels. A hotel can either include Internet service as part of its room charges, or have a separate charge. In general, low-price hotels include Internet service as part of the room charge, while high-price hotels have a separate charge. In a low-price hotel ($50 per night), a separate charge of $10 per day is a 20% surcharge, a relatively large surcharge in percentage term. Consumers subject to percentage bias are likely to react strongly to the seemingly large surcharge. In a hotel with a price $200 per night, a separate charge of $10 is only 5% of the price, a small enough percentage that the consumer response is likely to be relatively small.

SUMMARY

In this appendix to the chapter on consumer choice we've discussed some puzzling aspects of consumers' behavior. Here are the main points of the appendix.

1 Spending choices sometimes depend on the source of income.

2 The willingness to pay for a product sometimes is affected by irrelevant information.

3 Choices are sometimes influenced by irrelevant alternatives.

4 Decisions are sometimes based on percentage differences rather than absolute differences.

Production Technology and Cost

Consider the challenge of providing safe water to rural families in less developed countries.

In India, the conventional approach is for each family to use an individual carbon-activated filter, at a monthly cost of $2 per month. The alternative approach developed by the Byrraju Foundation exploits economies of scale in water filtration. A community filtration plant with a capital cost of $15,000 can provide clean water to 1,500 families at a monthly cost of only $1 per family. An added advantage of the filtration plant is that villagers can pay for water on a daily basis rather than being required to come up with large amounts of cash to buy the individual filter and replacement cartridges.[1]

*t*his chapter explores the relationship between the quantity of output produced and the cost of production. As we'll see, a firm's production cost is determined by its production technology—the way the firm combines capital, labor, and materials to produce output. After we explain the link between technology and costs, we'll look at the actual cost curves of several products, including aluminum, hospital services, wind power, truck freight, and airplanes.

Economists distinguish between the short run and the long run. The long run is a period long enough that a firm is perfectly flexible in its choice of all inputs, including its production facility. In contrast, when a firm cannot modify its facility, it is operating in the short run. In this chapter, we'll explore both short-run and long-run costs. In later chapters, we'll show how firms use short-run and long-run cost curves to make decisions about whether to enter a market and how much output to produce.

8.1   Economic Cost and Economic Profit

This is the first of several chapters on the decisions firms make. A firm's objective is to maximize its **economic profit**, which equals its total revenue minus its economic cost:

$$\text{economic profit} = \text{total revenue} - \text{economic cost}$$

As we saw earlier in the book, a firm's total revenue is the money it gets from selling its product. If a firm charges the same price to every consumer, its total revenue equals the price per unit of output times the quantity sold.

This chapter explores the firm's cost of production. A firm's **economic cost** equals the cost of all the inputs used in the production process; we measure it as the opportunity cost of the inputs. Recall the first key principle of economics.

> ## PRINCIPLE OF OPPORTUNITY COST
> The opportunity cost of something is what you sacrifice to get it.

To compute a firm's economic cost, we must determine what the firm sacrifices to use inputs in the production process. Economic cost is opportunity cost.

As shown in the first column of numbers in Table 8.1, a firm's economic cost can be divided into two types. A firm's **explicit cost** is its actual monetary payments for inputs. For example, if a firm spends a total of $10,000 per month on labor, capital, and materials, its explicit cost is $10,000. This is an opportunity cost because money spent on these inputs cannot be used to buy something else. A firm's **implicit cost** is the opportunity cost of the inputs that do not require a monetary payment. Here are two examples of inputs whose costs are implicit rather than explicit:

economic profit
Total revenue minus economic cost.

economic cost
The opportunity cost of the inputs used in the production process; equal to explicit cost plus implicit cost.

explicit cost
A monetary payment.

implicit cost
An opportunity cost that does not involve a monetary payment.

TABLE 8.1 Economic Cost versus Accounting Cost		
	Economic Cost	**Accounting Cost**
Explicit: monetary payments for labor, capital, materials	$10,000	$10,000
Implicit: opportunity cost of entrepreneur's time	5,000	—
Implicit: opportunity cost of funds	2,000	—
Total	17,000	10,000

- *Opportunity cost of the entrepreneur's time.* If an entrepreneur could earn $5,000 per month in another job, the opportunity cost of the time spent running the firm is $5,000 per month.
- *Opportunity cost of the entrepreneur's funds.* Many entrepreneurs use their own funds to set up and run their businesses. If an entrepreneur starts a business with $200,000 withdrawn from a savings account, the opportunity cost is the interest income the funds could have earned in the bank, for example, $2,000 per month.

a p p l i c a t i o n   1

OPPORTUNITY COST AND ENTREPRENEURSHIP

APPLYING THE CONCEPTS #1: What is the opportunity cost of an entrepreneur?

For many entrepreneurs, starting a new business means leaving paid employment. A study of Canadian workers showed that the lower a worker's earnings in paid employment, the more likely the worker was to become an entrepreneur. In other words, businesses are started by people with relatively low wages. After controlling for gender, age, education, marital status, and region, the wage gap between workers who become entrepreneurs and workers who remain in paid employment was about 12 percent. This is sensible because the lower the wage in paid employment, the lower the opportunity cost of leaving a job and starting a business. **Related to Exercise 1.8.**

SOURCE: Based on Rafael Amit, Eitan Muller, Iain Cockburn, "Opportunity Costs and Entrepreneurial Activity," *Journal of Business Venturing* 10 (1995), pp. 95–106.

Economic cost equals explicit cost plus implicit cost:

$$\text{economic cost} = \text{explicit cost} + \text{implicit cost}$$

In the first column of Table 8.1, the firm's economic cost is $17,000, equal to $10,000 in explicit cost plus $7,000 in implicit cost.

Accountants have a different approach to computing costs. Their narrower definition of cost includes only the explicit cost of inputs:

$$\text{accounting cost} = \text{explicit cost}$$

In other words, **accounting cost** includes the monetary payments for inputs, but ignores the opportunity cost of inputs that do not require an explicit monetary payment. In the second column of Table 8.1, the accounting cost is the $10,000 in monetary payments for labor, capital, and materials. **Accounting profit** equals total revenue minus accounting cost:

$$\text{accounting profit} = \text{total revenue} - \text{accounting cost}$$

A firm's accounting cost is always lower than its economic cost, so its accounting profit is always *higher* than its economic profit. For the rest of this book, when we refer to cost and profit, we mean *economic* cost and *economic* profit.

accounting cost
The explicit costs of production.

accounting profit
Total revenue minus accounting cost.

8.2   A Firm with a Fixed Production Facility: Short-Run Costs

Consider first the case of a firm with a fixed production facility. Suppose you have decided to start a small firm to produce plastic paddles for rafts. The production of paddles requires a workshop where workers use molds to form plastic material into paddles. Before we can discuss the cost of production, we need information about the nature of the production process.

Production and Marginal Product

The table in Figure 8.1 shows how the quantity of paddles produced varies with the number of workers. A single worker in the workshop produces one paddle per day. Adding a second worker increases the quantity produced to five paddles per day. The **marginal product of labor** is the change in output from one additional unit of

marginal product of labor
The change in output from one additional unit of labor.

Labor	Quantity of Output Produced	Marginal Product of Labor
1	1	1
2	5	4
3	8	3
4	10	2
5	11	1
6	11.5	0.5

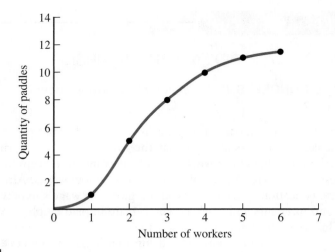

▲ **FIGURE 8.1**
Total-Product Curve
The total-product curve shows the relationship between the quantity of labor and the quantity of output, given a fixed production facility. For the first two workers, output increases at an increasing rate because of labor specialization. Diminishing returns occurs for three or more workers, so output increases at a decreasing rate.

labor. In the table, the marginal product of the first worker is one paddle, compared to a marginal product of four paddles for the second worker.

Why does the marginal product increase as output increases? As we saw earlier in the book, when a firm increases its workforce, workers can specialize in production tasks. Productivity increases because of the benefits of continuity—each worker spends less time switching between production tasks. In addition, there are benefits from repetition—each worker becomes more proficient at an assigned task. A two-worker operation produces more than twice as many paddles as a one-person operation because the two workers can specialize, one being responsible for preparing the plastic for the mold and the other for working the mold.

diminishing returns
As one input increases while the other inputs are held fixed, output increases at a decreasing rate.

Starting with the third worker, the production process is subject to **diminishing returns**, one of the key principles of economics.

PRINCIPLE OF DIMINISHING RETURNS
Suppose output is produced with two or more inputs and we increase one input while holding the other inputs fixed. Beyond some point—called the *point of diminishing returns*—output will increase at a decreasing rate.

The third worker adds three paddles to total output, down from four paddles for the second worker. As the firm continues to hire more workers, the marginal product drops to two paddles for the fourth worker and one paddle for the fifth worker. As we saw earlier in the book, diminishing returns occurs because each worker gets a smaller share of the production facility. In the paddle example, the workers share a mold; as the number of workers increases, they will spend more time waiting to use it.

total-product curve
A curve showing the relationship between the quantity of labor and the quantity of output produced, *ceteris paribus*.

Figure 8.1 shows the firm's **total-product curve**, which represents the relationship between the quantity of labor (on the horizontal axis) and output (on the vertical axis), *ceteris paribus*. The total-product curve shows the effects of labor specialization as well as diminishing returns. For the first two workers, output increases at an increasing rate because labor specialization increases the marginal product of labor. Starting with the third worker, however, total output increases at a decreasing rate because of diminishing returns.

Short-Run Total Cost

We've seen the production relationship between labor input and output, so we're ready to show the relationship between output and production cost. Suppose the opportunity cost of your time is $50 per day, and you can hire workers for your workshop at the market wage of $50 per day. You can purchase your workshop, including the building and the paddle mold, for $365,000. If the interest rate you could have earned on that money is 10 percent per year, the opportunity cost of tying up your $365,000 in the workshop is $36,500 per year, or $100 per day.

In the short-run analysis of costs, we divide production costs into two types, fixed cost and variable cost.

- **Fixed cost (FC)** is the cost that does not vary with the quantity produced. In our example, the fixed cost is the cost of the workshop, including the cost of the building and the mold. As shown in the third column of Table 8.2, the fixed cost is $100 per day, regardless of how much output is produced.

- **Variable cost (VC)** is the cost that varies with the quantity produced. For example, to produce more paddles, you must hire more workers. If the cost per worker is $50 per day, your daily variable cost is $50 times the number of workers, including you. As shown in the fourth column of Table 8.2, variable cost is $50 for one worker, $100 for two workers, and so on.

fixed cost (FC)
Cost that does not vary with the quantity produced.

variable cost (VC)
Cost that varies with the quantity produced.

TABLE 8.2 Short-Run Costs

1	2	3	4	5	6	7	8	9
Labor	Output	Fixed Cost (FC)	Variable Cost (VC)	Total Cost (TC)	Average Fixed Cost (AFC)	Average Variable Cost (AVC)	Average Total Cost (ATC)	Marginal Cost (MC)
0	0	$100	$ 0	$100	—	—	—	—
1	1	100	$ 50	150	$100.00	$50.00	$150.00	$ 50.00
2	5	100	100	200	20.00	20.00	40.00	12.50
3	8	100	150	250	12.50	18.75	31.25	16.67
4	10	100	200	300	10.00	20.00	30.00	25.00
5	11	100	250	350	9.09	22.73	31.82	50.00
6	11.5	100	300	400	8.70	26.09	34.78	100.00

To compute the firm's total cost, we simply add the fixed and variable costs. The firm's **short-run total cost (TC)** equals the sum of fixed and variable costs:

$$TC = FC + VC$$

The fifth column in Table 8.2 shows the total cost for different quantities of output. For example, one worker produces one paddle at a total cost of $150, equal to the fixed cost of $100 plus a variable cost of $50. Hiring a second worker increases output to five paddles and increases total cost to $200, equal to $100 in fixed cost and $100 in variable cost. Moving down the fifth column, the total cost rises to $250 for 8 units of output, $300 for 10 units, and so on.

Figure 8.2 shows the short-run cost curves corresponding to columns 3, 4, and 5 of Table 8.2. The horizontal line on the graph shows the fixed cost of $100. The lower of the two positively sloped curves shows the variable cost (VC), and the

short-run total cost (TC)
The total cost of production when at least one input is fixed; equal to fixed cost plus variable cost.

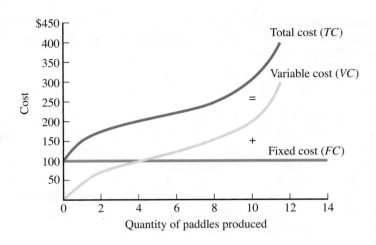

higher of the two positively sloped curves is total cost (*TC*). Total cost is the sum of fixed cost and variable cost, so the vertical distance between the *TC* curve and the *VC* curve equals the firm's fixed cost. Notice that this distance is the same at any level of output.

Short-Run Average Costs

average fixed cost (*AFC*)
Fixed cost divided by the quantity produced.

There are three types of average cost. **Average fixed cost (*AFC*)** equals the fixed cost divided by the quantity produced:

$$AFC = \frac{FC}{Q}$$

To compute *AFC* for our paddle company, we simply divide the fixed cost ($100) by the quantity of paddles produced. In Table 8.2, we divide the number in column 3 by the number in column 2. This calculation gives us the values for *AFC*, which are shown in column 6. For example, the output in the second row is one paddle, so the average fixed cost is $100 = $100/1. In the third row, output is five paddles, so the average fixed cost is $20 = $100/5. As output increases, the $100 fixed cost is spread over more units, so *AFC* decreases.

average variable cost (*AVC*)
Variable cost divided by the quantity produced.

A firm's **average variable cost (*AVC*)** incorporates the costs that vary with the quantity produced. Average variable cost equals the variable cost divided by the quantity produced:

$$AVC = \frac{VC}{Q}$$

To compute *AVC* for our paddle company, we simply divide the number in column 4 of Table 8.2 by the number in column 2. That calculation gives us the values for *AVC*, shown in column 7. For example, the output in the third row is five paddles and the variable cost is $100, so the average variable cost is $100/5 paddles, or $20 Notice that for small quantities of output, the *AVC* decreases as the quantity produced increases— from $50 for one paddle, $20 for two paddles, and so on. The *AVC* declines because of the benefits of labor specialization. Adding workers to a small workforce makes workers more productive on average, so the amount of labor required per unit of output drops, pushing down the average variable cost. In contrast, for large quantities of output, average variable cost increases as output increases because of diminishing returns. Adding workers to a large workforce makes workers less productive on average, pulling up the average variable cost. In Figure 8.3, the *AVC* curve is negatively sloped for small quantities, but positively sloped for large quantities.

A firm's total cost is the sum of its fixed cost and variable cost, so the **short-run average total cost (ATC)**, or what we'll simply call "average cost," is the sum of the average fixed cost and the average variable cost:

$$ATC = \frac{TC}{Q} = \frac{FC}{Q} + \frac{VC}{Q} = AFC + AVC$$

short-run average total cost (ATC)
Short-run total cost divided by the quantity produced; equal to AFC plus AVC.

In Figure 8.3, we go from the AVC to ATC by adding the average fixed cost to AVC. For example, for 5 paddles AFC is $20 and AVC is $20, so ATC is equal to $40, the sum of $20 + $20. For 10 paddles, the average fixed cost is lower—only $10—while the average variable cost is $20, so ATC is $30, the sum of $10 + $20. In Figure 8.3, the gap between the AVC and ATC curves is the average fixed cost.

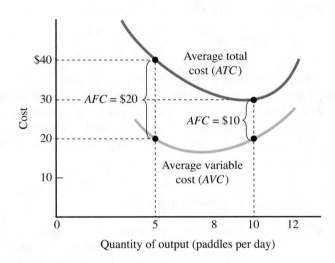

◄ FIGURE 8.3
Short-Run Average Costs
The short-run average-total-cost curve (ATC) is U-shaped. As the quantity produced increases, fixed costs are spread over more and more units, pushing down the average total cost. In contrast, as the quantity increases, diminishing returns eventually pulls up the average total cost. The gap between ATC and AVC is the average fixed cost (AFC).

The ATC curve in Figure 8.3 is negatively sloped at quantities less than 10 paddles. The negative slope results from two forces that work together to push average cost down as output increases:

- **Spreading the fixed cost.** For small quantities of output, a one-unit increase in output reduces AFC by a large amount because the fixed cost is pretty "thick," being spread over just a few units of output. For example, going from one paddle to five paddles decreases AFC from $100 to $20 per paddle.

- **Labor specialization.** For small quantities of output, AVC decreases as output increases because labor specialization increases worker productivity.

These two forces both push ATC downward as output increases, so the curve is negatively sloped for small quantities of output.

What happens once the firm reaches the point at which the benefits of labor specialization are exhausted? As the firm continues to increase output beyond that point, the average variable cost increases because of diminishing returns. There is a tug-of-war between two forces: The spreading of fixed cost continues to push ATC down, while diminishing returns and rising average variable cost pull ATC up. The outcome of the tug-of-war varies with the quantity produced, giving the ATC curve its U-shape:

- **Intermediate quantities of output, such as output between 3 and 10 paddles.** The tug-of-war is won by the spreading of fixed cost, because the fixed cost is still relatively "thick" and diminishing returns are not yet very strong. As a result, ATC decreases as output increases. For example, at 5 paddles ATC is $40, but at 10 paddles ATC drops to only $30.

• *Large quantities of output, such as 11 or more paddles.* The tug-of-war is won by diminishing returns and rising average variable cost. In this case, the reductions in *AFC* are relatively small because the fixed cost is already spread pretty thinly and diminishing returns are severe. As a result, *ATC* increases as output increases. For example, at 10 paddles *ATC* is $30, but at 11.5 paddles *ATC* jumps to $34.78.

Short-Run Marginal Cost

short-run marginal cost (*MC*)
The change in short-run total cost resulting from a one-unit increase in output.

The **short-run marginal cost (*MC*)** is the change in short-run total cost per unit change in output. In other words, it is the increase in total cost resulting from a one-unit increase in output. Mathematically, marginal cost is calculated by dividing the change in total cost (*TC*) by the change in output (*Q*):

$$MC = \frac{\Delta TC}{\Delta Q} = \frac{\text{change in TC}}{\text{change in output}}$$

The marginal cost of the first paddle is the increase in cost when the firm produces the first paddle. To produce the first unit of output, the firm hires a single worker at $50. As shown in column 9 of Table 8.2, the marginal cost of the first paddle is $50. Moving down the ninth column, hiring the second worker for $50 increases output to five paddles. A $50 increase in total cost increases output by four paddles, so the marginal cost is $12.50:

$$MC = \frac{\Delta TC}{\Delta Q} = \frac{\text{change in TC}}{\text{change in output}} = \frac{\$50}{4} = \$12.50$$

In this case, marginal cost decreases as output increases because of labor specialization and rising worker productivity. The first worker produces just one paddle, but adding a second worker increases output by four paddles. The $50 expense of adding the second worker translates into a $12.50 expense for each of the four extra paddles produced. We saw earlier that specialization leads to increasing marginal productivity. Now we know that specialization also leads to decreasing marginal cost. In Figure 8.4, the short-run marginal-cost curve is negatively sloped for the first five paddles.

▶ **FIGURE 8.4**
Short-Run Marginal and Average Cost
The marginal-cost curve (*MC*) is negatively sloped for small quantities of output because of the benefits of labor specialization, and positively sloped for large quantities because of diminishing returns. The *MC* curve intersects the average-cost curve (*ATC*) at the minimum point of the average curve. At this point *ATC* is neither falling nor rising.

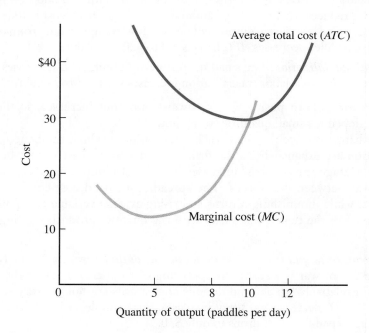

The positively sloped portion of the marginal-cost curve is a result of diminishing returns. Hiring the third worker increases output from 5 to 8, so the $50 expense translates into a $16.67 expense for each of the 3 extra paddles produced. Diminishing returns has set in, so marginal cost increases as output increases. The marginal cost increases to $25 for between 8 and 10 paddles ($50/2 paddles), then increases to $50 for between 10 and 11 paddles ($50/1 paddle), and so on. In general, diminishing returns decreases labor productivity and causes rising marginal cost.

The Relationship between Marginal Cost and Average Cost

Figure 8.4 shows the relationship between short-run marginal cost and short-run average total cost. Whenever the marginal cost is less than the average cost (for fewer than 10 paddles), the average cost is falling. In contrast, whenever the marginal cost exceeds the average cost (for more than 10 paddles), the average cost is rising. Finally, when the marginal cost equals the average cost, the average cost is neither rising nor falling. Therefore, the marginal-cost curve intersects the short-run average total cost curve at its minimum point.

We can use some simple logic to explain the relationship between average and marginal cost. Suppose that you start the semester with 9 completed courses and a cumulative grade-point average of 3.0. In the first row of Table 8.3, you have 27 grade points (4 points for each A, 3 points for each B, and so on), so your GPA is 3.0, which is 27 points divided by 9 courses. You enroll in a single course this semester—a history course. Your new GPA will depend on your grade in the history course, the marginal grade. There are three possibilities:

- *Marginal grade less than the average grade.* In the second row of Table 8.3, if you get a D in history, your grade point total increases from 27 points to 28 points. Dividing the new total by 10 courses, your new GPA is 2.80. It's lower because your marginal grade of 1.0 is less than the old average grade of 3.0.

- *Marginal grade equal to the average grade.* In the third row of Table 8.3, if you get a B in history, your grade point total increases from 27 points to 30 points. Dividing the new total by 10 courses, your new GPA is 3.0. It hasn't changed because your marginal grade of 3.0 equals the old average grade of 3.0.

- *Marginal grade greater than the average grade.* In the fourth row of Table 8.3, if you get an A in history, your grade point total increases from 27 points to 31 points, so your new GPA is 3.10. It's higher because your marginal grade of 4.0 is greater than the old average grade of 3.0.

To summarize, whenever the marginal grade is less than the average grade, the average will fall; whenever the marginal grade exceeds the average grade, the average will rise; and whenever the marginal grade equals the average grade, the average will not change.

TABLE 8.3 Marginal Grade and Average Grade				
	Marginal Grade	Number of Courses	Grade Points	Grade Point Average
Starting point	—	9	27	3.0 = 27/9
Marginal grade < GPA	D	10	28 = 27 + 1	2.8 = 28/10
Marginal grade = GPA	B	10	30 = 27 + 3	3.0 = 30/10
Marginal grade > GPA	A	10	31 = 27 + 4	3.1 = 31/10

application 2

IDLE CAPITAL AND SHORT-RUN MARGINAL COST

APPLYING THE CONCEPTS #2: Why is the marginal-cost curve positively sloped?

Consider the following simple production process. A firm that simply digs holes has a fixed amount of capital (10 standard shovels) and can vary the number of workers. Armed with a standard shovel, a worker requires two hours to dig one hole. To produce one hole per day, the firm hires a worker and uses only one of its 10 shovels. If the wage is $12 per hour, the marginal cost of the first dug hole is $24. As the quantity of output increases, the firm adds workers and uses more of its shovels, and the marginal cost remains at $24 for the first 10 holes. In this case, marginal cost is constant for the first 10 units of output because the firm doesn't experience diminishing returns. Normally, diminishing returns occurs because an increase in the number of workers means that each worker gets a smaller share of the production facility. But in this case, each worker gets one shovel, so for the first 10 units of output, the firm does not experience diminishing returns. As a result, marginal cost is constant, not increasing. Of course, beyond 10 units of output, the firm will experience diminishing returns and rising marginal cost.

The same logic applies to other sorts of firms that can adjust their utilization of capital. For example, a firm can vary the run time of its factory, choosing one, two, or even three 8-hour shifts per day. Going from a single shift to two shifts, the firm doubles its workforce and utilizes its factory for twice as many hours, but does not experience diminishing returns because each worker gets the same share of the production facility. In general, for a production process that can tap idle capital, marginal cost is constant over some range of output. Of course, diminishing returns sets in as soon as the capital is fully utilized, for example, once a factory is running 24/7. **Related to Exercise 2.8.**

SOURCE: Based on Richard Miller, "Ten Cheaper Spades: Production Theory and Cost Curves in the Short Run, *Journal of Economic Education* (2000), pp. 119–130.

8.3 Production and Cost in the Long Run

Up to this point, we've been exploring short-run cost curves, which show the cost of producing different quantities of output in a given production facility. We turn next to long-run cost curves, which show production costs in facilities of different sizes. The *long run* is defined as the period of time over which a firm is perfectly flexible in its choice of all inputs. In the long run, a firm can build a new production facility such as a factory, store, office, or restaurant. Another option in the long run is to modify an existing facility.

The key difference between the short run and the long run is that there are no diminishing returns in the long run. Recall that diminishing returns occur because workers share a fixed production facility, so the larger the number of workers in the facility, the smaller the share of the facility available for each worker. In the long run, a firm can expand its production facility as its workforce grows, so there are no diminishing returns.

Expansion and Replication

Continuing the example of paddle production, suppose you have decided to replace your existing workshop with a new one. You have been producing 10 paddles per day at a total cost of $300 per day, or an average cost of $30 per paddle. Suppose a company that sponsors rafting adventures orders new paddles, and you decide to produce twice as much output in your new facility. What should you do?

One possibility is simply to double the original operation. You could build two workshops identical to the original shop and hire two workforces, each identical to the original workforce. In the table in Figure 8.5, your firm moves from the third row of numbers (four workers and $100 worth of capital produces 10 paddles per day) to the fourth row, with twice as much labor, capital, and output. A firm's **long-run total cost (LTC)** is the total cost of production when the firm is perfectly flexible in choosing its inputs, including its production facility. As shown in column 5 of the table in Figure 8.5, if your firm doubles its output from 10 paddles to 20 paddles, the long-run total cost doubles too, from $300 to $600.

long-run total cost (LTC)
The total cost of production when a firm is perfectly flexible in choosing its inputs.

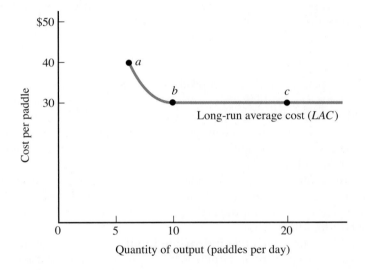

◄ **FIGURE 8.5**
The Long-Run Average-Cost Curve and Scale Economies
The long-run average-cost curve (LAC) is negatively sloped for up to 10 paddles per day, a result of indivisible inputs and the effects of labor specialization. If the firm replicates the operation that produces 10 paddles per day, the long-run average-cost curve will be horizontal beyond 10 paddles per day.

	1	2	3	4	5
Labor	Capital	Output	Labor Cost	Long-Run Total Cost (LTC)	Long-Run Average Cost (LAC)
1	$100	1	$ 50	$150	$150
2	100	5	100	200	40
4	100	10	200	300	30
8	200	20	400	600	30
12	300	30	600	900	30

The firm's **long-run average cost (LAC)** equals the long-run cost divided by the quantity produced. As shown in column 6 of the table in Figure 8.5, doubling output from 10 to 20 paddles doesn't change the long-run average cost because doubling output by doubling both labor and capital increases costs proportionately. In the graph in Figure 8.5, point *b* shows the average cost with 10 paddles and point *c* shows the average cost with 20 paddles. As the quantity produced increases, the average cost doesn't change, so the average-cost curve is horizontal over this range of output. This is the case of **constant returns to scale**: As a firm scales up its operation, costs increase proportionately with output, so average cost is constant.

long-run average cost (LAC)
The long-run cost divided by the quantity produced.

constant returns to scale
A situation in which the long-run total cost increases proportionately with output, so average cost is constant.

The same logic applies to larger output levels. Your firm could build a third workshop identical to the first two workshops, and its production costs will increase proportionately, from $600 to $900. In the table in Figure 8.5, the average cost for 30 paddles is $30, the same as for 10 and 20 paddles. In general, the replication process means the long-run total cost increases proportionately with the quantity produced, so the average cost is constant. In Figure 8.5, the long-run average-cost curve is horizontal for 10 or more paddles per day. In other words, there are constant returns to scale for output levels of 10 or more paddles.

We've seen that if a firm wants to double its output in the long run, replication is one option. By simply replicating an existing operation, a firm can double its output and its total costs, leaving average cost unchanged. Another possibility is to build a single larger workshop, one that can produce twice as much output at a lower cost than would be possible by simply replicating the original. If so, the long-run average cost of producing 20 or 30 paddles would be less than $30 per paddle.

long-run marginal cost (*LMC*)
The change in long-run cost resulting from a one-unit increase in output.

A firm's **long-run marginal cost (*LMC*)** is the change in long-run cost resulting from producing one more unit of output. In the long run, the firm is perfectly flexible in choosing its inputs. Therefore, *LMC* is the increase in cost when the firm can change its production facility as well as its workforce.

Reducing Output with Indivisible Inputs

What would happen if you decide to produce only 5 paddles per day instead of 10? Although it's tempting to think that your total costs would be cut in half, that's not necessarily the case. Remember that you use a single mold to produce 10 paddles per day. If you cut your output in half, you would still need the mold, so your capital costs won't be cut in half. In addition, if each mold requires a fixed amount of floor space, you would still need the same floor space. Therefore, cutting output in half wouldn't decrease the cost of your production facility at all. You would still have a cost of $100 per day for the mold and the workspace. Because cutting output in half doesn't cut capital costs in half, the average cost for producing 5 paddles will exceed the average cost for 10 paddles.

indivisible input
An input that cannot be scaled down to produce a smaller quantity of output.

The mold is an example of an **indivisible input**, one that we cannot scale down to produce a smaller quantity of output. When a production process requires the use of indivisible inputs, the average cost of production increases as output decreases, because the cost of the indivisible inputs is spread over a smaller quantity of output. Most production operations use some indivisible inputs, but the costs of these inputs vary. Here are some examples of firms and their indivisible inputs:

- A railroad company uses tracks to provide freight service between two cities. The company cannot scale down by laying a half set of tracks—a single rail.
- A shipping firm uses a large ship to carry TV sets from Japan to the United States. The company can't scale back by transporting TVs in rowboats.
- A steel producer uses a large blast furnace. The company can't scale back by producing steel in a toaster oven.
- A hospital uses imaging machines for X-rays, CAT scans, and MRIs. The hospital can't scale back by getting mini-MRI machines.

The second row of the table in Figure 8.5 shows labor and capital costs in the smaller operation. Suppose that to produce 5 paddles, you'll need two workers, including yourself. In this case, your labor cost will be $100. Adding the $100 cost of the indivisible input (the mold and shop space), the total cost of producing 5 paddles per day will be $200, or $40 per paddle. This cost exceeds the average cost of 10 paddles because in the smaller operation you still need the same amount of capital. In Figure 8.5, point *a* shows that the average cost of 5 paddles per day exceeds the average cost for larger quantities.

Scaling Down and Labor Specialization

A second possible reason for higher average long-run costs in a smaller operation is that labor will be less specialized in the small operation. As we saw earlier in the chapter, labor specialization—each worker specializing in an individual production task—makes workers more productive because of continuity and repetition. Reversing this process, when we reduce the workforce each worker will become less specialized, performing a wider variety of production tasks. The loss of specialization will decrease labor productivity, leading to higher average cost.

To see the role of labor specialization, consider the first row of numbers in the table in Figure 8.5. To produce one paddle per day, the firm needs a full day of work by one worker. The single worker performs all production tasks and is less productive than the specialized workers in larger operations. This is one reason for the relatively high average cost in a one-paddle operation ($150). The second reason is that the cost of the indivisible input is spread over fewer paddles.

Economies of Scale

A firm experiences **economies of scale** if the long-run average cost of production decreases as output increases, meaning that the long-run average-cost curve is negatively sloped. In Figure 8.5 on page 195, the paddle producer experiences economies of scale between points *a* and *b*. At point *a*, the long-run average cost is $40, compared to $30 at point *b* and beyond. An increase in output from 5 to 10 paddles decreases the long-run average cost of production because the firm spreads the cost of an indivisible input over a larger quantity, decreasing average cost. In other words, there are some economies—cost savings—associated with scaling up the firm's operation.

economies of scale
A situation in which the long-run average cost of production decreases as output increases.

One way to quantify the extent of scale economies in the production of a particular good is to determine the minimum efficient scale for producing the good. The **minimum efficient scale** is defined as the output at which scale economies are exhausted. In Figure 8.5, the long-run average-cost curve becomes horizontal at point *b*, so the minimum efficient scale is 10 paddles. If a firm starts out with a quantity of output below the minimum efficient scale, an increase in output will decrease the average cost. Once the minimum efficient scale has been reached, the average cost no longer decreases as output increases.

minimum efficient scale
The output at which scale economies are exhausted.

Diseconomies of Scale

A positively sloped long-run average-cost curve indicates the presence of **diseconomies of scale**. In this case, average cost increases as output increases. Diseconomies of scale can occur for two reasons:

diseconomies of scale
A situation in which the long-run average cost of production increases as output increases.

- *Coordination problems.* One of the problems of a large organization is that it requires several layers of management to coordinate the activities of the different parts of the organization. A large organization requires more meetings, reports, and administrative work, leading to higher unit cost. If an increase in the firm's output requires additional layers of management, the long-run average-cost curve may be positively sloped.

- *Increasing input costs.* When a firm increases its output, it will demand more of each of its inputs and *may* be forced to pay higher prices for some of these inputs.

For example, an expanding construction firm may be forced to pay higher wages to attract more workers. Alternatively, an expanding firm may be forced to hire workers who are less skilled than the original workers. An increase in wages or a decrease in productivity will increase the average cost of production, generating a positively sloped long-run average-cost curve.

Firms recognize the possibility of diseconomies of scale and adopt various strategies to avoid them. An example of a firm that adjusts its operations to avoid diseconomies of scale is 3M, a global technology company that produces products ranging from Post-it notes to pharmaceuticals and telecommunications systems. The company makes a conscious effort to keep its production units as small as possible to keep them flexible. When a production unit gets too large, the company breaks it apart.

Actual Long-Run Average-Cost Curves

Figure 8.6 shows the actual long-run average-cost curves for three products: aluminum production, truck freight, and hospital services.[2]

▶ **FIGURE 8.6**
Actual Long-Run Average-Cost Curves for Aluminum, Truck Freight, and Hospital Services

In each case, the long-run average cost curve is negatively sloped for small quantities of output and relatively flat—almost horizontal—over a large range of output. In other words, these curves are L-shaped. Other studies suggest that the long-run cost curves of a wide variety of goods and services have the same shape.

Why is the typical long-run average-cost curve L-shaped? The long-run average-cost curve is negatively sloped for small quantities of output because there are economies of scale resulting from indivisible inputs and labor specialization. As output increases, the average-cost curve eventually becomes horizontal and remains horizontal for a wide range of output. Over the horizontal portion of the cost curve, increases in inputs lead to proportionate increases in output, so the average cost doesn't change. In other words, the long-run average total cost (*LAC*) is constant and production is subject to constant returns to scale.

Short-Run versus Long-Run Average Cost

Why is the firm's short-run average-cost curve U-shaped, while the long-run average-cost curve is L-shaped? For large quantities of output, the short-run curve is positively sloped because of diminishing returns and the resulting decrease in labor productivity and increase in marginal cost. If a firm increases its output while at least one input is held fixed, diminishing returns eventually occur, pulling up the average cost of production.

The difference between the short run and long run is a firm's flexibility in choosing inputs. In the long run, a firm can increase all of its inputs, scaling up its operation by building a larger production facility. As a result, the firm will not suffer

---

application 3

INDIVISIBLE INPUTS AND THE COST OF FAKE KILLER WHALES

APPLYING THE CONCEPTS #2: How do indivisible inputs affect production costs?

Sea lions off the Washington coast eat steelhead and other fish, depleting some species threatened with extinction and decreasing the harvest of the commercial fishing industry. Rick Funk is a plastics manufacturer who has offered to build a life-sized fiberglass killer whale, mount it on a rail like a roller coaster, and send the whale diving through the water to scare off the sea lions, whales' natural prey. According to Funk, it would cost about $16,000 to make the first whale, including $11,000 for the mold and $5,000 for labor and materials. Once the mold is made, each additional whale would cost an additional $5,000. In other words, the cost of producing the first fake killer whale is more than three times the cost of producing the second. In terms of total cost, producing two whales would cost a total of $21,000, while three whales would cost a total of $26,000, and so on.

This little story illustrates the effects of indivisible inputs on the firm's cost curves. The mold is an indivisible input, because it cannot be scaled down and still produce whales. If Funk wants to cut his production from two whales per month down to one, he still needs the mold; he cannot simply produce half as many whales with half a mold or a mold that is half the size. The cost of producing the first whale, $16,000, includes the cost of the mold, the indivisible input. Once the firm has the mold, the marginal cost for each whale is only $5,000, so the average cost per whale decreases as the number of whales increases. **Related to Exercises 3.4 and 3.9.**

SOURCE: Based on Sandi Doughton, "Killer Whale Latest Idea on Sea Lions," *Oregonian*, January 7, 1995.

from diminishing returns. In most cases, the long-run average-cost curve will be negatively sloped or horizontal. In some cases, firms experience diseconomies of scale, so the long-run average-cost curve will be positively sloped for high output levels. Nonetheless, the long-run average cost will not be as steep as the short-run curve, which is relatively steep because of diminishing returns.

8.4   Examples of Production Cost

So far we've explored the links between production technology and the cost of production. We've seen the firm's short-run cost curves, which show how production costs vary with the quantity produced when at least one input is fixed. We've also seen the long-run average-cost curve, which shows how the average cost of production varies when the firm is perfectly flexible in choosing its inputs. In this part of the chapter, we look at actual production costs for several products.

Scale Economies in Wind Power

There are scale economies in the production of electricity from wind because electricity can be generated from turbines of different sizes. Although large wind turbines are more costly than small ones, the higher cost is more than offset by greater generating capacity. The scale economies occur because the cost of purchasing, installing, and maintaining a wind turbine increases less than proportionately with the turbine's generating capacity. Table 8.5 shows the costs of a small turbine (150-kilowatt capacity) and a large turbine (600-kilowatt capacity), each with an assumed lifetime of 20 years.

TABLE 8.5 Wind Turbines and the Average Cost of Electricity		
	Small Turbine (150 kilowatt)	**Large Turbine (600 kilowatt)**
Purchase price of turbine	$150,000	$420,000
Installation cost	$100,000	$100,000
Operating and maintenance cost	$75,000	$126,000
Total cost	$325,000	$646,000
Electricity generated (kilowatt-hours)	5 million	20 million
Average cost (per kilowatt-hour)	$0.065	$0.032

SOURCE: Based on Danish Wind Turbine Manufacturers Association, "Guided Tour of Wind Energy" (2003), www.windpower.dk (accessed June 27, 2006).

The large turbine has four times the generation capacity of the small turbine—20 million kilowatt hours versus 5 million kilowatt hours—but its purchase price is less than three times as much. The two turbines have the same installation cost, and the operating and maintenance cost of the larger turbine is less than twice as large. Adding the various costs, the larger turbine, with four times the generating capacity, has less than twice the cost. As a result, the average cost per kilowatt-hour is only $0.032 for the large turbine, compared to $0.065 for the smaller turbine.

The Average Cost of a Music Video

A music video is an information good—a product that is essentially a bundle of information. Most of the cost of producing an information good results from collecting the information and making a first copy. Once the information is organized and digitized, the marginal cost of reproduction is tiny. In other words, an information good has large first-copy cost, and a tiny marginal cost.

For a music video, the first-copy cost is the cost of putting images and sounds into a digital format. The typical music video has a first-copy cost of $223,000—an amount that includes $28,000 for the people responsible for the script or "treatment," $81,000 for two days of filming, $81,000 for editing, and $33,000 for other costs. Once the images and sounds are digitized, the marginal cost of making additional copies is small, or in the case of a music video distributed online, actually zero.

The average cost of a music video depends on how many copies are distributed. Suppose the music video can be distributed online, at zero marginal cost. The average cost is $223 if 1,000 copies are distributed, and drops to $0.23 if one million copies are distributed. In Figure 8.7, the average-cost curve is negatively sloped and gets closer and closer to the horizontal axis as the quantity distributed increases. The gap decreases as the fixed production cost is spread over a larger number of copies. If consumers can download the music video at a price of $1, the break-even quantity is 223,000 copies distributed.

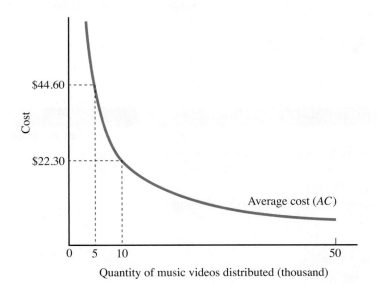

◄ FIGURE 8.7
Average-Cost Curve for an Information Good
For an information good such as a music video, the cost of producing the first copy is very high, but the marginal cost of reproduction is relatively low, and for products distributed online, the marginal cost is zero.

Solar versus Nuclear: The Crossover

In 1998, the cost of electricity produced with solar technology was $0.32 per kilowatt hour (Kwh), compared to $0.07 per Kwh for electricity produced with nuclear technology.[3] Recent innovations in photovoltaic technology have reduced the unit cost of solar power, to $0.21 per Kwh in 2005 and to $0.16 per Kwh in 2010. Over the same period, the unit cost of nuclear power increased, in large part because the capital cost of a nuclear reactor has increased, from $3 billion in 2002 to

$10 billion in 2010. For a new nuclear facility, the projected unit cost of electricity is about $0.16 per Kwh. In other words, the cost gap between solar and nuclear power has been eliminated: the cost of solar power is roughly the same as the unit cost of nuclear power.

SUMMARY

In this chapter, we explored the cost side of a firm, explaining the shapes of the firm's short-run and long-run cost curves. Table 8.6 summarizes the definitions of various types of costs. Here are the main points of the chapter:

1 The negatively sloped portion of the *short-run marginal-cost curve (MC)* results from input specialization that causes increasing marginal returns.

2 The positively sloped portion of the *MC* results from *diminishing returns*.

3 The *short-run average-total-cost curve (ATC)* is U-shaped because of the conflicting effects of (a) fixed costs being spread over a larger quantity of output and (b) diminishing returns.

4 The *long-run average-cost curve (LAC)* is horizontal over some range of output because replication is an option, so doubling output will no more than double long-run total cost.

5 The *LAC* is negatively sloped for small quantities of output because (a) there are indivisible inputs that cannot be scaled down and (b) a smaller operation has limited opportunities for labor specialization.

6 *Diseconomies of scale* arise if there are problems in coordinating a large operation or higher input costs in a larger organization.

TABLE 8.6 The Language and Mathematics of Costs

Type of Cost	Definition	Symbols and Equations
Economic cost	The opportunity cost of the inputs used in the production process; equal to explicit cost plus implicit cost	—
Explicit cost	The actual monetary payment for inputs	—
Implicit cost	The opportunity cost of inputs that do not involve a monetary payment	—
Accounting cost	Explicit cost	—
Short-Run Costs		
Fixed cost	Cost that does not vary with the quantity produced	FC
Variable cost	Cost that varies with the quantity produced	VC
Short-run total cost	The total cost of production when at least one input is fixed	$TC = FC + VC$
Short-run marginal cost		$MC = \Delta TC / \Delta Q$
Average fixed cost	Fixed cost divided by the quantity produced	$AFC = FC/Q$
Average variable cost	Variable cost divided by the quantity produced	$AVC = VC/Q$
Short-run average total cost	Short-run total cost divided by the quantity produced	$ATC = AFC + AVC$
Long-Run Costs		
Long-run total cost	The total cost of production when a firm is perfectly flexible in choosing its inputs	LTC
Long-run average cost	Long-run total cost divided by the quantity produced	$LAC = LTC/Q$
Long-run marginal cost	The change in long-run cost resulting from a one-unit increase in output	$LMC = \Delta LTC / \Delta Q$

accounting cost, p. 187

accounting profit, p. 187

average fixed cost (*AFC*), p. 190

average variable cost (*AVC*), p. 190

constant returns to scale, p. 195

diminishing returns, p. 188

diseconomies of scale, p. 197

economic cost, p. 186

economic profit, p. 186

economies of scale, p. 197

explicit cost, p. 186

fixed cost (*FC*), p. 189

implicit cost, p. 186

indivisible input, p. 196

long-run average cost (*LAC*), p. 195

long-run marginal cost (*LMC*), p. 196

long-run total cost (*LTC*), p. 195

marginal product of labor, p. 187

minimum efficient scale, p. 197

short-run average total cost (*ATC*), p. 191

short-run marginal cost (*MC*), p. 192

short-run total cost (*TC*), p. 189

total-product curve, p. 188

variable cost (*VC*), p. 189

EXERCISES

All problems are assignable in MyEconLab.

8.1 Economic Cost and Economic Profit

1.1 The computation of economic cost is based on the principle of _____.

1.2 A firm's implicit cost is defined as the _____ cost of nonpurchased inputs, such as the entrepreneur's _____ and _____.

1.3 Economic profit equals _____ minus _____.

1.4 Fill with "economic" or "accounting": Because _____ cost typically exceeds _____ cost, _____ profit typically exceeds _____ profit.

1.5 Suppose a person quits a job paying $40,000 per year and starts a business with $100,000 withdrawn from a money-market account earning 8 percent per year. The implicit cost of the business is _____ for the entrepreneur's time plus _____ for the entrepreneur's funds.

1.6 The _____ (long/short) run is defined as a period over which a firm cannot change its production facility.

1.7 When a firm is perfectly flexible in its choice of all inputs, the firm is operating in the _____ (long/short) run.

1.8 Workers who become entrepreneurs earn roughly _____ percent _____ (less, more) than workers who remain in paid employment. (Related to Application 1 on page 187.)

1.9 **Compute the Cost.** Edward the entrepreneur takes two hours to cut a lawn, and he cuts 1,000 lawns per year. He uses solar-powered equipment (truck and mower) that will last forever—and can be sold at any time for $20,000. Edward could earn $12 per hour as a pedicurist. The interest rate is 10 percent.

    a. Given his current output level, compute his marginal cost and average cost of cutting lawns.

    b. Suppose he decides to reduce the number of lawns cut by half, to 500 per year. Compute the new marginal cost and average cost.

8.2 A Firm with a Fixed Production Facility: Short-Run Costs

2.1 The short-run marginal cost curve is shaped like the letter _____ and the short-run average cost curve is shaped like the letter _____.

2.2 The negatively sloped portion of the short-run marginal-cost curve is explained by _____ and the positively sloped portion is explained by _____.

2.3 Over the positively sloped portion of the short-run average-cost curve, the effect of _____ dominates the effect of _____.

2.4 At the current level of output, the marginal cost of MP3 players exceeds the average cost. If you increase output, the average cost will _____ (increase/decrease).

2.5 If marginal cost equals average cost, we are at the minimum point of the _____ cost curve.

2.6 Arrows up or down. When marginal cost is less than average cost, an increase in output _____ average cost. When marginal cost exceeds average cost, an increase in output _____ average cost.

2.7 The short-run average cost of production is the same for two different quantities. _____ (True/False)

2.8 For a firm that doubles its workforce and adds a second shift at its factory, production _____ (is, is not) subject to diminishing returns, so marginal cost is _____. (Related to Application 2 on page 194.)

2.9 **Compute the Costs.** Consider a firm that has a fixed cost of $60. Complete the following table:

Output	Fixed Cost (FC)	Variable Cost (VC)	Total Cost (TC)	Marginal Cost (MC)	Average Fixed Cost (AFC)	Average Variable Cost (AVC)	Average Total Cost (ATC)
1		$10					
2		18					
3		30					
4		45					
5		65					

2.10 **Changing Costs.** Consider the paddle production example shown in Table 8.2 on page 189. Compute the short-run average cost for 10 paddles with the following changes.

   a. Your opportunity cost of work time triples, from $50 to $150.

   b. The interest rate for invested funds is cut in half, from 10 to 5 percent.

   c. Labor productivity—the quantity produced by each workforce—doubles.

2.11 **Compute the Short-Run Costs.** Consider a firm with the following short-run costs:

   a. What is the firm's fixed cost?

   b. Compute short-run marginal cost (MC), short-run average variable cost (AVC), and short-run average total cost (ATC) for the different quantities of output.

   c. Draw the three cost curves. Explain the relationship between the MC curve and the ATC curve and the relationship between the AVC curve and the ATC curve.

Quantity	Variable Cost (VC)	Total Cost (TC)	Marginal Cost (MC)	Average Variable Cost (AVC)	Average Total Cost (ATC)
1	$ 30	$ 90			
2	50	110			
3	90	150			
4	140	200			
5	200	260			

2.12 **Same Average Cost with Different Quantities?** Suppose there are two pencil producers with identical production facilities—identical factories and equipment. The firms pay the same wages and pay the same prices for materials. Sam has a small workforce and produces 1,000 pencils per minute; Marian has a medium-size workforce and produces 2,000 pencils per minute. The two firms have the same average total cost of 10 cents per pencil. Suppose you build a production facility identical to the ones used by the other firms and hire enough workers and buy enough materials to produce 2,500 pencils per minute. Would you expect your average cost to be 10 cents per pencil (like the other two firms), less than 10 cents, or more than 10 cents?

8.3 Production and Cost in the Long Run

3.1 The presence of _____ explains the negatively sloped portion of a long-run average-cost curve, and the notion of _____ explains the horizontal portion of the curve.

3.2 Consider the information provided in Figure 8.6 on page 198. Suppose the output of a large aluminum firm drops from two million pounds to one million pounds per year. The long-run average cost of producing aluminum will go from $_____ to $_____.

3.3 The typical *short-run* average-cost curve is shaped like the letter U, while the typical *long-run* average-cost curve is shaped like the letter L because _____ are not applicable in the _____ run.

3.4 The cost of producing the first fake killer whale is about three times the cost of producing the second because the firm uses _____ inputs. (Related to Application 3 on page 199.)

3.5 Deregulation and the Cost of Trucking. Suppose the government initially limits the number of trucking firms that can haul freight. The market for truck freight is served by a single firm that produces five million ton-miles of service per year, where one ton-mile is the hauling of one ton of freight one mile. The newly elected governor has proposed that other firms be allowed to enter the market. At a public hearing on the issue of eliminating the entry restrictions, the manager of the existing firm issued a grim warning: "If you allow entry into the market, four or five firms will enter, and the unit cost of truck freight will at least triple. There are big economies of scale in trucking services, so a single large firm is much more cost-efficient than several small firms would be." What's your reaction to this statement?

3.6 Draw the Long-Run Cost Curve. Consider the long-run production of shirts. The cost of the indivisible inputs used in the production of shirts is $400 per day. To produce 1 shirt per day, the firm must also spend a total of $5 on other inputs—labor, materials, and other capital. For each additional shirt, the firm incurs the same additional cost of $5.

    a. Compute the average cost for 40 shirts, 100 shirts, 200 shirts, and 400 shirts.

    b. Draw the long-run average-cost curve for 40 to 400 shirts per day.

3.7 Diminishing Returns versus Diseconomies of Scale. Explain the difference between diseconomies of scale and diminishing returns. Based on the cost curves you've seen in this chapter, which is more likely in firms?

3.8 Constant Marginal Cost. Consider a firm operating in the long run with an indivisible input that has a cost of $120. The marginal cost of production is constant at $3 per unit. Draw the firm's long-run average-cost curve for 1 to 12 units of output. The long-run average cost drops from $_____ for the first unit to $_____ for the twelfth unit.

3.9 A Better Whale Mold? Suppose a new mold is developed for producing fake killer whales. The new mold has twice the cost of the original mold, but cuts the marginal cost of whales to $1,000. (Related to Application 3 on page 199.)

    a. How does the cost of the first whale produced with the new mold compare to the cost with the original mold?

    b. At what quantity of whales will production with the new mold be less costly than production with the original mold?

8.4 Examples of Production Cost

4.1 The average cost of electricity _____ (increases/decreases) as the size of the wind turbine increases.

4.2 For information goods such as a music video distributed online, the cost of producing the first copy is very _____, but the marginal cost is _____.

4.3 The Average Cost of a Super-Sized Turbine. Suppose a new super-sized wind turbine is developed. Fill in the blanks in the following table.

	Super-Sized Turbine (1,000 kilowatt)
Purchase price of turbine	$500,000
Installation cost	$100,000
Operating and maintenance cost	$200,000
Total cost	
Electricity generated (kilowatt-hours)	40 million
Average cost (per kilowatt-hour)	

4.4 The Average Cost of a Music Video. In Figure 8.7 suppose a strike by wardrobe and makeup artists increases the cost of wardrobe and makeup by $17,000. Draw the average-cost curve for producing the video and distributing it online, with quantities up to 50,000.

4.5 The Average Cost of Drama DVDs. You have been hired to produce a DVD of a play put on by a high-school drama club. It will take you about 50 hours to make the master, which will be stored on a hard drive on your computer. The opportunity cost of your time is $20 per hour. The marginal cost of burning DVDs is constant at $2. Draw the average-cost curve for producing the DVD, with quantities up to 100 DVDs.

NOTES

1. Ashish Karamchandani, Michael Kubzansky, and Paul Franano, "Emerging Markets, Emerging Models: Market-Based Solutions to the Challenges of Global Poverty," Monitor Company Group L.P., 2009.

2. Laurits Christensen and William H. Greene, "Economies of Scale in U.S. Electric Power Generation," *Journal of Political Economy* 84 (1976): 655–676. Reprinted by permission of The University of Chicago Press; Joel P. Clark and Merton C. Flemings, "Advanced Materials and the Economy," *Scientific American* 255 (October 1986): 51–60. Copyright 1986 by Scientific American, Inc. All rights reserved; Roger Koenker, "Optimal Scale and the Size Distribution of American Trucking Firms," *Journal of Transport Economics and Policy* (January 1977): 62; Harold A. Cohen, "Hospital Cost Curves with Emphasis on Measuring Patient Care Output," in *Empirical Studies in Health Economics*, ed. Herbert E. Klarman (Baltimore, MD: Johns Hopkins University Press, 1970); John Johnson, *Statistical Cost Analysis* (New York: McGraw-Hill, 1960).

3. Diana Powers, Nuclear Energy Loses Cost Advantage, *The New York Times* July 26, 2010; John Blackburn and Sam Cunningham, "Solar and Nuclear Costs—The Historic Crossover" (July 2010).

Perfect Competition

In the award-winning 2004 movie *Sideways*, the main character raved about pinot noir wine, noting that the pinot grape requires special care and attention, and can be grown only in a few places. The character said that the payoff from all the attention is a wine whose subtle and brilliant flavors make it one of the best wines on the planet.[1]

This rave review increased the demand for pinot noir wine grown in the Willamette Valley in Oregon. As a result, the price of wine soared, and for some brands the price tripled. A few years later, growers competed fiercely for consumers by cutting prices, in many cases back to pre-*Sideways* prices. As we'll see in this chapter, this is a common pattern in markets that experience increases in demand, even if the higher demand persists.

LEARNING OBJECTIVES

- Distinguish between four market structures.
- Explain the short-run output rule and the break-even price.
- Explain the shut-down rule.
- Explain why the short-run supply curve is positively sloped.
- Explain why the long-run industry supply curve may be positively sloped.

- Describe the short-run and long-run effects of changes in demand for an increasing-cost industry.
- Describe the short-run and long-run effects of changes in demand for a constant-cost industry.

MyEconLab
MyEconLab helps you master each objective and study more efficiently.

perfectly competitive market

A market with many sellers and buyers of a homogeneous product and no barriers to entry.

price taker

A buyer or seller that takes the market price as given.

*t*his is the first of four chapters exploring the decisions firms make in different types of markets. Markets differ in the number of firms that compete against one another for customers. In this chapter, we'll look at a perfectly competitive market. In a **perfectly competitive market**, hundreds, or even thousands, of firms sell a homogeneous product. Each firm is such a small part of the market that it takes the market price as given: Each firm is a **price taker**. For example, each soybean farmer takes the market price as given. There is no reason to cut the price to sell more soybeans, because the farmer can sell as much as he wants at the market price. There is no reason to increase the price, because the farmer would lose all his customers to other farmers selling at the market price.

A perfectly competitive market has two other features. First, on the demand side of the market there are hundreds, or even thousands, of buyers, each of whom takes the market price as given. Second, there are no barriers to market entry, so firms can easily enter or exit the market. To summarize, here are the five features of a perfectly competitive market:

1 There are many sellers.
2 There are many buyers.
3 The product is homogeneous.
4 There are no barriers to market entry.
5 Both buyers and sellers are price takers.

If you're thinking that the model of perfect competition is unrealistic, you're right. Most firms actually have some flexibility over their prices. For example, when Target increases its price of DVDs, it will certainly sell fewer DVDs, but the quantity sold will probably not drop to zero. Although perfect competition is rare, it's a good starting point for analyzing a firm's decisions, because a price-taking firm's decisions are easy to understand. The firm doesn't have to pick a price; it just decides how much to produce, given the market price. Once you understand this simple case, you will be ready to tackle the more complex decisions made by firms that are *price makers*—able to affect prices. We'll discuss that scenario in later chapters.

In this chapter, we'll see how price-taking firms use information on revenues and costs to decide how much output to produce. The output decisions of price-taking firms underlie the market supply curve and the law of supply. In other words, this chapter reveals the economic logic behind the market supply curve and the law of supply.

firm-specific demand curve

A curve showing the relationship between the price charged by a specific firm and the quantity the firm can sell.

9.1   Preview of the Four Market Structures

Let's start by distinguishing between a market demand curve and the demand curve for an individual firm. As we saw earlier in the book, the market demand curve shows the relationship between the price and the quantity that suppliers can sell in the market, assuming all firms charge the same price. In contrast, the **firm-specific demand curve** shows the relationship between the price charged by a specific firm and the quantity that firm can sell. In a *monopoly*, a single firm serves the entire market, so the firm-specific demand curve is the same as the market demand curve. As shown in Panel A of Figure 9.1, the monopolist can choose any point on the market demand curve, recognizing that the higher the price, the smaller the quantity the firm will sell.

As shown in Panel B of Figure 9.1, things are different for a perfectly competitive firm. The firm-specific demand curve is horizontal—perfectly elastic. A perfectly competitive firm can sell as much as it wants at the market price of $12, but if it raises its price even a penny, it will sell nothing.

◀ FIGURE 9.1
Monopoly versus Perfect
Competition
In Panel A, the demand curve facing a
monopolist is the market demand curve.
In Panel B, a perfectly competitive firm
takes the market price as given, so the
firm-specific demand curve is horizontal.
The firm can sell all it wants at the market
price, but would sell nothing if it charged
a higher price.

(A) Firm-Specific Demand Curve of Monopolist

(B) Firm-Specific Demand Curve of Perfectly Competitive Firm

Most markets lie between the extremes of monopoly and perfect competition. Table 9.1 compares perfectly competitive markets with three alternative market structures, which we'll discuss in the next three chapters:

- **Monopoly.** A single firm serves the entire market. A monopoly occurs when the barriers to market entry are very large. This can result from very large economies of scale or a government policy that limits the number of firms. Some examples of monopolies that result from large economies of scale are local phone service, cable TV, and electric power transmission. Some examples of monopolies established by government policy are drugs covered by patents, the selling of firewood in national parks, and the U.S. Postal Service.

- **Monopolistic competition.** There are no barriers to entering the market, so there are many firms, and each firm sells a slightly different product. For example, coffee shops in your city provide slightly different goods and compete for customers. Your local grocery store sells many brands of toothbrushes, with slight differences in size, shape, color, and style.

- **Oligopoly.** The market consists of just a few firms because economies of scale or government policies limit the number of firms. Some product examples are automobiles, computer processor chips, airline travel, and breakfast cereals. The large economies of scale in automobile production result from the large startup costs, with billions of dollars required to build a factory or assembly plant. Similarly, a fabrication plant for computer processor chips costs several billion dollars.

TABLE 9.1 Characteristics of the Four Market Structures

Characteristic	Perfect Competition	Monopolistic Competition	Oligopoly	Monopoly
Number of firms	Many	Many	Few	One
Type of product	Homogeneous	Differentiated	Homogeneous or differentiated	Unique
Firm-specific demand curve	Demand is perfectly elastic	Demand is elastic but not perfectly elastic	Demand is less elastic than demand facing monopolistically competitive firm	Firm faces market demand curve
Entry conditions	No barriers	No barriers	Large barriers from economies of scale or government policies	Large barriers from economies of scale or government policies
Examples	Corn, plain T-shirts	Toothbrushes, music stores, groceries	Air travel, automobiles, beverages, cigarettes, mobile phone service	Local phone service, patented drugs

application 1

WIRELESS WOMEN IN PAKISTAN

APPLYING THE CONCEPTS #2: How do entry costs affect the number of firms in a market?

For another example of a competitive market, consider phone service in the developing world, where many people relied on pay phones until the recent development of mobile phones generated a new competitive industry. In Pakistan, phone service is now provided by thousands of "wireless women," entrepreneurs who invest $310 in wireless phone equipment (transceiver, battery, charger), a signboard, a calculator, and a stopwatch. Then they sell phone service to their neighbors, charging by the minute and second. On average, their net income is about $2 per day, about three times the average per capita income in Pakistan. The market for phone service has the features of a perfectly competitive market, with easy entry, a standardized good, and a large enough number of suppliers that each takes the market price as given. In contrast, to enter the phone business in the United States, your initial investment would be millions, or perhaps billions, of dollars, so the market for phone service is not perfectly competitive. **Related to Exercise 1.4.**

SOURCE: Based on TeleCommons Development Group, "Grameen Telecom's Village Phone Programme: A Multi-Media Case Study," 2000, www.telecommons.com/villagephone (accessed June 27, 2006).

9.2 The Firm's Short-Run Output Decision

We'll start our discussion of perfect competition with an individual firm's decision about how much output to produce. The firm's objective is to maximize *economic profit*, which, as we saw in the previous chapter, equals total revenue minus economic cost. Recall that economic cost includes all the opportunity costs of production, both explicit costs (cash payments) and implicit costs (the entrepreneur's opportunity costs). In the preceding chapter, we saw that the cost of production varies with the quantity produced. In this chapter, we'll see how economic profit varies with the quantity produced and then show how a firm can pick the quantity that maximizes its economic profit.

Remember that economic profit differs from the conventional notion of profit. Accountants focus on the flow of money into and out of a firm, so they ignore costs that do not involve explicit transactions. *Accounting profit* equals total revenue minus explicit costs. Because accountants ignore implicit costs, accounting profit usually exceeds economic profit.

We will use the market for plain T-shirts to illustrate decision making in a perfectly competitive market. Some plain T-shirts are sold directly to consumers, and others are sold to firms that imprint words and images on the T-shirts and then sell the finished shirts to consumers. Plain T-shirts are produced in countries around the world by a large number of producers.

The Total Approach: Computing Total Revenue and Total Cost

One way for a firm to decide how much to produce is to compute the economic profit at different quantities and then pick the quantity that generates the highest profit. As we've seen, economic profit equals total revenue minus economic cost. We looked at the cost side of the profit equation in Chapter 8. The revenue side for a perfectly competitive market is straightforward. A firm's total revenue is the money it gets by selling its product. Total revenue is equal to the price of the product times the quantity sold. For example, if a firm sells eight T-shirts at $12 per shirt, total revenue is $96 (equal to 8 × $12). If our T-shirt producer has an economic cost of $63, the firm's profit is $33 (equal to $96 – $63).

Table 9.2 shows the total revenue and total costs of a hypothetical producer of plain cotton T-shirts. Follow the row for an output of eight shirts. As shown in the second and third columns, the fixed cost is $17, and the variable cost increases with the amount produced. The fourth column shows total cost, the sum of the fixed and variable costs. As shown in the fifth column, at a price of $12 per shirt, the firm's total revenue is $12 times the number of shirts produced. The sixth column shows economic profit, equal to total revenue minus total cost.

TABLE 9.2 Deciding How Much to Produce When the Price Is $12

1 Output: Shirts per Minute (Q)	2 Fixed Cost (FC)	3 Variable Cost (VC)	4 Total Cost (TC)	5 Total Revenue (TR)	6 Profit = TR – TC	7 Marginal Revenue = Price	8 Marginal Cost (MC)
0	$17	$0	$17	$0	–$17		
1	17	5	22	12	–10	$12	$5
2	17	6	23	24	1	12	1
3	17	9	26	36	10	12	3
4	17	13	30	48	18	12	4
5	17	18	35	60	25	12	5
6	17	25	42	72	30	12	7
7	17	34	51	84	33	12	9
8	17	46	63	96	33	12	12
9	17	62	79	108	29	12	16
10	17	83	100	120	20	12	21

Figure 9.2 shows one way to choose the quantity of output that maximizes profit. We're looking for the largest profit, shown by the biggest gap between total revenue and total cost. For example, for five shirts the gap is $25: Total revenue (TR) equals $60, and total cost (TC) equals $35. Moving down the table and across the figure, we see that profit increases to $30 for six shirts:

$$TR - TC = \$72 - \$42 = \$30$$

Profit is maximized at $33 when the firm produces either seven or eight shirts:

$$TR - TC = 84 - 51 = \$33$$
$$TR - TC = 96 - 63 = \$33$$

When profit reaches its highest level with two different quantities (seven and eight shirts in this example), we assume the firm produces the larger quantity. When the firm produces eight shirts, its total revenue is $96 and its total cost is $63, leaving a profit of $33.

▶ **FIGURE 9.2**
Using the Total Approach to Choose an Output Level
Economic profit is shown by the vertical distance between the total-revenue curve and the total-cost curve. To maximize profit, the firm chooses the quantity of output that generates the largest vertical difference between the two curves.

The Marginal Approach

The other way for a firm to decide how much output to produce relies on the marginal principle, the general decision-making rule that is one of the key principles of economics.

> ## MARGINAL PRINCIPLE
> Increase the level of an activity as long as its marginal benefit exceeds its marginal cost. Choose the level at which the marginal benefit equals the marginal cost.

marginal revenue
The change in total revenue from selling one more unit of output.

Because our firm is in business to make money, the benefit it gets from producing shirts is revenue. The *marginal* benefit—or **marginal revenue**—of producing shirts is the change in total revenue that results from selling one more shirt. A perfectly competitive firm takes the market price as given, so the marginal revenue—the change in total revenue from one more shirt—is simply the price:

$$\text{marginal revenue} = \text{price}$$

The marginal principle tells us that the firm will maximize its profit by choosing the quantity at which price equals marginal cost:

To maximize profit, produce the quantity where price = marginal cost

In Figure 9.3, the horizontal line shows the market price for T-shirts, which our shirt producer takes as given. The price line intersects the marginal-cost curve at eight shirts per minute, so that's the quantity that satisfies the marginal principle and maximizes profit.

To see that an output of eight shirts per minute maximizes the firm's profit, imagine that the firm initially produced only five shirts per minute. Could the firm make more profit by producing more—that is, six shirts instead of five?

- From the seventh row of numbers in Table 9.2 on page 211 and point *c* in Figure 9.3, we know the marginal cost of the sixth shirt is $7.
- The price of shirts is $12, so the marginal revenue is $12.

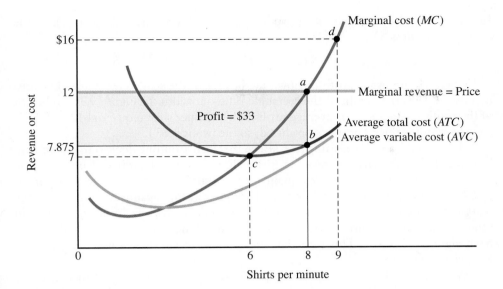

◀ **FIGURE 9.3**
The Marginal Approach to Picking an Output Level
A perfectly competitive firm takes the market price as given, so the marginal benefit, or marginal revenue, equals the price. Using the marginal principle, the typical firm will maximize profit at point *a*, where the $12 market price equals the marginal cost. Economic profit equals the difference between the price and the average cost ($4.125 = $12 − $7.875) times the quantity produced (eight shirts per minute), or $33 per minute.

Because the extra revenue from the sixth shirt (price = $12) exceeds the extra cost (marginal cost = $7), the production and sale of the sixth shirt increases the firm's total profit by $5 (equal to $12 − $7). Therefore, it is sensible to produce the sixth shirt. The same logic applies, with different numbers for marginal cost, for the seventh shirt. For the eighth shirt, marginal revenue equals marginal cost, so the firm's profit doesn't change. To be consistent with the marginal principle, we'll assume the firm produces to the point where marginal revenue equals marginal cost. In this case, the firm chooses point *a* and produces eight shirts.

If the firm produced more than eight shirts, it would earn less than the maximum profit. Imagine that the firm initially produced nine shirts. From Table 9.2 and the marginal-cost curve in Figure 9.3, we see that the marginal cost of the ninth shirt is $16 (point *d*), which exceeds the marginal revenue (the market price) of $12. The ninth shirt adds more to cost ($16) than it adds to revenue ($12), so producing the shirt decreases the firm's profit by $4. The marginal principle suggests that the firm should choose point *a*, with an output of eight shirts. The output decision is the same whether the firm uses the marginal approach or the total approach.

The advantage of the marginal approach is that it is easier to apply. To use the total approach, a firm needs information about the total revenue and total cost for all possible output levels. In contrast, a firm can apply the marginal principle by simply increasing its output by one unit and computing the marginal revenue (the price) and the marginal cost. Using the marginal principle, the firm should produce more output if the price exceeds the marginal cost, or produce less if the opposite is true. The firm can use the marginal principle to fine-tune its decision until the price equals the marginal cost.

Economic Profit and the Break-Even Price

We've seen that the perfectly competitive firm maximizes its profit by producing the quantity at which its marginal revenue (price) equals its marginal cost. How much profit does the firm earn? The firm's economic profit equals its total revenue minus its total cost. One way to compute a firm's total economic profit is to multiply the average profit per unit produced—the gap between the price and the average cost—by the quantity produced:

economic profit = (price − average cost) × quantity produced

In Figure 9.3, the average cost of producing eight shirts is $7.875 (point *b*), so the economic profit is $33:

$$\text{economic profit} = (\$12 - \$7.875) \times 8 = \$4.125 \times 8 = \$33$$

In Figure 9.3, the firm's profit is shown by the area of the shaded rectangle. The area of a rectangle is the height of the rectangle times its width. In Figure 9.3, the height of the profit rectangle is the average profit of $4.125 per shirt (equal to $12 – $7.875) and the width is the eight shirts produced, so the profit is $33.

How would a decrease in price affect the firm's output decision? A decrease in price shifts the marginal-revenue (price) line downward, so it will intersect the marginal-cost curve at a smaller quantity. In Figure 9.3, suppose the price drops to $7. The marginal-revenue line will shift downward, causing it to intersect the marginal-cost curve at point *c*, so the firm will produce only six shirts per minute. In other words, when the price decreases from $12 to $7 the quantity produced decreases from eight to six shirts. This is the law of supply in action: The lower the price, the smaller the quantity supplied.

break-even price

The price at which economic profit is zero; price equals average total cost.

What about the firm's economic profit at a price of $7? At point *c*, average total cost is $7, the same as the price. Therefore, economic profit is zero. We have discovered the **break-even price**, the price at which economic profit is zero. The

---

application 2

THE BREAK-EVEN PRICE FOR SWITCHGRASS, A FEEDSTOCK FOR BIOFUEL

APPLYING THE CONCEPTS #1: What is the break-even price?

In the search for alternatives to fossil fuels, a prominent contender is switchgrass, a perennial grass that is native to the U.S. plains states. The principal advantage of switchgrass and other cellulosic feedstocks for biofuels is their small carbon footprint. At what price will farmers convert their fields to switchgrass?

A recent study estimates the break-even price for growing switchgrass in North Dakota. The price per ton varies with the fertility of the land, from $56 on the least fertile land to $95 on the most fertile, or $76 on average. To compute the break-even price, the researchers started by adding up the explicit costs of production, including the costs of capital (machinery and equipment), labor, and raw materials. Then they added the opportunity cost of using land for switchgrass rather than another crop, for example, alfalfa, wheat, or soybeans.

We can illustrate the calculations with a simple example. Suppose the most profitable alternative to switchgrass is alfalfa, and the implicit rent on land used to grow alfalfa is $120 per acre—that's how much a farmer can earn in alfalfa production. If the switchgrass yield is 3 tons per acre, the opportunity cost of land per ton of switchgrass is $40 per ton (equal to $120/3). If the explicit cost of a ton of switchgrass (for capital, labor, and raw materials) is $36, the break-even switchgrass price is $76 = $36 + $40.

What are the implications for switchgrass biofuel? To get some North Dakota farmers to switch their crops to switchgrass, the price must be at least $56 per ton. And the higher the price, the larger the acreage devoted to switchgrass. To get the most fertile land in North Dakota switched to switchgrass, the price must be $95. **Related to Exercises 2.9 and 2.10.**

SOURCE: Based on Dean A. Bangsund, Eric A. DeVuyst, and F. Larry Leistritz, "Evaluation of Breakeven Farm-gate Switchgrass Prices in South Central North Dakota," *Agribusiness and Applied Economics Report* 632, North Dakota State University (2008).

break-even price is shown by the minimum point of the *ATC* curve, where marginal cost equals average total cost. Remember that zero economic profit means that the firm is making just enough money to cover all its costs, including the opportunity costs of the entrepreneur.

9.3   The Firm's Shut-Down Decision

Consider next the decisions faced by a firm that is losing money. Suppose the price of shirts drops to $4, which is so low that the firm's total revenue is less than its total cost. In Table 9.3, the marginal principle tells the firm to produce four shirts at this price, but the firm's total cost of $30 exceeds its total revenue of $16, so the firm will lose $14 per minute. Should the firm continue to operate at a loss or shut down?

| TABLE 9.3 Deciding How Much to Produce When the Price Is $4 | | | | | | | |
| 1 | 2 | 3 | 4 | 5 | 6 | 7 | 8 |
Output: Shirts per Minute (Q)	Fixed Cost (FC)	Variable Cost (VC)	Total Cost (TC)	Total Revenue (TR)	Profit = TR – TC	Marginal Revenue = Price	Marginal Cost (MC)
0	$17	$ 0	$17	$ 0	–$17		
1	17	5	22	4	–18	$4	$5
2	17	6	23	8	–15	4	1
3	17	9	26	12	–14	4	3
4	17	13	30	16	–14	4	4
5	17	18	35	20	–15	4	5
6	17	25	42	24	–18	4	7

Total Revenue, Variable Cost, and the Shut-Down Decision

The decision to operate or shut down is a short-run decision, a day-to-day decision to temporarily halt production in response to market conditions. Suppose our shirt factory hires workers by the day, so it makes the decision at the beginning of each day. The decision-making rule is

operate if total revenue > variable cost

shut down if total revenue < variable cost

As we saw in Chapter 8, a firm's variable cost includes all the costs that vary with the quantity produced. In the case of the shirt firm, it includes the costs of workers, raw materials such as cotton, and the cost of heating and powering the factory for the day. The variable cost does not include the $17 fixed cost of the production facility— for example, the cost of the machines or the factory itself—because these costs are not affected by the decision to operate or shut down.

Although the decision is made at the beginning of each day, we can use the revenue and costs per minute to compare total revenue to variable cost. From Table 9.3, when the price is $4, the best quantity is four shirts and the variable cost is $13. The total revenue from selling four shirts at $4 per shirt is $16, which exceeds the $13 variable cost. By operating the factory, the firm pays $13 in variable cost to generate $16 in revenue, so the firm is better off operating the facility. The benefit of operating the facility exceeds the variable cost, so it is sensible to produce four shirts per minute.

Figure 9.4 shows the firm's choice when the price of shirts is $4. The marginal principle is satisfied at point *a*, where the price equals the marginal cost. As shown by point *b*, the average cost of producing four shirts is $7.50, so the firm loses $3.50 per shirt. The shaded rectangle shows the firm's loss of $14. The height of the rectangle is the $3.50 loss per shirt, and the width of the rectangle is the four shirts produced.

▶ **FIGURE 9.4**

The Shut-Down Decision and the Shut-Down Price

When the price is $4, marginal revenue equals marginal cost at four shirts (point *a*). At this quantity, average cost is $7.50, so the firm loses $3.50 on each shirt, for a total loss of $14. Total revenue is $16 and the variable cost is only $13, so the firm is better off operating at a loss rather than shutting down and losing its fixed cost of $17. The shut-down price, shown by the minimum point of the *AVC* curve, is $3.00.

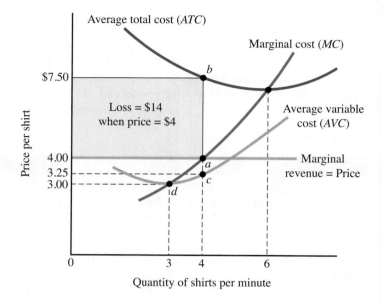

Of course, if the price drops to a low enough level, the firm will shut down the factory. For example, if the price drops to $1, the marginal principle is satisfied with two shirts per day. At this quantity, the variable cost is $6, which exceeds $2 revenue ($1 per shirt times two shirts). With this low price, the firm's total revenue is not high enough to cover the firm's variable cost from operating the facility, so it is better to shut down for the day.

The Shut-Down Price

There is a shortcut for determining whether it is sensible to continue to operate—compare the price to the average variable cost. Total revenue equals the price times the quantity produced, and the variable cost equals the average variable cost times the quantity produced. Therefore, total revenue will exceed variable cost if the price exceeds the average variable cost. If that happens, the firm should continue to operate. Otherwise, the firm should shut down.

operate if price > average variable cost

shut down if price < average variable cost

In Figure 9.4, with a price of $4, the marginal principle is satisfied at point *a*, and the average variable cost of producing four shirts is $3.25 (point *c*). The price exceeds the average variable cost, so it is sensible to continue operating, even at a loss.

shut-down price

The price at which the firm is indifferent between operating and shutting down; equal to the minimum average variable cost.

The firm's **shut-down price** is the price at which the firm is indifferent between operating and shutting down. To find the shut-down price, we find the minimum point on the *AVC* curve. In Figure 9.4, *AVC* reaches its minimum of $3 at a quantity of three shirts per minute, so the shut-down price is $3 (shown by point *d*). The average variable cost never drops below $3, so if the price drops below $3 it would be impossible to generate enough revenue to cover the firm's variable cost. When the price equals the shut-down price, the firm is generating just enough revenue to cover its variable costs, so it is just as well off operating as shutting down.

How long will a firm continue to operate at a loss? Let's think about what happens when the firm must decide whether or not to build a new production facility. The firm will build a new facility—and stay in the market—only if the price of shirts exceeds the average total cost of production. In other words, the firm will stay in the market only if the market price is high enough for its total revenue to cover *all* the costs of production, including the cost of the new facility. In other words, the price must be greater than or equal to the firm's break-even price. Although a firm might make a short-run decision to operate an existing facility at a loss, it won't replace the facility unless a new facility will be profitable.

Fixed Costs and Sunk Costs

Note that the decision whether to operate or shut down does not incorporate the fixed costs of the production facility. If we assume the facility cannot be rented out to some other firm while the shirt firm isn't using it, the fixed cost is a **sunk cost**, a cost the firm has already paid or committed to pay, so it cannot be recovered even by shutting down the factory. Therefore, the firm should ignore the cost of the facility when deciding whether to operate or shut down.

sunk cost
A cost that a firm has already paid or committed to pay, so it cannot be recovered.

Rent is just one example of an irrelevant sunk cost. The marginal principle tells us that decisions are based on the costs that depend on what we do, not on costs that we can do nothing about. Suppose a dairy farmer spills two-thirds of a 300-gallon load of milk on the way to an ice-cream plant. Should the farmer return to the farm or deliver the remaining 100 gallons? As long as the marginal cost of delivering the milk—the opportunity cost of the farmer's time and the cost of fuel—is less than the amount the farmer will be paid for the remaining 100 gallons, it is sensible to deliver the milk. The spilt milk is a sunk cost that is irrelevant to the farmer's delivery decision. The farmer should not cry over spilt milk, but deliver the rest.

application 3

STRADDLING THE ZINC COST CURVE

APPLYING THE CONCEPTS: What is the shutdown price?

Zinc is a vital input to the production of steel. Because the cost of mining zinc varies from one mine to another, the shutdown price varies too. The world price of zinc decreased from roughly $2,300 per ton in 2010–2011 to $1,900 in early 2012. The lower price was below the shutdown prices of Alcoa's mines in Italy and Spain: at a price of $1,900, the total revenue from the mines was less than the variable cost of operating the mines. The shutdown of Alcoa's mines decreased mining output by 531,000 tons. Although mines with lower production costs continued mining at a price of $1,900, many mines have shutdown prices in the range $1,500 to $1,900, and will shut down if the price continues to drop. **Related to Exercise 3.5.**

SOURCE: Based on Metal Bulletin, "No widespread shutdowns in zinc unless LME prices fall below $1,900," January 10, 2012; London Metal Exchange, LME Price Graph (lme.com/zinc_graph; accessed February 23, 2012).

Short-Run Supply Curves

Now that we've explored the output decision of a price-taking firm, we're ready to show how a firm responds to changes in the market price of its product. We'll show the relationship between price and quantity supplied with two short-run supply curves, one for the individual firm and one for the entire market.

The Firm's Short-Run Supply Curve

short-run supply curve
A curve showing the relationship between the market price of a product and the quantity of output supplied by a firm in the short run.

The firm's **short-run supply curve** shows the relationship between the market price and the quantity supplied by the firm in the short run, over a period of time during which one input—the production facility—cannot be changed. In the case of shirt producers, the firm's supply curve answers the following question: At a given market price for shirts, how many shirts will the firm produce? In Figures 9.3 and 9.4, we used the marginal principle to answer this question for several different prices: At a price of $3, the quantity is 3 shirts; at a price of $7, the quantity is 6 shirts; at a price of $12, the quantity is 8 shirts.

The firm's short-run supply curve is the part of the firm's short-run marginal-cost curve above the shut-down price. The shut-down price for the shirt firm is $3, so, as shown by point *a* in Figure 9.5, the short-run supply curve is the marginal-cost curve starting at $3. For any price above the shut-down price, the firm will choose the quantity at which price equals marginal cost, so we can read the firm's quantity supplied directly from its marginal-cost curve. If the price is $7, the firm will supply 6 shirts per minute (point *b*). As the price increases, the firm responds by supplying more shirts: 8 shirts at a price of $12 (point *c*) and 10 shirts at a price of $21 (point *d*).

What about prices below the shut-down price? If the price drops below the shut-down price, the firm's total revenue will not be high enough to cover its variable cost, so the firm will shut down and produce no output. In Panel A of Figure 9.5, the firm's supply curve starts at point *a*, indicating that the quantity supplied is zero for any price less than $3.

The Short-Run Market Supply Curve

short-run market supply curve
A curve showing the relationship between the market price and quantity supplied in the short run.

The **short-run market supply curve** shows the relationship between the market price and the quantity supplied by firms as a whole in the short run. Panel B of Figure 9.5 shows the short-run market supply curve when there are 100 identical shirt firms. For

▶ **FIGURE 9.5**
Short-Run Supply Curves
In Panel A, the firm's short-run supply curve is the part of the marginal-cost curve above the shut-down price. In Panel B, there are 100 firms in the market, so the market supply at a given price is 100 times the quantity supplied by the typical firm. At a price of $7, each firm supplies 6 shirts per minute (point *b*), so the market supply is 600 shirts per minute (point *f*).

(A) Firm's Supply Curve

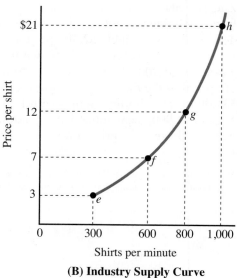

(B) Industry Supply Curve

each price, we get the quantity supplied for the entire market by multiplying the quantity supplied by the typical firm (from the individual supply curve) by 100. At a price of $7, each firm produces 6 shirts (point *b* in Panel A), so the market supply is 600 shirts (point *f* in Panel B). If the price increases to $12, each firm increases production to 8 shirts (point *c* in Panel A), so the market supply is 800 shirts (point *g* in Panel B).

What happens if firms are not identical but instead have different individual supply curves? To compute the market supply in this case, we add the quantities supplied by the hundreds of firms in the market. The assumption that firms are identical is harmless: It makes it easier to derive the market supply curve from the supply curve of the typical firm, but it does not change the analysis.

Market Equilibrium

Figure 9.6 shows a perfectly competitive market in equilibrium. For a short-run equilibrium, two conditions are satisfied:

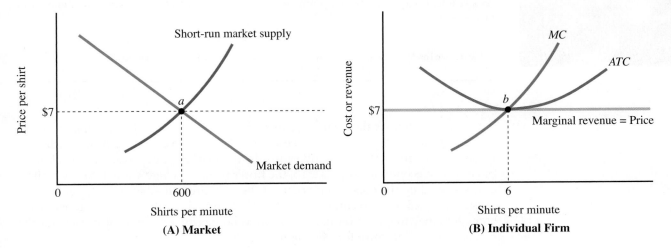

▲ **FIGURE 9.6**
Market Equilibrium
In Panel A, the market demand curve intersects the short-run market supply curve at a price of $7. In Panel B, given the market price of $7, the typical firm satisfies the marginal principle at point *b*, producing six shirts per minute. The $7 price equals the average cost at the equilibrium quantity, so economic profit is zero, and no other firms will enter the market.

1 At the market level, the quantity of the product supplied equals the quantity demanded. The demand curve intersects the short-run market supply curve at a price of $7 and a quantity of 600 shirts per minute (Panel A).

2 The typical firm in the market maximizes its profit, given the market price. Given the market price of $7, each of the 100 firms maximizes profit by producing 6 shirts per minute (Panel B).

In Figure 9.6, the market has reached a short-run equilibrium because the price of $7 generates a total of 600 shirts per minute, exactly the quantity demanded by consumers at this price.

In the long run, firms can enter or leave an industry, and existing firms can modify their facilities or build new facilities. The market reaches a long-run equilibrium when the two conditions for short-run equilibrium are met, and a third long-run condition holds as well:

3 Each firm in the market earns zero economic profit, so there is no incentive for existing firms to leave the market and no incentive for other firms to enter the market.

application 4

SHORT-RUN SUPPLY CURVE FOR CARGO

APPLYING THE CONCEPTS #4: Why is the short-run supply curve positively sloped?

Consider the supply of shipping services. The law of supply suggests that as the price of shipping increases, the quantity of shipping services will increase. At a relatively low freight rate of $2 per ton, only the most efficient ships operate, and they economize on fuel by traveling at a relatively low speed. As a result, the annual quantity of shipping services is only 70 units per year. At an intermediate freight price of $3 per ton, less efficient ships join the fleet. In addition, all the ships travel at a greater speed, using more fuel in the process. The combination of more ships and faster travel increases the quantity of shipping services provided to 85 units per year. At a high freight rate of $7 per ton, the least efficient ships join the fleet and all the ships run at full speed. As a result, the quantity of shipping services increases to 96 units per year. **Related to Exercise 4.6.**

SOURCE: Based on Martin Stopard, *Maritime Economics*, 3rd edition (New York: Routledge, 2007).

In Figure 9.6, at the quantity chosen by the typical firm (six shirts), the price ($7) equals the average total cost, so each firm makes zero economic profit, with total revenue equal to total cost. In other words, the market price equals the break-even price. When economic profit is zero, the firm's revenue is high enough to cover all its costs—including the opportunity costs of the entrepreneur—but not high enough to cause additional firms to enter the market. Each firm already in the market makes just enough money to stay in business, so there is no incentive for new firms to enter the market, and no incentive for existing firms to leave.

9.5 The Long-Run Supply Curve for an Increasing-Cost Industry

long-run market supply curve

A curve showing the relationship between the market price and quantity supplied in the long run.

Let's look at the **long-run market supply curve**, which shows the relationship between the market price and the quantity supplied by all firms in the long run, a period long enough that firms can enter or leave the market. Suppose the typical shirt firm produces six shirts per minute, using a standard set of inputs, including a factory, some workers, and raw materials of cotton and thread. In a perfectly competitive industry, there are no restrictions on entry, so anyone can use the standard set of inputs to produce six shirts per minute.

increasing-cost industry

An industry in which the average cost of production increases as the total output of the industry increases; the long-run supply curve is positively sloped.

We'll start with the case of an **increasing-cost industry**, in which the average cost of production increases as the total output increases, for two reasons:

- *Increasing input price.* As an industry grows, it competes with other industries for limited amounts of various inputs, and this competition drives up the prices of these inputs. For example, suppose the shirt industry competes against other industries for a limited amount of cotton. To get more cotton to produce more shirts, firms in the shirt industry must outbid other industries for the limited amount available, and this drives up the price of cotton.

- **Less productive inputs.** A small industry will use only the most productive inputs, but as the industry grows, firms may be forced to use less productive inputs. For example, a small shirt industry will use only the most skillful workers, but as the industry grows, it will hire workers with lower skills. As the average skill level of the industry's workforce decreases, the average cost of production increases: A firm will require more labor time—and pay more in labor costs—to produce each shirt.

Another example of progressively less productive inputs is the production of agricultural products such as sugar. Because of variation in climate and soil conditions, it is cheaper to grow sugar in some areas than in others. As the quantity of sugar produced increases, growers are forced to produce sugar in areas with less favorable climates and soil conditions, and this results in higher costs.

Production Cost and Industry Size

Table 9.4 shows hypothetical data on the cost of producing shirts. Let's start with the first row, which shows the firm's production costs in an industry with 100 firms and a total of 600 shirts produced per day (6 shirts per firm). To compute the total cost for the typical firm, we add the cost of the firm's production facility (the cost of the shirt factory), the cost of labor, and the cost of materials. In the first row, the total cost of the typical firm producing 6 shirts per minute is $42, and the average cost is $7 per shirt ($42 divided by 6 shirts). In the second row, if the number of firms doubles to 200 and each firm continues to produce 6 shirts per minute, the total output of the industry will double to 1,200 shirts per minute. For the two reasons listed earlier (higher input prices and less productive inputs), the total cost per firm increases to $60, so the average cost per shirt increases to $10. In the last row, when the total output of the industry increases to 1,800 shirts per minute, the average cost per shirt increases to $13.

TABLE 9.4 Industry Output and Average Production Cost

Number of Firms	Industry Output	Shirts per Firm	Total Cost for Typical Firm	Average Cost per Shirt
100	600	6	$42	$ 7
200	1,200	6	60	10
300	1,800	6	78	13

The shirt industry is an example of an increasing-cost industry. In the last column of Table 9.4, the average cost increases from $7 for an industry that produces 600 shirts, to $10 for an industry that produces 1,200 shirts, and so on. The average cost increases because firms in a larger industry pay higher input prices and use less productive inputs.

Drawing the Long-Run Market Supply Curve

The long-run supply curve tells us how much output will be produced at each price in the long run, when the number of firms in the market can change. Recall that in the long-run equilibrium, each firm makes zero economic profit, meaning that the price equals the average cost of production.

The data in Table 9.4 shows three points on the long-run supply curve. At a price of $7, a total of 100 firms will be in the market, with each producing 6 shirts per hour. This combination (price = $7 and quantity = 600 shirts) is on the long-run supply curve because the price equals the average cost. Each firm makes zero economic profit, so there is no incentive for firms to either enter or exit the market. This is shown by point *a* in Figure 9.7. Suppose the price of shirts increases. At the higher price, shirt making will be more profitable, and firms will enter the market, increasing total output. Firms will continue to enter the market until the economic profit becomes zero again, which happens when the average cost again equals the price. From Table 9.4, we see that entry will continue until the market reaches 200 firms producing 1,200 shirts at an average cost and price of $10. This is shown by point *b* in Figure 9.7. Point *c* shows another point on the long-run supply curve, with a price of $13 and a quantity of 1,800 shirts.

► **FIGURE 9.7**
Long-Run Market Supply Curve
The long-run market supply curve shows the relationship between the price and quantity supplied in the long run, when firms can enter or leave the industry. At each point on the supply curve, the market price equals the long-run average cost of production. Because this is an increasing-cost industry, the long-run market supply curve is positively sloped.

The long-run supply curve in Figure 9.7 is positively sloped, as it will be for any increasing-cost industry. This is another example of the law of supply. An increase in the price of shirts initially makes shirt production profitable, so firms enter the market and produce more shirts. As industry-wide output increases, the greater demand for cotton and labor increases input prices, which in turn increases the average cost of producing shirts. Firms will continue to enter the market until the average cost rises to the point where it equals the price of shirts. The positively sloped supply curve tells us the market won't produce a larger quantity of shirts unless the price rises to cover the higher average cost associated with the larger industry.

Examples of Increasing-Cost Industries: Sugar and Apartments

The sugar industry is an example of an increasing-cost industry. If the price of sugar is only 11 cents per pound, sugar production is profitable in areas with relatively low production costs, including the Caribbean, Latin America, Australia, and South Africa. At a price of 11 cents, the world supply of sugar equals the amount produced in these areas. As the price increases, sugar production becomes profitable in areas where production costs are higher, and as these areas enter the world market, the quantity of sugar supplied increases. For example, at a price of 14 cents per pound, sugar production is profitable in some countries in the European Union, too. At a price of 24 cents, production is profitable even in the United States.

application 5

CHINESE COFFEE GROWERS OBEY THE LAW OF SUPPLY

APPLYING THE CONCEPTS #5: How do producers respond to an increase in price?

Pu'er is a city in southern China that is famous for its tea, but is now getting a reputation for its coffee. Between 2009 and 2012, the world price of coffee beans nearly doubled. Farmers in Pu'er responded to the higher price by doubling the acreage of coffee, and cleared forested hillsides to grow more beans. At the relatively high world price, a hectare of coffee earns a family about $10,000 per year, which is three times the earnings from growing tea and five times the earnings from growing rice. The farmers' response illustrates the law of supply: an increase in price increases the quantity supplied. **Related to Exercise 5.7.**

SOURCE: Based on "For all the coffee in China," *The Economist*, January 28, 2012, pp. 44–45.

The market for apartments is another example of an increasing-cost industry with a positively sloped supply curve. Most communities use zoning laws to restrict the amount of land available for apartments. As the industry expands by building more apartments, firms compete fiercely for the small amount of land zoned for apartments. Housing firms bid up the price of land, increasing the cost of producing apartments. Producers can cover these higher production costs only by charging higher rents to tenants. In other words, the supply curve for apartments is positively sloped because land prices increase with the total output of the industry, pulling up average cost and necessitating a higher price for firms to make zero economic profit.

9.6   Short-Run and Long-Run Effects of Changes in Demand

We can use what we've learned about the short-run and long-run supply curves to get a deeper understanding of perfectly competitive markets. Let's use the two supply curves to explore the short-run and the long-run effects of a change in demand in a perfectly competitive market.

The Short-Run Response to an Increase in Demand

Figure 9.8 shows the short-run effects of an increase in the demand for shirts. Panel A shows what's happening at the market level. Let's start with the initial equilibrium shown by point *a*: The original demand curve intersects the short-run market supply curve at a price of $7 per shirt and a quantity of 600 shirts. When demand increases, the new demand curve intersects the supply curve at a price of $12 and a quantity of 800 shirts (point *b*). In Panel B, an increase in price from $7 to $12 increases the output per firm from 6 shirts to 8 shirts. At this quantity, the $12 price now exceeds the average total cost, so the typical firm makes an economic profit, as shown by the shaded rectangle.

Point *b* is not a long-run equilibrium because each firm is making a positive economic profit. Firms will enter the profitable market, and as they compete for customers the price of shirts will decrease. New firms will continue to enter the market until the price drops to the point at which economic profit is zero. How far will the price drop?

▲ **FIGURE 9.8**

Short-Run Effects of an Increase in Demand

An increase in demand for shirts increases the market price to $12, causing the typical firm to produce eight shirts instead of six. Price exceeds the average total cost at the eight-shirt quantity, so economic profit is positive. Firms will enter the profitable market.

The Long-Run Response to an Increase in Demand

We can use the long-run supply curve to determine the long-run price after an increase in demand. In Figure 9.9, the short-run effect of the increase in demand is shown by the move from point *a* to point *b*: The price increases from $7 to $12, and the quantity increases from 600 to 800. Economic profit is positive, so firms will enter the market. As shown by the long-run supply curve, entry will continue until

▶ **FIGURE 9.9**

Short-Run and Long-Run Effects of an Increase in Demand

The short-run supply curve is steeper than the long-run supply curve because of diminishing returns in the short run. In the short run, an increase in demand increases the price from $7 (point *a*) to $12 (point *b*). But in the long run, firms can enter the industry and build more production facilities, so the price eventually drops to $10 (point *c*). The large upward jump in price after the increase in demand is followed by a downward slide to the new long-run equilibrium price.

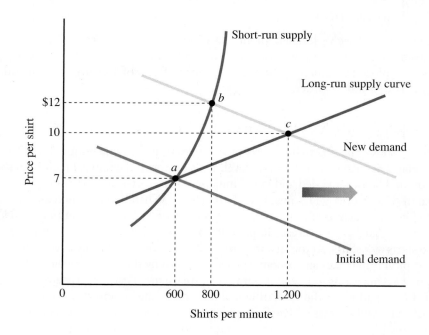

THE UPWARD JUMP AND DOWNWARD SLIDE OF WINE PRICES

APPLYING THE CONCEPTS #6: Why is the time path of market prices after an increase in demand?

As we saw in the chapter opener, the on-screen rave review of pinot noir wine increased the demand for pinot noir wine grown in the Willamette Valley in Oregon. In the short run, the supply of wine is inflexible, and eager consumers competed for the limited stock, causing prices to soar. For some brands, the price tripled. Producers responded to higher prices by expanding the vineyard acreage devoted to the pinot grape. A few years later, the new acreage came on line, increasing the quantity of wine produced. Eager growers competed for consumers by cutting prices, in many cases back to pre-*Sideways* prices. As we'll see in this chapter, when an increase in demand meets an inflexible short-run supply, prices rise in the short run. Eventually suppliers catch up with demand, and prices fall. **Related to Exercise 6.2.**

the price drops to $10 and the quantity is 1,200 shirts per minute. The new long-run equilibrium is shown by point *c*, where the new demand curve intersects the long-run supply curve. At this price and quantity, each of the 200 firms produces six shirts per minute and earns zero economic profit.

Figure 9.9 shows how the price of shirts changes over time. An increase in demand causes a large upward jump in the price from $7 to $12 in the short run, followed by a slide downward to the new long-run equilibrium price of $10. In the short run, firms respond to an increase in price by squeezing more output from their existing production facilities. Because of diminishing returns, it is very costly to increase output in the short run, so the price must increase by a large amount to cover these much higher production costs. The higher price causes new firms to enter the market and, as they enter, the price gradually drops to the point at which each firm makes zero economic profit. The long-run supply curve is relatively flat because firms enter the industry and build new factories, so there are no diminishing returns to increase production costs.

9.7 Long-Run Supply for a Constant-Cost Industry

So far we have examined products produced by increasing-cost industries, whose average cost increases as the industry expands. We turn next to a **constant-cost industry**, an industry whose average cost is constant—it doesn't change as the industry expands. That is, the prices of inputs such as labor and materials do not change as the total output of the industry increases. This happens when the industry uses a relatively small amount of the available labor and materials, meaning that events in the industry—increases or decreases in output—do not affect the price of the input. As a result, the average cost of production for the typical firm doesn't change as the industry grows. In Table 9.4, the shirt industry would be a constant-cost industry if the average cost of shirts was constant at $7 regardless of how many shirts were produced.

constant-cost industry
An industry in which the average cost of production is constant; the long-run supply curve is horizontal.

Long-Run Supply Curve for a Constant-Cost Industry

As an example of a constant-cost industry, consider the production of birthday cake candles. As the industry grows, it will use more workers, wicks, and wax, but because the industry is such a small part of the markets for labor and materials, the prices of these inputs won't change. As a result, the average cost of production won't change as the industry grows.

The long-run supply curve for a constant-cost industry is horizontal at the constant average cost of production. If the average cost of birthday cake candles is $0.05 per candle, the long-run supply curve for candles will be horizontal at $0.05, as shown by Figure 9.10. At any lower price, the quantity of candles supplied would be zero, because in the long run no rational firm would provide candles at a price lower than the average cost of production. At any higher price, firms would enter the candle industry in droves, and entry would continue until the price dropped to the constant average cost of $0.05 per candle.

► **FIGURE 9.10**

Long-Run Supply Curve for a Constant-Cost Industry
In a constant-cost industry, input prices do not change as the industry grows. Therefore, the average production cost is constant and the long-run supply curve is horizontal. For the candle industry, the cost per candle is constant at $0.05, so the supply curve is horizontal at $0.05 per candle.

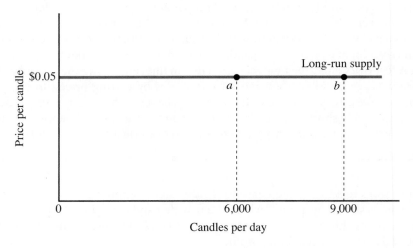

Hurricane Andrew and the Price of Ice

For an example of the effects of an increase in demand in a constant-cost industry, let's look at the short-run and long-run effects of a hurricane. In 1992, Hurricane Andrew struck the southeastern United States, leaving millions of people without electricity for several days. Figure 9.11 shows the short-run and long-run effects of the hurricane on the price of ice, which was used to cool and preserve food in areas without electricity. Before the hurricane, the market was at point *a*, with a price of $1 per bag of ice. The long-run supply curve is horizontal, indicating that the ice industry is a constant-cost industry.

In the short run (a day or two), the number of ice suppliers is fixed. The increase in demand caused by the hurricane moved the market from point *a* to point *b*, and the price rose to $5 per bag of ice. In the long run, firms responded to the higher price

► **FIGURE 9.11**

Hurricane Andrew and the Price of Ice
A hurricane increases the demand for ice, shifting the demand curve to the right. In the short run, the supply curve is relatively steep, so the price rises by a large amount—from $1 to $5. In the long run, firms enter the industry, pulling the price back down. Because ice production is a constant-cost industry, the supply is horizontal, and the large upward jump in price is followed by a downward slide back to the original price.

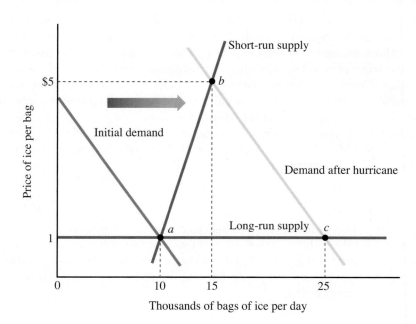

ECONOMIC DETECTIVE AND THE CASE OF MARGARINE PRICES

APPLYING THE CONCEPTS #7: How does a permanent decrease in demand affect the equilibrium price in a constant-cost industry?

Between 2000 and 2009, concerns about the health effects of trans-fatty acids decreased the demand for margarine. Although total consumption in the U.S. decreased by roughly half, the price of margarine in 2009 was roughly the same, in real terms, as the price in 2000. Why didn't the decrease in demand decrease the equilibrium price?

The margarine industry is an example of a constant-cost industry. As the total output of the industry changes, the prices of the key inputs to the production of margarine don't change, so the unit cost of production is unaffected by changes in total output. Of course a decrease in demand decreases the equilibrium price in the short run, but the exit of firms from the unprofitable industry causes the price to rise, and in the new long-run equilibrium, the original price—equal to the constant long-run marginal cost—will be restored. **Related to Exercises 7.3 and 7.5.**

SOURCE: Based on USDA/Economic Research Service, Food Availability Data Sets (http://www.ers.usda.gov/data/foodconsumption/FoodAvailDoc.htm). Accessed February 25, 2012.

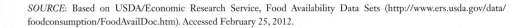

by entering the market. Many people trucked ice from distant locations and sold it from trucks parked on streets and highways. As these firms entered the ice market in the days after the hurricane, the price of ice gradually dropped, and the market eventually reached the intersection of the new demand curve and the long-run supply curve (point *c*), with a price equal to the pre-hurricane price. In the case of the retail ice industry, the long run is just a few days.

This pattern of price changes following the hurricane was observed in other markets. Immediately after the hurricane, $200 chain saws were sold for $900, but the price dropped steadily as new roadside firms entered the market. The same sort of price changes occurred for bottled water, tarpaper, and plywood. The basic pattern was a large upward jump in price followed by a downward slide to the long-run equilibrium price.

SUMMARY

In this chapter, we explored the decisions made by perfectly competitive firms and the implications of these decisions for the supply side of the market. In the short run, a firm uses the marginal principle to decide how much output to produce. In the long run, a firm will enter a market if the price exceeds the average cost of production. Here are the main points of this chapter:

1 A *price-taking* firm should produce the quantity of output at which the marginal revenue (the price) equals the marginal cost of production.

2 An unprofitable firm should continue to operate if its total revenue exceeds its total variable cost.

3 The long-run supply curve will be positively sloped if the average cost of production increases as the industry grows.

4 The long-run supply curve is flatter than the short-run supply curve because there are diminishing returns in the short run, but not in the long run.

5 An increase in demand causes a large upward jump in price, followed by a downward slide to the new long-run equilibrium price.

KEY TERMS

break-even price, p. 214

constant-cost industry, p. 225

firm-specific demand curve, p. 208

increasing-cost industry, p. 220

long-run market supply curve, p. 220

marginal revenue, p. 212

perfectly competitive market, p. 208

price taker, p. 208

short-run market supply curve, p. 218

short-run supply curve, p. 218

shut-down price, p. 216

sunk cost, p. 217

EXERCISES

All problems are assignable in MyEconLab.

9.1 Preview of the Four Market Structures

1.1 The firm-specific demand curve shows the relationship between the _____ charged by the firm and the _____ by the firm.

1.2 The firm-specific demand curve is _____ (horizontal/negatively) sloped for a perfectly competitive firm and _____ (horizontal/negatively) sloped for a monopolist.

1.3 For a monopolist, the firm-specific demand curve is the same as the _____ demand curve.

1.4 A perfectly competitive firm is a price _____, while a monopolist is a price _____.

1.5 In Pakistan, the market for phone service is perfectly _____, because a person can enter the market with a relatively small initial investment—only $310. (Related to Application 1 on page 210.)

9.2 The Firm's Short-Run Output Decision

2.1 Economic profit equals _____ minus _____.

2.2 Economic cost equals _____ cost plus _____ cost.

2.3 For a perfectly competitive firm, marginal revenue equals _____, and to maximize profit, the firm produces the quantity at which _____ equals _____.

2.4 The market price for wheat is $5. If a farmer's marginal cost is $7, the farmer should produce _____ (more/less) output.

2.5 At the current output level, a farmer's marginal cost of producing sugar is $0.30. If the price of sugar is $0.22 per pound, the farmer should _____ (increase/decrease) production. If the price of sugar is $0.32 per pound, the farmer should _____ (increase/decrease) production.

2.6 A firm produces 20 units of output at a market price of $5, a marginal cost of $5, and an average cost of $3. The firm's economic profit is $_____, and the firm _____ (is/is not) maximizing its economic profit.

2.7 If the market price equals a firm's break-even price, the firm earns _____ economic profit because _____ equals _____.

2.8 A decrease in price _____ (increases/decreases) a firm's marginal revenue, so it _____ (increases/decreases) the quantity supplied. This is the law of _____ in action.

2.9 The break-even price for switchgrass varies with _____, and on average is _____ per ton. (Related to Application 2 on page 214.)

2.10 Changes in the Break-Even Price. Consider a switchgrass farmer whose initial break-even price is $76 = $36 explicit cost + $40 opportunity cost for land. For each of the following changes, explain the effects on the farmer's production cost and break-even price. (Related to Application 2 on page 214.)

   a. The cost of fertilizer increases.

   b. The market price of alfalfa increases.

2.11 More or Fewer Deliveries? Consider a delivery firm that delivers packages by bicycle, charging $13 per package and paying each of its workers $12 per hour. One day, one of the workers was two hours late to work, and the number of packages delivered that day decreased by one package.

   a. Did the tardiness of the worker increase or decrease the firm's profit?

   b. Based on the new information provided by this experience, should the firm produce more deliveries by increasing its workforce, or produce fewer deliveries by reducing its workforce? Explain, using the marginal principle.

2.12 Advice for a Firm. You've been hired as an economic consultant by a price-taking firm that produces scarves. The firm already has a factory, so it is operating in the short run. The price of scarves is $9, the hourly wage is $24, and each scarf requires $1 worth of material. The following table shows the relationship between the number of workers and the output of scarves.

Workers	10	11	12	13	14	15
Output	5	29	41	47	50	52
Labor cost						
Material cost						
Fixed cost	$2	$2	$2	$2	$2	$2
Total cost						
Marginal cost						

a. Fill in the blanks in the table.
b. What is the profit-maximizing output?

9.3 The Firm's Shut-Down Decision

3.1 A firm will continue to operate an unprofitable business if _____ exceeds _____ cost.

3.2 Your firm has a total revenue of $500, a total cost of $700, and a variable cost of $600. You should _____ (operate/shut down) because _____ exceeds _____.

3.3 A firm that is losing money should continue to operate in the short run if the market price exceeds _____.

3.4 Your firm has a price of $5, an average total cost of $7, and an average variable cost of $4. In the short run, you should _____ (operate/shut down) because _____ exceeds _____. In the long run, you should _____ (stay in/exit) the market because _____ exceeds _____.

3.5 When the price of zinc dropped below $1,900, the price dropped below Alcoa's _____ price, the company _____. (Related to Application 3 on page 217.)

3.6 Advice for an Unprofitable Firm. You've been hired as an economic consultant by a price-taking firm that produces baseball caps. The firm already has a factory, so it is operating in the short run. The price of caps is $5, the hourly wage is $12, and each cap requires $1 worth of material. The firm has experimented with different workforces and the results are shown in the first two columns of the following table.

a. Fill in the blanks in the table.
b. Is it sensible to continue to operate at a loss with 14 workers?
c. Would it be better to operate with 15 workers? Explain, using the marginal principle.

Workers	Caps	Labor Cost	Material Cost	Variable Cost	Total Revenue	Marginal Cost of Caps
14	56					
15	60					

3.7 A Bluffing Farmer? Consider the following statement from a wheat farmer to his workers: "The price of wheat is very low this year, and the most I can get for the crop is $35,000. If I paid you the same amount as I paid you last year ($30,000), I'd lose money because I also have to worry about the $20,000 I paid three months ago for seed and fertilizer. I'd be crazy to pay a total of $50,000 to harvest a crop I can sell for only $35,000. If you are willing to work for half as much as last year ($15,000), my total cost will be $35,000, so I'll break even. If you don't take a pay cut, I won't harvest the wheat." Is the farmer bluffing, or will the farm workers really lose their jobs if they reject the proposed pay cut?

3.8 Operate or Shut Down? In Figure 9.4 on page 216, suppose the market price of shirts drops to $2. At this price, the marginal principle will be satisfied at a point below point _____ on the marginal-cost curve. Price is _____ (less/greater) than *AVC*, so the firm will be better off _____ (operating/shutting down).

9.4 Short-Run Supply Curves

4.1 A firm's short-run supply curve shows the relationship between _____ on the horizontal axis and _____ on the vertical axis.

4.2 To draw a firm's short-run supply curve, you need its _____ curve and its _____ price.

4.3 A perfectly competitive industry has 100 identical firms. At a price of $8, the typical firm supplies seven units of output, so the market quantity supplied is _____ units of output.

4.4 Figure 9.6 on page 219 shows a long-run equilibrium because (1) the quantity _____ equals the quantity _____; (2) the typical firm maximizes _____ by picking the quantity at which _____ equals _____; (3) each firm makes _____ economic profit because _____ equals _____.

4.5 A firm making zero economic profit stays in the market because total revenue is high enough to cover all the firm's costs, including the opportunity costs of the entrepreneur's _____ and _____.

4.6 As the price of shipping services increases, the quantity supplied _____ as firms deploy _____ ships and as each ship travels _____ (Related to Application 4 on page 220.)

4.7 **Soybeans versus Processor Chips.** Why is the market for soybeans perfectly competitive, with thousands of soybean farmers, while the market for computer processor chips is dominated by a few large firms? (Related to Application 2 on page 214.)

4.8 **Draw the Supply Curves.** The following table shows short-run marginal costs for a perfectly competitive firm:

Output	100	200	300	400	500
Marginal cost	$5	$10	$20	$40	$70

  a. Use this information to draw the firm's marginal-cost curve.

  b. Suppose the shut-down price is $10. Draw the firm's short-run supply curve.

  c. Suppose there are 100 identical firms with the same marginal-cost curve. Draw the short-run industry supply curve.

4.9 **Equilibrium and Break-Even Price.** Explain why the equilibrium price in a perfectly competitive industry is sometimes below the break-even price, sometimes above it, and sometimes equal to it.

4.10 **Maximizing the Profit Margin?** According to the marginal principle, the firm should choose the quantity of output at which price equals marginal cost. A tempting alternative is to maximize the firm's profit margin, defined as the difference between price and short-run average total cost. Use the firm's short-run cost curves to evaluate this approach. Draw the firm's short-run supply curve and compare it to the supply curve of a firm that maximizes its profit.

4.11 **Expand If Profit Margin Is Positive?** Consider a firm that uses the following rule to decide how much output to produce: If the profit margin (price minus short-run average total cost) is positive, the firm will produce more output. Use the firm's short-run cost curves to evaluate this approach. Draw the firm's short-run supply curve and compare it to the short-run supply curve of a profit-maximizing firm.

9.5 The Long-Run Supply Curve for an Increasing-Cost Industry

5.1 The long-run supply curve shows the relationship between _____ on the horizontal axis and _____ on the vertical axis.

5.2 Arrows up or down: As the total output of an increasing-cost industry increases, the average cost of production _____ because input prices _____ and the productivity of inputs used by firms _____.

5.3 As the total output of an increasing-cost industry increases, the average cost of production _____ (increases/decreases), so the supply curve is _____ (horizontal/positively sloped/ negatively sloped).

5.4 In Table 9.4 on page 221, suppose the relationship between industry output and the total cost for the typical firm is linear, and each firm produces six shirts. If there are 400 firms in the industry, the total cost for the typical firm is $_____, and the average cost per shirt is $_____. Another point on the supply curve is a price of $_____ and a quantity of _____ shirts.

5.5 An increase in the price of shirts will cause firms to _____ the industry, and as output increases the _____ cost of production increases. Entry will continue until _____ equals _____.

5.6 Land-use zoning that limits the amount of land for apartments generates a relatively _____ (flat/ steep) supply curve for housing, so an increase in the demand for apartments leads to a relatively _____ (large/small) increase in price.

5.7 An increase in the price of coffee increased the quantity supplied as land was converted from growing _____ to growing coffee. (Related to Application 5 on page 223.)

5.8 **Copper Price Elasticity of Supply.** Suppose the price of copper increases from $1,500 to $2,500 per ton and the quantity supplied increases from 9 million tons to 11 million tons. Use the midpoint formula to compute the price elasticity of supply for copper.

5.9 Sugar Import Ban. Suppose that initially there are no controls on sugar imported into the United States, so the price paid in the United States equals the prevailing world price.

   a. If the world price is 13 cents per pound, what areas of the world supply sugar to the world market and the United States?

   b. Suppose the United States bans sugar imports. The new price of sugar will be at least $_____.

5.10 Long-Run Supply Curve of Lamps. Suppose each lamp manufacturer produces 10 lamps per hour. Complete the following table. Then use the data in the table to draw the long-run supply curve for lamps.

Number of Firms	Industry Output	Total Cost for Typical Firm	Average Cost per Lamp
40		$300	
80		360	
120		420	

5.11 How Steep a Supply Curve? Consider two cities, one on a small island, and a second on a large plain.

   a. Draw a long-run supply curve for housing for each city, and explain any differences between the two supply curves.

   b. If demand for housing increases by the same amount in each city, which city will experience a larger increase in price?

9.6 Short-Run and Long-Run Effects of Changes in Demand

6.1 The short-run supply curve is steeper than the long-run supply curve because of the principle of _____.

6.2 Arrows up or down: Suppose the demand for shirts increases. In the short run, the price _____ by a relatively large amount. As firms enter the market, the price _____. In the new long-run equilibrium, there is a net _____ in price relative to the old equilibrium. (Related to Application 6 on page 225.)

6.3 An increase in demand causes a large initial upward (jump/slide) in price, followed by a downward (jump/slide) to the new long-run equilibrium price.

6.4 Increase in Housing Demand in Britain versus the United States. Suppose that in both Britain and the United States, the initial equilibrium price of housing is $200,000. Britain has more severe restrictions on residential development in the short run. Suppose the demand for housing increases by the same amount in the two countries.

   a. Draw a set of supply and demand curves showing the effects on housing prices in the short run.

   b. The price increase is larger in _____ because that country has a relatively _____ supply curve.

   c. Suppose the long-run supply curves in the two countries have the same slope. Show the long-run effects of the increase in demand.

   d. In the long run, Britain's price of housing is _____ (higher/lower/the same).

9.7 Long-Run Supply for a Constant-Cost Industry

7.1 As the total output of a constant-cost industry increases, the _____ cost does not change, so the long-run supply curve is _____ (horizontal/positively sloped/negatively sloped).

7.2 A constant-cost industry consumes a relatively _____ (small/large) amount of inputs such as labor and materials, so as industry output increases the prices of these inputs _____ (increase/decrease/don't change).

7.3 Arrow up, down, or horizontal: In a constant-cost industry, when demand increases the long-run equilibrium price _____ (Related to Application 7 on page 227.)

7.4 The Price of Haircuts. The haircutting industry in your city uses a tiny fraction of the electricity, scissors, and commercial space available on the market. In addition, the industry employs only about 100 of the 50,000 people who could cut hair.

   a. Draw a long-run supply curve for haircutting in your city.

   b. Suppose the initial equilibrium price of haircuts is $12. Draw demand and supply graphs to show the short-run and long-run effects of an increase in population. Does population growth affect the long-run equilibrium price of haircuts?

7.5 Margarine Prices. Several years ago, people became concerned about the undesirable health effects of eating margarine. The demand for margarine dropped, decreasing its price. Some time later, the price started rising steadily, although demand hadn't been changing. After several months of price hikes, the price of margarine reached the price observed before demand decreased. A blogger suggested that the rising price was evidence of a conspiracy on the part of margarine producers. Provide an alternative explanation for the rising price of and its eventual return to the original price. (Related to Application 7 on page 227.)

7.6 **The Price of Tattoos.** According to a market expert, tattooing in your city is a constant-cost industry. The initial equilibrium price is $24.

a. Arrows up or down: In the long run the wage of tattoo artists _____ as industry output increases.

b. If the demand for tattoos doubles and stays at the higher level for three years, the price of tattoos three years from now will be $_____.

c. Show the change in (b) using a supply-demand graph.

NOTES

1. *Sideways*, 2004 Twentieth Century Fox; written by Alexander Payne and Jim Taylor. Based on the novel *Sideways* by Rex Pickett; New York, St. Martin's Press, 2004.

Monopoly and Price Discrimination

On college campuses across the country, beverage companies like Coca-Cola and Pepsi pay cash in exchange for monopoly power— exclusive rights to sell beverages on campus.

For example, under the Coca-Cola agreement with the University of California Berkeley that expired in 2011, the company paid an average of $615,000 per year to support recreational sports, intercollegiate athletic programs, and various student groups. The exclusive agreement bans competing products on campus, and directs the university to "maximize the sale and distribution of (Coca-Cola) Products, including hawking Products . . . at all sporting events." As we'll see in this chapter, a firm is willing to pay for the rights to monopoly because the exclusion of competing products allows the monopolist to charge higher prices.

In recent years, the battles over campus beverage monopolies have become heated and more lucrative. In 2011, UC Berkeley responded to student concerns about the business practices of Coca-Cola by signing an exclusive contract with Pepsi. Under the new agreement, Pepsi will pay the university $1.6 million per year.

LEARNING OBJECTIVES

- Describe and explain a monopolist's output decision.

- Explain why a monopoly is socially inefficient.

- Identify the trade-offs associated with a patent.

- Describe the practice of price discrimination.

MyEconLab
MyEconLab helps you master each objective and study more efficiently.

monopoly

A market in which a single firm sells a product that does not have any close substitutes.

market power

The ability of a firm to affect the price of its product.

barrier to entry

Something that prevents firms from entering a profitable market.

patent

The exclusive right to sell a new good for some period of time.

network externalities

The value of a product to a consumer increases with the number of other consumers who use it.

*i*n the previous chapter we explored the decisions made by firms in a perfectly competitive market, a market in which there are many firms. This chapter deals with the opposite extreme: a **monopoly**, a market in which a single firm sells a product that does not have any close substitutes. In contrast with a perfectly competitive, or price-taking, firm, a monopolist controls the price of its product, so we can refer to a monopolist as a *price maker*. A monopolist has **market power**, the ability to affect the price of its product. Of course, consumers obey the law of demand, and the higher the monopolist's price, the smaller the quantity it will sell.

A monopoly occurs when a **barrier to entry** prevents a second firm from entering a profitable market. Among the possible barriers to entry are patents, network externalities, government licensing, the ownership or control of a key resource, and large economies of scale in production:

- A **patent** grants an inventor the exclusive right to sell a new product for some period of time, currently 20 years under international rules.

- When the value of a product to a consumer increases with the number of consumers who use it, **network externalities** are at work. For example, the larger the number of people on an online social network, the greater the opportunities for interaction. Similarly, the larger the number of people using a software application such as a word processor, the greater the opportunities to share files. Network externalities provide an advantage to existing firms and may inhibit the entry of new ones.

- Under a licensing policy, the government chooses a single firm to sell a particular product. Some examples are licensing for radio and television stations, off-street parking in cities, and vendors in national parks.

- If a firm owns or controls a key resource, the firm can prevent entry by refusing to sell the input to other firms. The classic example is DeBeers, the South African company that controls about 80 percent of the world's production of diamonds. Before the 1940s, the Aluminum Company of America—ALCOA—had long-term contracts to buy most of the world's available bauxite, a key input to the production of aluminum.

natural monopoly

A market in which the economies of scale in production are so large that only a single large firm can earn a profit.

- A **natural monopoly** occurs when the scale economies in production are so large that only a single large firm can earn a profit. The market can support only one profitable firm, because if a second firm entered the market, both firms would lose money. Some examples are cable TV service, electricity transmission, and water systems.

In this chapter, we will discuss "unnatural" monopolies, which result from artificial barriers to entry. Later in the book, we'll explore the reasons for natural monopolies and various public policies to control them.

This chapter examines the production and pricing decisions of a monopoly and explores the implications for society as a whole. As we'll see, monopoly is inefficient from society's perspective because it produces too little output. We'll also discuss the trade-offs with patents, which lead to monopoly and higher prices but also encourage innovation. We'll also explore the issue of price discrimination, which occurs when firms such as airlines and movie theaters charge different prices to different types of consumers. Although we discuss price discrimination in a monopoly, it also happens in markets with more firms, including oligopoly (a few firms) and monopolistic competition (many firms selling differentiated products).

10.1 The Monopolist's Output Decision

Like other firms, a monopolist must decide how much output to produce, given its objective of maximizing its profit. We learned about production costs in an earlier chapter, so we start our discussion of the monopolist's output decision with the revenue side of the profit picture. Then we show how a monopolist picks the profit-maximizing quantity.

Total Revenue and Marginal Revenue

A firm's total revenue—the money it gets by selling its product—equals the price times the quantity sold. In this part of the chapter, we'll assume that the monopolist charges the same price to each customer. The table in Figure 10.1 shows how to use a demand schedule (in columns 1 and 2) to compute a firm's total revenue (in column 3). At a price of $16, the firm doesn't sell anything, so its total revenue is zero. To sell the first unit, the firm must cut its price to $14, so its total revenue is $14. To get consumers to buy two units instead of just one, the firm must cut its price to $12, so the total revenue for selling two units is $24. As the price continues to drop and the quantity sold increases, total revenue increases for a while but then starts falling. To sell five units instead of four, the firm cuts its price from $8 to $6, and total revenue decreases from $32 to $30. The total revenue for selling six units is even lower, only $24.

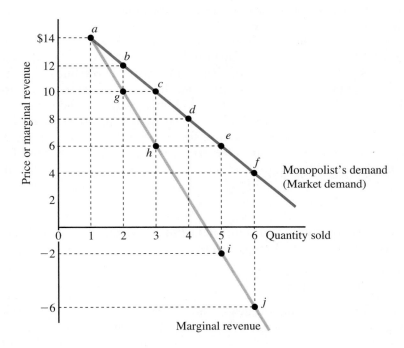

◄ **FIGURE 10.1**
The Demand Curve and the Marginal-Revenue Curve
Marginal revenue equals the price for the first unit sold, but is less than the price for additional units sold. To sell an additional unit, the firm cuts the price and receives less revenue on the units that could have been sold at the higher price. The marginal revenue is positive for the first four units, and negative for larger quantities.

(1) Price (P)	(2) Quantity Sold (Q)	(3) Total Revenue $(TR = P \times Q)$	(4) Marginal Revenue $MR = \Delta TR / \Delta Q$
$16	0	0	—
14	1	$14	$14
12	2	24	10
10	3	30	6
8	4	32	2
6	5	30	−2
4	6	24	−6

The firm's marginal revenue is defined as the change in total revenue that results from selling one more unit of output. You can see this in column 4 of the table in Figure 10.1. For example, the marginal revenue for the third unit is $6, equal to the total revenue from selling three units ($30) minus the total revenue from selling only two units ($24). As shown in the table, marginal revenue is positive for the first four units sold. Beyond that point, selling an additional unit actually decreases total revenue, so marginal revenue is negative. For example, the marginal revenue for the fifth unit is –$2, and the marginal revenue for the sixth unit is –$6.

The table in Figure 10.1 illustrates the trade-offs faced by a monopolist in cutting the price to sell a larger quantity. When the firm cuts its price from $12 to $10, there is good news and bad news:

- **Good news:** The firm collects $10 from the new customer (the third), so revenue increases by $10.
- **Bad news:** The firm cuts the price for all its customers, so it gets less revenue from the customers who would have been willing to pay the higher price of $12. Specifically, the firm collects $2 less from each of the two original customers, so revenue from the original customers decreases by $4.

The combination of good news and bad news leads to a net increase in total revenue of only $6, equal to $10 gained from the new customer minus $4 lost on the first two customers.

Our discussion of good news and bad news has revealed a key feature of a monopoly: *Marginal revenue is less than price.* To sell one more unit, the monopolist must cut its price, and the difference between marginal revenue and price is the bad news—the loss in revenue from consumers who would have bought the good at the higher price. In fact, this is true for any firm that must cut its price to sell more.

You may recall from the previous chapter that marginal revenue is different for a perfectly competitive firm, which can sell as much as it wants at the market price. If a perfectly competitive firm sells one unit at $12, it can sell a second unit at the same price, so its marginal revenue is $12 for the second unit sold, just as it was $12 for the first unit sold. For a perfectly competitive firm, marginal revenue is always equal to the price, no matter how many units the firm sells. A perfectly competitive firm does not cut the price to sell more, so there is no bad news associated with selling more.

A Formula for Marginal Revenue

We can use a simple formula to compute marginal revenue. The formula quantifies the good news and bad news from selling one more unit:

marginal revenue = new price + (slope of demand curve × old quantity)

The first part of the formula is the good news, the money received for the extra unit sold. The second part is the bad news from selling one more unit, the revenue lost by cutting the price for the original customers. The revenue change equals the price change required to sell one more unit—the slope of the demand curve, which is a negative number—times the number of original customers who get a price cut.

We can illustrate this formula with an example. Suppose the monopolist wants to increase the quantity sold from two to three, so it cuts the price from $12 to $10. The new price is $10, the old quantity is two units, and the slope of the demand curve is –$2, so marginal revenue is $6:

marginal revenue = $10 − ($2 per unit × 2 units) = $6

Similarly, to sell the fifth unit, the firm would cut the price from $8 to $6, and marginal revenue is actually negative:

marginal revenue = $6 − ($2 per unit × 4 units) = −$2

Marginal revenue is negative because the $8 revenue lost from the original customers exceeds the $6 gain from the new customer. This happens because there are so many original customers who get a price cut. If a monopolist continues to cut its price, marginal revenue will eventually become negative because there will be so many consumers who get price cuts.

The graph in Figure 10.1 shows the demand curve and marginal-revenue curve for the data shown in the table. For the first unit sold, the marginal revenue equals the price. Because the firm must cut its price to sell more output, the marginal-revenue curve lies below the demand curve. For example, the demand curve shows that the firm will sell three units at a price of $10 (point *c*), but the marginal revenue for this quantity is only $6 (point *b*). The firm will sell five units at a price of $6 (point *e*), but the marginal revenue for this quantity is –$2 (point *i*). The marginal revenue is positive for the first four units and negative for larger quantities.

Using the Marginal Principle

A monopolist can use the marginal principle to decide how much output to produce. Suppose a firm called Curall holds a patent on a new drug that cures the common cold and must decide how much of the drug to produce.

> ### MARGINAL PRINCIPLE
> Increase the level of an activity as long as its marginal benefit exceeds its marginal cost. Choose the level at which the marginal benefit equals the marginal cost.

The firm's activity is producing the cold drug, and it will pick the quantity at which the marginal revenue from selling one more dose equals the marginal cost of production.

In Figure 10.2, the first two columns of the table show the relationship between the price of the cold drug and the quantity demanded. We can use these numbers to draw the market demand curve, as shown in the graph in Figure 10.2. Because the firm is a monopolist—the only seller of the drug—the market demand curve shows how much the firm will sell at each price. The demand curve is negatively sloped, consistent with

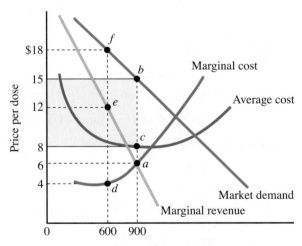

◀ **FIGURE 10.2**
The Monopolist Picks a Quantity and a Price
To maximize profit, the monopolist picks point *a*, where marginal revenue equals marginal cost. The monopolist produces 900 doses per hour at a price of $15 (point *b*). The average cost is $8 (point *c*), so the profit per dose is $7 (equal to the $15 price minus the $8 average cost) and the total profit is $6,300 (equal to $7 per dose times 900 doses). The profit is shown by the shaded rectangle.

(1) Price (*P*)	(2) Quantity Sold (*Q*)	(3) Marginal Revenue	(4) Marginal Cost	(5) Total Revenue (*TR* = *P* × *Q*)	(6) Total Cost (*TC*)	(7) Profit (*TR* − *TC*)
$18	600	$12	$4.00	$10,800	$5,710	$5,090
17	700	10	4.60	11,900	6,140	5,760
16	800	8	5.30	12,800	6,635	6,165
15	900	6	6.00	13,500	7,200	6,300
14	1,000	4	6.70	14,000	7,835	6,165
13	1,100	2	7.80	14,300	8,560	5,740
12	1,200	0	9.00	14,400	9,400	5,000

the law of demand. For example, at a price of $18 per dose, the quantity demanded is 600 doses per hour (point f), compared to 900 doses at a price of $15 (point b).

Like other monopolists, the firm must cut its price to sell a larger quantity, so marginal revenue is less than price. This is shown in the third column of the table as well as the graph. We can use the marginal-revenue formula explained earlier to compute marginal revenue for different quantities of output:

marginal revenue = new price + (slope of demand curve × old quantity)

The slope of the demand curve is –$0.01 per dose. To simplify the arithmetic, rather than using the "new" price and "old" quantity, we can use a matched pair of price and quantities from the demand curve to get an approximation of marginal revenue. When the change in price is relatively small (for example, $0.01) the difference between the new and old price is small enough to be ignored. For example, at a price of $18, the quantity sold is 600 doses, so marginal revenue is $12:

marginal revenue = $18 − ($0.01 × 600 doses) = $12

Similarly, at a price of $15, the quantity is 900 doses and marginal revenue is $6:

marginal revenue = $15 − ($0.01 × 900 doses) = $6

We're ready to show how a monopolist can use the marginal principle to pick a quantity to produce. To maximize its profit, the firm will produce the quantity at which the marginal revenue equals marginal cost. As shown in the fourth row in the table in Figure 10.2, this happens with a quantity of 900 doses. In the graph, the marginal-revenue curve intersects the marginal-cost curve at point a, with a quantity of 900 doses, so that's the quantity that maximizes profit. To get consumers to buy this quantity, the price must be $15 (point b on the demand curve). The average cost of production is $8 per dose (shown by point c).

We can compute the firm's profit in two ways. First, profit equals total revenue minus total cost:

profit = total revenue − total cost

profit = $15 per dose × 900 doses − $8 per dose × 900 doses = $6,300

Second, we can compute the profit per dose and multiply it by the number of doses:

profit = profit per dose × quantity of doses

The profit per dose is the price minus the average cost: $7 = $15−$8:

profit = $7 per dose × 900 doses = $6,300

To show that a quantity of 900 doses maximizes the firm's profit, let's see what would happen if the firm picked some other quantity. Suppose the firm decided to produce 599 doses per hour at a price just above $18 (just above point f on the demand curve). Could the firm make more profit by cutting the price by enough to sell one more dose? The firm should answer two questions:

- What is the extra cost associated with producing dose number 600? As shown by point d on the marginal-cost curve, the marginal cost of the 600th dose is $4.
- What is the extra revenue associated with dose number 600? As shown by point e on the marginal-revenue curve, the marginal revenue is $12.

If the firm wants to maximize its profit, it should produce the 600th dose because the $12 extra revenue exceeds the $4 extra cost, meaning the firm's profit will increase by $8. The same argument applies, with different numbers for marginal revenue and marginal cost, for doses 601, 602, and so on, up to 900 doses. The firm should continue to increase the quantity produced as long as the marginal revenue exceeds the marginal cost. The marginal principle is satisfied at point a, with a total of 900 doses.

Why should the firm stop at 900 doses? Beyond 900 doses, the marginal revenue from an additional dose will be less than the marginal cost associated with producing it. Although the firm could cut its price and sell a larger quantity, an additional dose would add less to revenue than it adds to cost, so the firm's total profit would decrease. As shown in the fifth row in the table in Figure 10.2, the firm could sell 1,000 doses at a price of $14, but the marginal revenue at this quantity is only $4, while the marginal cost at this quantity is $6.70. Producing the 1,000th dose would decrease the firm's profit by $2.70. For any quantity exceeding 900 doses, the marginal revenue is less than the marginal cost. Therefore, the firm should produce exactly 900 doses.

Let's review what we've learned about how a monopolist picks a quantity and how to compute the monopoly profit. The three-step process is as follows:

1 Find the quantity that satisfies the marginal principle, that is, the quantity at which marginal revenue equals marginal cost. In the example shown in Figure 10.2, marginal revenue equals marginal cost at point *a*, so the monopolist produces 900 doses.

2 Using the demand curve, find the price associated with the monopolist's chosen quantity. In Figure 10.2, the price required to sell 900 doses is $15 (point *b*).

3 Compute the monopolist's profit. The profit per unit sold equals the price minus the average cost, and the total profit equals the profit per unit times the number of units sold. In Figure 10.2, the profit is shown by the shaded rectangle, with height equal to the profit per unit sold and width equal to the number of units sold.

application 1

MARGINAL REVENUE FROM A BASEBALL FAN

APPLYING THE CONCEPTS #1: How does a monopolist maximize profit?

We expect the owner of a MLB (major-league baseball) team to choose the quantity (the number of fans at the game) at which marginal revenue equals marginal cost (MR = MC). The marginal cost of an additional fan is close to zero, so the profit-maximization rule simplifies to MR = 0. And yet for the typical team, it appears that MR is actually negative: adding fans by selling more tickets actually decreases total revenue from tickets. What explains this puzzling behavior?

We can illustrate the puzzle with a simple example. Suppose that with a ticket price of $24, the team sells 20,000 tickets. If the slope of the demand curve is –0.002, marginal revenue is –$16:

$$MR = \$24 - 0.002 \times 20,000 = -\$16.$$

In this case, cutting the price to sell one more ticket generates good news ($24 collected from the new fan) that is less than the bad news (the $40 lost on the 20,000 fans who would have paid the higher price). The marginal revenue is negative, so the team could increase its total revenue from tickets by increasing the price and decreasing the quantity of tickets sold. Why don't MLB teams increase their ticket prices?

The solution to this puzzle is concessions. Suppose the average MLB fan spends $20 per game on merchandise that costs the owner about $4 to provide. In this case, each ticket sold generates an additional $16 in net concession revenue to the owner, just enough to offset the $16 revenue loss on ticket sales. Once we expand the definition of marginal revenue to include the net revenue from concessions, the owner's choice is consistent with profit-maximization. What appears to be too low a price could be just about right. **Related to Exercises 1.8 and 1.9.**

SOURCE: Based on Anthony Krautmann and David Berri, "Can we find it at the concession? Understanding price elasticity in professional sports," *Journal of Sports Economics* 8 (2007), pp. 183–191.

10.2 The Social Cost of Monopoly

Why should we as a society be concerned about monopoly? Most people are not surprised to hear that a monopolist uses its market power to charge a relatively high price. If this were the end of the story, a monopolist would simply gain at the expense of consumers. In other words, a monopoly would change how we slice the economic "pie," with a bigger slice for producers and a smaller slice for consumers. As we'll see in this part of the chapter, the social consequences of monopoly go beyond a different slicing of the pie: A monopoly causes inefficiency and actually reduces the size of the pie, so there is less to divide among consumers and producers.

Deadweight Loss from Monopoly

How does a monopoly differ from a perfectly competitive market? To show the difference, let's consider an example of an arthritis drug that could be produced by a monopoly or a perfectly competitive industry. Let's take the long-run perspective—a period of time long enough that a firm is perfectly flexible in its choice of inputs and can enter or leave the market.

Consider the monopoly outcome first. Let's assume the long-run average cost of producing the arthritis drug is constant at $8 per dose. As we saw in the chapter on production and cost, if average cost is constant, the marginal cost equals the average cost. In Panel A of Figure 10.3, the long-run marginal-cost curve is the same as the long-run average-cost curve. Given the demand and marginal-revenue curves in Panel A of Figure 10.3, the monopolist will maximize profit where marginal revenue equals marginal cost (point *a*), producing 200 doses per hour at a price of $18 per dose (point *b*). The monopolist's profit is $2,000 per hour—a $10 profit per dose ($18 – $8) times 200 doses.

▲ FIGURE 10.3

Monopoly versus Perfect Competition: Its Effect on Price and Quantity

(A) The monopolist picks the quantity at which the long-run marginal cost equals marginal revenue—200 doses per hour, as shown by point *a*. As shown by point *b* on the demand curve, the price required to sell this quantity is $18 per dose. (B) The long-run supply curve of a perfectly competitive, constant-cost industry intersects the demand curve at point *c*. The equilibrium price is $8, and the equilibrium quantity is 400 doses.

Consider next the market for the arthritis drug under perfect competition. We're assuming the arthritis drug industry is a constant-cost industry: Input prices do not change as the industry grows, so the long-run market supply curve is horizontal at the long-run average cost of producing the drug, which is $8 per dose. In Panel B of Figure 10.3, the horizontal long-run supply curve intersects the demand curve at point c, with an equilibrium price of $8 and an equilibrium quantity of 400 doses per hour. Compared to a monopoly outcome, the perfectly competitive outcome has a lower price ($8 instead of $18 per dose) and a larger quantity (400 doses instead of 200).

To examine the social cost of monopoly power, let's imagine we start with a perfectly competitive market, and then switch to a monopoly. Consumers will be worse off under monopoly, and we can use the concept of consumer surplus to determine just how much worse off they will be. As we saw in the chapter on market efficiency, consumer surplus is shown by the area between the demand curve and the horizontal price line. In Figure 10.4, the monopoly price is $18, so the consumer surplus with a monopoly is shown by triangle A. In contrast, the perfectly competitive price is $8, so the consumer surplus with perfect competition is shown by the larger triangle consisting of triangle A, rectangle B, and triangle D. In other words, a switch from perfect competition to monopoly decreases consumer surplus by the areas B and D.

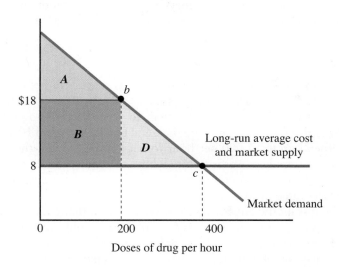

◄ **FIGURE 10.4**
The Deadweight Loss from a Monopoly
A switch from perfect competition to monopoly increases the price from $8 to $18 and decreases the quantity sold from 400 to 200 doses. Consumer surplus decreases by an amount shown by the areas B and D, while profit increases by the amount shown by rectangle B. The net loss to society is shown by triangle D, the deadweight loss from monopoly.

We can use some simple geometry to compute the reduction in consumer surplus. The formula for the area of a rectangle is

$$\text{area of rectangle} = \text{base} \times \text{height}$$

In Figure 10.4, the base of rectangle B is 200 and the height is $10, so the area is $2,000:

$$\text{area of rectangle } B = 200 \text{ doses} \times \$10 \text{ per dose} = \$2,000$$

The switch to monopoly increases the price by $10 per dose, so consumers pay $10 extra on the 200 doses they buy from the monopolist, resulting in a loss of $2,000. The other part of the consumer loss is triangle D. The formula for the area of a triangle is

$$\text{area of triangle} = 1/2 \times \text{base} \times \text{height}$$

In Figure 10.4, the base of triangle D is 200 and the height is $10, so the area is $1,000:

$$\text{area of triangle } D = 1/2 \times 200 \text{ doses} \times \$10 \text{ per dose} = \$1,000$$

The switch to monopoly increases the price and decreases the quantity demanded because consumers obey the law of demand. Consumers lose consumer surplus on the doses they would have consumed at the lower price, and this $1,000 loss is shown by triangle D. The total loss of consumers is the sum of the areas of rectangle B and triangle D, or $3,000.

It's clear that consumers lose from monopoly, but what about the monopolist? Under perfect competition, each firm makes zero economic profit. In contrast, the monopolist earns positive economic profit, shown by rectangle *B* in Figure 10.4. The monopolist's profit per dose is $10, the $18 price minus the $8 average cost. The monopolist's profit is $2,000:

$$\text{profit} = \$10 \text{ per dose} \times 200 \text{ doses} = \$2,000$$

This $2,000 gain by the monopolist comes at the expense of consumers.

Because the monopolist recovers only part of the loss experienced by consumers, there is a net loss from switching to monopoly. Consumers lose rectangle *B* and triangle *D*, but the monopolist gains only rectangle *B*. That leaves triangle *D* as the net decrease in the market surplus, or the **deadweight loss from monopoly**. The word *deadweight* indicates this loss is not offset by a gain to anyone. Triangle *D* measures the consumer surplus lost because the monopoly produces less output than a perfectly competitive market. The monopolist prevents consumers from getting consumer surplus for the 201st through the 400th units of output, meaning it reduces the size of the economic pie and causes inefficiency. The lesson is that monopoly is inefficient because it generates less output than a perfectly competitive market.

deadweight loss from monopoly
A measure of the inefficiency from monopoly; equal to the decrease in the market surplus.

Rent Seeking: Using Resources to Get Monopoly Power

Another source of inefficiency from a monopoly is the use of resources to acquire monopoly power. Because a monopoly is likely to earn a profit, firms are willing to spend money to persuade the government to erect barriers to entry that grant monopoly power through licenses, franchises, and tariffs. In Figure 10.4, a firm would be willing to spend up to $2,000 per hour to get a monopoly on the arthritis drug. One way to get monopoly power is to hire lobbyists to persuade legislators and other policymakers to grant monopoly power. **Rent seeking** is the process of using public policy to gain economic profit.

rent seeking
The process of using public policy to gain economic profit.

Rent seeking is inefficient because it uses resources that could be used in other ways. For example, the people employed as lobbyists could instead produce goods and services. In Figure 10.4, if the monopolist spent all its potential profit of $2,000 per hour on rent-seeking activity, the net loss to society would be areas *B* and *D*, not just area *D*. A classic study of rent seeking by economist Richard Posner found that firms in some industries spent up to 30 percent of their total revenue to get monopoly power.[1]

---

application 2

A CASINO MONOPOLY IN CRESWELL, OREGON?

APPLYING THE CONCEPTS #1: What is the value of a monopoly?

A developer interested in building a casino in Creswell, Oregon, placed a curious announcement in the local newspaper. If local voters approved the casino, the developer promised to give citizens a total of $2 million per year. With an adult population of about 1,600, each adult in Creswell would receive a cash payment of $1,250 per year. Why did the developers propose this deal? This is an example of rent seeking: The casino developer was seeking the profits that would come from having a monopoly in the casino market, and was willing to pay at least $2 million to get it. **Related to Exercises 2.5, 2.6, and 2.7.**

SOURCE: Based on Sherri Buri, "Creswell Casino Wins Few Friends," *Eugene Register Guard*, April 2, 1996, 1.

The chapter opener provides an example of rent seeking. Beverage companies pay millions of dollars to universities to get a monopoly on campus beverages. Like any monopolist, a beverage company will use its monopoly power to charge higher prices, so students pay, indirectly, for the programs supported by the beverage companies, for example recreational sports and intercollegiate athletic programs.

Monopoly and Public Policy

Given the social costs of monopoly, the government uses a number of policies to intervene in markets dominated by a single firm or likely to become a monopoly. We'll examine these policies later in the book. In the case of natural monopoly—a market that can support only a single firm—the government can intervene by regulating the price the natural monopolist charges. In other markets, the government uses antitrust policies to break monopolies into smaller companies and prevent corporate mergers that would lead to others. These policies are designed to promote competition, leading to lower prices and more production.

10.3 Patents and Monopoly Power

One source of monopoly power is a government patent that gives a firm the exclusive right to produce a product for 20 years. As we'll see, a patent encourages innovation because the innovators know they will earn monopoly profits on a new product over the period covered by the patent. If the monopoly profits are large enough to offset the substantial research and development costs of a new product, a firm will develop the product and become a monopolist. Granting monopoly power through a patent may be efficient from the social perspective because it may encourage the development of products that would otherwise not be developed.

Incentives for Innovation

Let's use the arthritis drug to show why a patent encourages innovation. Suppose a firm called Flexjoint hasn't yet developed the drug but believes the potential benefits and costs of doing so are as follows:

- The economic cost of research and development will be $14 million, including all the opportunity costs of the project.
- The estimated annual economic profit from a monopoly will be $2 million (in today's dollars).
- Flexjoint's competitors will need three years to develop and produce their own versions of the drug, so if Flexjoint isn't protected by a patent, its monopoly will last only three years.

Based on these numbers, Flexjoint won't develop the drug unless the firm receives a patent that lasts at least 7 years. That's the length of time the firm needs to recover the research and development costs of $14 million ($2 million per year times 7 years). If there is no patent and the firm loses its monopoly in 3 years, it will earn a profit of $6 million, which is less than the cost of research and development. In comparison, with a 20-year patent the firm will earn $40 million, which is more than enough to recover its $14 million cost.

Trade-Offs from Patents

Is the patent for Flexjoint's drug beneficial from the social perspective? The patent grants monopoly power to the firm, and the firm responds by charging a higher price and producing less than the quantity that would be produced in a perfectly competitive market. Looking back at Figure 10.4, a monopolist produces 200 doses per hour instead of 400. From society's perspective, 400 doses is better than 200 doses, but we don't have that choice. Flexjoint won't develop the drug unless a patent protects the firm from competition for at least seven years. Therefore, society's choice is between the monopoly outcome of 200 doses or 0 doses. Because a quantity of 200 doses is clearly better than none, the patent is beneficial from society's perspective.

What about a product a firm develops without the protection of a patent? Suppose we change the Flexjoint example by altering one number: The cost of research and development is only $5 million, not $14 million. Suppose it still takes Flexjoint's competitors three years to develop a substitute, and Flexjoint's profit per year is still $2 million. Without a patent, Flexjoint would earn an economic profit of $6 million during its three-year monopoly ($2 million per year times three years), which is more than the $5 million cost of research and development. Therefore, the firm would develop the new drug even without a patent. In this case, a patent would merely prolong a monopoly, and so it would be inefficient from society's perspective.

What are the general conclusions about the merits of the patent system? It is sensible for a government to grant a patent for a product that would otherwise not be developed, but it is not sensible for other products. Unfortunately, no one knows in advance whether a particular product would be developed without a patent, so the government can't be selective in granting patents. In some cases, patents lead to new products, although in other cases, they merely prolong monopoly power.

application 3

BRIBING THE MAKERS OF GENERIC DRUGS

APPLYING THE CONCEPTS #3: What happens when a patent expires and a monopoly ends?

When a patent expires, new firms enter the market, and the resulting competition for consumers decreases prices and increases quantities. In the pharmaceutical drug market, when the patent for a brand-name drug expires, other firms introduce generic versions of the drug. The generics are virtually identical to the original branded drug, but they sell at a much lower price. The producers of branded drugs have an incentive to delay the introduction of generic drugs and sometimes use illegal means to do so.

In recent years, the Federal Trade Commission (FTC) has investigated allegations that the makers of branded drugs made deals with generic suppliers to keep generics off the market. The alleged practices included cash payments and exclusive licenses for new versions of the branded drug. In 2003, the FTC ruled that two drug makers had entered into an illegal agreement when Schering-Plough paid Upsher-Smith Laboratories $60 million to delay the introduction of a low-price alternative to its prescription drug K-Dur 20, which is used to treat people with low potassium.

Another tactic is to claim that generics are not as good as the branded drug. DuPont has claimed that generic versions of its Coumadin (a blood thinner) are not equivalent to Coumadin and may pose risks to patients. Because generic versions are virtually identical to the branded drugs, such claims are not based on science. **Related to Exercises 3.4 and 3.5.**

SOURCE: Based on Federal Trade Commission, "Commission Rules Schering-Plough, Upsher, and AHP Illegally Delayed Entry of Lower-Cost Generic Drug," www.ftc.gov/opa/2003/12/schering.htm (accessed July 9, 2006).

10.4 Price Discrimination

Up to this point in the book, we've assumed a firm charges the same price to all its customers. As we'll see in this part of the chapter, however, a firm may be able to divide consumers into two or more groups and sell the good at a different price to each, a practice known as **price discrimination**. For example, airlines offer discount tickets to travelers who are flexible in their departure times, and movie theaters have lower prices for senior citizens. The only legal restriction on price discrimination is that a firm cannot use it to drive rival firms out of business.

Although price discrimination is widespread, it is not always possible. A firm has an opportunity for price discrimination if three conditions are met:

1   **Market power.** The firm must have some control over its price, facing a negatively sloped demand curve for its product. Although we will discuss price discrimination by a monopolist, any firm that faces a negatively sloped demand curve can charge different prices to different consumers. In fact, the only type of firm that cannot engage in price discrimination is a perfectly competitive price-taking firm. Such a firm faces a horizontal demand curve, taking the market price as given. For all other types of markets—monopoly, oligopoly, and monopolistic competition—price discrimination is possible.

2   **Different consumer groups.** Consumers must differ in their willingness to pay for the product or in their responsiveness to changes in price, as measured by the price elasticity of demand. In addition, the firm must be able to identify different groups of consumers. For example, an airline must be able to distinguish between business travelers and tourists, and a movie theater must be able to distinguish between seniors and nonseniors.

3   **Resale is not possible.** It must be impractical for one consumer to resell the product to another consumer. Airlines prohibit consumers from buying and reselling tickets. If airlines allowed consumers to sell discount tickets to each other, you could go into business as a ticket broker, buying discount airline tickets one month ahead and then selling them to business travelers one week before the travel date. In general, the possibility of resale causes price discrimination to break down.

One approach to price discrimination is to identify consumers who are not willing to pay the regular price and offer them a discount. Here are some examples:

- **Discounts on airline tickets.** Airlines offer discount tickets to travelers who spend Saturday night away from home because they are likely to be tourists, not business travelers. The typical tourist is not willing to pay as much for air travel as the typical business traveler. Airlines also offer discount tickets to people who plan weeks ahead, because tourists plan further ahead than business travelers.

- **Discount coupons for groceries and restaurant food.** The typical coupon-clipper is not willing to pay as much as the typical consumer.

- **Manufacturers' rebates for appliances.** A person who takes the trouble to mail a rebate form to the manufacturer is not willing to pay as much as the typical consumer.

- **Senior-citizen discounts on airline tickets, restaurant food, drugs, and entertainment.** Some seniors have more time to shop for bargains, and are thus more sensitive to prices. Other seniors have relatively low income, and are willing to pay less than the typical consumer.

- **Student discounts on movies and concerts.** The typical student has less income than the typical consumer, and is thus willing to pay less for movies.

The challenge for a firm is to figure out which groups of consumers should get discounts. Firms can experiment with different prices and identify groups of consumers

price discrimination
The practice of selling a good at different prices to different consumers.

that are most sensitive to price. In September 2000, Amazon.com started charging different prices for different types of consumers. For example, consumers who used Netscape's browser paid $65 for the *Planet of the Apes* DVD, while Internet Explorer users paid $75 for the same DVD.[2] Prices also varied with the consumer's Internet service provider and the number of previous purchases from Amazon. An Amazon spokeswoman said the company varied prices in a random fashion, as part of ongoing tests to see how consumers respond to price changes. In other words, it appears that Amazon was assessing the willingness to pay of different types of consumers. In principle, Amazon could use the data collected to develop systems of price discrimination, giving discounts to the most price-sensitive consumers. After widespread protests of the Amazon pricing experiments, the company stopped the practice and issued refunds to about 7,000 consumers who had paid relatively high prices.

Senior Discounts in Restaurants

Consider a restaurant whose patrons fall into two groups, senior citizens and others. In Figure 10.5, the demand curve for senior citizens is lower than the demand curve for other groups, reflecting the assumption that the typical senior is willing to pay less than the typical nonsenior. Their lower willingness to pay could result from having lower income or more time to shop for low prices.

► FIGURE 10.5
The Marginal Principle and Price Discrimination
To engage in price discrimination, the firm divides potential customers into two groups and applies the marginal principle twice—once for each group. Using the marginal principle, the profit-maximizing prices are $3 for seniors (point *b*) and $6 for nonseniors (point *d*).

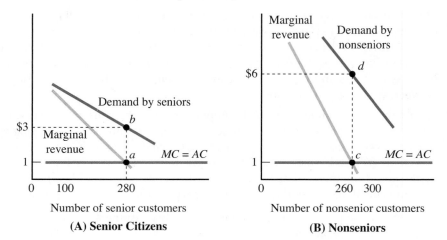

(A) Senior Citizens

(B) Nonseniors

Under a price-discrimination plan, the restaurant will simply apply the marginal principle twice, once for seniors and a second time for nonseniors. This approach is sensible, because the two groups have different demands for restaurant meals, so the restaurant should treat them differently. Panel A of Figure 10.5 shows how to pick a price for senior citizens. The marginal principle—marginal revenue equals marginal cost—is satisfied at point *a*, with 280 senior meals per day. Therefore, the appropriate price for seniors is $3, as shown by point *b* on the senior demand curve. In Panel B of Figure 10.5, the marginal principle is satisfied at point *c* for nonseniors, with 260 meals per day and a price of $6 per meal.

We know the application of the marginal principle maximizes profit in each segment of the market. Therefore, price discrimination—with a price of $3 for seniors and $6 for everyone else—maximizes the restaurant's total profit. If the restaurant were instead to charge a single price of $5 for both groups, the profit from each group would be lower, so the restaurant's total profit would be lower, too.

Price Discrimination and the Elasticity of Demand

We can use the concept of price elasticity of demand to explain why price discrimination increases the restaurant's profit. From the chapter on elasticity, we know that when demand is elastic ($E_d > 1$), there is a negative relationship between price and total revenue: When the price decreases, total revenue (price times quantity sold) increases because the percentage increase in the quantity demanded exceeds the percentage decrease in price.

Suppose the restaurant initially has a single price of $5 for both seniors and nonseniors. Compared to other consumers, senior citizens have more elastic demand for restaurant meals, in part because they have lower income and more time to shop for low prices. A price cut for senior citizens brings good news and bad news for the restaurant:

- **Good news:** Demand is highly elastic, so total revenue increases by a large amount.
- **Bad news:** More meals are served, so total cost increases.

If the senior demand for meals is highly elastic, that is, E_d is well above 1.0, the good news will dominate the bad news: The increase in revenue will more than offset the increase in cost. Consequently, a price cut will increase the firm's profit.

For nonseniors, the firm will have an incentive to increase the price above the initial common price of $5. Suppose nonseniors have a mildly elastic demand for meals, with E_d just above 1.0. A price hike for nonseniors brings bad news on the revenue side and good news on the cost side:

- **Bad news:** Demand is mildly elastic, so total revenue decreases by a small amount.
- **Good news:** Fewer meals are served, so total cost decreases.

If the demand by nonseniors is mildly elastic, the good news will dominate the bad news: The savings in production costs will exceed the revenue loss. Consequently, the price hike for nonseniors will increase the firm's profit.

Examples: Movie Admission versus Popcorn, and Hardback versus Paperback Books

Why do senior citizens pay less than everyone else for admission to a movie, but the same as everyone else for popcorn? As we've seen, a senior discount is not an act of generosity by a firm, but an act of profit maximization. Senior citizens are typically willing to pay less than other citizens for movies, so a theater divides its consumers into two groups—seniors and others—and offers a discount to seniors. This price discrimination in favor of senior citizens increases the theater's profit. Why don't theaters offer a senior discount for popcorn? Unlike admission to the theater, popcorn can be easily transferred from one customer to another. If senior citizens could buy popcorn at half the regular price, many nonseniors would get seniors to buy popcorn for them, so the theater wouldn't sell as much popcorn at the regular price and its profit would decrease. In contrast, as long as ticket takers check consumers' admissions tickets, admission to the movie is not transferable.

Why are hardback books so much more expensive than paperback books? Most books are published in two forms—hardback and paperback. Although the cost of producing a hardback book is only about 20 percent higher than producing a paperback, the hardback price is typically three times the paperback price. The hardback edition comes first, and the paperback edition is published months, or even years, later. Booksellers use hardbacks and paperbacks to distinguish between two types of consumers: those who are willing to pay a lot and those who are willing to pay a little. Some people are eager to read a book when it first comes out, and publishers provide them with high-price hardbacks. The more casual readers are willing to wait for the lower-priced paperback. The pricing of hardback and paperback books is another example of price discrimination, under which consumers with less elastic demand pay a higher price.

WHY DOES MOVIE POPCORN COST SO MUCH?

APPLYING THE CONCEPTS #4: When do firms have an opportunity to charge different prices to different consumers?

That $4 bucket of popcorn you get in the movie theater costs less than $0.10 to produce. What explains the 4,000 percent markup? Economists have struggled with this question for years, and now we have an answer. Moviegoers vary in their willingness to pay for seeing a movie, and a movie theater has an incentive to identify the high demanders and charge them more, while keeping the price low for the low demanders. It turns out that a reliable predictor of the willingness to pay for a movie is the consumption of movie popcorn: The people who buy a lot of popcorn are the consumers who are willing to pay the most for a movie experience. So a convenient way for the theater to charge more to the consumers who are willing to pay more is to jack up the price of popcorn. As a result, the low demanders simply pay the admission price, while the high demanders pay the admission price plus the jacked-up price of a bucket of popcorn.

We can illustrate with a simple example. Suppose a low demander is willing to pay $11 for a movie, while a high demander is willing to pay $15 for a movie and popcorn. If the theater charges $10 for admission and $4 for popcorn, each consumer will get a consumer surplus of $1 (equal to $11 – $10 for the low demander and $15 – $14 for the high demander), so both consumers will see the movie. If instead the theater charged $12 for admission and $0.10 for popcorn, the high demander will see the movie, but the low demander won't. The theater's pricing strategy gets the low demander into the theater at a price of $10, and because the marginal cost of an additional consumer is close to zero, the theater's profit increases. **Related to Exercise 4.3.**

SOURCE: Based on Ricard Gil and Wesley Hartman, "Why Does Popcorn Cost So Much at the Movies? An Empirical Analysis of Metering Price Discrimination" (Research Paper 1983, Stanford Graduate School of Business, 2008).

SUMMARY

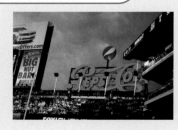

In this chapter, we've seen some of the subtleties of monopolies and their pricing policies. Compared to a perfectly competitive market, a monopoly charges a higher price, produces a smaller quantity, and wastes resources in the pursuit of monopoly power. On the positive side, some of the products we use today might never have been invented without the patent system and the monopoly power it grants. Firms with market power often use price discrimination to increase their profits. Here are the main points of the chapter:

1 Compared to a perfectly competitive market, a market served by a monopolist will charge a higher price, produce a smaller quantity of output, and generate a *deadweight loss* to society.

2 Some firms use resources to acquire monopoly power, a process known as *rent seeking*.

3 *Patents* protect innovators from competition, leading to higher prices for new products but greater incentives to develop new products.

4 To engage in *price discrimination*, a firm divides its customers into two or more groups and charges lower prices to groups with more elastic demand.

5 Price discrimination is not an act of generosity; it's an act of profit maximization.

KEY TERMS

barrier to entry, p. 234

deadweight loss from monopoly, p. 242

market power, p. 234

monopoly, p. 234

natural monopoly, p. 234

network externalities, p. 234

patent, p. 234

price discrimination, p. 245

rent seeking, p. 242

EXERCISES

All problems are assignable in MyEconLab.

10.1 The Monopolist's Output Decision

1.1 For a monopolist, marginal revenue is _____ (greater/less) than price.

1.2 A monopoly that cuts its price gains revenue from its _____ customers but loses revenue from its _____ customers.

1.3 At a price of $18 per CD, a firm sells 60 CDs. If the slope of the demand curve is –$0.10, marginal revenue for the 61st CD is $_____. The firm should cut the price to sell one more CD if the marginal cost is less than $_____.

1.4 Arrow up or down: As the quantity produced by a monopolist increases, the gap between the marginal-revenue curve and demand curve _____.

1.5 To maximize profit, a monopolist picks the quantity at which _____ equals _____.

1.6 Arrows up or down: At a price of $18 per CD, the marginal revenue of a CD seller is $12. If the marginal cost of CDs is $9, the firm should _____ its price to _____ the quantity.

1.7 You want to determine the profit-maximizing quantity for a monopolist. You can ask the firm's accountant to draw the firm's revenue and costs curves, but each curve will cost you $1,000. From the following list, indicate which curves you will request: average total cost, average fixed cost, average variable cost, marginal cost, demand, marginal revenue.

1.8 The marginal cost of an additional baseball fan is zero, so the profit-maximizing condition simplifies to _____. (Related to Application 1 on page 239.)

1.9 **Tickets and Merchandise.** Consider a baseball team that has a ticket price of $45 and sells 30,000 tickets at this price. The slope of the demand curve is –$0.002. The typical fan purchases $25 worth of merchandise that costs the owner $5 to provide.

  a. The marginal revenue from ticket sales is _____.

  b. Including both ticket sales and merchandise, the marginal fan contributes an additional _____ to the team's total revenue. (Related to Application 1 on page 239.)

1.10 **Book Pricing: Publishers versus Authors.** Consider the problem of setting a price for a book. The marginal cost of production is constant at $20 per book. The publisher knows from experience that the slope of the demand curve is –$0.20 per book: Starting with a price of $44, a price cut of $0.20 will increase the quantity demanded by one book. For example, here are some combinations of price and quantity:

Price per book	$44	$40	$36	$32	$30
Quantity of textbooks	80	100	120	140	150

  a. What price will the publisher choose?

  b. Suppose that the author receives a royalty payment equal to 10 percent of the total sales revenue from the book. If the author could choose a price, what would it be?

  c. Why would the publisher and the author disagree about the price for the book?

  d. Design an alternative author-compensation scheme under which the author and the publisher would choose the same price.

1.11 Restaurant Pricing. Consider a restaurant that charges $10 for all you can eat and has 30 customers at this price. The slope of the demand curve is –$0.10 per meal, and the marginal cost of providing a meal is $3. Compute the profit-maximizing price and quantity, and illustrate with a complete graph.

1.12 Empty Seats. Consider the Slappers, a hockey team that plays in an arena with 8,000 seats. The only cost associated with staging a hockey game is a fixed cost of $6,000: The team incurs this cost regardless of how many people attend a game. The demand curve for hockey tickets has a slope of –$0.001 per ticket ($1 divided by 1,000 tickets): Each $1 increase in price decreases the number of tickets sold by 1,000. For example, here are some combinations of price and quantity:

Price per ticket	$4	$5	$6	$7
Quantity of tickets	8,000	7,000	6,000	5,000

The owner's objective is to maximize the profit per hockey game (total revenue minus the $6,000 fixed cost).

a. What single price will maximize profit?

b. If the owner picks the price that maximizes profit, how many seats in the arena will be empty? Why is it rational to leave some seats empty?

c. Suppose the owner could engage in price discrimination. Would you expect the number of filled seats to increase or decrease? Explain.

1.13 Negative Marginal Revenue. The manager of your firm is puzzled because the larger the quantity of output sold, the lower its total revenue. The manager gets weekly data in a table with two columns of numbers: Quantity Sold and Total Revenue. After you do some computations and add a third and a fourth column of numbers, the manager looks at the new table and says, "Aha, now I see why selling more decreases total revenue."

a. The third column of numbers has data on _____, and the fourth column has data on _____.

b. How do the additional columns of numbers explain the negative relationship between quantity sold and total revenue?

10.2 The Social Cost of Monopoly

2.1 A monopoly is inefficient solely because the monopolist gets a profit at the expense of consumers. _____ (True/False)

2.2 To show the deadweight loss from monopoly, we compare the monopoly outcome to what would happen under _____.

2.3 The deadweight loss from monopoly is shown graphically by the area between the _____ curve and the _____ curve between the _____ quantity and the _____ quantity.

2.4 The average cost for providing off-street parking is $30 per space per day, and as a monopolist you could charge $35 per space per day for 200 spaces. The maximum amount that you are willing to pay for a monopoly is $_____.

2.5 The offer from casino developers to the citizens of Creswell, Oregon, is an example of _____. (Related to Application 2 on page 242.)

2.6 Ending a Casino Monopoly. Consider a state that initially has a single casino for gambling. Suppose the state allows a second casino to enter the market. How would you expect the entry of the second casino to affect (a) the variety of games offered in the casinos and (b) the payout (winnings) per dollar spent? (Related to Application 2 on page 242.)

2.7 Payoff for Casino Approval. Recall the Application on the casino developer's offer to pay citizens to approve a casino. Why aren't similar deals proposed for new clothing stores, music stores, or auto repair shops? (Related to Application 2 on page 242.)

2.8 Consumer Compensation. Consider the chapter opener about campus beverage monopolies. Your job is to fully compensate each student for the cost associated with a soft-drink monopoly. Suppose Coca-Cola increased the price of soft drinks by $0.20 per can and each student consumed 10 soft drinks before the monopoly was granted.

a. Kate continues to buy 10 soft drinks at the higher price. What is the appropriate compensation for her?

b. Elise buys only 4 soft drinks at the higher price. Her demand curve is linear. What is her appropriate compensation? Draw a graph that shows her change in consumer surplus.

2.9 Pricing with Zero Marginal Cost. Consider a natural spring that produces water with a unique taste. The monopolist who owns the spring has a fixed cost of installing plumbing to tap the water but no marginal cost. The demand curve for the spring water is linear. Draw a graph to show the monopolist's choice of a price and quantity. At the profit-maximizing quantity, what is the price elasticity of demand? If the spring were owned by a government that applied the marginal principle, what price would it charge?

2.10 Rules of Monopoly. In the board game Monopoly, a player who gets the third deed for a group of properties (for example, the third of three orange properties) doubles the rent charged to all other players who land on any property in the group. Similarly, a player who has a single railroad charges a rent of $25, while a player who has all four railroads charges a rent of $200 for each railroad.

    a. Are these pricing rules consistent with the analysis of monopoly in this chapter?

    b. In the game, is there a deadweight loss from monopoly? Why or why not?

2.11 The National Park Service Monopoly. The National Park service grants a single firm the right to sell food and other goods in Yosemite National Park.

    a. What are the trade-offs associated with this policy? Who gains and who loses?

    b. Does your answer to part (a) depend on whether the monopoly is granted as a political favor or auctioned to the highest bidder?

2.12 Deadweight Loss and Demand Elasticity. Using Figure 10.4 as a starting point, consider a similar product that has the same monopoly price and quantity ($18 and 200 doses), but a more elastic demand. The long-run marginal cost is the same ($8).

    a. A more elastic demand generates a _____ (flatter/steeper) market demand curve.

    b. Draw a graph like the one shown in Figure 10.4 and show the deadweight loss from the monopoly on the product.

    c. The deadweight loss is _____ (larger/smaller) than the loss shown in Figure 10.4 because the change in is _____ (larger/smaller).

10.3 Patents and Monopoly Power

3.1 A patent increases the incentive to develop new products because it _____ the price of the product and thus generates profit to cover a firm's costs of _____.

3.2 In some cases, a patent is socially inefficient because it merely _____; in other cases, a patent is socially beneficial because it _____.

3.3 Consider the arthritis drug example on page 240. If the research and development costs are $20 million, Flexjoint will develop the drug if it gets a patent that lasts at least _____ years.

3.4 To prolong their monopoly power, the producers of branded drugs pay millions of dollars to _____. (Related to Application 3 on page 244.)

3.5 Paying to Keep a Generic Out. Suppose your firm produces a branded drug at an average cost of $2 per dose and a price of $5 per dose. You sell 1,000 doses per day. If a generic version of the drug were introduced, your daily sales would decrease to 400 doses. How much are you willing to pay each day to prevent the entry of the generic version? (Related to Application 3 on page 244.)

3.6 Patent for NoSmak. A potential new drug, NoSmak, could cure lip-smacking with one dose, but research and development would cost $80 million. The monopoly profit (earned while a single firm produces the product) will be $10 million per year. After a patent expires, the original developer of the drug will have sufficient brand loyalty to earn $3 million per year for another 10 years.

    a. What is the shortest patent length required to induce a firm to develop the drug?

    b. How would your answer to part (a) change if you ignore the profit earned after the patent expires?

10.4 Price Discrimination

4.1 A price-discriminating firm will charge a higher price to consumers with a relatively _____ (elastic/inelastic) demand and a lower price to consumers with a relatively _____ (elastic/inelastic) demand.

4.2 The aspirin sold in airports is more expensive than aspirin sold in grocery stores because the demand for aspirin in airports is relatively _____.

4.3 A reliable predictor of a consumer's willingness to pay for a movie is the consumption of _____. (Related to Application 4 on page 248.)

4.4 Senior citizens pay less than everyone else for admission to a movie, but the same as everyone else for beverages because beverages are _____, while admission is not.

4.5 The price of a hardback edition of a best-selling book is typically three times the price of the paperback edition because the demand from the eager consumers who buy hardbacks is relatively _____ (elastic, inelastic).

4.6 Senior Discounts for Movies. Your movie theater charges a single price of $6. The marginal cost of each patron is $1. A recent marketing survey revealed the following information about senior citizens and nonseniors.

	Price	Number of Patrons	Slope of Demand Curve
Seniors	$6	100	–$0.01 per patron
Nonseniors	6	80	–0.10 per patron

a. The marginal revenue for senior citizens is $_____, while the marginal revenue for nonseniors is $_____.

b. If your objective is to maximize profit, the marginal principle tells you to _____ the price for seniors and _____ the price for nonseniors.

4.7 Book Pricing and Elasticity of Demand. A publisher initially prices both hardback books and paperback books at $20 per book. The hardback version comes out first, followed two months later by the paperback version. The publisher initially sells the same number of hardbacks and paperbacks (100 each). Each book costs $2 to produce.

a. Complete the following table.

	Price	Quantity	Total Revenue	Total Cost	Profit
Hardback	$20	100			
Paperback	20	100			
Total		200			

b. The price elasticity of demand for hardback (eager) buyers is 0.50, and the price elasticity of demand for paperback (patient) buyers is 2.00. Suppose the publisher increases the price for hardbacks by 10 percent and decreases the price of paperbacks by 10 percent. Complete the following table.

	Price	Quantity	Total Revenue	Total Cost	Profit
Hardback	$22				
Paperback	18				
Total					

c. Does price discrimination increase or decrease the publisher's profit?

4.8 Haircuts in Mulletville. The town of Mulletville has a single hairstylist. The marginal cost of a haircut is the same for men and women ($10). The quantity of haircuts is 100 for men and 100 for women. The profit-maximizing price for women is $35, compared to $15 for men.

a. What explains the price difference?

b. Illustrate with a complete graph.

4.9 Tax Cuts for Discounters? Consider the following statement from a member of a city council: "Several of the merchants in our city offer discounts to our senior citizens. These discounts obviously decrease the merchants' profits, so we should decrease the merchants' taxes to offset their losses on senior-citizen discounts." Do you agree or disagree? Explain.

4.10 Airline Pricing. Consider an airline that initially has a single price of $300 for all consumers. At this price, it has 120 business travelers and 80 tourists. The airline's marginal cost is $100. The slope of the business demand curve is –$2 per traveler, and the slope of the tourist demand curve is –$1 per traveler. Does the single-price policy maximize the airline's profit? If not, how should it change its prices?

ECONOMIC EXPERIMENT

PRICE DISCRIMINATION

An experiment shows how a monopolist—a museum—picks different prices for different consumer groups. Here is how the experiment works:

- The instructor picks a group of three to five students to represent the museum.

- Of the remaining students—potential museum patrons—half represent senior citizens with senior-citizen cards. Each consumer receives a number indicating how much he or she is willing to pay for a trip to a museum.

- In each round of the experiment, the museum posts two prices: one for senior citizens and one for nonseniors. Each consumer then decides whether to buy a ticket at the relevant posted price.

- A consumer's score in a particular round equals the difference between his or her given willingness to pay and the amount he or she actually paid for admission.

- The museum's score in each round equals its profit, or its total revenue minus its total cost. The total cost equals $2 per patron (for ticket-takers, guides, cleanup, and other tasks) times the number of tickets sold.

- The experiment runs for five rounds. After the fifth round, each consumer computes his or her score by adding up the consumer surpluses. The museum's score equals the sum of its profits from the five rounds.

MyEconLab

For additional economic experiments, please visit *www.myeconlab.com*.

NOTES

1. Richard A. Posner, "The Social Costs of Monopoly and Regulation," *Journal of Political Economy*, 83 (1975): 807–827.

2. Linda Rosencrance, "Amazon Charging Different Prices on Some DVDs," *Computerworld*, September 5, 2000, 23.

In the recession that started in 2008, some industries actually experienced increases in demand that caused market entry—new firms entered the markets.[1]

When total employment and income dropped, many consumers switched from buying new shoes to repairing old shoes, and the demand for shoe repair increased. In 2008 the sales of adult footwear decreased by about 3 percent, and the volume of shoe repairs increased dramatically; newspapers reported that in some shops sales increased by 40 to 50 percent. Some consumers purchased used shoes in thrift shops and brought them to cobblers for repairs and reconditioning. The surge in sales increased the profits of shoe-repair shops, and firms entered the market by opening new shops. The entry of new firms reversed—at least temporarily—a long decline of shoe-repair shops. The number of shops in the United States decreased from 120,000 during the Great Depression to 7,000 in 2008. As the economy comes out of the recession, the question is whether the long-term trend of disappearing cobblers will be restored, or whether a new consumer thriftiness will allow more cobblers to stay in business.

LEARNING OBJECTIVES

- Describe and explain the effects of market entry.

- List the conditions for equilibrium in monopolistic competition.

- Contrast monopolistic competition and perfect competition.

- Explain the role of advertising in monopolistic competition.

MyEconLab
MyEconLab helps you master each objective and study more efficiently.

*i*n this chapter, we explore a firm's decision to enter a market and examine the consequences of entry on prices and the profits of other firms. Firms will enter a market as long as they can make an economic profit. As we'll see, the entry of firms squeezes profit in three ways: The price decreases, the average cost of production increases, and the quantity sold per firm decreases. Eventually the entry process stops, and we can count the number of firms serving the market. If entry stops at a single firm, we have a natural monopoly, a topic we cover later in the book. If many firms enter the market, we have monopolistic competition, the topic of this chapter.

Monopolistic competition is a hybrid market structure, with features of both monopoly and perfect competition. The term may seem like an oxymoron—a pair of contradictory words—similar to "virtual reality" and "books on tape." However, the term actually conveys the two key features of the market:

monopolistic competition
A market served by many firms that sell slightly different products.

- Each firm in the market produces a good that is slightly different from the goods of other firms, so each firm has a narrowly defined *monopoly*.
- The products sold by different firms in the market are close substitutes for one another, so there is intense *competition* between firms for consumers. For example, your local grocery store may stock several brands of toothbrushes with different design features. If the price of one brand increases, some loyal customers will continue to buy the brand, but others will switch to different brands that are close substitutes.

Some other examples of monopolistic competition are the markets for bread, clothing, restaurant meals, and gasoline. In each case, firms in the market sell products that are close, but not perfect, substitutes.

The analysis in this chapter is based on two assumptions. First, we assume there are no barriers to entry: There are no patents or government licensing programs to restrict the number of firms. Second, we assume that firms do not act strategically: Each firm acts on its own, taking the actions of other firms as given. This means that firms already in the market do not conspire to fix prices and do not try to prevent other firms from entering the market. In the next chapter, we'll explore several types of strategic behavior in an oligopoly, a market with just a few firms.

11.1 The Effects of Market Entry

Consider a market served by a single profitable firm, a monopolist. As we saw earlier in the book, a firm in any market can use the marginal principle to decide how much output to produce.

MARGINAL PRINCIPLE

Increase the level of an activity as long as its marginal benefit exceeds its marginal cost. Choose the level at which the marginal benefit equals the marginal cost.

Consider a firm whose activity is producing toothbrushes. On the cost side, the firm has the conventional cost curves: For small quantities produced, the average-cost curve is negatively sloped and marginal cost is less than average cost. On the benefit side, the marginal benefit of producing toothbrushes is the marginal revenue from selling one more brush. In Panel A of Figure 11.1, if a single firm produces toothbrushes, the firm-specific demand curve (the demand curve applicable to a

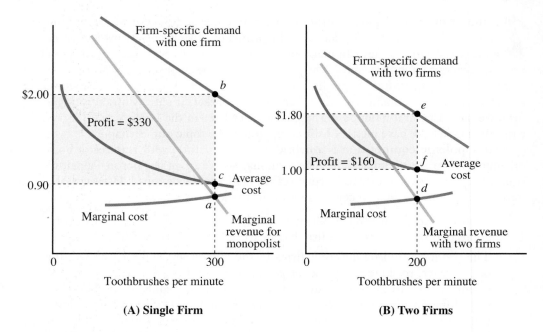

▲ **FIGURE 11.1**

Market Entry Decreases Price and Squeezes Profit

(A) A monopolist maximizes profit at point a, where marginal revenue equals marginal cost. The firm sells 300 toothbrushes at a price of $2.00 (point b) and an average cost of $0.90 (point c). The profit of $330 is shown by the shaded rectangle. (B) The entry of a second firm shifts the firm-specific demand curve for the original firm to the left. The firm produces only 200 toothbrushes (point d) at a lower price ($1.80, shown by point e) and a higher average cost ($1.00, shown by point f). The firm's profit, shown by the shaded rectangle, shrinks to $160.

specific firm) is the same as the market demand curve. As we saw in the chapter on monopoly, the firm's marginal-revenue curve lies below the demand curve because a monopolist must cut its price to sell more output.

As we saw in the previous chapter, a monopolist maximizes profit by picking the quantity at which marginal revenue equals marginal cost. In Figure 11.1, this happens at point *a*, with a quantity of 300 toothbrushes. From point *b* on the demand curve, the price associated with this quantity is $2.00. From point *c* on the average-cost curve, we see that the average cost of this quantity is $0.90. The firm's profit, shown by the shaded rectangle, is $330:

$$\text{profit} = (\text{price} - \text{average cost}) \times \text{quantity} = (\$2.00 - \$0.90) \times 300 = \$330$$

Given the large profits in the toothbrush market, will a second firm enter the market?

Entry Squeezes Profits from Three Sides

Suppose a second firm, producing a slightly different toothbrush, enters the market. When the second firm enters, the firm-specific demand curve for the original firm will shift to the left. At any particular price, some consumers will patronize the new firm, so there will be fewer consumers for the original firm: The original firm will sell fewer brushes at each price. In Panel B of Figure 11.1, the firm-specific demand curve for the original monopolist shifts to the left, and profit decreases for three reasons:

1 *The market price drops.* The marginal principle is satisfied at point *d*, so the original firm now produces 200 toothbrushes at a price of $1.80 (point *e*). The competition between the two firms causes the price to drop, from $2.00 to $1.80.

2 *The quantity produced by the first firm decreases.* The original firm produces only 200 toothbrushes, down from the 300 it produced as a monopolist.

3 *The first firm's average cost of production increases.* The decrease in the quantity produced causes the firm to move upward along its negatively sloped average-cost curve to a higher average cost per toothbrush, from $0.90 to $1.00 (point *f*).

The effects of entry are shown by comparing the profit rectangles in Panels A and B of Figure 11.1. Entry shrinks the firm's profit rectangle because it is squeezed from three directions. The top of the rectangle drops because the price decreases. The bottom of the rectangle rises because the average cost increases. The right side of the rectangle moves to the left because the quantity decreases. In this example, profit drops from $330 to $160:

$$\text{profit} = (\text{price} - \text{average cost}) \times \text{quantity} = (\$1.80 - 1.00) \times 200 = \$160$$

What about the second firm? If we assume the second firm has access to the same production technology as the first firm and pays the same prices for its inputs, the cost curves for the second firm will be the same as the cost curves for the first firm. If the product of the second firm is nearly identical to the product of the first firm, the firm-specific demand curve for the second firm will be nearly identical to the firm-specific demand curve of the first firm. As an approximation, we can use Panel B of Figure 11.1 to represent both firms. Each firm produces 200 toothbrushes at an average cost of $1.00 per toothbrush and sells them at a price of $1.80.

Examples of Entry: Car Stereos, Trucking, and Tires

To illustrate the effects of entry on price, cost, and profit, imagine that you just inherited enough money to start your own car-stereo business. Suppose that the existing monopolist sells 10 stereos per day at a price of $230 and an average cost of $200 per stereo, for a profit of $30 per stereo. If you enter the market, the increased competition will drop the price below $230, and if you sell fewer than 10 stereos (the monopoly quantity), your average will be greater than $200 because you will spread your fixed costs over fewer units. In other words, your entry squeezes profit per unit from both sides. For example, if the market price drops to $215 and the average cost increases to $205, your profit per stereo will be $10, significantly less than the monopolist's initial profit of $30 per stereo.

What happens when the government eliminates artificial barriers to entry? The Motor Carrier Act of 1980 eliminated the government's entry restrictions on the trucking industry, most of which had been in place since the 1930s. New firms entered the trucking market, and freight prices dropped by about 22 percent. The market value of a firm's trucking license indicates how much profit the firm can earn in the market. Deregulation increased competition and decreased prices and profits, and the average value of a trucking license dropped from $579,000 in 1977 to less than $15,000 in 1982.[2]

Empirical studies of other markets provide ample evidence that entry decreases market prices and firms' profits. In other words, consumers pay less for goods and services, and firms earn lower profits. In one study of the retail pricing of tires, a

SATELLITE v CABLE

APPLYING THE CONCEPTS #1: How does market entry affect prices?

Consider the market for television signals provided to residential consumers. How will an existing cable-TV provider respond to the entry of a firm that provides TV signals via satellite? In most cases, the entry of a satellite firm causes the cable firm to improve the quality of service and decrease its price, so consumer surplus increases. In some cases, the cable company improves the quality of service and *increases* price. Because the service improvement is typically large relative to the price hike, consumer surplus increases in this case too. On average, the entry of a satellite firm increases the monthly consumer surplus per consumer from $3.96 to $5.22, an increase of 32 percent. **Related to Exercises 1.6 and 1.8.**

SOURCE: Based on Chenghuan Chu, "The effect of satellite entry on cable television prices and product quality," *RAND Journal of Economics* 41 (2010), pp. 730–764.

market with only two tire stores had a price of $55 per tire, compared to a price of $53 in a market with three stores, $51 with four stores, and $50 with five stores. The larger the number of stores, the lower the price of tires.[3]

11.2 Monopolistic Competition

We've seen that the entry of a firm in a profitable market decreases the price and the profit per firm. Under a market structure called *monopolistic competition*, firms will continue to enter the market until economic profit is zero. Here are the features of monopolistic competition:

- *Many firms*. Because there are relatively small economies of scale, a small firm can produce its product at about the same average cost as a large firm. For example, a small donut shop can produce donuts and coffee at about the same average cost as a large shop. Because even a small firm can cover its costs, the market can support many firms.

- *A differentiated product*. Firms engage in **product differentiation**, the process used by firms to distinguish their products from the products of competing firms. A firm can distinguish its products from the products of other firms by offering a different performance level or appearance. For example, automobiles differ in horsepower and fuel efficiency, and toothpastes differ in flavor and their ability to clean teeth. Some products are differentiated by the services that come with them. For example, some stores provide informative and helpful salespeople, whereas others require consumers to make decisions on their own. Some pizza firms offer home delivery, and some software producers offer free technical assistance. As we'll see later in the chapter, some products are differentiated by where they are sold.

- *No artificial barriers to entry*. There are no patents or regulations that could prevent firms from entering the market.

product differentiation

The process used by firms to distinguish their products from the products of competing firms.

These characteristics explain the logic behind the label "monopolistic competition." Product differentiation means each firm is the sole seller of a narrowly defined good. For example, each firm in the toothbrush market has a unique design for its toothbrushes, so each is a monopolist in the narrowly defined market for that design. Because the products from different firms are close substitutes, there is keen competition for consumers. When one toothbrush maker increases its price, many of its consumers will switch to the similar toothbrushes produced by other firms. In other words, the demand for the product of a monopolistically competitive firm is very price elastic: An increase in price decreases the quantity demanded by a relatively large amount because consumers can easily switch to another firm selling a similar product.

When Entry Stops: Long-Run Equilibrium

We'll use the toothbrush example to illustrate the features of monopolistic competition. The producers of toothbrushes differentiate their products with respect to color, bristle design, handle size and shape, and durability. As we saw earlier, after a second firm enters the toothbrush market, both firms still make a profit. Will a third firm enter this lucrative market? The entry of a third firm will shift the firm-specific demand curve for each firm further to the left. As we saw earlier, a leftward shift of a firm's demand curve decreases the market price, decreases the quantity produced per firm, and increases the average cost per toothbrush. If after the third firm enters the market all three firms still earn positive profit, a fourth firm will enter.

Because there are no barriers to entering the toothbrush market, firms will continue to enter until each firm makes zero economic profit. Figure 11.2 shows the long-run equilibrium from the perspective of the typical firm. Suppose a total of six firms are in the toothbrush market. Given the firm-specific demand curve in a market with six firms, the typical firm satisfies the marginal principle

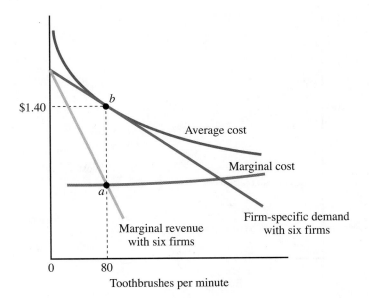

▲ FIGURE 11.2

Long-Run Equilibrium with Monopolistic Competition

Under monopolistic competition, firms continue to enter the market until economic profit is zero. Entry shifts the firm-specific demand curve to the left. The typical firm maximizes profit at point *a*, where marginal revenue equals marginal cost. At a quantity of 80 toothbrushes, price equals average cost (shown by point *b*), so economic profit is zero.

at point *a* by selling 80 brushes per minute at a price of $1.40 (point *b*) and an average cost of $1.40. Because the price equals the average cost, the typical firm makes zero economic profit. Each firm's revenue is high enough to cover all its costs—including the opportunity cost of all its inputs—but not enough to cause additional firms to enter the market. In other words, each firm makes just enough money to stay in business.

What are the implications of market entry for the market as a whole? In Figure 11.2, each of the six firms in the market produces 80 toothbrushes at a price of $1.40, so the total quantity produced is 480. In contrast, we started with a monopoly that had a price of $2.00 and a quantity of 300 toothbrushes. In other words, market entry decreased the price from $2.00 to $1.40 and increased the total quantity demanded from 300 to 480, consistent with the law of demand.

Differentiation by Location

In some monopolistically competitive markets, differentiation is simply a matter of location. Some examples are gas stations, music stores, bookstores, grocery stores, movie theaters, and ice-cream parlors. In each case, many firms sell the same product at different locations. Your city probably has several bookstores, each of which sells a particular book at about the same price. Everything else being equal, you are likely to purchase books from the most convenient store, but if a store across town offers lower prices, you might purchase your books there instead. In other words, each store has a monopoly in its own neighborhood, but competes with bookstores in the rest of the city.

Figure 11.3 shows the long-run equilibrium in the market for books. Because there are no barriers to entering the market, new bookstores will enter the market until each store makes zero economic profit. The typical bookstore satisfies the marginal principle at point *a*, selling 70 books per hour at a price of $14 per book

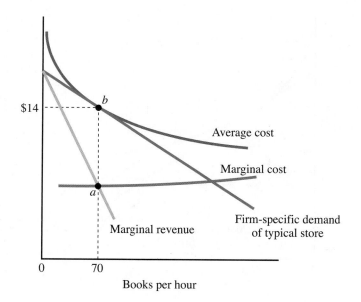

▲ **FIGURE 11.3**

Long-Run Equilibrium with Spatial Competition

Bookstores and other retailers differentiate their products by selling them at different locations. The typical bookstore chooses the quantity of books at which its marginal revenue equals its marginal cost (point *a*). Economic profit is zero because the price equals average cost (point *b*).

application 2

OPENING A DUNKIN' DONUTS SHOP

APPLYING THE CONCEPTS #2: Are monopolistically competitive firms profitable?

One way to get into a monopolistically competitive market is to get a franchise for a nationally advertised product. If you want to get into the donut market, you could pay a franchise fee of $40,000 to Allied Domecq, the parent company of Dunkin' Donuts. That gives you the right to sell donuts under the Dunkin' Donuts brand. You'll also get a few weeks of training at the corporate headquarters in Massachusetts and some help in organizing a grand opening. Once you start making money, you'll pay a royalty to the parent company equal to 5.9 percent of your sales.

How much money are you likely to make in your donut shop? You will compete for donut consumers with other donut shops, bakeries, grocery stores, and coffee shops. Given the small barriers to entering the donut business, you should expect keen competition for consumers. Although your brand-name donuts will give you an edge over your competitors, remember that you must pay the franchise fee and royalties. In the monopolistically competitive donut market, you should expect to make zero economic profit, with total revenue equal to total cost. Your total cost includes the franchise fee and royalties, as well as the opportunity cost of your time and the opportunity cost of any funds you invest in the business.

Table 11.1 shows the franchise fees and royalty rates for several franchising opportunities. The fees indicate how much entrepreneurs are willing to pay for the right to sell a brand-name product. **Related to Exercises 2.4 and 2.5.**

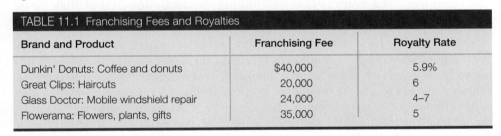

TABLE 11.1 Franchising Fees and Royalties

Brand and Product	Franchising Fee	Royalty Rate
Dunkin' Donuts: Coffee and donuts	$40,000	5.9%
Great Clips: Haircuts	20,000	6
Glass Doctor: Mobile windshield repair	24,000	4–7
Flowerama: Flowers, plants, gifts	35,000	5

SOURCE: Based on data from *www.entrepreneur.com* (accessed October 8, 2010).

(point *b*) and an average cost of $14 per book. The price equals the store's average cost, so the typical store makes zero economic profit. Each store's revenue is high enough to cover all its costs—including the opportunity cost of all its inputs—but not enough to cause additional stores to enter the market. In other words, the firm makes just enough money to stay in business.

11.3 Trade-Offs with Entry and Monopolistic Competition

We've seen that market entry leads to lower prices and a larger total quantity in the market. At the same time, entry decreases the output per firm and increases the average cost of production. As shown in Figure 11.2 and 11.3, monopolistically competitive firms operate on the negatively sloped portion of their average-cost curves, so average cost is higher than the minimum. In other words, the average cost of production would be lower if a single toothbrush firm served the entire market by providing a single type of toothbrush. What are the other consequences of entry and monopolistic competition?

Average Cost and Variety

There are some trade-offs associated with monopolistic competition. Although the average cost of production is higher than the minimum, there is also more product variety. In a market with many toothbrush firms, consumers can choose from a wide variety of designs, so the higher average cost is at least partly offset by greater product variety. Here are two other examples of the benefits of product variety:

- *Restaurant meals.* The typical large city has dozens of Italian restaurants, each of which has a different menu and prepares its food in different ways. Consumers can pick from restaurants offering a wide variety of menus and preparation techniques. Although a city with a single Italian restaurant would have a lower average cost of preparing Italian meals, consumers would get less variety.
- *Shoes and clothing.* Shoes are differentiated according to their style and performance. If we all wore the same type of shoes, the average cost of producing shoes would be lower, but consumers would be unable to match their shoe preferences with suitable shoes. Similarly, if we all wore uniforms, the average cost of clothing would be lower, but that would eliminate clothing choice.

What are the trade-offs when products are differentiated by location? When firms sell the same product at different locations, the larger the number of firms, the higher the average cost of production. But when firms are numerous, consumers travel shorter distances to get the product. Therefore, higher production costs are at least partly offset by lower travel costs. If a large metropolitan area had only one bookstore, the average cost of books would be lower, but consumers would spend more time traveling to get the books.

Monopolistic Competition versus Perfect Competition

Product differentiation is what makes monopolistic competition different from perfect competition. Perfectly competitive firms produce homogeneous products, while monopolistically competitive firms produce differentiated products. Panel A of Figure 11.4 shows the equilibrium for a perfectly competitive firm. Each price-taking firm has a horizontal demand curve. Point *a* shows the long-run equilibrium because the typical firm (1) satisfies the marginal principle, choosing the quantity where marginal revenue equals marginal cost, and (2) earns zero economic profit because price equals average cost:

$$price = marginal\ cost = average\ cost$$

The only place where price equals both marginal cost *and* average cost is the minimum point of the average-cost curve, shown by point *a*.

▲ **FIGURE 11.4**

Monopolistic Competition versus Perfect Competition

(A) In a perfectly competitive market, the firm-specific demand curve is horizontal at the market price, and marginal revenue equals price. In equilibrium, price = marginal cost = average cost. The equilibrium occurs at the minimum of the average-cost curve. (B) In a monopolistically competitive market, the firm-specific demand curve is negatively sloped and marginal revenue is less than price. In equilibrium, marginal revenue equals marginal cost (point *b*) and price equals average cost (point *c*).

Panel B shows the equilibrium for a monopolistically competitive firm. The firm has a differentiated product, so its demand curve is negatively sloped and marginal revenue is less than the price. With a negatively sloped demand curve, the zero-profit condition—price equals average cost—will be satisfied along the negatively sloped

application 3

HAPPY HOUR PRICING

APPLYING THE CONCEPTS #3: How does monopolistic competition compare to perfect competition?

Consider the phenomenon of "happy hour." Many bars and restaurants near workplaces face an increase in demand for food and drink around 5:00 p.m., and many cut their prices for an hour or two. According to the model of perfect competition, an increase in demand will lead to higher, not lower prices. What explains the happy-hour combination of higher demand and lower prices?

Bars are subject to monopolistic competition. Each bar has a local monopoly within its neighborhood, but faces competition from other bars outside its neighborhood. For an individual consumer, the higher the demand for food and drink, the greater the incentive to consider alternatives to the nearest bar. If you expect to purchase large quantities of bar food and drink, the savings achieved by finding a lower price at an alternative bar will be relatively large. In other words, when individual demand increases, each bar faces a more elastic demand for its products. In a market subject to monopolistic competition, the bar's rational response to more elastic demand (more sensitive consumers) is to decrease its price. In graphical terms, the demand curve facing each bar becomes flatter, and the demand curve will be tangent to the average-cost curve at a larger quantity and a lower price and average cost. **Related to Exercise 3.6.**

SOURCE: Based on Mark Fisher, "Happy Hour Economics, or How an Increase in Demand Can Produce a Decrease in Price," *Economic Review, Federal Reserve Bank of Atlanta* (Second Quarter 2005), pp. 25–34.

portion of the average-cost curve. In other words, the only place where a tangency can occur is along the negatively sloped portion of the average-cost curve. Compared to a perfectly competitive firm, a monopolistically competitive firm produces less output at a higher average cost. In Figure 11.4, the average cost for the monopolistically competitive firm is P_2, compared to P_1 for a perfectly competitive firm.

To illustrate the difference between the two market structures, imagine that product differentiation diminishes. Suppose, for example, that consumers decide that the distinguishing features of toothbrushes—color, shape, and bristle design—don't matter. As a result, the products of competing firms will become better substitutes, so the demand for a particular firm's product will become more elastic. In Panel B of Figure 11.4 the firm-specific demand curve will become flatter and will be tangent to the average-cost curve at a larger quantity, closer to the perfectly competitive quantity Q_1. As differentiation continues to diminish, the firm's demand curve will become flatter and flatter, and we will get closer and closer to the perfectly competitive outcome, where the average cost reaches its minimum.

11.4 Advertising for Product Differentiation

We've seen that product differentiation is a key feature of monopolistic competition. A firm can use advertising to inform consumers about the features of its product and thus distinguish its product from the products of other firms. In addition, advertisements can inform consumers about prices. A famous study of the eyeglass market found that advertising promoted price competition between firms and reduced eyeglass prices by about 20 percent.[4]

Some advertisements don't provide any real information about a product or its price. You've seen the advertisements featuring beer drinkers frolicking on the beach with attractive people, cigarette smokers riding horseback, drivers of sports cars impressing classmates at high-school reunions, and sports-drink

---

application 4

PICTURE OF MAN VERSUS PICTURE OF WOMAN

APPLYING THE CONCEPT #4: How does advertising affect consumer choices?

A South African consumer lender decided to use a mass mailing of 53,000 loan offers to test the sensitivity of consumers to variations in interest rates and other features of loan offers. The interest rates in the offer letters ranged from 3.75% to 11.75% *per month*. As expected, the uptake rate (the number of consumers who accepted a particular loan offer) was higher for offer letters with low interest rates. The elasticity of the uptake rate with respect to the interest rate was –0.34: a 10% decrease in the interest rate (from say an interest rate of 7.0% to 6.3%) increased the uptake rate by 3.4%.

More surprising was the finding that the uptake rate among men was much higher when the offer letter included a picture of a woman rather than a picture of a man. Replacing a male model with a female model was equivalent to cutting the interest rate by 25 percent, for example, from 7.0 percent to 5.25 percent. In contrast, the uptake rate for women consumers was unaffected by the gender of the model. **Related to Exercises 4.4 and 4.5.**

SOURCE: Based on Marianne Bertrand, Dean Karlan, Sendhil Mullainathan, Eddar Shafir, Jonathan Zinman, "What's Advertising Content Worth? Evidence from a Consumer Credit Marketing Field Experiment," *Quarterly Journal of Economics* 125 (2010), pp. 263–306.

consumers performing amazing athletic feats. These sorts of advertisements are designed to promote an image for a product, not to provide information about the product's features.

An advertisement that doesn't provide any product information may actually help consumers make decisions. Firms spend millions of dollars to get celebrities like Drew Brees and Kristen Stewart to endorse their products. When a famous athlete or actor appears in an advertisement for a product, everyone realizes the celebrity is doing the advertisement for money, not to share his or her enthusiasm for the advertised product. Nonetheless, these advertisements are effective in increasing sales. Why do they work?

By paying millions of dollars to run an advertisement featuring a celebrity, a firm sends a signal to consumers that the advertised product is appealing and likely to be popular. To illustrate this signaling effect, consider a firm that develops a new energy bar and picks a celebrity to endorse it. The purpose of a celebrity advertisement is to get people to try the product for the first time. After that, a consumer will base any repeat purchases on the taste and nutritional value of the energy bar. Suppose an advertisement with a cost of $10 million would cause 10 million consumers to try the energy bar. As shown in the first row of Table 11.2, energy bar A is an appealing product, and half the consumers who try it will become repeat consumers. If the firm makes a profit of $4 on each repeat customer, the firm's profit of $20 million exceeds the $10 million cost of the advertisement, so the firm will run the advertisement.

TABLE 11.2 Advertising Profitability and Signaling

Product	Number of Consumers Who Try the Product	Number of Repeat Customers	Profit per Repeat Customer	Profit from Repeat Customers	Cost of Advertisement
Energy bar A	10 million	5 million	$4	$20 million	$10 million
Energy bar B	10 million	1 million	4	4 million	10 million

What about a product that is less appealing? The second row of Table 11.2 shows the effects of an advertisement for energy bar B. Only 1 in 10 people who try energy bar B will become a repeat customer, so the firm's profit from an advertisement is only $4 million. That is not enough to cover the $10 million cost, so the firm won't advertise the less-appealing product. Notice that celebrity endorsements for the two products are equally effective in getting people to try the products, but what matters is repeat customers. The less-appealing product gets fewer repeat customers because it's an inferior product, and that's why it's not worthwhile to pay for an advertisement.

Celebrity endorsements and other expensive advertising send a signal to consumers that the producer expects many repeat customers. Firms undertake extensive marketing research to project the sales of their products and, when their research suggests the product will be popular, they have an incentive to spend money on advertising to send the signal to consumers. The signal tells consumers which new products are expected to have the greatest general appeal.

This chapter is about market entry and monopolistic competition. In a monopolistically competitive market, entry continues until each firm in the market makes zero economic profit. Firms can differentiate their products by design, level of service, location, or product image. Here are the main points of the chapter:

1 The entry of a firm into a market decreases the market price, decreases output per firm, and increases the average cost of production.

2 In a *monopolistically competitive* market, firms compete for customers by producing *differentiated products*.

3 In the long-run equilibrium with monopolistic competition, marginal revenue equals marginal cost, price equals average cost, and economic profit is zero.

4 Under monopolistic competition, the average cost of production is higher than the minimum, but there is also more product variety.

5 A firm can use celebrity endorsements and other costly advertisements to signal its belief that a product will be appealing.

KEY TERMS

monopolistic competition, p. 255   product differentiation, p. 258

EXERCISES

All problems are assignable in MyEconLab.

11.1 The Effects of Market Entry

1.1 A profit-maximizing firm picks the quantity of output at which _____ equals _____.

1.2 Arrows up or down: At a firm's current level of output, marginal revenue exceeds the marginal cost. The firm should _____ its output and _____ its price.

1.3 The entry of a second firm shifts the firm-specific demand curve of the first firm to the _____ (left/right).

1.4 Arrows up or down: The entry of a third firm into a market with two original firms _____ the market price, _____ the average production cost, _____ the quantity produced per firm, and _____ profit of each original firm.

1.5 Arrows up or down: Changes in regulatory policy in the 1980s _____ the price of trucking services and _____ the profits of trucking firms.

1.6 Arrows up or down: The entry of a satellite TV firm _____ consumer surplus, in part because the cable company _____ the quality of service while either _____ price or _____ price by a relatively small amount. (Related to Application 1 on page 258.)

1.7 **Bidding for Bookstore Licenses.** Paige initially has the only license to operate a bookstore in Bookville. She charges a price of $9 per book, has an average cost of $4 per book, and sells 1,001 books per year. When Paige's license expires, the city decides to auction two bookstore licenses to the highest bidders. Suppose the relevant variables (price, average cost, and output per firm) take on only integer values—no fraction or decimals.

   a. Suppose Paige is optimistic and imagines the best possible outcome with a two-firm market. What is the maximum amount she is willing to pay for one of the two licenses?

   b. Suppose Paige is pessimistic and imagines the worst possible outcome with a two-firm market. What is the maximum amount she is willing to pay for one of the two licenses?

1.8 **Draw the Cable TV Graph.** Consider the "Satellite versus Cable" Application. Use a graph to show that the entry of satellite TV decreases the profit-maximizing price of a cable TV company from $40 to $35 (Related to Application 1 on page 258.)

1.9 **Beware the Too-Easy Answer.** Your city initially restricts the number of pizzerias to one. The existing monopolist sells 3,000 pizzas per day. A pizzeria reaches the horizontal portion of its long-run average cost curve at an output of about 1,000 pizzas per day. Suppose the city eliminates the entry restrictions. Predict the equilibrium number of pizzerias. Beware of the TEC (too easy to be correct) answer.

1.10 Equilibrium? In your city, there are currently three firms providing oil changes. For each firm, there is a fixed cost of $80 per day and a marginal cost of $12 per oil change. Each firm currently maximizes its profit by providing 10 oil changes per day.

 a. For each firm, marginal revenue = $_____.

 b. This is a monopolistically competitive equilibrium if _____ equals $_____.

11.2 Monopolistic Competition

2.1 *Monopolistic competition* refers to a market in which old boys act naturally as they transport tight slacks in the back of Dodge Ram pickup trucks. _____ (True/False)

2.2 Perfectly competitive firms sell a _____ product, while monopolistically competitive firms sell a _____ product.

2.3 There are two conditions for a long-run equilibrium in a monopolistically competitive market:

 (1) _____ equals _____ and

 (2) _____ equals _____.

2.4 To enter the donut market as a seller of Dunkin' Donuts, you'll pay a one-time franchise fee of $_____ and then pay _____ percent of your sales. (Related to Application 2 on page 261.)

2.5 Willingness to Pay for a Dunkin' Donuts Franchise. You operate a Dunkin' Donuts shop under a franchise agreement. You pay a royalty of 6 percent of your sales revenue to the parent company. Your profit-maximizing quantity is 10,000 donuts per year, and at this quantity your price is $1.00 and your average cost per donut (including all the opportunity cost of production but not the 6 percent royalty) is $0.44. (Related to Application 2 on page 261.)

 a. Draw a graph with revenue and costs curves to show your profit-maximizing choice.

 b. What is the maximum amount you are willing to pay per year for the franchise?

2.6 How Many Bookstores? The city of Bookburg initially allows only one bookstore, which sells books at a price of $20 and an average cost of $11. Suppose the city eliminates its restrictions on bookstores, allowing additional stores to enter the market. According to an expert in the music market, "Each additional music store will decrease the price of books by $2 per book and increase the average cost of selling books by $1 per book." Predict the equilibrium number of bookstores.

2.7 Lawn-Cutting Equilibrium. Consider the market for cutting lawns. Each firm has a fixed daily cost of $18 for equipment, and the marginal cost of cutting a lawn is $4. Suppose each firm can cut up to three lawns per day. The market demand curve for lawn cuts is linear, with a vertical intercept of $70 and a slope of –$1 per lawn.

 a. If each firm in the market cuts three lawns, what is the average cost per lawn?

 b. What is the equilibrium price under monopolistic competition?

 c. How many lawns will be cut in total, and how many firms will be in the market?

2.8 Zero Price for a Permit. Consider a city that initially issues five licenses to pet groomers and does not allow the licenses to be bought and sold. Shortly after an economist joins the city licensing authority, the city decides to allow the licenses to be bought and sold on the open market. Much to the surprise of the licensers, the price of the licenses was zero: No one was willing to pay a positive amount for a pet grooming license.

 a. Explain why the price of grooming licenses was zero.

 b. Illustrate your answer with a complete graph.

2.9 Auctioning Business Licenses. The following table shows the relationships between the number of firms in the market, the market price, the quantity per firm, and the average cost of production.

Number of Firms	Price	Quantity per Firm	Average Cost
1	$20	38	$ 9
2	18	35	10
3	16	32	11
4	14	29	12
5	12	26	13
6	10	23	14
7	8	20	15

A business license allows a firm to operate the business for one day. The city will auction up to seven business licenses to the highest bidders, and the auctioning of licenses will continue as long as someone bids a positive amount for one of the licenses. Assume that each firm can buy only one license. What is the maximum amount you would be willing to pay for a license?

11.3 Trade-Offs with Entry and Monopolistic Competition

3.1 The trade-off with entry is that an increase in the number of firms leads to higher _____ but greater _____.

3.2 When products are differentiated by location, the entry of firms generates benefits for consumers in the form of _____.

3.3 A perfectly competitive firm has a _____ demand curve, whereas a monopolistic competitive firm has a _____ demand curve.

3.4 In the long-run equilibrium in a perfectly competitive market, price is equal to both _____ and _____.

3.5 Arrows up or down: As product differentiation diminishes, the price elasticity of demand for the product of a monopolistically competitive firm _____ and the average cost of production _____.

3.6 The phenomenon of "happy hour" pricing (_____ prices when demand is relatively high) results from relatively _____ (elastic/inelastic) demand. (Related to Application 3 on page 263.)

3.7 **Uniform Trade-Offs.** A prominent feature of Mao's Communist China in the 1940s through the 1970s was the blue uniform worn by all citizens.

  a. Explain the trade-offs associated with the use of uniforms. What were the benefits? What were the costs?

  b. Suppose people had a choice among five uniform colors rather than being required to wear blue. Would you expect the benefits of requiring uniforms to decrease by a little or a lot?

11.4 Advertising for Product Differentiation

4.1 Advertising for eyeglasses _____ (increases/decreases) the price of eyeglasses because advertising promotes _____.

4.2 An advertisement that succeeds in getting consumers to try the product will be sensible only if the number of _____ customers is large.

4.3 In Table 11.2 on page 265, the profit from repeat customers will equal the cost of the advertisement if there are _____ repeat customers.

4.4 Arrows up or down. In the application on consumer loans in South Africa, the loan uptake rate _____ as the interest rate decreased and _____ when the model on the offer was switched from a man to a woman. (Related to Application 4 on page 264.)

4.5 **Advertising for Loans.** Consider the numbers provided in Application 4 on South African consumer loans. Suppose a lender initially charges an interest rate of 10 percent and uses male models in its advertisements. The firm wants to increase its uptake rate among male consumers. Suppose the firm switches to female models in its advertisements. The male uptake rate will increase by _____ (1, 3, 8, 25) percent. (Related to Application 4 on page 264.)

4.6 **The Cost of Celebrities.** Consider a firm that hires an expensive celebrity to advertise its products. Does the firm have an incentive to prevent its customers from discovering how much it pays the celebrity?

4.7 **Word-of-Mouth Book Sales.** Consider a publisher who earns a profit of $2 per book sold. An advertisement that costs $320,000 would sell 100,000 books directly. To make the advertisement worthwhile, how many of the original buyers must each persuade just one other person to buy the book?

ECONOMIC EXPERIMENT

FIXED COSTS AND ENTRY

Here is an experiment that shows the implications of entry for prices and profits. Students play the role of entrepreneurs who must decide whether to enter the market for lawn cutting. If they decide to enter the market, they must then decide how much to charge for cutting lawns.

- There are eight potential lawn-cutting firms, each represented by one to three students. The firms have two sorts of costs: a fixed cost per day and a marginal cost of cutting each lawn. Each firm can cut up to two lawns per day.

- There are 16 potential consumers. Each potential consumer is willing to pay a different amount to have his or her lawn cut.

- The experiment has two stages. In the first stage, each potential firm decides whether to enter the market. The entry decision is sequential: The instructor will go down the list of potential firms, one at a time, and give each firm the option of entering the market. The entry decisions are public knowledge. When a firm enters the market, it incurs a fixed cost of $14.

- Each firm in the market posts a price for lawn cutting, and consumers shop around and decide whether to purchase lawn care at the posted prices.

- Each trading period lasts several minutes, and each firm can change its posted price up to three times each period.

- A consumer's score in a trading period equals the difference between the amount that the consumer is willing to pay for lawn care and the price actually paid.

- A firm's score equals its profit, which is its total revenue minus its total cost (the fixed cost of $14 plus the variable cost, equal to $3 per lawn times the number of lawns cut).

NOTES

1. Sarah Needleman, "In a Sole Revival, the Recession Gives Beleaguered Cobblers New Traction," *New York Times*, February 2, 2009, 1; Franco Capaldo, "Timpson Enjoys Shoe Repair Boom," *Financial Mail*, October 2008; Eric Apalategui, "Cobblers Step Up to Fill Need for Repair, Reuse," *The Oregonian*, January 8, 2010, B1.

2. Theodore E. Relate, "Deregulation and Scale Economies in the U.S. Trucking Industry: An Econometric Extension of the Survivor Principle," *Journal of Law and Economics* 32 (October 1989): 229–253; Thomas Gale Moore, "Rail and Truck Reform—The Record So Far," *Regulation* (November– December 1988): 57–62; Leonard W. Weiss, ed., *Concentration and Price* (Cambridge, MA: MIT Press, 1989).

3. Timothy F. Bresnahan and Peter C. Reiss, "Entry and Competition in Concentrated Markets," *Journal of Political Economy* 99 (October 1991): 977–1009.

4. Lee Benham, "The Effect of Advertising on the Price of Glasses," *Journal of Law and Economics* 15, no. 2 (1972): 337–352.

Oligopoly and Strategic Behavior

In an oligopoly, defined as a market with just a few firms, each firm has an incentive to act strategically, anticipating the possible actions and reactions of its fellow oligopolists.

In Brazil, a few firms dominate the market for cement, and the domestic cement producers are strategic oligopolists, with a twist.[1]

Although imported cement is just a tiny part of the market, it appears that importers are always poised to enter the market, and this constant threat of entry keeps prices lower than we would expect in an oligopoly. In a sense, the Brazilian cement firms are insecure oligopolists, keeping prices high enough to get a profit, but low enough to prevent importers from entering the market.

The prices of Brazilian firms depend on the degree of competition from importers. When imports become less costly and thus more competitive, the domestic firms cut their prices to protect their oligopoly power. On the other hand, when imports become more costly and thus less competitive, the domestic firms increase their prices and thus exploit their oligopoly power. For example, when an increase in the price of diesel fuel increases shipping costs and makes imports less competitive, domestic firms increase their prices. Domestic firms also charge relatively high prices in the interior area of Brazil, where the costs of importers are relatively high.

LEARNING OBJECTIVES

- Explain why a price-fixing cartel is difficult to maintain.

- Explain the effects of a low-price guarantee on the price.

- Describe the prisoners' dilemma.

- Explain the behavior of an insecure monopolist.

- Explain two advertisers' dilemmas.

MyEconLab
MyEconLab helps you master each objective and study more efficiently.

*t*his is the fourth chapter on decision making by firms. In this chapter, we look at an **oligopoly**, a market with just a few firms. Given the small number of firms in an oligopoly, the actions of one firm have a large effect on the other firms. Therefore, firms in an oligopoly act strategically. Before a firm takes a particular action, it considers the possible reactions of its rivals. For example, before Southwest Airlines cuts its fares in an attempt to sell more tickets, it will consider the possible reactions by other airlines. If the rivals maintain their old fares, Southwest's fare cut will increase its sales and profit. But if the rivals match the lower fare, Southwest is likely to gain only a few customers, and its profit may actually decrease.

Game theory is the study of decision making in strategic situations. We can apply the theory to the game of chess as well as the decisions of oligopolists. A chess player develops a strategy to win the game, anticipating his or her opponent's reaction to each of his or her moves. Similarly, an oligopolist develops a strategy to maximize profit, anticipating the reactions of rival firms. We'll use game theory to discuss three business strategies: conspiring to fix prices, preventing another firm from entering the market, and advertising.

In an oligopoly, a few firms have market power—the power to control prices. Economists use **concentration ratios** to measure the degree of concentration in a market, computed as the percentage of the market output produced by the largest firms. For example, a four-firm concentration ratio is the percentage of total output in a market produced by the four largest firms. In Table 12.1, the four-firm concentration ratio for house slippers is 97 percent, indicating that the largest four firms produce 97 percent of house slippers in the United States.

oligopoly
A market served by a few firms.

game theory
The study of decision making in strategic situations.

concentration ratios
The percentage of the market output produced by the largest firms.

TABLE 12.1 Concentration Ratios in Selected Manufacturing Industries

Industry	Four-Firm Concentration Ratio (%)	Eight-Firm Concentration Ratio (%)
Primary copper smelting	99	Not available
House slippers	97	99
Guided missiles and space vehicles	96	99
Cigarettes	95	99
Soybean processing	95	99
Household laundry equipment	93	Not available
Breweries	91	94
Electric lamp bulbs	89	90
Military vehicles	88	93
Primary battery manufacturing	87	99
Beet sugar processing	85	98
Household refrigerators and freezers	85	95
Small arms (weapons)	84	90
Breakfast cereals	82	93
Motor vehicles and car bodies	81	91
Flavoring syrup	Not available	89

SOURCE: U.S. Bureau of the Census, 2002 Economic Census, Manufacturing, *Concentration Ratios: 2002* (Washington, D.C.: U.S. Government Printing Office, 2006).

An alternative measure of market concentration is the *Herfindahl–Hirschman Index (HHI)*. It is calculated by squaring the market share of each firm in the market and then summing the resulting numbers. For example, consider a market with two firms, one with a 60 percent market share and a second with a 40 percent share. The HHI for the market is 5,200:

$$HHI = 60^2 + 40^2 = 3,600 + 1,600 = 5,200$$

In contrast, for a market with 10 firms, each with a 10 percent market share, the HHI is 1,000:

$$\text{HHI} = 10^2 \times 10 = 100 \times 10 = 1{,}000$$

According to the guidelines established by the U.S. Department of Justice in 1992, a market is "unconcentrated" if the HHI is below 1,000 and "highly concentrated" if it is above 1,800. For example, a market with five firms, each with a 20 percent market share, has an HHI of 2,000 and would be considered highly concentrated:

$$\text{HHI} = 20^2 \times 5 = 400 \times 5 = 2{,}000$$

An oligopoly—a market with just a few firms—occurs for three reasons:

1 *Government barriers to entry.* As we saw in Chapters 6 and 10, the government may limit the number of firms in a market by issuing patents or controlling the number of business licenses.

2 *Economies of scale in production.* As we saw in Chapter 10, a natural monopoly occurs when there are relatively large economies of scale in production, so a single firm produces for the entire market. In some cases, scale economies are not large enough to generate a natural monopoly, but are large enough to generate a natural oligopoly, with a few firms serving the entire market.

3 *Advertising campaigns.* In some markets, a firm cannot enter a market without a substantial investment in an advertising campaign. For example, the breakfast-cereal oligopoly results from the huge advertising campaigns required to get a foothold in the market. As in the case of economies of scale in production, just a few firms will enter the market.

12.1 Cartel Pricing and the Duopolists' Dilemma

One of the virtues of a market economy is that firms compete with one another for customers, and this leads to lower prices and larger quantities. But in some markets, firms cooperate instead of competing with one another. Eighteenth-century economist Adam Smith recognized the possibility that firms would conspire to raise prices: "People of the same trade seldom meet together, even for merriment and diversion, but the conversation ends in a conspiracy against the public, or in some contrivance to raise prices."[2] We'll see that raising prices is not simply a matter of firms getting together and agreeing on higher prices. An agreement to raise prices is likely to break down unless the firms find some way to punish a firm that violates the agreement.

duopoly
A market with two firms.

We'll use a market with two firms—a **duopoly**—to explain the key features of an oligopoly. The basic insights from a duopoly apply to oligopolies with more than two firms. Consider a duopoly in the market for air travel between two hypothetical cities. The two airlines can use prices to compete for customers, or they can cooperate and conspire to raise prices. To simplify matters—and to keep the numbers manageable—let's assume that the average cost of providing air travel is constant at $100 per passenger. As shown in Figure 12.1, the average cost is constant, which means that marginal cost equals average cost.

cartel
A group of firms that act in unison, coordinating their price and quantity decisions.

A **cartel** is a group of firms that act in unison, coordinating their price and quantity decisions. In our airline example, the two airlines could form a cartel and choose the monopoly price. In Figure 12.1, the firm-specific demand curve for a monopolist is the market-demand curve, and the marginal-revenue curve intersects the marginal-cost curve at a quantity of 60 passengers per day (point *a*). If the two airlines act as one, they will pick the monopoly price of $400 and split the monopoly output, so each will have 30 passengers per day. The average cost per passenger is $100, so each airline earns a daily profit of $9,000:

$$\text{profit} = (\text{price} - \text{average cost}) \times \text{quantity per firm} = (\$400 - \$100) \times 30 = \$9{,}000$$

A Cartel Picks the Monopoly
Quantity and Price
The monopoly outcome is shown by
point *a*, where marginal revenue equals
marginal cost. The monopoly quantity is
60 passengers and the price is $400. If
the firms form a cartel, the price is $400
and each firm has 30 passengers (half the
monopoly quantity). The profit per passenger is $300 (equal to the $400 price
minus the $100 average cost), so the
profit per firm is $9,000.

This is an example of **price fixing**, an arrangement in which firms conspire to fix
prices. As we'll see later in the chapter, cartels and price fixing are illegal under U.S.
antitrust laws.

    What would happen if the two firms competed rather than conspired to fix the
price? If they competed, each firm would have its own demand curve. As we saw in the
previous chapter, the firm-specific demand curve for the typical firm lies to the left of
the market demand curve because consumers can choose from two firms. At a particular
price, consumers will be divided between the two firms, so each firm will serve only part
of the market. In Figure 12.2, the demand curve for the typical duopolist is below the
market demand curve. For example, at a price of $300, point *d* shows that the market
quantity is 80 passengers, while point *b* shows that each firm has 40 passengers.

    Panel A in Figure 12.2 shows the quantity and price choice of an individual firm.
Given the firm-specific demand curve and marginal-revenue curve, the marginal

price fixing
An arrangement in which firms conspire
to fix prices.

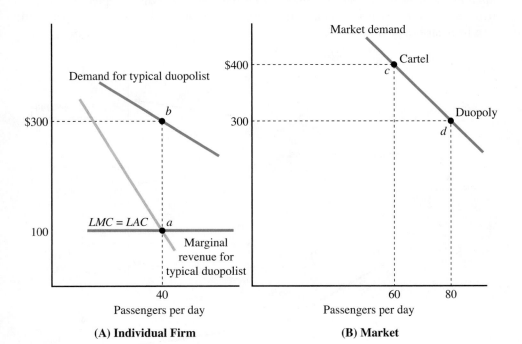

(A) Individual Firm **(B) Market**

Competing Duopolists Pick a Lower
Price
(A) The typical firm maximizes profit at
point *a*, where marginal revenue equals
marginal cost. The firm has 40 passengers. (B) At the market level, the duopoly
outcome is shown by point *d*, with a price
of $300 and 80 passengers. The cartel
outcome, shown by point *c*, has a higher
price and a smaller total quantity.

principle is satisfied at point *a*, where marginal revenue equals marginal cost. The firm has 40 passengers at a price of $300 (point *b*). The two firms are identical, so each has 40 passengers at a price of $300. Given an average cost of $100, each firm earns a profit of $8,000:

profit = (price − average cost) × quantity per firm = ($300 − $100) × 40 = $8,000

Price Fixing and the Game Tree

Clearly, each firm will earn more profit under a price-fixing cartel, but will a cartel succeed, or will firms cheat on a cartel agreement? We can answer this question with the help of a **game tree**, a graphical representation of the consequences of different actions in a strategic setting. Each firm must choose a price for airline tickets, either the high price (the $400 cartel price) or the low price (the duopoly price of $300). Each firm can use the game tree to pick a price, knowing that the other firm is picking a price too.

Figure 12.3 shows the game tree for the price-fixing game. Let's call the managers of the airlines Jack and Jill. The game tree has three components:

- The squares are decision nodes. Each square has a player (Jack or Jill) and a list of the player's possible actions. For example, the game starts at square *A*, where Jill has two options: high price or low price.

- The arrows show the possible paths of the game from left to right. Jill chooses her price first, so we move from square *A* to one of Jack's decision nodes, either square *B* or square *C*. If Jill chooses the high price, we move from square *A* to square *B*. Once we reach one of Jack's decision nodes, he chooses a price—high or low—and then we move to one of the rectangles. For example, if Jack chooses the high price too, we move from square *B* to rectangle 1.

- The rectangles show the profits for the two firms. When we reach a rectangle, the game is over, and the players receive the profits shown in the rectangle. There is a profit rectangle for each of the four possible outcomes of the price-fixing game.

We've already computed the profits for two payoff rectangles. Rectangle 1 shows what happens when each firm chooses the high price. This is the cartel or price-fixing outcome, with each firm earning $9,000. Rectangle 4 shows what happens when each firm chooses the low price. This is the duopoly outcome, when firms compete and each firm earns a profit of $8,000.

▶ **FIGURE 12.3**
Game Tree for the Price-Fixing Game
The equilibrium path of the game is square *A* to square *C* to rectangle *4*: Each firm picks the low price and earns a profit of $8,000. The duopolists' dilemma is that each firm would make more profit if both picked the high price, but both firms pick the low price.

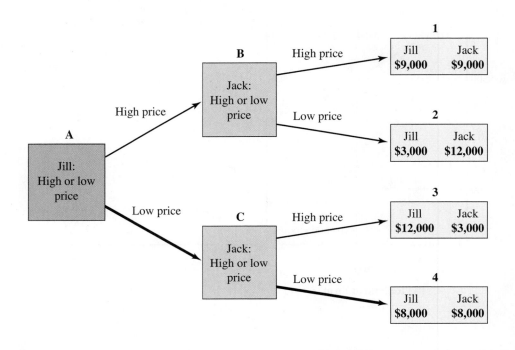

What would happen if the two firms chose different prices? If Jill chooses the high price and Jack chooses the low price, Jack will capture a large share of the market and gain at Jill's expense. In the first column of Table 12.2, Jill charges the high price and has only 10 passengers at a price of $400, so her profit is $3,000:

$$\text{profit} = (\text{price} - \text{average cost}) \times \text{quantity per firm} = (\$400 - \$100) \times 10 = \$3,000$$

TABLE 12.2 Duopolists' Profits When They Choose Different Prices		
	Jill: High Price	**Jack: Low Price**
Price	$ 400	$ 300
Average cost	$ 100	$ 100
Profit per passenger	$ 300	$ 200
Number of passengers	10	60
Profit	$3,000	$12,000

In the second column, Jack charges the low price and has 60 passengers at a price of $300, so his profit is $12,000:

$$\text{profit} = (\text{price} - \text{average cost}) \times \text{quantity per firm} = (\$300 - \$100) \times 60 = \$12,000$$

This is shown by rectangle 2 in Figure 12.3: The path of the game is square A to square B to rectangle 2. The other underpricing outcome is shown by rectangle 3. In this case, Jill chooses the low price and Jack chooses the high price, so Jill gains at Jack's expense. The roles are reversed, and so are the numbers in the profit rectangle.

Equilibrium of the Price-Fixing Game

We can predict the equilibrium of the price-fixing game by a process of elimination. We'll eliminate the rectangles that would require one or both firms to act irrationally, leaving us with the rectangle showing the equilibrium of the game:

- If Jill chooses the high price, we'll move along the upper branches of the tree and eventually reach rectangle 1 or 2, depending on what Jack does. Although Jill would like Jack to choose the high price too, this would be irrational for Jack. He can earn $12,000 profit by choosing the low price, compared to $9,000 with the high price. Therefore, we can eliminate rectangle 1.

- If Jill chooses the low price, we'll move along the lower branches of the tree and eventually reach rectangle 3 or 4, depending on Jack's choice. Jack won't choose the high price because he can earn $8,000 with the low price, compared to $3,000 with the high price. Therefore, we can eliminate rectangle 3.

We've eliminated the two profit rectangles that represent a high price for Jack—rectangles 1 and 3. For Jack, the low price is a **dominant strategy**: Regardless of what Jill does, Jack's best choice is the low price.

Two profit rectangles are left—2 and 4—and Jill's action will determine which rectangle is the equilibrium. Jill knows Jack will choose the low price regardless of what she does. She could choose the high price and allow Jack to capture most of the market, leaving her with a profit of only $3,000 in rectangle 2. A better choice is to pick the low price and get a profit of $8,000 in rectangle 4. In other words, it would be irrational for Jill to allow herself to be underpriced, so the outcome of the game is shown by profit rectangle 4: Each player chooses the low price. The thick arrows show the equilibrium path of the game, from square A to square C to rectangle 4.

Both firms will be unhappy with this equilibrium because each could earn a higher profit with rectangle 1. To get there, however, each firm must choose the high price. The **duopolists' dilemma** is that although both firms would be better off if they both chose the high price, each firm chooses the low price. The dilemma occurs because

dominant strategy

An action that is the best choice for a player, no matter what the other player does.

duopolists' dilemma

A situation in which both firms in a market would be better off if both chose the high price, but each chooses the low price.

there is a big payoff from underpricing the other firm and a big penalty from being underpriced, so both firms pick the low price. As we'll see later in the chapter, to avoid the dilemma, the firms must find some way to prevent underpricing.

Nash Equilibrium

Nash equilibrium

An outcome of a game in which each player is doing the best he or she can, given the action of the other players.

We have used a game tree to find the equilibrium in a price-fixing game. It is an equilibrium in the sense that each player (firm) is doing the best he or she can, given the actions of another player. The label for such an equilibrium is **Nash equilibrium**. This concept is named after John Nash, the recipient of the 1994 Nobel Prize in economics, who developed his equilibrium concept as a 21-year-old graduate student at Princeton University. Nash's life story, which includes a 25-year bout with schizophrenia and a dramatic recovery, is chronicled in the book *A Beautiful Mind*, later made into a movie starring Russell Crowe as Nash.[3]

In the Nash equilibrium for the price-fixing game, both firms pick the low price. Each firm is doing the best it can, given the action of the other firm:

- If Jill picks the low price, Jack's best action is to pick the low price.
- If Jack picks the low price, Jill's best action is to pick the low price.

What about the other potential outcomes? Consider first the possibility that both firms pick the high price. This is not a Nash equilibrium because neither firm is doing the best it can, given the action of the other firm:

- If Jill picks the high price, Jack's best action is to pick the low price.
- If Jack picks the high price, Jill's best action is to pick the low price.

Consider next the possibility that Jill picks the low price and Jack picks the high price. This is not a Nash equilibrium because Jack is not doing the best he can, given Jill's choice:

- If Jill picks the low price, Jack's best action is to pick the low price.

The concept of the Nash equilibrium has been applied to a wide variety of decisions. Analysts have used it to study the nuclear arms race, terrorism, evolutionary biology, art auctions, environmental policy, and urban development. Later in the chapter, we will use it to predict the outcomes of games of entry deterrence and advertising.

application 1

FAILURE OF THE SALT CARTEL

APPLYING THE CONCEPTS #1: Why do cartels sometimes fail to keep prices high?

At the beginning of the nineteenth century, high overland transportation costs protected salt producers from competition with one another, generating local salt monopolies. Over the course of the nineteenth century, decreases in overland transportation costs increased competition between salt producers and decreased prices. In response to the increased competition, salt producers colluded by forming salt pools, enterprises that set a uniform price and distributed the salt of all participating producers. Some pools established output quotas or paid firms not to produce salt for a year, a practice known as "dead-renting" a salt furnace. Every salt pool eventually broke down, usually within a year or two of its formation. In some cases, individual firms cheated on the cartel by selling salt outside the cartel. In other cases the artificially high price caused new firms to enter the market and underprice the salt pool. **Related to Exercise 1.9.**

SOURCE: Based on Margaret Levenstein, "Mass Production Conquers the Pool: Firm Organization and the Nature of Competition in the Nineteenth Century," *The Journal of Economic History* 55 (1995), pp. 575–611.

12.2   Overcoming the Duopolists' Dilemma

The duopolists' dilemma occurs because the two firms are unable to coordinate their pricing decisions and act as one. Each firm has an incentive to underprice the other because the low-price firm will capture a larger share of the market and earn a larger profit. Firms can avoid the dilemma in two ways: low-price guarantees and repetition of the pricing game, with retaliation for underpricing.

Low-Price Guarantees

The duopolists' dilemma occurs because the payoff from underpricing the other firm is too lucrative to miss. To eliminate the possibility of underpricing, one firm can guarantee it will match a lower price of a competitor. Suppose Jill places the following advertisement in the local newspaper:

> If you buy an airline ticket from me and then discover that Jack offers the same trip at a lower price, I will pay you the price difference. If I charge you $400 and Jack's price is only $300, I will pay you $100.

Jill's **low-price guarantee** is a credible promise because she announces it in the newspaper.

Suppose Jack makes a similar commitment to match a lower price from Jill. Figure 12.4 shows the effect of low-price guarantees on the game tree. Jill now has two decision nodes. As before, she starts the game in square *A*. If Jill picks the high price and then Jack picks the high price, we end up at rectangle 1, as before. But if Jill picks the high price and Jack picks the low price, we get to square *D*. Jill will issue a refund of $100 to each of her consumers. In effect, she has retroactively chosen the low price, and payoff rectangle 2 is the duopoly outcome, with both firms picking the low price. For the lower half of the game tree, recall that Jack has committed to match a lower price by Jill, so the old payoff rectangle 3 disappears, leaving us with rectangle 4, where both firms choose the low price and get the duopoly profit.

low-price guarantee
A promise to match a lower price of a competitor.

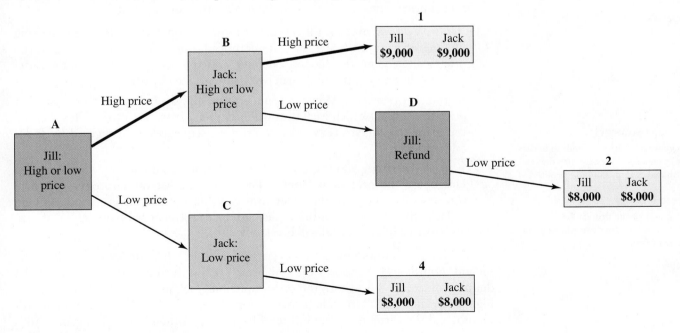

▲ FIGURE 12.4
Low-Price Guarantees Increase Prices
When both firms have a low-price guarantee, it is impossible for one firm to underprice the other. The only possible outcomes are a pair of high prices (rectangle 1) or a pair of low prices (rectangles 2 or 4). The equilibrium path of the game is square A to square B to rectangle 1. Each firm picks the high price and earns a profit of $9,000.

The thick arrows show the path of the game with low-price guarantees. Consider Jack's decision first:

- If Jill picks the high price, Jack chooses between payoff rectangles 1 and 2, a pair of high prices or a pair of low prices. His profit is higher at $9,000 with a pair of high prices (rectangle 1), so if Jill picks the high price, he will too.
- If Jill picks the low price, Jack is committed to the low price too.

Consider Jill's decision. She knows Jack will match her price—either high or low—meaning she chooses between profit rectangles 1 and 4. Profit is higher with rectangle 1, so she will pick the high price.

The low-price guarantee eliminates the possibility of underpricing, so it eliminates the duopolists' dilemma and promotes cartel pricing. The firms don't have to create a formal cartel to get the benefits from cartel pricing. The motto of a low-price guarantee is "Low for one means low for all," so both firms charge the high price. Once the possibility of underpricing has been eliminated, the duopoly will be replaced by an informal cartel, with each firm picking the price that a monopolist would pick.

To most people, the notion that a low-price guarantee leads to higher prices is surprising. After all, if Jill promises to give refunds if her price exceeds Jack's price, we might expect Jill to keep her price low to avoid handing out a lot of refunds. In fact, Jill doesn't have to worry about giving refunds because Jack will also choose the high price. In other words, the promise to issue refunds is an *empty* promise. Although consumers might think that a low-price guarantee will protect them from high prices, it means they are more likely to pay the high price.

Repeated Pricing Games with Retaliation for Underpricing

Up to this point, we've assumed the price-fixing game is played only once. Each firm chooses a price and keeps it for the lifetime of the firm. What happens when two firms play the game repeatedly, picking prices over an extended period of time? We'll see that repetition makes price fixing more likely because firms can punish a firm that cheats on a price-fixing agreement, whether it's formal or informal.

1 *A duopoly pricing strategy.* Jill chooses the lower duopoly price for the remaining lifetime of her firm. Once Jill is underpriced, she abandons the idea of cartel pricing and accepts the duopoly outcome, which is less profitable than the cartel outcome but more profitable than being underpriced by the other firm.

2 *A grim-trigger strategy.* When Jack underprices Jill, she responds by dropping her price to a level at which each firm will make zero economic profit. This is called the **grim-trigger strategy** because grim consequences are triggered by Jack's underpricing.

3 *A tit-for-tat strategy.* Starting in the second month, Jill chooses whatever price Jack chose the preceding month. This is the **tit-for-tat strategy**—one firm chooses whatever price the other firm chose in the preceding period. As long as Jack chooses the cartel price, the cartel arrangement will persist. But if Jack underprices Jill, the cartel will break down.

grim-trigger strategy
A strategy where a firm responds to underpricing by choosing a price so low that each firm makes zero economic profit.

tit-for-tat strategy
A strategy where one firm chooses whatever price the other firm chose in the preceding period.

Figure 12.5 shows how a tit-for-tat system works. Jack underprices Jill in the second month, so Jill chooses the low price for the third month, resulting in the duopoly outcome. To restore the cartel outcome, Jack must eventually choose the high price, allowing Jill to underprice him for one month. This happens in the fourth month, and the cartel is restored in the fifth month. Although Jack can gain at Jill's expense in the second month, if he wants to restore cartel pricing, he must allow her to gain at his expense during some other month. Under a tit-for-tat strategy, a duopolist does exactly what his or her rival did the last round. This encourages firms to cooperate rather than compete. Several studies have shown that a tit-for-tat strategy is the most effective strategy to promote cooperation.[4]

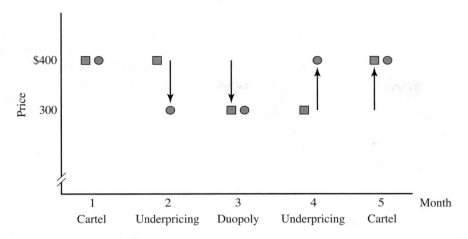

▲ **FIGURE 12.5**
A Tit-for-Tat Pricing Strategy
Under tit-for-tat retaliation, the first firm (Jill, the square) chooses whatever price the second firm (Jack, the circle) chose the preceding month.

These three pricing schemes promote cartel pricing by penalizing the firm that underprices the other firm. To decide whether to underprice Jill, Jack must weigh the short-term benefit against the long-term cost:

- The short-term benefit is the increase in profit in the current period. If Jack underprices Jill, he can increase his profit from the cartel profit of $9,000 to the $12,000 earned by a firm that underprices the other firm. Therefore, the short-term benefit of underpricing is $3,000.

- The long-term cost is the loss of profit in later periods. Jill will respond to Jack's underpricing by cutting her price, and this decreases Jack's profit. For example, if Jill retaliates with the duopoly price, Jack's future profit will be $8,000 per day instead of the $9,000 he could have earned by going along with the cartel price. The cost of underpricing is the daily loss of $1,000 in profit.

If the two firms expect to share the market for a long time, the long-term cost of underpricing will exceed the short-term benefit, so underpricing is less likely. The threat of punishment makes it easier to resist the temptation to cheat on the cartel.

Price Fixing and the Law

Under the Sherman Antitrust Act of 1890 and subsequent legislation, explicit price fixing is illegal. It is illegal for firms to discuss pricing strategies or methods of punishing a firm that underprices other firms. In one of the early price-fixing cases (*Addyston Pipe*, 1899), six manufacturers of cast-iron pipe met to fix prices. Several months after the Supreme Court ruled that their cartel pricing was illegal, the firms merged into a single firm, so instead of acting like a monopolist, they became a monopolist. Here are some other examples of price fixing:

1 *Electric generators (1961)*. Executives from General Electric and Westinghouse were convicted of fixing prices for electrical generators, resulting in fines of over $2 million and imprisonment or probation for 30 corporate executives.

2 *Carton-board pricing in Europe (1994)*. The European Union Commission fined 19 manufacturers of carton board a total of 132 million euros ($165 million) for operating a cartel that fixed prices at secret meetings in luxury Zurich hotels.

3 *Food additives (1996)*. An employee of Archer Daniels Midland (ADM), a huge food company, provided audio and videotapes of ADM executives conspiring to fix prices. ADM pleaded guilty to the charges of price fixing and was fined $100 million.

4 *Music distribution (2000).* In exchange for advertising subsidies, music retailers agreed to adhere to the minimum advertised prices (MAP) specified by distributors. Any retailer that advertised a CD for less than the MAP would lose all of its "cooperative advertising" funds from the distributor. In May 2000, the Federal Trade Commission reached an agreement with music distributors to end the MAP scheme. The FTC estimated that the MAP scheme imposed an annual cost of $160 million on U.S. music consumers.[5]

5 *Industrial diamonds (2004).* DeBeers, the world's largest diamond producer, plead guilty to conspiring with General Electric to fix the price of industrial diamonds, and paid a fine of $10 million.

Price Leadership

price leadership

A system under which one firm in an oligopoly takes the lead in setting prices.

Because explicit price fixing is illegal, firms sometimes rely on implicit pricing agreements to fix prices at the monopoly level. Under the model of **price leadership**, one of the oligopolists plays the role of price leader. The leading firm picks a price, and other firms match the price. Such an agreement allows firms to cooperate without actually discussing their pricing strategies.

The problem with an implicit pricing agreement is that it relies on indirect signals that are often garbled and misinterpreted. Suppose two firms have cooperated for several years, both sticking to the cartel price. When one firm suddenly drops its price, the other firm could interpret the price cut in one of two ways:

- **A change in market conditions.** Perhaps the first firm observed a change in demand or production cost and decides that both firms would benefit from a lower price.
- **Underpricing.** Perhaps the first firm is trying to increase its market share and profit at the expense of the second firm.

The first interpretation would probably cause the second firm to match the lower price of the first firm, and price fixing would continue at the lower price. In contrast, the second interpretation could trigger a price war, undermining the price-fixing agreement.

application 2

LOW-PRICE GUARANTEE INCREASES TIRE PRICES

APPLYING THE CONCEPTS #2: Do low-price guarantees generate higher or lower prices?

In two successive months (November and December), a Florida tire retailer listed prices for 35 types of tires in newspaper advertisements. In November the average price was $45, and in December the average price was $55. The December advertisement was different in another way: it included a low-price guarantee under which the retailer agreed to match any lower advertised price (and also pay the customer some percentage of the price gap). In fact, for each of the 35 types of tires, the December price was the same or higher than the November price. In this case, a low-price guarantee generated higher prices.

Is the relationship between low-price guarantees and prices apparent or real? A careful study of the retail tire market suggests that prices are generally higher in markets where firms offer low-price guarantees. On average, the presence of a low-price guarantee increases prices by $4 per tire, or about 10 percent of the price. **Related to Exercise 2.5.**

SOURCE: Maria Arbatskaya, Morten Hviid, Greg Shaffer, "Promises to Match or Beat the Competition," *Advances in Applied Microeconomics* 8 (1999), pp. 123–138.

12.3   Simultaneous Decision Making and the Payoff Matrix

So far we have considered a game with sequential decisions. Jill chooses her price first, and then Jack observes her choice and then makes his own. An alternative scenario is that the two firms make their decisions simultaneously, so each firm picks its price without knowing the other firm's price. The analysis of a simultaneous game requires a different tool. A **payoff matrix** shows, for each possible outcome of a game, the consequences—or payoffs—for each player.

payoff matrix
A matrix or table that shows, for each possible outcome of a game, the consequences for each player.

Simultaneous Price-Fixing Game

Figure 12.6 shows the payoff matrix for the price-fixing game. Each cell in the matrix shows the payoffs from a potential outcome of the game. In the northwest corner of the matrix, if both firms pick the high price, each firm earns a profit of $9,000. In the southeast corner, if both firms pick the low price, each firm earns a profit of $8,000. If one firm picks the low price and the other picks the high price, the low-price firm earns $12,000 and the high-price firm earns only $3,000. For example, in the northeast corner, if Jill picks the high price and Jack picks the low price, Jill earns a profit of $3,000 and Jack earns a profit of $12,000.

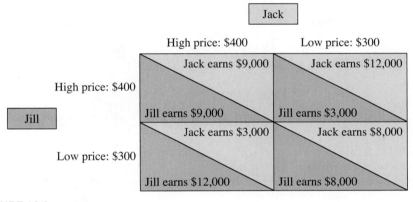

▲ FIGURE 12.6
Payoff Matrix for the Price-Fixing Game
Jill's profit is in red, and Jack's profit is in blue. If both firms pick the high price, each firm earns a profit of $9,000. Both firms will pick the low price, and each firm will earn a profit of only $8,000.

We can use the payoff matrix to predict the equilibrium of the price-fixing game. In a simultaneous-decision game, Jack doesn't know whether Jill will pick the low price or the high price. There are two possibilities:

- If Jill picks the high price, we will be in the upper half of the matrix, and Jack's best response is the low price. In the northeast corner of the matrix, he can earn $12,000 by picking the low price. This is better than the $9,000 he can earn by picking the high price in the northwest corner.

- If Jill picks the low price, we will be in the lower half of the matrix, and Jack's best response is the low price. In the southeast corner of the matrix, he can earn $8,000 by picking the low price. This is better than the $3,000 he can earn by picking the high price in the southwest corner.

In other words, the low price is the dominant strategy for Jack. Jill knows this, so she realizes that the equilibrium will be in the eastern half of the matrix. Her best response is the low price. In the southeast corner of the matrix, she can earn $8,000 by picking the low price. This is better than the $3,000 she can earn in the northeast corner by picking the high price. Therefore, the equilibrium is the same as with the game-tree approach: Both firms pick the low price.

The Prisoners' Dilemma

We can gain some insight into the duopolists' dilemma by examining the classic prisoners' dilemma. Consider two people, Bonnie and Clyde, who have been accused of committing a crime. The police give each person an opportunity to confess to the crime. The traditional version of the story is a simultaneous decision-making game: The two are put in separate rooms, and each makes a choice without knowing the other's choice.

The police confront Bonnie and Clyde with the payoff matrix in Figure 12.7. If both confess, each gets 5 years in prison, as shown in the southeast corner of the matrix. If neither confesses, the police can convict both of them on a lesser charge, and each gets 2 years, as shown in the northwest corner of the matrix. If only one confesses, he or she will implicate the other prisoner. The confessor is rewarded with a 1-year prison sentence, while the other prisoner gets 10 years. If Bonnie confesses and Clyde does not, we are in the southwest corner of the matrix. If the roles are reversed, we are in the northeast corner.

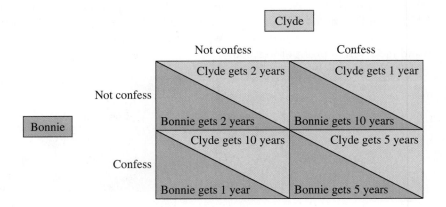

▲ **FIGURE 12.7**

Payoff Matrix for the Prisoners' Dilemma

The prisoners' dilemma is that each prisoner would be better off if neither confessed, but both people confess. The Nash equilibrium is shown in the southeast corner of the matrix. Each person gets five years of prison time.

We can use the payoff matrix to predict the equilibrium of the prisoner game. In a simultaneous-decision game, Clyde doesn't know whether Bonnie will confess or not:

- If Bonnie does not confess, we are in the upper half of the matrix, and Clyde's best response is to confess. In the northeast corner of the matrix, he gets one year in prison if he confesses. This is better than the two years he would get in the northwest corner by not confessing.

- If Bonnie confesses, we are in the lower half of the matrix, and Clyde's best response is to confess. In the southeast corner of the matrix, he gets 5 years in prison. This is better than the 10 years he would get in the southwest corner by not confessing.

In other words, confessing is the dominant strategy for Clyde. Bonnie knows this, so she realizes that the equilibrium will be in the eastern half of the matrix. Her best response is to confess. In the southeast corner of the matrix, she gets 5 years in prison. This is better than the 10 years she would get in the northeast by not confessing.

If both prisoners confess and each gets 5 years in prison, we have a Nash equilibrium because each prisoner is doing the best he or she can, given the actions of the other prisoner. Although both would be better off if they both kept quiet, they implicate each other because the police reward them for doing so. There is an incentive for squealing, just as there is an incentive for one duopolist to underprice the other.

application 3

CHEATING ON THE FINAL EXAM: THE CHEATERS' DILEMMA

APPLYING THE CONCEPTS #3: When does cooperation break down?

An economics professor discovered three students cheating on the final exam. Speaking to the students individually in his office, he gave each student two options:

1 If the student confessed, he or she would receive a zero on the final exam, but suffer no other consequences.

2 If the student did not confess, he or she would go before the Office of Student Judicial Affairs, and any confessions by the other two students would be used as evidence.

During the sessions in the professor's office, one of the accused said, "This feels like you put me in a prisoners' dilemma game." By the end of the day, the professor had three confessions. **Related to Exercise 3.3.**

12.4 The Insecure Monopolist and Entry Deterrence

We've seen what happens when two duopolists try to act as one, fixing the price at the monopoly level. Consider next how a monopolist might try to prevent a second firm from entering its market. We will use some of the numbers from our airline example, although we will look at a different city with a different cast of characters.

Suppose Mona initially has a secure monopoly in the market for air travel between two cities. When there is no threat of entry, Mona uses the marginal principle (marginal revenue equals marginal cost) to pick a quantity and a price. In Figure 12.8, we start at point c on the market demand curve, with a quantity of 60 passengers per day and a price of $400 per passenger. Her profit is $18,000:

$$\text{profit} = (\text{price} - \text{average cost}) \times \text{quantity per firm} = (\$400 - \$100) \times 60 = \$18,000$$

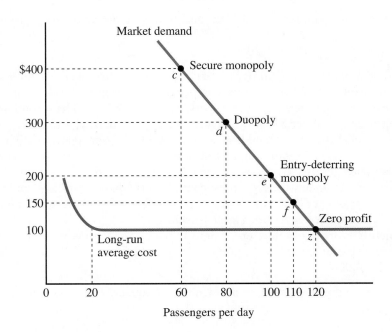

◀ **FIGURE 12.8**
Deterring Entry with Limit Pricing
Point c shows a secure monopoly, point d shows a duopoly, and point z shows the zero-profit outcome. The minimum entry quantity is 20 passengers, so the entry-deterring quantity is 100 (equal to $120 - 20$), as shown by point e. The limit price is $200.

If Mona discovers that a second airline is thinking about entering the market, what will she do? Now that her monopoly is insecure, she has two options: She can be passive and allow the second airline to enter the market, or she can try to prevent the other firm from entering the market.

The passive approach will lead to the duopoly outcome we saw earlier in the chapter. In Figure 12.8, if the second firm enters the market, we move downward along the market demand curve from point c to point d. In a duopoly, each firm charges a price of $300 and serves 40 passengers, half the total quantity demanded at a price of $300. For each duopolist, the daily profit is $8,000:

$$\text{profit} = (\text{price} - \text{average cost}) \times \text{quantity per firm} = (\$300 - \$100) \times 40 = \$8,000$$

Entry Deterrence and Limit Pricing

The second option is to take actions to prevent the second firm from entering the market. To decide whether to deter the entry of the other firm, Mona must answer two questions:

- What must she do to deter entry?
- Given what she must do to deter entry, is deterrence more profitable than being passive and sharing the market with the second firm?

To prevent the second firm from entering the market, Mona must commit herself to serving a large number of passengers. If she commits to a large passenger load, there won't be enough passengers left for a potential entrant to make a profit. Suppose there are economies of scale in providing air travel, and the minimum entry quantity is 20 passengers per day: That is, it would be impractical for a firm to serve fewer than 20 passengers. In Figure 12.8, the long-run average cost curve is negatively sloped for relatively low levels of output, and the average cost for the minimum entry quantity of 20 passengers is just over $100, say $101.

Mona must compute the quantity of output that is just large enough to prevent the second firm from entering the market. In Figure 12.8, point z shows the point of zero economic profit in the market: If the two firms serve a total of 120 passengers per day and split the market equally, with 60 passengers each, the price ($100) equals average cost, so each firm would earn zero economic profit. The quantity required to prevent the entry of the second firm is computed as follows:

$$\text{deterring quantity} = \text{zero profit quantity} - \text{minimum entry quantity}$$

$$100 = 120 - 20$$

If Mona commits to serve 100 passengers and a second firm were to enter with the minimum quantity of 20 passengers, the price would drop to $100. Mona, with an average cost of $100 to serve 100 passengers, would break even. The second firm, with an average cost just above $100, would lose money. Specifically, if the average cost of 20 passengers is $101, the second firm would lose $1 per passenger, or $20 in total.

Note that Mona cannot simply announce that she will serve 100 passengers. She must take actions that ensure that her most profitable output is in fact 100 passengers. In other words, she must commit to 100 passengers. She could commit to the larger passenger load by purchasing a large fleet of airplanes and signing labor contracts that require her to hire a large workforce.

Which is more profitable, entry deterrence or the passive duopoly outcome? The deterrence strategy, shown by point e in Figure 12.8, generates a price of $200 and a profit of $10,000:

$$\text{profit} = (\text{price} - \text{average cost}) \times \text{quantity per firm}$$

$$= (\$200 - \$100) \times 100 = \$10,000$$

This is larger than the $8,000 profit under the passive approach, so deterrence is the best strategy.

Figure 12.9 uses a game tree to represent the entry-deterrence game. Mona makes the first move, and she considers the consequences of her two options:

- If Mona is passive and commits to serve only 40 passengers, we reach the upper branch of the game tree. The best response for Doug, the manager of the second firm, is to enter to earn a profit of $8,000, as shown by rectangle 1.

- If Mona commits to serve 100 passengers, we reach the lower branch of the game tree. If Doug enters with the minimum entry quantity of 20 passengers, his average cost will be $101, which exceeds the market price of $100. Therefore, the best response is to stay out of the market and avoid losing money.

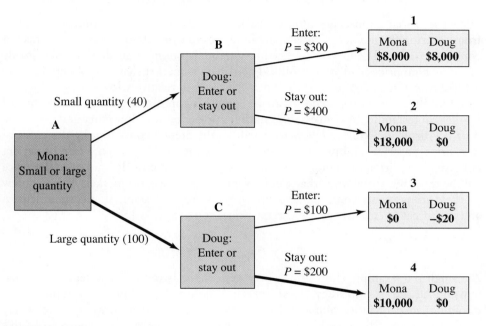

▲ **FIGURE 12.9**

Game Tree for the Entry-Deterrence Game

The path of the game is square *A* to square *C* to rectangle 4. Mona commits to the entry-deterring quantity of 100, so Doug stays out of the market. Mona's profit of $10,000 is less than the monopoly profit but more than the duopoly profit of $8,000.

Mona can choose between rectangles 1 and 4. Mona's profit is higher in rectangle 4, so that's the equilibrium. The equilibrium path of the game is square *A* to square *C* to rectangle 4.

Mona's entry-deterrence strategy generates a market price of $200, which is less than the $400 price charged by a secure monopolist and less than the $300 price with two competing firms. Mona can keep the second firm out of the market, but only by producing a large quantity and charging a relatively low price. This is known as **limit pricing**: To prevent a firm from entering the market, the firm reduces its price. The price that is just low enough to prevent entry is known as the **limit price**.

limit pricing
The strategy of reducing the price to deter entry.

limit price
The price that is just low enough to deter entry.

Examples: Aluminum and Campus Bookstores

For an example of limit pricing, consider the Aluminum Company of America (Alcoa). Between 1893 and 1940, Alcoa had a monopoly on aluminum production in the United States. During this period, Alcoa kept other firms out of the market by producing a large quantity and keeping its price relatively low. Although a higher price would have generated more profit in the short run, the entry of other firms would eventually have reduced Alcoa's profit.

We can apply the notion of entry deterrence to your favorite monopoly: your campus bookstore. On most college campuses, other organizations are prohibited, usually by the state government or the college, from selling textbooks on campus. Internet commerce has given students another option: Order textbooks online and have them shipped by mail, UPS, FedEx, or DHL. Several online booksellers charge less than the campus bookstore, and the growth of Internet book sales thus threatens the campus bookstore monopoly. If your campus bookstore suddenly feels insecure about its monopoly position, it could cut its prices to prevent online booksellers from capturing too many of its customers. If it does this, you will pay lower prices even if you don't patronize the Internet seller.

Entry Deterrence and Contestable Markets

We've seen that an insecure monopolist may cut its price to prevent a second firm from entering the market. The same logic applies to a market that has a few firms but could have many. The mere existence of a monopoly or oligopoly does not necessarily generate high prices and large profits. To protect its market share, an oligopolist may act like a firm in a market with many firms, leading to relatively low prices.

contestable market
A market with low entry and exit costs.

The threat of entry faced by an insecure monopolist underlies the theory of market contestability. A **contestable market** is a market with low entry and exit costs. The few firms in a contestable market will be threatened constantly by the entry of new firms, so prices and profits will be relatively low. In the extreme case of perfect contestability, firms can enter and exit a market at zero cost. In this case, the price will be the same as the price that would occur in a competitive market. Although few markets are perfectly contestable, many markets are contestable to a certain degree, and the threat of entry tends to decrease prices and profits.

When Is the Passive Approach Better?

Although our example shows that entry deterrence is the best strategy for Mona, it won't be the best strategy for all insecure monopolists. The key variable is the minimum entry quantity. Suppose that the scale economies in air travel were relatively small, so a second firm could enter the market with as few as 10 passengers. In this case, if Mona commits to serving only 100 passengers, that won't be enough to deter entry: A firm entering with 10 passengers will still make a profit. If the minimum entry quantity is 10 passengers, the entry-deterring quantity rises to 110 passengers:

$$\text{deterring quantity} = \text{zero profit quantity} - \text{minimum entry quantity}$$

$$110 = 120 - 10$$

Mona can commit to serving 110 passengers and thus prevent the second firm from entering the market, but is this the most profitable strategy? As shown by point f in Figure 12.8, the limit price associated with an entry-deterring quantity is $150. Mona's profit from entry deterrence would be $5,500:

$$\text{profit} = (\text{price} - \text{average cost}) \times \text{quantity per firm}$$

$$= (\$150 - \$100) \times 110 = \$5,500$$

This is less than the $8,000 profit she could earn by being passive and letting the second firm enter the market. In this case, the minimum entry quantity is relatively small, so the entry-deterring quantity is large and the limit price is low. As a result, sharing a duopoly is more profitable than increasing output and cutting the price to keep the other firm out.

For another example of the passive response to market entry, consider the ballpoint pen, introduced in 1945 by Reynolds International Pen Corporation.[6] For three years Reynolds earned enormous profits producing this revolutionary product and selling it for $12.50, about 16 times the average production cost of $0.80.

application 4

MICROSOFT AS AN INSECURE MONOPOLIST

APPLYING THE CONCEPT #4: How does a monopolist respond to the threat of entry?

Microsoft has a virtual monopoly in the market for personal-computer operating systems and business software. But there is a constant threat that another firm will launch competing products, so Microsoft engages in limit pricing to deter entry into its key markets. A recent study revealed some of the numbers behind the insecure monopoly.

1 The pure monopoly price for a software bundle of the Windows operating system and the Office Suite of business tools is about $354, but the actual price (the limit price) is about $143. The estimated cost for a second firm to develop, maintain, and market an alternative software bundle is about $38 billion, and Microsoft's actual price is just low enough to make such an investment unprofitable.

2 The pure monopoly profit would be about $191 billion, while the profit under Microsoft's limit pricing is about $153 billion. Although the profit under the entry-deterrence strategy is less than the pure monopoly profit, it is greater than the profit Microsoft would earn if it allowed a second firm to enter the market ($148 billion). In other words, entry deterrence is the best strategy. **Related to Exercise 4.8.**

SOURCE: Based on Robert E. Hall, "Potential Competition, Limit Pricing, and Price Elevation from Exclusionary Conduct," Chapter 18 in *Issues in Competition Law and Policy* 1 (2008, ABA Publishing Chicago), pp. 433–448.

Then in 1948, Reynolds stopped producing pens, dropping out of the market entirely. Why? Other producers could easily copy the simple production technology of the ballpoint pen. The limit price was thus so low that it was better for Reynolds to charge a high price and squeeze out as much profit as possible from a short-lived monopoly while it lasted. By 1948, a total of 100 firms had entered the ballpoint market, and the price had fallen to the average cost of production, so each firm made zero economic profit.

12.5 The Advertisers' Dilemma

We have explored two sorts of strategic behavior of firms in an oligopoly—price fixing and entry deterrence. A third type of strategy concerns advertising. As we'll see, firms in an oligopoly may suffer from an advertisers' dilemma: Although both firms would be better off if neither spent money on advertising, each firm advertises.

Consider the producers of two brands of aspirin. Each firm must decide whether to spend $7 million on an advertising campaign for its product. In Table 12.3, the first two columns show what happens if neither firm advertises. Each firm earns $8 million in net

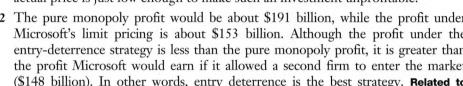

TABLE 12.3 Advertising and Profit						
	Neither Advertises		**Both Advertise**		**Adeline Advertises**	
	Adeline	Vern	Adeline	Vern	Adeline	Vern
Net revenue from sales ($ million)	$8	$8	$13	$13	$17	$5
Cost of advertising ($ million)	0	0	7	7	7	0
Profit ($ million)	8	8	6	6	10	5

revenue (revenue minus production cost) and spends no money on advertising, so each firm earns $8 million in profits. The third and fourth columns show what happens if each firm spends $7 million on advertising. The net revenue for each firm increases by only $5 million, so the profit of each firm drops by $2 million, to $6 million.

What happens if one firm advertises and the other does not? As shown in the last two columns in Table 12.3, a firm can increase its profit by advertising. If Adeline spends $7 million on advertising and Vern spends nothing, Adeline's net revenue increases to $17 million and her profit increases to $10 million. Adeline's advertisements cause some of Vern's consumers to switch to Adeline, and Vern's profit drops to $5 million.

We can use the data in Table 12.3 to construct a game tree for the advertising game. In Figure 12.10, Adeline makes her decision first, followed by Vern:

- If neither firm advertises, we go from square *A* to square *C* to rectangle 4, and each firm gets a profit of $8 million.

- If both firms advertise, we go from square *A* to square *B* to rectangle 1, and each firm earns a profit of $6 million.

- If Adeline advertises and Vern does not, we go from square *A* to square *B* to rectangle 2. Adeline earns $10 million, while Vern earns $5 million. If the roles are reversed, we end up in rectangle 3, with Vern the advertiser earning $10 million and Adeline earning only $5 million.

► **FIGURE 12.10**

Game Tree for the Advertisers' Dilemma

Adeline moves first, choosing to advertise or not. Vern's best response is to advertise no matter what Adeline does. Knowing this, Adeline realizes that the only possible outcomes are shown by rectangles 1 and 3. From Adeline's perspective, rectangle 1 ($6 million) is better than rectangle 3 ($5 million), so her best response is to advertise. Both Adeline and Vern advertise, and each earns a profit of $6 million.

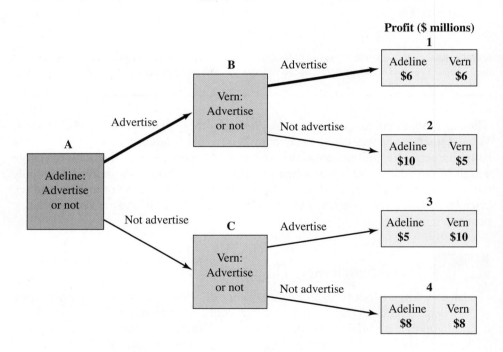

To determine the outcome of this advertising game, let's start with Vern's possible actions:

- If Adeline advertises, we move along the upper branches of the game tree from square *A* to square *B*. Vern will earn $6 million if he advertises (rectangle 1), but only $5 million if he does not advertise (rectangle 2). Therefore, Vern's best response is to match Adeline's campaign.

- If Adeline does not advertise, we move along the lower branches from square *A* to square *C*. Vern will earn $10 million if he advertises, but only $8 million if he does not. Therefore, if Adeline does not advertise, Vern's best response is to advertise.

Advertising is Vern's dominant strategy because it is the best response no matter what Adeline does.

Consider next the options faced by Adeline. She will figure out that advertising is a dominant strategy for Vern, so she realizes that the only possible outcomes are shown by rectangles 1 and 3. To get to rectangle 1, she advertises and gets a profit of $6 million. This is better than not advertising and going to rectangle 3, with a profit of $5 million. So Adeline's best response is to advertise. The thick arrows show the equilibrium path of the game, from square *A* to square *B* to rectangle 1. In equilibrium, both firms advertise and each earns a profit of $6 million.

What is the advertisers' dilemma? Both Adeline and Vern would be better off if neither advertised. Each would get a profit of $8 million, compared to $6 million when they both advertise. But each firm has an incentive to use advertising to increase its sales at the expense of the other. Stuck in the dilemma, each firm earns $2 million less than it would if neither advertised.

Why does the advertisers' dilemma occur? In general, it happens when advertising causes a relatively small increase in the total sales of the industry but allows a firm that advertises to gain at the expense of firms that don't. In our example, a pair of advertising campaigns costing a total of $14 million increases the net revenue of the entire industry by only $10 million. The increase in revenue is less than the cost of advertising, so advertising decreases total profit. Nonetheless, each firm has an incentive to advertise to take sales away from the other firm. If the increase in industry-wide net revenue were larger, advertising could benefit both firms.

application 5

GOT MILK?

APPLYING THE CONCEPTS #5: What is the rationale for generic advertising?

The Got Milk? advertisement campaign is run by the National Fluid Milk Producers, an industry group that is funded by a tax of $0.20 per hundredweight of processed milk. Milk producers pool their resources and run a generic (non-brand) advertising campaign. Why?

Milk is a standardized good, so advertising by one producer increases demand and benefits other producers. The Got Milk? campaign increases the demand for milk by about 6 percent, and the bang per buck (the increase in milk sales per dollar on advertising) is about $5. No single firm has an incentive to incur the cost of an advertising campaign, because the firm bears all the cost but experiences only a fraction of the benefits. The result is an advertisers' dilemma: All firms would benefit from an advertising campaign, but no single firm has an incentive to pay for a campaign. The solution to this advertisers' dilemma is to share the cost of an advertising campaign, along with the benefits. **Related to Exercise 5.6.**

SOURCE: Based on Noel Blisard, "Advertising and What We Eat: The Case of Dairy Products," in *America's Eating Habits: Changes and Consequences*, ed. Elizabeth Frazao (U.S. Department of Agriculture, 1999), chap. 10.

SUMMARY

In this chapter, we've seen that when a few firms share a market they have an incentive to act strategically. Firms in an oligopoly try to use cartel pricing—price fixing—to avoid competition and keep prices high. A monopolist may commit to a large quantity and a low price in order to prevent a second firm from entering the market. Oligopolists may use advertising to increase their sales at the expense of competitors. Here are the main points of the chapter:

1 Each firm in an oligopoly has an incentive to underprice the other firms, so price fixing will be unsuccessful unless firms have some way of enforcing a price-fixing agreement.

2 One way to maintain price fixing is a low-price guarantee: One firm chooses the high price and promises to match any lower price of a competitor.

3 Price fixing is more likely to occur if firms choose prices repeatedly and can punish a firm that chooses a price below the cartel price.

4 To prevent a second firm from entering the market, an insecure monopolist may commit itself to producing a relatively large quantity and accepting a relatively low price.

5 The advertisers' dilemma is that both firms would be better off if neither firm advertised.

KEY TERMS

cartel, p. 272

concentration ratio, p. 271

contestable market, p. 286

dominant strategy, p. 275

duopolists' dilemma, p. 275

duopoly, p. 272

game theory, p. 271

game tree, p. 274

grim-trigger strategy, p. 278

low-price guarantee, p. 277

limit price, p. 285

limit pricing, p. 285

Nash equilibrium, p. 276

oligopoly, p. 271

payoff matrix, p. 281

price fixing, p. 273

price leadership, p. 280

tit-for-tat strategy, p. 278

EXERCISES

All problems are assignable in MyEconLab.

12.1 Cartel Pricing and the Duopolists' Dilemma

1.1 A market is considered "unconcentrated" if the Herfindahl–Hirschman Index (HHI) is below _____ and is "highly" concentrated if the HHI is at least _____.

1.2 For a market with four firms, each with a 25 percent market share, the Herfindahl–Hirschman Index (HHI) is equal to _____.

1.3. Arrows up or down: If we move from the cartel outcome to the duopoly outcome, the price _____, the quantity per firm _____, and the profit per firm _____.

1.4 A dominant strategy is the strategy that allows one firm to dominate the market. _____ (True/False)

1.5 The duopolists' dilemma is that each firm would make more profit if both picked the _____ price, but both firms pick the _____ price.

1.6 In a Nash equilibrium, each player is doing the best he or she can, given _____.

1.7 In Figure 12.3 on page 274, rectangle 3 is not a Nash equilibrium because if _____ picks a(n) _____ price, the best response of _____ is to pick the _____ price.

1.8 In Figure 12.3 on page 274, suppose Jack promises Jill that if she picks the high price, he will too. Is this promise credible? Explain.

1.9 The salt cartels of the nineteenth century were _____ (short/long) lived, in part because individual firms _____ on the cartel. (Related to Application 1 on page 276.)

1.10 Buzz and Moe are duopolists in the lawn-care market. The following game tree shows the possible pricing outcomes and their payoffs. The outcome of the pricing game is that Buzz will pick the _____ price and Moe will pick the _____ price.

Use this figure to complete Exercise 1.10.

1.11 Vitamin Market Areas. Beta and Gamma produce vitamin A at a constant average cost of $5 per unit. Assume that low-price guarantees are illegal. Here are the possible outcomes:

- Price fixing (cartel). Each firm sells 30 units at a price of $20 per unit.
- Duopoly (no price fixing). Each firm sells 40 units at a price of $12 per unit.
- Underpricing (one firm charges $20 and the other charges $12). The low-price firm sells 70 units and the high-price firm sells 5 units.

  a. Suppose Beta chooses a price first, followed by Gamma. Draw a game tree for the price-fixing game and predict the outcome.

  b. Suppose the firms agree to pick the high price. Once Beta picks the high price, how much more could Gamma earn if it cheated on the price-fixing agreement?

  c. Suppose the firms divide the market into two areas of equal size and assign each firm one of the areas. Each firm agrees to sell only in its assigned areas. Will this arrangement generate a successful cartel?

1.12 Airporter Price Fixing? Hustle and Speedy provide transportation service from downtown to the city airport. Assume that low-price guarantees are illegal. The average cost per passenger is constant at $10. Here are the possible outcomes:

- Price fixing (cartel). Each firm has 15 passengers at a price of $25.
- Duopoly (no price fixing). Each firm has 20 passengers at a price of $20.
- Underpricing (one firm charges $20 and the other charges $25). The low-price firm has 28 passengers and the high-price firm has 5 passengers.

Hustle chooses a price first, followed by Speedy. Draw a game tree for the price-fixing game and predict the outcome.

1.13 Hotel Price Fixing? Waikiki Beach has two hotels, one run by Juan and a second run by Tulah. The average cost of providing rooms is constant at $30 per day. Assume that low-price guarantees are illegal. Here are the possible outcomes:

- Price fixing (cartel). Each firm has 30 customers at a price of $40.
- Duopoly (no price fixing). Each firm has 40 customers per day at a price of $37.
- Underpricing (one firm charges $40 and the other charges $37). The low-price firm has 50 customers and the high-price firm has 10 customers.

Juan chooses a price first, followed by Tulah. Draw a game tree for the price-fixing game and predict the outcome.

12.2 Overcoming the Duopolists' Dilemma

2.1 For firms with a low-price guarantee, the promise of matching a lower price is a(n) _____ promise, because all firms will charge the same _____ price.

2.2 Suppose that Jack and Jill use a tit-for-tat scheme to encourage cartel pricing. Jill chooses the low price for two successive months, and then switches to the high price. The two firms will deviate from cartel pricing for a total of _____ months.

2.3 If two firms expect to be in the market together for a long time, the _____ (cost/benefit) of underpricing will be large relative to the _____ (cost/benefit).

2.4 If a seller promises to refund any difference between its price and the price of its competitors, this practice will lead to _____ (higher/lower) prices.

2.5 A careful study of the retail tire market suggests that low-price guarantees _____ (increase/decrease) prices by about _____ (1, 10, 25, 37) percent. (Related to Application 2 on page 280.)

2.6 **Low-Price Guarantees for a Canopy Tour.** Dip and Zip provide canopy tours in a rain forest. The average cost per rider is constant at $10. Here are the possible outcomes:

- Price fixing (cartel). Each firm has 6 passengers at a price of $20.

- Duopoly (no price fixing). Each firm has 8 passengers at a price of $15.
- Underpricing (one firm charges $20 and the other charges $15). The low-price firm has 13 passengers and the high-price firm has 2 passengers.

Dip chooses a price first, followed by Zip.

a. Assume that the firms do not provide low-price guarantees. Draw a game tree and predict the outcome of the price-fixing game.

b. Suppose both firms provide low-price guarantees. Draw a new game tree and predict the outcome of the price-fixing game.

c. Is the promise to match any lower price a substantive promise or an empty promise?

2.7 **Going Out of Business Sales?** Many firms have going-out-of-business sales with remarkable bargains. What insights does the material in this chapter provide about such sales?

2.8 Under a price-leadership model, a sudden drop in price by the leader is unlikely to trigger a price war if other firms believe that the price cut was caused by higher _____.

12.3 Simultaneous Decision Making and the Payoff Matrix

3.1 Consider a market with two firms managed by Harry and Vera. Under a cartel (both firms pick the high price), each firm earns a profit of $80. Under a duopoly (both firms pick the low price), each firm earns a profit of $60. If the two firms pick different prices, the high-price firm earns a profit of $20 and the low-price firm earns a profit of $90.

a. Fill in the following payoff matrix.

b. The outcome of the pricing game is that Harry picks the _____ price and Vera picks the _____ price.

Use this figure to complete Exercise 3.1.

c. The outcome identified in part (b) is a Nash equilibrium because neither firm has an incentive to _____.

3.2 The prisoners' dilemma is that each prisoner would be better off if both prisoners _____, but both end up _____ .

3.3 The cheaters' dilemma is that all three cheaters would be better off if each _____, but each cheater has an incentive to _____ . (Related to Application 3 on page 283.)

12.4 The Insecure Monopolist and Entry Deterrence

4.1 Otto has a monopoly on limousine service, and Carla is thinking about entering the market. The outcome of the entry-deterrence game represented by the game tree on the following page is that Otto picks the _____ quantity and Carla _____ the market.

4.2 Use the game tree in the previous exercise as a starting point. If the minimum entry quantity increases, a single number in one of the profit rectangles changes from $_____ to a smaller number. If the relevant number is reduced by half, the new outcome of the entry-deterrence game is that Otto picks the _____ quantity and Carla _____ the market.

4.3 Consider a market with an insecure monopolist. The zero-profit quantity is 60 units and the minimum entry quantity is 5 units. The entry-deterring quantity is _____ units. The zero-profit price is $80. The slope of the market demand curve is –$2 per unit of output. The limit price is _____ .

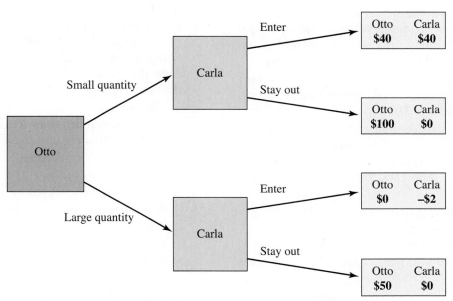

Use this figure to complete Exercise 4.1.

4.4 To deter entry, a monopolist can simply threaten that if a second firm enters, the monopolist will cut its price to the average cost. _____ (True/False)

4.5 Arrows up or down: As the minimum entry quantity decreases, the entry-deterring quantity _____, the limit price _____, and the profit from the entry-deterrence strategy _____.

4.6 In Figure 12.9 on page 285, rectangle 2 is not a Nash equilibrium because if _____ picks a small quantity, the best response for _____ is to _____.

4.7 A contestable market has relatively _____ (high, low) _____ costs.

4.8 Microsoft is a(n) _____ (secure/insecure) monopolist, and the limit price is roughly _____ (10, 20, 40, 60, 90, 100) percent of the pure monopoly price. (Related to Application 4 on page 287.)

4.9 **Ninja Turtles versus Tai Chi Frogs.** The demand for fantasy amphibians is linear, with a slope of –$0.01 per amphibian. The average cost of production is constant at $3. The demand curve intersects the horizontal average-cost curve at a quantity of 600 amphibians. A firm selling ninja turtles currently has a monopoly, selling 300 turtles at a price of $4. A second firm is considering entering the market with tai chi frogs, and the minimum entry quantity is 100 amphibians. If the turtle firm is passive and lets the frog firm enter, each firm will sell 200 amphibians at a price of $5.

a. Draw a graph like the one shown in Figure 12.8 on page 283 with all the relevant numbers.

b. Draw a game tree like the one shown in Figure 12.9 on page 285 and predict the outcome of the game. How will the turtle firm respond to the threat of entry? Will the frog firm enter the market?

c. How would your response to part (a) change if the minimum entry quantity dropped to 50 amphibians?

4.10 Take the Pen Money and Run? Consider the example of Reynolds International Pen and the ballpoint pen. Suppose the unit cost of a ballpoint pen is $1.00. Reynolds has two options:

1. *Passive.* Pick the monopoly price of $13. In the first year, Reynolds will sell 100,000 pens. Over time as other firms enter the market with lower prices, the quantity sold by Reynolds will decrease by 20,000 per year, to 80,000 in the second year and so on, down to zero in the sixth year.

2. *Deterrence.* Commit to produce one million pens per year, an amount large enough to deter entry. The limit price is $1.05.

   a. Under the passive strategy, the profit per year is $_____ in the first year, $_____ in the second year, and so on, down to zero in the sixth year. The total profit over the 6-year period would be $_____ .

   b. Under the deterrence strategy, the profit per year is $_____ . Over a 20-year period, total profit would be $_____ .

   c. Taking a 20-year perspective, which strategy is more profitable?

   d. How would your answer to part (c) change if the limit price were $1.50 rather than $1.05?

4.11 Shuttle Deterrence? Consider the market for air travel between Boston and New York. The long-run average cost is constant at $100 per passenger, and the demand curve is linear, with a slope of –$2 per passenger. The demand curve intersects the horizontal average-cost curve at a quantity of 120 passengers. The minimum entry quantity is

20 passengers. FirstShuttle currently has a monopoly, with 60 passengers at a price of $220. Another firm, SecondShuttle, is considering the market, and the minimum entry quantity is 20 passengers. If FirstShuttle is passive and lets the other firm enter, each firm will have 40 passengers at a price of $180.

a. Draw a graph like the one shown in Figure 12.8 on page 283 with all the relevant numbers.

b. Draw a game tree like the one shown in Figure 12.9 on page 285 and predict the outcome of the game. How will FirstShuttle respond to the threat of entry? Will SecondShuttle enter the market?

c. How would your response to (a) change if the minimum entry quantity dropped to 10 passengers?

4.12 Going off Patent. Consider the producer of a branded drug that will soon go off patent and compete with generic versions of the drug. The average cost of production is constant at $8 per dose. The producer could prevent the entry of generics by committing to a limit price of $10. At this price, the firm will sell 100 doses per day. Alternatively, the producer could charge a price of $12 and passively allow generics to enter the market. The price elasticity of demand for the branded drug is 2.0.

a. Under the passive approach (price = $12), the quantity of the branded drug demanded is _____ ; the firm's profit is _____ .

b. Under the entry-deterrence approach, the firm's profit is $_____ .

c. The best approach is (entry deterrence, passive).

d. If the price elasticity of demand for the branded drug were 3.0 instead of 2.0, the profit under the passive approach would be $_____ , so the best strategy is _____ (entry deterrence, passive).

12.5 The Advertisers' Dilemma

5.1 The advertisers' dilemma is that both firms would be better if _____ advertises, but each has an incentive to _____ .

5.2 The advertisers' dilemma shown in Figure 12.10 on page 288 occurs when advertising causes a relatively _____ increase in the total sales of an industry.

5.3 Consider a duopoly with two firms managed by Huck and Stella. A standard advertising campaign has a cost of $5 million per firm. If both firms run a standard campaign, the net revenue from sales increases by $4 for each firm. If only one firm runs a campaign, the advertiser's net revenue from sales increases by $8 million, and the other firm's net revenue from sales decreases by $7 million. Fill in the blanks in the following table, draw a game tree, and predict the outcome of the advertising game.

	Neither Advertises		Both Advertise		Huck Advertises	
	Huck	Stella	Huck	Stella	Huck	Stella
Net revenue from sales ($ million)	$10	$10				
Cost of advertising ($ million)	0	0	5	5	5	0
Profit ($ million)						

5.4 In Figure 12.10 on page 288, rectangle 2 is not a Nash equilibrium because if _____ advertises, the best response of _____ is to _____ .

5.5 **Automobile Advertising.** Consider two automobile companies that are considering advertising campaigns. If neither firm advertises, each will earn net revenue of $5 million. If each spends $10 million on advertising, each firm's net revenue will be $12 million. If one advertises and the other does not, the firm that advertises will earn $17 million in net revenue, while the firm that does not will earn $1 million. Draw a game tree and predict the outcome. From the industry perspective, do the benefits of advertising exceed the costs?

5.6 **Got Milk?** Bessie and George are milk producers, and each must decide whether to spend $7 million on an advertising campaign. If neither advertises, each will earn $10 million in net revenue from sales (net revenue). If both advertise, each will earn $20 million in net revenue and $13 million in profit ($20 million minus $7 million for advertising). If only one producer advertises, that firm will earn $16 million in net revenue, and the other firm will earn $15 million in net revenue. Prepare a game tree like Figure 12.10 on page 288. Assume that Bessie decides first. What is the outcome of this advertising game? If there is an advertisers' dilemma, how does it differ from the advertisers' dilemma discussed earlier in the chapter? How might the dairy industry solve this dilemma? (Related to Application 5 on page 289.)

ECONOMIC EXPERIMENT

PRICE-FIXING

Here is a price-fixing or cartel game for the classroom. You'll have an opportunity to conspire to fix prices in a hypothetical market with five firms. The instructor divides the class into five groups. Each group represents one of five firms that produce a particular good. Each group must develop a pricing strategy for its firm, recognizing that the other groups are choosing prices for their firms at the same time. Only two choices are possible: a high price (the cartel price) or a low price. The profit of a particular firm depends on the price chosen by the firm and the prices chosen by the four other firms. The profit matrix is shown below.

From the second row, if one of the five firms chooses the high price, and the other four firms choose the low price, the high-price firm earns a profit of $2, and each low-price firm

Number of High-Price Firms	Number of Low-Price Firms	Profit for Each High-Price Firm	Profit for Each Low-Price Firm
0	5	—	$ 5
1	4	$ 2	7
2	3	4	9
3	2	6	11
4	1	8	13
5	0	10	—

earns a profit of $7. The game is played for several rounds. In the first three rounds, the firms make their choices without talking to each other in advance. In the fourth and fifth rounds, the firms discuss their strategies, disperse, and then make their choices. The group's score equals the profit earned by the firm.

MyEconLab
For additional economic experiments, please visit *www.myeconlab.com*.

NOTES

1. Alberto Salvo, "Inferring market power under the threat of entry: The case of the Brazilian cement industry," *RAND Journal of Economics* 41 (2010), pp. 326–360.

2. Adam Smith, *An Inquiry into the Nature and Causes of the Wealth of Nations* (1776); Book 1, Chapter 10.

3. Sylvia Nassar, *A Beautiful Mind* (New York: Simon & Schuster, 1998).

4. Robert Axelrod, *The Evolution of Cooperation* (New York: Basic Books, 1984).

5. Federal Trade Commission, "Record Companies Settle FTC Charges of Restraining Competition in CD Music Market," Press Release, May 10, 2000.

6. Thomas Whiteside, "Where Are They Now?" *New Yorker*, February 17, 1951, 39–58.

Controlling Market Power: Antitrust and Regulation

In 1997, a U.S. court blocked the proposed merger of Staples and Office Depot, the nation's two largest office-supply retailers.

The judge in the case observed that the merger would eliminate Office Depot as a competitor and allow Staples to increase its prices by 13 percent. Where did the judge get that number?

When you buy groceries, hardware, or office supplies, a scanner at the checkout reads bar code information, recording the price you pay and the quantity you purchase. The scanner system helps retailers keep track of their stock and allows them to instantly change prices without putting new price tags on their products. The scanner data can also be used to observe the pricing patterns of firms such as Staples. Economists with the Federal Trade Commission (FTC) found an interesting pattern: The prices charged by Staples were lower in cities where Office Depot also had a store. The competition generated by Office Depot led to prices that were, on average, 13 percent lower.[1]

LEARNING OBJECTIVES

- Define a natural monopoly and explain the average-cost pricing policy.

- List three features of antitrust policy.

> **MyEconLab**
> MyEconLab helps you master each objective and study more efficiently.

*t*his chapter looks at various public policies dealing with markets that are dominated by a small number of firms. We'll start with the case of natural monopoly, which occurs when the scale economies in production are so large that only a single large firm can survive. In this case, the government can intervene by regulating the price charged by the natural monopolist. Then we'll look at markets in which the government can affect the number of firms in the market by using various policies to promote competition.

The government uses antitrust policies to break monopolies into several smaller companies, prevent corporate mergers that would reduce competition, and regulate business practices that tend to reduce competition. Sometimes prior government regulations actually end up inhibiting competition, so the government later deregulates an industry to promote more competition. In the last part of the chapter, we'll look at the recent deregulation of three markets: air travel, telecommunications, and electricity. In these three markets, the government reversed a long history of regulation, deregulating the industries to promote competition.

13.1 Natural Monopoly

In an earlier chapter, we considered monopolies that resulted from artificial barriers to entry, such as patents and government licenses. In this chapter, we'll look at natural monopolies, which occur when the economies of scale for producing a product are so large that only a single firm can survive. Some examples of natural monopolies are water systems, natural gas distribution, electricity transmission, and cable TV service. It is efficient for a city to have a single supplier of water service because a second supplier would install a second set of water pipes when a single set of pipes would suffice. Similarly, it is efficient to have a single set of transmission lines for electricity and a single set of cables for TV service.

Picking an Output Level

Figure 13.1 shows the long-run average-cost curve for water service in a particular city. The curve is negatively sloped and steep, reflecting the large economies of scale that occur because water service requires a costly system of pipes, and the cost is the same whether the firm pipes 70 or 70 million cubic meters of water. As the quantity of water increases, the average cost per unit decreases because the cost of the pipe system is spread over a larger volume of water.

What about the long-run marginal cost—the cost of an additional cubic meter of water delivered to a customer—once the system is built? For each additional unit, a water company incurs a cost for the energy required to pump the unit from the water source to a customer. The pumping cost depends on the distance (horizontal and vertical) from the source to the customer. To simplify matters, we'll assume that the marginal cost is constant at $0.80 per cubic meter.

Figure 13.1 shows how to use the cost curves and revenue curves to pick the output level that maximizes profit. Like other firms, the provider of water can use the marginal principle.

Million cubic meters of water

▲ **FIGURE 13.1**

A Natural Monopoly Uses the Marginal Principle to Pick Quantity and Price
Because of an indivisible input (the pipe system), the long-run average-cost curve is negatively sloped.
The monopolist chooses point *a*, where marginal revenue equals marginal cost. The firm sells 70 million
units of water at a price of $2.70 (point *b*) and an average cost of $2.10 (point *c*). The profit per unit of
water is $0.60 (equal to $2.70 – $2.10).

MARGINAL PRINCIPLE

Increase the level of an activity as long as its marginal benefit exceeds
its marginal cost. Choose the level at which the marginal benefit
equals the marginal cost.

If a single firm—a monopolist—provides water, the firm-specific demand
curve is the same as the market demand curve: The market demand curve shows,
for each price, the number of units sold by the monopolist. From the firm's
perspective, the marginal benefit of a cubic meter of water is the increase in
revenue—the marginal revenue. The marginal principle is satisfied at point *a*, with
70 million cubic meters. The price associated with this quantity is $2.70 per unit
(shown by point *b*), and the average cost is $2.10 per unit (shown by point *c*), so the
profit per unit is $0.60. The price exceeds the average cost, so the water company
will earn a profit.

Will a Second Firm Enter?

If there are no artificial barriers to entry, a second firm could enter the water market. What would happen if a second firm entered the market? In Figure 13.2, the entry of a second firm would shift the demand curve of the first firm—the former monopolist—to the left, from D_1 to D_2: At each price, the first firm will sell less water because it now shares the market with another firm. For example, at a price of $2.70, a total of 70 million units are sold, or 35 million for each firm (point d). In general, the larger the number of firms, the lower the demand curve for the typical firm.

▲ **FIGURE 13.2**

Will a Second Firm Enter the Market?

The entry of a second firm would shift the demand curve of the typical firm to the left. After entry, the firm's demand curve lies entirely below the long-run average-cost curve. No matter what price the firm charges, it will lose money. Therefore, a second firm will not enter the market.

Will a second firm enter the market? Notice that the demand curve of the typical firm in a two-firm market lies entirely below the long-run average-cost curve, so there is no quantity at which the price exceeds the average cost of production. No matter what price the typical firm charges, it will lose money. The firm's demand curve lies below the average-cost curve because the average-cost curve is steep, reflecting the large economies of scale for water provision. A second firm—with half the market—would have a very high average cost and wouldn't be able to charge a price high enough to cover the cost of building the pipe system in the first place. Therefore, the second firm will not enter the market, so there will be a single firm, a natural monopoly.

Price Controls for a Natural Monopoly

When a natural monopoly is inevitable, the government often sets a maximum price that the monopolist can charge consumers. There are many examples of natural monopolies that are subject to maximum prices. Local governments regulate utilities and firms that provide water, electricity, cable service, and local telephone service. Many state governments use public utility commissions (PUCs) to regulate the electric power industry.

We can use the water market to explain the effects of government regulation on a natural monopoly. Suppose the government sets a maximum price for water and requires the water company to serve all consumers who are willing to pay the maximum price. In other words, the government—not the firm—picks a point on the market demand curve. Under an *average-cost pricing policy*, the government picks the price at which the market demand curve intersects the monopolist's long-run average-cost curve. In Figure 13.3, the average-cost curve intersects the demand curve at point *e*, with a price of $1.20 per cubic meter. This is much lower than the profit-maximizing price of $2.70. As a result, the total quantity of water demanded is much larger—150 million units compared to 70 million. The purpose of the

▲ FIGURE 13.3
Regulators Use Average-Cost Pricing to Pick a Monopoly's Quantity and Price
Under an average-cost pricing policy, the government chooses the price at which the demand curve intersects the long-run average-cost curve. Regulation decreases the price and increases the quantity.

average-cost pricing policy is to get the lowest feasible price. The water company would lose money at any price less than $1.20, so a lower price isn't feasible.

How will this regulatory policy affect the monopolist's production costs? Under average-cost pricing, a change in the monopolist's production cost will have little effect on its profit, because the government will soon adjust the regulated price to keep the price equal to the average cost. The government will increase the regulated price when the monopolist's cost increases and decrease the price when the monopolist's cost decreases. Because the monopolist has no incentive to cut costs and faces no penalty for higher costs, its costs are likely to creep upward. As average cost increases, the regulated price will too.

application 1

PUBLIC VERSUS PRIVATE WATERWORKS

APPLYING THE CONCEPTS #1: What is the rationale for regulating a natural monopoly?

In the middle part of the nineteenth century, the British parliament staged an experiment in private enterprise. In the early part of the century, water was drawn from local rivers, stored in ponds on higher ground, and then distributed by wooden pipes to customers. In most urban areas, this primitive water system was run by local government. The Industrial Revolution caused the rapid growth of urban areas, and local governments lacked explicit powers to borrow money to finance the expansion of their water systems. The policies of Parliament caused many towns and cities to switch to private water companies, and by 1851 about three-fifths of the urban population got their water from private companies. There were many problems with the private provision of water, including low pressure that sometimes made firefighting ineffective, and water hardness (high mineral content) that damaged industrial boilers and reduced the quality of silk products. The control of the water supply gradually returned to local governments, and by 1891 only one-sixth of the urban population was served by private water companies. In addition to improving water pressure and water softness, the move to municipal provision increased total consumption of water and decreased the capital cost per unit of water.

What does the British experience with water privatization tell us? The distribution of water is a natural monopoly, meaning that although a single firm will be profitable, two firms will not. The private water companies established under the policies of Parliament were unregulated natural monopolies. As we've seen, an unregulated monopoly is socially inefficient. In this case, the inefficiency resulted in a low-quality product (hard water), low service (low pressure), low output (small quantity of water per capita), and high capital cost. If the water monopolies had been regulated in an efficient manner, the experience with privatization of the water supply might have been different. **Related to Exercises 1.5 and 1.9.**

SOURCE: J. S. Hassan, "The Growth and Impact of the British Water Industry in the Nineteenth Century," *The Economic History Review* 38 (1985): 531–547.

application 2

SATELLITE RADIO AS A NATURAL MONOPOLY

APPLYING THE CONCEPTS #2: When does a natural monopoly occur?

In 2008, the nation's only two satellite radio providers, Sirius Satellite Radio and XM Satellite Radio, merged into a single firm. Together the two firms had 14 million subscribers, each paying $13 per month for dozens of channels, most of which are free of advertisements. Both firms were losing money as they struggled to get enough subscribers to cover their substantial fixed costs. The cost of the infrastructure to set up a single system—satellites and ground stations—is about $2 billion. In addition, both firms added to their setup costs by signing contracts with radio personalities, news organizations, and sports information sources. One possible advantage of a merger was that the new firm could have a lower fixed cost per subscriber and thus could earn a profit. One possible disadvantage was that the new firm might charge higher prices.

Two years later, the new firm, Sirius XM, earned its first quarterly profit of $14.2 million, compared to a loss one year earlier of $245.8 million. The firm became profitable—just barely—by increasing the number of subscribers to 19 million and thus lowering its cost per subscriber. In other words, the merger transformed two unprofitable firms into a single profitable firm.

There was some concern that the merger would increase prices. Consumers choose from five packages of stations, including a limited set of stations for $10, the original Sirius stations for $13 (the same price as before the merger), a package that combines the original Sirius stations and a subset of the XM radio stations for $17, and a complete package for $19. In other words, the merger did not increase the price of the original Sirius package, but gave consumers more options for lower-priced and higher-priced packages. **Related to Exercises 1.6 and 1.10.**

SOURCES: Reuters, "Sirius XM Posts Profit, Its First Since Merger," *New York Times*, February 25, 2010; "They Cannot be Sirius," *Economist*, February 22, 2007.

13.2 Antitrust Policy

A **trust** is an arrangement under which the owners of several companies transfer their decision-making powers to a small group of trustees. The purpose of antitrust policy is to promote competition among firms, which leads to lower prices for consumers.

Two government organizations, the Antitrust Division of the Department of Justice and the Federal Trade Commission, are responsible for initiating actions against individuals or firms that may be violating antitrust laws. The courts have the power to impose penalties on the executives found to be in violation of the laws, including fines and prison sentences. In some cases, the government seeks no penalties but directs the firm to discontinue illegal practices and take other measures to promote competition. We'll explore three types of antitrust policies: breaking up monopolies, blocking mergers, and regulating business practices.

trust

An arrangement under which the owners of several companies transfer their decision-making powers to a small group of trustees.

Breaking Up Monopolies

One form of antitrust policy is to break up a monopoly into several smaller firms. The label "antitrust" comes from the names of the early conglomerates that the government broke up. The classic example is John D. Rockefeller's Standard Oil Trust, which was formed in 1882 when the owners of 40 oil companies empowered nine trustees to make the decisions for all 40 companies. The trust controlled over 90 percent of the market for refined petroleum products, and the trustees ran it like a monopoly. In 1911, the government ordered its breakup. The Supreme Court found that Rockefeller had used "unnatural methods" to maintain his monopoly power and drive his rivals out of business. In addition to forming the trust, he coerced railroads to give him special rates for shipping, and he spied on his competitors. The government broke up Standard Oil into 34 separate companies, including the corporate ancestors of Exxon, Mobil, Chevron, and Amoco.

The American Tobacco Company started in 1890 as a merger of several tobacco firms. By 1907, the company had acquired over 200 rival firms and controlled 95 percent of the U.S. cigarette market. The Supreme Court found that American Tobacco maintained its monopoly power by driving rivals out of business and agreeing to exclusive contracts with wholesalers that prevented them from purchasing cigarettes from other companies. The court-ordered breakup in 1911 led to new companies, including several of today's big cigarette companies: Reynolds, Liggett and Meyers, and P. Lorillard.

In 1982, the government broke up American Telephone and Telegraph (AT&T) into seven regional phone companies. AT&T had used its legal monopoly in local telephone service to prevent competition in the markets for long-distance service and communications equipment. After an eight-year legal battle, AT&T agreed to form seven Regional Bell Operating Companies, transforming "Ma Bell" into seven "Baby Bells." The new AT&T was allowed to compete in the market for long-distance service, where it faced competition from newcomers MCI and Sprint. AT&T was also allowed to operate in the market for communications equipment, where it faced competition from newcomers Mitel and Northern Telecom.

Blocking Mergers

merger

A process in which two or more firms combine their operations.

A **merger** occurs when two or more firms combine their operations. A *horizontal merger* involves two firms producing a similar product, for example, two producers of pet food. A *vertical merger* involves two firms at different stages of the production process, for example, a sugar refiner and a candy producer. A second type of antitrust policy is to block corporate mergers that would reduce competition and lead to higher prices. We saw in an earlier chapter that as the number of firms in a market increases, competition among firms drives down prices. Because a merger decreases the number of firms in a market, it is likely to lead to higher prices. In 1994, Microsoft tried to purchase Intuit, the maker of Quicken, a personal-finance software package that was a substitute for a similar Microsoft product. The merger would have reduced competition in the personal-finance software market, so the government blocked it.

Of course, the government does not oppose all corporate mergers. One possible benefit from a merger is that the new firm could combine production, marketing, and administrative operations, producing products at a lower average cost. Consumers might reap the rewards in the form of lower prices. In 1997, the Justice Department and the Federal Trade Commission (FTC) released new guidelines for proposed mergers. The new guidelines allow companies involved in a proposed merger to present evidence that the merger would reduce costs and lead to lower prices, better products, or better service. If the evidence for greater efficiency is convincing, the government might allow a merger that reduces the number of firms in a market. The chairman of the FTC assessed the effects of the new guidelines as follows:[2]

> There may be some deals that go through which otherwise would not have. But it won't change the result in a large number of cases [rather it will have] the greatest impact in a transaction where the potential anticompetitive problem is modest and efficiencies that would be created are great.

The new guidelines will bring the U.S. antitrust rules closer in line with those of Europe and Canada and could help U.S. companies compete in those markets.

In recent years, the analysis of proposed mergers has shifted from counting the number of firms in a market to predicting how a particular merger would affect prices. The data generated by retail checkout scanners provide an enormous amount of information about prices and quantities sold. Using these data, economists can determine how one firm's pricing policies affect the sales of that firm and its competitors. Economists can use this information to predict whether a merger would lead to higher prices.

As we saw in the chapter opener, the FTC used pricing data to support its decision to block a proposed merger between Staples and Office Depot. The data showed that Staples charged lower prices in cities where Office Depot also had stores. Figure 13.4 shows Staples' revenue and cost curves for one specific product: file folders. Panel A shows what happens when Staples faces no competition from an Office Depot, and Panel B shows what happens when it does. The demand curve of Staples is lower in the city where it faces competition with Office Depot because the two firms share the market. Using the marginal principle, Staples picks the quantity and price where its

▲ FIGURE 13.4
Pricing by Staples in Cities with and without Competition
Using the marginal principle, Staples picks the quantity at which its marginal revenue equals its marginal cost. In a city without a competing firm, Staples picks the monopoly price of $14. In a city where Staples competes with Office Depot, the demand facing Staples is lower, so the profit-maximizing price is only $12.

TABLE 13.1 A Merger Increases Prices						
	Wonder Brand		Interstate Brand		Total	
	1	2	3	4	5	6
	Before Merger	After Merger	Before Merger	After Merger	Before Merger	After Merger
>0	$1.50	$1.50	$1.50	$1.50		
Price	$2.00	$2.00	$2.00	$2.20		
Quantity	100	110	100	70	200	180
Profit	$ 50	$ 55	$ 50	$ 49	$100	$104

marginal revenue equals its marginal cost. The profit-maximizing price is $14 in a city without an Office Depot and $12 in a city with one.

The FTC used this logic to convince the court that the proposed merger of Staples and Office Depot would lead to higher prices. The judge in the case observed that,

> direct evidence shows that by eliminating Staples' most significant, and in many markets, only, rival, the merger would allow Staples to increase prices or otherwise maintain prices at an anticompetitive level.

Evidence from the companies' pricing data showed that the merger would have allowed Staples to increase its prices by about 13 percent. According to an FTC study, blocking the merger saved consumers an estimated $1.1 billion over five years.

Merger Remedy for Wonder Bread

In some cases, the government allows a merger to happen but imposes restrictions on the new company. In 1995, Interstate Bakeries, the nation's third-largest wholesale baker, tried to buy Continental Baking, the maker of Wonder bread. Based on grocery store scanner data, the government concluded that Wonder bread is a close substitute for Interstate's bread: The demand for Wonder bread increases when the price of Interstate's bread increases, and vice versa.[3] The scanner data showed that when Interstate increased its price, many consumers switched to Wonder bread, so their bread money went to Continental instead of Interstate. The substitutability of the two brands discouraged Interstate from increasing its prices.

Table 13.1 shows an example of a merger leading to higher prices and smaller quantities. Let's assume that the average cost per loaf of bread is $1.50, and this doesn't change with a merger. The situation before the merger is shown in columns 1 and 3: For each brand, the price per loaf of bread is $2.00, the quantity is 100 loaves, and the profit is $50 (the profit $0.50 per loaf times 100 loaves).

How would a merger affect the incentives to raise prices? After a merger, a single company would earn the profits from both brands (Wonder and Interstate) and pick both prices. Suppose the new company increased the price of Interstate bread to $2.20 but kept the price of Wonder bread at $2.00. The price hike would bring bad news and good news for the new company:

• Bad news: Less profit on Interstate Bread. As shown in columns 3 and 4, the price hike decreases the quantity of Interstate bread from 100 to 70 loaves. Although the profit per loaf increases to $0.70 (the new price of $2.20 minus the average cost of $1.50), only 70 loaves are sold, so the profit from the brand drops to $49, down from $50. The bad news is the $1 loss of profit on Interstate Bread.

- Good news: More profit on Wonder bread. As shown in columns 1 and 2, the increase in the price of Interstate Bread increases the quantity of Wonder bread sold from 100 to 110 loaves. The profit per loaf is still $0.50 per bread, so the profit on Wonder bread increases to $55, up from $50. The good news is the extra $5 of profit on Wonder bread.

In this case, the good news ($5 more profit from Wonder) exceeds the bad news ($1 less profit from Interstate), so the price hike increases the total profit of the merged company. This is shown in columns 5 and 6. Although the total quantity drops, total profit increases by $4. A merger means that the good news from a price hike stays within the larger firm, encouraging that firm to increase prices.

The lesson from this example is that a merger of two firms selling close substitutes may lead to higher prices. That's what the Department of Justice concluded in the case of Interstate Bakeries and Continental Bakery. The government allowed the merger between the two companies but forced Interstate to sell some of its brands and bakeries. For example, Interstate sold the rights to sell its Weber brand bread to Four-S Baking Company. The idea was to ensure that other companies would be able to compete with the newly merged company.

Regulating Business Practices

The third type of antitrust policy involves the regulation of business practices. As we saw in the previous chapter, price fixing—a cooperative agreement among firms to collude rather than compete—is illegal. Under the law, firms cannot discuss their pricing strategies with their competitors.

The government may intervene when a specific business practice increases market concentration in an already concentrated market. A **tie-in sale** occurs when a business forces the buyer of one product to purchase another product. The FTC recently charged a pharmaceutical company with tying the sale of clozapine, an antipsychotic drug, to a blood testing and monitoring system. Another illegal business practice is a cooperative agreement to limit advertising. The FTC recently charged a group of auto dealers with restricting comparative and discount advertising.

tie-in sale
A business practice under which a business requires a consumer of one product to purchase another product.

The Robinson–Patman Act prohibits the selling of products at "unreasonably low prices" with the intent of reducing competition, a practice known as **predatory pricing**. A firm engages in predatory pricing when it sells a product at a price below its production costs, with the objective of driving a rival out of business. Once the predator's rivals drop out of the market, the firm then charges a monopoly price, well above its production cost. This strategy will be profitable if the firm can charge the monopoly price for a long enough period to offset the losses it experienced while driving its rivals out of business.

predatory pricing
A firm sells a product at a price below its production cost to drive a rival out of business and then increases the price.

But is predatory pricing really practical? Consider a market with two firms, one of which is determined to have the market to itself. By cutting its price below its cost, the firm can drive its competitor out of business, losing perhaps $10 million in the process. If it increases its price next year, there may be nothing to prevent a new firm from entering the market. If so, it would have to cut its price below its cost again to drive the new firm out. The problem with predatory pricing is that it never ends. The firm must repeatedly lose money to drive out an endless series of competitors.

A Brief History of U.S. Antitrust Policy

Table 13.2 provides a brief summary of the history of antitrust policy. The first legislation was the Sherman Antitrust Act of 1890, which made it illegal to monopolize a market or to engage in practices that result in a restraint of trade. Because the act did not specify which practices were illegal, it led to conflicting court rulings.

TABLE 13.2 Key Antitrust Legislation		
Law	Date Enacted	Regulation Enacted
Sherman Act	1890	Made it illegal to monopolize a market or to engage in practices that result in a restraint of trade.
Clayton Act	1914	Outlawed specific practices that discourage competition, including tie-in sales contracts, price discrimination for the purpose of reducing competition, and stock-purchase mergers that would substantially reduce competition.
Federal Trade Commission Act	1914	Created a mechanism to enforce antitrust laws.
Robinson–Patman Act	1936	Prohibited selling products at "unreasonably low prices" with the intent of reducing competition.
Celler–Kefauver Act	1950	Outlawed asset-purchase mergers that would substantially reduce competition.
Hart–Scott–Rodino Act	1980	Extended antitrust legislation to proprietorships and partnerships.

Many of the ambiguities of the Sherman Act were resolved by the Clayton Act of 1914. The Clayton Act outlawed specific practices that discourage competition, including tie-in sales contracts and price discrimination that reduces competition. The act also outlawed mergers resulting from the purchase of a competitor's stock when such a merger would substantially reduce competition.

Subsequent legislation clarified and extended antitrust laws. The Robinson–Patman Act of 1936 prohibited predatory pricing. The Celler–Kefauver Act of 1950 closed a loophole in the Clayton Act by prohibiting one firm from purchasing another firm's physical assets, such as buildings and equipment, when the acquisition would reduce competition substantially. The Hart–Scott–Rodino Act of 1980 extended antitrust legislation to proprietorships and partnerships. Before this act, antitrust legislation applied only to corporations.

application 3

MERGER OF PENNZOIL AND QUAKER STATE

APPLYING THE CONCEPTS #3: How does a merger affect prices?

In 1998, Pennzoil Motor Oils purchased Quaker State Motor oils in an acquisition valued at $1 billion. The merger brought together two of the five brands of premium motor oil, with a combined market share of 38% (29% for Pennzoil and 9% for Quaker State). The antitrust agencies approved the merger without any modifications. A recent study of the merger concludes that the new company increased the price of the Quaker State products by roughly 5%, but did not change the price of Pennzoil products. The market share of Pennzoil products increased, while the market shares of Quaker State products decreased.

The study also examines the price effects of four other mergers. In three of four cases, the merger increased prices, with price hikes between 3 and 7 percent. The modest price effects might be surprising to (1) people who expect relatively large positive price effects as firms exploit their greater market power and (2) people who expect negative price effects as the firms become more efficient. **Related to Exercise 2.5.**

SOURCE: Based on Orley Ashenfelter and Daniel Hosken, "The effects of mergers on consumer prices: Evidence from five selected case studies," NBER Working Paper (2008).

FAQ ABOUT PREDATORY PRICING FROM THE FTC

APPLYING THE CONCEPTS: What is predatory pricing?

The Federal Trade Commission (FTC) is responsible for enforcing laws against predatory pricing. Consider the following FAQ dialog from the FTC web site.

> Q: The gas station down the street offers a discount program that gives members cents off every gallon purchased. I can't match those prices because they are below my costs. If I try to compete at those prices, I will go out of business. Isn't this illegal?
>
> A: Pricing below a *competitor's* costs occurs in many competitive markets and generally does not violate the antitrust laws. Sometimes the low-pricing firm is simply more efficient. Pricing below your own costs is also not a violation of the law unless it is part of a strategy to eliminate competitors, and when that strategy has a dangerous probability of creating a monopoly for the discounting firm so that it can raise prices far into the future and recoup its losses. In markets with a large number of sellers, such as gasoline retailing, it is unlikely that one company could price below cost long enough to drive out a significant number of rivals and attain a dominant position. **Related to Exercise 2.6.**

SOURCE: Federal Trade Commission, *FTC Guide to the Antitrust Laws* (Washington DC, 2010).

SUMMARY

In this chapter, we've explored public policies for markets with a few dominant firms. In the case of natural monopoly, the government can regulate prices. In other industries, the government uses antitrust policies to affect the number of firms in the market, encouraging competition that leads to lower prices. Here are the main points of the chapter:

1 A natural monopoly occurs when there are large-scale economies in production, so the market can support only one firm.

2 Under an average-cost pricing policy, the regulated price for a natural monopoly is equal to the average cost of production.

3 The government uses antitrust policy to break up some dominant firms, prevent some corporate mergers, and regulate business practices that reduce competition.

4 The modern approach to merger policy uses price data to predict the effects of a merger.

5 In most circumstances, predatory pricing is unprofitable because the monopoly power is costly to acquire and hard to maintain.

6 The deregulation of the airline industry led to more competition and lower prices on average, but higher prices in some markets.

EXERCISES   All problems are assignable in MyEconLab.

13.1   Natural Monopoly

1.1   Arrows up or down: At a natural monopolist's current level of output, marginal cost exceeds marginal revenue. The firm should _____ its output and _____ its price.

1.2   The entry of a second firm shifts the demand curve of the original firm to the _____, so that at each price the original firm will sell a(n) _____ quantity.

1.3   A natural monopoly occurs when the long-run cost curve lies entirely _____ (above/below) the demand curve of the typical firm in a two-firm market.

1.4   Under an average-cost pricing policy, the maximum price is shown by the intersection of the _____ curve and the _____ curve.

1.5   When the British switched from private water supply to public supply, the quality of water, consumption per capita _____, and capital cost per unit of output _____. (Related to Application 1 on page 302.)

1.6   Sirius XM Radio became profitable—just barely—with about _____ subscribers. (Related to Application 2 on page 303.)

1.7   **Decrease in Cable Demand.** Consider a cable TV company that has a fixed cost of $48 million and a marginal cost of $5 per subscriber. The company is regulated with an average-cost pricing policy.

   a.   The first two columns of the following table show three points on the initial demand curve. For example, at a price of $15 the quantity demanded is six million subscribers. For each $2 reduction in price, the number of subscribers increases by one million.

Fill in the blanks in the following table. The regulated price is _____.

Price	Subscribers (Millions)	Average Cost
$15	6	
13	7	
11	8	

   b.   Suppose the demand for the product decreases, with the demand curve shifting to the left by one million subscribers. Fill in the blanks in the following table. The new regulated price is $_____.

Price	Subscribers (Millions)	Average Cost
$15		
13		
11		

1.8   **Environmental Costs for Regulated Monopoly.** The Bonneville Power Administration (BPA) is a regulated monopoly in the Northwest that uses dozens of hydroelectric dams to generate electricity. Unfortunately, the BPA's dams block the paths of migrating fish, contributing to the decline of several species. Suppose that BPA spends $100 million to make its hydroelectric dams less hazardous for migrating fish. Who will bear the cost of this program?

1.9   **From Private to Public Water Supply.** Consider the British experience with water provision. Suppose that an unregulated private monopoly has a price of

$3 per unit, a quantity of 10 million units, an average cost of $2 per unit, and a constant marginal cost of $1. (Related to Application 1 on page 302.)

a. Use a graph to show the price, quantity, and average cost as an outcome of profit maximization.

b. Use your graph to show the effects of average-cost regulation on the price, the average cost, and the quantity of output.

1.10 Satellite Radio Merger. Suppose each of the two satellite radio firms initially has 9.5 million subscribers and generates negative economic profit: Average cost exceeds the $13 price. Assume that the marginal cost is constant at $2 per subscriber. (Related to Application 2 on page 303.)

a. Use a graph to show the average-cost curve and firm-specific demand curve for one of the two satellite firms.

b. Suppose the two firms merge into a single firm. The profit-maximizing price is $13 and the average cost is $12. Illustrate with a graph.

13.2 Antitrust Policy

2.1 The purpose of antitrust policy is to promote _____, which leads to lower _____.

2.2 There are three types of antitrust policies: (1) _____, (2) _____, and (3) _____.

2.3 In the Staples case discussed in this chapter, the data showed that competition with Office Depot led to _____ prices, suggesting that a merger would harm _____.

2.4 In the Interstate Baking case discussed in this chapter, scanner data showed that the products of Interstate and Continental Baking were _____, so a merger would lead to higher _____.

2.5 Predatory pricing provides a practical and effective means of getting and keeping a monopoly. _____ (True/False)

2.6 The merger of companies with two of the top five brands of motor oil (Pennzoil and Quaker State) increased the price of one of the brands by roughly _____ percent (1, 5, 20, 50) percent. (Related to Application 3 on page 308.)

2.7 Pricing below a competitor's cost is _____ (legal/illegal). Pricing below your own cost is illegal if

it is part of a strategy to _____ and then _____ prices. (Related to Application 4 on page 309.)

2.8 Incentive to Raise Prices after a Merger. Suppose the merger of two firms, Heinz and Beech-Nut, will reduce the price elasticity of demand for each firm's product from 3.0 to 1.50. For each firm, the average cost of production is constant at $5 per unit. Suppose Heinz initially has a price of $10 and is considering raising the price to $11.

a. Fill in the blanks in the following table, showing the payoffs from raising the price before the merger (elasticity = 3.0) and after the merger (elasticity = 1.50).

Price	Quantity	Total Revenue	Total Cost	Profit
Initial: $10	100	$1,000	$500	$500
New: $11 Before merger: Elasticity of demand = 3.0				
New: $11 After merger: Elasticity of demand = 1.50				

b. Before the merger, raising the price would _____ the firm's profit. After the merger, raising the price would _____ the firm's profit.

c. Why is it reasonable to assume that the merger will decrease the elasticity of demand for each firm's products?

2.9 Recovering the Acquisition Cost. The long-run average cost of production is constant at $6 per unit. Suppose firm X acquires Y at a cost of $24 million and increases the price to $14. At the new price, X sells 1.5 million units per year.

a. How does the acquisition affect X's annual profit?

b. How many years will it take for X to recover the cost of acquiring Y?

2.10 Check YellowPages.com? On Yellin's first day on the job as an economist with the FTC, she was put on a team examining a proposed merger between the country's second- and fourth-largest hardware store chains. Her job was to predict whether a merger would increase hardware prices. Her boss handed her some CDs with checkout scanner data from the second-largest chain. Each CD contained scanner data from one small town, listing the prices and quantities of hammers, wrenches, nuts, bolts, rakes, glue, drills, and hundreds of other hardware products. Her boss also gave her the Web address for YellowPages.com. How can she use the information in the disks and YellowPages.com to make a prediction?

2.11 Cost Savings from a Merger. Consider the following statement from a firm that has proposed a merger between two companies: "The two companies could save about $50 million per year by combining our production, marketing, and administrative operations. In other words, we could realize substantial economies of scale. Therefore, the government should allow the merger." In light of the new guidelines concerning mergers, how would you react to this statement?

2.12 Deadweight Loss from a Merger. Consider a market that is initially served by two firms, each of which charges a price of $10 and sells 100 units of the good. The long-run average cost of production is constant at $6 per unit. Suppose a merger increases the price to $14 and reduces the total quantity sold from 200 to 150. Compute the consumer loss associated with the merger. How does it compare to the increase in profit? What is the net loss from the merger?

NOTES

1. "The Economics of Antitrust: The Trustbuster's New Tools," *Economist*, May 2, 1998, 62–64; *Federal Trade Commission v. Staples, Inc.*, 970 F. Supp. 1066 (D.D.C. 1997, Hogan, J); U.S. Federal Trade Commission, *Promoting Competition, Protecting Consumers: A Plain English Guide to Antitrust Laws*, www.ftc.gov/bc/compguide/index.htm (accessed June 28, 2006).

2. John R. Wilke, "New Antitrust Rules May Ease Path to Mergers," *Wall Street Journal*, April 9, 1997.

3. "The Economics of Antitrust: The Trustbuster's New Tools," *Economist*, May 2, 1998, 62–64.

Imperfect Information: Adverse Selection and Moral Hazard

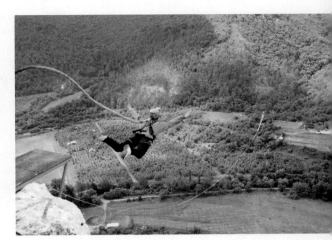

"So, why are you selling this used car?"

The buyers of used cars ask this question frequently and then listen carefully to the answer. Assuming the car seller is honest, the answer the buyer hopes for is "Because I need a different car for my new job," or "I buy a new car every three years." The buyer wants to avoid sellers who are trying to get rid of a "lemon"—a car that breaks down frequently and generates large repair bills. People don't ask this sort of question in other markets. For example, no one ever asks, "So, why are you selling this pizza?"

"Does my insurance policy cover accidental death from bungee jumping?"

Life is risky, and people buy insurance to decrease their financial losses from events such as theft, sickness, injury, and death. The question from the potential bungee jumper reveals an important fact about insurance: It causes people to take greater risks because they know insurance will cover part of the cost of an accident.

LEARNING OBJECTIVES

- Explain the notion of adverse selection for buyers.

- Discuss the possible responses to adverse selection for buyers.

- Explain the notion of adverse selection for sellers.

- Explain the notion of moral hazard.

- Use the marginal principle to describe optimal search by consumers.

MyEconLab
MyEconLab helps you master each objective and study more efficiently.

*t*his chapter explores the role of information in markets and what happens when one side of the market has better information than the other. In the market for used cars, sellers know more about the quality of the product than buyers do. In the market for life insurance, buyers know more about the risks they face than sellers do. As we saw earlier in the book, the model of supply and demand is based on several assumptions, one of which is that buyers and sellers have enough information to make informed choices. In a world of fully informed buyers and sellers, markets operate smoothly, generating an equilibrium price and an equilibrium quantity for each good. In a world with imperfect information, some goods will be sold in very small numbers or not sold at all. In addition, buyers and sellers will use resources to acquire information to help make better decisions. The 2001 Nobel Prize in economics was awarded to three economists—George Akerlof, Michael Spence, and Joseph Stiglitz—who studied the effects of imperfect information on all sorts of markets.

14.1   Adverse Selection for Buyers: The Lemons Problem

The classic example of a market with imperfect information is the market for used cars.[1] Suppose there are two types of cars, low quality and high quality. A low-quality car, also known as a "lemon," breaks down frequently and has relatively high repair costs. A high-quality car, also known as a "plum," is reliable and has relatively low repair costs. Suppose buyers cannot distinguish between lemons and plums. Although a buyer can get some information about a particular car by looking at the car and taking it for a test drive, the information gleaned from this kind of inspection is not enough to determine the quality of the car. In contrast, a person selling a car after owning it for a while knows from experience whether the car is a lemon or a plum. We say there is **asymmetric information** in a market if one side of the market— either buyers or sellers—has better information than the other side. Because buyers cannot distinguish between lemons and plums, there will be a single market for used automobiles: Both types of cars will be sold together in this **mixed market** for the same price.

asymmetric information
A situation in which one side of the market—either buyers or sellers—has better information than the other.

mixed market
A market in which goods of different qualities are sold for the same price.

Uninformed Buyers and Knowledgeable Sellers

How much is a consumer willing to pay for a used car that could be either a lemon or a plum? To determine a consumer's willingness to pay in a mixed market with both lemons and plums, we must answer three questions:

1 How much is the consumer willing to pay for a plum?

2 How much is the consumer willing to pay for a lemon?

3 What is the chance that a used car purchased in the mixed market will be of low quality?

Suppose the typical buyer is willing to pay $4,000 for a plum and $2,000 for a lemon. The buyer is willing to pay less for a lemon because it is less reliable and has higher repair costs. For someone willing to put up with the hassle and repair expense, a lemon is a reasonable car. That's why the typical buyer is willing to pay $2,000, not $0, for a low-quality car we tag with the label "lemon." Someone who pays $2,000 and gets a lemon is just as happy as someone who pays $4,000 and gets a plum.

Consumer expectations play a key role in determining the market outcome when there is imperfect information. Suppose half the used cars *on the road* are lemons, and consumers know this. A reasonable expectation for consumers is that half the cars *on the used-car market* will be lemons, too. In other words, buyers initially expect a 50–50 split between the two types of cars. A reasonable assumption is that a buyer in the mixed market is willing to pay the average value of the two types of cars, or $3,000. In other words, a buyer is willing to pay $3,000 for a 50–50 chance of getting either a plum or a lemon.

The current owner of a used car knows from everyday experience whether the car is a lemon or a plum. Given the single market price for all used cars, lemons and plums alike, the question for each owner is "Should I sell my car?" The answers to this question are shown by the two supply curves in Figure 14.1, one for lemons and one for plums:

- **Lemon supply.** As shown by the lower curve, the minimum supply price for lemons is $500: At any price less than $500, no lemons will be supplied. Lemons have a lower minimum price because they are worth less to their current owners. The number of lemons supplied increases with price. For example, 80 cars will be supplied at a price of $3,000 (point *b*).

- **Plum supply.** As shown by the upper curve, the minimum supply price for plums is $2,500: At any price less than $2,500, no plums will be supplied. Consistent with the law of supply, the higher the price of used cars, the larger the number of plums supplied. For example, 20 plums will be supplied at a price of $3,000 (point *a*).

◄ FIGURE 14.1
All Used Cars on the Market Are Lemons
If buyers assume that there is a 50–50 chance of getting a lemon or a plum, they are willing to pay $3,000 for a used car. At this price, 20 plums are supplied (point *a*) along with 80 lemons (point *b*). This is not an equilibrium because consumers' expectations of a 50–50 split are not realized. If consumers become pessimistic and assume that all cars on the market will be lemons, they are willing to pay $2,000 for a used car. At this price, only lemons will be supplied (point *c*). Consumer expectations are realized, so the equilibrium is shown by point *c*, with an equilibrium price of $2,000.

Equilibrium with All Low-Quality Goods

Table 14.1 shows two scenarios for our hypothetical used-car market, based on the supply curves shown in Figure 14.1. In the first column, we assume buyers have 50–50 expectations about the quality of used cars. As we saw earlier, if buyers expect a 50–50 split between lemons and plums, the typical buyer will be willing to pay $3,000 for a used car. From the supply curves in Figure 14.1, we know that at this price 20 plums and 80 lemons will be supplied, so 80 percent of the used cars (80 of 100) will be lemons. In this case, consumers are too optimistic and underestimate the chance of getting a lemon.

The experiences of these 100 consumers show that the actual chance of getting a lemon is 80 percent, not 50 percent as initially assumed. Once future buyers realize this, they will of course become more pessimistic about the used-car market. Suppose they assume that all the used cars on the market will be lemons. Under this assumption, the typical buyer will be willing to pay only $2,000 (the value of a lemon) for a used car. As shown in Figure 14.1, this price is less than the $2,500 minimum price for supplying plums, so plums will disappear from the used-car market. At a price of $2,000, the quantity of plums supplied is zero, but the quantity of lemons supplied is 45 (point *c*).

TABLE 14.1 Equilibrium with All Low-Quality Goods

	Buyers Initially Have 50–50 Expectations	Equilibrium: Pessimistic Expectations
Demand Side of Market		
Amount buyer is willing to pay for a lemon	$2,000	$2,000
Amount buyer is willing to pay for a plum	$4,000	$4,000
Assumed chance of getting a lemon	50%	100%
Assumed chance of getting a plum	50%	0%
Amount buyer is willing to pay for a used car in mixed market	$3,000	$2,000
Supply Side of Market		
Number of lemons supplied	80	45
Number of plums supplied	20	0
Total number of used cars supplied	100	45
Actual chance of getting a lemon	80%	100%

In other words, all the used cars will be lemons, so consumers' pessimism is justified. Because consumers' expectations are consistent with their actual experiences in the market, the equilibrium price of used cars is $2,000. The equilibrium in the used-car market is shown in the second column of Table 14.1.

In this equilibrium, no plums are bought or sold, so every buyer will get a lemon. People get exactly what they pay for: They are willing to pay $2,000 for a serviceable but low-quality car, and that's what each consumer gets. The domination of the used-car market by lemons is an example of the **adverse-selection problem**. The uninformed side of the market (buyers in this case) must choose from an undesirable or adverse selection of used cars. The asymmetric information in the market generates a downward spiral of price and quality:

adverse-selection problem
A situation in which the uninformed side of the market must choose from an undesirable or adverse selection of goods.

• The presence of low-quality goods on the market pulls down the price consumers are willing to pay.

• The decrease in price decreases the number of high-quality goods supplied, decreasing the average quality of goods on the market.

• This decrease in the average quality of goods on the market pulls down the price consumers are willing to pay again.

In the extreme case, the downward spiral continues until all the cars on the market are lemons.

A Thin Market: Equilibrium with Some High-Quality Goods

The disappearance of plums from our hypothetical used-car market is an extreme case. The plums disappeared from the market because informed plum owners decided to keep their cars rather than sell them at a relatively low price in the used-car market. This outcome would change if the minimum supply price of plums were lower, specifically if it were below $2,000. In this case, most but not all the used cars on the market will be lemons, and some lucky buyers will get plums. In this case, we say asymmetric information generates a **thin market**: Some high-quality goods are sold, but fewer than would be sold in a market with perfect information.

thin market
A market in which some high-quality goods are sold but fewer than would be sold in a market with perfect information.

Figure 14.2 shows the situation that leads to a thin market. The minimum supply price for plums is $1,833, and the quantity of plums supplied increases with the price of used cars. Suppose consumers are initially pessimistic, assuming all cars for sale will be lemons. This means consumers are willing to pay only $2,000 for a used car. Because the minimum supply price for plums ($1,833) is now less than the willingness to pay for a lemon, some plums will be supplied at a price of $2,000. In Figure 14.2, 5 plums and 45 lemons are supplied at this price, so 1 of every 10 buyers will get a plum. In this case, pessimism is not an equilibrium, because some buyers will get plums when they expect lemons. This is also shown in the first column of Table 14.2.

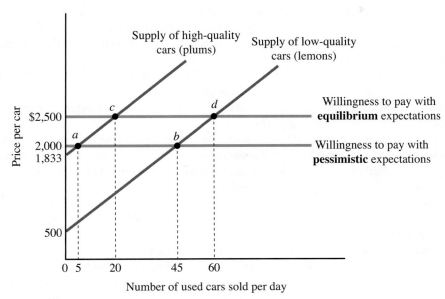

▲ FIGURE 14.2
The Market for High-Quality Cars (Plums) Is Thin
If buyers are pessimistic and assume that only lemons will be sold, they are willing to pay $2,000 for a used car. At this price, 5 plums are supplied (point a), along with 45 lemons (point b). This is not an equilibrium because 10 percent of consumers get plums, contrary to their expectations. If consumers assume that there is a 25 percent chance of getting a plum, they are willing to pay $2,500 for a used car. At this price, 20 plums are supplied (point c), along with 60 lemons (point d). This is an equilibrium because 25 percent of consumers get plums, consistent with their expectations. Consumer expectations are realized, so the equilibrium is shown by points c and d.

TABLE 14.2 A Thin Market for High-Quality Goods

	Initial Pessimistic Expectations	Equilibrium: 75–25 Expectations
Demand Side of Market		
Amount buyer is willing to pay for a lemon	$2,000	$2,000
Amount buyer is willing to pay for a plum	$4,000	$4,000
Assumed chance of getting a lemon	100%	75%
Assumed chance of getting a plum	0%	25%
Amount buyer is willing to pay for a used car in mixed market	$2,000	$2,500
Supply Side of Market		
Number of lemons supplied	45	60
Number of plums supplied	5	20
Total number of used cars supplied	50	80
Actual chance of getting a lemon	90%	75%

application 1

ARE BASEBALL PITCHERS LIKE USED CARS?

APPLYING THE CONCEPTS #1: What is adverse selection for buyers?

Professional baseball teams compete with each other for players. After six years of play in the major leagues, a player has the option of becoming a free agent and offering his services to the highest bidder. A player is likely to switch teams if the new team offers him a higher salary than his original team. A puzzling feature of the free-agent market is that pitchers who switch teams are more prone to injuries than pitchers who don't. On average, pitchers who switch teams spend 28 days per season on the disabled list, compared to only 5 days for pitchers who do not switch teams. This doesn't mean that all the switching pitchers are lemons; many are injury-free and are valuable additions to their new teams. But on average, switching pitchers spend five times longer recovering from injuries.

This puzzling feature of the free-agent market is explained by asymmetric information and adverse selection. Because the coaches, physicians, and trainers from the player's original team have interacted with the player on a daily basis for several years, they know from experience whether he is likely to suffer from injuries that prevent him from playing. In contrast, the new team has much less information. Its physicians can examine the pitcher, and the team can check league records to see how long the pitcher has spent on the disabled list, but these measures do not eliminate the asymmetric information. The original team has several years of daily experience with the pitcher and has better information about the pitcher's physical health.

Now consider the incentives for a team to outbid another team for a pitcher. Suppose the market price for pitchers is $1 million per year, and a pitcher who is currently with the Detroit Tigers is offered this salary by another team. If the Tigers think the pitcher is likely to spend a lot of time next season recovering from injuries, they won't try to outbid the other team for the pitcher: They will let the pitcher switch teams. But if the Tigers think the pitcher will be injury-free and productive, he will be worth more than $1 million to them, and they will outbid other teams and keep him. That's why an injury-prone pitcher is more likely to switch teams. As in the used-car market, there are many "lemons" on the used-pitcher market. The market for baseball players playing other positions does not suffer from adverse selection, perhaps because the injuries that affect their performance are easier for other teams to detect.

Although you may think it's bizarre to compare baseball pitchers to used cars, people in baseball don't think so. They recognize the similarity between the two markets. Jackie Moore, who managed a free-agent camp where teams looking for players can see free agents in action, sounded like a used-car salesman: "We want to get players off the lot. We want to cut a deal. How many camps can you go into where you can look at a player and take him home with you?" **Related to Exercises 1.7, 1.8, and 1.16.**

SOURCES: Based on Kenneth Lehn, "Information Asymmetries in Baseball's Free Agent Market," *Economic Inquiry* 22 (January 1984): 37–44; Associated Press, "Free Agents at End of Baseball's Earth," *Corvallis Gazette-Times*, April 15, 1995.

In equilibrium, consumer expectations about the chances of getting the two types of cars are realized. Suppose consumers expect one of every four cars to be a plum. Let's assume each consumer is willing to pay $2,500 for a used car under these circumstances. Consumers are willing to pay a bit more than the value of a lemon because there is a small chance of getting a plum. In Figure 14.2, at this price 20 plums are supplied (point *c*) and 60 lemons are supplied (point *d*), so in fact one in four consumers actually gets a plum. This is an equilibrium because 25 percent of the cars sold are plums and 75 percent are lemons, consistent with consumers' expectations. This is also shown in the second column of Table 14.2.

Evidence of the Lemons Problem

The lemons model makes two predictions about markets with asymmetric information. First, the presence of low-quality goods in a market will at least reduce the number of high-quality goods in the market and may even eliminate them. Second, buyers and sellers will respond to the lemons problem by investing in information and other means of distinguishing between low-quality and high-quality goods. What is the evidence for the lemons model?

Studies of the market for used pickup trucks have provided mixed results concerning the lemons problem.[2] It appears that for trucks less than 10 years old, those sold on the market are just as reliable, on average, as those that remain with their current owners. These studies provide support for the second implication of the theory of lemons, that people acquire information and develop effective means to deal with the problem of asymmetric information. In contrast, there does seem to be a lemons problem for trucks at least 10 years old, which represent about one-third of transactions. Compared to old trucks that remain with their current owners, old trucks that are sold have significantly higher repair costs, with a difference in cost of about 45 percent. Old trucks that are sold have a much higher probability of requiring engine and transmission repairs.

14.2 Responding to the Lemons Problem

In a market with asymmetric information, there are strong incentives for buyers and sellers to solve the lemons problem. In our example of a thin market, the price of a used car is $2,500, but consumers are willing to pay $4,000 for a plum. This $1,500 gap between the willingness to pay for a plum and the price in the mixed market provides an opportunity for mutually beneficial exchange. A person who owns a high-quality car may not be willing to sell it for $2,500, but might accept something closer to $4,000, an amount a buyer is willing to pay. The challenge is to identify a high-quality car in the mixed market.

Buyers Invest in Information

In our model of the thin market, one in four buyers pays $2,500 to get a plum worth $4,000. The more information a buyer has, the greater the chance of picking a plum from the cars in the mixed market. Suppose a buyer gets enough information to identify the plums in a market. The buyer could purchase a plum worth $4,000 at the prevailing price of $2,500, generating a gain of $1,500. A buyer can get information about individual cars by taking the car to a mechanic for a careful inspection. In addition, a buyer can get general information about the reliability of different models from magazines and the Internet. *Consumer Reports* publishes information on repair histories of different models and computes a "Trouble" index, scoring each model on a scale of 1 to 5. By consulting these information sources, a buyer improves the chances of getting a high-quality car. Another information source is Carfax.com, which provides information on individual cars, including their accident histories.

Consumer Satisfaction Scores from ValueStar and eBay

The problem of asymmetric information in consumer goods such as cars also occurs for some types of consumer services. Most consumers can't easily determine the quality of service they will receive from an auto repair shop, a landscaper, or a plumber. How can a high-quality service provider distinguish itself from low-quality providers?

Some organizations provide information about firms that provide consumers services such as landscaping, auto repair, and home improvement. ValueStar is a consumer guide and business directory that uses customer satisfaction surveys to determine how well a firm does relative to its competitors in providing quality service. To earn the right to display a Customer-Rated seal from ValueStar, a firm must prove that it has all the required licenses and insurance and must agree to pay for a survey of its past customers. ValueStar uses consumer surveys to compute a consumer-satisfaction score for each company. Any company receiving a score of at least 85 out of 100 has the right to display a Customer-Rated Gold seal for a one-year period. In New York City, servicemagic.com rates all kinds of contractors and household service providers, with scores based on reports from consumers.

Online consumers help each other by rating online sellers. On eBay, buyers must rely on sellers to honestly disclose the quality of the goods they are auctioning and to promptly ship them once a consumer pays. Buyers help other purchasers distinguish "good" from "bad" sellers on eBay by rating them online with "stars," indicating their satisfaction with their transactions. The same sort of information is provided by people who buy second-hand books.

Guarantees and Lemons Laws

Used-car sellers also have an incentive to solve the lemons problem. If a plum owner persuades a buyer that his or her car is a plum and then sells the car for $4,000 rather than $2,500, the seller's gain is $1,500. Sellers can identify a car as a plum in a sea of lemons by offering one of the following guarantees:

- *Money-back guarantees.* The seller could promise to refund the $4,000 price if the car turns out to be a lemon. Because the car is in fact a plum—a fact known by the seller—the buyer will not ask for a refund, so both the buyer and the seller will be happy with the transaction.

- *Warranties and repair guarantees.* The seller could promise to cover any extraordinary repair costs for one year. Because the car is a plum, there won't be any extraordinary costs, so both the buyer and the seller will be happy with the transaction.

Many states have laws that require automakers to buy back cars that experience frequent problems in the first year of use. For example, under California's Song-Beverly Consumer Warranty Act, also known as the "Lemons Law," auto dealers are required to repurchase vehicles that have been brought back for repair at least four times for the same problem or have been in the mechanic's shop for at least 30 calendar days in the first year following purchase. A vehicle repurchased under the lemons law must be fixed before it is sold to another customer and must be identified as a lemon with a stamp on the title and a sticker on the car that says "lemons law buyback." One problem with enforcing these laws is that lemons can cross state lines without a paper trail. The interstate commerce in lemons has led to new laws in some states requiring the branding of lemons on vehicle titles to follow the car when it crosses state lines.

application 2

REGULATION OF THE CALIFORNIA KIWIFRUIT MARKET

APPLYING THE CONCEPTS #2: How can government solve the adverse-selection problem?

Kiwifruit is subject to imperfect information because buyers cannot determine its sweetness—its quality level—by simple inspection. The sweetness level at the time of consumption is determined by the fruit's maturity—its sugar content at the time of harvest. Kiwifruit continues to convert starch into sugar after it is picked, but fruit that is picked early has a low sugar content at harvest time and never tastes sweet. There is asymmetric information because producers know the maturity of the fruit, but fruit wholesalers and grocery stores, who buy fruit at the time of harvest, cannot determine whether a piece of fruit will ultimately be sweet or sour.

Before 1987, kiwifruit from California suffered from the "lemons" problem. Maturity levels of the fruit varied across producers. On average, the sugar content at the time of harvest was below the industry standard, established by kiwifruit from New Zealand. Given the large number of "lemons" among California kiwifruit, grocery stores were not willing to pay as much for California fruit. In other words, the presence of low-quality (immature) fruit in the mixed market pulled down the price of California fruit. Mature kiwifruit is more costly to produce than immature fruit, and the low price decreased the production of mature fruit. This result is similar to the way low used-car prices decrease the number of high-quality used cars on the market. In general, adverse selection led to low prices and a relatively large volume of low-quality kiwifruit from California.

In 1987, California producers implemented a federal marketing order to address the lemon–kiwi problem. The federal order specified a minimum maturity standard, and as the average quality of California fruit increased, so did the price. Within a few years, the gap between California and New Zealand prices had decreased significantly. **Related to Exercises 2.3 and 2.6.**

SOURCE: Based on Christopher Ferguson and Hoy Carman, "Kiwifruit and the 'Lemon' Problem: Do Minimum Quality Standards Work?" (working paper, International Food and Agribusiness Management Association, 1999).

14.3 Adverse Selection for Sellers: Insurance

So far, we have explored the effects of asymmetric information when sellers are more knowledgeable than buyers. The same sort of problems occur when buyers are more knowledgeable than sellers. The best example of superior knowledge on the demand side of the market is insurance. A person who buys an insurance policy knows much more about his or her risks and needs for insurance than the insurance company knows. For example, when you buy an auto insurance policy, you know more than your insurance company about your driving habits and your chances of getting into an accident. We'll see that insurance markets suffer from the adverse-selection problem: Insurance companies get an adverse or undesirable selection of customers.

Health Insurance

To illustrate the information problems in the market for insurance, consider health insurance provided to individual consumers. Suppose there are two types of consumers: low-cost consumers with relatively low medical expenses of $2,000 per year and high-cost consumers with relatively high medical expenses of $6,000 per year. The amount a consumer is willing to pay for an insurance policy covering all medical expenses increases with the anticipated medical expenses, so high-cost people are willing to pay more for health insurance.

The insurance company cannot distinguish between high-cost and low-cost people, but it still must pick a price for its coverage. To simplify matters, let's assume there are no administrative costs, so the only cost for the insurance company is the medical bills it pays for its customers. Let's also assume the insurance company sets the price equal to its average cost per customer, equal to the total medical bills paid by the insurance company divided by the number of customers. These assumptions simplify the math without affecting the basic results.

What is the insurance company's average cost per customer? To determine the average cost in a mixed market, we must answer three questions:

- What is the cost of providing medical care to a high-cost person?
- What is the cost of providing medical care to a low-cost person?
- What fraction of the customers are low-cost people?

Suppose that half the population is high cost and the other half is low cost. Let's assume the insurance company is somewhat naive and initially assumes that the mix of insurance buyers will be the same as the population mix. In other words, the insurance company initially assumes that half its customers will be high cost and half will be low cost. In this case, the average cost per customer is $4,000, that is, the average of $2,000 for each low-cost customer and $6,000 for each high-cost customer.

There is asymmetric information in the insurance market because potential buyers know from everyday experience and family histories what type of customer they are, either low cost or high cost. For each person, the question is "Given the single market price for all insurance, for low-cost and high-cost people alike, should I buy insurance?" The answers to this question are shown in two demand curves in Figure 14.3. The demand curve for the high-cost people is higher than

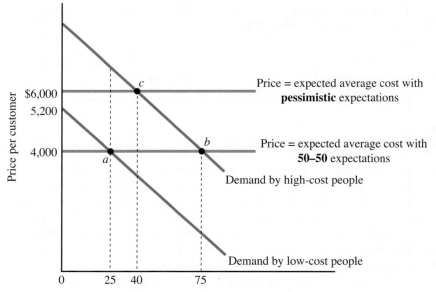

▲ FIGURE 14.3

All Insurance Customers Are High-Cost People

If insurance companies assume there will be a 50–50 split between high-cost and low-cost customers, the average cost of insurance and its price is $4,000. At this price, there are 25 low-cost customers (point *a*) and 75 high-cost customers (point *b*). This is not an equilibrium, because 75 percent of insurance buyers are high-cost customers, contrary to the expectations of a 50–50 split. If insurance companies become pessimistic and assume that all buyers will be high-cost consumers, the average cost and price is $6,000. The insurance company's expectations are realized, so the equilibrium is shown by point *c*.

the curve for the low-cost people, reflecting their larger benefits from having medical insurance.

Equilibrium with All High-Cost Consumers

Table 14.3 shows two scenarios for our hypothetical insurance market, with numbers based on the demand curves shown in Figure 14.3. In the first column, firms initially assume a 50–50 mix of customers. As we saw earlier, if sellers expect a 50–50 split between the two types, the average cost per customer is $4,000, and that's the price they charge for medical insurance. From the demand curves in Figure 14.3, we know that at this price 25 low-cost people will buy insurance (point *a*), along with 75 high-cost people (point *b*). In this case, insurance companies are too optimistic and underestimate the fraction of customers with large medical bills. The actual fraction of high-cost customers is 75 percent, and the actual average cost is $5,000 (equal to 0.25 times $2,000, plus 0.75 times $6,000). The company's average cost of $5,000 exceeds its price of $4,000, so the firm will lose money.

TABLE 14.3 Equilibrium with All High-Cost Customers		
	50–50 Expectations	**Equilibrium: Pessimistic Expectations**
Supply Side of Market		
Cost of serving a high-cost customer	$6,000	$6,000
Cost of serving a low-cost customer	$2,000	$2,000
Assumed fraction of high-cost customers	50%	100%
Assumed chance of low-cost customers	50%	0%
Expected average cost per customer (price)	$4,000	$6,000
Demand Side of Market		
Number of high-cost customers	75	40
Number of low-cost customers	25	0
Total number of customers	100	40
Actual fraction of high-cost customers	75%	100%
Actual average cost per customer	$5,000	$6,000

Suppose that after observing the outcome in the first column, insurance companies become very pessimistic. They assume that all their customers will be high-cost people. Under this assumption, the average cost per customer is $6,000, the average cost per high-cost customer, and that's the pessimistic price. As shown in Figure 14.3, this price exceeds the maximum that low-cost people are willing to pay for insurance ($5,200), so none of the low-cost consumers will buy insurance at this price. But a total of 40 high-cost consumers will buy insurance at this price (point *c*). In other words, all the customers will be high-cost people, so the company's pessimism is justified. The price chosen by the insurance company equals the actual average cost of providing service, so the equilibrium is shown by point *c*, with an equilibrium price of $6,000. This equilibrium is shown in the second column of Table 14.3.

The domination of the insurance market by high-cost people is another example of the adverse-selection problem. The uninformed side of the market (sellers in this case) must choose from an undesirable or adverse selection of consumers. The asymmetric information in the market generates an upward spiral of price and average cost of service:

- The presence of high-cost consumers in the market pulls up the average cost of service, pulling up the price.
- The increase in price decreases the number of low-cost consumers who purchase insurance.
- This decrease in the number of low-cost consumers pulls up the average cost of insurance.
- In the extreme case, the upward spiral continues until all insurance customers are high-cost people.

Our example of health insurance indicates that only high-cost people buy insurance. A more realistic outcome is a thin market, with a relatively small number of low-cost people buying insurance. The adverse-selection problem could be less severe, but it will still be present as long as insurance companies cannot distinguish perfectly between low-cost and high-cost people.

Responding to Adverse Selection in Insurance: Group Insurance

Insurance companies use group insurance plans to diminish the adverse-selection problem. By enrolling all the employees of an organization in one or two insurance plans, they ensure that all workers, not just high-cost people, join the pool of consumers.

In our example, group insurance would generate a 50–50 mix of low-cost and high-cost customers, and the break-even price would be $6,000. In contrast, when a firm sells insurance to individuals, the low-cost people have an incentive to go without insurance, leading to the adverse-selection problem and higher prices.

experience rating
A situation in which insurance companies charge different prices for medical insurance to different firms depending on the past medical bills of a firm's employees.

Most insurance companies use **experience rating** to set their prices for group insurance. They charge different prices to different firms, depending on the past medical bills of the firm's employees. A firm whose employees have low medical bills pays a low price for its employees' health insurance. Experience rating gives firms an incentive to decrease the health costs of their workers by investing in safety and health programs for them. Firms also have an incentive to avoid hiring applicants with health problems. Under experience rating, a firm that hires a worker with above-average medical costs will ultimately pay a higher price for its group insurance.

The Uninsured

One implication of asymmetric information in the insurance market is that many low-cost consumers who are not eligible for a group plan will not carry insurance. Given the adverse-selection problem, the price for an individual insurance plan is relatively high, and many consumers go without insurance. This is a contributing factor to the problem of the uninsured. In 2008, about 47 million people (about 14 percent of the U.S. population) were not covered by health insurance. About 70 percent of working-age people have private insurance, and another 10 percent have some sort of government insurance, leaving 20 percent without health insurance. In general, the uninsured are the people and their families who do not receive insurance through their employers, are unemployed or between jobs, or are poor but do not qualify for Medicaid. The uninsured obtain care for medical emergencies but typically do not receive routine—and ultimately less costly—preventive care.

In 2010 the U.S. Congress approved legislation to regulate the nation's health insurance markets and reduce the number of uninsured people. The new law will prevent insurance companies from denying coverage based on preexisting conditions and outlaws lifetime caps on reimbursement. In addition, the law requires individuals to get health insurance, and imposes penalties on people who remain uncovered. Other provisions impose penalties on employers that do not provide insurance to their employees. For small businesses and low-income individuals, the law provides subsidies and tax credits to partly offset the cost of insurance. The law is expected to significantly reduce the number of uninsured citizens.

Other Types of Insurance

The same logic of adverse selection applies to the markets for other types of insurance, including life insurance, home insurance for theft and property damage, and automobile insurance. Buyers know more than sellers about their risks, so there is adverse selection, with high-risk individuals more likely to buy insurance. Life insurance companies provide group coverage to get a broader base of consumers and also try to distinguish between high-risk and low-risk people with physical exams. However, because the companies are unable to distinguish between high-risk and low-risk people with sufficient precision, the adverse-selection problem persists.

application 3

UNISEX AUTOMOBILE INSURANCE IN THE EUROPEAN UNION

APPLYING THE CONCEPTS #3: What is adverse selection for sellers?

Starting in 2012, the European Union prohibits gender discrimination (different prices for men and women) in automobile insurance. On average, women are much safer drivers: in Britain, the average insurance claim of an 18-year-old woman is about £2,700, compared to £4,400 for an 18-year-old man. Before the unisex pricing policy, women paid lower prices because they were less costly for insurance companies. The ban on gender discrimination is expected to increase prices for women by about 25 percent and decrease insurance prices for men by about 10 percent.

Unisex insurance pricing will promote adverse selection in the insurance market. Some women will respond to the higher price by dropping out of the insurance pool, while some men will respond to the lower price by entering the pool. The pool will have a more costly (more adverse) mix of customers, leading to a higher average cost for insurance companies and a higher price. Unisex pricing promotes adverse selection because it eliminates one way to control adverse selection—a lower price for lower-cost customers. **Related to Exercise 3.3.**

SOURCE: Based on BBC News, "Insurance and pension costs hit by ECJ gender ruling," March 1, 2011.

14.4 Insurance and Moral Hazard

Does insurance affect people's risk-taking behavior? The answer is yes. Insurance causes people to take greater risks because they know part of the cost of an undesirable outcome will be borne by their insurance companies. Here are some examples of people taking greater risks because they have insurance:

- Will Irma buy a fire extinguisher for her kitchen? If she had to pay for any property damage caused by a fire, she would definitely buy a fire extinguisher. But because her homeowner's insurance covers property damage from fires, she doesn't buy a fire extinguisher.

- Will Harry drive his car carefully? If he had to pay for all repairs resulting from a collision out of his own pocket, he would drive very carefully. But because his auto insurance covers some of the repair costs, he drives fast and recklessly.

- Will Flo fly on a commercial airline or hitch a ride with her pilot friend in a four-seat airplane? Traveling in small airplanes is much riskier. If Flo dies in an airplane crash, her family will lose the income she would otherwise earn. If she didn't have life insurance to offset these income losses, she would be less likely to risk harming her family by flying on the small plane instead of the commercial airline. But because she knows her family will collect $1 million in life insurance, she is willing to take the risk.

moral hazard

A situation in which one side of an economic relationship takes undesirable or costly actions that the other side of the relationship cannot observe.

The risky behavior triggered by insurance is an example of the moral-hazard problem. **Moral hazard** occurs when one side of an economic relationship takes undesirable or costly actions that the other side of the relationship cannot observe. For example, Irma's insurance company doesn't know whether she has a fire extinguisher. If there is a fire, Irma's hidden action—going without an extinguisher—is costly for the insurance company. Similarly, Harry's insurance company doesn't know how fast and recklessly he drives, and insurance encourages him to drive recklessly. His hidden action of reckless driving increases the likelihood of a costly accident. Just as collision insurance encourages risky driving, life insurance encourages risky activities such as flying small airplanes, parachuting, and bungee jumping. Similarly, health insurance encourages risky behavior such as smoking, drinking, and unhealthy diets.

Insurance Companies and Moral Hazard

Insurance companies use various measures to decrease the moral-hazard problem. Many insurance policies have a deductible—a dollar amount that a policy holder must pay before getting compensation from the insurance company. For example, if your car insurance policy has a $500 deductible and the damage from a collision is $900, the insurance company will pay you only $400. You pay the other $500 as your deductible. Deductibles reduce the moral-hazard problem because they shift to the policy holder part of the cost of a claim on the policy. Like a deductible, an insurance copayment shifts part of the cost of risky behavior to policy holders and thus reduces the moral-hazard problem.

Savvy insurance companies anticipate moral hazard. To illustrate, suppose 1 of 10 bicycles on your campus was stolen in 2008. If you decide to be the first to offer bicycle theft insurance, you might naively assume that the theft rate wouldn't change. But the moral-hazard problem tells us that people with insurance take greater risks, so we'd expect a higher theft rate on a campus where insurance is widespread. Students who buy theft insurance are likely to be less careful in protecting their bikes, perhaps using flimsy locks or no locks at all. Or they might start leaving their bikes on campus overnight. A savvy insurance company would assume a theft rate higher than 10 percent and set its price accordingly.

Deposit Insurance for Savings and Loans

For another example of moral hazard, consider the insurance provided for bank deposits. When you deposit money in a Savings and Loan (S&L), the money doesn't just sit in a vault. The S&L will invest the money, loaning it out and expecting to make a profit when loans are repaid with interest. Unfortunately, some loans are not repaid, and the S&L could lose money and be unable to return your money. To protect people who put their money in S&Ls and other banks, the Federal Deposit Insurance Corporation (FDIC) insures the first $250,000 of your deposit, so if the S&L goes bankrupt, you'll still get your money back. The government enacted the federal deposit insurance law in 1933 in response to the bank failures of the Great Depression.

How does deposit insurance affect you and the people who manage the S&L? If you know you'll get your money back no matter what happens to the S&L, you may deposit your money there without evaluating the performance of the S&L and the riskiness of its loans to borrowers and investments in the stock market. The manager of an S&L will also be more likely to make risky investments knowing that if it doesn't pay off and the S&L goes bankrupt, the federal government will reimburse depositors. Recognizing this moral hazard problem, the federal government has historically limited S&Ls to relatively safe investments.

In the 1980s, the federal government loosened some of the investment restrictions on S&Ls, and S&L managers began investing in volatile securities, including high-risk commercial mortgages and junk bonds. When these risky investments failed, many of the S&Ls went into bankruptcy. The government then bailed out the failed S&Ls, at a total cost to taxpayers of about $200 billion.

application 4

CAR INSURANCE AND RISKY DRIVING

APPLYING THE CONCEPTS #4: What is moral hazard in car insurance?

The theory of moral hazard suggests that an insured driver, who bears less than the full cost of a collision, will drive less carefully than an uninsured driver. A recent study suggests that the moral-hazard cost of automobile insurance is substantial. When a state makes car insurance compulsory and thus decreases the number of uninsured drivers, roads become more hazardous: The number of collisions and the number of traffic deaths increase. Roads become more dangerous because the newly insured drivers drive less cautiously. The study estimates that a one percentage point decrease in the share of uninsured drivers increases the number of traffic fatalities by 2 percent. Of course, there are benefits associated with compulsory insurance, but in the interests of efficiency, we must compare the benefits to the costs, including the increase in fatalities on more hazardous roads. **Related to Exercises 4.5 and 4.11.**

SOURCE: Based on Alma Cohen and Rajeev Dehejia, "The Effect of Automobile Insurance and Accident Liability Laws on Traffic Fatalities," *Journal of Law and Economics* XLVII (2004): 357–393.

14.5 The Economics of Consumer Search

Suppose the price of a particular television model varies from one store to another. If you don't know which store has the lowest price, should you keep shopping until you find it? The short answer is "No." Searching is costly because it takes time to visit a store, make a phone call, or visit a Web site. We can apply the marginal principle to the problem of searching for low prices. It will be sensible to continue searching if the marginal benefit of search (the expected savings from finding a lower price) exceeds the marginal cost (the time cost). In most cases, it will be rational to stop shopping before you find the lowest possible price.

Search and the Marginal Principle

We can illustrate the economics of search with a simple example. Suppose the price of a television ranges from $100 at the lowest price store to $180 at the highest price store. In addition, suppose that for a randomly selected store, any price from the low price to the high price is equally likely. Let's assume that the opportunity cost of the time required to visit a store—the marginal cost of search—is constant at $0.90 per visit.

The marginal benefit of search depends on your **discovered price**—the lowest price you have found so far in your search. The first column in Table 14.4 shows how to compute the marginal benefit of another visit when the discovered price is $140. A price of $140 is at the 50th percentile of the price range of the television (from $100 to $180). In other words, half the stores have lower prices (from $100 to $139), and half have higher prices (from $141 to $180). We compute the marginal benefit of an additional visit as follows:

- Row 2: If you visit one more store, the probability of finding a lower price is 0.50. You have a 50–50 chance of finding a lower price.
- Row 3: If you actually find a lower price, it will be between the low price of $100 and your discovered price of $140. The best guess for a lower price is the midpoint of this range, or $120.
- Row 4: The best guess for the savings from a lower price is the gap between the discovered price ($140) and the lower price ($120), or $20.
- Row 5: The probability of finding a lower price is 0.50, so your expected savings from visiting another store is $10 (equal to the anticipated $20 price gap times 0.50). You have a 50–50 chance of saving $20, so on average a visit to another store will generate a $10 savings.

To summarize, the marginal benefit of search is $10, which exceeds the $0.90 marginal cost. Therefore, if your discovered price is $140, it is sensible to visit one more store.

discovered price
The lowest price observed so far in a search process.

TABLE 14.4 Marginal Benefit of Searching for a Lower Price				
Discovered price (lowest so far)	$140	$120	$110	$112
Probability of discovering lower price in next visit	0.500	0.250	0.125	0.150
Best guess of lower price	$120	$110	$105	$106
Best guess of savings from lower price	$ 20	$ 10	$ 5	$ 6
Marginal benefit: Expected savings	$ 10.00	$ 2.50	$ 0.625	$ 0.900

As shown in the second column of Table 14.4, if the discovered price is $120, the marginal benefit of another visit is only $2.50. This is lower than the marginal benefit shown in column 1 (discovered price = $140) for two reasons. First, a discovered price of $120 is in the 25th percentile of the price range of $100 to $180 (only one-fourth of stores have lower prices), so the probability of finding a lower price is only 0.25. Second, if you actually find a lower price, the savings will be smaller because you start with a lower discovered price. A lower price will be between $100 and $120, so your best guess of a lower price is $110 (the middle of the range) and your best guess of the savings from a lower price is only $10 (equal to $120 – $110). Multiplying the probability of finding a lower price (0.25) by the $10 price gap, the expected savings is $2.50. This marginal benefit still exceeds the $0.90 marginal cost, so it is sensible to visit an additional store to try to improve on your discovered price of $120.

As shown in the third column of Table 14.4, if the discovered price is only $110, visiting an additional store is not sensible. In this case, only one in eight stores has lower prices, meaning that the probability of finding a lower price at the store you visit is only 0.125. In addition, your best guess of a lower price is $105 (the middle of the range from $100 to $110), and your savings from a lower price is only $5. The expected savings from an additional visit is only $0.625 (equal to 0.125 times $5), which is less than the $0.90 marginal cost. In this case, the cost of an additional visit exceeds the expected benefit, so it is best to pay your discovered price of $110 rather than continuing to search for a lower price.

Figure 14.4 illustrates the application of the marginal principle to the search process. The horizontal axis shows the discovered price, and the vertical axis shows the marginal benefit and marginal cost. As we saw in Table 14.4, the higher

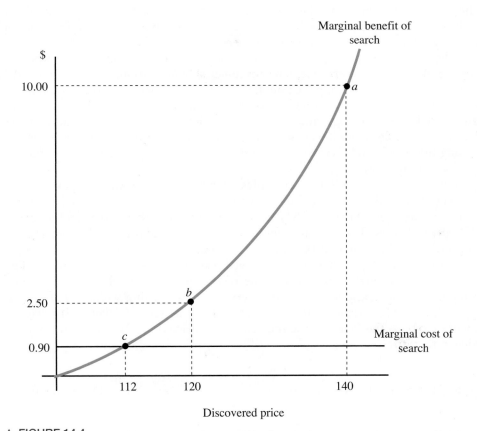

▲ **FIGURE 14.4**

Marginal Benefit and Marginal Cost of Search

The marginal benefit of search increases with the discovered price (the lowest price found so far), while the marginal cost of search is constant. If at a particular discovered price the marginal benefit exceeds the marginal cost, it is sensible to continue searching for a low price. The reservation price, defined as the price where the marginal benefit of search equals the marginal cost, is $112 (shown by point c).

the discovered price, the larger the marginal benefit of additional search, so the marginal-benefit curve is positively sloped. For example, the marginal benefit is $2.50 for a discovered price of $120 (point *b*), compared to $10 for a discovered price of $140 (point *a*). If the marginal cost is constant at $0.90 per visit (per unit of search), the marginal-cost curve is horizontal. If the discovered price is less than $112 (for example $110), the marginal benefit is less than the marginal cost, and it is not sensible to search for a lower price.

Reservation Prices and Searching Strategy

reservation price

The price at which a consumer is indifferent about additional search for a lower price.

A consumer's **reservation price** is defined as the discovered price at which the consumer is indifferent about additional search. If the discovered price exceeds the reservation price, additional searching is sensible, but if the discovered price is lower, additional searching is irrational. In Table 14.4, the reservation price is computed as $112.

- The probability of finding a lower price is 0.15 (a price of $112 is in the 15th percentile of the price range $100 to $180).
- The best guess of a lower price is $106 (the midpoint of the range $100 to $112).
- The marginal benefit (the expected savings over the discovered price) is $0.90, equal to 0.15 times $6.

The marginal benefit equals the marginal cost, so the consumer is indifferent about additional search. In Figure 14.4 the reservation price is shown by the intersection of the marginal-cost curve and the marginal-benefit curve at point *c*.

The reservation price provides consumers with a convenient rule for when to stop searching for a lower price. The consumer should continue to search until the discovered price (the lowest price found) is less than or equal to the reservation price. Some consumers will get lucky and discover a price below their reservation prices with just a little bit of searching, while others will take longer. But a consumer who knows the range of prices from lowest to highest can compute a reservation price before starting the search, and then search until the discovered price is less than or equal to the reservation price.

Figure 14.5 provides two examples of price searches that stop when the discovered price drops below the reservation price. The dots show one sequence of observed prices, starting at $174, followed by $175, then $165, and so on to $110 after 10 visits. The solid line connects the discovered prices—the lowest price observed over the course of the search. The dots above the line are the observed prices that, at the time they were observed, exceeded the discovered price. The discovered price finally drops below the reservation price in the 10th visit. The triangles show a second sequence of observed prices, starting with $151, followed by $152, then $162, then $130, and finally $107. The second (diamond) sequence is half as long as the first because the discovered price drops below the reservation price in the fifth visit.

The Effects of Opportunity Cost and Product Prices on Search Effort

Reservation prices and search efforts vary across consumers. A consumer with a relatively high opportunity cost of search time will have a higher marginal cost of search and will naturally spend less time searching for lower prices. In Figure 14.4 an increase in the marginal cost of search will shift the marginal-cost curve upward, increasing the reservation price. For example, if the cost per visit were $2.50 instead

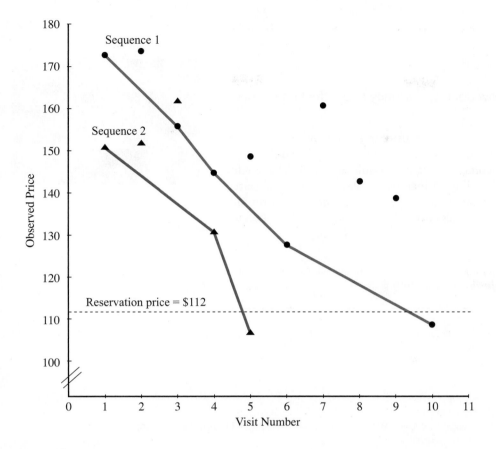

▲ FIGURE 14.5

Price Sequences and the Reservation Price

Each sequence (indicated by dots in #1 or triangles in #2) shows prices observed on visits to different stores. The lines connect the discovered prices (lowest price so far). A rational consumer stops shopping for lower prices when the discovered price is less than or equal to the reservation price ($112).

of $0.90, the reservation price would be $120 rather than $112. The higher the reservation price, the less time it will take, on average, to discover a price below the reservation price. Therefore, a consumer with a high opportunity cost of search won't spend as much time searching for low prices.

The amount of searching for low prices also depends on the price of the product. The higher the price, the bigger the payoff from discovering a price that is, say, 2 percent lower. For example, if an additional visit to a car dealer could save you 2 percent on a $10,000 car ($200), an additional visit will be sensible if your opportunity cost is less than $200. In contrast, if additional searching might save you 2 percent on a $10 pizza ($0.20), it is not sensible to continue searching unless your opportunity cost is less than $0.20. In general, the higher the price of a product, the greater the incentive to search for a lower price.

The amount of searching also depends on the range of prices, from lowest to highest. The smaller the gap between the low and high price, the smaller the possible savings from additional search. In our example, suppose the price range for the television is only $139 to $141, and suppose your discovered price is $140 (the average price). As before, there is a 50–50 chance that an additional visit will generate a lower price. But at most you'll save only $1, and your best guess for a lower price is $139.50 (the middle of the range $139 to $140). Given the relatively small anticipated savings, additional search will be rational only if your marginal cost is very low ($0.25). In general, the smaller the price range for a product, the less time consumers will spend searching for lower prices.

INCOME AND CONSUMER SEARCH

APPLYING THE CONCEPTS #5: How does opportunity cost affect consumer search?

A recent study explores the relationship between consumer search and income. The opportunity cost of search depends on income because one hour of search means one less hour available for earning income. The study examines search behavior for liquid detergents, and shows that a doubling of income increases the cost of search and decreases the amount of searching by about 14 percent. In addition, consumer search on workdays is more costly and thus less extensive than on weekends. **Related to Exercise 5.6.**

SOURCE: Based on Nitin Mehta, Surendra Rajiv, Kannan Srinivasan, "Price Uncertainty and Consumer Surplus: A Structural Model of Consideration Set Formation," *Marketing Science* 22 (2003), pp. 58–84.

SUMMARY

In this chapter, we've seen what happens when one of the assumptions underlying most supply and demand analysis—that people make informed decisions—is violated. If either buyers or sellers don't have reliable information about a particular good or service, the market will suffer from the adverse-selection problem. The uninformed side picks from an adverse selection of goods or customers. Here are the main points of the chapter:

1 The *adverse-selection problem* occurs when one side of the market cannot distinguish between high-quality and low-quality goods. The presence of low-quality goods pulls down the price that buyers are willing to pay, which decreases the quantity of high-quality goods supplied, which further decreases the average quality and the price. In the extreme case, only low-quality goods are sold.

2 A *thin* market occurs when the sellers of high-quality goods have a relatively low minimum supply price, so some high-quality goods are sold.

3 In a market subject to *asymmetric information*, buyers have an incentive to invest in information to help make better choices and sellers have an incentive to provide quality guarantees.

4 Insurance markets suffer from adverse selection because compared to insurance sellers, buyers have better information about the risks they face.

5 Insurance encourages risky behavior because part of the cost of an unfavorable outcome will be paid by an insurance company.

6 Searching for low prices is costly, and a rational consumer is likely to stop searching for low prices before finding the lowest possible price.

KEY TERMS

adverse-selection problem, p. 316

asymmetric information, p. 314

discovered price, p. 328

experience rating, p. 324

mixed market, p. 314

moral hazard, p. 326

reservation price, p. 330

thin market, p. 316

1.1 There is asymmetric information in the used-car market because _____ (buyers/sellers) cannot distinguish between lemons and plums but _____ (buyers/sellers) can.

1.2 The supply curve for high-quality used cars lies _____ (above/below) the supply curve for low-quality used cars.

1.3 The following table shows the prices and quantities in three different used-car markets. Complete the table by filling in the last two rows.

	Market A	Market B	Market C
Assumed chance of getting a lemon	60%	80%	95%
Willingness to pay for a used car	$6,000	$5,000	$4,500
Number of lemons supplied	70	40	90
Number of plums supplied	30	10	10
Total number of used cars supplied	100	50	100
Equilibrium: Yes or No?			
If disequilibrium, will price then rise or drop?			

1.4 We will have a thin market for used cars if the minimum supply price for plums (high quality) is _____ (greater than/less than) the willingness to pay for a lemon.

1.5 Arrows up or down: A decrease in the minimum supply price for a plum (high quality) shifts the plum supply curve _____ and the likelihood of buying a plum _____.

1.6 Suppose you are willing to pay $1,000 for a low-quality used car and $5,000 for a high-quality used car. If there is an 80 percent chance of getting a low-quality car and a 20 percent chance of getting a high-quality car, you are willing to pay _____ for a used car.

1.7 Professional baseball pitchers are like used _____ because there is _____ information: A player's _____ has better information about the pitcher's health and likelihood of injury. (Related to Application 1 on page 318.)

1.8 Your favorite baseball team just announced that it signed a new pitcher from the free-agent market. We expect the new pitcher to be injured _____ (more/less) often than free-agent pitchers who returned to their old teams. (Related to Application 1 on page 318.)

1.9 *Consumer Reports.* You want to buy a used car, specifically a 1999 Zephyr. According to *Consumer Reports*, half the 1999 Zephyrs now on the road are lemons, meaning they break down frequently and generate large repair bills. Consumers are willing to pay $2,000 for a lemon, but $5,000 for a plum. According to Ms. Wizard, "The equilibrium price of used 1999 Zephyrs will be $2,000 in Sourland but $2,600 in Sweetland."

   a. Illustrate with a complete graph for each market.

   b. What is the fundamental difference between the two markets?

1.10 **Fashion and Prices.** You are in the market for a used car and have narrowed your options to two types of cars, type F and type P. According to *Consumer Reports*, the two types of cars have roughly the same frequency of lemons (50 percent). Like other consumers, you are willing to pay $1,000 for a lemon and $7,000 for a plum. The people who buy new F cars are fashion-conscious and purchase a new car every three years. The people who buy new P cars are insensitive to the whims of fashion. Predict the equilibrium prices of the two types of cars and defend your answer with two graphs, one for each type of car.

1.11 **Double Ignorance.** Suppose both buyers and sellers of used cars are ignorant: No one can distinguish between lemons and plums. Would you expect the market to be dominated by lemons? Illustrate with a completely labeled graph.

1.12 **Groucho Club.** Consider a classic quip from Groucho Marx: "I won't join any club that is willing to accept me as a member." Suppose Groucho wants to associate with high-income people (the higher the income the better) and everyone else has the same preferences as Groucho.

   a. Use the notion of adverse selection to explain this quip.

   b. Relate the quip to the adverse-selection problem.

1.13 **Purchasing a Fleet of Used Cars.** You are responsible for buying a fleet of 10 used cars for your employees and must pick either brand B or brand C. For your purposes, the two brands are identical except for one difference: Based on your experience with the two brands, you figure that 50 percent of B cars in the market are lemons and only 20 percent of C cars in the market are lemons. You are willing to pay $1,000 for a known lemon and $3,000 for a known plum. If the price of B cars is $1,800 and the price of C cars is $2,200, which brand of car should you pick?

1.14 Adverse Selection of MP3 Players. Consider the market for used MP3 players, with knowledgeable sellers and ignorant buyers. Half the MP3 players in existence are plums and half are lemons. Each buyer is willing to pay $50 for a plum or $20 for a lemon. The minimum supply price for a plum is $10 and the minimum supply price for a lemon is $2.

  a. In equilibrium, will the market be "thin" or will all the used MP3 players in the market be lemons? Explain and illustrate your answer with a complete graph.

  b. Suppose that at a price of $26, the quantity of plums is 20 and the quantity of lemons is 80. Is this an equilibrium? Explain and illustrate your answer with a complete graph.

1.15 Mix of Lemons and Plums in the Week-Old Car Market. Suppose the value of a high-quality week-old car (a plum) is $20,000 (the same as the purchase price of a new car), while the value of a low-quality week-old car (a lemon) is $10,000. Suppose that at a price of $16,000 per car, 6 of 10 cars on the used market are plums and 4 of 10 are lemons.

  a. How much is the typical buyer willing to pay for a used car in the mixed market?

  b. Is the $16,000 price an equilibrium price? Why or why not?

  c. Suppose that for every 10 new cars sold by new-car dealers, 9 are plums and only 1 is a lemon. Why is the equilibrium mix in the used car market different from the mix of new cars sold?

1.16 Willingness to Pay for Used Baseball Pitchers. Suppose a healthy baseball pitcher is worth $5 million per year to his team, compared to only $1 million per year for an unhealthy pitcher. Suppose that half the pitchers in the league are healthy, and half are unhealthy. According to an executive of a baseball team, "If my assumptions are correct, our team is willing to pay a maximum of $3 million for a pitcher in the free-agent market." (Related to Application 1 on page 318.)

  a. What are the executive's assumptions?

  b. Are these assumptions realistic?

14.2   Responding to the Lemons Problem

2.1 Consider a thin used-car market. Someone just developed a device that can instantly identify the nearest plum in a used-car lot. The device works only once. The maximum amount that a consumer would be willing to pay for the device equals _____ minus _____.

2.2 A money-back guarantee will be provided by the owners of _____, but not by the owners of _____ (lemons/plums).

2.3 Arrows up or down: Government regulations for kiwifruit _____ the average quality and _____ the price of kiwifruit. (Related to Application 2 on page 321.)

2.4 Paying for Information. You are willing to pay $7,000 for a high-quality car—a plum. The current price of used cars is $4,000, and 4 of 5 cars in the market are lemons, meaning that 1 in 5 is a plum.

  a. Suppose you could pay a finder's fee to a personal shopper/mechanic who will find you a plum at a price of $4,000. What is the maximum you are willing to pay as a finder's fee?

  b. As you shop for a used car, you will bring each car you consider to your mechanic, who will thoroughly inspect the car and tell you for certain whether it is a plum or a lemon. If the price per inspection is $400, is it worth the money?

  c. How would your answer to part (b) change if only 1 out of 10 used cars was a plum?

2.5 Money-Back-Plus Guarantee. The equilibrium price in the thin market is $2,600. Suppose car sellers provide a special money-back-plus guarantee: A dissatisfied buyer can return a car for a refund plus $100.

  a. If a lemon owner sells his or her car for $5,000, the owner's gain from providing the guarantee is $_____.

  b. If a plum owner sells his or her car for $5,000, the owner's gain from providing the guarantee is $_____.

2.6 Equilibrium in the Kiwifruit Market. Consumers are willing to pay 10 cents for a sour kiwifruit and 30 cents for a sweet kiwifruit. The minimum supply price for sour kiwifruit is 6 cents and the minimum supply price for sweet kiwifruit is 18 cents. The slope of each supply curve is 1 cent per thousand kiwifruit. (Related to Application 2 on page 321.)

  a. Suppose consumers initially expect a 50–50 mix of sweet and sour kiwifruits. Is this an equilibrium? Illustrate with a graph.

  b. Suppose consumers are pessimistic, expecting all sour kiwifruit. Is this an equilibrium? Illustrate with a graph. What is the price of kiwifruit?

  c. Suppose the state outlaws sour kiwifruit, and they disappear from the market. What happens to the equilibrium price of kiwifruit? What is the equilibrium quantity of sweet kiwifruit?

3.1 Suppose the average annual malpractice cost is $40,000 for reckless doctors and $2,000 for careful doctors. If half of an insurance company's insured doctors are reckless, the company will earn zero economic profit if the price of insurance is $_____. If careful doctors are not willing to pay any more than $5,000 for insurance, the price required for zero economic profit is $_____.

3.2 Arrows up or down: In an insurance market, the presence of high-cost consumers _____ the average cost of providing insurance. The resulting _____ in the number of low-cost consumers _____ the average cost of providing insurance and _____ price.

3.3 Arrows up or down: The European Union ban on gender discrimination in automobile insurance will _____ insurance prices for women and _____ insurance prices for men. (Related to Application 3 on page 325.)

3.4 **Genetic Testing and Insurance Prices.** Suppose the likelihood that a person will get disease X is determined in large part (but not exclusively) by his or her genes. Initially, it is impossible to determine who carries the gene for the disease, and many people spend $500 on special health insurance to cover the costs of treatment for the disease. Suppose scientists uncover the gene responsible for the disease and develop a simple test for the gene.

    a. Suppose the government passes a law that prevents insurance companies from getting the results of a customer's genetic test for X. Will the new price of X insurance be greater than or less than $500?

    b. Suppose insurance companies have access to the results of genetic tests and they require all customers to get the test. How will the insurance company change its price of X insurance?

3.5 **Rising Insurance Rates.** Consider an insurance company that provides group medical coverage for university employees. The company discovered that some of its younger employees had switched to other insurance companies. The company responded to the loss of customers by increasing its price. This is puzzling because you might think the insurance company would drop its price to prevent other employees from switching to other companies.

    a. What is the rationale for increasing the price?

    b. If you change one word in the second sentence, it would be logical for the insurance company to decrease rather than increase its price. What is the word, and why is it decisive?

3.6 **State Auto Insurance Pool.** Consider a state in which automobile drivers are divided equally into two types of drivers: careful and reckless. The average annual auto insurance claim is $400 for a careful driver and $1,200 for a reckless driver. Suppose the state adopts an insurance system in which all drivers are placed in a common pool and allocated to insurance companies randomly. An insurance company cannot refuse coverage to any driver it is assigned, but a driver who is unhappy with the insurance company has the option of being randomly reassigned to another insurance company. By law, each insurance company must charge the same price to all its customers. Predict the price of auto insurance under the two alternative policy scenarios:

    a. Under Policy M, auto insurance is mandatory.

    b. Under Policy V, auto insurance is voluntary.

4.1 In the market for insurance, the moral-hazard problem is that _____ encourages _____.

4.2 While shopping for office equipment, an office manager sees a display of fire extinguishers. After making a single phone call, the manager decides not to buy a fire extinguisher. The manager had called her _____ and asked, "_____?"

4.3 Many professional athletes purchase insurance against career-ending injuries. We expect the insured players to experience _____ (more/fewer) injuries than uninsured players.

4.4 If the single firm providing bicycle theft insurance on campus disappears and is not replaced, we would expect bicycle theft rates on campus to _____.

4.5 Car insurance increases traffic _____ because insured drivers _____. (Related to Application 4 on page 327.)

4.6 **Selling iPod Insurance.** On the campus of Klepto College, half the iPods are expensive (replacement value is $400) and half are cheap (replacement value is $100). There is a 20 percent chance that any particular iPod—expensive or cheap—will be stolen in the next year. Suppose a firm offers iPod-theft insurance for $50 per year: The firm will replace any insured iPod that is stolen. Suppose the firm sells 20 insurance policies.

    a. Assume for the moment that the theft rate remains at 20 percent for both types of iPods. The firm's total revenue equals _____. The firm's cost—the money paid out to replace stolen iPods—will be $_____ to replace expensive iPods and $_____ to replace cheap iPods, for a total of $_____. The insurance firm will make zero economic profit with a price of $_____.

b. Is it realistic to assume that the introduction of insurance will not affect the theft rate? Which is a more plausible assumption, that the theft rate will decrease to 10 percent or that it will increase to 30 percent? For the more plausible theft rate, compute the zero-profit insurance price when insurance is purchased exclusively by the owners of expensive iPods.

4.7 Skydiver Question. Several of your friends have offered to take you on a tandem skydiving adventure: Strapped together with a single set of parachutes (main and emergency), you will all jump out of an airplane and then either float to earth or crash. All your skydiving friends are equally skillful, and none of them has the thrill-seeker gene. You can ask each of them a single question.

a. What's your question?

b. Provide the answer you're looking for in a skydiving mate.

4.8 Insurance and Fire Prevention. In a given year, there is a 10 percent chance that a fire in Ira's warehouse will cause $100,000 in property damage. If Ira spends $4,000 on a fire-prevention program, the probability of a fire would drop to zero.

a. If Ira doesn't have fire insurance, will he spend the money on the prevention program?

b. If Ira has an insurance policy that covers 80 percent of the property damage from a fire (covering $80,000 of the $100,000 worth of damage), will he spend the money on the prevention program?

4.9 Mandatory Insurance. Consider a city with 100 drivers and a perfectly competitive market for automobile insurance. The demand curve for auto insurance is linear and negatively sloped, with a slope of –$10 per customer. At the initial price of $1,500, half the city's drivers (50 drivers) buy insurance. The price is just high enough to cover all the costs of providing insurance, including a 50 percent premium to cover the costs associated with uninsured drivers. Suppose the city makes auto insurance mandatory. Predict the new equilibrium.

4.10 Crop Insurance. Consider a state in which farmers are divided equally into two types: high risk and low risk. The average annual crop loss (and possible insurance claim) is $200 for a low-risk farmer and $1,200 for a high-risk farmer.

a. If all farmers were to buy insurance, what is the break-even price for the insurance company?

b. Suppose a farmer will purchase insurance only if the price (the annual premium) is no more than 50 percent higher than his or her average crop loss. What is the equilibrium price?

4.11 Safety Rebate from the Insurance Company. In 2010 a leading insurance company started a policy that pays a policy holder a 5 percent rebate on his or her insurance premium in any year in which the driver does not file an insurance claim. For example, a household with an annual premium of $1,200 will get a $60 rebate check each year it does not file a claim. Explain the rationale for the rebate policy. What problem is the policy trying to solve? (Related to Application 4 on page 327.)

14.5 The Economics of Consumer Search

5.1 The reservation price is the price at which the consumer is _____ about additional search, meaning that the _____ of search equals the _____.

5.2 If a consumer knows that a product is available at some store at a price as low as $100, it is sensible to continue shopping until the consumer finds the lowest-price store. _____ (True/False)

5.3 Suppose the range of prices for a product is $10 to $20 and your discovered price (lowest price so far) is $16. If you visit one more store and discover a lower price, the best guess for a lower price is _____ and the savings if you discover this lower price is _____.

5.4 As the opportunity cost of search time increases, the reservation price _____ (increases, decreases) and the amount of search time _____ (increases, decreases).

5.5 A doubling of prices _____ (increases, decreases) the marginal benefit of search at a given _____ price, and the percentage gap between the reservation price and the lowest price _____ (increases, decreases).

5.6 A study of consumer search for liquid detergents estimated that a doubling of income decreased the amount of search by roughly _____ (1, 14, 50, 70) percent. (Related to Application 5 on page 332.)

5.7 Compute the Reservation Price. Suppose the range of prices for a consumer good is $20 to $60, and all prices in this range are equally likely.

a. Fill in the blanks in the table.

Discovered price (lowest so far)	$40	$30
Probability of discovering lower price in next visit	___	___
Best guess of lower price	___	___
Savings if lower price is discovered	___	___
Marginal benefit: Expected savings from additional visit	___	___

b. If the marginal cost of search is $1.25, the reservation price is _____.

5.8 Internet and Reservation Prices. Consider a country that initially has no Internet service or telephones, so consumers must travel to stores to get information about prices. Use a graph to show the effects of introducing Internet service on the reservation price for a consumer good.

ECONOMIC EXPERIMENT

ROLLING FOR LEMONS

In this experiment, students play the role of consumers purchasing used cars. Over half the used cars on the road (57%) are plums, and the remaining cars (43%) are lemons. Each consumer offers a price for a used car and then rolls a pair of dice to find out whether he or she gets a lemon or a plum. In general, rolling a big number is good news: To get a plum, you need to roll a big number. The higher the price you offer, the smaller the number you must roll to get a plum. Here is how the experiment works:

- Each consumer tells the instructor how much he or she is offering for a used car and then rolls the dice.

- The instructor tells the consumer whether the number rolled is large enough to get a plum. If the number is not large enough, the consumer gets a lemon.

- The consumers' scores equal the difference between the maximum amount they are willing to pay for the type of car they got ($1,200 for a plum and $400 for a lemon) and the price they actually paid. For example, if Otto offers $500 and gets a plum, his score is $700. If Carla offers $600 and gets a lemon, her score is –$200.

- The instructor announces the result of each transaction to the class.

- There are three to five buying periods. At the end of the last trading period, each consumer adds up his or her score.

ECONOMIC EXPERIMENT

BIKE INSURANCE

This experiment shows the effect of asymmetric information on the market for bicycle insurance. Consider a city with two types of bike owners: Some face a relatively high probability of bike theft, and others face a relatively low probability of bike theft. Bike owners know from experience whether they face a high probability or a low probability of theft, but the insurance company cannot distinguish between the two types of owners. For the city as a whole, 20 percent of bicycles are stolen every year. Here is how the experiment works:

- The class is divided into small groups. Each group represents an insurance company that must pick a price at which to offer bike-theft insurance. The insurance company must pay $100 for each insured bike that is stolen.

- The instructor has a table that shows for each price of bike insurance how many owners of each type (high probability and low probability) will purchase insurance. Using the numbers supplied by the instructor, each insurance company can compute its total revenue (the price per bike insured times the number of insured bikes), the number of bikes stolen, and the company's total replacement cost.

- The group's score for a trading period equals the company's profit, which is the total revenue less the total replacement cost for stolen bikes.

- The experiment runs for several trading periods, and a group's score equals the sum of its profits over these trading periods.

NOTES

1. George Akerlof, "The Market for 'Lemons': Quality Uncertainty and the Market Mechanism," *Quarterly Journal of Economics* (August 1970): 488–500.

2. Eric Bond, "A Direct Test of the Lemons' Model: The Market for Used Pickup Trucks," *American Economic Review* 72 (September 1982): 836–840; Michael Pratt and George Hoffer, "Test of the Lemons Model: Comment," *American Economic Review* 74 (September 1984): 798–800; Eric Bond, "Test of the Lemons' Model: A Reply," *American Economic Review* 74 (September 1984): 801–804.

Public Goods and Public Choice

Meteors regularly enter the earth's atmosphere, and most burn up before they reach the earth's surface or are too small do much harm.

But the impact of the occasional large meteorite—at least 200 meters in diameter—would have catastrophic global effects. In 2012 the European Union initiated NEOShield, a project that will explore alternative responses to the threats posed by large near-earth objects (NEOs). The cooperative project draws support and expertise from Germany, France, Britain, Spain, Russia, and the U.S.

Scientists are exploring three options for preventing an NEO impact: nudge, tug, and blast.

Nudge: Launch a kinetic impactor to strike the NEO and change its velocity so that it arrives at the crossing point with the earth's orbit at an earlier or later time, thus avoiding an impact. A nudge replaces an impact with a near miss.

Tug: Position a spacecraft close to the NEO and use long-term thrusters to maintain a constant distance between the objects and use the gravitational force between the two objects to pull the NEO off course.

Blast: Detonate a nuclear device close enough to the NEO to change its course.

The purpose of the NEOShield project is to study each of the three options and recommend a course of action.

LEARNING OBJECTIVES

- Define a public good and the free rider problem.

- Define an external benefit from a private good.

- Describe the median-voter rule and its consequences for public policy.

MyEconLab

MyEconLab helps you master each objective and study more efficiently.

*i*n this chapter, we'll see that if a particular good generates external benefits, government intervention can make beneficial transactions happen. For example, although everyone on Earth would benefit from a system to deal with NEOs, the cost is so high that no single person would provide it. We will never have such a program—even if its benefits exceed its costs—unless we make a collective decision about what sort of system to develop and how to pay for it. One purpose of government is to help make this kind of collective decision.

This chapter explores the challenges associated with providing goods that generate external benefits. After an overview of government spending programs and tax sources, we'll look at the differences between private goods, such as housing, and public goods, such as levees. We'll discuss various responses to the problem of free riders—people who benefit from public goods but don't pay for them. We'll also discuss the external benefits from education and other private goods. Then we'll show how the preferences of citizens affect elections and decisions in the public sector. Finally, we'll look at some alternative theories on government decision making.

Although it's convenient to talk about "the" government, there are thousands of governments in the United States, and each citizen deals with at least three different levels of government. Figure 15.1 shows the budget breakdown for the three levels of government. The United States has more than 80,000 local governments, including

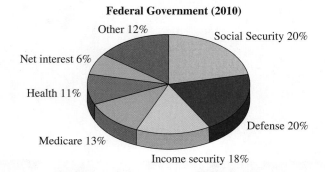

▲ **FIGURE 15.1**

Spending Programs for Local, State, and Federal Governments
SOURCE: Statistical Abstract of the United States, 2008.

municipalities (city governments), counties, school districts, and special districts responsible for providing services such as water, fire protection, and libraries. Local governments spend most of their money on education (kindergarten through high school), public welfare and health (payments to poor households and support for public hospitals), highways, fire protection, and police and corrections. For states, the biggest spending programs are education (including colleges and universities), public welfare, highways, health and hospitals, and corrections (state courts and prisons). For the federal government, the biggest spending programs are programs for the elderly (Social Security and Medicare), national defense, income security (payments to the poor), and interest on the national debt.

Figure 15.2 shows the revenue sources for local governments, states, and the federal government. About two-fifths of local government revenue comes from higher levels of government in the form of intergovernmental grants. The other major revenue source for local governments is the property tax, which is a fixed percentage of the value of residential, commercial, or industrial property. At the state level, the most important revenue sources are intergovernmental grants from the federal government, the sales tax, and the individual income tax. A person's state income tax liability is based on how much he or she earns, with tax rates that typically increase as income increases. At the federal level, the major revenue sources are individual income taxes and employment taxes, which include taxes collected to support Social Security and Medicare.

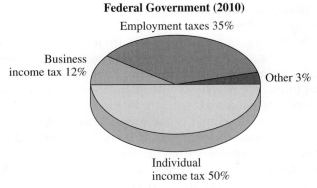

▲ FIGURE 15.2
Revenue Sources for Local, State, and Federal Governments
SOURCE: Statistical Abstract of the United States, 2008.

15.1 External Benefits and Public Goods

As we saw earlier in the chapter on market efficiency, when there are neither external benefits nor external costs, the market equilibrium is efficient. When a government intervenes in an efficient market, the result is inefficiency. In this chapter, we'll see that a market with external benefits is inefficient, so there is an opportunity for government to promote efficiency.

For most goods, the benefits of consumption are confined to the person who buys the good. The benefit experienced by a buyer is called a *private benefit*. In contrast, when someone else benefits from a good, the good generates an **external benefit**. To illustrate the idea of external benefits and inefficiency, consider a dam built for flood-control purposes. One thousand people would be protected by the dam, and each person would get a $50 benefit. If one person builds a dam, the private benefit is $50 and the external benefit is $49,950, or $50 for each of the 999 other people who benefit. If the cost of building the dam is $20,000, no single person will build it because the cost exceeds the $50 private benefit. In other words, if we rely on the forces of supply and demand, with each person considering only the private benefits and costs of the dam, it won't be built.

When there are external benefits from a good, collective decision making generates more efficient choices. In the case of the dam, the total benefit of $50,000 exceeds the $20,000 cost, so the dam is efficient and society as a whole will be better off if it is built. The government can solve this problem by collecting enough tax revenue to pay for the dam. Suppose the government proposes to collect $20 per person to pay for the dam. The tax raises $20,000 in tax revenue ($20 per person times 1,000 people), which is just high enough to pay the $20,000 cost of the dam. Most people will support this proposal because the $20 tax per person is less than the $50 benefit per person. The government can use its taxing power to provide a good that would otherwise not be provided.

> **external benefit**
>
> A benefit from a good experienced by someone other than the person who buys the good.

Public Goods and the Free-Rider Problem

The dam is an example of a *public good*. A **public good** is available for everyone to utilize, regardless of who pays for it and who doesn't. More precisely, a public good is *nonrival* in consumption: The fact that one person benefits from a good does not prevent another person from benefiting. For example, the fact that I benefit from a flood-control dam doesn't reduce your benefit from the dam. Public goods are also *nonexcludable*: It is impractical to exclude people who don't pay. Some examples of public goods are national defense, law enforcement, space exploration, the preservation of endangered species, the protection of the earth's ozone layer, and fireworks shows. If someone refuses to pay for one of these public goods, it would be impractical to prevent that person from consuming or benefiting from the good.

In contrast with public goods, each unit of a **private good** is consumed by a single person or household. For example, only one person can eat a hot dog, so it is a private good. If a government hands out free cheese, is the free cheese a public good or a private good? Although anyone can get in line for the cheese, only one person can actually consume a particular piece of cheese, so the free cheese is a private good that happens to be available free of charge from the government. Similarly, an apartment in a public housing project can be occupied by a single household, so it is a private good provided by the government.

Most public goods are supported by taxes. What would happen if we eliminated taxes and asked people to contribute money to pay for national defense, dams, city streets, and the police? Would people contribute enough money to support these

> **public good**
>
> A good that is available for everyone to consume, regardless of who pays and who doesn't; a good that is nonrival in consumption and nonexcludable.

> **private good**
>
> A good that is consumed by a single person or household; a good that is rival in consumption and excludable.

programs at the efficient level? The problem with using voluntary contributions to support public goods is known as the *free-rider problem*. A **free rider** is a person who gets the benefit from a good but does not pay for it. Each person has a financial incentive to try to get the benefits of a public good without paying for it. That is, some people will try to get a "free ride" at the expense of others who do pay. Of course, if everyone tries to get a free ride there will be no money to support the public good, so it won't be provided.

The flip side of the free-rider problem is the chump problem: No one wants to be the chump—the person who gives free rides to other people—so no one contributes any money. The free-rider problem suggests that if taxes were replaced with voluntary contributions, the government would be forced to cut back or eliminate many programs.

free rider
A person who gets the benefit from a good but does not pay for it.

Overcoming the Free-Rider Problem

Many organizations, including public radio and television, religious organizations, and charitable organizations, raise money through voluntary contributions. So it appears that some people overcome their inclination to be free riders and contribute voluntarily to organizations that provide public goods. The successful organizations use a number of techniques to encourage people to contribute:

- *Giving contributors private goods such as coffee mugs, books, musical recordings, and magazine subscriptions.* People are more likely to contribute if they get something for it.
- *Arranging matching contributions.* You are more likely to contribute if you know your $30 contribution will be matched with a contribution from another person or your employer.
- *Appealing to a person's sense of civic or moral responsibility.* People are more likely to contribute when they are reminded that they benefit from the service.

Note, however, that these organizations are only partly successful in mitigating the free-rider problem. Public radio is one of the success stories, even though the typical public-radio station gets contributions from fewer than a quarter of its listeners.

---

application 1

FREE RIDERS AND THE THREE-CLOCK TOWER

APPLYING THE CONCEPTS #1: How can we respond to the free-rider problem?

In the days before inexpensive wristwatches, most people did not carry their own timepieces. Many towns built clock towers to help their citizens keep track of time. The towns paid for the clock towers with voluntary contributions from citizens. One town in the northeastern United States built a four-sided tower but put clock faces on only three sides of the tower. To most people, this seems bizarre. If you build a clock tower, why not put clock faces on all four sides? It turns out that one of the town's wealthy citizens refused to contribute money to help build the clock tower. The town officials decided not to put a clock face on the side of the tower facing this citizen's house. In other words, the citizen tried—unsuccessfully—to get a free ride. The problem is that other citizens on the same side of town also suffered from not having a clock. In this case, preventing a free ride by one citizen caused problems for other citizens. It also caused inefficiency because the cost of a fourth clock was presumably much less than the foregone benefits to the excluded citizens. **Related to Exercises 1.4 and 1.5.**

application 2

GLOBAL WEATHER OBSERVATION

APPLYING THE CONCEPTS #2: What happens when external benefits spill across international borders?

As another example of a public good, consider global weather observation. In this case, information gathered by one country generates external benefits when it is shared with other countries. Satellites, nomadic buoys, and weather stations monitor weather in different parts of the world, but no single organization gathers all the information to reveal the big weather picture. Another problem is that the uninhabited parts of the world, in particular the vast oceans of the Southern Hemisphere, receive little monitoring. This makes it difficult to observe the interactions between oceans and atmosphere, and difficult to measure any changes in sea level that might be caused by global warming.

In recent years, the United States has taken the lead in encouraging cooperation and the sharing of data collected by different organizations around the world. The experience of coordination in monitoring El Niño, the intermittent ocean current that affects weather in the western United States, is encouraging. According to the National Oceanic and Atmospheric Administration (NOAA), early warnings of a change in the current in 1997–98 reduced damage to the California economy by about $1.1 billion. **Related to Exercise 1.6.**

SOURCE: Based on "Flying Blind: Earth Observation," *Economist,* July 26, 2003.

15.2 Private Goods with External Benefits

In contrast to a public good, a private good can be utilized by only a single person or household. However, some private goods generate benefits for people who do not directly consume the good. For example, suppose I replace the peeling paint on my house with a fresh coat of paint. I benefit from the new paint because it protects my house from decay and my house will look better. My neighbors will also benefit from the improved appearance of the neighborhood. Similarly, if I buy a fire extinguisher and install fireproof roofing, my neighbors benefit because a fire is less likely to spread to their houses.

External Benefits from Education

Education is another private good that generates external benefits. Most of the benefits of education go to the student because education increases productivity and income, and presumably it makes everyday life easier and more interesting. Education generates three kinds of external benefits:

1 *Workplace externalities.* In most workplaces, people work in groups and teamwork is important. A well-educated person understands instructions readily and is more likely to suggest ways to improve the production process. As a result, when a well-educated person joins a work team, the productivity of everyone on the team increases. Higher productivity generally leads to higher profits for firms, and members of the team are likely to earn higher salaries.

2 *Civic externalities.* Citizens in a democratic society make collective decisions by voting in elections, and each citizen must live with these decisions. A well-educated person is more likely to vote intelligently, so there are external benefits for other citizens.

3 *Crime externalities.* Educated people earn higher legal incomes and thus commit less crime. High-school dropouts have relatively low wages and high crime rates, so increasing the high-school graduation rate generates large reductions in crime.

A recent study estimates the external benefits of education related to lower crime rates.[1] For every high-school student who graduates rather than dropping out after 11th grade, the cost of crime decreases by about $1,600 per year for the rest of the graduate's working life. The average cost of one year of high school is about $6,000, so for a one-time expense of $6,000 society gets a crime-reduction benefit of $1,600 per year for 30 or 40 years.

External Benefits and the Marginal Principle

Consider a parent's decision about how much time and money to spend on a child's education. Suppose the parent bases the decision on his or her cost and the child's private benefits—the child's increase in potential earnings as an adult. To be specific, consider the decision on how many books to buy for the child. In Figure 15.3, the marginal private benefit curve shows the extra benefit to the child from each additional book, measured as the increase in future income. Assume the marginal cost of books is constant at $8 per book. Applying the marginal principle, the parent will choose point *a*, where the marginal benefit equals the marginal cost, and buy nine books.

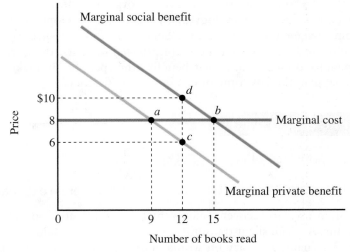

▲ **FIGURE 15.3**

External Benefits and the Marginal Principle

Education (represented here as the number of books read) generates external benefits, so the marginal social benefit exceeds the marginal private benefit. Using books as an example of education, an individual picks point *a*, where the marginal private benefit equals the marginal cost. Point *b* is the socially efficient point, where the marginal social benefit equals the marginal cost.

MARGINAL PRINCIPLE

Increase the level of an activity as long as its marginal benefit exceeds its marginal cost. Choose the level at which the marginal benefit equals the marginal cost.

The higher of the two negatively sloped curves is the marginal social benefit of education. The marginal social benefit equals the marginal private benefit plus the marginal external benefit. As we've seen, there are external benefits from education, so the social benefit exceeds the private benefit. From society's perspective, the best point is *b*, where the marginal social benefit equals the marginal cost. The socially efficient quantity is 15 books. As an illustration, consider the 12th book. The marginal private benefit is $6 (shown by point *c*) and the external benefit is $4, so the marginal social benefit is $6 plus $4, or $10 (shown by point *d*). The social benefit exceeds the $8 cost, so providing the book is efficient from the social perspective. The private benefit of $6 is less than the $8 cost, however, so the parent won't buy the 12th book, but instead will stop with 9 books. The lesson is that when there are external benefits, decisions based on private benefits will generate an inefficiently small quantity of the good.

Because of the external benefits from education, the government uses various policies to encourage people to become educated. Local governments provide free education through high school. States subsidize students at public colleges and universities, providing college education at a fraction of its actual cost. In addition, the federal government provides financial aid to students in both public and private schools.

Other Private Goods That Generate External Benefits

The government subsidizes other goods that generate external benefits. Subsidies for on-the-job training and education encourage workers and firms to invest in human capital and increase labor productivity. It is sensible for the government to subsidize training and education because some of the benefits are transferred to other firms when workers change employers. Another example of external benefits is research at universities and other nonprofit organizations. If a research project provides knowledge or technology that leads to the development of new products or the improvement of old ones, the benefits from the project spill over onto consumers and producers. When there are external benefits, the government can encourage people to take actions that benefit other people. By making beneficial transactions happen, the government can increase efficiency.

application 3

EXTERNAL BENEFITS FROM LOJACK

APPLYING THE CONCEPTS #3: What private goods generate external benefits?

LoJack, a system used to recover stolen vehicles, is a private good that generates external benefits. A small, silent transmitter hidden in a vehicle allows police to track a stolen car. The name is a play on words, meant to convey the idea that LoJack will recover vehicles that are hijacked or stolen. A thief who steals a LoJack-equipped car won't keep the car for long and is likely to get caught, so LoJack is an effective deterrent to car theft. Car thieves cannot distinguish between cars with and without LoJack, so the system decreases the payoff from car theft in general, and criminals steal fewer cars. People who install LoJack systems in their cars generate benefits for themselves and external benefits for other car owners who don't have LoJack.

A study by two economists estimated the private and external benefits from LoJack. The annual cost of a LoJack system is about $100. For a car owner who carries theft insurance, the benefit from a LoJack system is the discount offered by an insurance company, typically well below the $100 annual cost. For every three LoJack systems installed, the number of auto thefts decreases by one car per year. The external benefit from fewer vehicle thefts is about $1,300 per LoJack per year. The benefits are experienced by people who don't buy their own LoJack systems but who benefit because thieves can never be sure whether a particular car is protected by LoJack or not. **Related to Exercises 2.6 and 2.8.**

SOURCE: Based on Ian Ayres and Steven Levitt, "Measuring Positive Externalities from Unobservable Victim Precautions: An Empirical Analysis of Lojack," *Quarterly Journal of Economics* 113 (1998): 43–77.

application 4

THE PRIVATE AND EXTERNAL BENEFIT OF TREES

APPLYING THE CONCEPTS #4: What happens when neighbors benefit?

Mature trees in residential neighborhoods have private costs and both private and social benefits. The initial cost—to purchase a seedling and plant it is relatively low, but the owner's opportunity cost of upkeep (time and money spent watering, raking leaves, trimming) can be large. The benefits—from shade, improved air quality, and aesthetics—go to the property owner and the neighbors. A forest economist estimates that a mature tree adds about $7,000 to the value of the owner's house, and also increases the value of neighboring houses (within 100 feet) by a total of $13,000. Given the $13,000 external benefit, we anticipate that the equilibrium number of trees will be less than the socially efficient number. To address this problem, some cities subsidize the purchase of trees. For example, the city of Portland, Oregon, pays $50 for each new tree. In addition, some cities provide public services such as leaf pickup that reduce the cost of upkeep. **Related to Exercise 2.7.**

SOURCE: Based on Matthew Preusch, "The Money Trees," *The Oregonian*, February 12, 2010, E1.

15.3   Public Choice and the Median Voter

We have discussed the challenges associated with providing and paying for goods that generate external benefits. In this part of the chapter, we study **public-choice economics**, a field that uses models of rational choice to explore decision making in the public sector. We'll start with a model of government decisions based on voting and then look at some alternative models.

public-choice economics

A field of economics that uses models of rational choice to explore decision making in the public sector.

Voting and the Median-Voter Rule

As citizens in a democracy, we pick people to make public decisions. We vote for people to represent our viewpoints in legislative bodies (city council members, state legislators, and congressional representatives), and we vote for people in executive positions (mayors, governors, and presidents). The basic idea of a democracy is that the government will take actions that are approved by the majority of citizens. If governments are responsive to voters, the voting public ultimately makes all the important decisions, and the actions of the government will reflect their preferences.

One concept of public-choice economics is known as the **median-voter rule**. According to this rule, the choices made by the government will match the preferences of the median voter, defined as the voter whose preferences lie in the middle of the set of all voters' preferences: Half the voters want more of something (for example, a larger government budget) and half want less (a smaller government budget). As we'll see, this rule has some important implications for decision making and politics.

To see the logic of the median-voter rule, consider a state where there are two candidates for governor—Penny and Buck—and the only issue in the election is how much the state should spend on education. Each citizen will vote for the candidate whose proposed education budget is closest to the citizen's preferred budget. Figure 15.4 shows citizens' preferences for education spending, with different preferred budgets on the horizontal axis and the number of voters on the vertical axis. For example, two citizens have a preferred budget of $1 billion, four have a preferred budget of $2 billion, and so on. The median budget, which splits the rest of the voters into two equal groups (20 voters on each side), is $5 billion.

median-voter rule

The choices made by the government will match the preferences of the median voter.

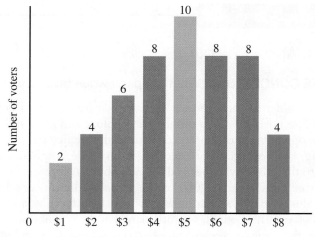

▲ **FIGURE 15.4**

The Median-Voter Rule

If Penny proposes a $3 billion budget and Buck proposes a $7 billion budget, the election will result in a tie. By moving toward the median budget, Penny can increase her chance of being elected. In equilibrium, both candidates will propose a budget close to the $5 billion preferred budget of the median voter.

Suppose the two candidates start out with very different proposed education budgets. Penny proposes a budget of $3 billion, and Buck proposes $7 billion. The 20 citizens with preferred budgets less than or equal to $4 billion will vote for Penny because her proposed budget is closest to their preferred budgets. Buck's supporters include the 20 citizens with preferred budgets greater than or equal to $6 billion. The two candidates will split the 10 voters with a preferred budget of $5 billion (halfway between the two proposed budgets), so each candidate will get a total of 25 votes, resulting in a tie.

Penny could increase her chance of being elected by increasing her proposed budget. Let's say she proposes $4 billion instead of $3 billion. All the voters with a preferred budget of $5 billion will vote for Penny because Penny's $4 billion proposal is now closer to their $5 billion preferred budget than Buck's $7 billion proposal. Penny won't lose any of her other votes either, so she will win the election by a vote of 30 (equal to 2 + 4 + 6 + 8 + 10) to 20 (equal to 8 + 8 + 4). If Buck is smart, he will realize that he could get more votes by moving toward the median budget. For example, if he decreases his proposed budget to $6 billion, the election would result in a tie vote again. Penny and Buck will continue to move their proposed budgets toward the median budget ($5 billion) until they both propose budgets that are very close to the median budget.

Powerful forces pull the two candidates toward the preferences of the median voter. As long as Penny proposes a smaller budget than Buck, the people with small preferred budgets will continue to vote for her. The benefit of moving toward the median is that she can take some votes from Buck. Similarly, Buck doesn't have to worry about people with large preferred budgets but can concentrate instead on the battle for voters in the middle. The result is that by election day the two candidates have adopted virtually the same position: The position of the median voter. Voters trying to choose between two candidates may feel they don't have much choice. In fact, the median-voter rule says the choices made by government will match the preferences of the median voter, regardless of who wins the election.

Although we usually think that people make political decisions by voting in elections, it is also possible to "vote with your feet." In 1956 economist Charles M. Tiebout suggested that a household's choice of which community to live in is based in part on the tax and spending policies of different communities.[2] Households express their preferences by moving to communities that offer the best package of services and taxes. A community with inefficient public services will experience a loss in population, perhaps causing the local officials to make public services more efficient to attract new residents.

It is clear that people vote with their ballots *and* with their feet. In both cases, citizens can express their preferences for public goods, taxes, and public policies. These two sources of citizen power limit the ability of governments to take actions that are inconsistent with the preferences of most voters.

The Median Voter and the Median Location

The logic of the median-voter result also applies to competition among some types of sellers. Imagine a one-mile stretch of beach with 120 swimmers and sunbathers distributed evenly along it. Suppose each person on the beach will purchase one ice-cream cone and is willing to travel up to a mile to get it. If there are two ice-cream vendors on the beach selling identical products, where will they locate?

The most efficient arrangement is to locate the two vendors a half mile apart. We could divide the beach into two half-mile territories and locate each vendor at the middle of a territory. As shown in Panel A of Figure 15.5, Lefty would be at the 1/4 mile mark, and Righty would be at the 3/4 mile mark. If beachgoers patronize the closer vendor, each vendor would sell 60 ice-cream cones. This arrangement will minimize the total travel costs of ice-cream patrons.

Is this an equilibrium arrangement? If Lefty were to move to the right—to the 1/2 mile mark, the median location that splits consumers into two equal halves—he would not lose any of his customers to his left but would capture part of Righty's market. As shown in Panel B of Figure 15.5, Lefty would then be the closer vendor for the people located between the 1/2 mile mark and the 5/8 mile mark. Therefore, Lefty would sell 75 cones (up from 60) and Righty would sell only 45 cones. To protect her market, Righty would move to the median location, too, locating right next to Lefty. By doing so, Righty can recover her 50 percent share of the market, again serving the consumers on the right half of the beach. At any other location, she would get less than half the market, given Lefty is at the median location. In equilibrium, shown in Panel C of Figure 15.5, both vendors pick the median location and each serves half the market.

The outcome of the ice-cream vendors' game is the same as for the politicians' game. Like politicians, the vendors have an incentive to move to the median location, so there is no real difference between the two vendors.

Alternative Models of Government: Self-Interest and Special Interests

Several economists, including Nobel Laureate James Buchanan, have suggested a model of government that focuses on the selfish behavior of government officials. According to this view, politicians and bureaucrats pursue their own narrow interests, which, of course, may differ from the public interest. For example, politicians or bureaucrats may gain prestige from starting a new spending program even if the cost of the program exceeds its social benefit. Because voters don't have much information about the costs and benefits of public services, they may not be in a position to evaluate the actions of politicians or bureaucrats and vote accordingly.

The *self-interest theory* of government explains why voters sometimes approve explicit limits on taxes and government spending. For example, many states have limits on property tax rates and total revenue, and many states also limit total government spending. According to the self-interest theory of government, limitations on taxes and spending are necessary safeguards against politicians and bureaucrats who benefit from larger budgets.

If the two sellers start at the 1/4 and 3/4 mile marks, each
has a territory of 1/2 mile and sells 60 cones:

If Lefty moves to the median location, his territory increases to the
5/8 mile mark, and he sells 75 cones, compared to 45 for Righty:

Righty can recover her lost territory by moving to the median
location. In equilibrium, both sellers locate at the median location
and each has half the market:

▲ FIGURE 15.5

Competition on a Beach Leads to a Median Location for Both Sellers

(A) If one seller starts at the 1/4 mile mark and the other starts at the 3/4 mile mark, each has a territory
of 1/2 mile and sells 60 cones. (B) If Lefty moves to the median location, his territory increases to the
5/8 mile mark, and he sells 75 cones, compared to 45 for Righty. (C) Righty can recover her lost territory
by moving to the median location. In equilibrium, both sellers locate at the median location and each has
half the market.

Another model of government is based on the idea that small groups of people
manipulate government for their own gain. Suppose the total benefit of a dam is
less than its total cost, so the project is inefficient, but a few farmers reap large
benefits from the dam, while the costs are spread over a million taxpayers. The
farmers have a strong incentive to spend time and money convincing policymakers
to build the dam. In contrast, if the tax is only $1 per person, few taxpayers will
make their preferences known to policymakers because the marginal benefit (the
$1 tax savings) is less than the marginal cost (the opportunity cost of their time).
If politicians listen to people who express their preferences and contribute money
to political campaigns, the inefficient project may be approved. This is an example
of a special-interest group (farmers) manipulating the government at the expense of a
larger group (all taxpayers). In general, when a few people share the benefit from
a project and a large number of people share the cost, the government is more likely
to approve inefficient projects.

Whenever benefits are concentrated on a few citizens but costs are spread out
over many, we expect special-interest groups to form. Special-interest organizations
often use lobbyists to express their views to government officials and policymakers.

application 5

THE MEDIAN VOTER IN THE NBA

APPLYING THE CONCEPTS #5: What is the median voter rule?

The National Basketball Association (NBA) uses labor agreements between players and owners to control player salaries. In the absence of a collective bargaining agreement regarding salaries, the market equilibrium would generate very high salaries for a small number of superstar players. Labor agreements are approved by majority rule, and as in other voting environments, the winning proposals reflect the preferences of the median voter, defined in this case as the player with the median salary. To predict the outcome of a vote between two competing labor agreements, we can ask, Which agreement does the median player prefer?

Recent NBA agreements use salary caps and other provisions to shift salary money away from the superstars in favor of less super players, including the median player. For the 1997 agreement, all players with salaries below the median salary gained from the agreement, and the largest gains went to players with salaries closest to the median salary. **Related to Exercise 3.5.**

SOURCE: Based on J. Richard Hill and Peter Groothuis, "The new NBA collective bargaining agreement, the median voter model, and a Robin Hood redistribution," *Journal of Sports Economics* 2 (2001), pp. 131–144.

Which Theory Is Correct?

Which of these theories or viewpoints best describes the actual practices of governments? This is a very difficult question. Economists and political scientists have studied many dimensions of the decision-making processes underlying tax policies and spending policies. There is evidence that people do vote with ballots and with their feet, and that these two forms of voting make a difference. There is also evidence that government officials sometimes pursue their own interests and those of special-interest groups. The field of public choice is a very active area of research for both economists and political scientists.

SUMMARY

In this chapter, we've seen why the government provides public goods. The free-rider problem means that we can't rely on voluntary contributions to support public goods and subsidies, so taxes are necessary to support public programs. We've also examined different views on how governments actually make decisions. Here are the main points of the chapter:

1 When a good generates *external benefits*, collective decision making generates more-efficient choices.

2 A *public good* is available for everyone to consume (nonrival in consumption), regardless of who pays and who doesn't (nonexcludable).

3 A system of voluntary contributions suffers from the *free-rider problem*: People do not have a financial incentive to support public goods.

4 Education generates external benefits in the workplace and in elections and reduces crime.

5 The *median-voter rule* suggests that government choices will match the preferences of the median voter, defined as the voter whose preferences lie in the middle of voter preferences.

external benefit, p. 342

free rider, p. 343

median-voter rule, p. 347

private good, p. 342

public-choice economics, p. 347

public good, p. 342

EXERCISES   All problems are assignable in MyEconLab.

15.1   External Benefits and Public Goods

1.1 Suppose 1,000 people would each get a benefit of $40 from a levee. Building the levee is socially efficient if its cost is less than $_____. If the cost is $30,000, a tax of $_____ per person would generate unanimous support for the levee.

1.2 An external benefit is experienced by _____.

1.3 A public good is _____ (rival/nonrival) in consumption and _____ (excludable/nonexcludable).

1.4 The three-clock tower—a response to the _____ problem—caused inefficiency because the _____ of a fourth clock was greater than its _____. (Related to Application 1 on page 343.)

1.5 **Paying for a Wi-Fi Network.** Consider a small town with 1,000 households. The town could install a wireless Wi-Fi network that would give everyone in town access to the Internet. Each household is willing to pay a maximum of $50 per year for the network, and the cost of the system is $20,000 per year. (Related to Application 1 on page 343.)

   a. Is the Wi-Fi system efficient?

   b. Suppose the town asks for voluntary contributions to support the network. Would you expect the total contributions to cover the $20,000 cost?

   c. Suppose the town keeps track of the contributions and issues passwords to people who contributed at least $20. Would you expect the total contributions to cover the $20,000 cost?

1.6 **Cost Sharing for Monitoring El Niño.** Suppose the monitoring of El Niño's current costs a total of $12 billion per decade. Over a decade, early warning of the current's path would reduce its damages by $9 billion in the United States, $6 billion in Canada, and $3 billion in Mexico. (Related to Application 2 on page 344.)

   a. Does any country, acting unilaterally, have an incentive to monitor El Niño?

   b. Do the social benefits of monitoring exceed the costs?

   c. Design a cost-sharing arrangement that will cause all three countries to support a monitoring system.

1.7 **Defenders of Wildlife.** Each of the 80,000 citizens in a particular county is willing to pay $0.10 to increase the number of wolf litters by one. Each litter of wolves imposes a cost of $5,000 in livestock losses to ranchers.

   a. Is the provision of an additional litter of wolves efficient from the social perspective?

   b. Visit the Web site of Defenders of Wildlife. Then design a system that will generate the socially efficient outcome.

1.8 **Class Participation.** Consider a course with 40 students, some of whom are confused after the professor explains a concept. The professor doesn't know whether students are confused but will clarify the concept if one student asks a question. A student who asks a question—and reveals his or her confusion—loses 10 utils. When the professor clarifies the concept in response to a question, each confused student gets a benefit of 2 utils.

   a. At what level of confusion (measured by the number of confused students) is a question from a confused student socially efficient?

   b. In the absence of participation incentives, will a confused student ask a question when it would be socially efficient to do so?

   c. Design an incentive system to generate efficient questioning.

1.9 **Fireworks as Public Goods.** A three-person city is considering a fireworks display. Bertha is willing to pay $100 for the proposed fireworks display, Marian is willing to pay $30, and Sam is willing to pay $20. The cost of the fireworks display is $120.

    a. Will any single citizen provide the display on his or her own?

    b. If the cost of the fireworks display is divided equally among the citizens, will a majority vote be in favor of the display?

    c. Describe a transaction that would benefit all three citizens.

1.10 **Stream Preservation.** Consider a trout stream that is threatened with destruction by a nearby logging operation. Each of the 10,000 local fishers would be willing to pay $5 to preserve the stream. The owner of the land would incur a cost of $20,000 to change the logging operation to protect the stream.

    a. Is the preservation of the stream efficient from the social perspective?

    b. If the landowner has the right to log the land any way he wants, will the stream be preserved?

    c. Propose a solution to this problem. Describe a transaction that would benefit the fishers and the landowner.

15.2 Private Goods with External Benefits

2.1 A fire extinguisher is an example of a(n) _____ good with a(n) _____ benefit.

2.2 Education generates three types of external benefits: _____ , _____ , and _____ .

2.3 The external benefit of transforming a high-school dropout into a graduate is about $ _____ per year.

2.4 A parent chooses the level of education at which the marginal _____ benefit equals marginal cost and chooses _____ (more/less) than the socially efficient level because the parent ignores the _____ .

2.5 It is sensible for the government to subsidize worker training and education because some of the benefits from training go to _____ .

2.6 The external benefit of a LoJack is about $ _____ per year, compared to an annual cost per LoJack of $ _____ . (Related to Application 3 on page 346.)

2.7 The external benefit of a tree is measured by the change in _____ , and is equal to about _____ . (Related to Application 4 on page 347.)

2.8 **LoJack and Insurance Companies.** Consider the application "External Benefits from LoJack." Suppose all vehicles in a state carry theft insurance. The benefit from reduced vehicle theft goes to insurance companies because they replace fewer stolen vehicles. Insurance companies do not offer any discounts for customers who install LoJack. The cost of LoJack is $100 per vehicle per year. To simplify matters, assume that the private benefit of LoJack is zero, so the social benefit equals the external benefit. (Related to Application 3 on page 346.)

    a. Suppose a single insurance company provides automobile insurance to all vehicles in the state. Will the insurance company provide free LoJacks to at least some of its customers? Explain.

    b. Suppose that there are 20 companies in the state, each with a market share of 5 percent. Will the insurance company provide free LoJacks?

    c. What is the threshold number of insurance companies—the number at which each insurance company will be indifferent about providing free LoJack systems?

2.9 **External Benefits from Education and Deadweight Loss.** Using Figure 15.3 on page 345 as a starting point, compute the deadweight loss associated with reaching the market equilibrium at point a rather than the socially efficient outcome at point b. Notice that the marginal external benefit is constant at $4 per book, so the gap between the marginal private benefit curve and the marginal social benefit curve is $4.

3.1 According to the model of voting developed in the chapter, the choices made by the government match the preferences of the _____ voter.

3.2 The self-interest theory of government explains why many states have limits on _____ and _____ .

3.3 The special-interest theory of government suggests a government will approve an inefficient project if the costs of the project are paid by a _____ (large/small) number of citizens and the benefits go to a _____ (large/small) number of citizens.

3.4 In the example of ice-cream vendors, the vendors choose the _____ location, and this is an _____ (efficient/inefficient) choice.

3.5 The labor agreements of the National Basketball Association favor players with close to the _____ (lowest/average/median/highest) salaries. (Based on Application 5 on page 351.)

3.6 Consider the application on the median voter and public education. (Based on Application 5 on page 351.)

a. Fill in the blanks in the following table.

	Income: Voter 1	Income: Voter 2	Income: Voter 3	Average income	Tax share of median (Voter 2)
A: Median Income < Average	10	30	80		
B: Median Income > Average	10	30	32		

b. Under what scenario is the median voter more likely to vote in favor of public schooling?

c. Consider the scenario that is least favorable to the median voter. Under what conditions will the median voter vote in favor of public schooling?

3.7 **Alienation and the Median-Voter Rule.** Consider the example of the ice-cream vendors on the beach. Suppose people are unwilling to walk more than 1/4 mile for an ice-cream cone. As a starting point, suppose both sellers locate at the median location, the 1/2 mile mark.

a. Fill in the blanks in the following table.

	Location Lefty	Location Righty	Quantity Lefty	Quantity Righty
Starting point: Median location	1/2	1/2		
Lefty moves to 1/4 mile mark	1/4	1/2		
Righty moves to 3/4 mile mark	1/4	3/4		

b. Does Lefty have an incentive to move to the left, to the 1/4 mile mark?

c. If Lefty moves to the 1/4 mile mark, does Righty have an incentive to move to the right, to the 3/4 mile mark?

d. What are the equilibrium locations for the two sellers? How does it differ from the equilibrium when everyone bought an ice-cream cone, regardless of the distance to the nearest seller?

e. Recall the discussion of the median-voter rule. Suppose voters are subject to alienation: A citizen will not vote in a budget election if the difference between the voter's preference and the politician's position is too large. Does the median-voter rule still hold?

3.8 **More Voters.** Consider the example of the gubernatorial election shown in Figure 15.4 on page 348. Suppose 18 new people move into the state and each newcomer has a desired education budget of $9 billion. Predict the proposed education budgets for the two candidates for governor.

3.9 **Change in Preferences and Proposed Budgets.** Consider the example of the election shown in Figure 15.4 on page 348. Suppose the preferences of the four voters who prefer a budget of $8 billion change, with each person preferring $15 billion instead. Will this change in preferences change the proposed budgets of the two candidates?

ECONOMIC EXPERIMENT

VOLUNTARY CONTRIBUTIONS

Do people really try to get free rides? Or would most people contribute at least some money to support a public good? Here is a classroom experiment that helps to answer this question:

- The instructor selects 10 students and gives each student 10 dimes.

- Each student can contribute money to support a public good by dropping 1, 2, or 3 dimes into a public-good pot. Each student has the option of keeping all the dimes and not contributing anything. The contributions are anonymous: No one knows how much a particular student contributes.

- For each dime in the pot, the instructor adds 2 dimes. For example, if the students contribute a total of 40 dimes, the instructor adds 80 dimes, for a total of 120 dimes in the pot. The two-for-one match represents the idea that the benefits of public goods exceed the costs. In this case, the benefit/cost ratio is three to one.

- The instructor divides the money in the public-good pot equally among the 10 students. For example, if there are 120 dimes in the pot, each student receives 12 dimes.

- Steps 2 through 4 can be repeated four or five times.

We can change the experiment to mimic the compulsory tax system. The instructor could require each student to contribute 3 dimes, the maximum amount. Would a switch to a compulsory tax system make the students better or worse off?

DEBRIEFING

After completing the experiment, do the following exercise: Consider the contribution incentives for Margie, one of the 10 students in the experiment. She thinks in marginal terms and asks herself, "If I contribute one more dime, how would that affect my payoff from the experiment?"

a. Answer Margie's question, assuming her contribution does not affect the contributions of other students.

b. If Margie uses the marginal principle to make all her decisions, will she contribute the extra dime?

MyEconLab

For additional economic experiments, please visit *www.myeconlab.com*.

NOTES

1. Lance Lochner and Enrico Moretti, "The Effect of Education on Crime: Evidence from Prison Inmates, Arrests, and Self Reports," *American Economic Review* 94 (2004): 155–189.

2. "A Pure Theory of Local Public Expenditures," *Journal of Political Economy* 64 (1956): 416–424.

CHAPTER 16

External Costs and Environmental Policy

Buildings account for about 40 percent of our consumption of raw materials and energy, and are responsible for about 30 percent of greenhouse gas emissions.

To encourage the construction of energy-efficient buildings, the U.S. Environmental Protection Agency (EPA) awards Energy-Star certificates to buildings that meet certain efficiency targets. In addition, a private organization awards LEED certificates (Leadership in Environmental and Energy Design) to buildings that meet energy-efficiency targets, among other "sustainability" goals. Many states and cities in the U.S. require LEED certification for new commercial buildings and renovations.

How do the market prices of Energy-Star and LEED buildings compare to the prices of less energy-efficient buildings? A recent study[1] shows that the typical building certified under one of the programs sells at a premium of about $5.7 million, or about 16 percent of the purchase price. A certified building sells at a premium because its greater energy efficiency means lower utility bills for its tenants. In addition, there are other unmeasured benefits such as higher worker productivity and a more favorable corporate image. The certified buildings vary in their energy efficiency, and the greater the energy efficiency, the larger the premium: a 10 percent decrease in the actual energy used in a building increases the market price by 1.2 percent.

LEARNING OBJECTIVES

- Use the marginal principle to describe the optimum level of pollution.

- Describe the role of taxation in promoting efficient environmental policy.

- Explain the superiority of taxation over traditional regulation.

- Describe the virtues of marketable pollution permits and the factors that determine their price.

- List three external costs associated with automobiles.

MyEconLab

MyEconLab helps you master each objective and study more efficiently.

*a*s we saw earlier in the chapter on market efficiency, one condition for market efficiency is that there are no external costs in production. The cost of producing a product is confined to the person who sells it. In contrast, when production generates external costs such as air or water pollution, we say there is market failure: Markets fail to allocate resources efficiently. The role of public policy is to intervene in the market to make it more efficient. As we'll see in this chapter, the best response to market failure is not to abandon markets, but instead to use them to reduce pollution in the most efficient manner. We'll discuss two market-oriented policies: pollution taxes and auctions for pollution permits. The chapter's theme is that often the economic solution to market failure is to create markets where they do not currently exist.

One of our most challenging environmental problems concerns climate change. The mission of the Intergovernmental Panel on Climate Change (IPCC), an organization that reports to the United Nations, is to provide comprehensive scientific assessments of the causes and consequences of rising levels of atmospheric greenhouse gases (GHGs). In a recent report[2], the IPCC presents three key conclusions.

1 *Observed changes in climate.* The warming of the climate system is unequivocal, as shown by increases in average air and ocean temperatures, widespread melting of snow and ice, and rising sea levels.

2 *Causes of change.* The energy balance of the climate system has been altered by changes in (a) atmospheric concentrations of greenhouse gases (GHGs) and aerosols, (b) land cover, and (c) solar radiation. Between 1970 and 2004, the GHG emissions from human activities increased by 70%.

3 *Projected climate change and its impacts.* Under current practices (including current climate-change mitigation policies), there is much evidence that global GHG emissions will continue to increase over the next few decades.

To summarize, IPCC concludes that the climate is warming, that human activities contribute to warming, and that under current practices, warming will continue.

The IPCC reports the most reliable projections of changes in surface temperatures and sea levels for the rest of this century. The projected changes are large enough to cause significant changes in economies throughout the world. The anticipated increase in sea level will inundate coastal land., and the anticipated changes in the climate will alter the patterns of winds and rainfall, affecting the production of food and other agricultural products. As we'll see in this chapter, the economic approach to the problem of global warming is to impose a unit tax on greenhouse gases such as CO_2. This approach ensures that any reduction in CO_2 emissions will be achieved in the most efficient way.

16.1 The Optimal Level of Pollution

Should we eliminate all pollution? Although a pristine environment with pure water and air sounds appealing, there would be some very unappealing consequences. To reduce air pollution, we could eliminate trucks, but shipping goods by horse-drawn wagon would result in higher freight costs and higher prices for most products—and a different sort of pollution. We could reduce water pollution by shutting down all the paper mills, but reverting to parchment and slate boards would be unwieldy. Given the consequences of eliminating pollution, it is sensible to allow some pollution to occur. What's the optimal level of pollution?

Using the Marginal Principle

The most convenient way to discuss pollution policies is in terms of pollution abatement, that is, reductions in pollution from some starting level. We can use the marginal principle to determine the optimal level of pollution abatement.

> MARGINAL PRINCIPLE
>
> Increase the level of an activity as long as its marginal benefit exceeds its marginal cost. Choose the level at which the marginal benefit equals the marginal cost.

According to this principle, we should cut pollution to the level where the marginal benefit of abatement equals its marginal cost.

The marginal principle focuses our attention on the trade-offs from pollution—its costs and benefits. From society's perspective, there are many benefits from pollution abatement:

- *Better health.* Cleaner water means less sickness from waterborne pollutants, and cleaner air means fewer respiratory problems and thus lower health-care costs and fewer sick days taken by workers.

- *Increased enjoyment of the natural environment.* Improving the air quality increases visibility and improves the health of trees. Improving the water quality enhances recreational activities, such as swimming, boating, and fishing.

- *Lower production costs.* Some firms are dependent on clean water for survival: Farmers use water for irrigation, and some manufacturers use clean water as part of the production process. Cleaner water means lower production costs for these firms.

On the other hand, pollution abatement is costly because resources—labor, capital, and land—are used in the abatement process. Using the marginal principle, we look for the level of pollution abatement at which the marginal benefit equals the marginal cost.

Example: The Optimal Level of Water Pollution

To illustrate the determination of the optimum level of pollution, consider a lake shared by a steel mill and a fishing firm. The mill dumps waste into the lake, and pollution degrades the fish habitat and decreases the fish harvest. Figure 16.1 shows

▶ **FIGURE 16.1**

Efficient Abatement and Coase Bargaining

The efficient level of pollution abatement, where the marginal benefit equals the marginal cost, is 300 tons (200 tons of waste). If the property rights are assigned to the polluter (steel mill), we start with zero abatement, and the other party (the fishing firm) pays to reach 300 tons of abatement. If the property rights are assigned to the other party, we start with zero pollution, and the polluter pays to increase pollution to 200 tons of waste.

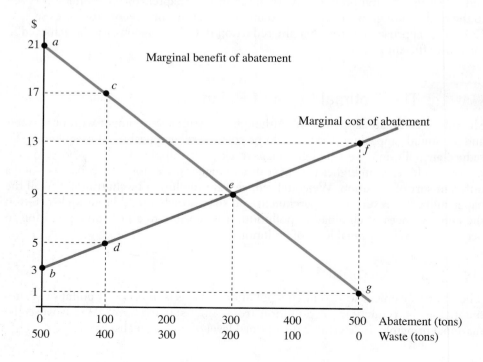

the marginal benefits and marginal costs of pollution abatement. The firm can abate pollution, and the positively sloped curve is the marginal cost of abatement, which increases from $3 for the first unit abated (point *b*) to $13 for the last unit abated (point *f*). The negatively sloped curve is the marginal benefit of abatement, equal to the increase in the fish harvest from a one-ton decrease in pollution. The marginal benefit decreases as abatement increases, from $21 for the first ton of abatement (point *a*) to $1 for the last ton abated (point *g*).

We can apply the marginal principle to determine the socially efficient outcome. The efficient outcome is shown by point *e*, where the marginal benefit of abatement equals the marginal cost at 300 tons of abatement and 200 tons of waste. For any smaller quantity of abatement, the marginal benefit exceeds the marginal cost, so increasing abatement is more beneficial than costly. For example, if we start with 100 tons of abatement (400 tons of waste), the marginal benefit is $17, compared to a marginal cost of $5. Abating an additional ton increases the fish harvest by $17 but costs the steel firm only $5, so additional abatement is socially efficient. At the other extreme, we could have a pristine lake, with zero waste and 500 tons of abatement (points *f* and *g*). This is inefficient because the last unit of abatement (decreasing pollution from 1 ton to 0) has a cost of $13 (point *f*) and a benefit of only $1 (point *g*). Stated another way, the first unit of pollution is less costly to experience ($1) than it is to prevent ($13), so it is efficient to have some pollution. The same logic applies to the 301st through the 500th units of abatement: The marginal benefit of abatement is less than the marginal cost.

Coase Bargaining

Under some circumstances, an external-cost problem can be resolved through bargaining among the affected parties. The Coase bargaining solution, named after economist Ronald Coase, applies to a situation when there is a small number of affected parties, and the transactions costs of bargaining are relatively low.

We can illustrate the bargaining solution with our example of a lake shared by a steel mill and a fishing firm. If the steel mill has the property rights to the lake, it can dump waste into the lake. The fishing firm benefits from abatement, and would be willing to pay the mill to reduce pollution. For the first ton of abatement, the fishing firm is willing to pay $21, the cost of abating the first ton is only $3, and the two parties can cut a deal. If they split the difference between the benefit and the cost, the fishing firm will pay $12 to the mill for one ton of abatement, and both will be better off. The fishing firm pays $12 to get $21 in additional fish, while the mill gets $12 to incur an abatement cost of $3. The same logic applies to the second ton of abatement: The marginal benefit (just below $21) exceeds the marginal cost (just above $3), so the two parties can cut a deal. As shown by points *c* and *d*, the marginal benefit of the 100th ton of abatement exceeds the marginal cost by $12, so there is still an opportunity for an abatement deal. The deal making continues until we reach point *e*, where the marginal benefit to the fishing firm equals the marginal cost to the mill. Beyond this point, the marginal benefit of abatement is less than the marginal cost: The amount the fishing firm is willing to pay for one more ton of abatement is less than the cost of abatement.

How would things change if we assigned the property rights to the fishing firm rather than the steel mill? In this case, we would start with a pristine lake, with 0 tons of pollution and thus 500 tons of abatement. In Figure 16.1, we start at points *f* and *g*. As shown by point *g*, the marginal benefit of the last unit of abatement (going from 1 ton of pollution to 0), is a $1 increase in the fish harvest. As shown by point *f*, the marginal cost of the last unit of abatement is $13. In other words, going from 1 ton of pollution to 0 generates a cost to the steel mill of $13. Reversing direction, allowing 1 ton of pollution would save the steel firm $13. In other words, allowing the first ton of waste would harm the fishing firm by only $1 and save the mill $13, so there is room to bargain. Splitting the difference between the $1 harm and $13 cost savings, if the steel mill paid $7 for the right to dump 1 ton of waste, both firms would be better off: The fishing firm would receive $7 to tolerate a $1 loss in harvest, while the steel mill would pay $7 to avoid $13

application 1

REDUCING METHANE EMISSIONS

APPLYING THE CONCEPTS #1: How do we determine the optimum level of pollution?

Methane is one of the greenhouse gases that contribute to global warming. It is released into the atmosphere from landfills, natural gas systems, coal mining, and livestock management. In this case, abatement of emissions requires methane recovery—capturing the gas before it is released into the atmosphere and then using it to generate heat or electricity. The marginal cost of abatement is less than $10 per ton for the first 36 million metric tons, and increases at an increasing rate, reaching $150 per ton at 69 million metric tons. It is relatively cheap to recover moderate amounts of methane from landfills and coal mines and to reduce leaks in the distribution of natural gas. As the volume recovered increases, however, the abatement systems become progressively more expensive. For example, it is relatively cheap to reduce natural-gas leakage by maintaining surface facilities such as pipelines, but relatively expensive to reduce venting at production sites.

What is the optimal level of methane abatement? It depends on the marginal benefit of abatement. For example, if the marginal benefit is $10, the optimum level is about 36 million metric tons. But if the marginal benefit is $150, the optimum level of abatement is about 69 million metric tons. **Related to Exercises 1.3 and 1.4.**

SOURCE: Based on U.S. Environmental Protection Agency, "U.S. Methane Emissions 1990–2020: Inventories, Projections and Opportunities for Reductions," EPA 430-R-99-013 (September 1999).

---

in abatement cost. The same logic applies to the second ton of pollution: The harm to the fishing firm (just above $1) is less than the cost savings to the steel firm (just below $13), so the fishing firm can cut a deal to allow 2 tons of waste. The bargaining stops at the socially efficient point (200 tons of waste and 300 tons of abatement) because an additional ton of pollution harms the fishing firm by more than it saves the steel firm.

We've seen that assigning property rights to either the steel mill or the fishing firm generates the socially efficient outcome. Once property rights are assigned, bargaining and side payments allow the firms to adjust the level of pollution as long as the marginal benefit exceeds the marginal cost. For efficiency purposes, it doesn't matter who owns the lake as long as *someone* owns it. Of course, the assignment of property rights has important equity implications: Whoever owns the lake collects the side payments from the party that doesn't.

Under what circumstances can we rely on Coase bargaining to generate the socially efficient outcome? In our example, bargaining is plausible because there are only two parties. In contrast, if there were several polluting and fishing firms, bargaining among all the affected parties would probably be unwieldy. In general, Coase bargaining requires a small number of affected parties and small transactions costs (the costs of arranging side payments). When the number of affected parties is large, the bargaining process won't work, and the solution to a spillover problem requires a centralized policy such as pollution taxes, regulations, or marketable permits.

16.2 Taxing Pollution

private cost of production

The production cost borne by a producer, which typically includes the costs of labor, capital, and materials.

The economic approach to pollution is to get producers to pay for the waste they generate, just as they pay for labor, capital, and materials. The costs of labor, capital, and materials are the **private cost of production**, the cost borne by the producer of the product. The **external cost of production** is the cost incurred by someone other than the producer, for example, the cost associated with health problems and premature deaths from sulfur dioxide. The **social cost of production** is the sum of the private cost and the external cost. The idea of a **pollution tax** equal to the external cost per unit of pollution is to "internalize" the externality—to make the producer responsible for the external cost of production. When the tax equals the external cost imposed on others, the externality is internalized. In the example of sulfur dioxide pollution, the appropriate pollution tax is the external cost of $3,500 per ton.

external cost of production
A cost incurred by someone other than the producer.

social cost of production
Private cost plus external cost.

pollution tax
A tax or charge equal to the external cost per unit of pollution.

A Firm's Response to a Pollution Tax

A polluting firm will respond to a pollution tax in the same way it responds to the prices of labor and materials. The firm will use the marginal principle to decide how much waste to generate and how much to abate. The firm will increase the level of abatement as long as the marginal benefit exceeds the marginal cost and stop when the marginal benefit equals the marginal cost.

Figure 16.2 shows an electricity producer's marginal benefits and costs of abating SO_2. The marginal cost is $2,200 for the first ton abated (point a), and the marginal cost increases with the level of abatement to $3,500 for the sixth ton abated (point c) and $4,500 for the seventh ton (point d). The marginal cost increases with the amount abated because the firm must use progressively more costly means to cut emissions. From the firm's perspective, the benefit of abating pollution is that it can avoid paying the pollution tax. The marginal benefit of abatement is the $3,500 savings in pollution taxes from abating a ton of SO_2 rather than discharging it into the air.

◀ **FIGURE 16.2**
The Firm's Response to an SO_2 Tax
From the perspective of a firm subject to a pollution tax, the marginal benefit of abatement is the $3,500 pollution tax that can be avoided by cutting pollution by one ton. The firm satisfies the marginal principle at point c, with six tons of abatement, leaving two tons of SO_2 discharged into the atmosphere.

The firm satisfies the marginal principle at point c, with six tons of abatement. For the first six tons abated, the marginal benefit of abatement—avoiding the $3,500 tax—is greater than or equal to the marginal cost. The firm stops at six tons because the marginal cost of abating a seventh ton ($4,500, as shown by point d), exceeds the marginal benefit (the $3,500 tax avoided). Instead of paying $4,500 to abate one more ton, the firm will instead pay the $3,500 tax.

The Market Effects of a Pollution Tax

Consider the effect of a pollution tax on the market for the product produced by polluting firms. For example, a tax on SO_2 increases the cost of producing electricity because firms pay for abatement and also pay pollution taxes on any remaining waste they generate. As we saw in an earlier chapter on market efficiency, a tax shifts the supply curve upward by the amount of the tax, decreasing the equilibrium quantity and increasing the equilibrium price.

Consider the effects of pollution taxes on the market for electricity. The production of electricity generates two major pollutants:

- **Sulfur dioxide.** Electric power plants are responsible for about two-thirds of SO_2 emissions. As we saw earlier in the chapter, the marginal damage from SO_2 is $3,500 per ton, so that's the appropriate pollution tax.

- **Nitrogen oxides (NO$_x$).** Power plants are also responsible for about one-quarter of the nation's NO_x emissions, a contributing factor in acid rain and the most important factor in urban smog. The study cited earlier in the chapter estimated that the appropriate tax for NO_x is about $1,100 per ton.

Figure 16.3 shows the effects of pollution taxes in the market for electricity. The taxes increase the cost of producing electricity, shifting the supply curve upward. The equilibrium moves from point *a* to point *b*, where the demand curve intersects the new supply curve. According to the electricity study, the pollution taxes would increase the price of electricity from $64.90 to $67.60 per megawatt-hour, an increase of 4 percent. The price elasticity of demand for electricity is 0.28, so the 4 percent increase in price decreases the quantity of electricity demanded by 1.1 percent, from 4,294 to 4,247 megawatt-hours. Like other taxes, the pollution tax is shifted forward to consumers in the form of a higher price, and they respond by consuming less of the polluting good. When consumers face the full cost of producing electricity, they buy less of it.

▶ **FIGURE 16.3**
The Effects of SO_2 and NO_x Taxes on the Electricity Market
The pollution tax increases the cost of producing electricity, shifting the market supply curve up. The equilibrium moves from point *a* to point *b*. The tax increases the equilibrium price from $64.90 to $67.60 per megawatt-hour and decreases the equilibrium quantity.

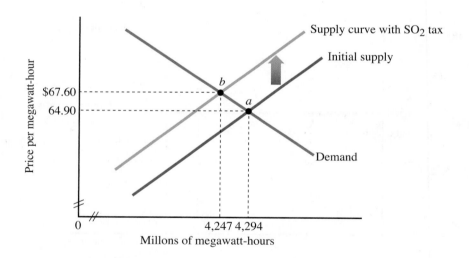

A pollution tax also changes the production process as firms switch to cleaner technology. Figure 16.4 shows the effects of pollution taxes on the energy sources used to generate electricity. Producers respond to the taxes by switching to low-sulfur coal, which is more expensive but reduces their SO_2 taxes. The share of power generated with low-sulfur coal increases from 0.43 to 0.53. The taxes increase the cost of using coal relative to the cost of using natural gas and nuclear power, so the share of electricity from these other sources increases while the share of power from coal decreases. As firms shift to cleaner energy sources, the amount of SO_2 and NO_x emissions per unit of electricity generated decreases.

These pollution taxes decrease the total amount of air pollution for two reasons. First, as shown in Figure 16.3, the increase in the price of electricity decreases the quantity of electricity demanded by 1 percent. Second, as shown in Figure 16.4,

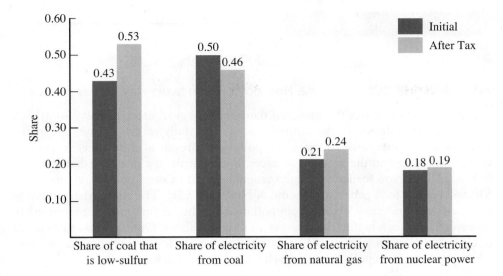

◀ **FIGURE 16.4**
Responses to SO_2 and NO_x Taxes on Electricity Generation
Taxes on SO_2 and NO_x cause electricity generators to switch to low-sulfur coal and to alternative energy sources that generate less SO_2 and NO_x.
SOURCE: Based on Spencer Banzhaf, Dallas Burtraw, and Karen Palmer, "Efficient Emission Fees in the U.S. Electricity Sector," *Resource and Energy Economics* 26 (2004): 317–341.

the shift to cleaner energy sources means that each unit of electricity generates less pollution. The combined effect of these two changes is a substantial reduction in pollution: SO_2 decreases to 11 percent of its initial volume, and NO_x decreases to 30 percent of its initial volume. An added bonus of the pollution tax is that the government could use the revenue from the tax to cut other taxes, for example, the payroll tax or the income tax.

Example: A Carbon Tax

An ongoing environmental issue is how to respond to the problem of global warming caused by greenhouse gases. One approach is to tax carbon-based fuels. A carbon tax of $100 per ton of carbon content would translate into taxes of $0.28 per gallon of gasoline, $12 per barrel of oil, and $70 per ton of coal. The tax on coal would be relatively high because of its higher carbon content.

A carbon tax would reduce greenhouse emissions in several ways:

- The price of gasoline would increase, causing people to drive less and buy more energy-efficient vehicles.
- The tax would increase the price of electricity, decreasing the quantity of electricity demanded and the quantity of fossil fuels burned.
- The higher price of home heating would cause people to turn down their thermostats and improve the heating efficiency of their homes, perhaps by installing energy-efficient windows or more insulation.
- Some electricity producers would switch from coal to natural gas, which has a lower carbon content, and thus a lower carbon tax. Others would switch to noncarbon energy sources such as wind power, solar power, and geothermal sources.

Carbon taxes have been imposed by governments around the world. In Canada, the province of British Columbia has a revenue-neutral carbon tax of $30 per ton of CO_2. The revenue raised from the carbon tax is returned to taxpayers through reductions in taxes on personal and business income. Since 2008, per-capita fuel consumption in the province has decreased by 4.5 percent, and citizens use less fuel—and pay lower income taxes—than elsewhere in Canada. According to local observers, the tax has been good for the environment and taxpayers, and hasn't harmed the economy.[3] In the U.S., the city of Boulder, Colorado has a tax on carbon emissions from electricity. In Europe, there are carbon taxes in Britain, Finland, and Sweden.

POLLUTION TAXES IN RURAL AND URBAN AREAS

APPLYING THE CONCEPTS #2: How do pollution taxes vary across space?

A recent study estimates the marginal damages (marginal external cost) for 10,000 sources of air pollution in the United States. The study reveals substantial spatial variation in the marginal damage from pollution, a result of differences in population densities around the pollution sources. For example, the marginal damage from SO_2 is $220 per ton for an electricity-generating unit in rural Oregon, compared to $10,860 per ton for a generator upwind of New York City. The appropriate pollution tax equals the marginal damage from pollution, so the tax on a polluter in an urban area would be much higher than the tax on a rural polluter. One response to a system of efficient pollution taxes would be to shift pollution to less densely populated areas, where damages from pollution are much lower. **Related to Exercise 2.6.**

SOURCE: Based on Nicholas Z. Muller and Robert Mendelsohn, "Efficient Pollution Regulation: Getting the Prices Right," *American Economic Review* 99, no. 5 (2009): 1714–1739.

16.3 Traditional Regulation

Although the economic approach to pollution is to get polluters to pay for the waste they generate, governments often take a different approach. Under a traditional regulation policy, the government tells each firm how much pollution to abate and what abatement techniques to use.

Uniform Abatement with Permits

To illustrate the effects of regulation, consider an area with two electricity generators, firm L (for low cost) and firm H (for high cost). Suppose that in the absence of pollution-abatement efforts, each firm would discharge two tons of pollution per hour. The government sets a target abatement level of two tons of SO_2 per hour, divided equally between the two firms. Under this *uniform abatement policy*, the government will issue four pollution permits to each firm, forcing each firm to cut pollution from two tons to one ton.

Table 16.1 shows the numbers behind the example. The marginal abatement cost of firm L is $2,000 and the marginal abatement cost for firm H is $5,000. Under the uniform-abatement policy, the total cost of abatement is $2,000 for firm L and $5,000 for firm H, for a total of $7,000. Suppose instead the government imposes a pollution tax of $3,000 per ton. Firm L will respond by abating two tons because the marginal cost of abatement ($2,000) is less than the tax. In contrast, firm H will pay the tax because the marginal cost of abatement ($5,000) exceeds the tax. When the low-cost firm does all the abating, the total cost of reducing pollution by two tons is only $4,000.

TABLE 16.1 Uniform Reduction versus Pollution Tax

		Abatement Cost	
	Marginal Abatement Cost	Uniform Abatement Policy	Pollution Tax = $3,000 per Ton
Low-Cost Firm	$2,000	$2,000	$4,000
High-Cost Firm	$5,000	$5,000	$ 0
Total		$7,000	$4,000

A policy of uniform abatement is inefficient because it does not take advantage of the differences in abatement costs between the two firms. In contrast, a pollution tax encourages abatement by the most efficient abaters. When we treat firms equally in terms of the consequences of their pollution (each pays the same tax per ton), we get an efficient response. The low-cost firm incurs abatement costs to avoid the tax, while the high-cost firm incurs tax costs to avoid costly abatement.

Command and Control

Traditional regulation policies have another dimension that contributes to higher compliance costs. Under a command-and-control policy, the government requires each firm to produce no more than a certain volume of pollution and requires the abatement be done with a particular technology. The problem with this approach is that the mandated abatement technology—the control part of the policy—is unlikely to be the most efficient technology for two reasons:

- The regulatory policy specifies a single abatement technology for all firms. Because the producers of a polluting good often use different materials and production techniques, an abatement technology that is efficient for one firm may be inefficient for others.
- The regulatory policy decreases the incentives to develop more efficient abatement technologies. The command part of the policy specifies a maximum volume of waste for each firm, so there is no incentive to cut the volume of waste below the maximum allowed. In other words, the benefit of developing new technologies is relatively small because there is no payoff from using them. In contrast, a pollution tax provides the right incentives: If the firm develops a new technology that cuts pollution, it will pay less in pollution taxes.

A command-and-control policy causes firms to use inefficient abatement technologies, so production costs will be higher than they would be under a pollution tax.

Market Effects of Pollution Regulations

How do the market effects of pollution regulation compare to the effects of a pollution tax? Recall that the uniform abatement policy achieves the same reduction in pollution at a higher cost because it doesn't exploit differences in abatement costs across firms. In addition, the control part of command and control may lead to relatively costly abatement techniques because there's no incentive to develop better ones. This will cause the supply curve for the polluting good to shift upward by a larger amount than it would with a tax. A larger supply shift causes a larger increase in the equilibrium price and a larger reduction in quantity. The inefficiency of regulations is passed on to consumers, who pay higher prices.

One advantage of the command-and-control policy is its predictability. The policy specifies how much waste each firm can produce, so we can predict the total volume of waste. In contrast, we don't know exactly how firms will respond to the pollution tax—they could pollute a little or a lot, depending on the tax and the cost of abating pollution—so it is difficult to predict the total volume of waste that will be emitted.

Lesson from Dear Abby: Options for Pollution Abatement

We've seen that one problem with traditional environmental policy is that it is inflexible. It doesn't allow firms to use the most efficient abatement methods available. An example of different abatement strategies comes from advice columnist Abigail Van Buren.[4] A person with the moniker "Dreading Winter" sought advice about how to deal with a pollution problem. Her neighbors heated their home with a wood-burning stove, and the smell and smoke from the wood fire gave Dreading Winter burning eyes, a stuffy nose, and painful sinuses. She offered the neighbors $500 to stop burning wood, but

application 3

OPTIONS FOR REDUCING CO_2 EMISSIONS FROM INTERNATIONAL SHIPPING

APPLYING THE CONCEPTS #3: What is the most efficient way to reduce pollution?

International shipping is responsible for about 3% of global CO_2 emissions, and there are many ways to reduce (abate) CO_2 emissions. As a tool for comparing the cost of alternative reduction methods, policy analysts compute the marginal abatement cost (MAC) of each method, defined as the cost per ton of CO_2 abated. For low-cost methods such as propeller maintenance and weather-sensitive routing, the fuel savings cover the cost of the abatement method, so the MAC for these methods is close to zero. For other abatement methods, the MAC are higher:

- Switch from diesel to gas-powered engines: $20 per ton
- Reduce speed and increase fleet size: $90 per ton
- Install fixed sails and wings to tap wind power: $105 per ton

Related to Exercise 3.7.

SOURCE: Based on Magnus Eide, Tore Longva, Peter Hoffmann, Oyving Endresen, Stig Balssoren, "Future cost scenarios for reduction of ship CO_2," *Maritime Policy Management* 38 (2011), pp. 11–37.

---

they declined the offer. The readers of "Dear Abby" offered the following suggestions to Dreading Winter:

- Buy the neighbors a catalytic add-on for the wood stove or a wood-chip gasifier for an oil furnace. In either case, there would be much less air pollution from burning wood.
- Soak a towel in water, swish it around the room, and watch the smoke disappear.
- Leave a saucer of vinegar in each room to eliminate the smoke odor.
- Pay your neighbors to hire a chimney sweep to clean their flue.
- Seal and caulk your windows to keep the smoke outside at a cost of less than $500.
- Use the $500 to purchase an air purifier for your home.

These suggestions demonstrate a fundamental idea behind environmental economics: There is usually more than one way to deal with a pollution problem. The economic question is "What is the most efficient and least costly way to reduce the problem?" In some cases, it may be more efficient to prevent pollution (by modifying the stove or switching to an alternative fuel) than to let pollution happen and then clean up the environment (by using an air purifier). In other cases, cleanup will be more efficient than prevention.

16.4 Marketable Pollution Permits

marketable pollution permits
A system under which the government picks a target pollution level for a particular area, issues just enough pollution permits to meet the pollution target, and allows firms to buy and sell the permits; also known as a *cap-and-trade system*.

In recent years, policymakers have developed a new approach to environmental policy. The approach uses **marketable pollution permits**, sometimes called *pollution allowances*. Here is how a government runs a system of marketable pollution permits:

- Pick a target pollution level for a particular area.
- Issue just enough permits to meet the pollution target.
- Allow firms to buy and sell the permits.

In the policy world, this is known as a *cap-and-trade system*: The government "caps" the total emissions by issuing a fixed number of permits, and then allows firms to trade the permits.

Voluntary Exchange and Marketable Permits

Making pollution permits marketable is sensible because it allows mutually beneficial exchanges between firms with different abatement costs. This is another illustration of the principle of voluntary exchange.

> ## THE PRINCIPLE OF VOLUNTARY EXCHANGE
>
> A voluntary exchange between two people makes both people better off.

Firms will buy and sell pollution permits only when an exchange will make both firms better off. This happens when the firms have different abatement costs.

To illustrate the effects of marketable permits, let's return to the example of the two electricity generators with different abatement costs shown in Table 16.1. Suppose the government issues each firm one permit (one less than the initial level of pollution). In other words, the government will reduce pollution by two tons. Can the two firms make a deal for a permit?

- Firm H is willing to pay a maximum of $5,000 for a permit because that's how much it costs to abate a ton of pollution.

- Firm L is willing to accept a minimum of $2,000 for a permit because that's how much it costs to abate a ton of pollution.

Firm H is willing to pay up to $5,000 and firm L is willing to accept as little as $2,000, so there is an opportunity for mutually beneficial exchange. If the two firms split the difference, the price of a permit is $3,500, and each firm gains $1,500 from the transaction. Firm H pays $3,500 to save $5,000 on abatement cost, for a savings of $1,500. Firm L gets $3,500 but pays an additional $2,000 in abatement cost, for a benefit of $1,500.

How does the marketability of permits affect the total cost of abatement? In our example, the total cost with nonmarketable permits is $7,000, including $2,000 for firm L and $5,000 for firm H. In contrast, when a single firm does all the abating, the cost for two tons of abatement is $4,000 (two tons times $2,000 per ton). The savings of $3,000 equals the gap between the abatement cost of the high-cost and low-cost firm. Making the permits marketable exploits differences in abatement costs across firms, so we get the same level of abatement at a lower total cost.

The first program of marketable pollution permits, started in 1976 by the U.S. Environmental Protection Agency, allowed limited trading of permits for several airborne pollutants. Trading was later extended to lead in gasoline (in 1985) and to the chemicals responsible for the depletion of the ozone layer (in 1988).

The Clean Air Act of 1990 established a system of marketable pollution permits (also known as *allowances*) for SO_2. Under the cap-and-trade program, in 1990 the government issued permits for SO_2 emissions based on a firm's emission levels 10 years earlier. Each company initially received enough permits to discharge between 50 and 70 percent of the volume it had discharged a decade earlier, and over time the number of permits will decrease. Firms can also trade the permits. For example, if one firm has an abatement cost of $140 and a second firm has an abatement cost of $180, the low-cost firm could sell a permit to the high-cost firm at a price of $160, giving each firm a benefit of $20: The low-cost firm gets $160 for a permit and incurs an abatement cost of $140; the high-cost firm pays $160 for a permit but saves $180 in abatement cost. A report from the National Acid Precipitation Assessment Program (NAPAP) showed that being able to buy and sell permits lowered firms' total cost of abatement by 15 to 20 percent.

Each year the Environmental Protection Agency issues permits to existing SO_2 sources but withholds some for auction on the Chicago Board of Trade. In 2008, a total of 125,000 permits were auctioned at an average price of $390 per ton. Individuals and environmental groups are allowed to buy the permits and, if they wish, reduce pollution by withdrawing them from the market. In 2001 a total of 31 permits went to schools and environmental groups.

Supply, Demand, and the Price of Marketable Permits

We can use a model of supply and demand to represent the market for pollution permits. Figure 16.5 depicts a trading system introduced in the Los Angeles basin for smog pollutants such as NO_x. The supply curve for permits is vertical at the fixed number of permits provided by the government. The demand for permits comes from firms that can use a permit to avoid paying for pollution abatement, and the willingness to pay for a permit equals the savings in abatement costs. In Figure 16.5 the demand curve for permits is negatively sloped, meaning that the larger the number of permits available, the lower the willingness to pay for a permit. This is sensible because with more permits and pollution, the marginal cost of abatement will be relatively low. With a fixed supply of 100 permits in 1994, the equilibrium price, shown by the intersection of the demand curve and the 1994 supply curve at point *a*, is $7.

Under Los Angeles's smog program, the number of NO_x permits decreased each year, and in 2003 reached its goal of cutting NO_x discharges to 30 percent of the level attained nine years earlier.[5] In Figure 16.5, the decrease in the number of permits from 100 to 30 shifts the supply curve to the left, increasing the equilibrium price of permits from $7 at point *a* to $21 at point *b*. Polluters in Los Angeles responded to the higher permit prices by abating more. The Los Angeles Department of Water and Power installed abatement equipment—at a cost of $40 million—because abatement was cheaper than buying pollution permits. Libbey Glass Company installed low-pollution burners in its plant, dropping its emissions below the volume allowed

▶ **FIGURE 16.5**

The Market for Pollution Permits
The equilibrium price of permits is shown by the intersection of the demand curve and the vertical supply curve. The supply curve is vertical because each year the government specifies a fixed number of permits. A decrease in the number of permits shifts the supply curve to the left, increasing the equilibrium price.

WEATHER AND THE PRICE OF POLLUTION PERMITS

APPLYING THE CONCEPTS #4: How is the price of pollution permits determined?

The European Climate exchange is a market for the CO_2 allowances issued to European Union (EU) countries under the EU cap-and-trade system. The equilibrium price of an allowance is determined by the interplay of supply and demand. The EU determines the total quantity of allowances issued, and distributes the allowances to organizations in the energy-intensive industries, including iron and steel production, building materials, pulp and paper, electricity generators, and heat generators. The demand for the allowances is determined by a number of factors, including the level of economic activity, fuel prices, and the weather.

The Nordic countries rely heavily on hydroelectric power to generate electricity. In a dry year, the amount of power generated by hydroelectric plants is relatively low, and the Nordic countries shift to coal-fired plants. For example, in the exceptionally dry year of 1996, the emissions from power and heat generation in Denmark were roughly 70 percent higher than the emissions in 1990, a relatively wet year. A dry year will generate a relatively high demand for CO_2 emissions and thus increase the equilibrium price of the allowances. **Related to Exercises 4.5 and 4.10.**

SOURCE: Based on European Climate Exchange (www.ecx.eu).

by its permits. The company sold its extra permits to other firms, generating income for Libbey. The firms that bought the permits from Libbey were able to continue production using their existing abatement equipment.

How do technological advances in abatement technology affect the price of pollution permits? A pollution permit allows a firm to avoid paying for abatement, and the higher the abatement cost that can be avoided, the larger the amount a firm is willing to pay for a permit. A technological innovation that decreases abatement costs will encourage firms to use the new technology to abate pollution rather than buying permits that allow pollution. As a result, the demand curve for permits shifts downward and to the left, and the equilibrium price of permits decreases.

16.5 External Costs from Automobiles

The use of automobiles generates three types of external costs. First, as we saw in Chapter 1, a person who uses a congested highway slows down other travelers, imposing time costs on other people. Second, automobiles generate air pollution, so drivers impose external costs on people sensitive to air pollutants. The third externality is motor-vehicle accidents—collisions with other vehicles, bicycles, and pedestrians. In this part of the chapter, we'll explore various policy responses to these externalities.

External Costs from Pollution

Ozone pollution, more commonly known as smog, is one of our most persistent environmental problems. Smog results from the mixing of several pollutants, including nitrogen oxides, sulfur dioxide, and volatile organic compounds. Smog causes health problems, triggering asthma attacks in the 15 million people in the United States who suffer from asthma and causing other respiratory problems, leading to premature deaths. Smog also retards plant growth and decreases agricultural productivity.

Because of health and other problems created by smog, the EPA has established standards for smog concentrations in urban areas. Nonetheless, in many cities ozone pollution levels rise above these healthful levels.

The Breathmobile provides a visible reminder of the health effects of smog. Started in Los Angeles in 2000, the mobile asthma clinic, housed in a 34-foot recreational vehicle, provides free diagnosis and treatment for asthmatic schoolchildren. The clinic identifies and treats children who experience aggravated asthma symptoms on smoggy days. The Breathmobile program started in low-income neighborhoods and has since spread to other cities.[6]

The automobile is by far the biggest source of smog-causing pollutants. We currently use a command-and-control approach to regulate automobile pollution: The EPA tells automakers what abatement equipment to install in cars. The equipment does not control the total emissions of the car, just the pollution per mile driven. If people buy cleaner cars but then drive more miles, total emissions can actually increase.

The economic approach to air pollution is to internalize the external cost with a pollution tax. Under such a tax, a car owner would have the car tested at the end of the year to determine how much pollution it generated per mile and then pay a tax equal to the miles driven times the external cost per mile. For example, if the external cost for a particular car is $0.02 per mile and the mileage for the year is 10,000 miles, the pollution tax for the year would be $200. The pollution tax would encourage people to buy cleaner cars, maintain their emissions equipment, drive less, and use alternative modes of transportation. The tax is consistent with the idea that people should pay the full cost of driving their automobiles, including the external costs.

One alternative to a direct pollution tax on automobile travel is a gasoline tax. According to a recent study, smog-related damages from automobiles average about $0.02 per mile driven, which translates to an average of $0.40 per gallon of gasoline.[7] Burning gasoline also contributes to global warming, and if the appropriate carbon tax is $100 per ton of carbon, the associated gasoline tax would be about $0.28 per gallon. Adding the $0.40 tax for smog damage and the $0.28 tax for global warming, the gasoline tax would be $0.68 per gallon. This tax would be added to the current gasoline taxes (a federal tax of $0.18 and state taxes that average about $0.22), which pay for highway construction and maintenance. A gasoline tax would be inferior to a real pollution tax because a driver's gasoline tax bill would not depend directly on pollution, so there would be less incentive to drive cleaner cars.

Figure 16.6 shows the market effects of a gasoline tax equal to $0.68 per gallon. The tax shifts the supply curve upward by the amount of the tax, as shown by points *a* and *b*. The new equilibrium is shown by point *c*, with an equilibrium price of $2.00 (up from $1.60) and an equilibrium quantity of 80 million gallons (down from 100 million

▶ **FIGURE 16.6**

The Market Effects of a Gasoline Tax
A gasoline tax of $0.68 per gallon shifts the supply curve upward by the amount of the tax and increases the equilibrium price by $0.40. The tax is shifted forward onto consumers, who pay $0.40 more per gallon, and backward onto input suppliers, who receive lower prices for crude oil.

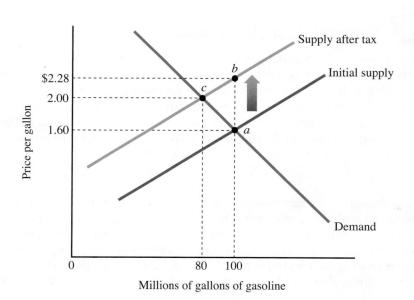

gallons). The increase in price decreases the quantity demanded as consumers drive fewer miles, switch to alternative travel modes—bus, train, bicycle, walking—and switch to more fuel-efficient cars.

The equilibrium price rises by $0.40, which is less than the $0.68 tax. As we saw earlier in the book, a tax is shifted forward to consumers in the form of a price hike ($0.40 in this example) and backward onto input suppliers in the form of lower prices for inputs. The decrease in the quantity of gasoline produced will decrease the demand for crude oil, decreasing its price. In other words, part of the gasoline tax will be borne by the people and governments who own crude oil.

External Costs from Congestion

As we saw in Chapter 1, the typical urban commuter wastes about 47 hours per year in slow traffic and wastes $84 worth of fuel. The economic approach to congestion is to internalize the external cost by imposing a tax on drivers equal to the external costs they impose on others. To compute the appropriate tax per mile driven, we compute the change in total travel time caused by one additional car on the highway and multiply the change in travel time by the opportunity cost of travel time. For peak travel in the typical large metropolitan areas, the external cost is about $0.21 per mile traveled, so a commuter who makes a 10-mile trip during peak travel times would pay a congestion tax of $2.10. During off-peak periods when highways are less crowded, the external cost is much lower, around $0.04 per mile driven. When traffic volume is low enough that everyone can travel at the legal speed limit, the external cost is zero, so there would be no congestion tax.

Modern technology allows the efficient collection of congestion taxes. Under a vehicle identification system (VIS), each car is equipped with a transponder—an electronic device that allows sensors along the road to identify a car as it passes. The system records the number of times a vehicle uses a congested highway and sends a congestion bill to the driver at the end of the month. For example, a driver who travels 10 miles along a congested highway 20 times per month would pay a monthly congestion bill of $42.00 (20 times $2.10). The alternative approach is to use anonymous debit cards to charge for driving on congested roads.

The use of congestion taxes and other time-sensitive pricing of highways is spreading. Singapore uses Electronic Road Pricing (ERP), a debit-card system with charges that increase with the level of congestion. In Toronto, users of the Express Toll Road pay fees that depend on the distance traveled and time of day. The per-kilometer toll is $0.10 (Canadian) during peak periods, $0.07 during other weekday times, and $0.04 on the weekend. Along some highways in Southern California, drivers can pay a fee to use lanes normally reserved for carpools. The toll varies in "real time" from $0.50 to $4.00, depending on the level of congestion, and is highest from 7 A.M. to 8 A.M. and 4 P.M. to 5 P.M.

External Costs from Collisions

A third externality from the use of the automobile comes from motor-vehicle accidents—collisions with other vehicles, bicycles, and pedestrians. In the United States, the annual cost of property damage, injuries, and deaths from traffic collisions is about $300 billion per year. On average, the driver who causes an accident incurs about two-thirds of the costs, leaving one-third as an external cost imposed on others. On average, the collision-related external cost of travel is about 4.4 cents per mile driven. By way of comparison, the fuel cost per mile is about 10 to 15 cents. The direct approach to internalize this externality would be to impose a tax of 4.4 cents per vehicle-mile traveled, a VMT tax. Such a tax would improve traffic safety by reducing the number of miles driven.

Consider two alternatives to the VMT tax. First, the premium for automobile insurance could be based on miles driven rather than being a fixed amount per year. A person who drove less would pay less for insurance, which is sensible because he or she would be less likely to have an accident and impose an external cost on someone else.

Second, a gasoline tax could be imposed. The basic problem is that a person's gas-tax bill depends on the amount of gasoline consumed, not the number of miles driven and the external cost of collisions. Gas mileage varies across vehicles, and a person in a car with better gas mileage would pay less than the external cost of collisions.

application 5

YOUNG DRIVERS AND COLLISIONS

APPLYING THE CONCEPTS #5: What is the external cost of young drivers?

A VMT tax of 4.4 cents per mile would internalize the external cost from collisions on average, but the external cost varies with the age of the driver. The external cost per mile is 11 cents for young drivers (age less than 25 years), 3.4 cents for middle-aged drivers (age 25 to 70), and 5.4 cents for older drivers. A precise VMT tax would involve a higher tax rate for young drivers and generate a relatively large decrease in the miles driven by drivers with the highest collision rates and external costs. **Related to Exercises 5.6 and 5.7.**

SOURCE: Based on Ian W.H. Parry, "Comparing Alternative Policies to Reduce Traffic Accidents," *Journal of Urban Economics* 56 (2004): 346–368.

TABLE 16.2 The External Accident Costs for Different Vehicles and Driver Ages

	Younger Than Age 25	Between the Ages of 25 and 70	Over Age 70
Cents per mile	11	3.4	5.4

SUMMARY

The theme of this chapter is that the best way to control pollution and other external costs is to rely on the exchange principle and markets. A *pollution tax* internalizes the external cost of pollution, causing firms to cut the pollution per unit of output and consumers to buy less of a polluting product. A *cap-and-trade system* for emissions achieves a pollution target at the lowest possible cost because the firms with the lowest cost do most of the abatement. The external costs from automobiles could be internalized with taxes on pollution, congestion, and miles driven. Here are the main points of the chapter:

1 The optimum level of pollution abatement is where the marginal benefit equals the marginal cost.

2 A tax on the emissions of electricity generators decreases total emissions as firms switch to cleaner fuels and consumers buy less electricity at the higher price.

3 Compared to a pollution tax, traditional pollution regulations lead to higher production costs and higher product prices.

4 Allowing firms to buy and sell pollution permits reduces the cost of abatement because low-cost firms do more of the abatement.

5 Urban smog is a continuing problem, in part because the traditional command-and-control policies are less effective than an annual automobile pollution tax.

6 The external cost from traffic congestion could be internalized with a tax that varies with the level of traffic congestion.

7 The external cost from traffic collisions could be internalized with a tax that varies with the likelihood of causing a collision.

external cost of production, p. 361   **pollution tax**, p. 361   **social cost of production**, p. 361
marketable pollution permits, p. 366   **private cost of production**, p. 360

EXERCISES

All problems are assignable in MyEconLab.

16.1 The Optimal Level of Pollution

1.1 The optimal level of pollution abatement is the level at which the _____ of abatement equals the _____ of abatement.

1.2 The marginal cost of abatement typically _____ (increases/decreases) with the level of abatement.

1.3 The marginal cost of abating methane _____ at a(n) _____ rate. If the marginal benefit of methane abatement is $150 per metric ton, the optimal level of abatement is about _____ million metric tons. (Related to Application 1 on page 360.)

1.4 **Optimal Pollution Abatement.** Suppose the marginal benefit of pollution abatement is constant at $12 per unit. The marginal cost of abatement is $2 for the first unit abated and increases by $2 for each additional unit, to $4 for the second unit, $6 for the third unit, and so on. Draw the marginal-benefit and marginal-cost curves and show the optimum level of pollution abatement. (Related to Application 1 on page 360.)

1.5 **Coase and Noise Pollution.** Vivian is trying to learn to play the violin, much to the dismay of her housemates. Vivian and her roommates are willing to bargain over her practice time, and will split the difference between the willingness to pay for noise reduction and the willingness to accept it. The following table shows her marginal benefits from playing for one to five hours as well as the marginal external cost incurred by her housemates (constant at $5 per hour).

Hour	1	2	3	4	5
Marginal benefit to Vivian	$10	$8	$6	$4	$2
Marginal external cost	$ 5	$5	$5	$5	$5

a. Suppose Vivian has the property rights to make as much noise as she likes. How many hours will Vivian practice? Who gets how much money?

b. Suppose the housemates have the property rights to a quiet house. How many hours will Vivian practice? Who gets how much money?

16.2 Taxing Pollution

2.1 The private cost of production includes the amount a firm pays for _____, _____, and _____.

2.2 The external cost of production is the cost incurred by _____.

2.3 The social cost of production equals the _____ cost plus the _____ cost.

2.4 A pollution tax will decrease the amount of pollution a firm generates if the tax exceeds the _____ of abatement.

2.5 A pollution tax decreases the volume of pollution in two ways, by decreasing _____ and decreasing _____.

2.6 The marginal damage from pollution varies with _____, so they are higher in _____ areas than in _____ areas. (Related to Application 2 on page 364.)

2.7 Arrows up or down: A carbon tax will shift the supply curve for home heating oil _____, causing the equilibrium price to _____ and the equilibrium quantity to _____.

2.8 **The Market Effects of a Carbon Tax.** Consider the market for gasoline. In the initial equilibrium, the price is $2.00 per gallon and the quantity is 100 million gallons. The price elasticity of demand is 0.70, and the price elasticity of supply is 1.0. Suppose a carbon tax shifts the supply curve upward by $0.34 and to the left by 17 percent.

a. Use a graph to show the effects of the tax on the equilibrium price and quantity of gasoline.

b. After reviewing the price-change formula in the earlier chapter on elasticity, compute the new price and quantity. The new price is $_____ per gallon and the new quantity is million _____ gallons.

c. Consumers pay $_____ of the $0.34 tax and producers pay the remaining $_____ of the tax.

2.9 Shifting a Tax on Home Heating Oil. You are an economic consultant to a member of Congress. Someone just introduced a bill that would impose a carbon tax of $100 per ton, which would shift the supply curve for heating oil upward by $0.30 per gallon and to the left by 15 percent. The initial (pretax) price of heating oil is $2.00.

a. Use a graph to show the effects of the tax on the price and quantity of heating oil. Will the entire tax be paid by consumers? If not, who else will bear part of the tax?

b. Suppose the price elasticity of the supply of heating oil is 1.0 and the price elasticity of demand is 0.50. Use the price-change formula developed in the chapter on elasticity to predict the new equilibrium price. What fraction of the tax is passed forward to consumers?

16.3 Traditional Regulation

3.1 Compared to a pollution tax, a uniform-abatement policy is _____ (more/less) efficient because it does not exploit differences in _____ across firms.

3.2 The "command" part of a command-and-control pollution policy specifies a _____ for each firm.

3.3 A command-and-control policy is likely to be inefficient because it requires firms to use _____.

3.4 A pollution tax encourages firms to develop more efficient abatement technology. _____ (True/False)

3.5 Arrows up or down: A switch from a pollution-tax policy to a uniform-reduction policy will shift the supply curve of the polluting product _____ and _____ the equilibrium price.

3.6 The lesson from the Dear Abby column is that sometimes _____ is more efficient than _____, and sometimes the reverse is true.

3.7 Arrange the following CO_2 abatement techniques for international shipping in order of increasing MAC (marginal abatement cost): reduce speed, switch to gas-powered engines, propeller maintenance, tap wind-power with sails and wings. (Related to Application 3 on page 366.)

3.8 Options for Abating Noise Pollution. Janis enjoys loud music and is willing to pay $9 for the first song and $1 less for each succeeding song ($8 for the second, $7 for the third, and so on). For her dormmates, the external cost from the noise pollution is $4 per song. (Related to Application 3 on page 366.)

a. Suppose initially the price of songs is $0. How many songs will Janis play? Illustrate with a graph.

b. Suppose the government imposes a pollution tax of $4 per song. How many songs will Janis play? Compute the loss in consumer surplus from the tax, which increases the price of songs from $0 to $4.

c. Janis could soundproof her room, eliminating the noise pollution and her responsibility to pay the pollution tax. If the soundproofing costs $30, is it worthwhile?

d. Janis could compensate her dormmates for each unit of noise pollution—each song played. How much compensation would be required? From her perspective, is paying compensation better than paying the tax, worse, or the same?

3.9 Regulations Eliminate a Market? Consider a market in which the initial equilibrium quantity of a polluting good is 20 tons.

a. Use a graph to show the effects of a pollution tax that decreases the equilibrium quantity to 12 tons.

b. Consider a command-and-control policy that generates the same volume of pollution as the pollution tax but decreases the equilibrium quantity of the polluting good to zero. Use a graph to show the effects of the command-and-control policy.

16.4 Marketable Pollution Permits

4.1 Under a system of marketable pollution permits, a firm with _____ (low/high) abatement costs will buy permits from a firm with _____ (low/high) abatement costs.

4.2 Arrow up or down: A switch from regular pollution permits to marketable permits _____ the total cost of abatement.

4.3 A decrease in the supply of marketable pollution permits will shift the supply curve for permits to the _____ and the _____ equilibrium price of permits.

4.4 Arrows up or down: A technological advance that decreases abatement costs will _____ the demand for marketable pollution permits and _____ the equilibrium price.

4.5 Dry weather in the Nordic countries will _____ the demand for CO_2 allowances and _____ the equilibrium price. (Related to Application 4 on page 369.)

4.6 Split the Difference for a Pollution Permit. Consider two firms, each of which is issued three marketable pollution permits. For firm H, the marginal cost of abatement is $190. For firm L, the marginal cost of abatement is $130.

  a. Is there room for a mutually beneficial exchange of one permit? If so, which firm will buy a permit and which firm will sell a permit?

  b. If the two firms split the difference, what's the price of a permit?

  c. Suppose that after the exchange of one permit, the marginal cost of abatement for the firm that sold the permit is $170 and the marginal cost of the firm that bought the permit is $150. Will the firms exchange another permit, or are they done trading?

  d. What is the savings in abatement cost from allowing firms to buy and sell a permit?

4.7 Reforestation versus Abatement. Suppose your firm commits to reducing greenhouse gases by 11 tons per year. You can pay for a reforestation project that offsets your emissions at a cost of $7 per ton of carbon offset. Or you can modify your production cost to abate pollution. Your marginal cost of abating the first ton is $3; the marginal cost increases by $1 for each additional ton, to $4 for the second ton, $5 for the third ton, and so on.

  a. What's the best combination of reforestation offsets and abatement?

  b. How much money does your firm save by using the offsets?

4.8 No Permits Exchanged? A state issued marketable permits for sulfur dioxide emissions to several electricity generators. Most of the permits were given to the utilities with the oldest generating facilities. One year later, none of the permits had been bought or sold. What could explain the absence of permit exchanges?

4.9 Lower Abatement Cost and Permit Prices. Suppose new technology decreases the cost of abating pollution by half. Depict graphically the implications of the decrease in abatement cost on the equilibrium price of marketable permits. Use Figure 16.5 on page 368 as a starting point, with an initial permit price of $21 (point *b*). What's the new equilibrium price?

4.10 Consider the demand for CO_2 allowances in the European Union. The supply of allowances is fixed, and the initial price is $20 per ton. Suppose that dry weather in the Nordic countries increases the demand for allowances by 6 percent, and the price elasticity of demand for permits is 2.0. Predict the new equilibrium price, and illustrate with a graph. (Related to Application 4 on page 369.)

16.5 External Costs from Automobiles

5.1 A pollution tax on automobiles provides an incentive to buy _____, maintain _____, drive _____, and use alternative _____.

5.2 Arrows up or down: A gasoline tax will shift the supply curve for gasoline _____, causing the equilibrium price to _____ and the equilibrium quantity to _____.

5.3 A gasoline tax will be shifted forward to _____ and backward to _____, such as the suppliers of _____.

5.4 To internalize the external cost associated with automobile emissions that cause urban smog, the appropriate gasoline tax is about _____ ($0.20/$0.40/$0.80/$1.00) per gallon.

5.5 To internalize the external cost associated with traffic collisions, the appropriate VMT tax is about _____ ($0.01/$0.02/$0.04/$0.20) per mile.

5.6 The external accident cost per mile for the typical young driver is about _____ (1/3/6/11/15) cents, compared to _____ (1/3/6/11/15) cents for a driver between the ages of 25 and 70. (Related to Application 5 on page 372.)

5.7 Youngsters Pay to Drive. The demand for automobile travel by the typical young driver (age less than 25 years) is linear, with a vertical intercept of $1.00 per mile and a horizontal intercept of 200 miles per week. Initially, the cost of automobile insurance is a fixed weekly sum, independent of mileage. The average cost of driving—for gasoline, oil, maintenance, and repair—is constant at $0.20 per mile. (Related to Application 5 on page 372.)

  a. Use a graph to show the driver's choice of how many miles to drive, labeled as point *a*.

  b. Use the data in Table 16.2 on page 372 in the application "Young Drivers and Collisions" to show the socially efficient outcome, labeled as point *b*.

POLLUTION PERMITS

In this pollution-permit experiment, students play the role of paper firms that buy or sell pollution permits. The class is divided into groups of three to five students, with each group representing a firm that produces one ton of paper per period. The instructor provides each firm with data about its cost of production. The cost depends on how much waste the firm generates: The smaller the volume of waste, the higher the production cost. Here is an example:

Each firm receives three pollution permits for each of the five trading periods. A firm that does not sell any of its permits to other firms has the right to generate three gallons of waste in that period. A firm that sells one of its three permits can generate only two gallons of waste, and a firm that buys a permit from another firm can generate four gallons of waste.

Gallons of waste generated	2	3	4
Production cost per ton	$36	$26	$20

At the beginning of each of the five trading periods, firms meet in the trading area to buy or sell pollution permits for that day. Each firm can buy or sell one permit per day. Once a transaction has been arranged, the buyer and the seller inform the instructor of the transaction, record the transaction on their report cards, and then leave the trading area. The firm's objective is to maximize profit, and in each trading period we compute the firm's profit with the following equation:

$$\text{profit} = \text{price of paper} - \text{production cost}$$
$$+ \text{revenue from permit sold} - \text{cost of permit purchased}$$

In each period, a firm will either buy or sell a permit, so we compute the firm's profit with just three numbers. For example, using the production cost numbers shown in the table, if the price of paper is $50 per ton and a firm buys a permit for $5 and generates four gallons of waste, the firm's profit is

$$\text{profit} = \$50 - \$20 + \$0 - \$5 = \$25$$

If another firm sells a permit for $5 and generates two gallons of waste, the firm's profit is

$$\text{profit} = \$50 - \$36 + \$5 - 0 = \$19$$

For the fourth and fifth trading periods, several environmental groups have the option of buying pollution permits. Each environmental group is given a fixed sum of money to spend on permits, and its objective is to get as many permits as possible, reducing the total volume of pollution in the process.

MyEconLab

For additional economic experiments, please visit
www.myeconlab.com.

NOTES

1. Piet Eichholtz, Nils Kok, John Quigley, "Doing Well by Doing Good? Green Office Buildings," *American Economic Review* 100 (2010), pp. 2492–2509.

2. Intergovernmental Panel on Climate Change, *Climate Change 2007: Synthesis Report and Summary for Policymakers* (2007).

3. Economist, "Greenery in Canada: We have a winner; British Columbia's carbon tax woos skeptics July 21st 2011, p. 33.

4. Abigail Van Buren, "Aid for Reader's Winter Woe," *Sacramento Bee*, February 15, 1984, http://www.epa.gov/airmarkets/auctions/ (accessed July 9, 2006).

5. Gary Polaroid, "Cost of Clean Air Credits Soars in Southland," *Los Angeles Times*, September 5, 2000.

6. South Coast Air Quality Management District, "New Mobile Asthma Clinic to Serve L.A. County Children," May 12, 2000.

7. Kenneth Small and Camilla Kazimi, "On the Costs of Air Pollution from Motor Vehicles," *Journal of Transport Economics and Policy* 29 (1995): 7–32.

The Labor Market and the Distribution of Income

A key factor in a worker's earnings is educational attainment.

In 2009, the median annual earnings of high-school graduates were $32,600, compared to $56,700 for college graduates.[1] In other words, the college premium—the increase in earnings from earning a college degree rather than stopping with a high school education—was 74 percent. Over a lifetime, the payoff from a college degree was $964,000. Over the last several decades, the college premium has almost doubled.

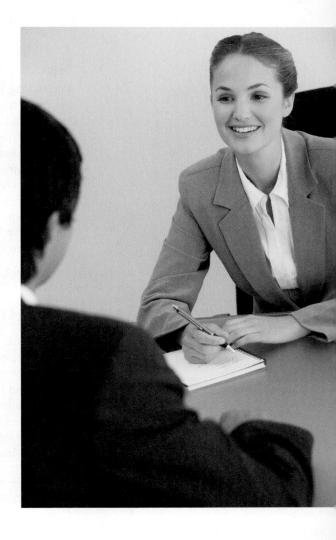

LEARNING OBJECTIVES

- Explain why competition generates wages equal to marginal revenue product.

- Explain why an increase in the wage could increase, decrease, or not change hours worked.

- Explain why wages differ across occupations and levels of human capital.

- Describe recent changes in the distribution of income.

- Describe the effects of government policies on poverty and the distribution of income.

MyEconLab
MyEconLab helps you master each objective and study more efficiently.

*u*p to this point in the book, we have discussed the markets for final goods and services. In this chapter, we switch to the market for one of the factors of production—labor. Labor costs are responsible for about three-fourths of production costs, and for most people labor income is by far the most important source of income. We'll use a model of demand and supply to see how wages are determined and why wages differ between college graduates and high-school graduates, men and women, and people in different occupations. We'll also take a look at recent changes in the distribution of income and the effects of government tax and transfer policies on poverty and the distribution of income.

17.1 The Demand for Labor

We can use demand and supply curves to show how wages are determined and examine how changes in the labor market affect wages and employment. We'll start with the demand side of the labor market, looking first at how an individual firm can use the key principles of economics to decide how many workers to hire.

The demand for labor and other productive inputs is different from the demand for consumer products such as iPods, books, haircuts, and pizza. Firms use workers to produce the products demanded by consumers, and so economists say that labor demand is a "derived demand." That is, it is determined by, or derived from, the demand for the products that workers produce. As we'll see in this chapter, the demand for labor is determined by the demand for consumer products and the price of those products.

Labor Demand by an Individual Firm in the Short Run

Consider a perfectly competitive firm that produces rubber balls. Because this firm is perfectly competitive, it takes the price of its output and the prices of its inputs as given. Because it hires a tiny fraction of the workers in the labor market, it takes the market wage as given and can hire as many workers as it wants at that wage. In addition, the firm produces a tiny fraction of the rubber balls sold in the market, so it takes the price of its output as given. Let's say the price of rubber balls is $0.50.

Consider the firm's hiring decision in the short run, defined as the period during which at least one input—for example, its factory—cannot be changed. We can use two of the key principles of economics to explain the firm's hiring decision. Recall the marginal principle.

MARGINAL PRINCIPLE

Increase the level of an activity as long as its marginal benefit exceeds its marginal cost. Choose the level at which the marginal benefit equals the marginal cost.

The firm will pick the quantity of labor at which the marginal benefit of labor equals the marginal cost of labor. It can hire as many workers as it wants at the market wage, so the marginal cost of labor equals the hourly wage. If the wage is $8 per hour, the extra cost associated with one more hour of labor—the marginal cost—is $8, regardless of how many workers the firm hires.

What is the marginal benefit of labor? The firm hires labor to produce balls, so the marginal benefit equals the monetary value of the balls produced with an additional hour of labor. Table 17.1 shows how to compute the marginal benefit associated with different quantities of labor. The first two columns show the relationship between the number of workers and the quantity of balls produced. Recall the principle of diminishing returns.

TABLE 17.1 Using the Marginal Principle to Make a Labor Decision					
(1) Workers	(2) Balls	(3) Marginal Product of Labor	(4) Price	(5) Marginal Revenue Product of Labor (*MRP*)	(6) Marginal Cost When Wage = $8
1	26	26	$0.50	$13	$8
2	50	24	0.50	12	8
3	72	22	0.50	11	8
4	92	20	0.50	10	8
5	108	16	0.50	8	8
6	120	12	0.50	6	8
7	128	8	0.50	4	8
8	130	2	0.50	1	8

PRINCIPLE OF DIMINISHING RETURNS

Suppose that output is produced with two or more inputs and we increase one input while holding the other inputs fixed. Beyond some point—called the *point of diminishing returns*—output will increase at a decreasing rate.

As we saw earlier in the book, the **marginal product of labor**, the change in output from one additional unit of labor, typically rises for the first few workers and then eventually decreases. To simplify matters, we'll assume diminishing returns start to occur with the second worker. As shown in the third column of Table 17.1, the marginal product of labor decreases as the number of workers increases, from 26 for the first worker, to 24 for the second worker, and so on.

The marginal benefit of labor equals the **marginal-revenue product of labor** (***MRP***), which is defined as the extra revenue generated by one additional unit of labor. To compute the *MRP*, we multiply the marginal product of labor by the price of output ($0.50 per ball in this example):

$$MRP = \text{marginal product} \times \text{price of output}$$

Figure 17.1 shows the marginal-revenue product curve. Because the marginal product drops as the number of workers increases, the *MRP* curve is negatively sloped, falling from $11 for the third worker (point *a*) to $8 for the fifth worker (point *b*), and so on.

marginal product of labor
The change in output from one additional unit of labor.

marginal-revenue product of labor (*MRP*)
The extra revenue generated from one additional unit of labor; *MRP* is equal to the price of output times the marginal product of labor.

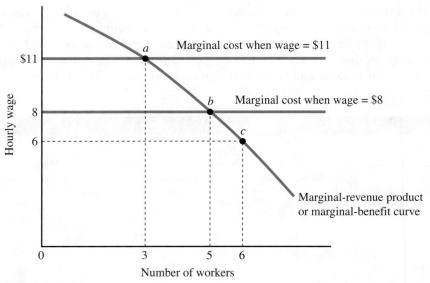

▲ **FIGURE 17.1**

The Marginal Principle and the Firm's Demand for Labor
Using the marginal principle, the firm picks the quantity of workers at which the marginal benefit (the
marginal-revenue product of labor) equals the marginal cost (the wage). The firm's short-run demand
curve for labor is the marginal-revenue product curve.

A firm can use its *MRP* curve to decide how much labor to hire at a particular
wage. In Figure 17.1, the marginal-cost curve is horizontal at the market wage ($8).
The perfectly competitive firm takes the wage as given, so the marginal-cost curve
is also the labor-supply curve faced by the firm. The marginal principle is satisfied
at point *b*, where the marginal cost equals the marginal-revenue product. The firm
will hire five workers because for the first five workers, the marginal benefit (the
MRP) is greater than or equal to the marginal cost (the $8 wage). It would not
be sensible to hire another worker, because the additional revenue from the sixth
worker ($6) would be less than the $8 additional cost of that worker. If the wage
increases to $11, the firm will satisfy the marginal principle at point *a*, hiring only
three workers.

short-run demand curve for labor

A curve showing the relationship between
the wage and the quantity of labor
demanded over the short run, when the
firm cannot change its production facility.

The *MRP* curve is also the firm's **short-run demand curve for labor**, which
shows the relationship between the wage and the quantity of labor demanded in the
short run, when the firm cannot change its production facility. The demand curve
answers the following question: At each wage, how many workers does the firm
want to hire? We've already used the *MRP* curve to answer this question for two
different wages ($11 and $8), and we can do the same for any other wage. Because the
MRP curve is a marginal-benefit curve, and the firm uses the marginal principle to
decide how much labor to hire, the *MRP* curve is the same as the firm's demand curve
for labor. If you pick a wage, the *MRP* curve tells you exactly how much labor the firm
will demand at that wage.

What sorts of changes would cause the demand curve to shift? To draw the labor-demand curve, we fix the price of the output and the productivity of workers. Therefore, an increase in the price of the output will increase the *MRP* of workers, shifting the entire demand curve for labor to the right: At each wage, the firm will hire more workers. This is shown in Figure 17.2. An increase in the price of balls shifts the labor-demand curve to the right. At a wage of $8, the firm hires seven workers instead of five. Similarly, if workers become more productive, the increase in the marginal product of labor will increase the *MRP* and shift the demand curve to the right. Conversely, a decrease in price or labor productivity will shift the demand curve to the left.

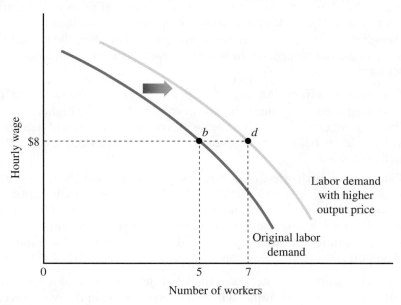

▲ **FIGURE 17.2**
An Increase in the Price of Output Shifts the Labor-Demand Curve
An increase in the price of the good produced by workers increases the marginal revenue product at each quantity of workers, shifting the demand curve to the right. At each wage, the firm will demand more workers. For example, at a wage of $8, the demand for labor increases from five workers (point *b*) to seven workers (point *d*).

Market Demand for Labor in the Short Run

To draw the short-run market demand curve for labor, we add the labor demands of all the firms that use a particular type of labor. In the simplest case, all firms are identical, and we simply multiply the number of firms by the quantity of labor demanded by the typical firm. If there were 100 firms and each hired 5 workers at a wage of $8, the market demand for labor would be 500 workers. Similarly, if the typical firm hired 3 workers at a wage of $11, the market demand would be 300 workers. In the more realistic case of non-identical firms, we use the same technique used for the market demand for a consumer good. We draw the individual demand curves and then sum them horizontally to get the market demand curve. In other words, for each wage we add up the labor demands of all the firms to get the aggregate or market demand.

Labor Demand in the Long Run

long-run demand curve for labor

A curve showing the relationship between the wage and the quantity of labor demanded over the long run, when the number of firms in the market can change and firms can modify their production facilities.

output effect

The change in the quantity of labor demanded resulting from a change in the quantity of output produced.

input-substitution effect

The change in the quantity of labor demanded resulting from an increase in the price of labor relative to the price of other inputs.

Recall that in the long run, firms can enter or leave the market and firms already in the market can change all their inputs, including their production facilities. The **long-run demand curve for labor** shows the relationship between the wage and the quantity of labor demanded over the long run, when the number of firms in the market can change and firms in the market can modify their production facilities.

Although there are no diminishing returns in the long run, the market demand curve is still negatively sloped. As the wage increases, the quantity of labor demanded decreases for two reasons:

• The **output effect**. An increase in the wage will increase the cost of producing balls, and firms will pass on at least part of the higher labor cost to their consumers: Prices will increase. According to the law of demand, firms will sell fewer balls at the higher price, so they will need less of all inputs, including labor.

• The **input-substitution effect**. An increase in the wage will cause the firm to substitute other inputs for labor. At a wage of $4, it may not be sensible to use much machinery in the ball factory, but at a wage of $20, it may be sensible to mechanize the factory, using more machinery and fewer workers. This substitution of other inputs for labor decreases the labor input per unit of output.

The input-substitution effect decreases the labor input per unit of output while the output effect decreases total output. The two effects operate in the same direction, so the market demand curve is negatively sloped.

The notion of input substitution applies to other labor markets as well. For the most graphic examples of factor substitution, we can travel from a developed country, such as the United States, Canada, France, Germany, or Japan, to a less-developed country in South America, Africa, or Asia. Wages are much lower in the less-developed countries, so production tends to be more labor intensive. In other words, labor is less costly relative to machinery and equipment, so labor is substituted for these other inputs. Here are some examples:

• *Mining*. U.S. firms use huge earthmoving equipment to mine for minerals; firms in some less-developed countries use thousands of workers digging by hand.

• *Furniture*. Firms in developed countries manufacture furniture with sophisticated machinery and equipment; firms in some less-developed countries make furniture by hand.

• *Accounting*. Accountants in developed countries use computers and sophisticated software programs; some accountants in less-developed countries use simple calculators and ledger paper.

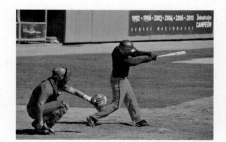

application 1

MARGINAL REVENUE PRODUCT IN MAJOR LEAGUE BASEBALL

APPLYING THE CONCEPTS #1: Are workers paid their marginal revenue product (MRP)?

In 2011, the average salary in Major League Baseball (MLB) was $3.3 million. Are players really worth that much? A team will pay $3.3 million for a player only if the player's marginal revenue product (MRP) is at least $3.3 million. The MRP of a player equals his contribution to the firm's total revenue from ticket sales and television contracts. People are willing to pay for winners, and a player whose performance increases the team's winning percentage increases its revenue from tickets and TV. For example, a player with a relatively high slugging percentage increases the team's winning percentage, increasing the revenue from ticket sales and TV.

A recent study shows that for some types of players, the salary is less than the player's MRP. Some MLB players are free agents, meaning that they are free to negotiate a contract with any MLB team. Given the competition between teams for the services of free agents, their salaries are close to their MRPs. In contrast, two types of players are not allowed to change teams, and the limited competition for their services means that they earn relatively low salaries.

1 Journeymen (3–6 years in the league) are restricted to a single team, but can enter salary arbitration to change their salaries.

2 Apprentices (up to 3 years in the league) are restricted to a single team and cannot change their salaries.

Given the immobility of journeymen and apprentices, we expect them to be paid less than their MRPs. According to a recent study, the average MRP of journeymen is about $1.08 million, which is about 17 percent higher than the average journeyman salary. For apprentices, the average MRP is about $810,000, which is about 3.6 times the average apprentice salary. **Related to Exercise 1.7.**

SOURCE: Based on Anthony Krautmann, "What's Wrong with Scully-Estimates of a Player's Marginal Revenue Product," *Economic Inquiry* 37 (1999), pp. 369–381.

Short-Run versus Long-Run Demand

How does the short-run demand curve for labor compare to the long-run demand curve? There is less flexibility in the short run because firms cannot enter or leave the market and they cannot modify their production facilities. As a result, the demand for labor is less elastic in the short run. That means the short-run demand curve is steeper than the long-run demand curve. In the chapter on perfect competition we used the same logic to explain why the short-run supply curve for a product (plain cotton T-shirts) was steeper than the long-run supply curve for the product.

17.2 The Supply of Labor

The labor-supply curve answers the following question: How many hours of labor will be supplied at each wage? When we speak of a labor market, we are referring to the market for a specific occupation in a specific geographical area. Consider the supply for nurses in the hypothetical city of Florence. The supply question is "How many hours of nursing services will be supplied at each wage?" To answer that question, we must think about how many nurses are in the city and how many hours each nurse works.

The Individual Labor-Supply Decision: How Many Hours?

Let's start with an individual's decision about how many hours to work. The decision to work is a decision to sacrifice some leisure time for money: Each hour of work reduces leisure time by one hour. Therefore, the demand for leisure is the flip side of the supply of labor. The price of leisure time is the income sacrificed for each hour of leisure, that is, the hourly wage. We know from earlier chapters that an increase in the price of a good has two effects: a substitution effect and an income effect. An increase in the wage—the price of leisure—has two effects on the demand for leisure.

substitution effect for leisure demand

The change in leisure time resulting from a change in the wage (the price of leisure) relative to the price of other goods.

Consider first the **substitution effect for leisure demand**. The worker faces a trade-off between leisure time and consumer goods such as music, books, food, and entertainment. For each hour of leisure time Leah takes, she loses one hour of work time, and her income drops by an amount equal to the wage. Therefore, she has less money to spend on consumer goods. For example, if the wage is $8 per hour, each hour of leisure decreases the amount of income available to spend on consumer goods by $8. When the wage increases to, say, $10, Leah will sacrifice more income—and consumer goods—for each hour of leisure she takes. Given the larger sacrifice of consumer goods per hour of leisure time, she will demand less leisure. That means she will work more hours and earn more money for consumer goods. In other words, as the wage increases, she will substitute income—and the consumer goods it buys—for leisure time.

income effect for leisure demand

The change in leisure time resulting from a change in real income caused by a change in the wage.

Consider next the **income effect for leisure demand**. For most people, leisure is a normal good in the sense that the demand for leisure increases as real income increases. An increase in the wage increases Leah's real income in the sense that she can afford more of all goods, including leisure time. Suppose Leah has a total of 100 hours per week to divide between leisure and work. At a wage of $10, she works 36 hours and has 64 hours of leisure. She also earns $360 ($10 per hour times 36 hours of work) and spends that amount on consumer goods. If her wage increases to $15, her real income increases because she can have more consumer goods and more leisure time. For example, if she worked only 30 hours, she could buy $450 worth of consumer goods ($15 per hour times 30 hours) and have 70 hours of leisure (100 hours per week minus 30 hours of work). The increase in real income causes Leah to consume more of all normal goods, including leisure time. The increase in real income causes her to demand more leisure and supply less labor.

In the labor market, the income and substitution effects of an increase in wages operate in opposite directions. The substitution effect decreases the desired leisure time, while the income effect increases the desired leisure time. Therefore, we can't predict whether an increase in the wage will cause a worker to demand more leisure time (supply less labor) or less leisure (supply more labor).

An Example of Income and Substitution Effects

A simple example will show why we can't predict a worker's response to an increase in the wage. Suppose each nurse in Florence initially works 36 hours per week at an hourly wage of $10 and the wage increases to $12. The following are three reasonable responses to the higher wage:

1 *Lester works fewer hours*. If Lester works 30 hours instead of 36 hours, he gets 6 hours of extra leisure time and still earns the same income per week ($360 = 30 hours × $12 per hour).

2 *Sam works the same number of hours*. If Sam continues to work 36 hours per week, he gets an additional $72 of income ($2 per hour × 36 hours) and the same amount of leisure time.

3 *Maureen works more hours*. If Maureen works 43 hours instead of 36 hours, she sacrifices 7 hours of leisure time but earns a total of $516, compared to only $360 at a wage of $10 per hour.

Empirical studies of the labor market confirm that each of these responses is reasonable. When the wage increases, some people work more, others work less, and others work about the same amount. At the market level, the aggregate response to an increase in the wage varies across markets.

The Market Supply Curve for Labor

Now that we know how individual workers respond to changes in wages, we're ready to consider the supply side of the labor market. The **market supply curve for labor** shows the relationship between the wage and the quantity of labor supplied. In Figure 17.3, the market supply curve for labor is positively sloped, consistent with the law of supply: There is a positive relationship between the wage (the price of labor) and the quantity of labor supplied, *ceteris paribus*. An increase in the wage affects the quantity of nursing supplied in three ways:

market supply curve for labor
A curve showing the relationship between the wage and the quantity of labor supplied.

1 **Hours worked per employee.** When the wage increases, some nurses will work more hours, some will work fewer hours, and some will work the same number of hours. We don't know for certain whether the average number of work hours will increase, decrease, or stay the same, but the change in the average number of hours worked is likely to be relatively small.

2 **Occupational choice.** An increase in the nursing wage will cause some workers to switch from other occupations to nursing and motivate more new workers to pick nursing over other occupations.

3 **Migration.** Some nurses in other cities will move to Florence to earn the higher wages offered there.

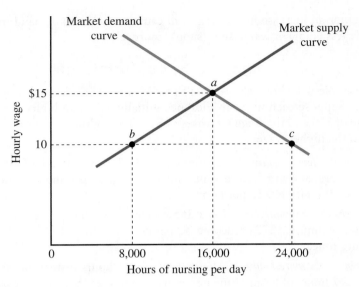

▲ FIGURE 17.3

Supply, Demand, and Labor Market Equilibrium

At the market equilibrium shown by point *a*, the wage is $15 per hour and the quantity of labor is 16,000 hours. The quantity supplied equals the quantity demanded, so there is neither excess demand for labor nor excess supply of labor.

application 2

CABBIES RESPOND TO AN INCREASE IN THE WAGE

APPLYING THE CONCEPTS #2: When the wage increases, will the typical person work more hours or fewer hours?

Taxi drivers have a lot of flexibility in choosing their work hours, and we can readily observe their response to an increase in the wage. An increase in the taxi fare, which is regulated by cities, represents an increase in the wage earned by taxi drivers. A recent study of the taxi market in New York City shows that an increase in the regulated fare (an increase in the wage) actually decreases the quantity of labor supplied. In 2004 a 19 percent increase in the regulated fare decreased the miles driven per cabbie by 5.6 percent. Overall, the elasticity of miles driven (quantity of labor supplied) with respect to the fare per mile (the wage) is –0.22. In other words, a 10 percent increase in the wage decreases the quantity of labor supplied by 2.2 percent. **Related to Exercises 2.6 and 2.11.**

SOURCE: Based on Orley Ashenfelter, Kork Doran, Bruce Schaller," A Shred of Credible Evidence on the Long Run Elasticity of Labor Supply" (working Paper 551, Industrial Relations Section, Princeton University, 2009).

The second and third effects reinforce one another, so an increase in the wage causes movement upward along the market supply curve. If the wage of Florence nurses increases from $10 to $15 per hour, the quantity of nurses supplied increases from 8,000 hours per day (point *b*) to 16,000 hours per day (point *a*). Although individual workers may not work more hours as the wage increases, the supply curve is positively sloped because an increase in the wage changes workers' occupational choices and causes migration.

17.3 Labor Market Equilibrium

We're ready to put demand and supply together to think about equilibrium in the labor market. A market equilibrium is a situation in which there is no pressure to change the price of a good or service. Figure 17.3 shows the equilibrium in the market for nurses. The supply curve intersects the demand curve at point *a*, so the equilibrium wage is $15 per hour and the equilibrium quantity is 16,000 hours of nursing per day. At this wage, there is neither an excess demand for labor nor an excess supply of labor, so the market has reached an equilibrium.

Changes in Demand and Supply

How would a change in the demand for nurses affect the equilibrium wage of nurses? We know from Chapter 4 that a change in demand causes the equilibrium price and the equilibrium quantity to move in the same direction: An increase in demand increases the equilibrium price and quantity, whereas a decrease in demand decreases the equilibrium price and quantity. For example, suppose the demand for medical care increases. Nurses help to provide medical care, so an increase in the quantity of medical care demanded will shift the demand curve for nurses to the right: At each wage, firms will demand more hours of nursing services. As shown in Figure 17.4, an increase in demand increases the equilibrium wage and the equilibrium quantity of nursing services.

▲ FIGURE 17.4
The Market Effect of an Increase in Demand for Labor
An increase in the demand for nursing services shifts the demand curve to the right, moving the equilibrium from point *a* to point *b*. The equilibrium wage increases from $15 to $17 per hour, and the equilibrium quantity increases from 16,000 hours to 19,000 hours.

How would a change in supply of nurses affect the equilibrium wage of nurses? We know from Chapter 4 that a change in supply causes price and quantity to move in opposite directions: An increase in supply decreases the equilibrium price but increases the equilibrium quantity, whereas a decrease in supply increases the equilibrium price but decreases the equilibrium quantity. Suppose a new television program makes nursing look like an attractive occupation, causing a large number of young people to become nurses rather than accountants, lawyers, or doctors. The supply curve for nurses will shift to the right: At each wage, more nursing hours will be supplied. The equilibrium wage will decrease, and the equilibrium quantity will increase.

The Market Effects of the Minimum Wage

We can use the model of the labor market to show how various public policies, such as the federally mandated minimum wage, affect total employment. In 2012 the federal minimum wage was $7.25 per hour. Figure 17.5 shows the effects of a minimum wage on the market for restaurant workers. The market equilibrium is shown by point *a*: The supply of restaurant workers equals demand at a wage of $6.05 and a quantity of 50,000 worker hours per day. Suppose a minimum wage is established at $7.25 per hour. At this wage, the quantity of labor demanded is only 49,000 hours (point *b* on the demand curve). In other words, the minimum wage decreases the quantity of labor restaurants use by 1,000 hours per day.

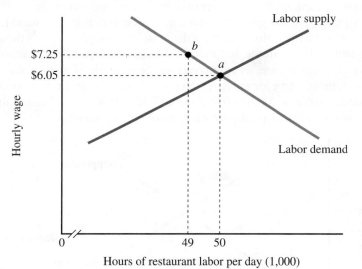

▲ FIGURE 17.5

The Market Effects of a Minimum Wage

The market equilibrium is shown by point *a*: The wage is $6.05 per hour, and the quantity of labor is 50,000 hours. A minimum wage of $7.25 decreases the quantity of labor demanded to 49,000 hours per day (point *b*). Although some workers receive a higher wage, others lose their jobs or work fewer hours.

What are the trade-offs associated with the minimum wage? For restaurant workers and restaurant diners, there is good news and bad news:

- *Good news for some restaurant workers.* Some workers keep their jobs and receive a higher wage ($7.25 per hour instead of $6.05 per hour).

- ***Bad news for some restaurant workers.*** Some workers lose their jobs. If the typical workday for restaurant workers is 5 hours, the loss of 1,000 hours of restaurant work per day translates into a loss of 200 jobs.
- ***Bad news for diners.*** The increase in the wage increases the cost of producing restaurant meals, increasing the price of meals.

There are winners and losers from the minimum wage. Workers who keep their jobs gain at the expense of other workers and at the expense of diners. A recent study suggests that a 10 percent increase in the minimum wage decreases the number of minimum wage jobs by about 1 percent.[2]

Why Do Wages Differ across Occupations?

There is substantial variation in wages across occupations. Most professional athletes earn more than medical doctors, who earn more than college professors, who earn more than janitors. We'll see that the wage for a particular occupation will be high if the supply of workers in that occupation is small relative to the demand for those workers. This is shown in Figure 17.6, where the supply curve intersects the demand curve at a high wage. The supply of workers in a particular occupation could be small for four reasons:

1 ***Few people with the required skills.*** To play professional baseball, people must be able to hit balls thrown at them at about 90 miles per hour. The few people who have this skill are paid a lot of money, because baseball owners compete with one

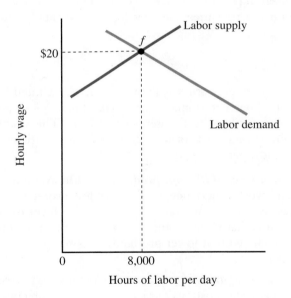

▲ FIGURE 17.6

The Equilibrium Wage When Labor Supply Is Low Relative to Demand

If supply is low relative to demand—because few people have the skills, training costs are high, or the job is undesirable—the equilibrium wage will be high.

another for skillful players, bidding up the wage. The same logic applies to other professional athletes, musicians, and actors. The few people who have the skills required for these occupations are paid high wages.

2 *High training costs.* The skills required for some occupations can be acquired only through education and training. For example, the skills required of a medical doctor call for medical school training, and legal skills must be acquired in law school. If it is costly to acquire these skills, a relatively small number of people will become skilled, and they will receive high wages. The higher wage compensates workers for their training costs.

3 *Undesirable working conditions.* Some occupations have undesirable working conditions, and workers demand higher wages as compensation. Wages are higher for jobs that are dirty or stressful or require people to work at odd hours.

4 *Danger.* Some jobs are dangerous, and wages are higher to compensate for the risk of injury or death. The workers with the greatest risk of losing their lives on the job are lumberjacks, boilermakers, taxicab drivers, and mine workers. To compensate for the higher risk of getting killed on the job, steelworkers receive a wage premium of 3.7 percent. In the United States, the average job fatality rate is 1 in 25,000 workers per year. For a worker who faces twice the average fatality rate, the wage is about 1 percent higher. The wage premium for jobs with an annual injury rate of 2 percent is 1.15 percent for men and 3.68 percent for women.[3]

5 *Artificial barriers to entry.* As we'll see in the next chapter, government and professional licensing boards restrict the number of people in certain occupations, and labor unions restrict their membership. These supply restrictions increase wages.

The Gender Pay Gap

Why do women, on average, earn less than men? In the United States, the typical woman earns about 80 percent as much as the typical man.[4] A recent study explored several factors that contribute to the gender pay gap.[5] The study observed a gap of about 20 percent among workers aged 26 to 34, and identified four factors that contribute to the gender gap:

• *Difference in worker skills and productivity.* On average, women have less education and work experience, so they are less productive and thus receive lower wages. An important factor in the lower level of work experience among women is that many women interrupt their careers to raise children. The study concluded that lower productivity is the most important factor in the gender gap.

• *Differences in occupational preferences.* Wages vary across occupations: Clerical and service occupations receive lower wages than craft and professional occupations. Compared to men, women express stronger preferences for low-wage occupations, such as clerical and service occupations, and weaker preferences for some high-wage occupations, such as craft and operator occupations. In contrast, men have slightly stronger preferences for high-wage professional and technical occupations. On balance, the general orientation of women toward low-wage occupations contributes to the gender gap.

- *Occupational discrimination.* Given the variation in wages across occupations, if employers have a bias against hiring women for high-paying occupations, women will receive lower wages. The study shows that on average, women are less successful than men in attaining their desired occupations, and this occupational discrimination by employers explains between 7 and 25 percent of the gender gap.
- *Wage discrimination.* If employers pay women less than their equally productive male counterparts, women's wages will be lower. The results of the study on this issue are mixed, with some evidence that wage discrimination is a significant factor in the gender pay gap.

The general conclusion of the study is that differences in productivity and occupational status are the most important factors in the gender pay gap. It appears that the relatively large number of women in low-paying occupations results both from the occupational preferences of women and employer discrimination that inhibits occupational attainment for women.

Racial Discrimination

What about differences in earnings by race? African-American males who work full-time earn 73 percent as m as their white counterparts, while African-American females earn 85 percent as much as their white counterparts. Hispanic males earn 65 percent as much as white males, while Hispanic females earn 78 percent as much as white females.[6] For both males and females, part of the earnings gap is caused by differences in productivity: On average, whites have more education and work experience, so they are paid higher wages. However, part of the wage gap is caused by racial discrimination. Some African-American and Hispanic workers are paid lower wages for similar jobs, and others are denied opportunities to work in some high-paying jobs.

How much of the earnings gap is caused by discrimination? Recent studies suggest that racial discrimination decreases the wages of African-American men by about 13 percent and that these earnings differences have decreased over the last few decades and are now small enough that "most of the disparity in earnings between blacks and whites in the labor market of the 1990s is due to the differences in skills they bring to the market, and not to discrimination within the labor market."[7] The differences in skills brought to the labor market are caused by a number of factors, including past discrimination that has inhibited the acquisition of job skills and differences in educational opportunities. For example, in urban areas about one-third of African-American high-school students have above-average scores on reading and math exams, compared to about two-thirds of white students.

Why Do College Graduates Earn Higher Wages?

In 2009, the college premium—the increase in earnings from a college degree—was 74 percent. A college education provides the skills necessary to enter certain occupations, so a college graduate has more job options than a high-school graduate. Both high-school grads and college grads can fill jobs that require only a high-school education, so the supply of workers for these low-skill jobs is plentiful, and the equilibrium wage for these jobs is low. In contrast, there is a smaller supply of workers for jobs that require a college education, so the wages in these high-skill jobs are higher than the wages for low-skill jobs. This is the **learning effect** of a college education: College students learn the skills required for certain occupations, increasing their human capital.

learning effect
The increase in a person's wage resulting from the learning of skills required for certain occupations.

A second explanation of the college premium requires a different perspective on college and its role in the labor market. Suppose certain skills are required for a particular job, but an employer cannot determine whether a prospective employee has these skills. For example, most managerial jobs require the employee to manage time efficiently, but it is impossible for an employer to determine whether a prospective employee is a good manager of time. Suppose that these skills are also required to complete a college degree. For example, to get passing grades in all your classes, you must be able to use your time efficiently. When you get a college degree, firms will conclude that you have some of the skills they require, so they may hire you instead of a high-school graduate. This is the **signaling effect** of a college education: People who complete college provide a signal to employers about their skills. This second explanation suggests that colleges simply provide a testing ground where students can reveal their skills to potential employers.

signaling effect
The information about a person's work skills conveyed by completing college.

The most important factor in the doubling of the college premium over the last few decades is technological change. Changes in technology have increased the demand for college graduates relative to the demand for other workers. In all sectors of the economy, firms are switching to sophisticated machinery and equipment that require highly skilled workers. Consequently, the share of jobs that require a college education has increased steadily, increasing the demand for college graduates. Of course, the supply of college graduates has increased too, but not by as much as demand. Because the increase in demand is large relative to the increase in supply, the wages of college graduates have increased. Another factor in the growing college premium is the pace of technological change. Workers with more education can more easily learn new skills and new jobs, so firms are willing to pay more for college graduates.

Labor Unions and Wages

A **labor union** is a group of workers organized to increase job security, improve working conditions, and increase wages and fringe benefits.[9] Acting as a group, union members have some control over the wages and fringe benefits they receive. In the U.S., about one in eight workers in the United States belongs to a union, down from about one in three workers in the 1950s. The unionization rate is 8.2 percent for private-sector workers, compared to 39.8 percent for public-sector workers. In the rest of the world, unionization rates vary widely, from 2 percent in India to 78 percent in Sweden.

There is evidence that unions raise the wages of union workers. For the United States, the consensus is that union workers earn 10 to 20 percent more than nonunion workers doing the same work. As we saw earlier in the chapter, an increase in the wage decreases the quantity of labor demanded because of the output effect and the input-substitution effect. Given the trade-off between wages and employment, an increase in the union wage increases the income of the workers who keep their jobs, but also decreases the number of union jobs.

One response to the trade-off between wages and jobs is to impose work rules that increase the amount of labor required to produce a given quantity of output.

labor union
A group of workers organized to increase job security, improve working conditions, and increase wages and fringe benefits.

application 3

THE BEAUTY PREMIUM

APPLYING THE CONCEPTS #3: What explains differences in wages?

How does physical attractiveness affect earnings? Studies of the U.S. labor market show that beautiful people earn more than people of average looks, and unattractive people earn less. The beauty premium is 5 percent for the 33 percent of workers who are considered beautiful or handsome, and the beauty premium is larger for men than for women. The penalty for bad looks is about 8 percent for the 10 percent of workers who are considered plain or unattractive. The beauty premium and the plain penalty have been observed in other countries and within specific occupations such as lawyers.

Why do beautiful people earn more income? According to biologists, beauty is a marker for underlying characteristics such as health and intelligence, and beautiful people start with a slight edge in the labor market. Beautiful people get more opportunities to learn through experience, and they also acquire better professional contacts. Because of these wider opportunities, a small difference in innate characteristics can be amplified into a large difference in earnings. Another factor in the beauty premium is that some workers and consumers simply like dealing with attractive people, so there is a higher demand for beautiful workers, resulting in higher wages. **Related to Exercises 3.10 and 3.11.**

SOURCES: Based on Daniel Hamermesh and Jeff Biddle, "Beauty and the Labor Market," *American Economic Review* 84 (2001): 1174–1194; "To Those That Have, Shall Be Given," *Economist*, December 22, 2007, 53–54.

featherbedding

Work rules that increase the amount of labor required to produce a given quantity of output. Featherbedding may actually decrease the demand for labor.

This is called **featherbedding**. One example of featherbedding is requiring a minimum crew size, which forces a firm to hire more workers than it needs to perform a particular task. For example, the typical unionized airline hires three workers to guide an airplane into the gate, while nonunion airlines use only two workers. In the past, railroad unions forced railroads to use firemen (whose job was to shovel coal) on diesel-powered engines, which don't use coal.

Although featherbedding forces the firm to use more labor per unit of output, it also decreases the quantity of output produced. A firm that hires workers it doesn't need will have higher production costs, resulting in a higher price for its product. Consumers respond to a higher price by purchasing less output, so although the firm may use more labor per unit of output, it sells less output. If output falls by a large amount, the quantity of labor demanded by the firm will actually decrease.

We've seen that unions lead to higher wages and may impose work rules that reduce productivity. In other words, unions increase production costs. What are the possible benefits of unions? First, unions may increase worker productivity by facilitating communication between workers and managers. A second possible benefit of unions is lower turnover among workers. If a worker is unhappy with a job, one option is to quit. From the firm's perspective, this is costly because the firm loses an experienced worker and must train a new one. A dissatisfied worker who belongs to a union has a second option: The worker can use the union as an intermediary to discuss job issues with managers. This sort of communication can solve problems before they become so severe that the worker quits. There is evidence that firms whose workers are in unions have lower turnover rates, in part because they facilitate communication between workers and managers. These lower turnover rates lead to lower training costs and a more experienced workforce. The savings from less turnover is equivalent to a 1 to 2 percent reduction in costs.

17.4 The Distribution of Income

In 2009 the median household income in the United States was $49,777. In other words, half of households earned more than $49,777, and half earned less. There is substantial variation in household income, with some households earning much more and others earning much less. In this part of the chapter, we'll discuss the extent of income inequality in the United States and recent trends in the distribution of income. We'll also explore the effects of several government policies on the distribution of income.

Income Distribution in 2007

Market income is defined as all earnings received from labor and capital markets. It includes wages and salaries, as well as earnings from bonds, stocks, and real estate. Market income does not account for the effects of government tax and transfer payments. We'll discuss the effects of government tax and transfer programs in the next section of the chapter.

Table 17.2 shows the distribution of market income in 1979 and 2007. Both years were peak economic years, when the nation's economy was thriving. To compute the numbers in a column of the table, we take four steps:

1 Rank the nation's households according to market income: The household with the highest income is at the top of the list, and the household with the lowest income is at the bottom of the list.

2 Divide the households into five groups, or "quintiles": The lowest fifth includes the poorest 20 percent of households (the lowest 20% of the list); the second fifth is the next poorest 20 percent, and so on.

3 Compute each group's income by adding up the income received by all the households in the group.

4 Compute each group's share of market income (the numbers in the second and third columns of the table) by dividing the group's income by the nation's total income.

In the case of perfect income equality, each quintile would earn 20 percent of income.

TABLE 17.2 Distribution of Market Income, 1979–2007			
Group	Share of Market Income, 1979	Share of Market Income, 2007	Percentage growth in income, 1979–2007
Quintile 1 (percentiles 0–20)	2.9	2.5	18.3
Quintile 2 (percentiles 20–40)	10.1	7.3	27.5
Quintile 3 (percentiles 40–60)	15.3	12.2	35.2
Quintile 4 (percentiles 60–80)	22.4	19.0	43.3
Quintile 5 (percentiles 80–100)	49.6	59.9	75.6
Percentiles 80–99	39.1	38.6	65.0
Top 1 percent	10.5	21.3	277.5

SOURCE: Congressional Budget Office, Trends in the Distribution of Household Income between 1979 and 2007 (Washington, DC, 2011).

The third column of Table 17.2 shows the distribution of market income in 2007. As shown near the top of the table, the lowest fifth earned only 2.5 percent of the total income. If we combine the first two quintiles, the lowest 40 percent of households earned 9.8 percent of total income. In contrast, the top quintile (percentiles 80–100) earned about 60 percent of total income. At the very top, households in the top 1 percent earned 21.3 percent of market income. In other words, the one percenters get over 20 times the income they would get in the case of perfect income equality. In contrast, households in the first quintile get one-eighth of the income they would get in the case of perfect equality.

What explains the substantial differences in market income? There are three key reasons for income inequality in a market-based economy.

1 ***Differences in labor skills and effort.*** Some people have better labor skills—more human capital—than others, so they earn higher wages. Labor skills are determined by innate ability, education, and work experience. In addition, some people work longer hours or at more demanding jobs, so they earn more income.

2 ***Luck and misfortune.*** Some people are luckier than others in investing their money, starting a business, or picking an occupation. Among the unlucky people are those who develop health problems that make it difficult to earn income. Among the lucky people are those who inherit wealth and earn income by investing their inheritance.

3 ***Discrimination.*** Some people are paid lower wages or have limited opportunities for education and work because of their race or gender.

Recent Changes in the Distribution of Income

Table 17.2 shows changes in market income between 1979 and 2007. The last column shows the percent growth in income over the 28-year period for different groups of households. As we move down through the column to progressively higher income, the growth rate of market income increases. For example, the growth rate for the poorest quintile was 18.3 percent, compared to 43.3 for the fourth quintile and 75.6 percent for the top quintile. For the one percenters, the growth rate was 277.5 percent.

The second and third columns in the table show the changes in the income shares over the 28-year period. The shares of the bottom 99 percent of households (quintiles 1 through 4 and percentiles 80–99) decreased, while the share of the top one percent increased. Although the income share of the top quintile increased (from about 50 percent to about 60 percent), the increase in income was concentrated among the top one percent of households.

Over the period 1979–2007, all major sources of income became less evenly distributed. Consider the income share of the bottom 80 percent of households. As shown in Table 17.2, the share of *overall* income earned by the 80 percenters decreased from 51.4 percent to 41.1 percent. This group's share of *labor* income decreased from 60 percent to 50 percent, while its share of income from capital, business, and capital gains decreased from 41 percent to 25 percent. Another factor in the increased concentration of income is that the share of income from capital gains (the most concentrated source of income) increased.

Why has labor income become less evenly distributed? It appears that the most important reason for growing inequality is what labor economists call an "increase in the demand for skill."[8] In the labor market, the demand for highly skilled (highly educated) workers has increased relative to the demand for less-skilled (less-educated) workers. As a result, the wage gap between the two groups has widened. Over the last few decades, the college premium doubled, and the advanced-degree premium—the increase in earnings from getting post-graduate degrees—has increased as well. At

application 4

TRADE-OFFS FROM IMMIGRATION

APPLYING THE CONCEPTS #2: Who benefits from the immigration of low-skilled workers?

Since about 1850, international migration has played an important role in labor markets. In the first wave of immigration, from 1850 to 1913, over a million people migrated to the Americas each year. Most were from European countries. After several decades of war and economic depressions, massive immigration resumed in 1945, and most of the immigrants were from less-developed countries. The most recent wave of immigration started in 1990 and has increased the supply of labor to the U.S. economy by about 10 percent per decade.

Immigration creates winners and losers within the economy. The increase in the supply of labor decreases wages for the native workers who have the same skill level as the immigrants. Because the average U.S. immigrant has less education and earns less income than the average native, immigrants compete with low-skill natives, decreasing their wages. On the benefit side, the decrease in the wages of low-skill labor decreases production costs and product prices, so consumers benefit. In general, we expect low-skill workers to lose as a result of immigration because the lower wages will dominate the benefits of lower consumer prices. In contrast, we expect high-skill workers to benefit from lower prices.

Economists have estimated the net effect of immigration on the U.S. economy. George Borjas shows that immigration to the United States has a small positive effect, with the losses in wages of low-skilled workers more than offset by gains to consumers and firms. This conclusion is consistent with the idea that exchange increases efficiency and the size of the overall economic pie. Studies of the most recent wave of immigration suggest that immigration decreases the wages of high-school dropouts and other low-skilled workers. **Related to Exercises 4.5, 4.6, and 4.7.**

SOURCES: Based on George Borjas, "The Economics of Immigration," *Journal of Economic Literature* 32 (1994): 1667–1717; George Borjas, "The Labor Demand Curve Is Downward Sloping: Reexamining the Impact of Immigration on the Labor Market," *Quarterly Journal of Economics* 108 (2003): 1335–1374; Gianmarco Ottaviano and Giovanni Peri, "Rethinking the Gains from Immigration: Theory and Evidence from the U.S." (working paper 11672, NBER, 2005).

the low end of educational attainment, the dropout penalty—the income loss from dropping out of high school, rather than simply graduating from high school—has nearly doubled.

Why did the demand for skill increase over the last three decades? Economists have explored this issue, and provide evidence for two key factors.

- *Technological change.* Advances in technology have simultaneously decreased the demand for less-educated workers and increased the demand for college graduates and people with advanced degrees. While the new technology has made it possible to replace many low-skilled workers with "smart" machines and computers, it has also increased the demand for workers who have the education and skills required to produce the new technology and use it.

- *Increased international trade.* An increase in international trade means more exports and imports. Trade allows developed countries like the United States to easily export goods produced with high-skilled labor and import goods produced with low-skilled labor. As a result, the expansion of international trade in the last three decades has increased the demand for high-skilled workers and decreased the demand for low-skilled workers in the United States.

Economists have not yet reached a consensus on the relative importance of these two factors.

17.5 Public Policy and the Distribution of Income

Government policies affect the distribution of income through taxes and transfer policies. In this part of the chapter, we explore the broad effects of federal tax and transfer policies on the distribution of income. We also discuss specific policies designed to boost the income and economic prospects of the poor.

Effects of Tax and Transfer Policies on the Distribution of Income

Table 17.3 shows the shares of income for the five quintiles before and after accounting for federal taxes and transfers. The federal policies redistribute income from the top fifth, whose income share decreases by about 7 percentage points (from 59.9 percent to 52.7 percent) to the lowest four-fifths, which collectively gain about 7 percentage points. The largest gain occurs for the lowest fifth (2.6 percentage points), and the other three quintiles gain between 0.9 and 1.9 percentage points.

In the last few decades, the redistributional effects of federal tax and transfer policies have diminished. Between 1979 and 2007, the government took less from high-income households and gave less to low-income households because:

1 Although the total amount of transfer payments was roughly constant over the period, a decreasing share of payments were for means-tested programs (eligibility is determined by income) such as Temporary Assistance to Needy Families

TABLE 17.3 Government Policies and the Distribution of Income			
Group	Share of Market Income, 2007	Share of Income After Federal Tax and Transfers, 2007	Change in Share from Federal Tax and Transfers
Quintile 1 (percentiles 0–20)	2.5	5.1	+2.6
Quintile 2 (percentiles 20–40)	7.3	9.2	+1.9
Quintile 3 (percentiles 40–60)	12.2	14.0	+1.8
Quintile 4 (percentiles 60–80)	19.0	19.9	+0.9
Quintile 5 (percentiles 80–100)	59.9	52.7	−7.2
Percentiles 80–99	38.6	35.6	−3.0
Top 1 percent	21.3	17.1	−4.2

SOURCE: Congressional Budget Office, Trends in the Distribution of Household Income between 1979 and 2007 (Washington, DC, 2011).

(TANF). In contrast, an increasing share was spent on Medicare, a program that is not means-tested. Households in the lowest quintile received only 36 percent of all federal transfer payments in 2007, down from 54 percent in 1979.

2 The overall average federal tax rate decreased from 22 percent in 1979 to 20 percent in 2007. The average rate for the individual income tax, which is responsible for bulk of the redistributional effects of federal taxes, decreased from over 11 percent in 1979 to less than 10 percent in 2007.

Poverty and Public Policy

The U.S. government defines a poor household as one with a total income less than the amount required to satisfy the "minimum needs" of the household. The government estimates a minimum food budget for each type of household and multiplies the food budget by three to get the official poverty budget. A household with income lower than the official poverty budget is considered poor. In 2010 the poverty budget was $22,113 for a two-adult, two-child household, which is less than half of the median household income. In 2010, almost 47 million people were below the poverty line, or 15.2 percent of the population.

Table 17.4 shows the incidence of poverty among different groups of people. For each group, the poverty rate equals the percentage of people in that group who live in households with incomes lower than the official poverty budget.

TABLE 17.4 Poverty Rates for Different Groups, 2009	
Characteristic	Poverty Rate in 2010
All Races	15.2%
White	13.1
Black	27.5
Hispanic	26.7
Asian	12.1
Type of Family	
Married couple	7.6
Female-headed household	28.7
Age	
Under 18 years	22.5
65 years and older	9.0

SOURCE: U.S. Census Bureau, Current Population Reports:. Report P60-241 (November 2011).

1 *Race.* The poverty rates for both Blacks and Hispanics are more than twice the poverty rates for whites.

2 *Type of family.* The poverty rate for female-headed households is about five times the poverty rate for households headed by a married couple.

3 *Age.* The poverty rate is relatively low for the aged, and relatively high for children.

Education is a key factor in determining wages, and poverty rates are lower for more-educated workers. As we saw earlier in the chapter, college graduates earn 74 percent more than high-school graduates. The poverty rate for college graduates is 3 percent, compared to 9 percent for high-school graduates. For high-school dropouts, the poverty rate is 22 percent.

The government uses a number of programs to provide assistance to the poor. In decreasing order of spending, they include medical care (about half of spending), cash assistance (about one-fifth of spending), food assistance, and housing assistance. These programs, broadly defined as "welfare programs," are **means-tested programs**, meaning that only people whose incomes fall below a certain level receive assistance. These programs reduce the poverty rate by a substantial margin. The poverty rates shown in Table 17.4 account for cash transfers to poor households. Cash transfers decrease the overall poverty rate by about one-third. The poverty rates listed in Table 17.4 do not account for the value of noncash programs such as food stamps, which decrease poverty rates by roughly two percentage points.

In 1996, the overhaul of federal antipoverty programs ended decades of policy based on the notion that poor families are entitled to cash and in-kind assistance. The Personal Responsibility and Work Opportunity Reconciliation Act of 1996 eliminated the entitlement of poor families to receive cash assistance. The federal government now provides block grants to states to provide Temporary Aid to Needy Families (TANF), with restrictions on what recipients must do to qualify for assistance and limits on how long they can receive assistance:

- A recipient must participate in work activities, defined as employment, on-the-job training, work experience, community service, or vocational training.

- After a total of 60 months of cash assistance (consecutive or nonconsecutive), assistance stops. States can allow exceptions to the 60-month rule for up to 20 percent of recipients.

The general thrust of welfare reform was to change an entitlement program into a program that requires work in exchange for time-limited assistance. Since the implementation of welfare reform, the number of people receiving assistance has decreased dramatically.

How does cash assistance to the poor affect their incentives to work? Two features of an assistance program affect work incentives.

- **Base cash payment.** The larger the amount provided as a base—the payment to someone who earns no market income—the lower the incentive to work to supplement the base income.

- **Benefit reduction rate.** When a recipient earns market income, the welfare payment decreases by a rate that varies from state to state. The reduction rate is 100 percent in about one-third of states ($1 of market income decreases the welfare payment by $1), and less than 50 percent in about one-third of states ($1 of market income decreases the welfare payment by less than $0.50). The lower the reduction rate, the larger the payoff for each hour of market income, and the greater the incentive for the recipient to earn additional income.

The Earned Income Tax Credit

The government also provides assistance to low-income households through the tax system. In 2010, federal spending on the earned income tax credit (EITC) was $55 billion, which was more than twice the spending on TANF. EITC is an earnings subsidy for low-income households that is determined by the number of children

means-tested programs
A government spending program that provides assistance to those whose income falls below a certain level.

in the household. Here is how the EITC works for a household with two children (roughly two-fifths of EITC recipients).

- Phase in: For the first $12,590 of earnings, the subsidy rate is 0.40: for each $1 of earnings, the government provides a subsidy of $0.40.

- Flat spot: The credit reaches its maximum of $5,036, when household earnings reach $12,590. For the next $2,410 of income, the credit remains at the maximum.

- Phase out. For income above $15,000, the phase-out rate is 0.21: for each additional dollar of earnings, the credit decreases by $0.21. The earnings subsidy reaches zero at an income of $40,363.

The subsidy rate and the phase-out rate are lower for households with fewer children.

The EITC is a successful anti-poverty policy on two counts.[10] First, the policy encourages participation in the workforce. For a $1,000 increase in the maximum credit, the employment rate of single mothers increases by about 3.6 percentage points. Between 1992 and 1999, the employment rate for single mothers increased

application 5

STATE LOTTERIES AND THE DISTRIBUTION OF INCOME

APPLYING THE CONCEPTS #5: How do government policies affect the distribution of income?

A total of 41 states use lotteries to raise money for government programs. In 2003, lottery ticket sales totaled over $40 billion. Roughly half of lottery revenue is paid out as prizes, leaving 20 percent for administrative costs and 30 percent as net revenue to the state. On average, every dollar spent on a lottery ticket pays out only $0.50, so buying a lottery ticket is equivalent to a voluntary contribution of $0.50 to the state. How is this lottery contribution distributed across income groups?

According to a recent study, the average annual spending on lotteries ($212 per adult in lottery states) is roughly constant across income groups. On average, a low-income household spends about the same per year on lotteries as a medium-income household and a high-income household. In other words, the lottery contribution is regressive in the sense that a low-income household contributes a larger percentage of its income. **Related to Exercise 5.5.**

SOURCE: Based on Melissa Kearney, "The Economic Winners and Losers of Legalized Gambling," *National Tax Journal* 58 (2005), pp. 281–302.

from 71 percent to 86 percent, and increases in the maximum credit over this period were responsible for a large share of the increase in the employment rate. Second, the EITC reduces poverty. In 2003, the program lifted 4.4 million people in low-income working families out of poverty. For the period 2002–2004, the EITC decreased the poverty rate among participants from 57 percent to 49 percent. For households below the poverty line, the EITC filled 31 percent of the gap between income and the poverty line.

SUMMARY

In this chapter, we've seen how wages are determined in perfectly competitive labor markets and why wages differ from one occupation to another. We've also looked at the distribution of income in the United States and explored possible reasons for growing inequality. Here are the main points of the chapter:

1 The *long-run demand curve for labor* is negatively sloped because the output and input-substitution effects operate in the same direction: An increase in the wage decreases labor per unit of output and decreases the total output produced.

2 An increase in the wage triggers *income* and *substitution effects* that operate in opposite directions, so an increase in the wage has an ambiguous effect on the quantity of labor supplied.

3 The wage in a particular occupation will be relatively high if supply is small relative to demand. This will occur if (1) few people have the skills required for the occupation, (2) training costs are high, or (3) the job is dangerous or stressful.

4 College graduates earn more than high-school graduates because a college education provides new skills and allows people to reveal their skills to employers.

5 The trade-off with a minimum wage is that some workers earn higher income, but others lose their jobs.

6 In the last few decades, the distribution of income has become more unequal. Federal tax and transfer policies diminish income inequality, but the redistributional effect has diminished in recent decades.

7 Poverty rates are relatively high among Blacks, Hispanics, high-school dropouts, and female-headed households.

KEY TERMS

featherbedding, p. 394

income effect for leisure demand, p. 384

input-substitution effect, p. 382

labor union, p. 393

learning effect, p. 392

long-run demand curve for labor, p. 382

marginal product of labor, p. 379

marginal-revenue product of labor (MRP), p. 379

market supply curve for labor, p. 385

means-tested programs, p. 401

output effect, p. 382

short-run demand curve for labor, p. 380

signaling effect, p. 392

substitution effect for leisure demand, p. 384

17.1 The Demand for Labor

1.1 The marginal revenue product of labor equals _____ times _____.

1.2 A profit-maximizing firm will hire the number of workers where _____ equals _____.

1.3 Your favorite professional team is considering hiring a new player for $3 million per year. It will be sensible (profitable) to hire the player if his _____ is greater than the $3 million cost.

1.4 Arrows up or down: The logic of the output effect is that a decrease in the wage will _____ production costs, so the price of output will _____ and the quantity of output demanded will _____. As a result, the quantity of labor demanded will _____.

1.5 The input-substitution effect is that a decrease in the wage _____ (increases/decreases) the quantity of labor per unit of _____, so the quantity of labor demanded _____ (increases/decreases).

1.6 The short-run market demand curve for labor is _____ (steeper/flatter) than the long-run demand because _____ occur(s) in the short run.

1.7 Fill the blanks with 75, 100, 117, 200, or 360. In major league baseball, the marginal revenue product of the typical free agent is roughly _____ percent of his salary, compared to _____ percent for a journeyman and _____ percent for an apprentice. (Related to Application 1 on page 383.)

1.8 Demand for News Kids. Consider the market for newspaper delivery kids in Kidsville. Each news kid receives a piece rate of $2 per subscriber per month and has a fixed territory that initially has 100 subscribers. The price elasticity of demand for subscriptions is 2.0. Suppose the new city council of Kidsville passes a law that establishes a minimum piece rate of $3 per subscriber per month. As a result, the publisher increases the monthly price of a subscription by 20 percent. How will the new law affect the monthly income of the typical news kid?

1.9 **Demand for Airline Pilots.** Comment on the following: "There is no substitute for an airline pilot: Someone has to fly the plane. Therefore, an increase in the wage of airline pilots will not change the number of pilots used by the airlines."

17.2 The Supply of Labor

2.1 Arrows up or down: An increase in the wage _____ the opportunity cost of leisure time, which tends to _____ leisure time and _____ labor time.

2.2 Arrows up or down: An increase in the wage _____ real income, and if leisure is a normal good this tends to _____ leisure time and _____ labor time.

2.3 We _____ (can/cannot) predict a worker's response to an increase in the wage because the _____ effect and the _____ effect work in _____ (the same/opposite) direction(s).

2.4 Your objective is to earn exactly $120 per week. If your wage decreases from $6 to $4 per hour, you respond by working _____ hours instead of _____ hours. In other words, your labor-supply curve is _____ sloped.

2.5 If every worker in a particular occupation works exactly 40 hours per week, regardless of the wage, the individual supply curve is vertical. _____ (True/False)

2.6 For cabbies in New York City, the elasticity of supply of labor is _____ (positive/negative/zero). (Related to Application 2 on page 386.)

2.7 Income and Substitution Effects. Sabrina works for a workers' cooperative that initially pays her a lump sum of $200 per week (as long as she works at least 15 hours per week) and a wage of $20 per hour of work. She initially works 40 hours per week. Suppose the cooperative changes its pay plan by increasing the lump-sum payment to $280 and decreasing the hourly wage to $18.

   a. If Sabrina continues to work 40 hours per week, how does the change in the pay plan affect her total income?

   b. Use the concepts of the income and substitution effects to predict whether Sabrina will work more hours, fewer hours, or the same number of hours. (*Hint:* Is there an income effect to consider?)

2.8 City versus National Carpenter Supply. Draw two supply curves for carpenters: one for the market in the city of Portland and one for the market in the United States. In which market would you expect a more elastic supply of carpenters?

2.9 Tax Rate and Tax Revenue. Critically appraise the following statement: "The law of supply says that an increase in price increases the quantity supplied. A decrease in the income tax rate will increase the worker's net wage, so each worker will work more hours. As a result, the revenue from the income tax will increase."

2.10 Personal Labor Supply. We discussed the responses of Lester, Sam, and Maureen to a wage increase. Which person's response is closest to your own? If your wage increased, would you work more hours, fewer hours, or about the same number of hours?

2.11 Cabbie Wages and Income. Suppose New York City increases the taxi fare by 20 percent. (Related to Application 2 on page 386.)

   a. For the typical cabbie, daily income will increase by _____ (more than/less than/exactly) 20 percent. Explain.

   b. Suppose the initial fare per mile is $0.60 and the initial miles per day is 100. Compute the percentage change in daily income.

17.3 Labor Market Equilibrium

3.1 Arrows up or down: A decrease in the supply of nurses will _____ the equilibrium wage and _____ the equilibrium quantity of nursing services.

3.2 Arrows up or down: An increase in the demand for nursing services will _____ the equilibrium wage and _____ the equilibrium quantity of nursing services.

3.3 Arrows up or down: A minimum wage _____ the quantity of labor demanded and _____ the quantity of labor supplied.

3.4 A minimum wage for restaurant workers brings good news to _____, but bad news to _____ and _____.

3.5 In Figure 17.5 on page 388, an increase in the wage decreases the quantity of labor demanded. Using the simple approach to computing percentage changes (see the Appendix to Chapter 1), the implied elasticity of demand for labor is _____.

3.6 The wage for a particular occupation will be relatively low if labor _____ (demand/supply) is small relative to labor _____ (demand/supply).

3.7 If a city has a relatively high crime rate, we would expect the wage for taxi drivers to be relatively _____ (high/low).

3.8 In some countries, it is customary to tip restaurant waiters. We would expect the wages paid to waiters to be _____ (higher/lower/the same) in countries where tips are customary.

3.9 If a worker switches from a relatively safe factory job to a job in a steel mill, the wage will increase by roughly _____ (2/4/10/30) percent.

3.10 The wage premium for beautiful people is about _____ percent, while the wage penalty for unattractive people is about _____ percent. (Related to Application 3 on page 393.)

3.11 Beautiful workers get wider opportunities to _____ , so a small difference in innate characteristics can lead to a large difference in _____ . (Related to Application 3 on page 393.)

3.12 Living Wage and Labor Income. Consider a university that has sweatshirts bearing its logo produced overseas by a contractor who initially pays a wage of $8 per sweatshirt and has other costs of $12 per sweatshirt, resulting in a price of $20 per sweatshirt. At this price, the university sells 100 sweatshirts per week. Suppose a student group succeeds in getting the contractor to increase the wage to $10 per shirt and the other costs of production don't change.

  a. The price per sweatshirt will increase from _____ to _____ , an increase of _____ percent.

  b. Suppose the price elasticity of demand for the university's sweatshirts is 3.0. At the higher price, a total of _____ sweatshirts will be purchased and the total spending on sweatshirt labor (total labor income) will change from $_____ to $_____ .

  c. Suppose consumers are willing to pay a higher price for sweatshirts made by workers receiving a higher wage. How would this change the numbers in part (b)? Provide an example in which the higher wage actually increases the total spending on sweatshirt labor.

3.13 Payroll Tax. You are an economic consultant to a city that just imposed a payroll tax of $1 per hour of work. This payroll tax is paid by workers through a payroll deduction: For each hour of work, the employer deducts $1 and sends the money to the city government. The initial wage (before the tax) is $10, and total employment is 20,000 hours per day. Use a graph to show the effect of the tax on the equilibrium wage and employment.

3.14 Higher Teacher Salaries. Advocates of higher salaries for teachers point out that most teachers have college degrees and that teaching children is an important job.

  a. Why aren't teachers' salaries higher, given the importance of the job and the education required?

  b. Suppose a new law establishes a minimum teacher salary that is 20 percent higher than the prevailing salary. How would you expect this law to affect the average quality of teachers and the taxes paid by the typical household?

3.15 Improved Safety and Wages. Consider an occupation that initially has a relatively high rate of nonfatal injuries. The equilibrium wage is $20 per hour, and the equilibrium quantity is 100,000 hours. Suppose a new safety device cuts the injury rate in half, and the supply of labor increases by 12 percent: The labor supply curve shifts to the right by 12 percent.

  a. Use a graph to show the effects of the safety device on the equilibrium wage and employment.

  b. Suppose the elasticity of supply of labor is 3.0 and the elasticity of demand is 1.0. Use the price change formula discussed in an earlier chapter on elasticity to compute the change in the equilibrium wage.

  c. Suppose the demand curve you've drawn is a long-run demand curve. Explain the roles of the output effect and substitution effect on the change in the quantity of labor demanded.

3.16 Waiter Tips and Income. Consider a city where the typical waiter has a five-hour shift and daily "sales" (total bills presented to customers) of $400. The customary tip is 15 percent, so tips add up to $60 per day (15% of $400). The initial wage is $10 per hour, so the typical waiter initially earns $50 in wages paid directly by the restaurant. Suppose a local waiter association runs a successful campaign to get the city's restaurant patrons to increase the average tip from 15 to 20 percent.

  a. Use a supply and demand graph with wage (excluding tips) on the vertical axis to show the effects of the new tip rate on the labor market.

  b. How will the new tip rate affect the daily income (wages plus tips) of the typical waiter?

4.1 Government transfer and tax policies increase the income share of the lowest quintile of the income distribution from about _____ percent to about _____ percent.

4.2 The college premium is defined as the percentage difference between the incomes of _____ and _____ . It is currently about _____ percent.

4.3 Arrows up or down: Since 1970, the income share of the top fifth of the income distribution has _____ , while the shares of the lowest and middle fifths have _____ .

4.4 Arrows up or down: An important factor in growing inequality over the last 30 years is technological change that has _____ the demand for college graduates and _____ the demand for less-educated workers.

4.5 The average immigrant has _____ (less/more) education than the average native, so immigration _____ (increases/decreases) the wages of _____ (low/high) skill natives. (Related to Application 4 on page 397.)

4.6 The immigration of low-skill workers generates net benefits for _____ workers because they benefit from lower _____ without bearing the cost associated with lower _____ . (Related to Application 4 on page 397.)

4.7 Wage and Price Effects of Immigration. In the initial equilibrium in the market for farm workers, the wage is $10 per hour. The elasticity of supply of farm workers is 2.0, and the elasticity of demand for farm workers is 1.0. Suppose that immigration increases the supply of farm workers by 12 percent: The supply curve shifts to the right by 12 percent. (Related to Application 4 on page 397.)

a. Use the price-change formula discussed in an earlier chapter on elasticity to compute the change in the equilibrium wage.

b. Suppose that farm workers are responsible for one-fourth of the production cost of food. What are the implications of immigration for the cost of producing food and its price?

17.5 Public Policy and the Distribution of Income

5.1 For each of the following pairs of population groups, indicate which group has a higher poverty rate:

a. _____ White vs. _____ Hispanic

b. _____ White vs. _____ Asian

c. _____ Married couple vs. _____ Female-headed household

d. _____ Under 18 years vs. _____ 65 years and older

5.2 Government spending and tax policies reduce the overall poverty rate from roughly _____ (25/20/15/10) percent to roughly _____ (15/10/5/2) percent.

5.3 Cash aid to the poor makes up roughly _____ (90/50/30/20) percent of the total spending on means-tested programs.

5.4 A low-income person receiving cash aid under TANF receives a fixed sum per month for an unlimited length of time. _____ (True/False)

5.5 On average, a low-income household spends _____ (more, less, the same) on lotteries as a high-income household. (Related to Application 5 on page 402.)

1. Anthony Carnevale, Stephen, Rose, Ban Cheah, *The College Payoff: Education, Occupations, and Lifetime Earnings* (2009: Georgetown University Center on Education and the Workforce)

2. Victor R. Fuchs, Alan B. Krueger, and James M. Poterba, "Why Do Economists Disagree about Policy? The Role of Beliefs about Parameters and Values," *Journal of Economic Literature* 36, no. 3 (1998): 1387–1426.

3. Craig Olson, "An Analysis of Wage Differentials Received by Workers on Dangerous Jobs," *Journal of Human Resources* 16 (Spring 1981): 167–185; John Leeth and John Ruser, "Compensating Wage Differentials for Fatal and Nonfatal Injury Risk by Gender and Race," *Journal of Risk and Uncertainty* 27 (2003): 257–277; Michael French and Laura Dunlap, "Compensating Wage Differentials for Job Stress," *Applied Economics* 30 (1998): 1067–1075; Ronald Ehrenberg and Robert Smith, *Modern Labor Economics* (Boston: Pearson Addison Wesley, 2005).

4. U.S. Department of Labor, Bureau of Labor Statistics, www.bls.govdata/ (accessed August 5, 2008).

5. Eric J. Solberg, "Occupational Assignment, Hiring Discrimination, and the Gender Pay Gap," *Atlantic Economic Journal* 32 (2004): 11–27.

6. U.S. Department of Labor, Bureau of Labor Statistics, www.bls.govdata/ (accessed August 5, 2008).

7. William Darity and Patrick Mason, "Evidence on Discrimination in Employment: Codes of Color, Codes of Gender," *Journal of Economic Perspectives* 12, no. 2 (1998): 63–90; James Heckman, "Detecting Discrimination," *Journal of Economic Perspectives* 12, no. 2 (1998): 101–116.

8. Finis Welch, "In Defense of Inequality," *American Economic Review* 89, no. 2 (1999): 1–17.

9. Ronald Ehrenberg and Robert Smith, *Modern Labor Economics: Theory and Public Policy* (Boston: Pearson Addison Wesley, 2006); Richard B. Freeman and James Medoff, *What Do Unions Do?* (New York: Basic Books, 1985).

10. Nicole Simpson, Jill Tiefenthaler, Jameson Hyde, "The Impact of the Earned Income Tax Credit on Economic Well-Being: A Comparison Across Household Types," *Population Research Policy Review* 29 (2010), pp. 84–864; Nada Eissa, Hilary Hoynes, "Redistribution and Tax Expenditures: The Earned Income Tax Credit," *National Tax Journal* 64 (2011), pp. 689–730; Jeffrey Grogger, "The Effects of Time Limits, the EITC, and Other Policy Changes on Welfare Use, Work, and Income among Female-Headed Families," *Review of Economics and Statistics* 85 (2003), pp. 394–408.

International Trade and Public Policy

Countries always want to have foreign markets open for their exporters.

But if a country limits access to its own markets, foreign countries may take action to limit access to their own markets. The United States, despite an overall strong record in trade, is no exception. Here are a few examples.

As part of the North American Free Trade Agreement, the United States was required to open its borders to trucks from Mexico, although it resisted allowing this. As a result, in 2009 Mexico imposed tariffs on over $2 billion of U.S. goods, reducing employment in U.S. export industries.

In 2010 the United States accused China of selling aluminum products below their fair market value and imposed sanctions on the Chinese. In turn, China decided that the United States was doing precisely the same thing with nylon products and imposed its own tariffs on these products.

Two years later, the United States again charged China with selling solar cells below costs and unfairly providing subsidies to its producers. It imposed steep tariffs on Chinese imports. The Chinese did not look upon this favorably and began investigating other U.S. products on which to impose their own sanctions.

Trade agreements can help lower barriers to international commerce, but countries still have to believe that other countries are "playing fair." Otherwise, two can tango.

LEARNING OBJECTIVES

- Explain carefully the terms *comparative advantage* and *terms of trade*.

- List the common protectionist policies.

- Describe the rationales that have been offered for protectionist policies.

- Summarize the history of international trade agreements.

- Analyze one recent controversy in trade policy.

MyEconLab
MyEconLab helps you master each objective and study more efficiently.

*a*s the world economy grows, U.S. policies toward international trade become ever more important. Many people view trade as a "zero-sum game." They believe that if one country gains from international trade, another must lose. Based on this belief, they advocate restricting trade with other countries. The United States does restrict trade to protect U.S. jobs in many sectors, such as those in the apparel and steel industries. One lesson from this chapter is that free trade could make all countries better off. The challenge for government officials is to create policies that accomplish, or come close to accomplishing, this goal.

In this chapter, we discuss the benefits of international trade and the effects of policies that restrict trade.

18.1 Benefits from Specialization and Trade

What if you lived in a nation that could produce everything it consumed and didn't depend on any other country for its economic livelihood? If you were put in charge of your nation, would you pursue a policy of national self-sufficiency? Although self-sufficiency might sound appealing, it would actually be better for your country to specialize in the production of some products and then trade some of those products to other countries. You saw in Chapter 3 that specialization and exchange can make both parties better off. In this chapter, we use a simple example to explain the benefits of specialization and international trade between two nations.

Let's say there are two nations, Shirtland and Chipland. Each nation produces computer chips and shirts, and each consumes computer chips and shirts. Table 18.1 shows the daily output of the two goods for the two nations. In a single day, Shirtland can produce a maximum of either 108 shirts or 36 computer chips, whereas Chipland can produce a maximum of either 120 shirts or 120 computer chips. The last two rows of the table show the opportunity costs of the two goods. Recall the principle of opportunity cost.

TABLE 18.1 Output and Opportunity Cost			
	Quantity Produced Per Day	Opportunity Cost of Shirts	Opportunity Cost of Chips
Shirtland	108 shirts	1/3 chip	3 shirts
	36 chips		
Chipland	120 shirts	1 chip	1 shirt
	120 chips		

PRINCIPLE OF OPPORTUNITY COST
The opportunity cost of something is what you sacrifice to get it.

In Chipland, the trade-off between shirts and chips is one to one: The opportunity cost of one shirt is one chip, and the opportunity cost of one chip is one shirt. In Shirtland, people can produce three times as many shirts as chips in a given amount of time: The opportunity cost of one chip is three shirts. Conversely, the opportunity cost of one shirt is one-third of a chip.

Production Possibilities Curve

Let's start by seeing what happens if Shirtland and Chipland are each self-sufficient. Each nation can use its resources (labor, land, buildings, machinery, and equipment) to produce its own shirts and chips. The *production possibilities curve* shows all the possible combinations of products that an economy can produce, given that its productive resources are fully employed and efficiently used. This curve, which we discussed in Chapter 2, provides a menu of production options. To keep things simple, we assume the curve is a straight line, indicating a constant trade-off between the two goods. As shown by Shirtland's production possibilities curve in Figure 18.1, the following combinations of chips and shirts are possible:

1 *All shirts and no chips*: point *a*. If Shirtland uses all its resources to produce shirts, it will produce 108 shirts per day.

2 *All chips and no shirts*: point *d*. If Shirtland uses all its resources to produce chips, it will produce 36 chips per day.

3 *Equal division of resources*: point *b*. Shirtland could divide its resources between shirts and chips to produce 54 shirts and 18 chips each day.

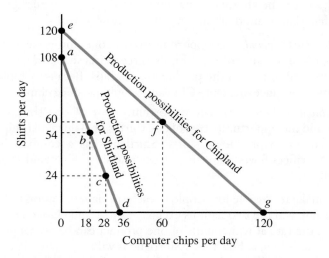

Shirtland Possibilities

Point	Shirts	Chips
a	108	0
b	54	18
c	24	28
d	0	36

Chipland Possibilities

Point	Shirts	Chips
e	120	0
f	60	60
g	0	120

▲ FIGURE 18.1

Production Possibilities Curve

The production possibilities curve shows the combination of two goods that can be produced with a nation's resources. For Chipland, the trade-off between the two goods is one to one. For Shirtland, the trade-off is 3 shirts for every computer chip. In the absence of trade, Shirtland can pick point *c*—28 chips and 24 shirts—and Chipland can pick point *f*—60 chips and 60 shirts.

All the other points on the line connecting points *a* and *d* are also feasible. One option is point *c*, with 28 chips and 24 shirts. The steepness of the curve's slope—negative 3.0—shows the opportunity cost of computer chips: 1 chip per 3 shirts. Figure 18.1 also shows the production possibilities curve for Chipland. Chipland can daily produce 120 shirts and no chips (point *e*), 120 chips and no shirts (point *g*), or any combination of chips and shirts between these two points. In Chipland, the trade-off is 1 shirt per computer chip: The opportunity cost of 1 chip is 1 shirt, so the slope of the production possibilities curve is negative 1.0.

Each nation could decide to be self-sufficient, picking a point on its production possibilities curve and producing everything it wants to consume. For example,

Shirtland could pick point *c*, daily producing 28 chips and 24 shirts, and Chipland could pick point *f*, daily producing 60 chips and 60 shirts. In the language of international trade, this is a case of *autarky*, or self-sufficiency (in Greek, *aut* means "self" and *arke* means "to suffice").

Comparative Advantage and the Terms of Trade

Would the two nations be better off if each specialized in the production of one good and traded with the other nation? To decide which nation should produce a particular good, we need to look at each good and figure out which nation has the lower opportunity cost of producing it. As you saw in Chapter 3, the nation with the lower opportunity cost has a *comparative advantage* in producing that good. As we emphasized in Chapter 3, it is comparative advantage that matters for trade—not *absolute advantage*, the ability of a nation to produce a particular good at a lower absolute cost than that of another nation. Let's see how it works.

1 *Chips produced in Chipland.* The opportunity cost of one chip is one shirt in Chipland, and the opportunity cost of one chip is three shirts in Shirtland. Chipland has a comparative advantage in the production of chips. Because Chipland sacrifices fewer shirts to produce one chip, Chipland should produce chips.

2 *Shirts produced in Shirtland.* The opportunity cost of one shirt is one chip in Chipland, and the opportunity cost of one shirt is one-third of a chip in Shirtland. When it comes to producing shirts, Shirtland has a comparative advantage because it sacrifices fewer chips to produce one shirt. Shirtland should therefore produce shirts.

terms of trade

The rate at which units of one product can be exchanged for units of another product.

Trade will make it possible for people in each specialized nation to consume both goods. At what rate will the two nations exchange shirts and chips? To determine the **terms of trade**, the rate at which units of one product can be exchanged for units of another product, let's look at how much Shirtland is willing to pay to get one chip and how much Chipland is willing to accept to give up one chip.

1 To get one chip, Shirtland is willing to pay up to three shirts. That's how many shirts it would sacrifice if it produced its own chip. For example, if the nations agree to exchange two shirts per chip, Shirtland could rearrange its production, producing one fewer chip but three more shirts. After exchanging two of the newly produced shirts for one chip, Shirtland will have the same number of chips but one additional shirt.

2 To give up one chip, Chipland is willing to accept any amount greater than one shirt. For example, if the nations agree to exchange two shirts per chip, Chipland could rearrange its production, producing one more chip and one fewer shirt. After it exchanges the newly produced chip for two shirts, Chipland will have the same number of chips but one additional shirt.

The potential for mutually beneficial trade between the two countries is possible because the willingness to pay—three shirts by Shirtland—exceeds the willingness to accept—one shirt by Chipland. It's possible for Shirtland and Chipland to split the difference between the willingness to pay and the willingness to accept, exchanging two shirts per chip. This will actually make both countries better off in terms of the total amount of goods they can consume. We'll see why next.

The Consumption Possibilities Curve

consumption possibilities curve

A curve showing the combinations of two goods that can be consumed when a nation specializes in a particular good and trades with another nation.

A nation that decides to specialize and trade is no longer limited to the options shown by its own production possibilities curve. The **consumption possibilities curve** shows the combinations of two goods (computer chips and shirts in our example) that a nation can consume when it specializes in one good and trades with another nation.

Figure 18.2 shows the consumption possibilities curve for our two nations, assuming that they exchange two shirts per chip:

- In Panel A, Chipland specializes in chip production, the good for which it has a comparative advantage. It produces 120 chips and no shirts (point *g*). Given the terms of trade, Chipland can exchange 40 of its 120 chips for 80 shirts, leading to point *h*. At point *h*, Chipland can consume 80 chips and 80 shirts.

- In Panel B, Shirtland specializes in shirt production. It produces 108 shirts and no chips (point *a*). Given the terms of trade, it can exchange 80 of its 108 shirts for 40 chips, leading to point *k* on its consumption possibilities curve. Shirtland can consume 28 shirts and 40 chips.

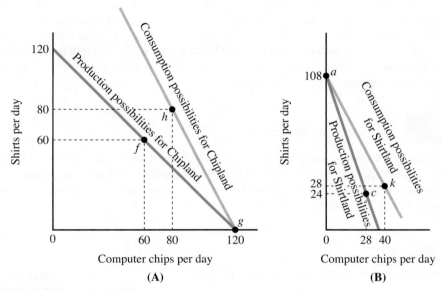

▲ **FIGURE 18.2**
Consumption Possibilities Curve
The consumption possibilities curve shows the combinations of computer chips and shirts that can be consumed if each country specializes and trades. In Panel A, Chipland produces 120 chips and trades 40 of these chips to Shirtland for 80 shirts. In Panel B, Shirtland produces 108 shirts and trades 80 of these shirts to Chipland for 40 chips. The trade allows each nation to consume more.

How do the outcomes with specialization and trade compare to the autarky outcomes? Chipland moves from point *f* (autarky) to point *h*, so trade increases the consumption of each good by 20 units. Shirtland moves from point *c* to point *k*, so this nation consumes 12 additional chips and 4 additional shirts.

In Figure 18.2, each consumption possibilities curve lies above the nation's production possibilities curves, meaning each nation has more options about how much to consume under specialization and trade. In most cases, a nation picks a point on the consumption possibilities curve that provides more of each good. Of course, this is a very simple example. In the actual world market, many countries produce and trade many goods. The marketplace determines what the terms of those trades will be, depending upon supply, demand, and pricing.

How Free Trade Affects Employment

You've now seen that trade allows each nation to consume more of each good. But we haven't yet discussed the effects of trade on employment. Under free trade, each nation will begin to specialize in a single good, causing considerable changes in the country's employment in different industries. In Chipland, the chip industry doubles in size—output increases from 60 to 120 chips per day—while the shirt industry disappears. Workers and other resources will leave the shirt industry and move to the chip industry. In Shirtland, the flow is in the opposite direction: Workers and other resources move from the chip industry to the shirt industry.

Is free trade good for everyone? Switching from self-sufficiency to specialization and trade increases consumption in both nations, so on average, people in each nation benefit from free trade. But some people in both nations will be harmed by free trade. In Chipland, for example, people in the shirt industry will lose their jobs when the shirt industry disappears. Some workers can easily move into the expanding computer chip industry. For these workers, free trade is likely to be beneficial. However, other shirt workers will be unable to make the move to the chip industry and will be forced to accept lower-paying jobs or face unemployment. Free trade is likely to make these displaced workers worse off. There is a saying, "Where you stand on an issue depends on where you sit." In our example, a worker sitting at a sewing machine in Chipland is likely to oppose free trade because that worker is likely to lose a job. A worker sitting at a workstation in a computer chip fabrication facility is likely to support free trade because the resulting increase in computer chip exports will generate more employment opportunities in that industry.

18.2 Protectionist Policies

Now that you know the basic rationale for specialization and trade, we can explore the effects of public policies that restrict it. All the restrictions we explore limit the gains from specialization and trade. We will consider four common import-restriction policies: an outright ban on imports, an import quota, voluntary export restraints, and a tariff.

Import Bans

To show how an import ban affects the market, let's start with an unrestricted market—no import ban. Figure 18.3 shows the market for shirts in Chipland, a nation with a comparative advantage in producing computer chips, not shirts. The domestic

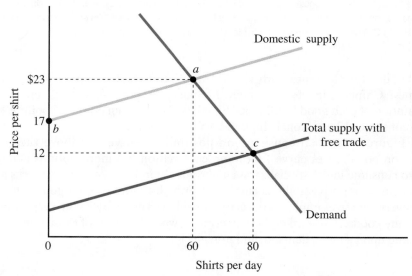

▲ **FIGURE 18.3**

Effects of an Import Ban

In the free-trade equilibrium, demand intersects the total supply curve at point *c*, with a price of $12 and a quantity of 80 shirts. If shirt imports are banned, the equilibrium is shown by the intersection of the demand curve and the domestic supply curve (point *a*). The price increases to $23.

supply curve shows the quantity of shirts supplied by firms in Chipland. Looking at point *b*, we see that Chipland firms will not supply any shirts unless the price is at least $17 per shirt. The total supply curve for shirts, which shows the quantity supplied by both domestic firms and foreign firms (in Shirtland), lies to the right of the domestic supply curve. At each price, the total supply of shirts exceeds the domestic supply because foreign firms supply shirts, too. Point *c* shows the free-trade equilibrium. The demand curve from domestic residents intersects the total supply curve at a price of $12 per shirt and a quantity of 80 shirts. Because this price is below the minimum price for domestic firms, domestic firms produce no shirts, and all the shirts in Chipland are imported from Shirtland.

What will happen if Chipland bans imported shirts? Foreign suppliers will disappear from the shirt market, so the total supply of shirts will be the domestic supply. In Figure 18.3, point *a* shows the equilibrium when Chipland bans imported shirts: The domestic demand curve intersects the domestic supply curve at a price of $23 per shirt and a quantity of 60 shirts. In other words, the decrease in supply resulting from the import ban increases the price consumers have to pay for shirts and decreases the quantity available for them to buy.

Quotas and Voluntary Export Restraints

An alternative to an import ban is an **import quota**—a government-imposed limit on the quantity of a good that can be imported. An import quota is a restrictive policy that falls between free trade and an outright ban: Imports are cut, but not eliminated. For example, if a quota were put on shirts, the price consumers would have to pay would fall somewhere between the price they would pay with free trade ($12 per shirt, as in our example) and the price they would pay if imported shirts were banned ($23 per shirt). Where exactly the price would fall would depend on how high or low the quotas are.

Import quotas are illegal under international trading rules. To get around these rules, an exporting country will sometimes agree to a **voluntary export restraint (VER)**. VERs are similar to import bans. When an exporting nation adopts a VER, it decreases its exports to avoid having to face even more restrictive trade policies importing countries might be tempted to impose on them. Although VERs are legal under global-trade rules, they violate the spirit of international free-trade agreements. In any case, quotas and VERs have the same effect. Like a quota, a VER increases the price of the restricted good, making it more feasible for domestic firms to participate in the market.

Figure 18.4 shows the effect of an import quota or VER. Starting from the free-trade equilibrium at point *c*, an import quota will shift the total supply curve to the left: At each price there will be a smaller quantity of shirts supplied because foreign suppliers aren't allowed to supply as many. The total supply curve when there is an import quota or VER will lie between the domestic supply curve and the total supply curve under free trade. The equilibrium under an import quota or VER occurs at point *d*, where the demand curve intersects the total supply curve under an import limitation. The $20 price per shirt with the import quota exceeds the $17 minimum price of domestic firms, so domestic firms supply 22 shirts (point *e*). Under a free-trade policy, they would have supplied no shirts.

A quota or a VER produces winners and losers. The winners include foreign and domestic shirt producers. In our example, foreign firms can sell shirts at a price of $20 instead of $12 each, and the price is high enough for domestic firms to participate in the market. This generates benefits for the firms and their workers. The losers are consumers, who pay a higher price for shirts. In some cases, the government issues **import licenses** to some citizens, who can then buy shirts from foreign firms at a low price, such as $12, and sell the shirts at the higher domestic price, $20. Because import licenses provide profits to the holder, they are often awarded to politically powerful

import quota
A government-imposed limit on the quantity of a good that can be imported.

voluntary export restraint (VER)
A scheme under which an exporting country voluntarily decreases its exports.

import licenses
Rights, issued by a government, to import goods.

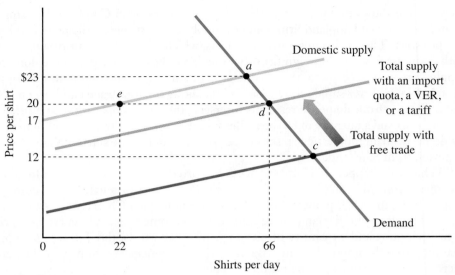

▲ **FIGURE 18.4**

Market Effects of a Quota, a VER, or a Tariff

An import quota shifts the supply curve to the left. The market moves upward along the demand curve to point *d*, which is between point *c* (free trade) and *a* (an import ban). We can reach the same point with a tariff that shifts the total supply curve to the same position.

firms or individuals. Moreover, because they are so valuable, some people may bribe government officials to obtain them.

We know consumers pay higher prices for goods that are subject to protectionist policies, but how much more? Here is one example. In the United States, voluntary export restraints on Japanese automobiles in 1984 increased the price of a Japanese car by about $1,300 and the price of a domestic car by about $660.[1]

tariff

A tax on imported goods.

An alternative to a quota or a VER is an import **tariff**, which is a tax on an imported good. Tariffs have the same effect as quotas and VERs. We know from our earlier discussions that a tax shifts the supply curve to the left and increases the equilibrium price. In Figure 18.4, suppose the tariff shifts the total supply curve with free trade so that it intersects the domestic demand curve at point *d*. In other words, we reach the same point we reached with the quota: Consumers pay the same $20 price per shirt, and domestic firms produce the same quantity (22 shirts).

There is one fundamental difference between a quota and a tariff. An import quota allows importers to buy shirts from foreign suppliers at a low price—say, $12 per shirt—and sell them for $20 each, the artificially high price. In other words, importers make money from the quota. Under a tariff, the government gets the money, collecting $8 per shirt from foreign suppliers. Citizens in Chipland will prefer the tariff to the quota because the government can use the revenue from the tariff to cut other taxes or expand public programs.

In the real world, tariffs can have major effects. One trade expert estimated that cutting industrial tariffs by 50 percent would increase the output of the world's economy by $270 billion per year. Similar easing of tariffs on agricultural products would cut the world's food bill by $100 billion.[2]

Tariffs also appear to disproportionately affect the poor.

Responses to Protectionist Policies

A restriction on imports is likely to lead to further restrictions on trade. For example, if Chipland bans shirt imports, Shirtland might retaliate by banning computer chips from Chipland. A trade war of this sort could escalate to the point where the two nations return to self-sufficiency. If this happens, the two countries would be forced

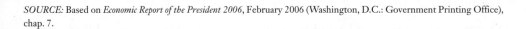

application 1

THE IMPACT OF TARIFFS ON THE POOR

APPLYING THE CONCEPTS #1: Do tariffs (taxes) on imported goods hurt the poor disproportionately?

Economists have found that tariffs in the United States fall most heavily on lower-income consumers. In the United States, tariffs are very high on textiles, apparel items, and footwear. These goods represent a higher fraction of the consumption of lower-income households than higher-income households. For example, footwear accounts for 1.3 percent of the expenditure of lower-income households, as compared to 0.5 percent for higher-income households.

Moreover, even within these categories of goods for which tariffs are high, the highest tariffs fall on the cheapest products—precisely those that will be purchased by lower-income consumers. For example, low-price sneakers face a 32 percent tariff whereas expensive track shoes face only a 20 percent tariff. In general, to protect U.S. industries, tariffs are highest on labor-intensive goods; goods that use relatively more labor than capital. But these goods tend to be lower priced. That is why tariffs do fall disproportionately on the poor. **Related to Exercise 2.7.**

SOURCE: Based on *Economic Report of the President 2006*, February 2006 (Washington, D.C.: Government Printing Office), chap. 7.

to scale back their consumption. We can see that by looking back at Figure 18.2: Chipland will move from point *h* to point *f*, and Shirtland will move from point *k* to point *c*. This sort of retaliatory response is common. Because it is, we know that protecting one industry in a nation is likely to harm that nation's other exports. Chipland's shirt industry, if protected from imports, may grow, but it will be at the expense of its computer-chip industry.

Many import restrictions have led to retaliatory policies and substantially lessened trade. The most famous was the Smoot–Hawley Tariff Act of 1930. When the United States increased its average tariff on imports to 59 percent, its trading partners retaliated with higher tariffs on U.S. products. The resulting trade war reduced international trade and deepened the worldwide depression of the 1930s.

The threat of retaliatory policies may persuade a nation to loosen its protectionist policies. For example, in 1995 the United States announced it would impose 100 percent tariffs on Japanese luxury cars if Japan didn't ease its restrictions on imported auto parts. Just hours before the tariffs were to take effect, the two nations reached an agreement that was expected to increase the sales of U.S. auto parts to Japanese firms. In 2002, President Bush imposed tariffs on steel. However, when faced with the threat of retaliatory policies in Europe, he ended the sanctions in 2003.

Import restrictions also create an incentive to smuggle goods. The restrictions create a gap between the cost of purchasing the restricted goods abroad and the price goods can be sold for in the protected economy, so there is a profit to be made.

18.3 What Are the Rationales for Protectionist Policies?

Why would a government impose protectionist policies such as an import ban, quota, VER, or tariff? We'll look at three possible reasons:

1 To shield workers from foreign competition

2 To nurture infant industries until they mature

3 To help domestic firms establish monopolies in world markets

To Shield Workers from Foreign Competition

One of the most basic arguments for protectionism is that it shields workers in industries that would be hurt by trade. Suppose, relative to the United States, nations in the Far East have a comparative advantage in producing textiles. If the United States were to reduce existing tariffs on textiles, domestic manufacturers could not compete. They would have to close their factories and lay off workers. In an ideal world, the laid-off workers would take new jobs in other sectors of the economy. In practice, this is difficult. Many workers don't immediately have the skills to go to work in other sectors, and obtaining those skills takes time. Moreover, the textile industry is heavily concentrated in the southeastern part of the United States. Politicians from that region will try to keep tariffs in place to prevent temporary unemployment and changes in employment patterns in their areas—they have an incentive to protect their own constituents, even though it may cause major economic losses for the economy. The result of this protection will be less-efficient production, higher prices, and lower consumption for the United States. How much does it cost to protect a job?

To Nurture Infant Industries until They Mature

learning by doing
Knowledge and skills workers gain during production that increase productivity and lower cost.

infant industries
Industries that are at an early stage of development.

During World War II the United States built hundreds of boats, called Liberty ships, for the navy. As more and more of these ships were built, each required fewer hours to complete because workers acquired knowledge during the production process and got better at it. Engineers and economists call this phenomenon **learning by doing**. To learn a new game, such as Ping-Pong, you learn by doing. At first, you may find it difficult to play, but your skills improve as you go along.

Tariffs and other protectionist policies are often defended on the grounds that they protect new or **infant industries** that are in the early stages of development and can benefit from learning by doing. A tariff shields a young industry from the competition of its more mature rivals. After the infant industry "grows up," the tariff can eventually be eliminated because the industry is able to compete. In practice, infant industries rarely become competitive with their foreign rivals. During the 1950s and 1960s, many Latin American countries used tariffs and other policies to protect their young manufacturing industries from foreign competition. Unfortunately, the domestic industries never became as efficient as foreign suppliers, and the Latin American countries that tried this policy suffered. Another problem with protecting an infant industry is that once a government gives an industry tariff protection, it is difficult to take that protection away. More generally, even some established companies also complain about "unfair competition," but this concept does not always make sense.

To Help Domestic Firms Establish Monopolies in World Markets

If the production of a particular good requires extremely large economies of scale, the world market will support only a few, or perhaps just one, firm. In this case, a nation might be tempted to adopt policies to ensure a company within its borders will end up being the world monopolist. Suppose the commercial aircraft industry can support only one large firm. If two firms enter the industry, both will lose money. A nation could agree to provide financial support to a domestic firm to guarantee the firm will make a profit. With such a guarantee, the domestic firm will enter the industry. Knowing this, a foreign firm will be reluctant to enter, so the domestic firm will capture the monopoly profit. The country where the successful firm is located will benefit from higher production and more jobs for its citizens.

application 2

CHINESE IMPORTS AND LOCAL ECONOMIES

APPLYING THE CONCEPTS #2: What have been the local effects of Chinese imports?

Do imports from China really make a difference in U.S. labor markets? Economists David Autor, David Dorn, and Gordon Hanson examined detailed data on Chinese imports into local communities. Some local communities are more heavily impacted by Chinese imports than others depending on the mix of products produced locally. The authors found that the pace of Chinese import growth was so rapid from 1990 to 2007 that it often had a strong and negative effect on local economies. Those communities that were more exposed to imports had larger increases in workers receiving unemployment insurance, food stamps, and disability payments.

These findings do not mean that trade with China was ultimately beneficial. Displaced workers can find new jobs and import competition lowers prices for all consumers. But it does mean that the burden of adjustment to imports varies by region. Some regions will have a more difficult time adjusting than others to a sudden influx of imports. The study also does not measure the indirect benefits from trade with China. As the Chinese economy expanded during this period, it created more export opportunities for producers in the United States. Those benefits were not measured in this study. **Related to Exercise 3.7.**

SOURCE: Based on David H. Autor, David Dorn, and Gordon H. Hanson, "The China Syndrome: Local Labor Market Effects of Import Competition in the United States," MIT Working Paper, May 2012, Available at: http://economics.mit.edu/faculty/dautor/papers/inequality (Accessed May 28, 2012).

One famous example is Airbus, an airplane-manufacturing consortium in Europe that competes with the U.S. firm Boeing. Several European countries provided large subsidies for the firms producing the Airbus line of planes. These subsidies allowed the consortium firms to underprice their rivals in the United States, and at least one U.S. manufacturer of commercial airplanes was forced out of business.

What could go wrong with these monopoly creation policies? First, if both nations subsidize their domestic firms, both firms will enter the market and lose money. The taxpayers in both countries will then have to pay for the subsidies. Second, a nation may pick the wrong industry to subsidize. Together, the British and French subsidized an airplane known as the Concorde, which flew at supersonic speeds, rapidly shuttling passengers between Europe and the United States. Although the Concorde captured the market, the market was not worth capturing. The venture lost money because the Concorde was very costly to develop and fly, and few people were willing to pay a large premium for supersonic travel. The Concorde stopped flying in 2003. Finally, the subsidized firm may not perform well. As an example, in 2006, Airbus was facing severe problems with its planes and losing business to its competitor, Boeing.

18.4 A Brief History of International Tariff and Trade Agreements

Today, the average U.S. tariff is 4.6 percent of the value of imported goods, a rate close to the average tariffs in Japan and most European nations but very low by historical standards. When the Smoot–Hawley tariffs were implemented in the

General Agreement on Tariffs and Trade (GATT)

An international agreement established in 1947 that has lowered trade barriers between the United States and other nations.

World Trade Organization (WTO)

An organization established in 1995 that oversees GATT and other international trade agreements, resolves trade disputes, and holds forums for further rounds of trade negotiations.

1930s, the average U.S. tariff was a whopping 59 percent of a product's price. Tariffs are lower today because several international agreements subsequently reduced them.

The first major international trade agreement following World War II was the **General Agreement on Tariffs and Trade (GATT)**. This agreement was initiated in 1947 by the United States and 23 other nations and now has over 149 members. Nine rounds of GATT negotiations over tariffs and trade regulations have taken place, resulting in progressively lower tariffs for the member nations. The last completed set of negotiations, the Uruguay round (1994), decreased tariffs by about one-third of the previous level. In 1995, the **World Trade Organization (WTO)** was formed to enforce GATT and other international trade agreements. Under GATT's "most favored nation" provision, a country that reduces tariffs for one nation must do so for all members of GATT. This provision helps reduce tariffs throughout the world.

The most recent round of trade negotiations began in Doha, Qatar, in 2001 but major negotiations collapsed in 2008, although the negotiations still continue on a smaller scale. This round was billed as an attempt to benefit developing countries that exported agricultural goods. The idea was that reductions in subsidies and tariffs on agriculture goods in developed countries would promote exports of agriculture goods for developing countries. In turn, developed countries wanted lower tariffs for industrial goods in developing countries. Why did the negotiations fail? One reason was that China and India, rapidly growing countries each with populations over a billion, were more interested in promoting their industrial bases than their agricultural exports. Perhaps a second reason was that previous trade negotiations had been successful, leaving less room for "grand bargains" that would motivate all countries to embrace new agreements.

If global negotiations do not work, what alternatives are there? In addition to the large group of nations in the WTO, other groups of nations have formed trade associations to lower trade barriers and promote international trade. Here are some of the best-known agreements:

- The North American Free Trade Agreement (NAFTA) took effect in 1994 and was implemented over a 15-year period. It eliminates all tariffs and other trade barriers between Canada, Mexico, and the United States.

- The European Union (EU) was designed to remove all trade barriers within Europe and create a single market. Initially, the EU consisted of just six countries: Belgium, Germany, France, Italy, Luxembourg, and the Netherlands. Denmark, Ireland, and the United Kingdom joined in 1973; Greece in 1981; Spain and Portugal in 1986; and Austria, Finland, and Sweden in 1995. In 2004, the biggest ever enlargement took place with 10 new countries joining the EU.

- The leaders of 18 Asian nations have formed an organization called Asian Pacific Economic Cooperation (APEC). In 1994, APEC signed a nonbinding agreement to reduce trade barriers among these nations.

- The Dominican Republic–Central America Free Trade Agreement (DR-CAFTA) promotes trade liberalization between the United States, the Dominican Republic, and five Central American countries: Costa Rica, El Salvador, Guatemala, Honduras, and Nicaragua. DR-CAFTA is modeled after NAFTA.

Some economists are concerned that these regional trade agreements may stand in the way of broader international trade agreements under GATT. Although regional agreements may lead to reduced tariffs for neighboring or member countries, they do little to promote efficiency across the globe. For example, a Belgian firm may find it easier to sell goods in France than does a firm from South America that has a lower cost of production.

18.5 Recent Policy Debates and Trade Agreements

We're now ready to discuss three recent policy debates concerning international trade:

1 Are foreign producers dumping their products?
2 Do trade laws inhibit environmental protection?
3 Do outsourcing and trade cause income inequality?

Are Foreign Producers Dumping Their Products?

Although tariff rates have been reduced in recent years, a number of controversies surrounding free trade remain. One of these relates to *dumping*. A firm is **dumping** when the price it charges in a foreign market is either lower than the price it charges in its home market or lower than its production cost. Dumping is illegal under international trade agreements. Hundreds of cases of alleged dumping are presented to WTO authorities each year. Here are some cases in which the WTO concluded that dumping had indeed occurred: Hong Kong VCRs sold in Europe; Chinese bicycles sold in the United States; Asian TV sets sold in Europe; steel from Brazil, India, Japan, and Spain sold in the United States; U.S. beef sold in Mexico; and Chinese computer disks sold in Japan and the United States. Under the current provisions of the WTO,

dumping

A situation in which the price a firm charges in a foreign market is lower than either the price it charges in its home markets or the production cost.

application 3

ARE THEY REALLY DUMPING?

APPLYING THE CONCEPTS #3: How does the Commerce Department try to determine whether countries are dumping their products?

Dumping is selling a product in a foreign market at a lower price than a firm's own domestic market. You might think that this would require a comparison of *actual* prices charged in home markets compared to foreign markets. But that is rarely the case in the United States. For example, from 1995 to 1998, only 4 out of 141 cases of dumping used actual prices.

Instead, the U.S. Department of Commerce typically uses a "constructed value" method where it makes its own estimates of what prices in countries' own markets *would be* based on available data on production costs, transportation, and other expenses and also a margin for profit and administration. In many cases, these are very crude and dated estimates. In other cases, they rely solely on the information provided by the parties who filed the complaint, who clearly have a vested interest in the outcome.

Perhaps this is why the Commerce Department virtually always finds that foreign countries are in fact guilty of dumping their products. Chinese companies have been accused of dumping for a wide array of products including crawfish, paint brushes, sodium nitrate, and plastic shopping bags. Critics of dumping believe that "constructed values" calculations overstate prices in domestic markets and inevitably lead to the conclusion that firms are in fact guilty of dumping their products. **Related to Exercise 5.7.**

SOURCE: Based on Douglas A. Irwin, *Free Trade under Fire* (Princeton, New Jersey: Princeton University Press, 2009), chap. 5.

price discrimination
The practice of selling a good at different prices to different consumers.

predatory pricing
A firm sells a product at a price below its production cost to drive a rival out of business and then increases the price.

a nation can impose antidumping duties, a tax, on products that are being dumped within its borders.

Why would a firm dump—charge a low price in the foreign market? The first reason is price discrimination. **Price discrimination** occurs when a firm charges a different price to different customers buying the same product. If a firm has a monopoly in its home market but faces strong competition in a foreign market, it will naturally charge a higher price in the home market. What the firm is doing is using its monopoly power to charge higher prices to consumers at home and charge lower prices to consumers abroad where it faces competition. This strategy maximizes the firm's profits.

To illustrate how international price discrimination works, let's look at the case of Korean VCRs.[3]

In the 1980s there were only three firms, all Korean, selling VCRs in Korea, but there were dozens of firms selling VCRs in Europe. The lack of competition in Korea generated very high prices for Korean consumers, who paid much more than European consumers paid for identical Korean VCRs and VCRs produced by firms in other countries. Essentially, Korean firms used their market power to discriminate against consumers in their own country. When international trade authorities concluded these companies were, indeed, dumping VCRs in Europe, the Korean firms responded by cutting prices in their home market. However, they didn't increase their prices in Europe—much to the delight of European consumers and the dismay of European producers, who had sought relief from the dumping in the first place.

The Korean VCR example brings up a second reason for dumping: **predatory pricing**—cutting prices in an attempt to drive rival firms out of business. The predatory firm sets its price below its production cost, low enough that both the predator and its prey (a firm in the foreign market) lose money. After the prey goes out of business, the predator increases its price to earn a monopoly profit.

Although the rationale for antidumping laws is to prevent predatory pricing, it is difficult to determine whether low prices are the result of this or price discrimination. Many economists are skeptical about how frequently predatory pricing actually occurs, as opposed to price discrimination. They suspect many nations use their antidumping laws as protectionist policies in disguise. Because WTO rules limit tariffs and quotas, some nations may be tempted to substitute antidumping duties for these protectionist policies.

Until the 1990s, antidumping cases were brought almost exclusively by Australia, New Zealand, Europe, Canada, and the United States. However, starting in the 1990s, the number of antidumping cases alleged by developing countries began to rise. Today, approximately half the cases are brought by developing countries. Professor Thomas Prusa of Rutgers University has studied antidumping and has found it is a potent weapon for protecting domestic industries. If an antidumping case is settled and a tariff is imposed as a result, imports typically fall by 50 to 70 percent during the first three years of the protection period. Even if a country loses a claim, imports still fall by 15 to 20 percent.[4]

Do Trade Laws Inhibit Environmental Protection?

In recent trade negotiations, a new player—environmental groups—appeared on the scene. Starting in the early 1990s, environmentalists began to question whether policies that liberalized trade could harm the environment. They were concerned that increased trade would lead to worldwide environmental degradation. An important issue that attracted their attention was the killing of dolphins by tuna fishers.

Anyone who catches tuna with a large net will also catch the dolphins that swim with the tuna, and most of the dolphins will die. In 1972, the United States outlawed the use of tuna nets by U.S. ships. However, ships from other nations, including Mexico, were still catching tuna with nets and selling that tuna in the United States. The United States responded with a ban of Mexican tuna caught with nets. The Mexican government complained to an international trade authority that the tuna boycott was an unfair trade barrier. The trade authority agreed with Mexico and forced the United States to remove the boycott.

Under current WTO rules, a country can adopt any environmental standard it chooses, as long as it does not discriminate against foreign producers. For example, the United States can limit the exhaust emissions of all cars that operate in the United States. As long as emissions rules apply equally to all cars, domestic and imports, the rules are legal according to the WTO. An international panel upheld U.S. fuel efficiency rules for automobiles on this principle.

The tuna boycott was a violation of WTO rules because killing dolphins does not harm the U.S. environment directly. For the same reason, the United States cannot ban imported goods produced by factories that generate air or water pollution in other countries. It is easy to understand why WTO rules do not allow countries to restrict trade on the basis of the methods that are used to produce goods and services. Countries differ in the value they place on the environment. For example, a poor nation may be willing to tolerate more pollution if it means attaining a higher standard of living for its citizens.

If trade restrictions cannot be used to protect the dolphins and deal with other global environmental problems, what else can we do? Shouldn't we have the right to protect dolphins? International agreements have been used for a variety of different environmental goals, from limiting the harvest of whales to reducing the chemicals that deplete the ozone layer. These agreements are difficult to reach, however, so some nations will be tempted to use trade restrictions to pursue environmental goals. If they do, they will encounter resistance because WTO rules mean that a nation can pursue its environmental goals only within its own borders. In recent years, environmentalists have lobbied Congress not to approve bilateral trade deals unless sufficient environmental standards are in place. This trend is likely to continue.

Trade disputes about environmental issues are part of a larger phenomenon that occurs when trade issues and national regulations collide. At one time, most trade disputes were simply matters of protecting domestic industries from foreign competition. Agriculture, textile, and steel industries around the world frequently benefited from various forms of protection. But in recent years, a new breed of trade disputes has erupted revolving around social problems and the role that government regulation should play in solving them.

The EU, for example, has banned imports of hormone-treated beef. The United States and Canada successfully challenged this ban with the WTO. They argued there was no scientific evidence that hormone-treated beef adversely affected human health. The EU refused to rescind the ban and, as a consequence, the United States and Canada were permitted to impose retaliatory tariffs on a wide range of European products that affected many EU industries.

The EU's ban on hormone-treated beef was intended to protect European farmers from imports, but it also reflected Europeans' nervousness about technology. After all, Europe banned all hormone-treated beef, not just imported beef. Shouldn't a country have a right to pursue this policy, even if it is not based on the best science of the day? Although the costs of the policy are straightforward in terms of higher beef prices, the benefits, in terms of potential safety and peace of mind, are much more difficult to assess. Similar issues have arisen as genetically modified crops have become more commonplace. As a world trading community, we will have to decide at what point we allow national policy concerns to override principles of free trade.

application 4

TRADE, CONSUMPTION, AND INEQUALITY

APPLYING THE CONCEPTS #4: Why might international trade reduce measured inequality in the United States?

While it is conventional wisdom now that inequality in the United States has increased in the last several decades, until recently no one had taken a careful look at the actual living standards of different income groups, taking into account the goods they purchase. Two economists from the University of Chicago, Christian Broda and John Romalis, discovered that the prices low-income groups paid for goods and services increased substantially less than for high-income groups. As a result, living standards have not become more unequal.

The key to understanding this result is that consumption patterns of the rich and poor differ. The poor consume a higher ratio of nondurable goods (such as cosmetics, toys, and sporting goods) to services than the rich, while prices for nondurable goods have risen less than prices for services. Prices for the nondurable goods purchased by the poor, which are typically sold in grocery, drug, and mass merchandise stores, also increased less than the prices of nondurable goods purchased by the rich. And the poor typically consume a higher fraction of new goods, whose prices have often fallen.

Trade with China is an important part of this story. About one-third of the change in relative prices that has helped the poor can be accounted for by an increase in imports from China. These are the goods that stock the shelves of Walmart and other lower-end stores where the poor shop. Sam Walton and his successors effectively ran their own antipoverty program.

The moral of the story: Trade does not just affect employment patterns—it also changes prices. We must take both factors into account to understand how living standards have changed for the rich and poor. **Related to Exercise 5.9.**

SOURCE: Based on Christian Broda and John Romalis, "Inequality and Prices: Does China Benefit the Poor in America?" March 26, 2008, http://siteresources.worldbank.org/INTMACRO/Resources/June5&62008MGConferencePAPERBRODA.pdf (accessed May 29, 2012).

Do Outsourcing and Trade Cause Income Inequality?

Inequality in wages has been growing in the United States since 1973. The wages of skilled workers have risen faster than the wages of unskilled workers. World trade has also boomed since 1973. Could there be a connection between the two?

Trade theory suggests a link between increased trade and increased wage inequality. Here is how they might be linked. Suppose the United States produces two types of goods: one using skilled labor (say, airplanes) and one using unskilled labor (say, textiles). The United States is likely to have a comparative advantage in products that use skilled labor, and developing countries are likely to have a comparative advantage in products that use unskilled labor. An increase in world trade will increase both exports and imports. An increase in U.S. exports means we'll need to produce more goods requiring skilled labor, so the domestic demand for skilled labor will increase, and so will the wages of these workers. At the same time, an increase in U.S. imports means we'll be buying more goods produced by unskilled laborers abroad, so the demand for unskilled workers here will decrease, and these people's wages will fall. As a result, the gap between the wages of the two types of workers in the United States will grow.

In addition, U.S. firms will produce some components of their goods and services overseas, which is known as **outsourcing**. If a firm outsources products that use unskilled labor, the demand for unskilled labor in the United States will decline, and this will also increase the gap between wages for the skilled and the unskilled.

Economists have tried to determine how much trade has contributed to growing wage inequality in the United States. As usual, other factors make such a determination difficult. It is difficult, for example, to distinguish between the effects of trade and the effects of technical progress. Technical change, such as the rapid introduction and use of computers, will also tend to increase the demand for skilled workers and decrease the demand for unskilled workers. Economists have noted, however, that the exports of goods using skilled labor and the imports of goods using unskilled labor have both increased, just as the theory predicts. Nonetheless, at least some of the increased wage inequality is caused by international trade. Trade, however, may also reduce the prices of goods and services purchased by consumers in different income classes. We must take this factor into account in assessing trade and inequality.

One response to this undesirable side effect of trade is to use trade restrictions to protect industries that use unskilled workers. Another approach is to make the transition to an economy with more skilled than unskilled jobs less traumatic. In the long run, of course, workers will move to industries that require skilled labor, and they will eventually earn higher wages. However, in the short run the government could facilitate the transition by providing assistance for the education and training of unskilled workers.

More recently, there has been another concern. In recent years, jobs in call centers for airlines and credit card companies, customer service and technical support for computers, and the work of writing computer code have been relocated overseas. Some of these jobs require considerable skill, and therefore not all jobs that are outsourced will be low-skilled jobs. Nor can all services be outsourced, particularly those that are less routine. In the coming years, we will gain better insights into how international trade and outsourcing affect the wages of skilled workers.

outsourcing
Firms producing components of their goods and services in other countries.

Why Do People Protest Free Trade?

We have seen some of the important policy issues surrounding trade. Under current international trade rules, a country cannot dictate the terms under which another country actually produces the goods and services it sells—even if production harms the environment. It is also possible that free trade can contribute to inequality within the United States, although lower prices for goods consumed partially offset this effect. But do these reasons explain the passion we sometimes see in protests against free trade, such as the riots in 1999 in Seattle at a WTO meeting or the protestors dressed in death masks gathering at world trade meetings? Possibly, but protestors are more likely driven by something very basic. As we have seen in this chapter, trade and specialization provide important opportunities to raise living standards throughout the globe. But they also mean individuals and nations surrender some of their independence and sovereignty. By not producing precisely what we consume, we become dependent on others to trade with us. By cooperating with other nations, we need to develop agreed-upon rules that, at times, limit our own actions.

The protestors may simply not understand the principles of trade, but they also may fear loss of cultural identity and independence. In today's world, "no man is an island." Nations have become increasingly dependent on one another. Multinational corporations are the ultimate symbol of this interdependence, producing and distributing goods on a global scale. Thus companies such as McDonald's, Starbucks, or Nike can come under attack by protestors. The benefits of trade, however, are so vast that countries will need to find ways to address issues of sovereignty and control while retaining an open and prosperous trading system.

In this chapter, we discussed the benefits of specialization and trade, and we explored the trade-offs associated with protectionist policies. There is a basic conflict between consumers who prefer free trade because free trade decreases prices and workers in the protected industries who want to keep their jobs. Here are the main points of the chapter:

1 If one country has a *comparative advantage* vis-à-vis another country in producing a particular good (a lower opportunity cost), specialization and trade will benefit both countries.

2 An import ban or an *import quota* increases prices, protecting domestic industries, but domestic consumers pay the price.

3 Because the victims of protectionist policies often retaliate, the protection of a domestic industry can harm an exporting industry.

4 A *tariff*, a tax on imports, generates revenue for the government, whereas an *import quota*—a limit on imports—generates revenue for foreigners or importers.

5 In principle, the laws against *dumping* are designed to prevent *predatory pricing*. In practice, predatory pricing laws are often used to shield domestic industries from competition. Allegations of it are hard to prove.

6 Under *World Trade Organization (WTO)* rules, each country may pursue its environmental goals only within its own borders.

7 International trade has contributed to the widening gap between the wages of low-skilled and high-skilled labor. However, it also has reduced the relative prices facing the poor, offsetting some of the effects on inequality.

KEY TERMS

consumption possibilities curve, p. 412

dumping, p. 421

General Agreement on Tariffs and Trade (GATT), p. 420

import licenses, p. 415

import quota, p. 415

infant industries, p. 418

learning by doing, p. 418

outsourcing, p. 425

predatory pricing, p. 422

price discrimination, p. 422

tariff, p. 416

terms of trade, p. 412

voluntary export restraint (VER), p. 415

World Trade Organization (WTO), p. 420

EXERCISES

All problems are assignable in MyEconLab.

18.1 Benefits from Specialization and Trade

1.1 A country has a comparative advantage if it has a lower _____ cost of producing a good.

1.2 The terms of trade is the rate at which two goods can be _____ for one another.

1.3 Suppose a country has a comparative advantage in shirts but not computer chips. Workers in the chip industry will be _____ with trade.

1.4 Countries will always export the goods in which they have absolute advantage. _____ (True/False)

1.5 **Finding Comparative Advantage.** In one minute, Country B can produce either 1,000 TVs and no computers or 500 computers and no TVs. Similarly, in one minute Country C can produce either 2,400 TVs or 600 computers.

   a. Compute the opportunity costs of TVs and computers for each country. Which country has a comparative advantage in producing TVs? Which country has a comparative advantage in producing computers?

   b. Draw the production possibilities curves for the two countries.

1.6 **Benefits from Trade.** In Country U, the opportunity cost of a computer is 10 pairs of shoes. In Country C, the opportunity cost of a computer is 100 pairs of shoes.

   a. Suppose the two countries split the difference between the willingness to pay for computers and the willingness to accept computers. Compute the terms of trade, that is, the rate at which the two countries will exchange computers and shoes.

   b. Suppose the two countries exchange one computer for the number of shoes dictated by the terms of trade you computed in part (a). Compute the net benefit from trade for each country.

1.7 **Measuring the Gains from Trade.** Consider two countries, Tableland and Chairland, each capable of producing tables and chairs. Chairland can produce the following combinations of chairs and tables:

All chairs and no tables: 36 chairs per day

All tables and no chairs: 18 tables per day

Tableland can produce the following combinations of chairs and tables:

All chairs and no tables: 40 chairs per day

All tables and no chairs: 40 tables per day

In each country, there is a fixed trade-off of tables for chairs.

a. Draw the two production possibilities curves, with chairs on the vertical axis and tables on the horizontal axis.

b. Suppose each country is initially self-sufficient and divides its resources equally between the two goods. How much does each country produce and consume?

c. Which country has a comparative advantage in producing tables? Which country has a comparative advantage in producing chairs?

d. If the two countries split the difference between the buyer's willingness to pay for chairs and the seller's willingness to accept, in terms of chairs per table, what are the terms of trade?

e. Draw the consumption possibilities curves.

f. Suppose each country specializes in the good for which it has a comparative advantage, and it exchanges 14 tables for some quantity of chairs. Compute the consumption bundles—*bundles* mean the consumption of tables and chairs—for each country.

1.8 **Who Benefits in the Short Run?** Suppose a country is about to open its markets for trade. In the short run, would you rather be employed in an industry with a comparative advantage or a comparative disadvantage? What about in the long run?

18.2 Protectionist Policies

2.1 If a country bans the importation of a particular good, the market equilibrium is shown by the intersection of the _____ curve and the _____ curve.

2.2 The equilibrium price under an import quota is _____ (above/below) the price that occurs with an import ban and _____ (above/below) the price that occurs with free trade.

2.3 From the perspective of the government, a _____ (tariff/quota) is better.

2.4 Threatening to impose a tariff on a country's exports if it doesn't open up its markets to trade is an example of a _____ policy.

2.5 **Incentives for Smuggling.** If a country bans imports, smugglers may try to penetrate its markets. Suppose Chipland bans shirt imports, causing some importers to bribe customs officials who "look the other way" as smugglers bring shirts into the country. Your job is to combat shirt smuggling. Use the information in Figure 18.3 on page 414 to answer the following questions:

a. Suppose importers can sell their shirts on the world market at a price of $12 per shirt. How much is an importer willing to pay to get customs officials to look the other way?

b. What sort of change in trade policy would make your job easier?

2.6 **Tariffs on Computer Chips.** Suppose a country imposed tariffs on computer chips to protect its chip-making industries. What other types of firms in that economy might object to this policy?

2.7 **Tariffs and the Poor.** Historically, apparel and textiles were subject to high tariffs. Explain why this might hurt low-income consumers more than high-income consumers. (Related to Application 1 on page 417.)

2.8 **Auctioning Import Licenses.** In the text we explained that tariffs can be set to have the same effects as import quotas. However, if the government gives import licenses to producers, it will not collect any revenues. Suppose the government auctions the import licenses to the highest bidders. How will the revenue from the auction compare to the revenue raised by tariffs?

18.3 What Are the Rationales for Protectionist Policies?

3.1 The _____ industry argument is often given to provide a rationale for tariffs for new firms.

3.2 Knowledge gained during production is known as _____ by doing.

3.3 If only one firm can exist in a market, a government may try to subsidize the firm so that the country can share in the _____ profits.

3.4 In the 1950s and 1960s, countries in _____ used tariffs and other policies to nurture domestic industries.

3.5 **Learning by Doing?** An industry has been operating for 10 years under protection. The government wants to remove the trade protection, but the industry claims that it needs the protection because of learning by doing. Evaluate its claim. Can you think of a circumstance where it could be true?

3.6 **Two Countries Fighting over Airplane Production.** Suppose there are monopoly profits in the production of airplanes, but two countries are each determined to capture the industry. When one country subsidizes its domestic firm, the other country matches the tactic. As a result, both firms stay in business. Who gains and who loses? Consider the effects on the firms, consumers, and taxpayers.

3.7 Why the Pace of Imports May Matter. If it rains very hard during a major storm, the drains in the streets may not be able to handle all the water and flooding will temporarily occur. Use this analogy to explain why the pace of imports into a community may be important in the short run for economic adjustment. (Related to Application 2 on page 419).

3.8 Protection for Candle Makers. In a famous tale, the French economist Frédéric Bastiat (1801–1850) wrote a fake petition for relief from trade for the candle makers. They were complaining that the sun was hurting their business. What lesson do you draw from this tale?

18.4 A Brief History of International Tariff and Trade Agreements

4.1 The latest trade round is called the _____ round.

4.2 The _____ was formed in 1995 to oversee GATT.

4.3 NAFTA is a free-trade agreement between the United States, Mexico, and _____.

4.4 The average tariff rate in the United States is roughly _____ percent.

4.5 A Major Change in U.S. Trade Policy? In Chapter 7 of the 2006 *Economic Report of the President* (www.gpoaccess.gov/eop/download.html), the authors of the report discuss the important changes that occurred in 1934 under the Reciprocal Trade Agreements Act. They contend that it began to move the United States to a policy of more open trade after the Smoot–Hawley tariffs. Identify the key changes enacted in 1934.

4.6 Expansion in the European Union. When the EU originated, member countries generally had similar standards of living. However, with the most recent expansion of the EU, countries that were less developed joined the developed countries. What implications might the entry of the new countries have for wage inequality within the more established European countries?

4.7 Trade in Intellectual Property. Trade in international property (for example, patents, licenses, royalty agreements) has been particularly controversial. Go to the intellectual property section of the WTO's Web site (http://www.wto.org/english/tratop_e/trips_e/trips_e.htm) and explore some of

its case studies. Do developing countries, as well as developed countries, have an interest in protecting intellectual property?

18.5 Recent Policy Debates and Trade Agreements

5.1 Pricing below production cost or selling at prices in foreign markets less than those in domestic markets is known as _____.

5.2 Under global trade rules, the United States was allowed to ban Mexican tuna because Mexico used fishing nets that killed dolphins. _____ (True/False)

5.3 Suppose the United States has a comparative advantage in goods that use skilled labor. If we trade with a country that has a comparative advantage in goods using unskilled labor, the wage differences between skilled and unskilled labor in the United States will _____.

5.4 Under a scheme of _____ pricing, a firm cuts its price to drive out rivals and then raises its price later.

5.5 Trade in Genetically Modified Crops. Suppose the residents of a country become fearful of using genetically modified crops in their food supply. Consider the following two possible scenarios:

a. Aware of consumer sentiment, the largest supermarket chains in the country vow they will not purchase food products that use genetically modified crops.

b. The government, aware of voter sentiment during an election year, bans the import of the food products that use genetically modified crops.

In both cases, no genetically modified crops enter the country. Does either of these cases run afoul of WTO policies?

5.6 Blinder versus Bhagwati on Outsourcing of Services. In an essay in the journal *Foreign Affairs*, Princeton economist Alan Blinder warned that the United States potentially faces great dangers from outsourcing of services. Columbia economist Jagdish Bhagwati was highly skeptical of this argument. Read both articles and come to your own assessment. The Blinder article, "Offshoring: The Next Industrial Revolution," *Foreign Affairs*, March/April 2006, is available at http://www.foreignaffairs.com/articles/61514/alan-s-blinder/offshoring-the-next-industrial-revolution (Accessed October 29, 2012). The Bhagwati article, "Don't Cry for Free Trade," New York: Council of Foreign Relations, October 15, 2007, is available at http://www.cfr.org/trade/dont-cry-free-trade/p14526 (Accessed October 29, 2012).

5.7 A Dumping Calculation. To produce 100 units of a good, a firm needs $40,000 in labor, $60,000 in material and capital cost, and requires a 10 percent profit rate. What would be the hypothetical price calculated for this firm? Suppose the profit rate was 20 percent—how would the price change? (Related to Application 3 on page 421.)

5.8 To Whom Should China Be Compared? Under U.S. dumping rules, China is classified as a non-market economy so other market economies are used to calculate prices for dumping. Until recently, China was compared to India, but now it is compared to Thailand. Using Thailand rather than India as a comparison country was one of the key reasons that China was found to be dumping solar panels. Why does the choice of country matter?

5.9 What Do the Poor and the Rich Buy? In Application 4, we highlighted research showing that the nondurable goods the poor buy have gone up in price less than those purchased by the rich and that the poor buy a higher percentage of newer goods than the rich. Can you give some examples of these price differences from your experience at normal and upscale supermarkets? Visit a couple of same-industry stores such as Walmart and Whole Foods to collect data if necessary. (Related to Application 4 on page 424.)

NOTES

1. *A Review of Recent Developments in the U.S. Automobile Industry, Including an Assessment of the Japanese Voluntary Restraint Agreements* (Washington, D.C.: U.S. International Trade Commission, February 1985).

2. Gary C. Hufbauer, "The Benefits of Open Markets and the Costs of Trade Protection and Economic Sanction," ACCF Center for Policy Research, www.accf.org/publications/reports/sr-benefits-openmarkets1997.html (accessed June 2006).

3. Taeho Bark, "The Korean Consumer Electronics Industry: Reaction to Antidumping Actions," in *Antidumping: How It Works and Who Gets Hurt*, ed. J. Michael Finger (Ann Arbor, MI: University of Michigan Press, 1993), chap. 7.

4. Virginia Postrel, "Curb Demonstrates Faults of Courting Special Interests," *New York Times*, June 14, 2001.

Glossary

absolute advantage The ability of one person or nation to produce a product at a lower resource cost than another person or nation.

accounting cost The explicit costs of production.

accounting profit Total revenue minus accounting cost.

adverse-selection problem A situation in which the uninformed side of the market must choose from an undesirable or adverse selection of goods.

asymmetric information A situation in which one side of the market—either buyers or sellers—has better information than the other.

average fixed cost (AFC) Fixed cost divided by the quantity produced.

average variable cost (AVC) Variable cost divided by the quantity produced.

barrier to entry Something that prevents firms from entering a profitable market.

break-even price The price at which economic profit is zero; price equals average total cost.

cartel A group of firms that act in unison, coordinating their price and quantity decisions.

centrally planned economy An economy in which a government bureaucracy decides how much of each good to produce, how to produce the good, and who gets the good.

ceteris paribus The Latin expression meaning that other variables are held fixed.

change in demand A shift of the demand curve caused by a change in a variable other than the price of the product.

change in quantity demanded A change in the quantity consumers are willing and able to buy when the price changes; represented graphically by movement along the demand curve.

change in quantity supplied A change in the quantity firms are willing and able to sell when the price changes; represented graphically by movement along the supply curve.

change in supply A shift of the supply curve caused by a change in a variable other than the price of the product.

comparative advantage The ability of one person or nation to produce a good at a lower opportunity cost than another person or nation.

complements Two goods for which a decrease in the price of one good increases the demand for the other good.

concentration ratios The percentage of the market output produced by the largest firms.

constant returns to scale A situation in which the long-run total cost increases proportionately with output, so average cost is constant.

constant-cost industry An industry in which the average cost of production is constant; the long-run supply curve is horizontal.

consumer surplus The amount a consumer is willing to pay for a product minus the price the consumer actually pays.

consumption possibilities curve A curve showing the combinations of two goods that can be consumed when a nation specializes in a particular good and trades with another nation.

contestable market A market with low entry and exit costs.

cross-price elasticity of demand A measure of the responsiveness of demand to changes in the price of another good; equal to the percentage change in the quantity demanded of one good (X) divided by the percentage change in the price of another good (Y).

deadweight loss The decrease in the total surplus of the market that results from a policy such as rent control.

deadweight loss from monopoly A measure of the inefficiency from monopoly; equal to the decrease in the market surplus.

deadweight loss from taxation The difference between the total burden of a tax and the amount of revenue collected by the government.

demand schedule A table that shows the relationship between the price of a product and the quantity demanded, *ceteris paribus*.

diminishing returns As one input increases while the other inputs are held fixed, output increases at a decreasing rate.

discovered price The lowest price observed so far in a search process.

diseconomies of scale A situation in which the long-run average cost of production increases as output increases.

dominant strategy An action that is the best choice for a player, no matter what the other player does.

dumping A situation in which the price a firm charges in a foreign market is lower than either the price it charges in its home markets or the production cost.

duopolists' dilemma A situation in which both firms in a market would be better off if both chose the high price, but each chooses the low price.

duopoly A market with two firms.

economic cost The opportunity cost of the inputs used in the production process; equal to explicit cost plus implicit cost.

economic model A simplified representation of an economic environment, often employing a graph.

economic profit Total revenue minus economic cost.

economics The study of choices when there is scarcity.

economies of scale A situation in which the long-run average cost of production decreases as output increases.

efficiency A situation in which people do the best they can, given their limited resources.

elastic demand The price elasticity of demand is greater than one, so the percentage change in quantity exceeds the percentage change in price.

entrepreneurship The effort used to coordinate the factors of production—natural resources, labor, physical capital, and human capital—to produce and sell products.

excess burden of a tax Another name for deadweight loss.

excess demand A situation in which, at the prevailing price, the quantity demanded exceeds the quantity supplied.

excess supply A situation in which the quantity supplied exceeds the quantity demanded at the prevailing price.

experience rating A situation in which insurance companies charge different prices for medical insurance to different firms depending on the past medical bills of a firm's employees.

explicit cost A monetary payment.

export A good or service produced in the home country (for example, the United States) and sold in another country.

external benefit A benefit from a good experienced by someone other than the person who buys the good.

external cost of production A cost incurred by someone other than the producer.

factors of production The resources used to produce goods and services; also known as *production inputs* or *resources*.

featherbedding Work rules that increase the amount of labor required to produce a given quantity of output. Featherbedding may actually decrease the demand for labor.

firm-specific demand curve A curve showing the relationship between the price charged by a specific firm and the quantity the firm can sell.

fixed cost (*FC*) Cost that does not vary with the quantity produced.

free rider A person who gets the benefit from a good but does not pay for it.

game theory The study of decision making in strategic situations.

game tree A graphical representation of the consequences of different actions in a strategic setting.

General Agreement on Tariffs and Trade (GATT) An international agreement established in 1947 that has lowered trade barriers between the United States and other nations.

grim-trigger strategy A strategy where a firm responds to underpricing by choosing a price so low that each firm makes zero economic profit.

human capital The knowledge and skills acquired by a worker through education and experience and used to produce goods and services.

implicit cost An opportunity cost that does not involve a monetary payment.

import A good or service produced in a foreign country and purchased by residents of the home country (for example, the United States).

import licenses Rights, issued by a government, to import goods.

import quota A government-imposed limit on the quantity of a good that can be imported.

income effect for leisure demand The change in leisure time resulting from a change in real income caused by a change in the wage.

income elasticity of demand A measure of the responsiveness of demand to changes in consumer income; equal to the percentage change in the quantity demanded divided by the percentage change in income.

increasing-cost industry An industry in which the average cost of production increases as the total output of the industry increases; the long-run supply curve is positively sloped.

individual demand curve A curve that shows the relationship between the price of a good and quantity demanded by an individual consumer, *ceteris paribus*.

individual supply curve A curve showing the relationship between price and quantity supplied by a single firm, *ceteris paribus*.

indivisible input An input that cannot be scaled down to produce a smaller quantity of output.

inelastic demand The price elasticity of demand is less than one, so the percentage change in quantity is less than the percentage change in price.

infant industries Industries that are at an early stage of development.

inferior good A good for which an increase in income decreases demand.

input-substitution effect The change in the quantity of labor demanded resulting from an increase in the price of labor relative to the price of other inputs.

labor Human effort, including both physical and mental effort, used to produce goods and services.

labor union A group of workers organized to increase job security, improve working conditions, and increase wages and fringe benefits.

law of demand There is a negative relationship between price and quantity demanded, *ceteris paribus*.

law of supply There is a positive relationship between price and quantity supplied, *ceteris paribus*.

learning by doing Knowledge and skills workers gain during production that increase productivity and lower cost.

learning effect The increase in a person's wage resulting from the learning of skills required for certain occupations.

limit price The price that is just low enough to deter entry.

limit pricing The strategy of reducing the price to deter entry.

long-run average cost (LAC) The long-run cost divided by the quantity produced.

long-run demand curve for labor A curve showing the relationship between the wage and the quantity of labor demanded over the long run, when the number of firms in the market can change and firms can modify their production facilities.

long-run marginal cost (LMC) The change in long-run cost resulting from a one-unit increase in output.

long-run market supply curve A curve showing the relationship between the market price and quantity supplied in the long run.

long-run total cost (LTC) The total cost of production when a firm is perfectly flexible in choosing its inputs.

low-price guarantee A promise to match a lower price of a competitor.

macroeconomics The study of the nation's economy as a whole; focuses on the issues of inflation, unemployment, and economic growth.

marginal benefit The additional benefit resulting from a small increase in some activity.

marginal change A small, one-unit change in value.

marginal cost The additional cost resulting from a small increase in some activity.

marginal product of labor The change in output from one additional unit of labor.

marginal revenue The change in total revenue from selling one more unit of output.

marginal-revenue product of labor (MRP) The extra revenue generated from one additional unit of labor; *MRP* is equal to the price of output times the marginal product of labor.

market demand curve A curve showing the relationship between price and quantity demanded by all consumers, *ceteris paribus*.

market economy An economy in which people specialize and exchange goods and services in markets.

market equilibrium A situation in which the quantity demanded equals the quantity supplied at the prevailing market price.

market power The ability of a firm to affect the price of its product.

market supply curve A curve showing the relationship between the market price and quantity supplied by all firms, *ceteris paribus*.

market supply curve for labor A curve showing the relationship between the wage and the quantity of labor supplied.

marketable pollution permits A system under which the government picks a target pollution level for a particular area, issues just enough pollution permits to meet the pollution target, and allows firms to buy and sell the permits; also known as a *cap-and-trade system*.

means-tested programs A government spending program that provides assistance to those whose income falls below a certain level.

median-voter rule The choices made by the government will match the preferences of the median voter.

merger A process in which two or more firms combine their operations.

microeconomics The study of the choices made by households, firms, and government and how these choices affect the markets for goods and services.

minimum efficient scale The output at which scale economies are exhausted.

minimum supply price The lowest price at which a product will be supplied.

mixed market A market in which goods of different qualities are sold for the same price.

monopolistic competition A market served by many firms that sell slightly different products.

monopoly A market in which a single firm sells a product that does not have any close substitutes.

moral hazard A situation in which one side of an economic relationship takes undesirable or costly actions that the other side of the relationship cannot observe.

Nash equilibrium An outcome of a game in which each player is doing the best he or she can, given the action of the other players.

natural monopoly A market in which the economies of scale in production are so large that only a single large firm can earn a profit.

natural resources Resources provided by nature and used to produce goods and services.

negative relationship A relationship in which two variables move in opposite directions.

network externalities The value of a product to a consumer increases with the number of other consumers who use it.

nominal value The face value of an amount of money.

normal good A good for which an increase in income increases demand.

normative analysis Answers the question "What *ought to be*?"

oligopoly A market served by a few firms.

opportunity cost What you sacrifice to get something.

output effect The change in the quantity of labor demanded resulting from a change in the quantity of output produced.

outsourcing Firms producing components of their goods and services in other countries.

patent The exclusive right to sell a new good for some period of time.

payoff matrix A matrix or table that shows, for each possible outcome of a game, the consequences for each player.

perfectly competitive market A market with many sellers and buyers of a homogeneous product and no barriers to entry.

perfectly elastic demand The price elasticity of demand is infinite.

perfectly elastic supply The price elasticity of supply is equal to infinity.

perfectly inelastic demand The price elasticity of demand is zero.

perfectly inelastic supply The price elasticity of supply equals zero.

physical capital The stock of equipment, machines, structures, and infrastructure that is used to produce goods and services.

pollution tax A tax or charge equal to the external cost per unit of pollution.

positive analysis Answers the question "What *is*?" or "What *will be*?"

positive relationship A relationship in which two variables move in the same direction.

predatory pricing A firm sells a product at a price below its production cost to drive a rival out of business and then increases the price.

price ceiling A maximum price set by the government.

price discrimination The practice of selling a good at different prices to different consumers.

price elasticity of demand (Ed) A measure of the responsiveness of the quantity demanded to changes in price; equal to the absolute value of the percentage change in quantity demanded divided by the percentage change in price.

price elasticity of supply A measure of the responsiveness of the quantity supplied to changes in price; equal to the percentage change in quantity supplied divided by the percentage change in price.

price fixing An arrangement in which firms conspire to fix prices.

price floor A minimum price set by the government.

price leadership A system under which one firm in an oligopoly takes the lead in setting prices.

price taker A buyer or seller that takes the market price as given.

private cost of production The production cost borne by a producer, which typically includes the costs of labor, capital, and materials.

private good A good that is consumed by a single person or household; a good that is rival in consumption and excludable.

producer surplus The price a producer receives for a product minus the marginal cost of production.

product differentiation The process used by firms to distinguish their products from the products of competing firms.

production possibilities curve A curve that shows the possible combinations of products that an economy can produce, given that its productive resources are fully employed and efficiently used.

public good A good that is available for everyone to consume, regardless of who pays and who doesn't; a good that is nonrival in consumption and nonexcludable.

public-choice economics A field of economics that uses models of rational choice to explore decision making in the public sector.

quantity demanded The amount of a product that consumers are willing and able to buy.

quantity supplied The amount of a product that firms are willing and able to sell.

real value The value of an amount of money in terms of what it can buy.

rent seeking The process of using public policy to gain economic profit.

reservation price The price at which a consumer is indifferent about additional search for a lower price.

scarcity The resources we use to produce goods and services are limited.

short-run average total cost (ATC) Short-run total cost divided by the quantity produced; equal to *AFC* plus *AVC*.

short-run demand curve for labor A curve showing the relationship between the wage and the quantity of labor demanded over the short run, when the firm cannot change its production facility.

short-run marginal cost (MC) The change in short-run total cost resulting from a one-unit increase in output.

short-run market supply curve A curve showing the relationship between the market price and quantity supplied in the short run.

short-run supply curve A curve showing the relationship between the market price of a product and the quantity of output supplied by a firm in the short run.

short-run total cost (TC) The total cost of production when at least one input is fixed; equal to fixed cost plus variable cost.

shut-down price The price at which the firm is indifferent between operating and shutting down; equal to the minimum average variable cost.

signaling effect The information about a person's work skills conveyed by completing college.

slope of a curve The vertical difference between two points (the *rise*) divided by the horizontal difference (the *run*).

social cost of production Private cost plus external cost.

substitutes Two goods for which an increase in the price of one good increases the demand for the other good.

substitution effect for leisure demand The change in leisure time resulting from a change in the wage (the price of leisure) relative to the price of other goods.

sunk cost A cost that a firm has already paid or committed to pay, so it cannot be recovered.

supply schedule A table that shows the relationship between the price of a product and quantity supplied, *ceteris paribus*.

tariff A tax on imported goods.

terms of trade The rate at which units of one product can be exchanged for units of another product.

thin market A market in which some high-quality goods are sold but fewer than would be sold in a market with perfect information.

tie-in sale A business practice under which a business requires a consumer of one product to purchase another product.

tit-for-tat strategy A strategy where one firm chooses whatever price the other firm chose in the preceding period.

total revenue The money a firm generates from selling its product.

total surplus The sum of consumer surplus and producer surplus.

total-product curve A curve showing the relationship between the quantity of labor and the quantity of output produced, *ceteris paribus*.

trust An arrangement under which the owners of several companies transfer their decision-making powers to a small group of trustees.

unit elastic demand The price elasticity of demand is one, so the percentage change in quantity equals the percentage change in price.

variable A measure of something that can take on different values.

variable cost (*VC*) Cost that varies with the quantity produced.

voluntary export restraint (VER) A scheme under which an exporting country voluntarily decreases its exports.

willingness to accept The minimum amount a producer is willing to accept as payment for a product; equal to the marginal cost of production.

willingness to pay The maximum amount a consumer is willing to pay for a product.

World Trade Organization (WTO) An organization established in 1995 that oversees GATT and other international trade agreements, resolves trade disputes, and holds forums for further rounds of trade negotiations.

Photo Credits

CHAPTER 01: Pages 1 and 13, Ulrich Niehoff/Alamy; Page 9, Alamy; Page 10, Photos.com; Page 24, Stefan Witas/iStockphoto.

CHAPTER 02: Pages 28 and 43, Puwanai/Shutterstock, Page 33, Fotolia, Page 36, Shutterstock; Page 38, Alamy; Page 40, Navarone/Dreamstime.

CHAPTER 03: Pages 49 and 62 (bottom), Bill Bachman/Alamy; Page 55, Fotolia; Page 59, Joyce/Photo Researchers, Inc.; Page 62, Charles Sturge/Alamy (top).

CHAPTER 04: Pages 67 and 91, Steshkin Yevgeniy/Shutterstock; Page 71, Michal Bednarek/Shutterstock; Page 76, Diether Endlicher/AP Images; Page 78, Hemis/Alamy; Page 82, J JAVA/Fotolia; Page 89, Shutterstock.

CHAPTER 05: Pages 97 and 120 (bottom), Oleg - F/Shutterstock; Page 103, Justin Sullivan/Getty Images; Page 107, Mike Kahn/Alamy; Page 110, Fotolia; Page 112, Economic Research Service; Page 116, Dennis Donohue/Shutterstock; Page 120 (top), Shutterstock.

CHAPTER 06: Pages 127 and 116, Andy Kropa/Redux; Page 131, Shutterstock; Page 134, Owe Andersson/Alamy; Page 137, Coprid/fotolia; Page 140, Shutterstock; Page 145, Oleg Golovnev/Shutterstock.

CHAPTER 07: Pages 152 and 176 (bottom), Mike Kemp/AGE Fotostock; Page 160, Stephanie Pilick/Newscom; Page 164, Martin Shields/Alamy; Page 169, Tim Pannell/Alamy; Page 176 (top), Shutterstock.

CHAPTER 08: Pages 185 and 202, Appujee/Fotolia; Page 187, Anthony Lee/AGE Fotostock; Page 194, Alamy; Page 199, Juniors Bildarchiv/Alamy.

CHAPTER 09: Pages 207 and 227 (bottom), David Espin/Fotolia; Page 210, Getty Images; Page 214, Jim Parkin/Alamy; Page 217, Timothy Epp/Shutterstock; Page 220, Dedi/Fotolia; Page 223, Joachim E Röttgers/AGE Fotostock; Page 225, Alamy; Page 227 (top), Fotolia.

CHAPTER 10: Pages 233 and 248 (bottom), Doug Schneider/Alamy; Page 239, Rhona Wise/Newscom; Page 242, John Reddy/Alamy; Page 244, John Reddy/Alamy; Page 248 (top), Larry Mulvehill/The Image Works.

CHAPTER 11: Pages 254 and 266, Ariel Skelley/Alamy; Page 258, Lexaarts/Fotolia; Page 261, Judith Collins/Alamy; Page 263, Dutourdumonde/Shutterstock; Page 264, Kurhan/Shutterstock.

CHAPTER 12: Pages 270 and 290, SeanPavonePhoto/Shutterstock; Page 276, LianeM/Fotolia; Page 280, Tony Freeman/PhotoEdit, Inc.; Page 283, Lisa F. Young/Shutterstock; Page 287, Lightworks Media/Alamy; Page 289, Michael Siluk/The Image Works.

CHAPTER 13: Pages 297 and 309 (bottom), Sheila Halsall/Alamy; Page 302, Samuel Wheeler/Alamy; Page 303, Earth Observing System/NASA; Page 308, Joe Belanger/Shutterstock; Page 309 (top), Glow Images.

CHAPTER 14: Pages 313 and 322 (bottom), Vitalii Nesterchuk/Shutterstock; Page 318, Duane Burleson/AP Images; Page 321, Ron Redfern/Dorling Kindersley, Ltd.; Page 325, Andrey Kekyalyaynen/Alamy; Page 327, Nick Lylak/Alamy; Page 332 (top), Iofoto/Shutterstock.

CHAPTER 15: Pages 339 and 351 (bottom), Detlev van Ravenswaay/Photo Researchers, Inc.; Page 343, Duncan Smith/Getty Images; Page 344, National Oceanic and Atmospheric Administration; Page 346, Mitch Kezar/Getty Images; Page 347, Frank Tozier/Alamy; Page 351 (top), Action Plus/Alamy.

CHAPTER 16: Pages 356 and 372 (bottom), Elxeneize/Shutterstock; Page 360, Repina Valeriya/Shutterstock; Page 364, Anne Kitzman/Shutterstock; Page 366, Chris Cheadle/Alamy; Page 369, FB-Rose/Alamy; Page 372 (top), Lisa F. Young/Shutterstock.

CHAPTER 17: Pages 377 and 403, WavebreakmediaMicro/Fotolia; Page 383, Cstyle/Fotolia; Page 386, Shutterstock; Page 393, Stephen Coburn/Shutterstock; Page 397, Michael Newman/PhotoEdit, Inc.; Page 402, Gabe Hernandez/AP Images.

CHAPTER 18: Pages 409 and 426, Stephen Barnes/Alamy; Page 417, Dior Azcuy/AP Images; Page 419, Arkadiusz Komski/Shutterstock; Page 421, Lawrence Manning/Alamy; Page 424, Jason Turner/AP Images.

Index

A

Absolute advantage, 52, 55
Accounting, 382
Accounting cost, 186, 187
Accounting profit, 187
Accounting rules, 56
Adverse-selection problem, 316, 321, 324
Advertisers' dilemma, 287–289
Advertising
  consumer choice and, 264
  generic, 289
  oligopoly and, 287–289
  for product differentiation, 264–265
Affordability, 158, 161, 171
Africa, poverty in, 5–6
African Americans, wage discrimination and, 391–392
Agriculture policy, 78
Airbus, 419
Airline ticket discounts, 245
Air pollution, 362–363, 369–371
Akerlof, George, 314
Alcoa, 217
Aluminum Company of America (Alcoa), 285
Amazon.com, 246
American Telephone and Telegraph (AT&T), 304
American Tobacco Company, 304
Amygdala, 167
Anchoring, 182
Antidrug policies, 107
Antitrust policy, 61, 303–308
Apartment market, 223

Archer Daniels Midland (ADM), 279
Artificial barriers to entry, 258, 300
Asian Pacific Economic Cooperation (APEC), 420
Assumptions, use of, for simplification, 7, 9
Asymmetric information, 314–317
  insurance and, 321–325
  lemons problem and, 314–317
Automobile collisions
  external costs from, 371–372
  young drivers and, 372
Automobile emissions standards, marginal principle and, 35–36
Automobile insurance, 325, 371–372
Automobiles, external costs from, 369–372
Average-cost curves, 198–199
Average-cost pricing, 301–302
Average costs, 190–192, 198–200
  of information goods, 201
  marginal costs and, 193
  variety and, 262
Average fixed cost (AFC), 190
Average variable cost (AVC), 190

B

Bar graphs, 15
Barrier to entry, 234
  artificial, 257, 258, 300
Baseball pitchers, 318
Beef, hormone-treated, 423

Beer prices, highway death and, 104
Benefit valuation, 165–166
Bentham, Jeremy, 153
Biofuels, 214
Boeing, 419
Brain, energy for, 168–169
Brand elasticity, 106–107
Brazil, cement industry in, 270
Break-even price, 213–215
Breathmobile, 370
Broda, Christian, 424
Buchanan, James, 349
Buchholz, Todd, 54
Budget line, 153–155
Budget set, 154
Bumper crops, 107
Bundling, 181–182
Bus fares, deficits and, 107
Bush, George W., 417
Business decisions, using macroeconomics to make, 11
Business licenses, 137–139
Buyers
  knowledgeable, 321–323
  uninformed, 314–315

C

Campus bookstores, 286
Cap-and-trade system, 366–369
Capital
  human, 2
  idle, 194
  physical, 2
Carbon tax, 363

Cargo ships
  short-run supply curve
    for, 220
  speeds, marginal principle
    and, 36
Car insurance, 327
Cars, resale value of, 320
Car stereos, 257
Cartel, 272–273
Cartel pricing, 272–276, 279
Carton-board pricing, 279
Cash assistance, to the poor, 401
Celebrity endorsements, 265
Celler-Kefauver Act, 308
Cement industry, 270
Centrally planned economy, 56
Ceteris paribus, 8, 10, 69–70, 72,
    73, 78, 83, 98
Change in demand, 79
  vs. change in quantity
    demanded, 78–79
  market effects of, 90
Change in quantity
    demanded, 70
  vs. change in demand, 78–79
Change in quantity supplied, 73
  vs. change in supply, 83–84
Change in supply, 83
  vs. change in quantity
    supplied, 83–84
  effects of, across markets, 89
Changes
  marginal, 8, 10
  using microeconomics to
    predict, 12
Cheaters' dilemma, 283
Cheating, 136
China
  demand for pecans in, 82
  imports from, 419
  trade sanctions on, 409
  trade with, 424

Choice, cognition and, 167–168
Chump problem, 343
Cigarette prices, law of demand
    and, 62
Cigarette prices, teenagers and,
    104–105
Cigarette taxes, 143, 176
Civic externalities, 344
Civil liberties, 62
Clayton Act, 308
Clean Air Act, 367
Climate change, 357
  carbon tax and, 363
Clinton, Bill, 143
Clock towers, 343
Clothing, 262
Coase bargaining, 358–360
Cobblers, 254
Coca-Cola, 233
Coffee growers, law of supply
    and, 223
Cognition
  and choice, 167–168
  fuel for, 168–170
  vs. gut feelings, 170
Cognitive weighting, 168
College campuses, monopolies
    on, 233, 243
College degree
  higher wages and, 377, 392
  opportunity cost of, 29–30
College facilities rental, marginal
    principle and, 35–36
Colony collapse disorder
    (CCD), 89
Command-and-control
    policy, 365
Commerce Department, 421
Common Agricultural Policy
    (CAP), 78
Comparative advantage, 52
  vs. absolute advantage, 52

exchange and, 50–55
  international trade and, 53–54
  in Latvia, 55
  terms of trade and, 412
Competition
  imperfect, 60
  in market economy, 61
  monopolistic, 209, 255,
    258–261
  perfect, 207–227
  pricing and, 305–306
  spatial, 260–261
  unfair, 418–419
Complements, 70, 80, 81
Concentration ratios, 271
Concorde, 419
Conservation, of rainforests, 28
Constant-cost industry, 225
  long-run supply for, 225–227
Constant returns to scale, 195
Consumer choice, 152–176
  advertising and, 264
  cognition and, 171
  dietary choices, 170–171
  mental shortcuts and, 181–184
  neuroscience of, 153, 165–176
  predicting, 168
  price decreases and, 160–163
  utility theory and, 153–160
Consumer constraints, 153–155
Consumer decisions, 170–176
Consumer groups, 245
Consumer preferences, shifts
    in, 80, 82
Consumer products, information
    about, 60–61
Consumer satisfaction
    scores, 320
Consumer search
  economics of, 328–332
  marginal principle and,
    328–330

opportunity cost and, 330–332
prices and, 330–332
reservation prices and searching strategy, 330
Consumer services, asymmetric information and, 320
Consumer surplus, 128–130
demand curve and, 129–130
of Internet service, 131
Consumption, inequality, trade, and, 424
Consumption possibilities curve, 412–413
Contestable markets, 286
Continuity, 53
Contracts, 56
Coordination problems, 197
Corporate mergers. *See* Mergers
Cost curves, long-run, 198–199
Costs
accounting, 186, 187
average, 190–193, 198–200, 262
economic, 186–187
entry, 210
explicit, 186
fixed, 189, 191, 217
implicit, 186
input, 197–198
labor, 378
language and mathematics of, 202
long-run, 194–200
marginal, 33, 192–194, 196
opportunity. *See* Opportunity cost
production technology and, 185–202
short-run, 187–194
sunk, 217
total, 189–190, 195
variable, 189, 215–216

Cost savings, from outsourcing, 54
Cost valuation, 166
Coupons, 245
Credit cards, present bias and, 173
Crime externalities, 345
Crop yields, fertilizer and, 40
Cross-price elasticity of demand, 111
Curves. *See also* Demand curve; Production possibilities curve; Supply curve
consumption possibilities, 412–413
moving along vs. shifting, 20–21
nonlinear, 22–23
slope of, 19
supply, 71–76
total-product, 188–189

D

Deadweight loss, 135–136, 138
Deadweight loss from monopoly, 240–242
Deadweight loss from taxation, 143–145
DeBeers, 280
Decision making
in market economy, 57
simultaneous, 281–282
using microeconomics for, 12
Decoy effect, 182–183
Deflation, 42
Demand, 68
change in, 78–79
derived, 378
elastic, 100–101, 105–106, 142
excess, 76–77

increases in, 79–81
inelastic, 100–101, 105–106, 142
for labor, 378–381
law of, 68–70, 98, 160–165
for leisure, 384–385
market effects of changes in, 78–82
perfectly elastic, 100–101
perfectly inelastic, 100–101
for pollution permits, 368–369
price decrease and, 160–163
price elasticity of, 98–104
price increase and, 161
simultaneous changes in supply and, 87–89
unit elastic, 100–101, 106
Demand and supply model, 78–89
Demand changes
long-run response to, 224–225
price effects of, 116–118
short-run response to, 223–224
Demand curve, 68–71
budget line vs., 154–155
consumer surplus and, 129–130
decreases in, 81–82
firm-specific, 208–209
individual, 68–70, 163–165
law of demand and, 68–70
linear, 108–110
long-run demand curve for labor, 382–383
marginal-revenue curve and, 235
market, 70–71
movement along, 70
price elasticity and, 100–101, 108–110
shifts in, 79–81

short-run demand curve for labor, 381–382

Demand increase
long-run response to, 224–225
short-run response to, 223–224

Demand schedule, 68–69

Deposit insurance, 327

Derived demand, 378

Diamonds, price fixing of, 280

Dietary choices, 170–171

Differentiation
advertising and, 264–265
by location, 260–261
product, 258

Diminishing marginal utility, 156, 160

Diminishing returns, 39, 188

Diminishing returns principle, 39, 157, 188, 379

Discounts, 245–246

Discovered price, 328

Diseconomies of scale, 197–198

Division of labor, exchange and, 53

Doha trade negotiations, 420

Dolphins, tuna fishing and, 422–423

Domestic industries
helping, with protectionist policies, 418–419
protection of, 139–140

Dominant strategy, 275

Dominican Republic-Central America Free Trade Agreement (DR-CAFTA), 420

Dopamine, 165–166, 174–175

Dorsal-lateral portion of the PFC (DLPFC), 168, 171
economic, 170

Driving speed, marginal principle and, 36

Drug prices, 90

Dumping, 421–422

Dunkin' Donuts, 261

Duopolists' dilemma, 275–276
overcoming, 277–280

Duopoly, 272

E

Earned income tax credit (EITC), 401–403

Earnings gap, 389–394

eBay, 320

Economic analysis
of government intervention in efficient markets, 133–134
problem solving and, 5–7

Economic cost, 186–187

Economic fluctuations, using macroeconomics to understand, 11

Economic growth, using macroeconomics to understand, 11

Economic models, 4–5

Economic principles, 30. See also Diminishing returns principle; Marginal principle; Opportunity cost; Real-nominal principle; Voluntary exchange principle

Economic profit, 186–187, 213–215

Economic questions, 4

Economic rate of return, civil liberties and, 62

Economics, 1, 2
public-choice, 347–351

Economic uncertainty, 61

Economic way of thinking elements of, 7–9

example, 9–10

Economies of scale, 195–196, 197

Economy, centrally planned, 56

Edison, Thomas, 1

Education
external benefits from, 344–346
wages and, 377

Efficiency, 1, 128
invisible hand and, 133
licensing and, 138
market equilibrium and, 131–134

Elastic demand, 100–101, 105–106, 142

Elasticities
computing, 99–100
market vs. brand, 106–107
predicting changes in equilibrium price using, 116–120

Elasticity of demand. See also Price elasticity of demand
along linear demand curve, 108–109
cross-price, 111
estimates of, 112
for gasoline, 103–104
income, 110–111
price, 98–104
price discrimination and, 246–247
for vanity plates, 107

Electric generators, price fixing and, 279

Electricity, 362

Email, spam, 10

Employment, free trade and, 413–414

Employment taxes, 341

Energy efficiency, 356

Entrepreneurs, role of, 58
Entrepreneurship, 2, 6
    opportunity cost and, 187
Entry barriers, 234
Entry costs, 210
Entry deterrence, 283–287
    contestable markets and, 286
    examples of, 285–286
    limit pricing and, 284–285
    passive approach to, 283–284, 286–287
Environmental protection, trade laws and, 422–423
Environmental Protection Agency (EPA), 356, 367
Equations, using, to compute missing values, 25
Equilibrium
    with all high-cost consumers, 323–324
    with all low-quality goods, 315–317
    labor market, 387–389
    long-run, 259–260
    market, 128
    Nash, 276
    of price-fixing game, 275–276
    with some high-quality goods, 316–319
Equilibrium price
    consequences of price above, 78
    decrease in demand and, 81–82
    decrease in supply and, 87
    increase in demand and, 80–81
    increase in supply and, 85–86
    for pollution permits, 368
    predicting changes in, using elasticities, 116–120

simultaneous changes in demand and supply and, 87–89
    total surplus and, 132–133
Equilibrium quantity, simultaneous changes in demand and supply and, 87–89
Equilibrium wage, 389
Equimarginal rule, 156–159, 161, 171
European Climate Exchange, 369
European Community (EC), 49, 55
European Union (EU), 420
Excess burden of a tax, 145
Excess demand, 76–77
Excess supply, 77–78
Exchange
    comparative advantage and, 50–55
    division of labor and, 53
Expansion, 195–196
Experience rating, 324
Explicit cost, 186
Exports, 54
External benefits, 340, 342
    across international borders, 344
    from education, 344–346
    marginal principle and, 345–346
    private goods with, 344–347
    public goods and, 342–344
External cost of production, 361
External costs
    from automobiles, 369–372
    Coase bargaining and, 358–360
    from collisions, 371–372

from congestion, 371
    of pollution, 357–360
    regulation of, 364–366
    of young drivers, 372
Externalities
    negative, 59–60
    network, 234

F

Factors of production, 2
Featherbedding, 394
Federal Deposit Insurance Corporation (FDIC), 327
Federal government, 340–341. *See also* Government
    revenue sources for, 341
    spending by, 340
Federal Trade Commission (FTC), 303, 304–305, 309
Federal Trade Commission Act, 308
Fertilizer, crop yields and, 40
Financial crises, economic view of, 6–7
Firm-specific demand curve, 208–209
Fixed costs, 189, 191, 217
Fixed production facility, 187–194
Food additives, 279
Foreign competition, workers and, 418
Foreign producers, dumping by, 421–422
Franchises, 261
Freedom House, 62
Free rider, 343
Free-rider problem, 342–343

Free trade, 409, 410
dumping and, 421–422
employment and, 413–414
reasons for protests
against, 425
Funk, Rick, 199
Furniture manufacture, 382

G

Gambling, as consumer good,
174–175
Game theory, 271
Game tree, 274–275, 285, 288
Gasoline
elasticity of demand for,
103–104, 120
prices, 97
prices and, 120
tax on, 164, 370–371, 372
GATT. *See* General Agreement on Tariffs and Trade
(GATT)
Gender pay gap, 390–391
General Agreement on Tariffs
and Trade (GATT), 420
Generic advertising, 289
Generic drugs, 244
Genetically modified crops, 423
Global economy, 53–54
Global warming. *See* Climate
change
Global weather observation, 344
Glucose, 168–169
Goods
complement, 80
complementary, 81
inferior, 80, 81
nondurable, 424
normal, 79, 81
private, 342
public, 60, 342–344

smuggled, 417
substitute, 80, 81, 101–102
Got Milk? campaign, 289
Government
alternative models of,
349–350
enforcement of rules of
exchange by, 60–61
levels of, 340–341
revenue sources for, 341
role of, in market economy,
59–62
self-interest theory of, 349
Government intervention
in efficient markets, 133–134
through import restrictions,
139–140
through price controls,
134–137
through quantity controls,
137–140
Government regulations
on business practices, 307
on natural monopoly, 301–302
on pollution, 364–366
Government spending, on welfare programs, 400–401
Government subsidies, 346
Graphs
of negative relationships,
21–22
of nonlinear relationships,
22–23
of single variable, 15–17
of two variables, 17–19
using, 15–23
Greenhouse gases (GHGs), 357
Grim-trigger strategy, 278
Group insurance, 324
Guarantees, 320
Gut feelings, 166, 167, 168,
170, 171

H

Hanseatic League, 49
Happy hour pricing, 263
Hardback books, 247
Hart-Scott-Rodino Act, 308
Hayek, Friedrich, 56
Health insurance, 321–323,
324–325
Herfindahl-Hirschman Index
(HHI), 271–272
Heuristics, 181
Highway deaths, beer prices
and, 104
Honeybees, price of ice cream
and, 89
Horizontal mergers, 304
Hormone-treated beef, 423
Housing prices
controls on, 134–136
increase in, 67
supply restrictions and, 127
Humana index, 62
Human capital, 2
Hurricane Andrew, price of ice
and, 226–227
Hybrid vehicles, incentives to
buy, 9

I

Ice cream prices, honeybee
population and, 89
Idle capital, 194
Immigration, trade-offs
from, 397
Imperfect competition, 60
Imperfect information, 60
Implicit cost, 186
Import bans, 414–415
Import licenses,
415–416
Import quotas, 415

Import restrictions, 139–140
Imports, 54, 419
Incentives, 8–9
Income
    cross-price elasticities
      and, 111
    decrease in, 80, 81
    differences in, 389–394
    increase in, 79, 81
    market, 394
    relationship between hours
      worked and, 17–18
Income distribution, 394–399
    in 2007, 394–396
    lotteries and, 402
    public policy and, 398–399
    recent changes in, 396–398
    tax policy and, 398–399
Income effect, 163, 165, 385
    of price change, 161–162
Income effect for leisure
    demand, 384
Income elasticity of demand,
    110–111
Income inequality,
    outsourcing and trade
    and, 424–425
Income tax, 341, 399
Increasing-cost industry, 220
    examples of, 222–223
    long-run supply curve for,
    220–223
India, water filtration in, 185
Individual demand curve, 68–70,
    163–165
Individual supply curve, 72–73
Indivisible inputs, 196, 199
Industrial diamonds, price fixing
    of, 280
Industrial Revolution, 302
Industry size, production costs
    and, 221

Inefficiencies, 1
Inelastic demand, 100–101,
    105–106, 142
Inelastic supply, 112
Inequality, international trade
    and, 424
Infant industries, 418
Inferior good, 80, 81
Inflation
    effect on real minimum wage,
    41–42
    repayment of student loans
    and, 42
Information
    about consumer products,
    60–61
    asymmetric, 314–317
    buyers invest in, 319–320
    imperfect, 60
    role of, in markets, 314
Information goods, cost
    structure for, 201
Innovation, 53
    incentives for, 243
Input costs, 197–198
Input prices, 220–221
Input-substitution effect, 382
Insourcing, 54
Insula, 169
Insurance, 56, 61
    adverse selection and,
    321–325
    asymmetric information and,
    321–325
    automobile, 325, 327,
    371–372
    deposit, 327
    group, 324
    health, 321–323, 324–325
    moral hazard and, 326–327
    risk and, 313
Insurance companies, 326–327

Intergovernmental Panel on
    Climate Change
    (IPCC), 357
International trade, 410. *See also*
    Free trade; Trade
    comparative advantage and,
    53–54
    income distribution and, 398
    inequality and, 424
Internet service, consumer sur-
    plus of, 131
Interstate Bakeries, 306–307
Inventions, patents on, 56
Invisible hand, 57, 133
Iowa Gambling Task, 167
iPod Shuffle, 1

J

Jam experiment, 170
Japan, protectionist policies, 417
Job loss, costs of protecting
    against, 140
Job loss, from outsourcing, 54

K

Kiwifruit market, 321
Knowledgable sellers, 314–315
Knowledgeable buyers, 321–323
Koppel, Ted, 90

L

Labor, 2
    division of, and exchange, 53
    marginal benefit of, 378–381
    marginal product of,
    187–188, 379

skilled, 425
unskilled, 425
Labor agreements, 351
Labor costs, 378
Labor demand, 378–381
  by individual firm in short
    run, 378–381
  labor market equilibrium and,
    387–389
  in long run, 382–383
  marginal principle and, 378
  market, in short run, 381–382
  market effect of increase in,
    387–388
  short-run vs. long-run, 383
Labor demand curve
  long-run, 382–383
  short-run, 381–382
Labor market, 2
  equilibrium, 387–389
  income and substitution effects
    in, 385
Labor specialization, 191, 197
Labor supply, 384–387
  labor market equilibrium and,
    387–389
Labor supply curve, 384–387
Labor unions, wages and,
  393–394
Latvia, 49, 55
Law of demand, 69–70, 98
  cigarettes and, 71
  individual demand curve and,
    160–165
Law of diminishing marginal
  utility, 156, 160
Law of supply, 73, 76, 223
Laws, against price fixing,
  279–280
Learning by doing, 418
Learning effect, 392
LEED certification
Leisure demand, 384–385

Lemons laws, 320
Lemons problem, 314–321
  evidence for, 319
  responding to, 319–320
Liberty ships, 418
Licensing, 137–139
Limit price, 285
Limit pricing, 284–285
Lincoln, Abraham, 54
Linear demand curve, price
  elasticity along,
    108–109, 110
Living standards, 1
  trade and, 424
Loan repayment, effect of
  inflation and deflation
  on, 42
Local government, 340–341
  revenue sources for, 341
  spending by, 340
LoJack, 346
Long run
  labor demand in, 382–383
  production costs in, 194–200
Long-run average cost (LAC),
  195, 199–200
Long-run average-cost curves,
  198–199
Long-run demand curve for
  labor, 382–383
Long-run equilibrium
  in monopolistic competition,
    259–260
  with spatial competition, 260
Long-run marginal cost
  (LMC), 196
Long-run market supply curve,
  220–223
Long-run supply, for constant
  cost industry, 225–227
Long-run supply curve, 225–227
Long-run supply elasticity, 114
Long-run total cost (LTC), 195

Lotteries, 402
Low-price guarantees,
  277–278, 280
Low-skilled workers, immigration
  of, 397
Luxury boat tax, 143

M

Macroeconomics, 10
  use of, 11
Major League Baseball
  (MLB), 383
Manufacturers' rebates, 245
Manufacturing firms,
  concentration ratios
  in, 271
Margarine prices, 227
Marginal approach, to
  determining output,
    212–213
Marginal benefit, 33
  of consumer search, 328–329
  of labor, 378–381
Marginal change, 8, 10
Marginal cost, 33
  average cost and, 193
  of consumer search, 329–330
  short-run, 192–193
Marginal principle, 33–36,
  73, 255
  automobile emissions
    standards and, 35–36
  consumer search and, 328–
    330
  driving speed and, 36
  external benefits and, 345–346
  labor demand and, 378
  movie sequels and, 34–35
  output decisions and, 299
  pollution and, 357–358
  price discrimination and, 246

of renting facility, 35–36
taxes and, 156–158
using, 237–239
Marginal product of labor, 187–188, 379
Marginal revenue, 212–213
formula for, 236–237
total revenue and, 235–236
Marginal-revenue curve, 235
Marginal-revenue product of labor (MRP), 379–381
Marginal revenue product of labor (MRP), 383
Marginal utility, 155–156
Marketable pollution permits, 366–369
Market changes, predicting and explaining, 90–91
Market demand, for labor in short run, 381–382
Market demand curve, 70–71
Market economy, 55–56
risk in, 61
role of government in, 59–62
Market effects
of changes in demand, 78–82
of changes in supply, 83–89
of gasoline tax, 370–371
of import restrictions, 139–140
of increase in labor demand, 387–388
of licensing, 138–139
of pollution regulation, 365
of pollution tax, 361–363
of simultaneous changes in demand and supply, 87–89
of taxes, 141–145
Market efficiency
external costs and, 357
licensing and, 138
Market elasticity, 106–107
Market entry, 254, 255

effects of, 255–257
examples of, 257–258
franchises and, 261
trade-offs with, 261–264
Market equilibrium, 76–78, 128
efficiency and, 131–134
perfect competition and, 219–220
price controls and, 135
Market-equilibrium price. *See* Equilibrium price
Market failure, role of government and, 59–61
Market income, 394
Market power, 234, 245, 271
Markets, 2, 50, 55–59. *See also* Labor market
development of, 58–59
emergence of, in POW camps, 58
government intervention in efficient, 133–134
perfectly competitive, 68, 75
role of entrepreneurs in, 58
role of information in, 314
thin, 316–319
using microeconomics to understand, 12
virtues of, 56–58
voluntary exchange and, 37–38
Market structures, 208–209
Market supply curve, 74–75
long-run, 220–223
short-run, 218–219
slope of, 75
Market supply curve for labor, 385–387
Maximum prices, 134–136
Means-tested programs, 400–401
Median location, 349
Median-voter rule, 347–349, 351
Medicare, 399

Mental accounting, 181–182
Mental shortcuts, 181–184
Mergers, 304
blocking, 304–306
horizontal, 304
prices and, 308
restrictions on, 305–306
vertical, 304
Meteorite market, 59
Meteors, 339
Methane, 360
Microeconomics, 12–13
Microsoft, 287
Military spending, opportunity cost of, 30–31
Milk prices, in short run and long run, 116
Mill, John Stuart, total, 153
Minimum efficient scale, 197
Minimum prices, 136
Minimum supply price, 73
Minimum wage
market effects of, 388–389
value of the, 41–42
Mining industry, 67, 382
Mixed market, 314
Mobile phones, entry costs and, 210
Money
nominal value of, 41
real-nominal principle and, 40–42
real value of, 41
Money-back guarantees, 320
Monopolies, 209, 234
antitrust policies and, 61, 303–308
breaking up, 303–304
deadweight loss of, 240–242
entry deterrence by, 283–287
helping domestic firms establish, in world markets, 418–419

natural, 234, 298–303
output decisions by, 234–239, 298–299
patents and, 243–244
vs. perfect competition, 209, 240
profit maximization by, 237–239
public policy and, 243
rent seeking by, 243–244
social cost of, 240–243
value of, 242
Monopolistic competition, 209, 255, 258–261
advertising and, 264–265
differentiation by location and, 260–261
features of, 258–259
long-run equilibrium and, 259–260
vs. perfect competition, 262–264
trade-offs with, 261–264
Moral hazard, 326
insurance and, 326–327
Movie popcorn, 247–248
Movie sequels, marginal principle and, 34–35
Mozambique, 6
Music distribution, 280
Music videos, average cost of, 201

N

Nash equilibrium, 276
National Basketball Association (NBA), 351
Natural monopoly, 234, 298–303
examples of, 302–303
output decisions by, 298–299
price controls for, 301–302
regulation of, 301–302

Natural resources, 2
Near-earth objects (NEOs), 339
Negative externalities, 59–60
Negative relationship, 19
graphing, 21–22
NEOShield, 339
Network externalities, 234
Neuroscience
of benefit valuation, 165–166
consumer choice and, 153, 165–176
of cost valuation, 166
of diminishing marginal utility, 160
New York City, housing market in, 127
Nitrogen oxide, 362, 363
Nominal value, 41
Nondurable goods, 424
Nonlinear relationships, graphing, 22–23
Normal good, 79, 81
Normative analysis, 3–4
North American Free Trade Agreement (NAFTA), 409, 420
Nuclear power, 201–202
Nucleus Accumbens (NAcc), maximization, 165–166

O

Occupational discrimination, 391
Occupations, wages differences across, 389–390
Office Depot, 297, 305
Offshoring, 54
Oil industry, 67
Oil pipelines, 97, 120
Oligopoly, 209, 270, 271–272
advertising and, 287–289
pricing by, 272–276

Online games, market exchange and, 38
Online retailers, tax on, 169
Opportunity cost, 29, 50
of college degree, 29–30
consumer search and, 330–332
of entrepreneurship, 187
of military spending, 30–31
production possibilities curve and, 31–33
productivity and, 50, 55
of running a business, 33
Opportunity cost principle, 157, 166, 186, 410
Output
marginal approach to determining, 212–213
reducing with indivisible inputs, 196
short-run output decisions, 210–215
Output decisions, for monopoly, 234–239, 298–299
Output effect, 382
Output prices, labor demand and, 382
Outsourcing, 54, 424–425
Ozone pollution, 369–371

P

Pakistan, wireless phone service in, 210
Paperback books, 247
Patents, 56, 234
expiration of, 244
as incentive for innovation, 243
monopolies and, 243–244
trade-offs from, 243–244
Payoff matrix, 281–282
Pecan prices, 82
Pennzoil Motor Oils, 308

Percentage changes
  appeal of, 183–184
  computing, 23–25, 99–100
  in equilibrium price, 117–118, 119
  in price, 112
  in quantity demanded, 104–105
  in quantity supplied, 112, 115
Perfect competition, 207–227
  effects of changes in demand in, 223–225
  market equilibrium and, 219–220
  monopolistic competition vs., 262–264
  vs. monopoly, 209, 240
  short-run output decisions, 210–215
  short-run supply curves and, 218–220
Perfectly competitive markets, 68, 75, 208
Perfectly elastic demand, 100–101
Perfectly elastic supply, 114–115
Perfectly inelastic demand, 100–101
Perfectly inelastic supply, 114–115
Permits, 364–365
  marketable pollution permits, 366–369
Pharmaceutical industry, patents and, 244
Physical attractiveness, wages and, 393
Physical capital, 2
Pie graphs, 15
Point of diminishing return, 39
Pollution, 59–60
  air, 362–363

automobile, 369–371
marketable permits for, 366–369
optimal level of, 357–360
regulation of, 364–366
taxing, 360–364
water, 358–359
Pollution tax, 360–364
Poor
  impact of tariffs on, 417
  redistribution programs for, 400–401
Population, decreases in, 82
Population increases, 80
Positive analysis, 3–4
Positive relationship, 19
Poverty, 1
  in Africa, 5–6
  public policy and, 399–401
Predatory pricing, 307, 309
Prefrontal cortex (PFC), 167–168
Present bias
  credit cards and, 173
  smoking and, 174, 176
  spending vs. saving, 171–173
Price ceiling, 77, 132
Price-change formula, 117–118
Price changes, response of producers to, 223
Price controls
  effect on market, 137
  maximum prices, 134–136
  minimum prices, 136
Price controls, for natural monopoly, 301–302
Price discrimination, 245–248, 422
  conditions for, 245
  discounts, 245–246
  elasticity of demand and, 246–247

examples of, 247
marginal principle and, 246
senior discounts and, 246
Price effects
  of changes in demand, 116–118
  of changes in supply, 118–120
Price elasticity of demand, 98–104
  along linear demand curve, 108–110
  availability of substitutes and, 101–102
  computing, 99
  demand curve and, 100–101
  determinants of, 102–104
  predicting changes in equilibrium price using, 116–118
  predicting changes in quantity using, 104–105
  predicting revenue effects of price changes using, 106–107
  price discrimination and, 246–247
  tax shifting and, 142–143
  total revenue and, 105–106
Price elasticity of supply, 112–115
  determinants of, 113
  short-run vs. long-run, 114
Price fixing, 272–273
  equilibrium of, 275–276
  examples of, 279–280
  game tree and, 274–275
  laws on, 279–280
  simultaneous, 281–282
Price floor, 78, 132–133
Price leadership, 280
Price makers, 208

Prices
  break-even, 213–215
  changes in demand and, 90
  of complementary goods, 80
  consumer search and, 330–332
  controls on, 134–137
  decreases in, 90
  demand schedule and, 68–69
  effect of decrease in, 160–163
  effect of increases in, 161
  effect of market entry on, 255–257
  equilibrium, 80–82, 85–89
  excess demand and, 76–77
  excess supply and, 77–78
  expectations of higher, 80
  expectations of lower, 82
  happy hour, 263
  import restrictions and, 139–140
  input, 220–221
  low-price guarantees and, 277–278
  in market economy, 57
  market entry and, 258
  maximum, 134–136
  mergers and, 308
  minimum, 136
  minimum supply price, 73
  for pollution permits, 368–369
  reservation, 330
  scarcity and, 57
  shut-down, 216–217
  of substitutes, 80
  supply schedule and, 72
  tax cuts and, 145
  trade and, 424
Price taker, 208
Pricing
  average-cost, 301–302
  cartel, 272–276, 279
  competition and, 305–306
  limit, 284–285

  low-price guarantees and, 277–278
  predatory, 307, 309
  repeated pricing games, 278–279
Prisoner of war (POW) camps, emergence of markets in, 58
Prisoners' dilemma, 282
Private cost of production, 360–361
Private goods, 342, 344–347
Problem solving, economic analysis and, 5–7
Producer surplus, 130–131
Product differentiation, 258, 262
  advertising for, 264–265
Production
  diseconomies of scale in, 197–198
  economies of scale in, 197
  factors of, 2
  long-run costs, 194–200
  marginal product and, 187–189
  scale economies in, 200
  scaling down, 196–197
  short-run costs, 187–194
  short-run output decisions, 210–215
Production costs
  examples of, 200–202
  external, 357
  indivisible inputs and, 199
  industry size and, 221
  long-run, 194–200
  price elasticity of supply and, 113
  short-run, 187–194
Production facilities, sharing, and diminishing returns, 39
Production possibilities curve, 31, 410–412
  opportunity cost and, 31–33

  scarcity and, 31
  shifting the, 32
Production technology, 185–202
Productivity
  increased, from specialization, 53
  opportunity cost and, 50, 55
Profit maximization, by monopoly, 237–239
Profits
  economic, 186–187, 213–215
  effect of market entry on, 256–257
Property crime, 107
Property taxes, 341
Prosperity, 1
Protectionist policies, 414–419
  import bans, 414–415
  import restrictions, 139–140
  quotas, 415–416
  rationales for, 417–419
  responses to, 416–417
  tariffs, 416
  voluntary export restraints, 415–416
Protests, against free trade, 425
Public choice, 347–351
Public-choice economics, 347–351
  median location and, 349
  median-voter rule and, 347–349
Public goods, 60, 342–344
  free-rider problem and, 342–343
  global weather observation as, 344
Public policies
  monopoly and, 243
  poverty and, 399–401
  using microeconomics to evaluate, 12–13
Public utility commissions (PUCs), 301

Q

Quaker State Motor Oils, 308
Quantities, controlling, 137–140
Quantity demanded, 68, 78–79
Quantity supplied, 71–72
Quotas
  import, 415
  vs. tariffs, 416

R

Racial discrimination, wages and, 391–392
Rainforest conservation, 28
Real-nominal principle, 40–42
Real value, 41
Real wages, 41
Rebates, 245
Recessions, economic view of current, 6–7
Redistribution programs, 400–401
Regulations
  housing market, 127
  on pollution, 364–366
Rent control, 134–136
Rent seeking, 243–244
Repair guarantees, 320
Repetition, 53
Replication, 195–196
Resale, 245
Reservation price, 330
Resources, scarcity of, 2
Restaurant meals, 262
Revenue. *See also* Total revenue
  marginal, 212–213
Reynolds International Pen Corporation, 286–287
Risk
  insurance and, 56, 61, 313
  in market economy, 61
Robinson-Patman Act, 307, 308
Romalis, John, 424

S

Safety, driving speed and, 36
Sales taxes, 341
Salt cartels, 276
Satellite radio, 303
Saving, vs. spending, 171–173
Savings and loan crisis, 327
Scale economies, 195–196, 200
Scarcity, 2
  prices and, 57
  production possibilities curve and, 31
  trade-offs and, 2–3
Search. *See* Consumer search
Search costs, 136
Seat belts, marginal principle and, 36
Self controls, 152
Self-imposed penalties, 174
Self-interest, 37, 57–58, 349
Self-sufficiency, 37, 50, 51
Sellers
  knowledgeable, 314–315
  uninformed, 321–323
Senior discounts, 246
Sherman Antitrust Act, 279, 308
Shipping services
  reducing pollution from, 366
  short-run supply curve for, 220
Shirt industry, 221–222
Shoe-repair firms, 254
Shoes, 262
SHOP experiment, 168
Shortage, 76–77
Short run, labor demand in, 381–382
Short-run average costs, 190–192, 199–200
Short-run average total cost (ATC), 191
Short-run costs, 187–194
Short-run demand curve for labor, 381–382

Short-run marginal cost (MC), 192–193
Short-run market supply curve, 218–219
Short-run output decisions, 210–215
Short-run supply curves, 218–220
Short-run supply elasticity, 114
Short-run total costs, 189–190
Shut-down decision, 215–217
Shut-down price, 216–217
Signaling, 265
Signaling effect, 392
Simultaneous decision making, 281–282
Sirius Satellite radio, 303
Skilled labor, 425
Slope, of supply curve, 113
Slope of a curve, 19, 73, 75
Smith, Adam, 8–9, 37, 53, 57
Smog, 369–371
Smoking, present bias and, 174, 176
Smoot-Hawley Tariff Act, 417
Smoot-Hawley tariffs, 419–420
Smuggling, 417
Social cost of production, 361
Social costs, of monopoly, 240–243
Social safety net, 61
Social Security, real-nominal principle and, 41
Solar power, 201–202
Spam, 10
Spatial competition, 260–261
Special interest, 350
Specialization
  benefits of, 410–414
  gains from trade and, 50–52
  increased productivity and, 53
  rationale for, 55
  voluntary exchange and, 37, 38
Speed, marginal principle and, 36

Spence, Michael, 314
Spending, vs. saving, 171–173
Standard of living. *See* Living standards
Standard Oil Trust, 304
Staples, 297, 305
State government, 340–341
  revenue sources for, 341
  spending by, 340
State lotteries, 402
Steel tariffs, 417
Stiglitz, Joseph, 314
Stores, vs. online retailers, 169
Student discounts, 245
Student loans, inflation and cost of repaying, 42
Sub-Saharan Africa, 1, 5–6
Subsidized firms, 419
Substitutes, 70, 80, 81
  price elasticity and, 101–102
Substitution effect, 165, 385
  of price change, 161–162, 164
Substitution effect for leisure demand, 384
Sugar industry, 222
Sulfur dioxide, 362, 363
Sunk costs, 217
Supply
  decrease in, and equilibrium price, 87
  excess, 77–78
  increase in, and equilibrium price, 85–86
  inelastic, 112
  of labor, 384–387
  law of, 73, 76, 223
  long-run, 225–227
  market effects of changes in, 83–89

perfectly elastic, 114–115
perfectly inelastic, 114–115
of pollution permits, 368–369
price effects of changes in, 118–120
price elasticity of, 112–115
simultaneous changes in demand and, 87–89
Supply curve, 71–76
  decreases in supply and shifts in, 86
  downward shift in, 83
  of firm, 218
  increase in supply and shifts in, 83–85
  individual, 72–73
  labor, 384–387
  long-run, 225–227
  long-run market, 220–223
  market, 74–75
  movement along, 73
  producer surplus and, 130–131
  rightward shift, 83
  short-run, 218–220
  short-run market, 218–219
  slope of, 73, 75
Supply schedule, 72
Surplus, 77–78
  consumer, 128–130
  producer, 130–131
  total, 131
Switchgrass biofuel, 214

T

Tariffs, 409, 416
  history of, 419–420
  impact of, on poor, 417
Tax burden, 143–145

Tax cuts, prices and, 145
Taxes
  cigarette, 143, 176
  congestion, 371
  earned income tax credit, 401–403
  employment, 341
  on gasoline, 164, 370–371, 372
  income, 341, 399
  income distribution and, 398–399
  luxury boat, 143
  market effects of, 141–145
  pollution, 360–364
  property, 341
  revenue-neutral, 164
  as revenue source, 341
  sales, 341
  value-added, 145
  VMT, 371–372
Taxi drivers, wage increases and, 386
Taxi medallions, 137–138
Tax shifting, 141–143, 145
Technological progress, income distribution and, 398
Teenagers, cigarette prices and, 104–105
Temporary Assistance to Needy Families (TANF), 398–399, 401
Terms of trade, 412
Thin market, 316–319
Tie-in sale, 307
Time-series graph, 16–17
Tires, 257–258
Tit-for-tat strategy, 278–279
Tobacco land, 143

Total cost
    computing, 210–211
    short-run, 189–190
Total-product curve, 188–189
Total revenue, 105–106
    computing, 210–211
    marginal revenue and, 235–236
    price elasticity and, 105–106,
        108–110
    shut-down decision and,
        215–216
Total surplus, 131
    equilibrium price and,
        132–133
Total utility, 155–156
Trade. *See also* Free trade;
        International trade
    benefits of, 410–414
    comparative advantage and
        terms of, 412
    gains from, and specialization,
        50–52
    income inequality and,
        424–425
    inequality and, 424
    international, comparative
        advantage and, 53–54
    policy debates, 421–425
    protectionist policies and,
        414–419
    rationale for, 55
Trade agreements, history of,
        419–420
Trade laws, environmental pro-
        tection and, 422–423
Trade sanctions, 409
Traffic congestion, 371
    economic view of, 5
    economic way of thinking
        about, 9–10
Trampolines, 110

Transcranial magnetic
        stimulation (TMS),
        indifference, 168
Transfer payments, 398–399
Trees, external benefits
        from, 347
Trucking, 257
Truman, Harry S., 3
Trusts, 303
Tuna fishing, dolphins and,
        422–423
Two-variable graphs, 17–19

U

Underpricing, 278–279, 280
Unemployment insurance, 61
Unfair competition, 418–419
Uniform abatement policy,
        364–365
Uninformed buyers,
        314–315
Uninformed sellers, 321–323
Uninsured, 324–325
Union workers, 393–394
Unisex automobile
        insurance, 325
United States, prosperity in, 1
Unit elastic demand,
        100–101, 106
Unskilled labor, 425
Used car sales, 313,
        314–317, 320
Utilitarianism, 153
Utility
    marginal, 155–156
    maximization, 156–157,
        158–160, 172
    total, 155–156
Utility companies, 301–302
Utility theory, 153–160

V

Value-added tax (VAT), 145
ValueStar, 320
Van Buren, Abigail, 365–366
Vanity plates, 107
Variable costs, 189, 215–216
Variables, 7
    graphs of single, 15–17
    graphs of two, 17–19
    isolation of, 7–8, 10
    negative relationships
        between, 21–22
    nonlinear relationships
        between, 22–23
Variety, average cost and, 262
VAT. *See* Value-added tax (VAT)
Vehicle-mile traveled (VMT)
        tax, 371–372
Vertical intercept, 18
Vertical mergers, 304
Voluntary exchange principle,
        37–38, 52, 128, 136
    marketable permits and,
        367–368
    markets and, 37–38
    online games and, 38
    specialization and, 38
Voluntary export restraint
        (VER), 415
Voting, 347–351

W

Wages
    across occupation, 389–390
    attractiveness and, 393
    college degree and, 377, 392
    differences in, 389–394
    education and, 377
    equilibrium, 389

gender gap in, 390–391
immigration of low-skilled
    workers and, 397
inequalities, and outsourcing,
    424–425
labor unions and, 393–394
in less-developed
    countries, 382
racial discrimination and,
    391–392
real-nominal principle and, 41
supply of labor and, 386
Wal-Mart, 424
Warranties, 320
Water filtration, 185
Water pollution, 358–359
Water privatization, 302
Wealth of Nations (Smith), 53
Weather, pollution permits
    and, 369

Weather observation, as public
    good, 344
Welfare programs, 400–401
Welfare reform, 400–401
Willingness to accept, 130
Willingness to pay, 129, 131
Wind power, scale economies
    in, 200
Wine prices, 225
Wonder Bread, 306–307
Wool industry, 76
Worker productivity, 55
Workers
    foreign competition and, 418
    immigration of low-skilled, 397
    skilled, 425
    unskilled, 425
Work hours, relationship
    between income and, 17–18
Workplace externalities, 344

World Bank, 62
World Trade Organization
    (WTO), 420

X

XM Satellite radio, 303

Z

Zinc cost curve, 217

Applying the Concepts
Questions and Applications

Chapter 1   Introduction: What Is Economics?

Applying the Concepts #1:   How do people respond to incentives?
Application 1:   *Incentives to Buy Hybrid Vehicles*

Applying the Concepts #2:   What is the role of prices in allocating resources?
Application 2:   *The Economic Solution to Spam*

Applying the Concepts #3:   How do we compute percentage changes?
Application 3:   *The Perils of Percentages*

Chapter 2   The Key Principles of Economics

Applying the Concepts #1:   What is the opportunity cost of running a business?
Application 1:   *Don't Forget the Costs of Time and Invested Funds*

Applying the Concepts #2:   How do people think at the margin?
Application 2:   *How Fast to Sail?*

Applying the Concepts #3:   What is the rationale for specialization and exchange?
Application 3:   *Jasper Johns and Housepainting*

Applying the Concepts #4:   Do farmers experience diminishing returns?
Application 4:   *Fertilizer and Crop Yields*

Applying the Concepts #5:   How does inflation affect lenders and borrowers?
Application 5:   *Repaying Student Loans*

Chapter 3   Exchange and Markets

Applying the Concepts #1:   What is the rationale for specialization and trade?
Application 1:   *Absolute Disadvantage and Comparative Advantage in Latvia*

Applying the Concepts #2:   Why do markets develop?
Application 2:   *The Market for Meteorites*

Applying the Concepts #3:   What is the role of government in a market economy?
Application 3:   *Civil Liberties and Efficiency of Government*

Chapter 4   Demand, Supply, and Market Equilibrium

Applying the Concepts #1:   What is the law of demand?
Application 1:   *Law of Demand and Cigarettes*

Applying the Concepts #2:   What is the law of supply?
Application 2:   *Law of Supply and Woolympics*

Applying the Concepts #3:   What are consequences of a price above the equilibrium price?
Application 3:   *Shrinking Wine Lakes*

Applying the Concepts #4:   How does a change in demand affect the equilibrium price?
Application 4:   *Chinese Demand and Pecan Prices*

Applying the Concepts #5:   How does a change in supply affect the equilibrium price?
Application 5:   *Honeybees and the Price of Ice Cream*

Applying the Concepts #6:   What explains a decrease in price?
Application 6:   *Why Lower Drug Prices?*

Chapter 5   Elasticity: A Measure of Responsiveness

Applying the Concepts #1:   How does the price elasticity of demand vary over time?
Application 1:   *A Closer Look at the Elasticity of Demand for Gasoline*

Applying the Concepts #2:   How does an increase in price affect total expenditures?
Application 2:   *Vanity Plates and the Elasticity of Demand*

Applying the Concepts #3:   Will a firm choose a point on the lower half of a linear demand curve?
Application 3:   *Trampolines and the Lower Half of a Linear Demand Curve*

Applying the Concepts #4:   Where do I find estimates of elasticities of demand?
Application 4:   *I Can Find that Elasticity in Four Clicks!*

Applying the Concepts #5:   Why is supply more price-elastic in the long run?
Application 5:   *The Short-Run and Long-Run Elasticity of Supply of Milk*

Applying the Concepts #6:   How does a decrease in supply affect the equilibrium price?
Application 6:   *A Broken Pipeline and the Price of Gasoline*

Chapter 6   Market Efficiency and Government Intervention

Applying the Concepts #1:   How do we compute consumer surplus?
Application 1:   *Consumer Surplus of Internet Service*

Applying the Concepts #2:   Why does the market equilibrium maximize the value of a market?
Application 2:   *Rent Control and Mismatches*

Applying the Concepts #3:   How do price controls affect the market?
Application 3:   *Price Controls and the Shrinking Candy Bar*

Applying the Concepts #4:   What are the effects of import restrictions?
Application 4:   *The Cost of Protecting a Luggage Job*

Applying the Concepts #5:   How does a tax cut affect prices?
Application 5:   *Response to Lower Taxes in French Restaurants*

Chapter 7   Consumer Choice: Utility Theory and Insights from Neuroscience

Applying the Concepts #1:   How does marginal utility change with the quantity consumed?
Application 1:   *Measuring Diminishing Marginal Utility*

Applying the Concepts #2:   How would a simultaneous increase in the gasoline tax and a decrease in the income tax affect gasoline consumption?
Application 2:   *A Revenue-Neutral Gasoline Tax*

Applying the Concepts #3:   How do the sales strategies of conventional stores and online retailers differ?
Application 3:   *Stores vs. Online Retailers*

Applying the Concepts #4:   What is the appropriate cigarette tax?
Application 4:   *Taxing Cigarettes to Offset Present Bias*

Chapter 8   Production Technology and Cost

Applying the Concepts #1:   What is the opportunity cost of an entrepreneur?
Application 1:   *Opportunity Cost and Entrepreneurship*

Applying the Concepts #2:   Why is the marginal-cost curve positively sloped?
Application 2:   *Idle Capital and Short-Run Marginal Cost*

Applying the Concepts #3:   How do indivisible inputs affect production costs?
Application 3:   *Indivisible Inputs and the Cost of Fake Killer Whales*

Chapter 9   Perfect Competition

Applying the Concepts #1:   How do entry costs affect the number of firms in a market?
Application 1:   *Wireless Women in Pakistan*

Applying the Concepts #2:   What is the break-even price?
Application 2:   *The Break-Even Price for Switchgrass, a Feedstock for Biofuel*

Applying the Concepts #3:   What is the shutdown price?
Application 3:   *Straddling the Zinc Cost Curve*

Applying the Concepts #4:   Why is the short-run supply curve positively sloped?
Application 4:   *Short-Run Supply Curve for Cargo*

Applying the Concepts #5:   How do producers respond to an increase in price?
Application 5:   *Chinese Coffee Growers Obey the Law of Supply*

Applying the Concepts #6:   Why is the time path of market prices after an increase in demand?
Application 6:   *The Upward Jump and Downward Slide of Wine Prices*

Applying the Concepts #7:   How does a permanent decrease in demand affect the equilibrium price in a constant-cost industry?
Application 7:   *Economic Detective and the Case of Margarine Prices*

Applying the Concepts Questions and Applications *(continued)*

Chapter 10   Monopoly and Price Discrimination

Applying the Concepts #1:   How does a monopolist maximize profit?
Application 1:   *Marginal Revenue from a Baseball Fan*

Applying the Concepts #2:   What is the value of a monopoly?
Application 2:   *A Casino Monopoly in Creswell, Oregon?*

Applying the Concepts #3:   What happens when a patent expires and a monopoly ends?
Application 3:   *Bribing the Makers of Generic Drugs*

Applying the Concepts #4:   When do firms have an opportunity to charge different prices to different consumers?
Application 4:   *Why Does Movie Popcorn Cost So Much?*

Chapter 11   Market Entry and Monopolistic Competition

Applying the Concepts #1:   How does market entry affect prices?
Application 1:   *Satellite v Cable*

Applying the Concepts #2:   Are monopolistically competitive firms profitable?
Application 2:   *Opening a Dunkin' Donuts Shop*

Applying the Concepts #3:   How does monopolistic competition compare to perfect competition?
Application 3:   *Happy Hour Pricing*

Applying the Concepts #4:   How does advertising affect consumer choices?
Application 4:   *Picture of Man versus Picture of Woman*

Chapter 12   Oligopoly and Strategic Behavior

Applying the Concepts #1:   Why do cartels sometimes fail to keep prices high?
Application 1:   *Failure of the Salt Cartel*

Applying the Concepts #2:   Do low-price guarantees generate higher or lower prices?
Application 2:   *Low-Price Guarantee Increases Tire Prices*

Applying the Concepts #3:   When does cooperation break down?
Application 3:   *Cheating On the Final Exam: The Cheaters' Dilemma*

Applying the Concepts #4:   How does a monopolist respond to the threat of entry?
Application 4:   *Microsoft as an Insecure Monopolist*

Applying the Concepts #5:   What is the rationale for generic advertising?
Application 5:   *Got Milk?*

Chapter 13   Controlling Market Power: Antitrust and Regulation

Applying the Concepts #1:   What is the rationale for regulating a natural monopoly?
Application 1:   *Public versus Private Waterworks*

Applying the Concepts #2:   When does a natural monopoly occur?
Application 2:   *Satellite Radio as a Natural Monopoly*

Applying the Concepts #3:   How does a merger affect prices?
Application 3:   *Merger of Pennzoil and Quaker State*

Applying the Concepts #4:   What is predatory pricing?
Application 4:   *FAQ about Predatory Pricing from the FTC*

Chapter 14   Imperfect Information: Adverse Selection and Moral Hazard

Applying the Concepts #1:   What is adverse selection for buyers?
Application 1:   *Are Baseball Pitchers Like Used Cars?*

Applying the Concepts #2:   How can government solve the adverse-selection problem?
Application 2:   *Regulation of the California Kiwifruit Market*

Applying the Concepts #3:   What is adverse selection for sellers?
Application 3:   *Unisex Automobile Insurance in the European Union*

Applying the Concepts #4:   What is moral hazard in car insurance?
Application 4:   *Car Insurance and Risky Driving*

Applying the Concepts #5:   How does opportunity cost affect consumer search?
Application 5:   *Income and Consumer Search*

Chapter 15   Public Goods and Public Choice

Applying the Concepts #1:   How can we respond to the free-rider problem?
Application 1:   *Free Riders and the Three-Clock Tower*

Applying the Concepts #2:   What happens when external benefits spill across international borders?
Application 2:   *Global Weather Observation*

Applying the Concepts #3:   What private goods generate external benefits?
Application 3:   *External Benefits from LoJack*

Applying the Concepts #4:   What happens when neighbors benefit?
Application 4:   *The Private and External Benefit of Trees*

Applying the Concepts #5:   What is the median voter rule?
Application 5:   *The Median Voter in the NBA*

Chapter 16   External Costs and Environmental Policy

Applying the Concepts #1:   How do we determine the optimum level of pollution?
Application 1:   *Reducing Methane Emissions*

Applying the Concepts #2:   How do pollution taxes vary across space?
Application 2:   *Pollution Taxes in Rural and Urban Areas*

Applying the Concepts #3:   What is the most efficient way to reduce pollution?
Application 3:   *Options for Reducing CO_2 Emissions from International Shipping*

Applying the Concepts #4:   How is the price of pollution permits determined?
Application 4:   *Weather and the Price of Pollution Permits*

Applying the Concepts #5:   What is the external cost of young drivers?
Application 5:   *Young Drivers and Collisions*

Chapter 17   The Labor Market and the Distribution of Income

Applying the Concepts #1:   Are workers paid their marginal revenue product (MRP)?
Application 1:   *Marginal Revenue Product in Major League Baseball*

Applying the Concepts #2:   When the wage increases, will the typical person work more hours or fewer hours?
Application 2:   *Cabbies Respond to an Increase in the Wage*

Applying the Concepts #3:   What explains differences in wages?
Application 3:   *The Beauty Premium*

Applying the Concepts #4:   Who benefits from the immigration of low-skilled workers?
Application 4:   *Trade-Offs from Immigration*

Applying the Concepts #5:   How do government policies affect the distribution of income?
Application 5:   *State Lotteries and the Distribution of Income*

Chapter 18   International Trade and Public Policy

Applying the Concepts #1:   Do tariffs (taxes) on imported goods hurt the poor disproportionately?
Application 1:   *The Impact of Tariffs on the Poor*

Applying the Concepts #2:   What have been the local effects of Chinese imports?
Application 2:   *Chinese Imports and Local Economies*

Applying the Concepts #3:   How does the Commerce Department try to determine whether countries are dumping their products?
Application 3:   *Are They Really Dumping?*

Applying the Concepts #4:   Why might international trade reduce measured inequality in the United States?
Application 4:   *Trade, Consumption, and Inequality*